Philip Roth

Philip Roth

A Counterlife

IRA NADEL

OXFORD

UNIVERSITY PRESS

OXFORD
UNIVERSITY PRESS

Oxford University Press is a department of the University of Oxford. It furthers
the University's objective of excellence in research, scholarship, and education
by publishing worldwide. Oxford is a registered trade mark of Oxford University
Press in the UK and certain other countries.

Published in the United States of America by Oxford University Press
198 Madison Avenue, New York, NY 10016, United States of America.

Library of Congress Cataloging-in-Publication Data
Names: Nadel, Ira Bruce, author.
Title: Philip Roth : a counterlife / Ira Nadel.
Description: New York : Oxford University Press, [2021] |
Includes bibliographical references.
Identifiers: LCCN 2020045582 (print) | LCCN 2020045583 (ebook) |
ISBN 9780199846108 (hardback) | ISBN 9780190656768 (epub) |
ISBN 9780197514450
Subjects: LCSH: Roth, Philip. | Authors, American—20th century—Biography. |
Jewish authors—United States—Biography.
Classification: LCC PS3568.O855 Z8254 2021 (print) |
LCC PS3568.O855 (ebook) | DDC 813/.54—dc23
LC record available at https://lccn.loc.gov/2020045582
LC ebook record available at https://lccn.loc.gov/2020045583

DOI: 10.1093/oso/9780199846108.001.0001

1 3 5 7 9 8 6 4 2

Printed by LSC Communications, United States of America

For Anne
&
Gideon and Levi

People are unjust to anger—it can be enlivening and a lot of fun.

—Philip Roth, *The Counterlife*, 1986

Contents

Preface

> If Yahweh wanted me to be calm, he would have made me a goy.
> —Philip Roth, *Sabbath's Theater*, 1995

By Philip Roth's own definition, a counterlife "is one's own anti-myth." It is the opposite of a public persona; it is, as Roth called it, "the real thing, the thing *in the raw*." To identify this "real" self is to go behind the curtain, the mask, and roadblocks that Roth repeatedly put out to protect his real life (CL 147; AL 204). *Philip Roth: A Counterlife* looks for this hidden Roth, looking beyond his many disguises in an effort to go backstage to understand the cry "I am a theater" (CL 325).

The task, of course, is not easy given Roth's disenchantment with biography. Roth distrusted it, yet despite his belief that getting things wrong is what actually makes a life (see Nathan Zuckerman in *American Pastoral*, 35), he assiduously worked to get *his* details right, in both his fiction and his life. He hired not one but two official biographers.[1] In his fiction, biographers are satirized: Richard Kliman's effort in *Exit Ghost* to write the life of E. I. Lonoff becomes a source of ridicule, Zuckerman putting him off, Amy Bellette not talking. But Kliman persists and believes he has uncovered the secret that will explain why Lonoff stopped writing. But his pursuit confirms Roth's view that "our understanding of people must always be at best slightly wrong" (HS 22). Still, in the last six or so years of his life, Roth struggled to ensure that his story would be told right, preparing documents and meeting often with his newly appointed biographer. Yet he also understood that "the truth about us is endless. As are the lies" (HS 315).

This account of Roth's life, sourced in archives, interviews, and readings, is thematic, focusing on a number of crucial topics: insecurity, anger, betrayal; a debate with Jewish and American life; health; the emergence of a fluid style capturing the sexual (and other) dilemmas faced by his characters and himself; a growing awareness of the possibilities of narrative to mask his own counterlife; the critical role of women and their power; the incorporation of European oppression and the inescapable fate of death. Overall is the theme of discontent—becoming anger—and shaping his emotional and literary life. It is Alex Portnoy recognizing that "*In*-dig-*na*-tion fills the hearts of all of our coun-try-*men!*" (PC 169). Indignation, he adds, is his "favorite word in the English language" (PC 169). The narrative focus here is on Roth's psychological experiences, beginning with his family and youth, and how they formed his writing life.

The Roth in these pages runs counter to the personae Roth offered to readers and interviewers. Behind the public smiles (and glowers, often seen in his author photos) were inner doubts, uncertainties, and confusions, as well as difficult relationships with his parents, his wives, his girlfriends, his editors, his publishers, and, finally, his audience. We also see his determination to avenge those who offended or insulted him, even after they died, even after *he* died. "Let the intensity out! Let the belligerence out" is his rallying cry and the key to reading him (EG 103). It is also the all-clear to look at the backstory and recognize, as he once noted of Zuckerman, that "everybody is full of cracks and fissures, but usually we see people trying very hard to hide the places where they're split." The error is that hiding them is "sometimes taken for healing them."[2] In actuality, Roth could not heal his cracks but fashioned a complex positioning of difficult literary movements to hide them. Yet at the same time, his aim was disclosure: "Disclosure IS WHAT IT'S ALL ABOUT. IT'S WHY WE LIVE. DISCLOSE IT. TELL IT."[3] To hide and disclose is the Rothian paradox, embodying Kierkegaard's aphorism "Existence is after all a debate."[4]

But why tell this story? Zuckerman in *The Ghost Writer* explains: "When you admire a writer you become curious. You look for his secret. The clues to his puzzle" (GW 50). This narrative searches for clues to uncover what Roth behind the masks reveals through the origins of his writing life expressed by his narrative art, anatomy of his culture, and uneasy relationship with himself. It is parallel to Zuckerman's critical stance at the end of *The Facts*, where he challenges the pitfalls and mistakes Roth has made in telling his story, explaining that "what you choose to tell in fiction is different from what you're permitted to tell when nothing's being fictionalized" (FAC 162). It is an attempt to find some order in "the blizzard of details that constitute the confusion of a human biography" (HS 22).

A passage in *I Married a Communist* explicitly identifies the challenge. Leo Glucksman, proletarian writer, lectures Nathan Zuckerman, emphasizing nuance as the artist's task: you must not "erase the contradiction, not . . . deny the contradiction but to see where, within the contradiction, lies the tormented human being. To allow for the chaos, to let it in. You *must* let it in" (IMC 223). To understand the reasons for the contradictions is the goal that connects with what Virginia Woolf identified as the actual concern of a biography: "the record of the things that change rather than of the things that happen." But it is also to be aware of Roth's corollary: "your mistakes are how your life changes."[5]

Secrets have a critical part in Roth's life, beginning with his family. His mother's prosperous upbringing and financial fall were kept secret, as was his father's preemptory act of giving away Roth's treasured stamp collection when he went off to college, kept a secret from Roth for some ten years (PAT 29–30). Further devastating secrets include Margaret (Maggie) Williams's lying about her pregnancy to trick Roth into marriage; his depressions of 1974, 1987, and 1993; his secret affairs in New York, Connecticut, and London; his quintuple bypass operation, kept a secret from his father; his increasing disaffection from Claire Bloom; and, finally, his decision to stop writing, not made public until 2012, two years after his private resolution.

The story of Coleman Silk's secret family, his black family, embodies the thread of secrets in Roth's literary lives, preceded by the short story "Epstein" in *Goodbye, Columbus*, Henry Zuckerman's affairs in *The Counterlife*, Amy Bellette's possible secret identity as Anne Frank and Lonoff's relation with her in *The Ghost Writer*, and succeeded by the secret and missing manuscript at the center of *The Prague Orgy* and the multiple secrets in *Operation Shylock*, accelerated and exposed in *Sabbath's Theater*, but hidden again in *American Pastoral* and *I Married a Communist*, only to be revealed by their endings.

Secrets are often connected to sex as recounted in *The Counterlife*, *Everyman*, and *The Dying Animal*, where the sixty-two-year-old David Kepesh keeps secret his affair with the twenty-four-year-old Cuban American Consuela Castilla. Alex Portnoy, along with Mickey Sabbath, joyously expose their sexual and fantasy secrets, but others, like Nathan Zuckerman, keep theirs private, as do Lonoff in *The Ghost Writer*, Swede Levov in *American Pastoral*, and Silk in *The Human Stain*. "There's a huge popular appetite for secrets," Zuckerman tells Kliman, enticing the biographer to search for more, even if the tips are misleading (EG 47). It is no surprise to learn from Roth's friend Ben Taylor that "secrets and deceptions of every kind appealed to Roth."[6] Their exposure, too, fascinated Roth, although their purpose may have been self-transformative, decentering reality, while simultaneously generating a form of creativity necessary to survive.

Roth writes to simultaneously hide and tell secrets, explaining to his editor David Rieff in 1987 that he possesses an "irrepressible tendency to distort and then to give shape, not to the actuality, but to the accumulated distortions" in his work.[7] Writing is secret-making or at the very least disguising secrets, as Roth takes elements of his past and refashions them into literature, biography into narrative art. Lives may be understood incorrectly—the Roth mantra—because their secrets are never revealed.

But why should one need to keep secrets? From a fear of exposure, betrayal, or even shame. To be exposed is to have one's private, intimate life unexpectedly revealed, resulting in shame and humiliation, precisely what Portnoy fears: headlines revealing one's "filthy secrets to a shocked and disapproving world" (PC 175). Roth's seeing a psychiatrist was a secret, but continuing to see that psychiatrist after he exposed his early traumas in a 1967 article was an embarrassment. To continue his marriage with Maggie, despite her lying about her pregnancy, and then later with the often distraught Claire Bloom, was similarly shameful (although he may have orchestrated her breakdowns). Later in life he suffered more shame from his impotence, caused by drugs required for his back and heart problems. "Shame in this guy operated *always*," as did the effort to hide it, says a bearded mourner at Zuckerman's funeral midway in *The Counterlife*. The comment pinpoints Roth (CL 219, 216).

Earlier, in *My Life as a Man*, Zuckerman identifies the impact of humiliation, citing the final line of Kafka's *The Trial*, "it was as if the shame of it must outlive him," acknowledging his embarrassment at continuing life with the underaged Monica (Moonie) Ketterer. In therapy, however, the writer Peter Tarnopol in the novel transfers his feelings back to his mother, recognizing that she was anything but a loving figure. Her discipline, while generating obedience, also created fear, and he secretly loathed her, according to Dr. Spielvogel (MLM, 213, 216). This fear carried over to Tarnopol's inability to leave Maureen, the residue of maternal obedience. It is a secret he didn't know he kept until his therapy. Tarnopol's , and likely Roth's, evolving narcissism became the means to shield himself from rejection, separation, and a sense of helplessness (MLM 215, 217-18). To guarantee such a relationship would not happen again, Tarnopol protects himself (as does Roth) through anger knowing that "people are unjust to anger – it can be enlivening and a lot of fun" (CL 150).

Hiding, but also revealing, shameful acts was the impetus for the enigmatic narratives Roth constructed not only about masturbation, marriages, and misalliances but often about his personal relations, protectively casting himself (inaccurately) as a blameless victim. When trouble loomed, he blamed others: his ex-wives were either emotionally unwell (Maggie) or pathologically needy (Bloom). He became intensely litigious and distrustful, ensuring his isolation from the feelings of others.

Fear of failure might have been a factor. Failure implies weakness, so to counter it, he became aggressive, even hostile. His characters repeatedly faced failure, from Neil Klugman's failure to sustain his relationship with Brenda Patimkin, to the various failures of Peter Tarnopol, David Kepesh, Mickey Sabbath, Swede Levov, and Bucky Cantor, each of them voicing some form of discontent. Every Roth text is a site of failure, every relationship a failure, in his personal life as well. This may be related to the repeated failure of identity experienced by Zuckerman when he realizes about himself, "You are no longer any man's son, you are no longer some good woman's husband . . . you don't come from anywhere anymore, either" (ZU 404–5). To overcome this void, you impersonate, put on a mask, become a character named "Philip Roth" who appears in *Operation Shylock.*

"What the hell happened?" one may legitimately ask, as Murray Ringold does of Zuckerman in *I Married a Communist.* Why did you become so adversarial, so angry, and so removed from life to live in the country (IMC 320)? Murray succinctly answers for Zuckerman and Roth, "All those antagonisms and then the torrent of betrayals" (IMC 262). Roth, like Zuckerman, felt under siege and often betrayed, especially if he let his guard down. His Jamesian devotion to art, isolating himself in the country, was not only an excuse to remove himself from literary gossip and public attention but a self-protective act against failure.

Ironically, Roth himself may have actually sought out betrayal, especially when in love. With few exceptions, he chose younger women who, almost by definition, would leave; an older man, even one with as large a reputation as Roth, could not be attractive forever. When they wanted to stay, he was shocked, and when they wanted to leave, he was pleased. He may have chosen younger women precisely because he knew they would depart. To get the jump on any breakup, he would act first, writing a letter or meeting in person to say "It's over," because you want a lasting relationship and I do not. To protect himself from an attachment that might lead to betrayal, he had to move. As he paradoxically offered in a 1995 essay, "I seem always to need to be emancipated from whatever has liberated me."[8]

Curiously, he felt even language might betray him, as Kafka anticipated. In a letter to Max Brod, Kafka wrote, "My whole body puts me on my guard against each word; each word, even before letting itself be put down, has to look round on every side; the phrases positively fall apart in my hands, I see what they are like inside and then I have to stop quickly."[9] Roth's energetic expressive style, piling phrases upon phrases, may be his defense against such a betrayal (or failure), his strategy to overcome the possible disloyalty of individual words.

Complicating the story is that while Roth fed his own courage—on a yellow Post-it note he jotted down, "When God wants to say fuck, he says it through me"—he also reveled in mischief. At one point Sabbath, put on trial for disorderly conduct, boisterously declares, "I am disorderly conduct" (ST 323).[10] Roth explained his satisfaction with such a position when Hermione Lee asked him if he had a particular reader in mind: no, he said, he had "an anti-Roth reader in mind. I think, 'How he is going to hate this!' That can be just the encouragement I need."[11] Such hostility brought delight: "Let the re-pellent in! That's your achievement, Mr. Zuckerman," the biographer Kliman declares to the writer in *Exit Ghost* (EG 272). One of Roth's favorite essays might have been William Hazlitt's "The Pleasures of Hating."[12] As Daphna knowingly says in *The Counterlife*, "Bad Jews make better copy. . . . Bad Jews sell newspapers just the way they sell books" (CL 128).

Such intensity naturally brought criticism, occasionally scandal, and dis-tress to readers, critics, and friends. Alan Lelchuk, a young writer Roth met at Yaddo in the late 1960s and promoted, objected to Roth using him as the partial source for the renegade, predatory poet Ralph Baumgarten in *The Professor of Desire*. Roth didn't care, saying anyone who knows you will know you are not Baumgarten.[13] Their friendship paused, although Lelchuk later returned the favor in his novel *Ziff: A Life?* (2003), a satire of a Roth-like char-acter.[14] That brought their friendship to an end, although Roth claimed he never read it, which Lelchuk doubted.[15]

Only in opposition, Roth believed, can the writer write the truth, opposing sanctity, falsity, self-righteousness, and hypocrisy. Refuting orthodox sexual mores and social behavior provided the imaginative energy Roth required to write: "A writer needs to be driven round the bend, needs his poisons. He battens on them."[16] The anger and outrage over "Defender of the Faith" (his story of Jewish soldiers) and *Portnoy's Complaint* meant he was con-necting with his readers. In fact, in a 1971 article for the *New York Times*, he admitted that it would have been impossible for Jews to react to his early stories without fear or outrage "only five thousand days after Buchenwald and Auschwitz" (RMY 215).

The prototype is Céline, the often rejected anti-Semitic French writer deemed a collaborator but of whom Roth said, "Céline is my Proust!" To read him he had to suspend his Jewish conscience, although he argued that Céline's anti-Semitism was not "the heart of his books." "Céline is a great liberator," he insisted.[17] The misanthropy, dark comedy, and invective in his work appealed to Roth, notably in *Journey to the End of the Night*. What appealed was his "outlaw side," his writing drawing its power from his strangely "demotic voice." Roth read Céline in his twenties and then taught him at the University of Iowa.[18]

Roth's story is complicated. In Janet Hobhouse's fictional portrait of him in her novel *The Furies*, the narrator, who has an affair with Jack, the Rothian character (as Hobhouse did), writes that he couldn't directly deal with intense emotions but that "it was not convention that made him so fearful of emotional excess . . . but that self-protective center of his: the *in-there*." There was always conflict, not only between the characters but within Roth. Recklessness was in conflict with conventionality; there was always "the woeful *I* that seemed always to be saying this isn't me. I don't do this sort of thing."[19] Flaubert expressed it clearly when he wrote in a letter, "Be regular and orderly in your life, so that you may be violent and original in your work."[20] Roth pasted the comment near his computer, as did Zuckerman in *My Life as a Man*.

This biography, then, is an effort to explore the "in-there" and penetrate the fortress of Roth's protective self, to peer over the ramparts to see the multifaceted person, and to uncover some of the secrets. Several critics have suggested that given his insulated, protective, chameleon-like self-preservation, Roth is unbiographical. But the realignment of the pieces of his life may allow us to see the figure in new ways. Or grasp what "She," in Zuckerman's play in *Exit Ghost*, means when the character says, "You strike me as a person who was spoiling for adventure but didn't know it." You prefer to construct stories, she continues, of "unreasonable wishes. Yet that is what it is to be in life, isn't it?" "Rash moments" creating "perilous choices" becomes the measure of living or the guide to how Roth chose to define at least half of his engagement with life (EG 290–91). But his "self-protective center" prevented such "rash moments" from ruling his everyday life.

This account of the writer might be thought of as its own "anti-myth" or countertext, asking if he was too hard on his first wife, to whom he dedicated *Letting Go*, too harsh on his second, the dedicatee of *The Professor of Desire* and *Operation Shylock*, too antagonistic toward his enemies, too insistent on his own righteousness. He constantly torpedoed friendships over slights, insults, or criticism. Offenses could not be forgotten: "No one can leave anything without hating it first."[21]

The sting of life electrified Roth's literary antennae and became the necessary fuel to his fictional fire. As Zuckerman acknowledges in *Exit Ghost*, he—and by extension Roth—could not escape from his own intensity (EG 59). "Turning up the flame" was a requirement, the hotter the better.[22] Being "*stung* by life" both accelerated and shaped his writing but also left scars which he and his fiction rarely forgot.[23]

An example of Roth's anger galvanized was his response to what he believed to be the underhanded actions of Francine du Plessix Gray, a Cornwall Bridge neighbor. The novelist, autobiographer, and feminist embodied all that Roth resented: unwarranted female influence. At one time she and her husband were close friends, but when Roth discovered her gossiping about his personal behavior with another woman and accusing him of breaking up a marriage, he turned against her. He also believed Bloom was "enslaved" to her (Roth's term). The perceived slander was too much, and his anger accelerated when he thought that she, and not Bloom, wrote *Leaving a Doll's House*. At that point, he did all he could to expose the person he referred to as "Francine Duplicitous Gray." In letters and other documents, Roth excoriated Gray, holding her partly accountable for ending his marriage to Bloom. He put her on a list of those forbidden from attending his memorial service. But then she died before him.[24]

Roth's love life was marked by fear as much as by pleasure. The contested survival of love, assaulted by distrust and disloyalty, remains an open portal through which to enter Roth's writing, beginning with Neil Klugman in *Goodbye, Columbus* and ending with Bucky Cantor in *Nemesis*. In Roth, love rarely, if ever, brings fulfillment. Frustration, disappointment, and even disaster are more likely outcomes. Think of the car crash that ends the lives of Coleman Silk and Faunia Farley at the end of *The Human Stain* or Simon Axler's suicide in *The Humbling*. Generalities and big ideas did not concern Roth: individual behavior did. As he once explained to his close friend Ben Taylor, "I aim only at specifics."[25]

Those specifics were often of his own life, his most consistent and convenient subject. Autofiction became his specialty, with numerous narrative games added to distract the reader and perhaps himself. Critics responded in kind, calling *Sabbath's Theater* "a nervous breakdown in the form of a novel," while others railed against his unrepentant narcissism.[26] And those who called him out would never be forgiven: Irving Howe, Marie Syrkin, Claire Bloom, Francine du Plessix Gray, Ross Miller, and others became obvious targets. No insult went unreturned. As Taylor remarks in his memoir of Roth, "he couldn't stop litigating the past." He couldn't "get enough of getting even."[27]

Roth's career rebounded from disappointment to triumph, competing directly or indirectly with Bellow and Updike, while Mailer shadowboxed in the corner. Following his early success with *Goodbye, Columbus* was the tepid reception of both *Letting Go* and *When She Was Good.* But the sensational triumph of *Portnoy's Complaint,* branding him a sex-crazed anti-Semite, caused him to retreat to rural New York and then to Connecticut, duplicated by Zuckerman and his response to the success of his novel *Carnovsky.*

After *Portnoy*, Roth had modest bestsellers with *Operation Shylock, Sabbath's Theater,* and then the American trilogy, followed by the surprise success of *The Plot Against America.* A more restrained response greeted his final three works. Awards, yes, but then retirement capped not by the final novel, *Nemesis,* but by a collection with the curious, almost melancholic title *Why Write?* Even when not provoking others, he was the subject of unwarranted insults: walking with Taylor in New York not far from his apartment, they passed a monument to American winners of the Nobel Prize in the park adjacent to the American Museum of Natural History. The two stopped for a moment when a woman suddenly approached and yelled, "Looking for your name? It's not there!" She then dashed off.[28]

Throughout his career, life never left him alone.

Abbreviations

By Philip Roth

AL	*The Anatomy Lesson*. New York: Farrar, Straus and Giroux, 1983.
AP	*American Pastoral*. Boston: Houghton Mifflin, 2004.
BR	*The Breast*. New York: Holt, Rinehart and Winston, 1972.
CL	*The Counterlife*. New York: Farrar, Straus and Giroux, 1986.
CWPR	*Conversations with Philip Roth*, ed. George J. Searles. Jackson: University Press of Mississippi, 1992.
DA	*The Dying Animal*. Boston: Houghton Mifflin, 2001.
DE	*Deception: A Novel*. New York: Simon and Schuster, 1990.
EG	*Exit Ghost*. Boston: Houghton Mifflin, 2007.
EV	*Everyman*. Boston: Houghton Mifflin, 2006.
FAC	*The Facts*. New York: Farrar, Straus and Giroux, 1988.
GAN	*The Great American Novel*. New York: Holt, Rinehart and Winston, 1973.
GBC	*Goodbye, Columbus*. Boston: Houghton Mifflin, 1959.
GW	*The Ghost Writer*. New York: Farrar, Straus and Giroux, 1979.
HS	*The Human Stain*. Boston: Houghton Mifflin, 2000.
HUM	*The Humbling*. Boston: Houghton Mifflin Harcourt, 2009.
IMC	*I Married a Communist*. Boston: Houghton Mifflin, 1998.
IND	*Indignation*. Boston: Houghton Mifflin, 2008.
JB	"The Jewish Blues." *New American Review* 1 (1967) 136–64.
LG	*Letting Go*. New York: Random House, 1962.
MLM	*My Life as a Man*. New York: Holt, Rinehart Winston, 1974.
MM	"Marriage à la Mode," box B-1209, folder 5, Taylor/Roth Archive, Rare Books and Special Collections, Firestone Library, Princeton University.
NAR	*New American Review*
NEM	*Nemesis*. Boston: Houghton Mifflin, 2010.
NOT	"Notes for My Biographer," box B-1209, folders 10–12, Taylor/Roth Archive, Rare Books and Special Collections, Firestone Library, Princeton University.
NP	"Novotny's Pain." *New Yorker*, 27 October 1962; in *A Philip Roth Reader*, rev. ed., ed. Martin Green. Farrar, Straus and Giroux, 1980, 261–80.
OG	*Our Gang*. New York: Random House, 1971.

ONA	"On the Air." *New American Review* 10 (August 1970): 7–49.
OPS	*Operation Shylock: A Confession.* New York: Simon and Schuster, 1993.
PAA	*The Plot Against America.* Boston: Houghton Mifflin, 2004.
PAT	*Patrimony.* New York: Simon and Schuster, 1991.
PC	*Portnoy's Complaint.* New York: Random House, 1969.
PD	*The Professor of Desire.* New York: Farrar, Straus and Giroux, 1977.
PIH	"Pain and Illness History." box B-1209, folder 9, Taylor/Roth Archive, Rare Books and Special Collections, Firestone Library, Princeton University.
PR80	*Philip Roth at 80: A Celebration.* New York: Library of America, 2014.
REC	"Recollections from Beyond the Last Rope." *Harper's Magazine* 219 (July 1959): 42–48.
RMY	*Reading Myself and Others.* New York: Vintage, 2001.
SHP	*Shop Talk: A Writer and His Colleagues and Their Work.* Boston: Houghton Mifflin, 2001.
ST	*Sabbath's Theater.* Boston: Houghton Mifflin, 1995.
WR?	*Why Write? Collected Nonfiction, 1960–2013.* New York: Library of America, 2017.
WSWG	*When She Was Good.* New York: Random House, 1967.
ZB	*Zuckerman Bound.* Contains *The Ghost Writer, Zuckerman Unbound, The Anatomy Lesson, Epilogue: The Prague Orgy.* New York: Farrar, Straus, Giroux, 1985; New York: Library of America, 2007.
ZUB	*Zuckerman Unbound.* New York: Farrar, Straus and Giroux, 1981.

By Claire Bloom

LA	*Limelight and After: The Education of an Actress.* New York: Harper & Row, 1982.
LDH	*Leaving a Doll's House: A Memoir.* Boston: Little, Brown, 1996.

Other

LC	Library of Congress.
FSG	Farrar, Straus and Giroux.
NYPL	New York Public Library.

Introduction

The History of My Discontent

> How far back must you go to discover the beginning of trouble?
> —Philip Roth, "Epstein," 1959

In July 1967, Philip Roth began a letter to his first agent, Candida Donadio, with a curious phrase: "the history of my discontent, as I remember it." A two-page, single-spaced litany of complaints followed. So much was wrong with his second novel, *When She Was Good*, starting with the book jacket, the size of the first printing, advertising copy, galleys, promotion budget, incorrect sales reports, and the blurbs. Roth was fed up with his editor (Joe Fox) and publisher (Random House): both were incompetent.[1] Such accusations of ineptitude, his belief that *he* could do much better, would be repeated throughout his literary career.

Discontent defined Roth from the very beginning of his literary life: the production of *Goodbye, Columbus* was inept, the advertising budget inadequate, the marketing nonexistent. Roth was twenty-five when he made these complaints about Houghton Mifflin; he would repeat them about each of his subsequent publishers. Unsurprisingly, he titled a lengthy excerpt of *Portnoy's Complaint* "Civilization and Its Discontents." It appeared in the *New American Review* volume 3 (1968), edited by Theodore Solotaroff. The seventy-four-page excerpt startled and absorbed readers who encountered Portnoy's unleashed libido and fornicatory universe, as Roth repeatedly provided what his character demanded: "Details! Actual details" about sexual adventures (NAR 81)![2] As Roth later remarked, Portnoy wasn't a character, "he was an explosion, and I wasn't finished exploding after *Portnoy's Complaint*" (CWPR 175).[3]

Roth's allusion to Freud's classic text, and Roth's own explosions, heralded his literary rebellions. Freud was explaining how the individual, with his intense, primal desires, struggles to function in a repressive, rule-bound society. Portnoy, of course, venerates personal freedom, especially sexual freedom, in the face of restrictive laws and social codes. The individual's own pursuit of happiness entails flouting or dismantling society's repressive rules. In fact, Roth was somewhat obsessed with how society stifles the individual's emotional energy and realized that to achieve well-being, one had to rebel, to liberate oneself, even letting the unconscious loose. Zuckerman's mother does this when a doctor asks her, lying with a brain tumor in a Miami hospital, to write her name. With pen to paper, she perfectly spells not "Selma" but "Holocaust" (AL 41).[4] Memory and anger cross: writing, as Roth understood, "is an act of imagination [that] seems to perplex and infuriate everyone" (AL 44).

Of course, it wasn't just "society" or feckless publishers that provoked Roth's discontent. To Roth, betrayal was a fact of life, if an ugly one; as Murray Ringold says in *I Married a Communist*, "You control betrayal on one side and you wind up betraying somewhere else" (IMC 318). Indeed, *I Married a Communist* is a bible of betrayal, a fictionalized account of real-life betrayals. Roth certainly had many to draw on.

In 1967, an article appeared by Roth's psychiatrist, Dr. Hans J. Kleinschmidt, entitled "The Angry Act: The Role of Aggression in Creativity." More than breaching Roth's privacy, it was a major betrayal, revealing secrets and intimacies, beginning with worry about the size of his penis and fantasies of his teachers as his mother. At eleven he wanted a bathing suit with a jock strap, but his mother said, out loud, that he didn't need one: "You have such a little one that it makes no difference." This devastating remark caused adolescent fury and shame and the feeling of betrayal. Anger became a natural reaction to such humiliation. Kleinschmidt, however, widened its application to art. Anger, he wrote, "may be the prime mover or the unconscious motivating force for a creative push; it can find poetic, literary, graphic or musical expression, and thus channel and dissipate that which otherwise might be intolerable to the ego. The successful channeling of aggression into creativity restores equilibrium within the ego."[5] Nevertheless, Roth reacted angrily to this egregious breach of trust, satirizing Kleinschmidt in *My Life as a Man* as the therapist Dr. Spielvogel (the very same from *Portnoy*).

The appearance of "The Angry Act" in the *American Imago,* a widely read psychoanalytic journal, was, in fact, the signal betrayal of Roth's thirties, matched only by Maggie Williams's earlier trickery concerning her supposed pregnancy. But Kleinschmidt, the most trusted person in his life at that time, publicly exposed him; haunting Roth and his writing would, in fact, be fear of exposure.

Once every decade, it seems, Roth suffered a major betrayal. At age six, his mother locked him out of the house: he had threatened to leave in response to her discipline. She packed him a bag and told him to go. He stepped outside, took a few steps, turned around, and found the door locked. He cried and pounded the door, and it opened. Twenty or thirty years later, Roth was still thinking about this unhappy event, reliving it in his therapist's office. The episode remained a key moment in his early childhood, representing the betrayal of maternal love, if only temporarily, generating an unconscious aggression to battle any rejection. Proust suggested the psychological reaction in a sentence quoted by Kleinschmidt: "We always end up by betraying mother."[6] But it was repeated during Roth's year at Rutgers University in Newark: angry with his father over the question of a curfew, he came home one night after midnight to find the front door locked; only after beating and beating the door was it opened, again by his mother.[7]

At eleven, he confronted a second betrayal from his mother, that of the bathing suit and her remark that a jock strap was unnecessary. In his midtwenties, the deceptive Maggie betrayed him through the trickery of her false pregnancy, used as leverage to marry; in his thirties, Kleinschmidt's revealing article of 1967 appeared; and then in 1972, a turncoat article by Irving Howe denounced him. These early betrayals forged a determination never to allow them to occur again, his self-protection aggression. But he often failed.

In his forties, love and eventually marriage to Claire Bloom turned into a hostile relationship defined by her fear of abandonment and his feeling of entrapment; in his fifties, his own body began to betray him with increasing back and heart problems; in his sixties, age and depression, intensified by the death of friends and enemies (Veronica Geng, C. H. Huvelle, Irving Howe), began to betray his youthful sense of life. In his seventies, shadowed by death, writing itself betrayed him: he lost his vocation and in 2010 decided to stop, a decision he did not make public until 2012. In his eighties, rejected again for the Nobel Prize (won by Bob Dylan in 2016), he encountered failing health and finally death: life itself betrayed him.

Further betrayals included Saul Bellow insulting him in an interview; James Atlas criticizing his writing behind his back; continued attacks by feminists for his representation of women, the sale of his private correspondence, manuscripts, and autographed presentation copies by several of his closest friends.[8] Fiction writers freely used his life (Janet Hobhouse,

Lisa Halliday), while several of his lovers publicly exposed their romance (Alice Denham). He even became a character in a play, James Lapine's *The Moment When*, and the implied subject of the film *Listen Up Philip*. Publishers, once keen supporters, criticized his failure to earn back advances; his bestsellers were few: only *Portnoy's Complaint* and *The Plot Against America*. The cascade of personal and professional betrayals that hounded Roth likely led to Ringold's reflection in *I Married a Communist*: "Betrayal is an inescapable component of living—who doesn't betray?" (IMC 265). The title of one of Harold Pinter's most successful plays at this time was *Betrayal*.[9]

The betrayal by his analyst confirmed that a lifetime of distrust began literally at Roth's front door, one of a series of deceptions that led to his sustained unhappiness and anger and that filtered through his life and defined his work.[10] To find someone he could trust was perhaps a more important quest than finding someone to love. Intensity and even rage soon became hallmarks of his "emotional history," evident from his earliest publications to his last. Portnoy, he explained in 2014, is "as rich with ire as with erotic desire."[11] *My Life as a Man, Operation Shylock, Sabbath's Theater*, plus *The Plot Against America* through to *Nemesis* expose betrayal on political, social, sexual, and romantic levels. Illness became the ultimate betrayer because neither anger nor action can stop it. Zuckerman's "persecution mania" should be no surprise, confirmed when he receives an envelope addressed to "Kike, Apt. 2B," or his father's final word to him: "Bastard" (see ZUB 129, 176, 193, 199–200, 217). Such a betrayal of paternal love confirmed Roth's belief that "every soul [is] its own betrayal factory" (IMC 262).

But what character or literary work does not have an element of anger or displeasure? Roth once asked. The first word of the *Iliad*, in the Robert Fagles translation, is "rage" Roth pointed out: "Rage—Goddess, sing the rage of Peleus' son Achilles, / murderous, doomed, that cost the Achaeans countless losses."[12] Roth then added, "This is how the whole of European literature begins: singing the virile rage of Achilles, who wants his girlfriend back."[13] He recognized the potency of the subject and continued to emphasize it throughout his writing life, expressing anger and impatience with the restraints and taboos of individual social and sexual life. Murray Ringold, speaking to his brother, tells him, "The menace to you is not imperialist capitalism. . . . The menace to you is your private life" (IMC 87). As Roth wrote in his 1986 story "His Mistress's Voice," his desire was to cling "to hatred for dear life."[14] This was a more extreme and honest declaration than the pseudo-philosophical statement from *Sabbath's Theater*: "the law of living: fluctuation. For every thought a counterthought, for every urge a counterurge" (ST 158).

Roth himself tried to counter the "angry" label, writing that the term had been misapplied by others, notably Ross Miller, Claire Bloom, and Francine du Plessix Gray, to what they saw as his confrontational, excessive, and sometimes unreasonable reactions. He claimed that his relation to anger was more like that of Mickey Sabbath than of Alex Portnoy, closer to amusement, mischief, high jinks, satire, mimicry, self-mockery, and self-sabotage. Sabbath's "delectable layer cake of anger" is what Roth believed he possessed; he was seriously angry with only two "screwballs" in his life, he claimed: his first and second wives. They each nearly wrecked his life, he asserted. He admitted he had a talent for anger in his fiction but also that "anger isn't just anger—it's a helluva lot more." It's the "more" that is of importance in this account. Solipsistically, he then argued that those with a real stake in anger are always deadly serious and that their seriousness causes their anger—but in a circular manner. He believed that it's their anger that makes them serious. Writing retrospectively, Roth wanted to identify himself with the "great *clown* of anger," Mickey Sabbath, denying any of the deep-seated psychological events in his life that actually made him angry and discontent. He, furthermore, believed anger is a rich human emotion that can be justifiable or not in an effort to "remake the world." But you cannot, he wrote, "make me into a Norman Mailer," whose anger always turned vicious, "without doing critical violence to my work."[15]

A week-long conference in Aix-en-Provence in 1999 was called "The Roth Explosion," unintentionally evoking the idea of a volatile Roth, as did Christa Maerker's documentary of 1998, *The Roth Explosion: Confessions of a Writer*. "Explosion," of course, could connote expanding readership and a burst of European popularity but also the implication, for Roth and his characters, of detonating, blasting, and overturning convention in an effort to celebrate the rude or obscene as normal.

A literal explosion occurs in *American Pastoral* when the radicalized Merry Levov sets off a bomb at the Hamlin post office, accidentally killing Dr. Fred Conlon in February 1968. An explosion as an eruption. Rabelais rather than Jane Austen. And even Roth recognized the danger, warning his friend David Plante that "he needs to see people, but when he does, he becomes very intense." At a certain point, Roth explained, even "I can't bear my own intensity. I have to leave. I have to get back to Connecticut."[16]

One response to his own intensity was to perform, his comic entertainments a hallmark of his personality applauded by friends. Editors, writers, wives, girlfriends, interviewers, reporters, and family praised his mimicry, his acting out constantly displaying his comic powers. But his drive to perform may have masked a search for a deeper self compounded by his knowledge that, as Zuckerman knows, "I am a theater and nothing more than a theater" (CL 321). Being Zuckerman is itself "one long performance" and the opposite of "what is thought of as being oneself" (CL 319). But there is an element of the fraudulent to this which Roth disliked. The irony is that Roth understood that he possessed only a "variety of impersonations . . . and not only of myself" (CL 321). Propelling his discontent and anger was frustration at being unable to locate an inner self, leaving him only with impersonations. "[I] have no self independent of my imposturing," Zuckerman, and by extension Roth, confesses (CL 321). But that did not stop his search.

Anger and Roth are almost synonymous, sometimes a righteous anger, as seen in Swede Levov's reaction to his daughter's undoing all that he had sought for in modern America, or Ira Ringold in *I Married a Communist*, betrayed by his wife Eve Frame. It is not without note that the root of the name Ira is "ire" or "anger," although it can also mean "watchful." And there is the quiet anger of Coleman Silk, removed from his university position because of political correctness, and the anger of Marcus Messner against the dean in *Indignation*. The critic Alfred Kazin located this anger in the determination of Jewish writers *not* to be goys: "the Jewish writer as outrager, provocateur, 'shameless' fellow, his way of saying 'I am *not* a goyim!' "[17]

But the origin of Roth's singular anger may be difficult to pinpoint. It was certainly grounded in reaction to the behavior of his mother and the moral authority of his father, Herman Roth. In "His Mistress's Voice," the protagonist writes that his entire life "has been an attempt to get away from my mother. Enraged with her since babyhood. She implanted guilt in me which is a loathsome trick."[18] Roth's friend and editor Aaron Asher knew that Roth was "a stubborn little boy."[19] The Declaration of Independence, hanging in the hallway of the Roth home, was a sign to the aspirational young man that you could be free, a desire accelerated by the rigid rules set down by a watchful and anxious father, witness to the crude reality learned in the apartments and streets and businesses of Newark. Establishing his own identity separate from the family's became essential for Roth. The enclosed world of his parents needed to be dismantled, which Roth began to do in his stories of the 1950s.

Deception or entrapment by women made Roth furious, and when girlfriends suggested marriage or children, he adamantly refused and broke off the relationship out of fear rather than dislike. He would not be imprisoned again, no matter how strong the love, and then betrayed. In his fiction, this anger took the form of a relentless drive for sexual control—conquest, really—which expressed itself in hostile pleasures. Sex in Roth is angry sex, rarely resisted, except by the Israeli Sabra Naomi at the end of *Portnoy*: she kicks Portnoy in the chest in response to his pursuit of her, "rich with rage," in a hotel room (PC 270).

For Roth, acrimony supported discontent, which, in his mature years, became an active, litigious nature, as his friend Solotaroff explained: "What certainly comes through in *The Human Stain* is the kind of rage that he was carrying around from the whole affair with Claire Bloom and her book. He's found a very strong fire hose for all that pressure."[20] But anger is also a response to rejection despite its violation of decorum and behavior. It becomes a form of self-protection. To be confrontational is implicitly to triumph, but also a response to real life colliding with art, something Roth encountered throughout his life and work.

Another source of Roth's discontent, although it did not at first emerge in his idyllic, self-mythologizing childhood, was his Jewishness, not so much anger at the Holocaust or the destruction of the Jews as what he saw as Jewish self-satisfaction with material success and moral hypocrisy, presented in his first collection, *Goodbye, Columbus*. Yes, Jewish men had affairs; yes, Jewish boys questioned the title "the chosen people"; yes, Jews discriminated against other Jews. But swim clubs, not concentration camps, became his focus when outcast Orthodox European Jews threatened the integration of Judaism into suburban American life. The controversy surrounding "Defender of the Faith," his story about Jewish soldiers working against each other, led to charges of anti-Semitism and initiated a set of attacks by rabbis, critics, and readers, bursting into an onslaught later led by such figures as Gershom Scholem over *Portnoy*. The battlefield became public, causing resentment and anger, which he confronted in such essays as "Writing About Jews" and "Imagining Jews." "America," the sarcastic Murray Ringold admits in *I Married a Communist*, "was paradise for angry Jews" (IMC 164).

Anger actually brought more success as the outrage against *Portnoy* increased sales—but also brought worry; his next title, and the next after that, had to be equal to or greater than his hit novel. The need to repeat his success became a public expectation and private burden which triggered his withdrawal from public view. He preferred the writing colony of Yaddo, a rented house in Woodstock, and finally a home in northwestern Connecticut where he could be free from the publicity and attention. He also turned away from the novel of comic manners to satire—*Our Gang, The Breast,* and *The Great American Novel*—as refuge from public expectations that there would be a *Portnoy II,* another oversexed Jewish man in pursuit of *shiksas.* He could not, and did not, want to repeat *Portnoy,* much as Norman Mailer, reflecting on his brush with fame, did not want to write a sequel to his bestseller to be called *The Naked and the Dead Go to Japan.*[21]

From the start, Mailer was a public personality; Roth chose the opposite path, protecting himself from his success and mistaken identity as Portnoy. But for the public, the association was impossible to overcome, as Jacqueline Susann made clear in her quip on the Johnny Carson show that she'd like to meet the author of *Portnoy's Complaint* but not shake his hand. Roth receded into a private writing life, less a Jamesian retreat into artistic isolation than a response to Portnovian frenzy.

Portnoy was an author's nightmare but a columnist's dream, and the papers soon reported that Roth was an escort of Barbra Streisand's (false) and a date of Jackie Kennedy's (true). Retreating to the country, like E. I. Lonoff in *The Ghost Writer,* gave Roth protection and the freedom to write and reclaim his identity away from the gossip and Portnoy connection. ("In Gossip We Trust," the narrator in *I Married a Communist* claims, is America's motto [IMC 284].) Yet ironically, his absence from the stage increased his celebrity status: when he did appear, more stories of his sightings (and companions) made the press. But gradually the city became less of a need, until in 1981 he claimed, "One week in New York will take care of me for a year," although in *Exit Ghost,* Zuckerman visits the city regularly, mostly for medical matters.[22]

Roth expressed his insecurity with his identity through the presentation of the mature Zuckerman in *The Counterlife,* repeatedly establishing and then undermining his presence as characters die but then return and merge with another. If that novel was an attempt to show how literature could get him out of his identity crisis, *The Facts* put him right back in. The game continued with *Operation Shylock* and its Roth doppelgänger as history, biography, and fiction interacted, all part of his resistance to fame by employing slippery voices and multiple personalities.[23]

Psychologically, the result of Roth's failure to satisfy the demands of a series of traumatic incidents (worked out in his fiction) meant the continued experience of unsuccessful relationships in his life. He resisted meaningful romantic involvements. The agency of events, like his first wife's betrayal, marrying under fraudulent pretenses, became inextricable and brought on only anger.

The purpose of this account, then, is to examine Roth's strategies in dealing with the events that flamed up throughout his life, while testing several, often extreme assertions by Kleinschmidt, notably that Roth "acted out his anger in his relationships with women, reducing all of them to masturbatory sexual objects."[24] In his private "Notes for My Biographer," Roth candidly admitted that he loved neither Maggie nor Claire, and that he married Maggie because of a lurid deception and Claire because of sympathy for her needs. But these negative views need correction, or at least context. Maggie appealed because she allowed Roth to experience the "other," and Claire was an attractive movie star who was also Jewish. In his retrospective and defensive essay "Marriage à la Mode," he says he chose to marry them because of what he labeled the emotional instability of his second wife and the criminal actions of his first.[25] But when other women with whom he had loving relations wanted to formalize their connection and begin a family, he immediately backed away.[26] The idea of permanency scared him because it could always disappear. He had had the experiences to prove it.

A further source of Roth's overall discontent originated in his sense of personal injustice: acting the good son in the face of his father's authority was never quite enough. In the conclusion of his conflicted memoir *Patrimony*, there is a moment that unravels a lifetime of being the good son when Herman Roth returns to his son in a dream. Following Jewish tradition, the son buried the father in a simple shroud, but standing in his "hooded white shroud," the father reproaches him: "I should have been dressed in a suit. You did the wrong thing" (PAT 237). All that peered out from the covering, Roth writes, was "the displeasure in his dead face. And his only words were a rebuke: I had dressed him for eternity in the wrong clothes" (PAT 237). This is equally comic and tragic, showing that a Jewish son simply can't win, that something will always be wrong; only guilt will survive.

Roth would always remain the "little son," while his father would remain alive not just as a father "but as *the* father, sitting in judgment on whatever I do" (PAT 238). Against that, Roth sought liberation. But Jewish sons, even after the death of their parents (or themselves), still seek approval. The urge is always to be "good," as Roth made pointedly clear in *Portnoy* when the young Ronald Nimkin, about to commit suicide, nevertheless pins to his newly laundered sport shirt a note to his mother: "'*Mrs. Blumenthal called. Please bring your mah-jongg rules to the game tonight.'* Now, how's *that* for good to the last drop?" the narrator cynically asks (PC 120).

The contradictions for the Jewish son turned writer would never stop, evident when Zuckerman's father tells him that he's not the kind of boy who could ever write an insulting story about money and their family. "But I *did* write it," Nathan bravely replies. His father then puts his arms around his son as a sign of sympathy bordered by sentiment, but the opposite occurs: hostility (GW 95). Refusing his father's entreaties, Zuckerman hops on a bus to New York, leaving the father standing alone on a street corner in the gathering darkness, while Zuckerman thinks of how "all of Jewry [was] gratuitously disgraced and jeopardized by my inexplicable betrayal" (GW 96). Betrayal: once more, inescapable. A Jewish man just can't win.

But neither could the critics. When the *New York Times* book critic Christopher Lehmann-Haupt criticized, he attacked. Roth alluded to the critic's paucity of imagination and contradictory reading of *Portnoy* in "Imagining Jews,"[27] to which Lehmann-Haupt sarcastically replied in four paragraphs in the *New York Review of Books* of 12 December 1974. Roth then doubled his attack with a multiparagraph and multipronged response, gaining points for nastiness: for example, Lehmann-Haupt "does not have any critical standards . . . or position that it is possible to take seriously." But the key word of his attack is that as a reader, Lehmann-Haupt is "insensate." Roth's indictment is twice as long as Lehmann-Haupt's initial reply and three times as nasty, although "vengeful" might be more appropriate.[28] But Roth resists going as far as Henry Bech, age seventy-four, in Updike's "Bech Noir" from *Bech at Bay* (1998). There, the writer murders four critics for decades-old attacks he has remembered word-for-word. Words like "prolix" and "voulu" could not be forgotten.

Aggression, discontent, and anger are key concepts in the lexicon and life of Philip Roth, even if he minimized the importance of his psychoanalytic sessions, quipping that "the experience of psychoanalysis was probably more useful to me as a writer than as a neurotic, although there may be a false distinction there" (CWPR 170). Nevertheless, Roth did acknowledge that the anger awakened in him toward his mother, discovered in his sessions with Kleinschmidt which began as early as 1962, allowed him to confront it in *Portnoy's Complaint* and *My Life as a Man*. But he also recognized, as Updike's Rabbit Angstrom knew, that "if you have the guts to be yourself, other people'll pay [the] price."[29] Portnoy can admit, "Have I got grievances! Do I harbor hatreds I didn't even know were there," but he and Roth would also learn the cost of such complaining, even as Portnoy comically asks whether "*kvetching* for people like me [is] a *form* of truth," to which Mickey Sabbath would instantly shout, "Yes!" (PC 94).

Roth believed his anger was justified; there was always a reason, in contrast to figures like Mailer or Pinter, who he thought were habitually angry about everything and often without cause. But soon, even Roth comically believed that the rationale of life was only to get angry. Upsetting Bloom once in Connecticut by something he said, she angrily replied, "I didn't come here to be insulted." Roth laughed and said, "But of course you did . . . we all did," adding that that's what he wanted carved on his gravestone: "Philip Roth. He came here to be insulted."[30] Such a declaration would ensure his perpetual anger and register his protest against the humiliations of life. Anger shows that we can fight back against those disfiguring moments life imposes.

But as Roth made clear in his 1984 *Paris Review* interview, it's not only Jews who get angry, explaining to Hermione Lee that Lucy Nelson in *When She Was Good* is justifiably hostile: "The dirty little secret is no longer sex; the dirty little secret is hatred and rage. It's the tirade that's taboo. Odd that this should be so a hundred years after Dostoyevsky (and fifty after Freud) but nobody likes to be identified with the stuff" (CWPR 173).[31] Except Roth. He then explains that the novel examines the nature of the anger and the depth of Lucy's wound.

Roth transferred his "discontent" to his many characters and their expanding anger, whether it is Lucy Nelson, Alex Portnoy, Mickey Sabbath, Coleman Silk, or Bucky Cantor (undone by polio in *Nemesis*). Old age, death, and disease became fixations in his late writing, which intensified his anger to such a rage that in the final line of *Sabbath's Theater* Mickey Sabbath asks how he could die. "How could he leave? How could he go? Everything he hated was here" (ST 451). To end hate is to end life.

All of this, of course, is a further reaction to betrayal, but one Roth greedily and repeatedly explored in his fiction. And in his life, where they piled up: first, it was the incident at six with the locked door; then with the bathing suit and his virility at eleven; then the U.S. Army, where instead of a medal after approximately eleven months he got a backache; then his marriage to the deceptive Maggie; followed by repeated misgivings concerning his editors; then Bloom's deceptive attachment (she seemed more in love with her daughter than Roth), followed by her vengeful autobiographical narrative. His first biographer soon betrayed the trust Roth placed in him, confirmed by the negative interpretations of his attitude toward his mother, money, and women. And then there was the betrayal of his own body by illness. But Roth was not entirely blameless in these betrayals, having committed a number himself, including a series of affairs while married to Maggie and then to Bloom, and even while attached to other women. He also worked to undermine the work, if not careers, of others, such as Alan Lelchuk, Francine du Plessix Gray, and James Atlas.

In his fiction, the theme of betrayal is relentless, creating a sustained emotional insecurity and distrust to be met with anger, simultaneously aggressive and yet defensive. It ranges from Lucy Nelson to Peter Tarnopol, Ira Ringold, Herman Roth (in *The Plot Against America*), and Marcus Messner, who when challenged by the patronizing dean of his college over his multiple campus dorm moves and failure to attend chapel, responds with his own aggressive reply: "Fuck you!" (IND 231). Roth's characters do not retreat: they protest, and boldly; they fight, sometimes at the cost of their lives.

Sabbath's Theater, Roth's angriest text, was his favorite, keeping an oversized poster of the lurid Otto Dix cover painting in his Connecticut home. It was also the text he chose to read at his eightieth birthday celebration at the Newark Museum on 19 March 2013. The passage? An account of the inscriptions on Jewish gravestones in a South Jersey cemetery offering a chronicle of Jewish lives and revealing his own sense of an ending (ST 363–70). Read with sympathy but also an undertone of anger at the finality of death, it provided a capsule summary of Jewish history that had ended. Mickey Sabbath, Roth said in a preface to the passage, does not live with his back turned to death, and neither did Roth (PR80 58). Roth also said that he was the happiest when composing this novel, explaining that he was not genuinely angry: "I write about angry characters. When I'm doing that, I'm happy."[32] This transference of his anger on to that of his characters relieved Roth of the immediate pressures of his own aggressive behavior, the transference one of the principal accomplishments of his creative life, or why he turned to writing fiction rather than perhaps prizefighting and found it so satisfying.[33]

Illness, however, compounded Roth's discontent, the physical playing havoc with the psychological. Ever since he was ten, he had had medical problems, originating with a hernia, followed by an injured knee running into a first baseman during a summer softball game on the playground behind Chancellor Avenue School. The result was six weeks in a cast, leaving him with a protrusion below the knee. Next was his back injury while in the army at Fort Dix, New Jersey, caused by trying to right a tilting kettle of potatoes when his partner dropped his side and Roth instinctively jerked his end upward. One result, after hospitalization, was the need to wear a steel brace when he began to teach at the University of Chicago after his discharge—and a lifetime of back pain.

A burst appendix in the fall of 1967 initiated a series of mature health problems. New pain emerged in the 1970s caused not by lumbar spine problems but in the cervical section, described in *The Anatomy Lesson*, requiring a soft neck brace and relief by lying on the floor. Soon, further medical challenges: in the summer of 1982, an irregular EKG led to the discovery of a coronary blockage at only forty-nine. He began to take a beta blocker, which debilitated him and led to impotence. He sought surgery, but his doctors advised against it.

Leaving a swimming pool in January 1986, he developed a sore knee and soon couldn't climb stairs. This led to disastrous knee surgery at the Hospital for Special Surgery in New York, resulting in depression and paranoia brought on by painkillers and a new sleeping pill, Halcion, which led to an emotional slide, although his letters at the time suggest depression before he began taking the drug. Pain from the unsuccessful operation combined with the drug resulted in an extreme psychotic reaction, generating what Roth would call a suicidal depression in an essay he wrote on his pain and illness.

Next, an emergency quintuple coronary bypass in August 1989, what he had wanted seven years earlier. This was in the midst of his father's debilitating health caused by a brain tumor. More back pain followed, and various stents to open his carotid artery; soon he required more stents. In his last year of life, he claimed to have sixteen, an American League record, David Remnick joked in an appreciation of Roth shortly after his death on 22 May 2018.[34] He even experienced a silent heart attack. It is no surprise that the narrator of *Everyman* imagines writing an autobiography entitled *The Life and Death of the Male Body* (EV 52). Nor is it a surprise to learn that Roth's brother had two coronary bypass surgeries and died of congestive heart failure. His mother had died of a sudden heart attack in October 1981.

In the spring of 1993, depression set in again, his third encounter. His first occurred in 1974 because of his abrupt breakup with Barbara Sproul. By the summer of 1993, Roth was back at Silver Hill Hospital feeling desperate. At the same time, his marriage with Bloom was ending, and when she visited, he told her he wanted a divorce. What saved him was not the hospital, the Prozac, or the lithium, but a woman he met. He was there a total of thirty-six days over the two visits, the medical intervention, support of friends, and a new life without Bloom contributing to his recovery. At Silver Hill, he likely plotted how to extricate himself from Bloom and, despite his psychic distress, anticipated a new kind of freedom.[35] It is even possible he was orchestrating a kind of Sherwood Anderson departure from Bloom, a crafty breakdown that ends a marriage.[36] Bloom narrates this period and their painful encounters that August at the hospital in *Leaving a Doll's House* (200–204). In September, he had a second bout of depression and returned to the hospital unable to live alone in his farmhouse but definitely opposed to being with Bloom.

But occasionally, farce intervened. In September 2003, transferred from the Hungerford Hospital in Torrington, Connecticut, to Lenox Hill Hospital in New York for further tests, he traveled in a rickety ambulance driven by an orderly with an accompanying medic. Neither the driver nor the medic had ever been to New York, so Roth had to shout directions from the back. When they finally arrived, they were convinced they would be mugged. Too distracted to find the hospital entrance, they decided to stop at the corner of Lexington and 70th and slid Roth out, leaving him strapped to his gurney in a hospital gown at a crosswalk while they drove off to find parking. For fifteen minutes Roth remained "on view," while the public rushed by on a sunny Sunday afternoon in the fall with not a single New Yorker recognizing the Pulitzer Prize–winning novelist. Once they returned, they pulled Roth from the intersection and then pushed him up nearly six blocks to the hospital at 77th and Park before the driver and medic hastily and happily took off (PIH). They, like others, did not ask for an autograph.

These and other medical details underscore how persistently illness, pain, and medication contributed to Roth's distress, impeding his writing and behavior. For example, his withdrawal from the pain reliever Vicodin intensified his back pain to such an extent that he would break down and cry. Sleepless nights were common, and he remembered wandering his New York apartment recalling the death of his Aunt Ethel dying of cancer in the twin bed of his Leslie Street home when he was a teenager. Roth's back pain was wearing him out, so he eventually underwent a second back surgery in May 2005.

Illness has a tenacious presence in his fiction. *The Breast* may be its satiric expression, but *The Anatomy Lesson* is not. Nor is the unsuccessful heart surgery of Henry Zuckerman, who miraculously survives in *The Counterlife* (where Nathan also undergoes a heart operation in order to sustain his new relationship with the twenty-seven-year-old Maria—the thinly disguised writer Janet Hobhouse) or the cancer of Drenka Balich in *Sabbath's Theater*,

or the breast cancer of Consuela in *The Dying Animal,* or the heart operations of the seventy-one-year-old *Everyman,* who, though dead, narrates the
tale. The brain tumor of Amy Bellette in *Exit Ghost,* echoed in the appendicitis attack of Marcus Messner in *Indignation* and the polio that runs through
Nemesis, extend Roth's preoccupation with illness and pain. The despair pain
generates becomes so deep that Millicent Kramer in *Everyman* commits suicide, the shame of infirmity overpowering her ability to survive (EV 92).[37]

"Old age isn't a battle: old age is a massacre," Roth wrote in *Everyman,*
adding, "Life's most disturbing intensity is death. It's because death is so
unjust" (EV 156, 169). Unfairness, again. The novel begins and ends in a
cemetery, increasingly the site of choice for Roth: his encounter in the text
with a gravedigger is a memorable discussion of the meaning of death and
disappearance echoing Hamlet in Act V Scene 1 (EV 171–80). And a cemetery is where Zuckerman in *The Anatomy Lesson* falls and breaks his jaw.
A cemetery is also where Mickey Sabbath eulogizes the many Jewish lives
represented by the multiple gravestones he reads and where Roth's characters
even write their own imaginary obituaries (ST 195). In late Roth, one cannot
escape them.

Roth's writing is a testament to and an accounting of a militant discontent expressed through his characters and their rebellions, rejections, and
refusals. Its origin is multiple; during his early writing years in Chicago he
began each morning by shouting at the young face peering out from the
mirror at him, "'Attack! Attack!' certain that I would prevail, if only by sheer
perseverance" (WR 316). This aggressive attitude sustained him through
eighty-five years, alienating some, while enlivening others in his search for
honesty.

Nowhere was this more evident than in his decision to have a biography.
He despised the idea and often satirized the accuracy of narrated lives, seen
in the pursuits of Richard Kliman in *Exit Ghost.* But the apparent distortions
and lies offered up by Bloom demanded a response. A biography that
exposed her errors and set the record straight would be the answer and prevent anyone else from seizing her account and using it as the basis of a life.
Her autobiography of 1996 had already turned the public against the dismis-
sive, self-serving, aggravating, and money-conscious Roth. A documented
life would counter the distortions.

At first, Ross Miller would be the author. Miller had been editing the
Library of America edition of Roth's works, but the inadequacy of Miller's
editing of volume 3 of the series plus inaction concerning interviews and

research and a growing lack of sympathy for Roth's past behavior, especially with women, led to Roth's breaking their contact. But he was still determined to have his story told and, after vetting Hermione Lee and Steven Zipperstein, settled on Blake Bailey, author of biographies of John Cheever, Richard Yates, and Charles Jackson. Following several meetings, they agreed on a contract, with Roth giving Bailey carte blanche and full access to his archive. Roth also prepared several lengthy documents for Bailey in response to distortions he believed Miller was promoting, especially concerning Roth, money, and women.[38]

During his life Roth seems to have become a character of his own invention, whether Portnoy, Tarnopol, or Sabbath, the figure he chose to cite at his final public reading, held at the 92nd Street Y in New York on 8 May 2014. His construction of alternate selves (see *The Facts, Operation Shylock, The Plot Against America*) may have been a proactive escape from his actual self. His photographs suggest a divided self: in formal photos, he appears stern and serious and rarely smiles, but in candid pictures he laughs, smiles, and enjoys himself, the thoughtful author in contrast with the comic individual. Every cover in the Library of America series has a black-and-white photograph of an aging (and unsmiling) Roth staring out on its cover; only the last, as a finale, is in color. Under each three-quarter-page image is his name in large Baskerville type stretching across the cover in case we don't recognize the face. The format never changed throughout the ten volumes, only Roth's picture oddly echoing Dorian Gray, whose portrait aged, but not the person.

In many ways, Roth became the Rashomon of his own life, creating a set of intersecting subjective narratives. What was in balance was the struggle between "the rawness and the mess," the "embarrassment and the shame," and a desire for regular, everyday life brought into relief at Zuckerman's funeral in *The Counterlife,* when a bearded mourner rails against a sanitized eulogy (more like a book review, he complains), while he thinks of the writer who broke taboos and "fucked around" (CL 218–19).

The concern of this narrative is with the biographical roots and evolution of Roth's anger and corresponding need for control, its causes and expression, which continued even after his death. Not only did he specify the nature of his nondenominational burial at Bard College, but he also detailed the order and speakers at his memorial service held several months later at the New York Public Library, including the music and the food to be provided by the Russian Samovar, one of his favorite restaurants. He also made it clear who was, and was *not*, to be invited.[39] To the end, he remained, and remains, in control, directing his story and how it should be told. Longfellow originally outlined the scheme: to a friend he wrote, "I suppose you think I am dead. But it is not so; I am only *buried*."[40]

1

Newark, Newark, Newark

I once reminded Philip Roth that the Jews were born in the desert, not in Newark. I don't think this made any impression at all.
—Alfred Kazin, *Journal*, 20 January 1990

The story of Newark is America's story.
—Lyndon B. Johnson on the three-hundredth anniversary of the city, 1966

Establishing his credentials in *The Anatomy Lesson*, Nathan Zuckerman proudly announces that he is "not an authority on Israel. I'm an authority on Newark. Not even on Newark. On the Weequahic section of Newark. If the truth be known, not even on the whole of the Weequahic section. I don't even go below Bergen Street" (AL 99).

The source of this knowledge was not just Roth's remembrance of everyday encounters in the neighborhood he lovingly re-creates in *I Married a Communist* and *The Plot Against America*, but his father, who would return nightly with tales of the city. Herman Roth's business with the ethnic population of the city to whom he pitched life insurance resulted in endless stories for the young Philip and his slightly older brother, Sandy.

I

The Facts describes Roth's early life in Weequahic and the bounded, segregated life of the neighborhood: "Not only did growing up Jewish in Newark in the thirties and forties . . . feel like a perfectly legitimate way of growing up American but, what's more, growing up Jewish as I did and growing up American seemed to me indistinguishable" (FAC 122). The neighborhoods were as insulated and protected as a rural Indiana community, something

Roth seems to have tested with his later time in Iowa and the Midwest, the setting for *When She Was Good* (FAC 30). But Newark was a set of gated communities: Weequahic the Jewish ghetto, the North Ward the Italian, and the Central Ward the Black. The city was made up of small, self-contained towns, and each had its own taverns, stores, and churches, according to one Newark historian.[1] What is important to note is that Roth's Newark evolved: initially a safe and functional city of workers, it became a dangerous, riot-prone enclave of almost uncontrollable poverty and anger. Initially a fictional, atmospheric backdrop in "Goodbye, Columbus," by the time of *American Pastoral* it had become a tragic character in the story. What engages Roth in the city of the Levovs is what has been destroyed. And after *American Pastoral*, the city languishes until its capitulation to polio in his final novel, *Nemesis*.

At one point in *The Anatomy Lesson*, Roth's hero remarks that he wants "an active connection to life and I want it now. I want an active connection to *myself*" (AL 204). Roth's story, his connection to life, begins in Newark, a mixed community of roughly 420,000 Germans, Italians, Slavs, and Irish, where he was born on 19 March 1933 (the same year as James Brown, Roman Polanski, and Susan Sontag).[2] The Blacks and Jews formed minorities, with the Jews living mainly in the Weequahic section, an up-and-coming lower-middle-class neighborhood in the southeast corner of the city. In 1971, Roth referred to the area as his "nation-neighborhood," a "demi-Israel in a Newark that was our volatile Middle East" (RMY 213). Revisiting the neighborhood in 2010, Roth quipped that its name derived "from an old Lenape word meaning 'Is it good for the Jews?'"[3] Port Newark was an active, international port, while Newark itself was a manufacturing hub. The psychological impact of Newark, however, became one of insularity, unreality, and protectiveness, especially for the Jews. While there were frequent, often physical encounters with Italians, Germans, and others, the Jews essentially felt shielded from genuine threats. But for Roth, next to the inhibiting influence of family, especially his authoritarian father, Newark meant restrictions rather than freedoms. (Later, guided by nostalgia, he'd fictionalize the city as a place of positive Jewish identity and social reinforcement—a Jewish Arcadia.) Newark segregated and divided even the Jews, as "Goodbye, Columbus" makes clear. One neighborhood did not mix with another, and Newarkers had no business being in Short Hills or West Orange.

Newark became less an idyllic reminiscence than an early source of his discontent and disenchantment. It also accelerated his resolve to be independent. Newark became the dark world Nathan Zuckerman revisits at the end of *Zuckerman Unbound*. Protected by a driver with a gun, he senses the socially destructive space later described in *American Pastoral* and the fiery city attacking Jews and others in *The Plot Against America*. Remembered, Newark meant safety, but experienced, it brought anxiety and warnings, frequently pronounced by Alex Portnoy's oracle-like mother in *Portnoy's Complaint*.

Defining the Jewish context for inescapable Newark, one might begin in its cemeteries. In *Patrimony*, Roth accidentally passes by the cemetery where his mother was buried when he misses the exit to take him to North Avenue in Elizabeth and his father's apartment (PAT 19). He then refers to two earlier visits to the cemetery, one at his mother's funeral in 1981 and then a year later to show his father her headstone. This third visit he doesn't quite call "mystical," but he is amazed to realize that twenty minutes from New York he could be at this Jewish burial ground. With wonder and a sense of the macabre, he writes that even though he wasn't searching for the cemetery consciously or unconsciously, "on the morning when I was to tell my father of the brain tumor that would kill him, I had flawlessly traveled the straightest possible route from my Manhattan hotel to my mother's grave and the grave site beside hers where he was to be buried" (PAT 20).

Although he didn't want to keep his father waiting, he paused at his mother's graveside. He sought neither comfort nor courage there but realized, at the foot of her grave, that he had "to bow to its impelling force" (PAT 20). Thoughts of death and burial follow and the realization that overshadowing any emotional power is that the "dead seem even more distant and out of reach than they did" before, although you can do "some pretty crazy things to make the dead seem something other than dead." But even if you can somehow "*feel their presence*, you still walk away without them." Cemeteries only reinforce the feeling that although the dead are gone, we, "as yet, aren't" (PAT 21). Death and memory, whether of people or place, are inextricable.

In the triangulated cemetery area, now administered by the Gomel Chesed Cemetery Association, Bess and later Herman Roth are buried alongside Joseph and Mildred Komisar, Roth's mother's sister and her husband. The four headstones are neatly aligned. The headstones of the Roths read "Bess Roth / 1904–1981" and "Herman Roth / 1901–1989." Buried not far from the Roths are Allen Ginsberg and his parents.

Newark itself originated when Puritans seeking land with easy access to major waterways on which to establish their own theocracy purchased property along the Passaic River from the Hackensack Indians in May

1666 to found "New-Ark" or "Our Town on Passaick River." Abundant raw materials such as the tamarack tree's bark for tannin, the hides of wild animals for leather, and iron, as well as natural resources such as water for drinking, drainage, agriculture, livestock, transportation, and commerce, played a crucial role not only in transforming Newark into an industrial center and transportation hub but in pulling several industries to its location. Leatherworkers, for example, quickly developed a collective expertise for shoe and boot production because of their unlimited access to tannin.[4]

Jewish immigrants to Newark began to arrive early, the first Jewish resident (Louis Trier) settling in 1844. The major wave of Jewish immigrants from Europe, largely from Russia, Poland, Germany, and the Austro-Hungarian Empire, occurred in 1881–1882, and they continued to settle in the city through the 1920s. Roth's grandparents arrived during this wave of immigration from Poland. Prince Street was often the first point of residence, but as their economic conditions improved, Jews headed toward Clinton Hill and, finally, Weequahic, where the Roths lived. At its height in 1948, the Jewish population of Newark topped 56,800, the seventh largest Jewish population in the U.S., roughly 12 percent of the city's residents.[5]

Early immigrants, concentrated in the Third Ward and around Prince Street, had their own Yiddish-English weekly newspaper. For almost two decades, beginning in 1921, the *Jewish Morning Star/Yiddisher Morgenstern*, edited by Dr. Isaac Unterman, a rabbi, attorney, author, and noted scholar, appeared. Headquarters for the paper was 163 Prince Street, in the heart of Newark's heavily Jewish Third Ward. Each issue ranged from four to twelve pages and contained local Jewish news, plus the opinions of its editor-publisher about Hebrew events and religion—subjects on which Dr. Unterman had written numerous books in English, Yiddish, and Hebrew.

At one time, Newark could boast of fifty-three synagogues; by 1948 the number had fallen to just over forty; by 1998 there were only two within the city limits, and neither occupied a building from the previous century.[6] The fate of the buildings changed often: the Prince Street synagogue, built in 1884 by the Oheb Shalom congregation, founded in 1860 (the third synagogue organized in Newark), conducted services in German until sometime in the 1880s. English then became standard. The Moorish-style building was transferred to the Adas Israel congregation in 1911 and later sold to the Metropolitan Baptist Church, whose members worshiped there from 1940 to 1993. It was scheduled for demolition when it was rescued at the last moment and restored by the Greater Newark Conservancy.

Despite the intensity of synagogue life in Newark—at one time there were seventeen in Weequahic—the Roths attended irregularly.[7] They likely went twice a year to the Schley Street Synagogue, two blocks north but parallel with Leslie Street. Newark's *Jewish Chronicle* of 20 June 1941 featured this small but important synagogue in its twentieth-anniversary issue. "Schley Street Synagogue Is Pioneer Congregation in Weequahic Section" was the headline. (Ironically, Albert Schley was the local leader of the Friends of the New Germany, a pro-Nazi Newark organization of the 1930s and 1940s.) Founded in 1932, the Schley Street Synagogue was officially known as the Torah Chaim Jewish Center. The original rabbi was Herman L. Kahan, and the Hebrew teacher, who might have taught Roth, was Rabbi Gedaliah Convissor, indirectly cited in *The Facts* (FAC 121).

In his quasi-autobiography, Roth also cites a Mr. Rosenblum, a refugee teacher who escaped Nazism and the *shamash,* and a Mr. Fox, who would collar young pinball-playing boys at the local candy store and drag them to be part of a *minyan* (FAC 120–21). The Schley Street Synagogue's Talmud Torah was where Dr. Franz Kafka teaches in Roth's essay-fiction "Looking at Kafka" (RMY 301). In an interview discussing the Library of America edition of his novels, Roth recalled two refugees who taught at his Hebrew school who, despite numerous American distractions, were dedicated to the ancient language. "I thought 'what if one of them had been Franz Kafka?' Thus the metamorphosis from a biographical essay into biographical fantasy."[8]

A 1981 letter to Roth from Marcia Kahan Rosenthal, niece of Rabbi Kahan, recalled Weequahic days. A year or two behind Roth at Weequahic High, she remembered walking with Roth along Chancellor Avenue while he chatted up her friend Natalie Cornfield, also known as "Red." He headed to Leslie Street, Rosenthal to Schley. She suggests that her uncle was, indeed, as pompous and affected as described in *Portnoy,* although other members of her family were upset with *Goodbye, Columbus* and for the same reasons as Mr. Zuckerman: its unflattering portrait of Newark Jews. Nevertheless, she tells Roth that his work has reminded her constantly of the Leslie Sweet Shoppe, Rubin's Drug Store, Syd's, The Annex, Mrs. Lappe's class, and Mr. Castellucio's lab. In a brief reply, Roth writes that he does, indeed, remember her and Natalie Cornfield: "I can't forget any of it either."[9]

Roth attended Hebrew School for three years and had his Bar Mitzvah at the Schley Street Synagogue, an experience more formative for the impression made by the elderly, often European teachers out of step with their younger students than for the impact of Jewish learning. This emerged in his

1973 essay-story, "I Always Wanted You to Admire My Fasting; or Looking at Kafka," where Kafka becomes Roth's fictitious 1942 Hebrew teacher. "The Conversion of the Jews" and "Eli, the Fanatic" from *Goodbye, Columbus* may also have Schley Street origins. Nevertheless, retrospectively Roth claims that growing up Jewish and growing up American in the 1930s and 1940s were indistinguishable, more wish fulfillment than fact given the rise of anti-Semitism, marked by the 1939 Nazi rally at Madison Square Garden in February 1939. More than twenty thousand attended. Israel had not yet formed, nor the nostalgia for the world of Sholom Aleichem. And in Roth's family, there was a "willful amnesia" about their Eastern European past, especially when he queried aunts and uncles (FAC 123).

But the Newark Jewish community did have several important religious leaders during Roth's youth, beginning with Rabbi Joachim Prinz, expelled from Germany in 1937 after many arrests for his outspoken views of Jewish nationalism and telling many to leave Nazi Germany for Palestine. In 1934, he had published *Wir Juden* (We Jews), expressing a popular, nationalist theology. But America did not impress: during a short visit in March 1937 Rabbi Prinz complained about the indifference of American Jews to Hitler's new power and abuse of German Jews. He also felt America, with its racism and naïve political views, could not match the intellectual appeal of Germany—and he felt the country was ugly. But new threats on his return to Germany made his final departure imperative.

In Prinz's autobiography, he describes a huge farewell lecture he gave on 26 June 1937 in Berlin, which Adolf Eichmann, then a minor official in the Gestapo, attended. In a long report for his superior, Heinrich Himmler, Eichmann noted that Prinz's going to America meant he could now head an international Jewish propaganda bureau. Himmler promoted Eichmann for his convincing report.[10]

But the night before his departure, Prinz was arrested for treason; miraculously, he was released at 4:00 a.m. and allowed to depart for Paris with his family, where they remained for several days. Interestingly, their passports had a stamp that forbade them from attending the Paris World's Fair: "Jews are not permitted there" it read.[11] Realizing that the Germans had no control over them in France, they went anyway. From Le Havre they sailed for New York, traveling with the Folies Bergère, then making *their* first trip to America. Prinz arrived ostensibly as a representative of The United Palestine Appeal to promote Zionism in America but quickly became a spokesperson for the fate of the Jews in Germany.

To the high-minded Prinz, America was "an empty land," a description reinforced by his unsympathetic view of American Jews and rabbis, who possessed, it seemed, no intellect.[12] Particularly surprising was his realization that Jews lived in their own neighborhoods, in contrast to Berlin, where they were integrated throughout the city. The very thing Roth would celebrate— the Jewish nature of Weequahic—Prinz would despise, unable to understand why Jews wanted to live only among themselves.[13] Unwilling to accept a rabbinical post in his new country, Prinz took a position as educational director of the American Jewish Congress, but the offer was withdrawn because of internal politics. In 1958, however, he became president of the organization and invited Martin Luther King Jr. as the keynote speaker.[14]

As a Jewish refugee from Hitler, Prinz had few opportunities, but despite his criticisms of American Jewry, and American Jewry's criticism of him for his pessimistic view of the fate of European Jews, he accepted the pulpit of Temple B'nai Abraham in Newark in 1939, which had fallen on difficult financial times. The massive circular building designed in a "Greek style" could hold nearly one thousand on the High Holidays. His pulpit allowed him to reinforce his role as a bellwether for the Jewish situation in Europe, while vocally opposing all social and religious prejudice in America.[15] He would remain the rabbi for some thirty-eight years and in the early 1960s facilitated Roth's first visit to Israel, where he met David Ben-Gurion.

Taking over the largest synagogue in Newark, once known for its wealthy members and imposing structure (Roth calls it an "oval fortress" in *The Plot Against America,* the novel where Prinz makes his own appearance), was a challenge. Although the building contained a social hall, gym and swimming pool, and a large sanctuary, the congregation was financially and religiously bankrupt (PAA 133, 247, 268). By contrast, Newark at that time was thriving as the center of the costume jewelry and hat-making business. In addition, breweries, tanneries, and national insurance companies were prospering.

Roth understood Prinz as an important Jewish spokesperson with a singular past, but he also admired another of his attributes: Prinz's attitude toward sex. The rabbi objected to monogamy and in his autobiography detailed his premarital sexual adventures, especially with Lucie, who would become his first wife. He refers to her as sexually adventurous, inventive, and almost deviant. With unintentional humor he recalls that after their first night of sex, in a field, he responded (in an almost a Woody-Allenesque manner) to the moon and the stars by thinking of Kant and his line in *Critique of Pure Reason* where he discusses "the relationship of the moon, stars and moral conscience."[16] Experiences with his second wife were as momentous. It seemed natural that he would become an early admirer of Roth.

Ironically, one of Prinz's strongest Jewish allies was the gangster and bootlegger Abner "Longy" Zwillman, who grew up in the Third Ward on Charlton Street. Over six feet tall (hence the nickname), Zwillman willingly contributed to helping Jewish immigrants when asked by Prinz, who initially seemed unaware of Zwillman's extortion and bootlegging activities; he was also thought to be a founding member of the Murder Incorporated crime syndicate and made steady payments to the helpful Newark Police Department. He organized the Third Ward Gang, led by the Jewish boxer Nat Arno, which regularly battled Nazi supporters. In Newark, he controlled the telephone union and within twenty-four hours obtained a phone for Prinz when no one else could. Sam Teiger, who owned the well-known Tavern Restaurant (partly supported by Zwillman because he had a speakeasy on the second floor), facilitated the deal.

Prinz, Zwillman's spiritual advisor, reports in his autobiography that he aided Zwillman by marrying his "triggerman," supposedly a Kohen, to a divorced woman, traditionally not allowed.[17] Another friend of Prinz was Mayor Meyer Ellenstein, a childhood buddy friend of Zwillman and twice tried on charges of corruption but never convicted.[18] It was Prinz who officiated at Zwillman's funeral. These and other Jewish figures, such as Dutch Schultz (Arthur Flegenheimer), gunned down in a Newark toilet on 23 October 1935, represent the underside of Newark Jewish life, glossed over by Roth in his upbeat portrayal of Weequahic.

While at B'nai Abraham, Prinz remained an outspoken critic of German anti-Semitism and Nazi atrocities, warning not only the community but the country of the danger. Prinz was an activist and a dominating Jewish figure in Newark and the nation, and young Roth could hardly have avoided him. Yet, he repeatedly denied that Prinz was the model for Rabbi Bengelsdorf in *The Plot Against America* who becomes an apologist for Lindbergh. Prinz and Bengelsdorf were political adversaries in the novel, and Prinz is the only Newark rabbi to boycott the wedding of Bengelsdorf's daughter; he never "flinched in his opposition to Lindbergh"(PAA 247). And late in the novel it is Prinz who stops an imagined anti-Semitic attack against Newark's Jews (PAA 343).

Other Jewish public figures underscoring the predominance of Jewish life in Newark and the state were Oscar R. Wilensky, the first Jewish state senator elected in New Jersey, in 1940, and Rabbi Horace Zemel, who in 1942 became the first Jewish chaplain of the Newark police and fire departments.[19] Jewish philanthropists were also notable, beginning with the Baltimore-born Louis Bamberger of department store fame, who donated the buildings for the Newark Museum and the New Jersey Historical Society while supporting the new Jewish Y and establishing Princeton University's Institute of Advanced Study. Leonard Dreyfus gave the planetarium to the Newark Museum. In 1922, Bamberger, with Felix Fuld, launched a building drive that led to the erection and opening of the magnificent new Hebrew Y at 652 High Street in 1924. Soon membership soared to 4,500, with the High Street facility becoming the second largest YM-YWHA in the United States. This center of culture in a Jewish setting offered concerts, lectures, rallies, and occasionally Broadway shows. From 1924 to 1954, it remained on High Street, now Martin Luther King Boulevard. It also became a hangout for Herman Roth and his son, as would the YMHA in Elizabeth, New Jersey, where, to his son's dismay, years later his father would leave his *tefillin* (used in weekday morning prayer) in a locker for anyone to inherit (PAT 92–97).

Weequahic was not the only Jewish neighborhood of Newark. The Third Ward was another, less established, and rougher area but home to a series of Jewish notables, the best known the playwright and MGM producer Dore Schary, whose family operated a kosher catering business. Ed Koch, three-time mayor of New York and five-term New York congressman, who once worked with Herman Roth in the checkroom of the Krueger Auditorium on Belmont Avenue, was another. Curtis Lucas, a novelist, wrote a crime novel entitled *Third Ward Newark* (1946) set in the district. It dealt with the rape of a Black woman by white men because she witnessed a murder. Nathan Heard published *Howard Street* (the name of a crime-ridden street in the Third Ward) in 1968, written while doing time for armed robbery in the Trenton State Penitentiary. The population of the Third Ward dropped from 36,910 in 1910 to 25,830 in 1940, with just 2,300 Jewish residents (mainly grandparents to Roth's generation or working class).

The Third Ward was also the home for a good number of Jewish boxers, the sons of immigrants. The years from 1910 to 1940 were often called "The Golden Age of the American Jewish Boxer." During that period, when boxing was the most popular sport in America, Jewish boxers dominated, with twenty-six world champions. At one point, there were more than twenty thousand registered Jewish boxers nationally.[20] Roth, with his father and brother, often attended matches (PAT 201–3).

One boxer, Hymie Kugel, went on to be a respected referee, while the former Third Warder Dr. Max Novich won entry into medical school on a boxing scholarship and created sports medicine as a new medical specialty, founding the Association of Ringside Physicians in 1971. Additional notables among Newark's Jewish boxers included the two-term Depression-era mayor, Meyer C. Ellenstein, and the Newark bagel king, Sonny Amster.[21] The professional boxing sites in Newark in the 1920s and 1930s were Laurel Garden, the Newark Velodrome, Dreamland Park, the Newark Armory, and the Broad Athletic Club.

Jewish boxers soon had another role: combating the pro-Nazi groups springing up in the city. In the mid- to late 1930s, many of Newark's Jewish boxers from the Third Ward were recruited into an organization designed to counter the pro-Nazi activities of a Newark-area group called The Friends of New Germany. The name of the anti-Nazi organization was The Minutemen; Arno organized them with the backing of the Third Ward's crime boss, Longy Zwillman.[22]

The Minutemen provided the necessary resolve and muscle to prevent or break up pro-Hitler meetings and propaganda efforts. Organized in 1933, the group lasted until the start of World War II, combating the Friends of New Germany and its successor, the German-American Bund. Zwillman offered men, money, and, when necessary, political influence in the battle against anti-Semitic gangs who would regularly infiltrate the Third Ward. It was Zwillman and his gang who provoked a fight on 16 October 1933 at the Schwabenhalle, a meeting hall on Springfield Avenue for German American societies decorated with a large swastika banner for the event, a mile west of the Third Ward. With Hymie "The Weasel" Kugel, Julius "Skinny" Markowitz, "Primo" Weiner, and others, Zwillman's gang, numbering nearly two hundred, wrapped iron pipes in newspapers, hid them in an alley adjacent to the hall, and, following a diversion, attacked. Soon, twelve city blocks were involved in the melee marked by stink bombs, tear gas, and physical injuries.[23] The seeds of anti-Nazi protest were sprouting.

The Third Ward, with a growing Black population in the 1930s and 1940s, was where Herman Roth almost daily sought clients for the Metropolitan Insurance Company, recalled in *Patrimony*. He knew the neighborhood well and remembered Longy Zwillman and his gang, who defended, when necessary, the peddlers and Orthodox Jews. All of this action, turning into Jewish lore, was part of Roth's upbringing, even if he did not write about it.

II

Both of Roth's parents were first-generation Americans: they were each born in the U.S., Herman Roth in Newark in 1901, the middle child of seven born to Sender and Bertha Roth, immigrants from Polish Galicia. He had no more than an eighth grade education and began working early, attempting at one point a shoe store and then becoming a city marshal. His hard work provided for his family through a long career at the Metropolitan Life Insurance Company, rising to be manager of a district office in South Jersey with fifty-two employees. His self-discipline and determination, supported by will-power, drove him—as well as an implacable sense of duty toward those for whom he was responsible (PAT 79). That meant his family.

Herman Roth also had what his son called a "peremptory personality," who constantly admonished others, unaware of its damaging impact. Badgering can be effective, he believed; all you need to do is constantly *hock mir ein*

Figure 1.1 Philip Roth at four months old at Belmar, New Jersey, with his parents, Herman and Bess Roth, and his brother, Sandy, 1933. Credit: Newark Public Library.

chinick, literally "bang me with a teapot." The popular Yiddish phrase means "drive them crazy with talk." Why do I continue hocking, the father asked once in a letter to his son, Sandy. Because "if its [*sic*] people I *care for* I will try to cure, even if they object or won't disciplin [*sic*] themselves[.] I including myselve [*sic*]." He signed the letter "The Hocker, Misnomer / it should be the carer / Love / Dad." And then, in a final flourish, "Hock and Care. That's me / to people I care / for" (PAT 81–82). His advice was relentless. He never procrastinated. "I am a doer," he proclaimed, a practice transferred to his younger son (PAT 81).

All of this was in contrast to Herman's laconic father, Sender, authoritarian and remote, who had trained to be a rabbi in Galicia but in America worked in a hat factory. But even if the father was remote and emotionally austere, the son, Herman, kept his father's shaving cup, a kind of totem of his presence as a person, not a patriarch (PAT 27).

Neighborhoods were central for the first generation of Jewish immigrants, and Prince Street, as well as Springfield Avenue and Broome Street, was the center of Eastern European Newark Jewish life. Many chose Newark because of work: during the first two decades of the new century there were more than two thousand factories plus public works projects.[24] But as soon as Jewish families could afford to, they moved on to Clinton Hill and then Weequahic.

In 1901 Beth Israel Hospital was founded, partly because Jewish doctors were barred from working in other hospitals. In 1929 it moved to Lyons Avenue and a new structure with three hundred beds. It was the first hospital in the state to allow Jewish and African American doctors to practice medicine, and it was where Roth was born on 19 March 1933. Dr. Ira Flaxman was the obstetrician, whose given name Roth favored. Ira Posner, a retired psychiatrist, appears in *American Pastoral* (53–54) and Ira Ringold is the central figure of *I Married a Communist*.[25]

Newark also had a strong Zionist movement with such clubs as Young Judea, Mizrachi, and Poale Zion. In September 1922, more than eight thousand Jews marched up Broad Street to celebrate the ratification of the Palestine Mandate. Figures from Chaim Weizmann to Ze'ev Jabotinsky spoke in Newark. Part of the support was reaction against anti-Semitism. In 1930 the owner of a service station in Troy, New York, was ordered to remove a sign that read "No Jews or dogs allowed." That same year a man from Irvington, New Jersey, adjacent to Newark, was refused a rental at a nearby New Jersey resort on the grounds that he was Jewish.[26] Anti-Semitism was real.

Socialism also held sway for many in Newark, the result of labor man-agement conflicts, poverty, and a concern for social justice. The Workmen's Circle vied with Bundists to sway the workers. Bootleg liquor was another thriving "industry." *Der Langer,* Yiddish for "Longy" or "the tall one," con-trolled things, with Zwillman (who began as a teenager in the numbers racket) and his associate Joe Reinfeld dominating the liquor business with additional tentacles in Florida and Nevada gaming activities.[27] At his peak, Zwillman supposedly imported 40 percent of the illegal liquor entering the U.S.[28]

The war also increasingly brought social protest. Alarm over the rise of National Socialism in Germany and support for the Nazis in Newark saw a protest as early as 1933, when more than two thousand Jews organized at the Y on High Street in March. On that day Prince Street merchants closed their shops five hours early after a day of fasting and prayer in sympathy with Germany's Jews. That same day twenty-two thousand Jews held a rally in Madison Square Garden.[29] As Roth would later comment, awareness of the war was something he grew up with: ten years old in 1943, he was alert to Allied advances, German defeats, and the fate of the Jews. The radio gave constant updates, and war remained *the* topic of conversation in his family. At Weequahic High, once a week they sang songs in the auditorium that supported the armed forces, including the classics "Off We Go, into the Wild Blue Yonder" and "When the Caissons Go Rolling Along."

Herman Roth's work at the insurance company (starting around $82 a week) was considered a well-paying job at the time, but when he was not working, his interests were family, politics, the newspapers, boxing, and sto-rytelling. "Narrative is the form that his knowledge takes," Roth wrote in 1988, the year before his father died, and it was never large: "family, family, family, Newark, Newark, Newark, Jew, Jew Jew" (FAC 16). But he could also be stubborn and determined, as various domestic confrontations confirmed.

Undermining Herman Roth's authority in October 1944, when he was forty-three, was an emergency appendectomy. Most worrisome was that two of his brothers had died in the 1920s from complications following a sim-ilar operation. Ironically, the night he was to go to the hospital, after waiting for his two sons to come home to tell them directly, his wife was in Atlantic City at a Parent-Teacher Association convention. Told on the phone of his condition, she made immediate plans to return. Although he was given to worrying constantly about daily uncertainties, Herman was now in a posi-tion where he had to assure everyone that he would be well. Doctors were less confident. Six weeks later, he came home and began a recovery that was slow and saw swift swings in mood (FAC 12). What drove him to health, however, was sheer determination to overcome all obstacles.

Bess (Beatrice) Finkel, Roth's mother, born in Elizabeth, New Jersey, in 1904, was the second of five children born to Philip and Dora Finkel, immigrants from near Kiev. According to Roth in *The Facts*, she adored her mother but feared her tyrannical father. She helped to raise two younger sisters and loved her only brother, Mickey, who became an artist in Philadelphia and survived financially through photography. Bess, trained as a typist who also knew shorthand, worked as a secretary in a law office after her graduation from Battin High on Broad Street in Elizabeth in 1922. She lived at home with her parents. She grew up in a prosperous family in a large home on North Broad Street in Elizabeth, her father and his three brothers running a fuel supply company, initially coal and then oil. Finkel Fuels appeared on trucks all over the city, but the prosperity ended when the brothers feuded.

She married Herman Roth on 22 February 1927, and they spent their honeymoon weekend at the Riviera Hotel at 169 Clinton Avenue. Built in 1922, it became a Newark residence for businessmen and legal figures doing business with the county and city. It becomes the location of Dr. Kotler's office in *The Anatomy Lesson*, and in *The Plot Against America* is his (Roth's) parents' honeymoon headquarters (PAA 133).

After the marriage and the birth of Sandy, born 26 December 1927, named after his grandfather Sender, Bess stayed at home. Reserved and reticent, loving but emotionally restrained, her behavior may have partly originated in her family's traumatic past, which she wanted to hide. She was anxious that the financial failure of her father and ruin of the family might spill out if she let her emotions reign in either love or anger. After her father lost the money from his share of the fuel business and then the family home, the entire issue of patriarchal authority was undone. She likely wanted to see it restored and knew that only through female passivity would a male be able to reassert such confidence, hence her giving way to Herman's forceful manner.[30] She was also too embarrassed to ever mention these events to either son. Bess kept both the prosperity and the decline a secret; Roth did not learn of either until very late in his life, long after her death.

By comparison, Uncle Mickey seemed downright rebellious, even Bohemian. No accountancy for him: only art. And when he could afford it, he would regularly close his studio and head to Europe to copy paintings and sculptures in the museums, an act Herman thought completely irresponsible.

Nevertheless, Bess believed the artistic interests of Roth and his brother derived from their uncle. Art in the Roth home meant paintings by Uncle Mickey. The unconventional uncle stood out among family members for both Roth and his brother. And when Sandy expressed an interest in art, the sardonic Mickey tried to discourage him but did give him several books to study, including George B. Bridgman's *Constructive Anatomy,* first published in 1920. When Sandy brought the book home, it was the first time Roth saw any nudes. Soon Sandy went to New York on Saturdays to take a course in life drawing at the Art Students' League, where Bridgman taught, only to be quizzed by a fascinated Roth when he returned: What did the nude models look like? How did they pose? What did they say? And how could he sit in a room with a nude woman and only draw?

Music also had a minor role in the home. Although they did not have a record player, Bess and Herman were expert whistlers, which was popular on the radio at that time. One of Roth's strongest memories was arriving home at lunchtime, walking up the driveway to the back door at 81 Summit Avenue, and, as he sprung up the stairs to their second-floor flat, hearing his mother whistle in the kitchen. It meant more than a happy parent: it meant domestic security. Hearing her whistle ensured his return to a personal world of stability (NOT 4–5).

Bess was a renowned organizer of the household, whether finances, clothes, or their health. Indeed, Roth praised the neatness, orderliness, and cleanliness of their home, in contrast to his brother, who felt uncomfortable with the restrictive sense of order and constant cleaning. When Roth was about ten, his mother taught him to type, typing the method to organize one's thoughts. In 1943, Roth began one of his earliest writing ventures, "Storm Off Hatteras," an action-filled story written on his mother's typewriter in the kitchen. He did not put his own name on the page, believing it was not a writer's name. He preferred the more courageous and heroic "Eric Duncan." "I sometimes wish I had hid behind that name," he later comically said, considering the scandalized responses to several of his books. "Storm" was a sea adventure off Cape Hatteras, reflecting the influence of Howard Pease, a young adult adventure writer, among others.[31]

Bess was a devoted homemaker who looked after her boys, becoming at one point president of the Chancellor Avenue Parent-Teacher Association. She knew all of Roth's instructors. She kept a kosher kitchen, lit Shabbos candles, and carried out the responsibilities of Passover, although more because of ties to her childhood than any deeply held religious obligation.

She also took pleasure in doing the right thing and was well-spoken, with studied social graces (FAC 44, 119). Her principal reading consisted of the *Ladies' Home Journal, Redbook,* and *Woman's Home Companion.* In those she found confirmation of how to dress, furnish a home, recipes that worked, and details on rearing children. Pearl S. Buck was her favorite author, Eleanor Roosevelt her cherished heroine. She was consistently proud of her son's writing and couldn't fathom why he might be considered anti-Semitic. Her fulfilled life was challenged only when the two boys went away, the first to the navy, the second to university. According to Roth, she felt abandoned, almost devastated.[32]

But being American-born meant that the parents lacked a visceral, imme-diate experience with European Jewry and culture, especially Yiddish. Other than when he visited his grandmothers, Roth did not grow up with Yiddish spoken at home, in contrast to, say, Saul Bellow. Although the Old World of the *shtetl* might reside in certain parts of Weequahic—Yiddish signs reg-ularly appeared on Hawthorne Avenue—it did not find refuge on Summit Avenue. The late critic Mark Shechner, who spent his early youth in Newark, said that Yiddish nourished him partly because one of his grandmothers lived with him; it was shouted, sung, and spoken in the apartment. Shechner grew up over a grocery store at the corner of Hawthorne Avenue and Clinton Place, but like many Jewish families, money was always a problem. With en-terprise, his mother solved the dilemma by renting out his room to bookies when he was at school, something he learned only when he had to share the room during a sick day.

The year and day Roth was born—19 March 1933 (a Sunday)—was also the first year of FDR's presidency, his inauguration occurring on 4 March. Five days later, Congress began one hundred days of enacting New Deal legislation and on the twelfth, Roosevelt addressed the nation on the radio for the first time as U.S. president. The day after Roth was born, Germany completed construction of the Dachau concentration camp (opening on 22 March 1933) and on the twenty-third the Reichstag passed the Enabling Act, giving Hitler, by then chancellor of Germany, the power to rule by decree. It was a paradoxical time, one of anticipation as America took early steps to recover from the Depression, while Europe began to experience the threat of Hitler's increasing control. Two worlds faced different conflicts.

That same year, Newark elected its first (and only) Jewish mayor, Meyer "Doc" Ellenstein. A former boxer turned dentist turned lawyer, Ellenstein served two terms (1933–41) representing the city's large Jewish population in the Ironbound and Weequahic areas, plus the heavily Jewish Third Ward. Some claim, however, that Longy Zwillman handpicked Ellenstein because he would overlook the city's rampant political corruption—including election fraud and frequent embezzlement of city funds.[33] As the popular joke went, Newark politicians left office in one of two ways: death or conviction.

The city's Jewish population in 1933 was close to seventy-five thousand.[34] Contrary to Roth's rosy recall, Jewish life declined after the war as Jews moved to the suburbs. In 1948, Newark had approximately fifty-eight thousand Jews; ten years later, only forty-one thousand. Meanwhile, West Orange's Jewish population increased from sixteen hundred to seven thousand.[35] Newark's manufacturing base—home to multiple industries, with an ample labor supply—had also taken a hit: in the eight years up to Ellenstein's election as mayor, six hundred Newark factories had closed. Industries such as Ronson (started by Louis V. Aronson), Westinghouse, Mennen, Waterman, and General Electric cut back. Other industries on the decline included furriers, jewelry manufacturers, leather tanners, and other manufacturers, many summarized in Roth's *American Pastoral*.

In 1837 there were 155 patent-leather manufacturers in the city, producing an amount of leather then valued at $899,200. Besides the production of leather for shoes, Newark manufactured carriages, coaches, lace, and hats. Beer was also big: founded in Newark in 1840, the Ballantine Brewing plants covered twelve acres by the 1880s, making it the sixth largest brewer in the nation. The city was also known for its cider and quarries. African Americans began moving to Newark in the late 1800s, and especially during the World War I factory boom. Almost twenty-two thousand Blacks arrived between 1920 and 1930. War-related industry prompted another boom in the African American community, which tripled in size between 1940 and 1960, at that point 34 percent of Newark's population. As many former Newarkers moved to the suburbs, by 1970 African Americans composed 54 percent of the city's population.

When Roth was born, his parents lived at 81 Summit Avenue, two houses from the corner of Kerr. The two-and-a-half-story family house is currently clad in faux stone siding on the first floor, yellow cladding on the second. On the five-step stoop, Roth would play aces up, throwing the ball against the edge of the step so that it would bounce into the street with singles, doubles, or even a home run across the street. The rent for the Roths' flat (apartments were called flats then) was $48 a month. Their second-floor, five-room flat was part of a block of two-and-a-half-story wood-frame houses with gabled roofs and stoops of red brick. This tended to be the favored style north of Bergen Street and Osborne Terrace. Near the large Weequahic Park, designed by Frederick Law Olmsted, who did Central Park in New York City, were luxury apartment houses.[36]

The Roth home, now adorned with a plaque, is adjacent to the renamed Philip Roth Plaza, the intersection dedicated in October 2005 at a ceremony attended by Roth, the Newark historian Charles Cummings, and former Newark mayor Sharpe James. Organized by the Newark Preservation and Landmarks Committee, the ceremony occurred on 25 October, on the fifty-fifth anniversary of Roth's graduation from Weequahic High School. At the naming ceremony, the owner of the house, a Mrs. Roberta Harrington, got dressed up and came to the stairs, and Roth went over to say hello and shake her hand. She said, "Step up here and give me a kiss." Later, there was a reception at the Weequahic branch library, and she was with him for the rest of the day.[37]

To the east of their home, Summit Avenue ended at the intersection with Chancellor Avenue, a three-minute walk to the Chancellor Avenue Elementary School at 321 Chancellor Avenue. Roth attended from January 1938 until his graduation in January 1946. The oldest standing Newark school, going back to 1784, the original old stone schoolhouse was located on Lyons Farms on a lane that connected Newark and Elizabethtown. George Washington was said to have visited the school on his way to the Battle of Elizabeth. The original building was gifted to the Newark Museum in 1938, when the current three-story school with its Art Deco entranceway was built, dominating the intersection of Summit and Chancellor avenues.

Roth enjoyed elementary school and recalled a youthful fascination, possibly in first grade, with an alphabet frieze that ran around the top of the blackboards. The capital A and small a and the other letters captivated him. Bright and eager as a student, he skipped grade four and skipped again in grade eight. Adjacent to the school was a playing field—the same field where Bucky Cantor would triumphantly throw the javelin in the final pages of *Nemesis* and where a Bucky Harris supervised the playground and coached at Weequahic High, although he was not the model for Cantor, according to Roth.[38]

Before Roth graduated the Chancellor Avenue School in January 1946, a protest in the eighth grade made that year memorable. Roth and his classmates refused to participate in an essay-writing contest sponsored by the Daughters of the American Revolution. The reason? The DAR controlled bookings for Constitutional Hall in Washington and would not allow the Black pianist Hazel Scott, the wife of Congressman Adam Clayton Powell and the first woman of color to have her own TV show, to perform there on 20 October 1945. Powell took up the cause with President Harry Truman, who replied that democracy by definition was inclusive but that he would not interfere. The protest by Roth and his fellow students became a Newark newspaper story, and soon another eighth grade class, at the Maple Avenue School, joined in the protest. What was remarkable was that there was not a single Black student in the group: they were largely twelve-year-old Jewish kids. Roth alludes to the event in *Portnoy's Complaint* (PC 229).

One result was an invitation to the class to send representatives to a convention of the Congress of Industrial Organizations Action Committee, a labor union, perhaps the most left-wing labor union in the States at the time. Roth was one of the student delegates who sat on the stage and applauded with others when introduced. Frank Kingdon, a journalist and speechwriter for Roosevelt and later blacklisted, congratulated them and told them they were watching democracy in action, which thrilled Roth in particular. This was a direct introduction to politics and its effects, reinforcing some of the themes outlined by a writer the young Roth admired, Howard Fast, and his novel *Citizen Tom Paine*.

Roth cowrote the elementary school graduation play with a female classmate and starred in it, performing with fellow classmates and beginning a drama career at least through university. Entitled *Let Freedom Ring*, it plotted "Tolerance," played by a classmate, against "Prejudice," played by Roth. At the end of the play, Tolerance wins the day and Prejudice skulks away, exiting stage left while the cast sings "The House I Live in," a popular 1940s hit recorded by Frank Sinatra. "It's not such a stretch to say [that] that 12-year-old gave birth to the man of today," Roth told Columbia University News on 16 April 2008. In an eighth grade autograph album owned by Sandy Goldberg, a Chancellor Avenue classmate, Roth wrote, "Don't suck lollipops, suck-cess."[39]

While in grade four, Roth discovered the local branch of the public library, known as Osborne Terrace, where he would borrow such books as John Tunis's *The Kid from Tom Kinsville*. Books in his own home were limited: he recalled only four, largely gifts either to his father, when he had his serious appendectomy operation in October 1944, or to his mother. The books were three novels by Sir Walter Scott, including *Kenilworth* and *Ivanhoe,* and William L. Shirer's *Berlin Diary*. Roth read them all, although he was unsure of their subjects. His mother would occasionally acquire Pearl S. Buck titles from a nearby rental library in a pharmacy (actually just a few shelves of bestsellers) costing 5 cents a day. Roth often went to obtain the cellophane-wrapped books for his mother, and he could remember occasionally going to New York with her to see film versions of *The Good Earth* and *Dragon Seed* at Radio City Music Hall. One reason for such few books was largely that his parents, and those of his friends, did not have college educations and were themselves children of immigrants whose English was subpar. There was no culture (or money) to buy books. His own father rarely read a book; newspapers were his textbooks and pleasure reading.

When he got a bike, Roth would cycle to the Osborne Terrace library and return with a basketful of books. His brother had done the same. These were kids' books, Howard Pease one of his favorite authors. Pease wrote romantic adventure stories for boys. From Stockton, California, Pease set many of his stories in the West, often revolving around a young protagonist, Joseph Todhunter Moran, who shipped out on tramp freighters in the 1920s and 1930s. Mysterious adventure stories often at sea were a favorite, such as *Night Boat and Other Tod Moran Mysteries*. The first story takes place on a night boat going from San Francisco to Stockton; others occur in Caracas, Tahiti, and Mexico City.

Supplementing, if not replacing, reading at the Roth household was the radio, both Roth and his brother fans of popular music and radio comedies, especially on Sunday nights. The radio was an information and entertainment center, his father constantly tuned to the news and Roth, later, to Norman Corwin, the radio writer a great influence (Roth and Corwin actually became friends later in life; although they never met, they spoke frequently by phone.) Corwin appears in *I Married a Communist*, his radio play *On a Note of Triumph* for the young Zuckerman (and perhaps Roth) providing him with his "first sense of the conjuring *power* of art" (IMC 38). Another voice was that of the anti-Semitic Father Coughlin, whose weekly radio sermon became a *cause célèbre*. Roth's father, who would occasionally listen to Coughlin's show, would become livid and indict not only Coughlin but Henry Ford and Charles Lindbergh as outright anti-Semites.

The radio became a likely source for Roth's colloquial, readable, auditory style. It was American speech that he paid attention to and that became for him a schoolroom of voices. Writing may have been his way of transmitting his own radio signals to an audience. As Zuckerman remarks in *I Married a Communist*, a novel where radio and radio stardom become *the* subject, "The book of my life is a book of voices" (IMC 222). In answering the question of how he got to where he was, Zuckerman simply says, "Listening" (IMC 222). Whether from announcers or characters in radio drama, the fluidity of voices from the radio, mostly reading from scripts, taught Roth an American vernacular which he mastered, along with dialogue. One of his early but un-reprinted stories, "On the Air," is about radio: a talent agent seeks wacky new radio shows and imagines one featuring Einstein as the Answer Man.[40]

Roth's brother became quite attached to radio drama and later in life listened to popular old radio programs on tapes. A radio was always on in the kitchen of the Roth home, even when the family ate; his mother listened to it during the day and evening. Eventually, he and his brother had a radio of their own in their bedroom, believing that the height of childhood transgression was listening to the radio after 10 o'clock in bed with the lights out. Pages 41 to 43 of I Married a Communist intensely record the impact of the radio as a source of one's political consciousness and moral sensibility.

In Roth's fiction, the radio is ubiquitous. In The Anatomy Lesson, when Zuckerman visits his late mother's empty apartment, he turns on the radio to her favorite FM station: "show tunes smothered in strings" (AL 49). Coleman Silk listens to big-band music on his radio at his home near Athena College in The Human Stain and enjoys the songs of Dick Haymes, Helen O'Connell, and the young Frank Sinatra. The Plot Against America vividly renders the role of radio in 1940 in communicating politics as well as entertainment, heard throughout the neighborhood (PAA 15).

Radio also brought with it politics, which Roth began to follow quite carefully, hearing broadcasts about the war, political campaigns, and debates. His early interest in politics at this time included a youthful awareness of Roosevelt defeating Willkie in 1940 and then Truman defeating Dewey in the 1948 presidential election. Encouraged by his father, who was constantly alert to political corruption and conservative restrictions, Roth was introduced to political posturing, rhetoric, and bombast through the radio. Early in I Married a Communist, for example, he incorporates family debates of the 1948 election, his father arguing at length over the dangers of a Dewey presidency, while young Nathan Zuckerman celebrates Wallace. The bitterness of the dispute in the novel echoes frequent discussions in the Roth household (IMC 28–32).

Another source of political ideas was the daily newspaper P.M., which stood for "Picture Magazine." This leftist publication, which Roth began to read at fourteen, was published in New York City by Ralph Ingersoll from June 1940 to June 1948 and financed by Chicago millionaire Marshall Field

III. The paper borrowed many elements from weekly news magazines, such as enlarged photos. In an attempt to be free of pressure from business interests, it did not accept advertising. I. F. Stone was the Washington correspondent; Dr. Seuss contributed more than four hundred cartoons. Other contributors included Erskine Caldwell, McGeorge Bundy, Heywood Hale Broun, James Thurber, Dorothy Parker, Ernest Hemingway, Malcolm Cowley, and Ben Hecht. This political exposure solidified young Roth's liberal leanings and helped him understand his father's later hatred of the McCarthy hearings and the intense witch-hunts for Communists in America. His father's anger at the hearings intensified Roth's sense of battle between liberal and right-wing factions in the country.

Interestingly, Roth grew up without music. His Newark home had no phonograph nor records. The radio was his only source, and that was tuned mostly to pop music of the 1940s. In the living room was a large console radio, in the kitchen something smaller. During dinner, the radio first played the news and then music. But neither of his parents had any interest in classical music, and only one of his friends had a phonograph.[41] Surprisingly, however, music has been present from the beginning of his writing, notably in the André Kostelanetz version of "Night and Day" and the Glee Club's rendition of "Goodbye, Columbus" (GBC 73–74, 102–3). Music remains throughout Roth's late work, returning at one point in *Nemesis* to Native American roots in the camp songs at Indian Hill. In *Indignation* it's Beethoven, the favorite of one of Marcus Messner's roommates.

Letting Go epitomizes the increasing status of music that becomes more sophisticated as his fiction progresses. In *Letting Go* Roth offers a characteristic blend of classical and pop. Martha Reganhart and her "ex" listen to Mozart's *The Magic Flute* while they decide on the custody of their two children, but when Gabe Wallach drives Theresa Haug (Martha's friend, who will give up her child to Libby and Paul Herz) home to Gary, Indiana, Fabian and Frankie Avalon are on the radio. The two contrasting styles seem appropriate to the characters' contrasting situations and even social class. But in *Portnoy*, *The Human Stain*, and *The Dying Animal* music becomes exclusively classical. Reflecting Roth's personal love of chamber music (discovered during his time in the army) was his choice of Fauré's "Élégie," Op. 24, as his final words—or rather notes—at his Memorial Service in September 2018.[42]

In 1942, while Roth was still in grade school, the family moved to a second-floor flat at 359 Leslie Street, three blocks west of Summit Avenue and closer to the boundary with Irvington. The reason for the move was an increase in rent on Summit Avenue. In 1947, the year after he graduated elementary school, the family again moved, this time to a first-floor flat at 385 Leslie Street, closer to the commercial activity on Chancellor Avenue.

This area, only a few blocks from Summit Avenue, introduced him to several non-Jewish families. Roth remembered two of them on Leslie Street, one an Italian family next door; down the street was another gentile family with a young boy named Whitey Sable, who became one of Roth's closest friends. But aside from them, the entire street was Jewish, although Roth realized that the neighborhood was not a *shtetl* or ghetto but a community. They knew and experienced discrimination, of course, but matching that threat was the feeling of security emanating from their sense of a Jewish community. The bigotry, indirectly experienced by his father in his failure to get ahead in his insurance company, reinforced the threats to Jewish life locally and, of course, internationally during the war. Roth was aware of this overall situation, although his fictional reminiscences of Jewish life in Newark downplay or diminish such knowledge.

The Weequahic section, the Roths' neighborhood in the southwestern corner of Newark, began to grow in the late 1920s through the 1940s in part because of its excellent high school. Non-Jews soon moved westward as Jews from the Third Ward and the Ironbound section moved up to the more lower-middle-class Weequahic neighborhood, which was almost entirely Jewish, emphasizing a kind of withdrawn existence, not quite a ghetto but a small community sharing common knowledge and customs. The need to break out of restrictive practices originating in close-knit Jewish community life becomes especially clear in *Portnoy's Complaint*, contributing to Portnoy's rejection of Jewish women in favor of the more liberated non-Jewish women.

After his January 1946 graduation—midyear graduations were common then because elementary and high school populations were so large—Roth went almost next door to Weequahic High, which he attended from 1946 until January 1950.[43] The building, on the site of the home of Newark's fourth mayor, Oliver Spencer Halstead, opened on 11 September 1933 with an enrollment of 2,056 students. Expressing its Art Deco style, marked by a chandelier in the lobby, were staircases and even decorative handrails. The marble facing and dramatic tile floors echoed the Art Deco elements, which found dramatic expression in the mural just inside the entrance. Entitled *The History of the Enlightenment of Man* and painted by Michael Lenson in 1939, it covered three walls and dramatically retold the story of man's accomplishments. Lenson, a Russian-born muralist, was at the time in charge of the Mural and

Easel Division of the Works Progress Administration of the Federal Arts Project. That same year he did *New Jersey Agriculture and Industry* for the New Jersey Pavilion at the 1939 New York World's Fair and then *The History of Newark* for Newark's City Hall in 1941.

The reputation of Weequahic High reached national stature when it received a letter from Albert Einstein in 1934. The letter appeared on the front page of *The Calumet*, the school paper, on 11 March and was reprinted in almost thirteen hundred papers around the world. In his letter, Einstein offered his thoughts on education and the American school system. He encourages independence of mind and personal initiative, which schools should not suppress. Schools should also foster a social consciousness and sense of social responsibility. By contrast, he notes that European schools downplay independent thought and creativity. He concludes by stating that the "the cultural ideal of present-day America is not so much knowledge, as it is the desire and the ability for accomplishment." Einstein composed the letter on 8 February 1934.

Nineteen-forty-six, the year Roth started high school, was also the year of his Bar Mitzvah, which occurred on 9 March. He wanted to do well and had studied Hebrew in the afternoon Hebrew school at the Schley Street Synagogue for three years. But after reading his Haftarah and celebrating, he never, or almost never, visited a synagogue again. "I was one Jew at ten and another at twenty," he later said. Limited exposure to Yiddish-speaking grandparents, aunts, and uncles was his only contact with the *shtetl* world of Eastern Europe. It seemed alien as well as foreign, not really "Jewish" as understood by an ambitious Newark teenager more interested in girls and sports than in Torah study.

At high school, his friends would often gather at the playing field and share this cheer, recalled in *Portnoy's Complaint*:

> Ikey, Mikey, Jake and Sam,
> We're the boys who eat no ham,
> We play football, we play soccer—
> And we keep matzohs in our locker!
> Aye, aye, aye, Weequahic High! (PC 56)

Satire, not sanctity, was the focus. The school's actual fight song was "We're on Our Way," an important phrase considering the embattled ethnic groups Roth describes in both *Portnoy's Complaint* and *American Pastoral*.

Roth took particular pleasure in English taught by Hilde Lutzke, who taught there from 1937 to 1975. Roth was also supposedly taught English by Allen Ginsberg's aunt.[44] *The Legend*, the 1950 yearbook of Weequahic High, describes Roth as "a boy of real intelligence, combined with wit and common sense." It notes that he was assistant editor of the *Annex News*, class vice president, a member of the General Language Club, the Student Council, the Contemporary Club, and the Prom Committee.[45] His early interests were politics and law, supplemented by Romance languages, especially French.

Robert "Doc" Lowenstein was his beloved homeroom teacher and a French instructor met on his first day of high school in February 1946. Lowenstein became the inspiration for Murray Ringold in *I Married a Communist*.[46] Hilde Lutzke recalled in 2010 the chilling effect Senator Joseph McCarthy and his hunt for Communists had on local educators, particularly Lowenstein, who, with two others, lost his job in 1955.

Lowenstein fought the charges for six years and was eventually reinstated with back pay, rising to become chair of Weequahic's Foreign Languages Department. Multitalented, he also taught algebra and had a PhD from Johns Hopkins. Still alive in 2010, he wrote a letter to be read at a reunion in which he corrected a common fallacy—that he was 103 years old. "I am only 102," he wrote, while expressing the hope that the former student who contacted him still had the "spit and vinegar" he remembered.[47] Lowenstein would exchange postcards and notes with Roth for over twenty years, and at his death at 105, Roth wrote an appreciation of him.

In his account, Roth recalls that he was twelve when he first met Lowenstein. It was at the Hawthorne Avenue Annex in February 1946, where freshmen at Weequahic High went because of overflow at the main building. Fresh from serving as a master sergeant in the army air corps in North Africa and Italy, Lowenstein was impressive. Although he never took a class from him, Roth saw him every day for a year. At university and later, Roth followed Lowenstein's battle with the House Un-American Activities Committee and the Newark school board, having his parents mail him news clippings. Some forty years later, in the 1990s, they came together again. Roth had recently returned to the States after living in England with Claire Bloom, and they soon began to see each other and began a long exchange of poems (Lowenstein) and letters (Roth). The author even sent him a final draft of *American Pastoral* before it was published for him to review the Newark sections. When Roth turned sixty and gave a reading at New Jersey's Seton Hall University, Lowenstein, then eighty-five, introduced him. In his

memoir, Roth celebrates Lowenstein's courage and strength in resisting injustice and, in the words of the narrator of *I Married a Communist*, bringing
into the classroom "a charge of visceral spontaneity that was a revelation to
tamed, respectablized kids." His "special talent was for dramatizing inquiry"
(IMC 1).[48]

A picture from a high school prom party at Billy Rose's Diamond
Horseshoe nightclub in Manhattan to celebrate his graduation shows a
beaming Roth dressed in a dark jacket and tie. Divided by the table, the men
sit on one side in tuxedos and suits, the young women, all in fancy dresses, on
the other (Figure 1.2).

Roth long felt attached to the school, in October 2009 surprising a group
of fiftieth-anniversary graduates when he stepped onto the bus taking the
alumni on the fourth "Philip Roth's Newark Tour" organized by Liz Del Tufo,
herself a Newark historian and president of the Newark Preservation and
Landmarks Committee. On the first tour, in 2005, Roth was honored with
the placement of a historic plaque on his home on Summit Avenue: "Newark

Figure 1.2 Roth (fifth in on the right) with friends celebrating his high school
prom at Billy Rose's Diamond Horseshoe Club, New York City, January 1950.
Credit: Newark Public Library.

is my Stockholm and that plaque is my prize," he reportedly told Del Tufo at the ceremony.[49]

Herman Roth made a decent, lower-middle-class living as an insurance agent for the Metropolitan Life Insurance Company starting in 1932 and retiring in 1964. At one point, he earned $125 a week but often worked twelve to fourteen hours a day (FAC 35). He would be gone by 7:30 a.m., return by 5:00 p.m., when the family had an early dinner, and then head out again to call on prospects until 9:00 or 10:00, six and sometimes seven days a week. He was conscientious, hard-working, and generally uncomplaining. He had strong ideas about politics, morality, and family. He was a liberal and a strict moralist who believed in human and political rights. Any infringement of either brought out his anger. He would listen to Father Coughlin's insults to Jews just to get worked up, an anger repeatedly witnessed by his son. His views were fixed and dominated the home conversations, his wife again avoiding any controversy. He was above all a pragmatist in human relations and was unafraid to sidestep facts—but he wanted facts, not opinions or emotions. He reasoned from facts, not feelings.

Nowhere was this more evident than his actions following his wife's funeral. Back at the apartment, rather than greet mourners in the living room, he went to the bedroom and vigorously began to dispose of Bess's clothes and mementoes. He saw this act as another "difficult job" that had to be done, and he never turned away from such challenges (PAT 31). Emotions had no part. It was work, and he believed he was doing something "generous, helpful, and morally . . . efficacious" (PAT 30). A primitive determination controlled his actions.

Family practice meant that Roth and his brother spent almost every Sunday visiting their fraternal and maternal grandmothers, one in the morning, the other in the afternoon. Both were widows who spoke little English and had no money. Family issues were front and center, and, according to Roth, the visits were intense, surrounded by pathos for their situation, which gave him a strong emotional education. Aunts and uncles also played a vital role in his upbringing, especially an Uncle Irv who had fought in the war, a subject that fascinated the young Roth, who had studied battles, aircraft, and strategy. He built model planes that hung from the ceiling of his bedroom.

Married to his older cousin Florence, Uncle Irv Cohen talked to Roth repeatedly about the fighting, a subject Roth had followed closely. Roth would later dramatize Uncle Irv as Ira Ringold in *I Married a Communist*. Irv never killed anyone, as Ira did, but he was quick-tempered and strong. Irv's opposition to everything American, especially the status quo and capitalism, appealed to the young, left-leaning Roth. Driving a truck to make deliveries for an uncle, Irv occasionally invited Roth, who enjoyed every moment of the adventure, talking and seeing life on the road: "The heroic rhetoric of the war and the heroic rhetoric of the left-wing popular front had gotten into my head. . . . The manliness of the guys who'd been in the war" matched the heroism implicit in Wolfe's *Look Homeward, Angel,* a title Roth would use for a section of *Zuckerman Unbound.* Roth's appetite to be a man was fed by the stories and actions of Uncle Irv and the heroic rhetoric of the war and the Popular Front.[50]

In the area of Clinton Hall and Weequahic, there was a natural blend of the commercial and the criminal. Roth captures a portion of this in the action of Cousin Alvin in *The Plot Against America,* who comes home from the war injured and takes a series of shady jobs. Not all Weequahic children and young adults played chess, collected stamps, and read Thomas Wolfe. And if they did, their fathers often ran numbers. "Hustler" in Newark at that time was a term of praise. The boisterous literary critic Leslie Fiedler, Newark-born, recalled seeing Zwillman's mother walking the streets with the diamonds her son bought her and remembered that Dutch Schultz was shot in a local tavern.[51]

A dominating father, displayed in the first section of *Portnoy,* initiates the father-son relationship Roth will portray throughout his work. In the novel, the father is plagued by constipation and rages and suffers and drinks, not whiskey but mineral oil and milk of magnesia. His "blockaded body" becomes a metaphor for his relationship with his son, blockaded in *his* quest for freedom. Even the explosion of the atomic bomb didn't have an effect on the father's bowels (PC 5). His overbearing love had the effect of suffocating his son, who rebels.

As Roth documents the father's failings, the father creates a kind of aura of failure, working hard for a future "he wasn't slated to have. Nobody ever really gave him satisfaction," a development that would later play into the theme of discontent in Roth's fiction, condemning the son at least in fiction to impotence and bachelorhood (PC 6). In Roth no characters are able to have a happy marriage. If they do marry, they are never completely satisfied.

The terror behind Roth's fiction "is the realization that the father is impotent," one critic has written, adding that for Roth, enmity of the father was preferable to his adoration: "There is no escape from the ineffectual father, for the son's oedipal guilt is renewed daily by the father's failure."[52] Exploited by his employer, laughed at by his clients, Portnoy Senior persevered, not as a hero but as an embarrassment to his son, no less because, while mistreated by the company and critical of them in private, he praised them in public (PC 8). Young Portnoy's life, and those of later Roth characters, is a "history of disenchantment" (PC 9).

Roth's own father suffered several business failures, notably a shoe store and a frozen food distribution business undertaken with several partners. But he countered the disaster—the food venture not only used up their savings, but he had a debt of $8,000 borrowed from relatives—with a renewed determination to work harder at his insurance business. In turn, he stressed hard work to his sons—that alone could bring success. Roth's later discipline and approach to writing as an everyday labor likely reflects his father's rock-hard commitment to *his* work. Above all, one does not give up. Roth in many ways was determined to become "the hero [his] father failed to be" (FAC 17).

Roth began what would be a lifetime as a reader after his brother, one summer, brought home the student newspaper from Pratt Institute of Art in Brooklyn, where he had been studying. It included a list of recommended summer reading. Roth took it to the library and started: *Portrait of the Artist as a Young Man, Ulysses, Babbitt, Winesburg, Ohio,* and *Look Homeward, Angel.* Reading Wolfe in particular "transported" him, admiring the hero of *Look Homeward, Angel,* Eugene Gant, who was sensual, intellectual, and adventurous, marked by his wanderings through cities. The subtitle alone may have stimulated Roth's hopes: *A Story of the Buried Life.* Wolfe was a colossus to young Roth, who read all four of Wolfe's major novels: *Look Homeward, Angel, Of Time and the River, The Web and the Rock,* and *You Can't Go Home Again.* He even got his friends to read them.

At the time, Roth had no intention of being a writer, but the list was tremendously stimulating, various texts emphasizing the independence and self-discovery that he himself was seeking. Family was support, but independence was a necessity. Roth was then thirteen or fourteen.

Soon, however, it was Howard Fast, the popular 1940s leftist writer who wrote about American history. *Conceived in Liberty* about Valley Forge and then *Citizen Tom Paine* (published in 1943, the year Fast joined the Communist Party) were two inspiring favorites emphasizing justice and moral courage which Roth read in the seventh and eighth grades. Later, Fast became known as the author of *Spartacus* (1951), about a Roman slave revolt. He wrote it while in jail for contempt of the House Committee on Un-American Activities. He has an important role in *I Married a Communist,* where *Citizen Tom Paine* is a constant reference and model of the moral agency of fiction (IMC 24–26).

By now, Roth regularly visited the main branch of the Newark Public Library, where Neil Klugman works in "Goodbye, Columbus" to put himself through Rutgers. Located at 5 Washington Street across from the triangular Washington Park, the Italianate building, completed in 1901 (with additions in 1922 and 1931), displays the architectural influence of the Palazzo Strozzi in Florence (Figure 1.3). Large glass lanterns and Roman iron gates flank the entrance. Nine large rounded windows provide natural light on the second floor, its balcony overlooking the marbled main entrance hall. A set of Corinthian columns surround the balcony on the third floor, which completes the three-story atrium. The Centennial Hall stretches across the entire front of the building's second floor.

Leslie Fiedler, who also grew up in Newark, remembered that characterless city taking on meaning only when he visited the library. It was *the* focal point of Newark, a city that in the 1940s was gritty with college boys working in shoe stores, workers wearing "Vote Communist" buttons, and

Figure 1.3 The main branch of the Newark Public Library, which opened in 1901. Building based on the fifteenth-century Palazzo Strozzi in Florence. Credit: Newark Public Library

neighborhoods redolent with the smell of lox and the noise of *cheders*. He also recalled the Little Theater across Washington Park from the library, where Hedy Lamarr played in *Ecstasy* in 1933, the year Roth was born. But by the 1950s, as prosperity emerged, families went from brick stoops to the swim clubs of Livingston and Short Hills. In Fiedler's words, success "had removed the sons of leatherworkers and the owners of candy stores to Bucknell or Ohio State."[53] Life transformed from the multiple and squalid areas of "switchmen shacks, lumberyards and Dairy Queens" expressing a kind of drab horror to the middle class of vacations at "the Shore," cars, and shopping at Bergdorf Goodman in Manhattan (GBC 8).

Today a light rail station stands across from the Newark Public Library on Broad Street, while the new building housing the Rutgers University Business School towers over the three-story Italianate structure. To the library's left, the New Jersey Historical Society at 52 Park Place remains, formerly the location of the Essex Club. Nearby is the Newark Museum, all three buildings (library, historical society, and museum) bordering Washington Park, originally laid out in 1666 and intended to be a marketplace.

The information desk where Neil Klugman gives advice to the young African American seeking a work on Gauguin in "Goodbye, Columbus" still stands on the second floor. Roth's appreciation of the library led to a 1 March 1969 editorial in the *New York Times* opposing proposed budget cuts by the Newark City Council to the library and Newark Museum, effectively shutting them down. Public outcry essentially reversed the decision; Roth wrote before that action, somewhat in the vein of Jonathan Swift, satirically wondering if scholars would take up sniping positions in the reference room while schoolchildren would seize the main building to complete their term papers.[54]

Repeating that his family did not own many books in his 1969 defense, he stressed that it was essential to know that the city had a library that offered knowledge to the entire community and was owned by the community. The very place was civilizing, teaching order and restraint, as he learned to decode systems in the library catalogue and then wandered in the open stacks to locate his books. This is a satisfying form of discovery for a ten-year-old, he writes. The freedom to read anything anywhere in the building was nourishing—almost as much as knowing that a book brought home possessed "a family tree of Newark readers" (RMY 217). How bizarre, then, to learn that the City Council believed that the books do not belong to the public. In a city still reeling from the riots of 1967, the library was even more essential for civilized discourse, he concludes.

Roth consistently supported the library and often appeared for book signings and celebrations. In 1991, for example, in lieu of a speaking fee he asked to have his library card renewed. Eight years later, he participated in a three-day series entitled "Newark through the Prism of Philip Roth: Artistry, Imagery, Reality." How Roth presented and understood Newark in his work was the focus. Introducing him was Charles Cummings, then assistant director of the Newark Public Library and a distinguished Newark historian. Roth had developed a close friendship with the Puerto Rico–born, southern-educated Cummings.[55] The author increasingly relied on him for details of Newark's past, although it was initially the former journalist and historian John T. Cunningham, author of almost ninety books on Newark, who renewed Roth's knowledge of the city. It was Cunningham, in fact, who took Roth around Mendham, a borough in Morris County, forty miles west of Manhattan (and northwest of Newark), which became Rimrock in *American Pastoral.*

But it was Cummings who encouraged Roth to walk the neighborhoods and re-explore both old and new areas of Newark, and it was Cummings who soon became Newark's expert, not only through his "Knowing Newark" articles in the papers but also in his authoring and coauthoring several books, including a pictorial history of Essex County and three histories of Newark. As head of the Newark Public Library's New Jersey Information Center, he fielded questions from the public, scholars, and children eager to track down details of the city and its past. And it was Cummings who gave Roth the framed "Street and House Number Map of Newark" that became the backdrop for one of the most iconic photos of Roth, taken by Nancy Crampton in 2004 and used as the author photo on the back jacket flap for *The Plot Against America*: Roth in tie and jacket and with a slight smile sitting in front of the enlarged Newark map.

Following Cummings's death on 21 December 2005, Roth wrote a short piece for the Newark *Star-Ledger,* which appeared on Christmas Day. In it, Roth celebrated Cummings's desire to educate everyone about their city, whether as archivist, journalist, lecturer, teacher, student, librarian, or tour guide. Roth generously acknowledged Cummings as the source of his Newark knowledge, including helping him search for an appropriate building to serve as the location for the Levov glove factory in *American Pastoral.* They eventually found it on Central Avenue; Cummings photographed the abandoned structure from ten different vantage points: "Fewer than 10 perspectives on anything in Newark would not do," Roth remarked. While writing the novel,

Roth walked with Cummings about the city; he later said that the Pulitzer Prize for the book was as much Cummings's as his. According to Roth, Cummings was a tremendous Newark resource and "a great Newark hero."[56] Appropriately, the city had earlier recognized Cummings as its official historian. And in recognition of Roth's role in promoting Newark in his books, he received the third annual Charles Cummings Award in May 2009. Roth's praise of Cummings as "the living encyclopedia of Newark" confirms his importance for the writer.[57]

As Roth wrote in *American Pastoral*, Newark had density: no well-born child of Renaissance Florence could "have a held a candle to growing up within aromatic range of Tabachnik's pickle barrels" (AP 42). The "ocean of details" about the city and neighborhoods which suffuse the novel, and his other works, convey the depth, as well as surface, of the city.

Earlier, Newark's industrial boom had attracted enterprising inventors like Thomas Edison, who created the ticker-tape machine while there. Seth Boyden invented the process for making patent leather and malleable iron, in addition to developing a hat-forming machine and an inexpensive process for manufacturing sheet iron. John W. Hyatt developed celluloid (for camera film). Edward Weston's Weston Electrical Instrument Company created the Weston standard cell, the first accurate portable voltmeters and ammeters, the first portable light meter, and many other electrical developments. Such advances helped the city enter early into the manufacture of plastics, electrical goods, and chemicals.

And then there were the insurance companies: Prudential, Firemen's, Merchants, and Mutual Benefit, plus the Metropolitan. Insurance companies in Newark (America's fourth oldest city) had a long history, beginning in 1804 with the opening of the Newark Banking and Insurance Company, followed by the Newark Mutual Assurance Company (the Newark Fire Insurance Company) in 1810, and the Mutual Benefit Life Insurance Company in 1845. John F. Dryden founded the Prudential Insurance Company in Newark in 1875. Metropolitan Life opened in Newark in 1882, Herman Roth joining the district sales office in 1932.[58]

The slogan of Metropolitan Life, "The light that never fails," resonated with Americans seeking protection offered by life insurance. By 1930, Metropolitan Life insured every fifth man, woman, and child in the United States and Canada. During the 1930s, the company grew and diversified its holdings; it had financed the construction of the Empire State Building in 1929, as well as providing capital to build Rockefeller Center in 1931.

During World War II, Metropolitan Life placed more than 51 percent of its total assets in war bonds and was the largest single private contributor to the Allied cause.

In New York, Met Life was headquartered at One Madison Avenue, at Madison Square Park, the first New York street address Roth knew. It had an Essex County office in Newark, where Herman Roth worked. A modest but steady living during the beginning of the Depression was invaluable. When Roth accompanied his father on Saturday mornings to the office in downtown Newark, he would spend time learning about pregnancy, diabetes, and tuberculosis from a set of company-produced brochures designed to educate its policy holders and encourage them to buy more coverage. Occasionally, he would sit in his father's swivel chair at his desk and work on his penmanship using Metropolitan Life stationery.

One clear sign of his father's accomplishments was the framed Declaration of Independence hanging above the telephone table in the family hallway. It was awarded to men of his father's district for a successful year. Seeing it there daily "forged an association" between the founders of American democracy and equality and "our benefactors, the corporate fathers at Number One Madison Avenue," where its president was, incidentally, named Mr. Lincoln (FAC 21–22).

Admired for his good work by a Mr. Wright in New York, superintendent of agencies, Herman Roth slowly rose in the ranks, maintaining respect for these non-Jews while aware that they both permitted his advancement and yet prevented Jews from assuming positions of importance. His own manager, however, was Jewish: Sam Peterfreund, who recognized early Herman's drive and promoted him to assistant manager. And when Mr. Peterfreund made a rare visit to the Roth household, fresh linen, the good dishes, and use of the dining room was mandatory (FAC 22). It was an occasion, since the guest was responsible for Herman's "occupational well-being and our family fate" (FAC 23). Met Life received respect.

Besides baseball and basketball, another preoccupation for the teenage Roth was the movies. With his buddies, he would often go to double features at the Roosevelt Theater on Friday nights. A lobby area led to a kind of tunnel to the auditorium, the interior of the narrow building at 796 Clinton Avenue white with a gold-colored arch over the middle of the screen and stage area and similarly colored columns on either side. Saturday matinees cost 25 cents. In his fiction, Roth refers to a number of Newark movie theaters, from the Roosevelt and the Park to the Newsreel downtown at the intersection of Broad and Market streets (FAC 31; AP 25). Additional movie houses included Proctor's, the Paramount, the Branford, the Goodwin, the Rialto, the Loews, the Little, and the Mosque, where the young Nathan Zuckerman meets Paul Robeson and Henry Wallace in *I Married a Communist.*[59]

And for Roth, the impact of the movies lasted. When he and his brother accompany their parents to Union, New Jersey, in advance of a possible transfer for his father and a family move early in *The Plot Against America*, he identifies the homes as "looking a lot like the little white houses in the movies about small-town salt-of-the-earth America" (PAA 8). Early in his writing career, Roth wrote movie reviews for the *New Republic.*[60]

The most important movie house in his fiction is the Newsreel in *The Plot Against America*, offering a visual register of the political upheavals occurring around the world with implications for the freedom of Americans. The projectionist, Shepsie Tirschwell, was a boyhood friend of Herman and edited daily news footage into a one-hour summary of world events. Opening in 1935, the theater was Newark's only all-news movie house. By 1942, when nine-year-old Philip visits, his father had been a regular for years and had recounted to his family the cast of newsreel characters—ranging from Tojo, Pétain, Batista, De Valera, Gandhi, Rommel, and King George to La Guardia and Pope Pius—all figures who were shaping history. Shepsie would entertain Philip and Sandy in the projection booth, identifying the parts of the projector and showing them photographs of the luminaries who attended shows there. *I Married a Communist* has similar scenes.

Narrow, with perhaps 100 to 150 seats, the Newsreel was located on the ground floor of the City Investment Building at 800 Broad Street, next door to the American Shops men's clothing store and a few steps from the Belmore Cafeteria. Five newsreel companies—Fox Movietone News, News of the Day, Paramount, RKO-Pathé, and Universal—provided footage. But since newsreels did not usually fill out a full hour, to round out the program the Newsreel Theater would also run several short subjects, often dealing with current politics, movie stars, sporting events, foreign news, or technology. These shows were updated twice a week.

In the *The Plot Against America* (and reflecting Roth's own memories), what the young Philip enjoys most are the well-spaced seats, the soundproof projectionist booth, and the carpet design of motion picture reels you can step on. On consecutive Saturdays, the Roth boys and father would attend showings that became increasingly more political: the Bund rally in Madison Square Garden or FDR addressing the anti-Ribbentrop rally. But what the young Roth remembered best was the voice of Lowell Thomas narrating the political news and Bill Stern reporting sports. And audience participation: patrons would frequently boo or hiss or clap depending on their allegiances (PAA 180–81). The darkness of the theater permitted the expression of emotions and attachments that the daylight did not.

Another favorite hangout was Syd's. This hot dog and soda haunt at 340 Chancellor Avenue, between Summit and Hobson Street near Weequahic High, was a landmark for kids, and both Roth and his brother worked there part time (FAC 29). In 1941, Syd Goldstein, whose family was in the dairy business in Bayonne, New Jersey, bought a small restaurant at the 340 Chancellor Avenue address, renamed it Syd's, and introduced a menu that featured hot dogs and hamburgers, rolled beef, ham, cheese sandwiches, tuna and egg salad, and potato and kasha knishes. In 1941, you could buy a hot dog at Syd's in two sizes: 3 cents or 6 cents. The war, however, meant changes: near the end of 1941, the 3-cent hot dog was dropped and the larger one shot to 10 cents. When the woman who supplied Syd's with knishes died in 1942, Goldstein replaced them on his menu with "Syd's Homemade French Fries," which became an instant hit with many patrons, but not Alex Portnoy's mother. Early in *Portnoy's Complaint* she is convinced the French fries are giving her son diarrhea, which explains why he locks himself in the family bathroom so often. And hamburgers? Another sin: " '*Hamburgers*,' she says bitterly, just as she might say '*Hitler*' " (PC 33). Syd's becomes "Harold's Hot Dog and *Chazerai* Palace," *chazerai* Yiddish for "disgusting," "horrid," or "garbage" (PC 23–24).

In 1947 Syd Goldstein sold his popular Weequahic luncheonette to Mort Bratter, who continued with the original Syd's menu until 1957, when he too sold the business. During those years, Roth would often be there with such friends as Jack Kirsten, later a judge, or Bernie Marcus, who founded Home Depot. In Roth's novels, Syd's is a beacon of both pleasure and danger. In *American Pastoral* it is remembered as *the* gauge of social behavior; in *Nemesis,* it is mistakenly thought to be the breeding ground for polio (AP 43; NEM 58). A more recent study replaces the nostalgic view of Syd's with something more sinister: as a location for dealing drugs, overlooked in Roth.[61]

With his buddies, Roth would also stop at the twenty-four-hour Watson Bagel Company (280 Clinton Place) after a movie and often hang out on the wooden bleachers along the sidelines of the asphalt playground adjacent to the large dirt playing field at the Chancellor Avenue Elementary School. The conversation would be carefree and wide-ranging, from family to radio programs, sports, and sex. Politics tended to be praise for Roosevelt and the New Deal and a celebration of Americanness, an important element of Roth's character (FAC 31–32). Later, at Bucknell, Roth would stand up in a Shakespeare class following the 1952 defeat of Adlai Stevenson and excoriate the American public (and, by inference, the Bucknell student body) for choosing a war hero (Eisenhower) over an intellectual statesman. Roth was actually supposed to explicate a passage in the class about the mob in *Coriolanus* (FAC 63).

Summers for Roth and his family were spent at Belmar or Bradley Beach, just south of Asbury Park on the Jersey Shore (Figure 1.4). (Asbury Park is where Mickey Sabbath returns at the end of *Sabbath's Theater* to visit his family's graves and meet the hundred-year-old cousin, Fish.) In rented rooms, sometimes a cabin, or sometimes a small house shared with three other families, the Roths vacationed free from the humid, often mosquito-populated Newark. For several weeks, they joined other lower-middle-class Jews from their neighborhood. Herman would come for his two-week vacation and then drive down on weekends in their old Pontiac after his work in the city (FAC 23). It was at the beach where Roth found romance, adventure, and an awareness of a world beyond New Jersey marred by concern about the war.

Roth felt "snug" and protected in what he called the "homey hubbub" of Bradley Beach (FAC 23–24), although surrounding him and visible on the beach were signs of war: barbed wire, Coast Guard bunkers, blacked-out boardwalk lights, blackout shades on rooming-house windows, and occasional skirmishes with anti-Semitic gangs from neighboring Neptune. At nine, he feared that he might emerge from under a wave amid dead bodies. But by ten and free from homework, he had an idyllic time.

In 1959, Roth would publish a brief memoir of those days swimming and sunbathing entitled "Recollections from Beyond the Last Rope."[62] Celebrating the freedom and carefree quality of the seashore, he also noted the "unprivate" nature of life at the shore, where you shared everything, from the bathroom to the kitchen. Chaos had to be met with "communal authoritarianism" (REC 43). But as the years passed, it was thrilling for the children to discover that they had actually been sabotaging "the guardianship of our parents" (REC 43).

Summer at the beach, Roth writes, was educational in other ways because it was there that he learned not only to swim and dive "but to flirt, to drink, to pose, to swindle, to do everything," including explore female bodies (REC

Figure 1.4 Philip Roth, age eight, at Bradley Beach with his brother, Sandy, 1942. Credit: Newark Public Library.

43).[63] Girls upended any thoughts of improvement, physical or mental. And it was there he learned to dance in the white-pillared pavilions, pounded on their pillars by the sea, while the favorite summer song played and the couples kissed, Roth confessing, "I think I kissed more kisses between the ages of thirteen and seventeen than I will kiss the rest of my life. And I'm only talking about summers" (REC 44). "For entire summers kissing was like baseball: an end in itself," until it became a prelude to groping and perhaps sex, always with Vaughn Monroe, Billy Eckstine, or Sinatra in the background (REC

44). The girls changed, but the mood was constant. And during the last few summers there, Roth had a girl.

But his memoir ends with a chilling sense of mortality: entering the water with his girlfriend, he suddenly realizes, "If I am old enough for her, my parents are suddenly older than I like to imagine" (REC 45). Learning that a fellow vacationer had gotten married and entered the trucking business signals a new maturity and awareness of mortality but not before an elegiac description of his father unexpectedly arriving midweek and immediately heading for a swim. The image of Herman happily entering the water anticipates the lyrical and eulogistic moment at the end of *Patrimony*, when Roth recalls being on a pier with his father and Uncle Ed at the Port of Newark to see the ships anchored in the harbor and the sudden vastness of the scene. But it also evokes another image, of ghostly ships and the absence of his recently deceased father (REC 47–48; PAT 234–36).

Newark would also have a stylistic influence on Roth. Rob Steinbaum, publisher of the *New Jersey Law Journal*, remembers Roth once saying, "My sentences are like a Hobby's sandwich. First you slap on the pastrami, then you slap on the coleslaw, then you put on the Russian dressing, and pretty soon the whole thing gets soggy." The reference is to the overstuffed pastrami and corned beef sandwiches at Newark's venerable Jewish delicatessen and restaurant, Hobby's, at 32 Branford Place, corner of Halsey. Metaphorically, this description of piling up phrases, clauses, verbs, and nouns accurately describes the exuberant style of Roth, which has, one might argue, a Newark origin if not taste to it.[64]

But soon an exodus took place. Dr. Charles Kotler from *The Anatomy Lesson* has moved from Newark to New York, a reaction to the 1967 riots that saw the city burn, re-created in *I Married a Communist* when Murray Ringold, longtime English teacher at South Side High, reveals to Zuckerman at the end of the novel that he finally left the city. It wasn't because of union politics or a vengeful school board but because he persisted in staying on even after he was mugged twice—until his wife was murdered in a robbery attempt (IMC 317). His determination not to betray his students or Newark backfired: he betrayed his wife, who became the victim of his "civic virtue" (IMC 317). Scenes in *American Pastoral* describe similar devastation.

The decline of Newark is the obverse of Roth's memories and praise, part of his evolving narrative of the city. While he generally locates his urban portrait in the 1933–50 period, he also exposes its demise and violence, seen most vividly in the actions of *American Pastoral*, with its narration of the

Levov family's rise from a Prince Street tenement, the first stop for Newark's immigrant Jews, to the pastoral pleasantness of Old Rimrock, the idyllic homestead of Swede Levov, but also with accounts of threats to individual security in the city. Roth himself did not return to Newark once he left to attend Bucknell.

The Plot Against America cements the destruction of Newark: in the searing atmosphere of anti-Semitic Newark, one needs weapons to defend oneself. To protect themselves against the riots in the city following the assassination of the presidential candidate Walter Winchell, the new neighbor of the Roths on Summit Avenue (where the Roth family *did* live), the night watchman Mr. Cucuzza, visits with his son (the Roths *did* have Italian neighbors). Joey, the son, brings a cake, the father a gun. But Mr. Roth instantly rejects the pistol, believing there will not be any disruption: born in Newark in 1901 (the actual year of birth of Herman Roth), the fictitious father emphasizes that he has always been a good citizen, as if that would protect him (PAA 284). But he does admit there is a new danger because America has elected a fascist (Lindbergh) and Winchell has been killed.

Anti-Semitic riots begin, but Mr. Roth still rejects the protection of a gun. Why do I need it, he asks? I am a law-abiding U.S. citizen, and that alone will protect me. A radio bulletin outlining Winchell's funeral after his body has lain in state in New York's Penn Station and the expected appearance of FDR, who lost to Lindbergh, appearing at the funeral, takes attention away from the gun but not the question posed by Mr. Cucuzza: "How you gonna protect?" (PAA 282–86).

The destruction of Newark, in the words of Lou Levov, Swede's father, has turned the city into "a carcass" (AP 235): "Used to be the city where they manufactured everything. Now it's the car-theft capital of the world" (AP 24). Newark has become a battleground: it's no longer Uncle Max in his undershirt. "What do you know about Newark, Mama's Boy! . . . Moron! *Moron!* Newark is a nigger with a knife!" is the new cry (ZUB 218). Ironically, the rant and report is by Alvin Pepler, a self-proclaimed genius and former game show champ. But when Zuckerman drives up and down the streets of his past—Lyons Avenue, Chancellor Avenue—and his schools, he and his armed driver observe a ruined city and change; the synagogue where he had taken Hebrew lessons has become an African Methodist Episcopal Church (ZUB 262).

Topophilia, the love of place, characterizes Roth's return to his haunted sites, but each return is with a difference, epitomized perhaps by a stop near an alleyway on Chancellor Avenue. A young African American emerges from a house with a German shepherd and slowly approaches the limousine. He asks, "Who you supposed to be?" Defeated by his own ego and the destitution of his city and withdrawal of his own family, Zuckerman answers "No one" and drives off into the night (ZUB 262).

Ironically, Roth had not lived in Newark since he left for Bucknell in September 1951, but neither had his parents who, in 1951, moved, first, to a garden apartment in Elizabeth, then to Moorestown in southern New Jersey, and finally back to Elizabeth once Herman Roth retired. But for Philip Roth, it's Newark from first to last, from "Goodbye, Columbus" (1959) to *Nemesis* (2010). In between, there is the Newark of *The Anatomy Lesson* and *Operation Shylock* and *I Married a Communist*, plus the Newark threaded throughout *Patrimony* and revived in both *American Pastoral* and *The Plot Against America*. Zuckerman is at one point mockingly called "Nathan of Newark" by Sylphid, the daughter of Eve Frame in *I Married a Communist*. Earlier, in *Zuckerman Unbound*, Pepler identifies the fictitious Roth as "the Marcel Proust" of New Jersey (ZUB 127).

In *Zuckerman Unbound*, Pepler of Newark badgers the hero about facts, details, and trivia about Newark life, a delight for the reader but work for the writer. Even Roth seems to feel enough is enough: in March 1980, while working on the novel, he wrote to the biographer and critic James Atlas, "If I write the word Newark one more time in my life I'll shoot the Mayor. I know you can't go home again, but you do anyway."[65]

Roth himself expressed disbelief at his own fascination with Newark. In an interview about *I Married a Communist*, he said:

> I, myself, am surprised I'm so mesmerized by this place, because I left younger than any of my friends. I was sixteen or so when I went off to college, just seventeen. And I never went back. And many of my high school friends went back after college, were professionals, doctors, lawyers in Newark, hung on until they couldn't hang on there any longer and then moved to the suburbs. But close to Newark, when I lived all over. On the other hand, the place has come to represent for me, I suppose, modern times in America, and the fate of Newark has been the fate of many other cities.[66]

What was America like beyond Weequahic, he wondered? To find out he went to Bucknell after Newark Rutgers. But Newark remained, providing the breeding ground of experience and memory. It was also his laboratory and workshop, offering him the tools to remake his life and America into something new.

Newark dropped out of Roth's fiction of the 1970s, although not out of his life. In that decade, he does not set a single work in the city, immersed in his new life with Claire Bloom and dividing his time between London and Connecticut. He returned to it in the 1980s, however, initially in *Zuckerman Unbound* and then *The Facts* and *Patrimony*, preparatory to its central role in his American Trilogy. But a walk through the city in 1990, a year after his father's death, introduced him to a waste land, the African Americans so miserable that they don't even play basketball on his old playground, he wrote. He came away thinking he had the most privileged of childhoods, the city in its heyday and the Jews at "the height of their energy." Who could ask for anything more?[67]

Roth's use of Newark may be analogous to Walter Benjamin's well-known depiction of the angel of history in a 1920 painting by Paul Klee. Klee's *Angelus Novus* shows an angel looking as though he is about to move away from something he is fixedly contemplating in the past while moving forward. Benjamin writes, "His face is turned toward the past. Where we perceive a chain of events, he sees one single catastrophe which keeps piling wreckage upon wreckage and hurls it in front of his feet. The angel would like to stay, awaken the dead, and make whole what has been smashed."[68] Roth's presentation of Newark is his attempt to "make whole what has been smashed," a looking back to a past that compels him forward.

2

Declaration of Independence

I was a countervoice, an antitheme.

—Philip Roth, *The Facts*, 1988

Roth's declaration of independence was not a document signed by fifty-six Americans, including two future presidents, three vice presidents, and ten members of the U.S. Congress. It was not a document at all, but a shouting match between himself and his father over his independence and family restrictions. Reminded by the framed Declaration of Independence in the Roth hallway given to his father by the Metropolitan Life Insurance Company, Roth felt that at age eighteen it was time to go (FAC 21; PAA 275). But challenging "a tycoon in the moral-authority racket" was not easy, as Roth would discover from his reading of Kafka (IMC 85). Yet his determination to be "an absolutely independent, self-sufficient man" overrode everything (FAC 160). It is no surprise that the title of Peter Tarnopol's first novel, cited in *My Life as a Man*, is *A Jewish Father* and uses as its epigram the portentous quote from Thomas Mann Roth employed in *his* first novel, *Letting Go*.[1]

Reference to the Declaration of Independence anticipates that moment in "The Conversion of the Jews" from *Goodbye, Columbus*, when the thirteen-year-old Hebrew student Ozzie Freedman asks Rabbi Binder why he calls the Jews "'The Chosen People' if the Declaration of Independence claimed all men to be created equal" (GBC 141). The rabbi tries to distinguish between political equality and spiritual legitimacy, but what Ozzie wants to know is different. How can Jews be different people from everyone else in the U.S.? Already, the American document had pragmatic and fictional currency for Roth, reinforced by a family trip to Washington, D.C., in 1941 to tour the nation's monuments (Figure 2.1).

Roth's mother never had to duplicate Ozzie's mother pleading with Ozzie not to jump off the roof of the synagogue, where he has dramatically demanded obedience from his audience beneath him. This was

Figure 2.1 The Roth family on a trip to Washington, D.C., in the summer of 1941. Photo taken at the Arlington Memorial Amphitheater, Arlington National Cemetery. *Left to right:* Philip, Bess, Herman, Sandy. Credit: Newark Public Library.

largely because Bess Roth never opposed her son or his stubborn nature. She hesitated to challenge her quick and generally obedient son, who did his homework and hung out with the right guys, even if he did eat hamburgers at Syd's. But his father became unnerved when Roth became independent during his last year of high school and first at college in downtown Newark.

Herman Roth's career was difficult, earning a modest salary and commission as an assistant manager in the Essex County office of Metropolitan Life. To improve, he took a risk that wiped out the family savings. Believing that his Jewishness would hold him back from advancement with Metropolitan Life, the forty-five-year-old sought a new beginning. He borrowed money to join friends in a frozen food distribution business. It didn't work out, and when Philip was ready to begin Rutgers Newark, the father was still paying off debts. But in 1949, Herman was unexpectedly promoted to manage an office in Union City, just outside of Newark, with an increase in salary.

Roth himself began working as soon as he graduated Weequahic High in January 1950, spending six months as a clerk at the S. Klein department store, while living at home and reading Wolfe, Anderson, Lardner, Caldwell, and Dreiser. These were formative writers for the young Roth, more for their theme of self-discovery than as inspiration to become a writer. Particularly important were the themes of independence and self-awareness, leading to his own departure from home to find his purpose in life. At the time, Roth was leaning toward law and actually enrolled in the prelaw program when he began Rutgers Newark several months later. But the emotional power, especially of Wolfe (he read all four of Wolfe's autobiographical novels) and his lyrical sense of ordinary American life, combined with the moral passion of the patriotic Howard Fast, influenced his determination to find his own way. The moral quandaries outlined by literature were inescapable. Wolfe, along with Henry James and later Hawthorne, would be the most influential early writers of Roth's career. Later, it would be Kafka.

Daily trips to the heart of Newark also had an impact, his experience at the department store exposing him to consumerism at a discount. The department store slogan, "S. Klein on the Square," referred to its flagship New York store on Union Square at 14th Street but also to the square or honest deal it offered every customer. The New York store used a carpenter's square as its logo. Roth recalled that after his high school graduation, he worked briefly at the Union Square store and ate lunch quickly so that he could rush to Fourth Avenue and buy Modern Library books at 25 cents each. The Modern Library Giants were 75 cents. Suddenly he began to amass his own library, one hour of work equaling one Modern Library Giant. For forty hours, he made $30.[2] Soon he transferred to the Newark branch of S. Klein, which stood across from the Military Park on Broad Street. Taking the No. 14 Clinton Place bus to downtown, he often passed the park, while the Traffic tower at Broad and Market (recalled in *The Plot Against America*) acted as the center of the city.

The store positioned itself as a more affordable but fashionable option to Macy's or even Newark's own Bamberger's, where Roth also worked part time in the late 1940s in the shoe department during Christmas.[3] S. Klein stores were full-line department stores, with furniture departments, fur salons, and pet departments. They were steps above discount regional stores like Two Guys from Harrison or E. J. Korvettes, venerable New Jersey retailers.

Another neighborhood attraction often passed by Roth was the Empire Theater, with its burlesque. The Empire opened in 1912 at 265 Washington Street, at the corner of Branford Place, just one block in from Market Street. It quickly got a reputation as a vaudeville house, adding striptease and burlesque when vaudeville began to feel competition from the movies. Suddenly the Empire was a mix of girls, gags, and music. Strippers and dancing chorus lines were the draw, exposing as much as the law permitted (and sometimes more).[4]

In *The Facts*, Roth recalls how he entertained friends like the Wheatcrofts and the Maurers, young academic couples at Bucknell, with comic routines learned at the Empire, while Zuckerman in *The Anatomy Lesson* recounts with delight the vaudeville houses of Newark (FAC 59; AL 115–16). Vaudeville may have influenced not only the comic monologues in *Portnoy's Complaint* but more directly Roth's short story "On the Air," which unites vaudeville and radio.

In September 1950, Roth entered Newark College of Rutgers as a prelaw student; he had wanted to go to the New Brunswick campus but failed to get an entrance scholarship there. Rutgers Newark, founded in 1946, was the amalgamation of the New Jersey Law School plus four others, including the Newark Institute of Arts & Sciences. An alliance became a merger in 1936 to create the University of Newark; a decade later, Rutgers University in Newark was formed when the New Jersey State Legislature voted to make the University of Newark part of Rutgers University.

Although Roth wanted desperately to go away to college, he spent his first year at Rutgers Newark, commuting to downtown by bus, hardly the college life on a bucolic campus he imagined. In *Indignation*, he alludes to his experience there, the school disguised as Robert Treat (the name of the colonial leader who started what would become Newark), admiring the excitable manner of the few Jewish professors there. Their combative style and sharp, hard attitude was more vital than anything he or the character Marcus Messner encounters in the midwestern college he attends in *Indignation* (IND 85–86).

Located at 40 Rector Street (which runs from Broad Street to the McCarter Highway and then the Passaic River) in the former Ballantine brewery and a bank, the campus was only a twenty-minute bus ride from Roth's home. He felt grown up to be going downtown not for the movies or a Sunday dinner with the family but with a purpose: education, supported by new textbooks, a new briefcase, and a pipe (FAC 36–37). Alongside Irish and Italian students, he felt exposed to a world he had not known in the Weequahic enclave. His studies and his new associates elevated him above distinct social differences. He, too, was different, but he felt accepted by the working-class boys from Newark's Ironbound district (see GBC 30–31).

With his new range of gentile friends from high schools like Barringer and South Side, he began to feel American in ways not possible in Weequahic. The diversity he experienced emboldened him to explore and learn an America other than that of the striving Jews of Weequahic. This would be where Neil Klugman would go to school, to the chagrin of Brenda Patmikin and her parents, Neil mentioning that he had actually taken a course in Contemporary Moral Issues in the former waiting room of the bank's president. The bank itself had become a main campus building (GBC 30). He majored in philosophy.

Roth's first-year curriculum for the BA degree at Rutgers Newark had a set of required courses that included English composition and literature, the development of Western civilization, science (either biology, chemistry, geology, or the Principles of Science), language, and physical education. The required scholastic average to graduate was 3.4. The year Roth entered Rutgers Newark, officially the Newark College of Arts and Sciences, the university instituted a new combined Bachelor of Arts and Law degree, requiring only three years of undergraduate study. On completion of the first year of law school, one received the BA degree.[5]

When Roth attended, there were 1,170 students in the Arts and Sciences Division, although by the second term 135 had dropped out, a reflection of the working-class nature of the student body and financial demands of family competing with attendance.[6] Instead of continuing, Roth decided to transfer to a school the complete opposite of Rutgers Newark, gritty with students striving to get ahead. His selection was the pristine campus and neatly manicured lawns of Bucknell in rural Pennsylvania.

The reason was less academic than familial, recognizing that if he stayed any longer in their Leslie Street home, the friction between himself and his father would only increase. In *The Facts,* he skirts the issue by writing that he could "no longer truthfully account to him" or to his mother (FAC 38). He would feel suffocated by the father's restrictions on his private life, especially now that he was a college student. He had outgrown the family dinner table but admitted that the main reason he had to get away was to protect this self-sacrificing father and devoted son from "a battle that they were equally ill equipped to fight" (FAC 38). In *Indignation*, the hero is more candid: "I left because my father's surveillance had become insufferable" (IND 9).

His mother was not a problem: she acknowledged the growing independence of both Roth and his brother and accepted (reluctantly) their new maturity. Sandy, born when their mother was twenty-three, felt more constrained by her mothering than Roth, born five years later, when the father's weekly Metropolitan paycheck mitigated some of their earlier financial anxieties. But, beginning at sixteen, Roth began energetically to seek his freedom.

The decision to attend Bucknell was as accidental as it was purposeful. He knew nothing of the school and only wanted a decent university away from home that would prepare him to become an "idealistic lawyer," something he had thought of since he was twelve (FAC 39). But he had no guidance nor model. Until then, only ex-GIs were his neighborhood tutors, and most of them became rumba dancers, short-order cooks, or gas station attendants. They instructed only in five-card stud, craps, or petty thievery. His brother, who had been a Saturday student at the Art Students League in New York during high school, studied at Pratt Institute for three years after two in the navy. On weekends, he would set up his easel in the dining room and paint or draw. Often, he would leave about their apartment paperback books he had read on the subway or train home, so at fifteen or sixteen, his younger brother began reading in earnest. Curiosity took hold of him. (FAC 39–40).

From a youthful visit to Princeton to see a football game with his Uncle Ed, a dealer in cardboard cartons, Roth had an idealized vision of what a campus should be. But he (correctly) sensed that the Ivy League was anti-Semitic and had quotas. To a young man who championed the Four Freedoms, opposed the DAR, and supported Henry Wallace, the idea of a privileged class that discriminated against minorities was an anathema. He also did not want to struggle against prejudice as his father had done at Metropolitan Life, no doubt a source of Roth's views to fight such opposition. Listening to football scores on the radio, he learned the names of hundreds of other universities and read additional names in the sports pages of the *Newark Evening News* and saw them on football-pool cards. Such a pool was illegal, but when he was eleven Roth bought the cards, and when he was thirteen stared selling them with some friends on the playground for the owner of a candy store, his only connection with organized crime, he claimed (FAC 41). Through the pool he became familiar with more institutions of higher learning than through his college advisor at high school.

A Leslie Street neighbor, Marty Castlebaum, was a quiet student with an enthusiasm for baseball who became a studious piano player (which, Roth writes, separated himself from other friends, who counterbalanced good grades and good conduct with shooting craps and storing sealed condoms in their wallets [FAC 42]). Marty attended Bucknell, a name that meant nothing to Roth, but Marty displayed exactly what Roth sought: "the sort of poise and savoir fare that encouraged a boy to run for student-council president" (FAC 42). Marty's new, confident manner appealed to Roth, who was astonished that he was still on Leslie Street "keeping my father at bay by heeding high school rules of conduct" (FAC 43).

At Newark Rutgers, Roth might become more of a Newarker and an American from the working middle class, but what he really wanted to be was a college undergraduate dressed in the chino pants and sport jacket or blazer that identified the purposeful sophomore. A button-down shirt under a V-neck sweater would finish the look, supported on the ground by the penny loafer. Bucknell, with its nubile coeds, seemed to make that look possible.

In March 1951, Roth and his parents drove to Bucknell, located in a farming valley of the Susquehanna River in Lewisburg, a town of some five thousand. Interviewed by an assistant director of admissions, he was told he would receive full credit for his Rutgers year, but was less assured about receiving financial assistance. His father's recent promotion and their solid appearance made him an unlikely candidate for financial aid, although the school did not know Herman Roth was still paying off his business debt; Herman forbade its reporting on the financial form under "debts." At forty-seven Bess Roth looked very much the American mother in a navy-blue dress. A small gold pin marked her two years as president of the PTA, and her comportment and dress showed her to be "thoroughly Americanized" (FAC 44).

Roth did not receive the scholarship that seemed so necessary. But his father, sensing the attraction and importance of the school to his son, simply told him on the evening of their visit that if he wanted to go, he could go (FAC 47). Being away from home, hundreds of miles from everything that was constraining, allowed Roth the freedom to become a new person.

But relocation did not eliminate the father-son battles, and Roth reports that he had a second major fight with his father on his first midyear vacation home, a fight that was bitter and resentful (FAC 47). And his father still shadowed him, an "intellectual homunculus" on his shoulder; Roth actually, secretly, physically on occasion, brought him to class (PAT 225). He educated not only himself but his father, his independence strangely tying him to his family and city, which would form the paradox at the center of his work: his escape from Newark ironically pulled him back to the city and his family in his writing. But he felt the strain as having more to do with saving and rescuing rather than advancing and eliminating. This, however, was not unusual in his parents' generation: you carried the limitations of the preceding generation with you and wanted "to redeem them from their shame" by completing "their ascendance." Removal from one environment to another was necessary for each generation: if his father had not left the slums of his parents and moved to Weequahic, if Roth had not left Leslie Street and headed to Pennsylvania, he couldn't have completed the "family mission" of education and success in America. Leaving was not abandoning but continuing the ascent.[7]

Replacing the commuter school that was Rutgers was the quiet, manicured campus of well-behaved, upwardly mobile, largely white students with only a sprinkling of Jews, far from back alleys and bus lines. At Bucknell, Roth threw himself into campus life. Living in room 409 of the West Wing of Main College for his first two years, he moved to 238 South 4th Street for his last, only blocks from the campus. Entering as a prelaw student, he switched to English in 1952. He worked in his first year for *L'Agenda*, the yearbook, and continued in his second year, when he also became involved with the literary magazine, *Et Cetera*. The first issue was published in March 1952; it sold for 25 cents and appeared four times a year. He was a member of Cap and Dagger and University Players all three years at Bucknell and for one year was a member of the International Relations Club and the Booster Club. He was also a member of Sigma Tau Delta, the honorary English society; Theta Alpha Phi, the National Theater Honors Fraternity; and Pi Sigma Alpha, the National Political Science Honor Society, of which he was secretary treasurer.

For a year he was also a member of the Jewish fraternity Sigma Alpha Mu but resigned with two friends (Peter Tasch from Baltimore and Dick Minton from Mount Vernon, New York) in the winter of 1952 to work at *Et Cetera*, which they had helped to start (Figure 2.2). They resigned from the fraternity to protest its anti-intellectual atmosphere, which divided students into either commerce and finance majors or prelaw types. Roth and his friends were in the arts.

Roth's selection as editor-in-chief of *Et Cetera* made news on the campus, the headline of the school paper, the *Bucknellian*, for 2 October 1952 reading "Roth, Pincus Chosen to Head *Et Cetera*." They planned to release their first issue on Homecoming weekend. The news story listed Roth as an English

Figure 2.2 Roth (*left*) in the office of Bucknell's literary magazine *Et Cetera* with Robert Pincus, 1953. Credit: Special Collections/University Archives, Bucknell University.

and Political Science major in his junior year who was also assistant editor of *L'Agenda*. The paper reported that in addition to his campus activities, he was a participant in intramural sports, especially tennis. Another headline in the same issue announced "Brown, Roth, Have Leading Roles for Cap and Dagger's Madwoman." The story reported that Jane Brown and Philip Roth would have the leading roles in the November production of Jean Giraudoux's *The Madwoman of Chaillot*, Roth to play a ragpicker, "a tattered philosopher who sees beauty in every garbage can."

The *Bucknellian*, however, was also the source of a contretemps at the school. *Et Cetera* was meant to be an alternative to the weekly school paper, displaying wit, whimsy, and good writing loosely based on the *New Yorker*, with a nonchalant tone and dissident position toward conventional collegiate behavior. The first issue, in October 1952, the first under Roth as editor-in-chief, did not comment on the presidential race between Stevenson and Eisenhower, although a year later the magazine published a prose poem Roth had written that summer, a monologue by a coward too worried to object to McCarthyism. The piece received no response. During the actual McCarthy hearings, Roth would visit his campus friends, the Maurers, and become upset listening to the proceedings on the radio with Bob Maurer.

In the spring of 1953, however, Roth chose to take on the low-brow campus enthusiasms expressed in the weekly *Bucknellian* and publish a sarcastic attack on the banal paper then edited by the innocent captain of the cheerleading squad. (A year earlier he had dated two members of the squad.) He attacked the paper for its banality and published a centerfold facsimile of their front page burlesquing the *Bucknellian* and its vapid stories. His taste for mimicry overwhelmed any sense of good taste. Indignation became performance, as he later wrote (FAC 65–66). Admonishment by the Dean of Men was one result, and then censure before the Board of Publications, while several students threatened Roth for his attack on the other editor, Bobby Roemer.

As he notes, the incident revealed his own talent for "comic destruction" in his fiction, but he was so upset by the Board's reprimand that he rushed to his admired English professor Mildred Martin distraught (FAC 66–67). It was an early encounter with opposition to his writing which would come fully into bloom when his Jewish readers attacked *Goodbye, Columbus* and then *Portnoy's Complaint*. Bucknell at the time still had protocols, and one was weekly attendance at chapel, underscored by the Dean of Men. Roth responded by bringing his Schopenhauer and reading it in his pew.

Robert Maurer, academic advisor to *Et Cetera,* was an instructor in American literature at Bucknell and completing a PhD at Wisconsin. His subject was ee cummings. His wife, Charlotte, had been a secretary to William Shawn at the *New Yorker.* The Maurers had little income, which, in an odd way, appealed to Roth: they were independent from convention, "free, levelheaded Americans" unconcerned with "position and appearances" (FAC 57). Robert had a midwestern openness about him, even if he came from industrial New Jersey. Charlotte, educated at Antioch College, was attractive and well-read, and Roth fell for her after he graduated from Bucknell, especially after he spent a week with them in their cabin on a tiny Maine island (FAC 58).

Another mentor was John (Jack) Wheatcroft, English instructor and poet. He was twenty-six and Roth nineteen when they met in 1952. Roth and he hit it off immediately, and Roth would often visit and sometimes babysit with his girlfriend at the Wheatcrofts' home. Most important, Wheatcroft enjoyed listening to Roth's re-creation of Newark life, its characters and contradictions, and believed he had a real talent in fashioning that world, something he also described to the Maurers—the first non-Jewish family with whom he shared his inside view of his Jewish neighborhood, including stories of the Seltzer King and Mickey Pasteelnik, Newark's three-hundred-pound Apple King, a family friend. Someone's shady uncle, a bookie, or an illicit relationship involving a Jewish husband—all this color was a prelude before retelling the same stories to Richard Stern at Chicago years later (FAC 59).

Stern, of course, told Roth to write them down. The result was *Goodbye, Columbus*. But at Bucknell, he had not realized how such a substratum of experience could become literary material. How could art be rooted in Jewish Newark he asked himself (FAC 59)? Comics, confidence men, and crooks populated his stories, and those witnessed on the streets became his narrative heroes. It was Wheatcroft who first encouraged Roth to "mimic" the idiosyncratic manner of self-presentation from his neighborhood. With no other faculty member did Roth experience such freedom.

Wheatcroft was a World War II navy veteran who received a Purple Heart for his service in the Pacific. Although he rarely spoke of his experiences, there were hints at what he went through, which may have influenced Roth's early short story about two surviving but forgotten marines on an isolated atoll in the Pacific, "Expect the Vandals." It appeared in *Esquire* in December 1958. Possibly more important was Wheatcroft's dedication to literature, both as a teacher and a creative writer. The idea of literature as a mission to which one devoted oneself, even if it meant isolation, was something Roth embraced throughout his career. Wheatcroft treated writing with gravity and concentration. He had the "severity of [a] cleric" when addressing the big issues of life, whether mortality, morality, or meaning. But he could also laugh and displayed a remarkable sense of humor, the two qualities developed by the mature Roth in his personality and his writing. Literature was not a subject but a calling, Roth wrote, and Wheatcroft was no less than its "priest."[8] This aspirational posture became an ideal for Roth, later isolated in his Cornwall Bridge studio, completing, or perhaps struggling, with his latest project.

At Bucknell, Roth enthusiastically turned to drama as well as writing. He was a performer, noting that he and fellow student Dick Denholtz, also from New Jersey, would produce coarse and uninhibited humor. One of their successes, a work they wrote and directed together, was a musical skit for the interfraternity Mid-Term Jubilee, a condensed version of *Guys and Dolls* set at Bucknell. They also starred in the work. It was, Roth said, genuine low comedy (FAC 53). But he also acted on stage (while the classroom became his intellectual stage), initially in supporting roles in productions of *Oedipus*, *School for Scandal*, and *Death of a Salesman* (Figure 2.3).

His role as the ragpicker in *The Madwoman of Chaillot* earned respectable reviews. By then he was a member of Cap and Dagger, the theatrical society, and was elected to the National Theater Honors Fraternity. Cap and Dagger and *Et Cetera* had become his substitute family, replacing the social fraternity, from which he had resigned.

It was through Cap and Dagger that Roth found a steady girlfriend he names Paula Bates in *The Facts*, nicknamed Polly, who was actually Betty Powell. She would come to rehearsals and occasionally act as prompter or director's assistant. She transferred to Bucknell her junior year and was to Roth the most sophisticated and sardonic girl he had ever met. Not only did she drink martinis but she chain-smoked. Her frail blonde appearance, not conventionally pretty, appealed to him—as would later Margaret (Maggie) Martinson Williams, similar in stature and looks.

Figure 2.3 Roth (*right*) performing in *Death of a Salesman* at Bucknell, 1953. Credit: Special Collections/University Archives, Bucknell University.

"Polly" was complicated, balancing an independent, no-nonsense wit with a passion that made her susceptible to Roth's intensity. A love affair quickly developed, although they had difficulty finding a place to be intimate. When they babysat for faculty, they used their beds. Whether in the laundry room at her mother's home in Scotch Plains, New Jersey, or in his father's car, they found room for love. In the summer of 1953, they worked as counselors at a Jewish summer camp, Pocono Highland Camps in Marshalls Creek, Pennsylvania, where the summer before Roth had been the counselor for Bunk 18. A photo of the teenage campers shows a robust, fit, healthy Roth. In *The Facts*, he writes that their erotic life had the thrill of adultery, the product of concealment and secrecy.

For his senior year at Bucknell, Roth rented a room from a Mrs. Nellenback at 238 South 4th Street. It was on a corner close to the women's quadrangle. He saw it as a love nest, despite being warned that women were allowed only on Sunday afternoons for tea. His front room opened onto a summer porch. Peter Tasch, managing editor of *Et Cetera*, lived upstairs. "Polly" came in through the front porch window. Unsurprisingly, they were caught at the beginning of second semester. An elaborate ruse to hide her from the suddenly returned Mrs. Nellenback backfired. She discovered Polly hiding under the bed, while Roth left the house with a book as an unsuccessful diversion. A fight with Mrs. Nellenback ensued, one threatening the other, while Roth saw his future and that of Polly's in pieces. Only some ten years later did he exploit the scene in an episode in his second novel, *When She Was Good*. Fearful that he would be expelled, Roth was relieved to discover that neither he nor Polly would be penalized other than with their embarrassment at being caught. He thought that Mrs. Nellenback did not report him because she needed his rent.

But a new worry emerged: for six weeks in the spring of 1954, they thought that Polly was pregnant. If so, they would both have to give up graduate school plans (she wanted to go on in French, Roth in English), marry, and stay on at Bucknell as teaching assistants. It was a possibility, although certainly not their first choice. Roth had applied to go to Oxford or Cambridge as a Fulbright or Marshall scholar, and if that didn't work out, he had also applied for fellowships at Chicago and Penn, where Polly hoped to study. They were shocked to think they might not be able to go forward with their lives and careers.

They met regularly for dinner at the men's dining hall and buoyed each other up about their future as a married couple "with a child and no money"

(FAC 76). At least as a new father he would not be drafted, although he had dropped out of ROTC despite a colonel's urging him to seek a commission in the post-Korea army. He quit because he opposed military training on college campuses. They did not consider an abortion. When they found out she was *not* pregnant, it was Roth's second pardon of the term (after the failure of Mrs. Nellenback to report him to the university authorities). But following his enormous relief, their affair waned. Premature domesticity did not appeal to him. In a neat set of sentences in *The Facts*, he summarizes what he had escaped: at eighteen his father's rules; at nineteen a meaningless relationship to a Jewish fraternity; at twenty the ordinariness of the campus student community; and at twenty-one monogamous love (FAC 77).

Escape to England would have been the easy answer, but he did not win a Fulbright or a Marshall. He did, however, win a full fellowship to the University of Pennsylvania and a similar offer from the University of Chicago. To Polly's astonishment and even Roth's, he chose to go to Chicago. And by the summer after graduation, he was involved with someone else, a girl he had met at a Newark day camp where he was working until he left for Chicago. His affair with Polly was over. She went on to marry a professor from Penn and became, herself, a professor of French at New York University. She tragically died from cancer at forty-seven.

That Roth goes into such detail in recounting this early romantic episode in his life attests to its seriousness in almost derailing his career but setting him on a path of erotic adventure. During his period at Bucknell, his parents left Newark and moved to a garden apartment in Elizabeth, on the same street where they were married in 1927 and where Roth as a child would regularly make Sunday visits to his widowed maternal grandmother after visiting his widowed paternal grandmother in Newark the same day.

During his senior year at Bucknell, Roth became involved with *L'Agenda*, the yearbook, and began to write critically serious papers, encouraged in part by his favorite English professor, Mildred Martin (1904–1995), an important figure in his literary and personal development and largely the reason for his shift from prelaw studies to English.

Martin had joined the Bucknell faculty in 1940 (retiring in 1972) after completing a PhD at the University of Illinois. She was an outstanding teacher, and many students remembered her interest, commitment, and encouragement, not the least, Roth. Her seminar on English literature began with *Beowulf* and ended with T. S. Eliot, on whom she published an early but important bibliography. Often held at her home beginning in the late

afternoon, her senior honors seminar was for Roth one of the most stimulating experiences of his university life. He had previously taken her writing
tutorial.

Her influence on him was large, Roth explaining in a 1981 commemora-
tive booklet for Martin, when she received an Award of Merit Citation from
Bucknell at their September graduation, that her attention to stylistic precision was unparalleled. She demanded it in reading, writing, and speech: "In
that class, the unexamined line wasn't worth uttering. We were merciless with
one another about 'unsubstantiated' argument and 'subjective' criticism." She
was the first of his "scrupulous editors—the sternest, the most relentless, the
best."[9]

Martin's honors seminar began in September 1953 with an ambitious
reading list: at least two books a week plus fifty pages in Albert C. Baugh's
monumental, hefty, and once admired *Literary History of England*. A weekly
critical essay added to the workload, intensified by Martin's attention to
verbal and written accuracy. Her businesslike, midwestern, practical manner
combined with rimless glasses and solid learning made her precisely the kind
of "humane intellectual disciplinarian" Roth was ready for (FAC 68). There
were eight in the seminar, but Roth, Tasch, and Minton dominated.

Roth provides great detail about the weekly seminar meetings between
1:30 and 4:30 every Thursday in the front room of an eighteenth-century clapboard house. Like the young Zuckerman visiting Lonoff's study in *The Ghost
Writer*, Roth would admire the dark paneling, bookshelves, and Oriental
carpet and think "This is how *I* shall live once I have my PhD and a decent
tenured position" (FAC 68). To him, this seemed a more viable (and secure)
life than that of a novelist, and to reinforce the excitement of discovery, he
includes three excerpts from Martin's diary for that year in *The Facts* (FAC
69). She, in turn, found Roth an eager and attractive student; there is a story
that one afternoon she may have made advances toward him, having invited
him for extra sessions.[10] In *The Facts*, he quotes her comment when he was
upset over the reprimand from the school's Board of Publications for a satire
he published in *Et Cetera* and rushed to her to be consoled: "When you came
to my house you were nearly in tears" (FAC 67).[11]

Eloise Mallinson, a graduate student of Martin's, recalled that she "was a
brilliant woman, and as I say, the best questioner I ever sat under. She, by
questioning, could lead you to the answer of her first question so deftly
that you felt you'd done it all yourself. But she was really awfully good at
it. I admired her immensely. It was an experience to have a class with her."

Another of her students, Katherine Wheatcroft, remembered how demanding were her courses.[12]

Martin was one of the few female professors in the department but achieved success with only one publication, an annotated bibliography of Eliot criticism. But Miss Martin, as she was known, was the epitome of a teacher and mentor and became head of the department for a time. But she was after only one thing, truth, and she questioned students until she felt they faced it, something Roth transferred in later years to his fiction. His characters may dissemble, evade, and hide, but in the end they recognize the truth of their situation, whether it is Ira Ringold or Swede Levov.

Martin's candor was relentless. As one of her former students wrote, "She made you love the truth more than you loved yourself. She scared nine-tenths of the student body." She possessed a "practical reflexive integrity that affected you." The very day she died, at age ninety in 1995, she had made her way through most of Faulkner's *Absalom, Absalom.*[13] When Roth returned to Bucknell in 1979 to receive an honorary degree, he stayed with the emeritus professor, who accompanied him to the platform in her academic robes. He also revisited the house on South 4th Street, recalling how difficult it was to enter and exit through those front porch windows. He would dedicate *Our Gang* to her, along with two other important teachers, Robert Maurer and Napier Wilt.[14]

His earliest short stories, most written at Bucknell, contained none of his Newark outspokenness and certainly not Jews. His early attempts focused on sensitive adolescents seeking a refined life away from the lower middle class of Newark. Not art but earning a living and raising a family became the goals. There was neither comedy nor Newark in his early prose efforts. Salinger, Capote, and Wolfe were his early influences in these allegories of displacement. At Rutgers Newark, he was just another lower-middle-class boy from an ambitious minority striving for something better through education; at Bucknell he was unique, feeling out of place as a Jew with a focus not on commerce or finance but the arts. A career and a solid income seemed to be the only interests of his fellow students. But he began to wonder, "How could Art be rooted in a parochial Jewish Newark neighborhood?" (FAC 59).

Roth graduated in June 1954 *magna cum laude* and was elected to Phi Beta Kappa and listed in *Who's Who in American Colleges and Universities.*[15] Zuckerman celebrates what Roth experienced at Bucknell, perhaps too optimistically, in *The Anatomy Lesson*: "To be raised as a post-immigrant Jew in America was to be given a ticket out of the ghetto into a wholly unconstrained world of thought. . . . Alienated? Just another way to say 'Set Free!' A Jew set free even from Jews—yet only by steadily maintaining self-consciousness as a Jew. That was the thrilling paradoxical kicker" (AL 74).

This, in many ways, was Roth's situation, although he didn't fully realize it until he hit Chicago and began to take stock of his freedom, which began at Bucknell, where he combined a resistance to his father's control with a liberated college life. The combination affected his Jewish identity and Newark past. No longer the Weequahic kid, he became the liberal, sweater-wearing, college student of the 1950s on the Dean's List and enjoying campus clubs, publications, and non-Jewish coeds. Life in a non-Jewish, rural college in central Pennsylvania allowed him to discover an America unbordered by Jews or family. In contrast to the determined, get-ahead approach at Newark Rutgers and the strong-minded, I'm-gonna-make-it attitude of its less privileged students, Bucknell meant tradition, success, and professional careers.

With a fellowship to Chicago, however, a new phase was to begin, the city of Augie March replacing the repose of central Pennsylvania and the noisy Jewish *shtetl* of Newark. The city was rough and ready, with factories and manufacturing plants surrounding a downtown where art and culture could coexist with grime and grunting. "In Chicago you got a sense of all the streams that America could contain," wrote the poet and University of Chicago graduate Charles Simic.[16] University would quickly become Roth's natural habitat, going on not only for a second stint at Chicago, when he returned in 1956 after an MA in August 1955 and time in the army, to teach English composition and briefly enter the PhD program, but accepting later appointments at Iowa, Princeton, Stony Brook, the University of Pennsylvania, Hunter, and Bard.

For Roth the classroom was his second home, where the serious discussion of literature and writing could take place. It provided an intellectual and creative atmosphere that stimulated the writer, as well as offering him the settings and situations that mattered. The appearance of numerous academics in his fiction confirms the university as his everyday world, whether it is the graduate student world of *Letting Go,* the academic pursuits of David Kepesh in *The Professor of Desire,* Kepesh's later romance with his former student Consuela in *The Dying Animal,* or the life of the intelligent but disgraced former dean and classics professor Coleman Silk in *The Human Stain.*

But the classroom was also an almost unlimited sexual arena. Incidents and relationships exist throughout Roth's work, epitomized, perhaps, by Kepesh in *The Dying Animal* and his affair with a Cuban American student, preceded by the sexual parody of *The Breast*, where teaching Kafka and Gogol may have accelerated Kepesh's transformation into a sexual appendage. Academe is a hotbed of sexual adventure even out of the classroom: the protagonist in *The Professor of Desire* prepares lectures in the dining room of a Prague hotel under the alluring gaze of several attractive prostitutes; in *The Human Stain*, the mature Silk happily pursues a relationship with a much younger and less educated woman; in *The Humbling*, same-sex relations flourish in a university environment. In Roth, sex is never left at the classroom door. And the pattern repeats itself: the smart intellectual appeals to the admiring and nubile student, an activity Roth himself experienced numerous times, as later chapters will show. But disappointment if not disaster often results. As he writes in *The Human Stain*, "Every mistake that man can make usually has a sexual accelerator," later referred to as "the chaos of eros" (HS 35; DA 20).

Universities also initiate social distinctions. In "Goodbye, Columbus," Radcliffe emphasizes Brenda Patimkin's social status, as Rutgers Newark does for Neil Klugman. The final scene in Harvard Yard with Neil standing in front of the Lamont Library (with its Patimkin bathroom sinks) is symbolic not only of his remaining an outsider but of Roth's awareness that labels can easily mask individual identity. Roth began his writing career *in* a university, first at Bucknell and then at the University of Chicago, and was a professor of creative writing at Iowa, Princeton, and Penn.

Roth was unfamiliar with Chicago before he went there in September 1954. Aware of its long literary history—Dreiser, Norris, Anderson, Sandburg, Wright, and Algren—he prepared by reading Bellow's *The Adventures of Augie March*, the sensation of 1953. But he likely had some sense of the city that Harriet Monroe, editor of Chicago's famed *Poetry* magazine, aptly described as "boiling and bubbling." And he might have understood what the well-known Chicago journalist and writer Ben Hecht meant when he called Chicago "a prose town." In the first issue of Hecht and Max Bodenheim's *Chicago Literary Times*, they declared Chicago to be "the reeking, cinder-ridden, joyous . . . chewing gum center of the world, the bleating, slant-headed rendezvous of half-witted newspapers, sociopaths and pants makers."[17] Only Nelson Algren said it better: Chicago "used to be a writer's town and it's always been a fighter's town. For writers and fighters and furtive torpedoes, cat bandits, baggage thieves, hallway head-lockers on the prowl, baby photographers and stylish coneroos, this is the spot."[18]

After Roth arrived and rented a room in International House in Hyde Park, adjacent to the university, he began to explore the city through Augie's eyes, wandering and discovering. Its mix of high and low culture appealed to him: stockyards and the Art Institute of Chicago, South Side jazz bars and the North Side's Gold Coast. It was the birthplace of Walt Disney, Edgar Rice Burroughs, and Benny Goodman, as well as the home of *Playboy* magazine, which celebrated its first anniversary in 1954.

The university, located some eight miles south of the city in Hyde Park and on the former fairgrounds of the 1893 Chicago World's Fair, already had an international reputation and numbered among its faculty Nobel Prize winners and writers. At first, it also seemed to Roth like a "utopian extension" of the Jewish world of his origins. The gift of "satiric irony" seemed seeded in the Jews, who were unabashedly Jewish: contentious, excitable, fueled by intellectual energy (FAC 114). Friends like Arthur Geffen from Brooklyn and Ted Solotaroff from Elizabeth often debated Jewish elements in Henry James at the University Tavern, where Geffen bartended, a perfect blend of the high and low life. A playful confidence in their Jewishness provided intellectual resilience, as well as being a counterweight to intellectual over-refinement. They did not eliminate but accepted their Jewishness, often expressed in a direct if not coarse language and behavior originating in their own lower-class neighborhoods and streets.

Chicago's Department of English had a host of heavyweights: George Williamson, seventeenth-century scholar; James Sledd, a one-eyed Texas linguist; Ronald Crane, a stocky, mustachioed, remarkably self-confident eighteenth-century scholar; Fredson Bowers, the *doyen* of bibliography, who would offer summer seminars in book history; plus Stuart M. Tave, Napier Wilt, Morton Dauwen Zabel, and Norman Maclean, with younger figures like Elder Olson and Gwin Kolb.

Program requirements for the MA were straightforward and included English 301, Methods of Literary Study, taught by the departmental chair, Walter Blair, and English 302, History of Culture and Bibliography and Literary Historiography, taught by Gwin Kolb. Napier Wilt, a florid, gay, *bon vivant* who would become dean of the Humanities Division and who would take a special interest in Roth, taught the seminar Contemporary American Literature and directed the research seminar in American literature (he also taught Melville and Whitman); Morton Zabel taught 19th Century Criticism and 20th Century Poetry; Elder Olson, the History of Criticism and Form, and Structure in Contemporary British Literature. The catalogue stated that the degree was to cover the broad areas of literary study: "advanced training in the criticism of imaginative works, in the analysis of rhetorical, intellectual and historical works, in linguistics, and in the methods of literary research."[19]

Roth clearly had rigorous and comprehensive training for the MA, evident in his constant referencing of major figures in the literary tradition of the day and, especially, as noted in his early writing, Henry James. Both he and Solotaroff took Wilt's James seminar, which initiated an engagement with the Jamesian tragic vision marked by Isabel Archer's decision to return to her oppressive husband, Gilbert Osborne, rather than follow a new life with Caspar Goodwood in *The Portrait of a Lady*. The ethics of her decision becomes the situation room, so to speak, of *Letting Go* (1962), Roth's first novel, where he attempts release from the "intellectual baggage of the previous generation but has no means [to] let it go altogether."[20] His unresolved encounter with the "moral realism" of characters engaged with Jamesian seriousness and responsibility led to an unsteady first novel, later solved by his full rejection of such virtues, as demonstrated in *Portnoy's Complaint*, *Sabbath's Theater*, and his American Trilogy.[21]

The maverick history teacher Murray Ringold in *I Married a Communist*, whose mantra of subversion was "cri-ti-cal thinking," embodies Roth's growing intellectual independence and celebration of identity "uncorrected by piety" in Chicago (IMC 2). This Chicago freedom, especially after he returned to begin a PhD following a short period in the army, and defined by his decision after one term to leave the program to write and to begin a relationship with a midwestern divorced mother of two, underline his newly fashioned rebellious life.

But before he began his relationship with Maggie Martinson Williams, Roth had another, with a black woman, a student from a different Chicago college. Daughter of a professional family, she introduced Roth to the black middle class, of which he later admitted he knew nothing. He dated the woman for some time and met her light-skinned family, the mother especially so. And he vividly remembered the mother saying that "there were relatives of hers who'd been lost to all their people." The phrase stuck with him, the girl later explaining that it meant "passing" as white: they gave up identifying themselves as Black and joined the white world.[22] He later fashioned this idea into the pivotal theme of his 2000 novel, *The Human Stain*, and the character of Coleman Silk.

When not engaged with the "moral realism" of literary lives, Roth enjoyed campus life, living initially in the dorms; a photo from 1954 shows a smiling Roth with fellow graduate students Herb Haber and Barry Targan.

"Bibliography by day, women by night" was the way Roth remembered it (CWPR 142).

Richard Stern, novelist and critic, joined the department in 1955 from the University of Iowa, where he received a PhD and taught in the Iowa Writers' Workshop. He became the first writer hired at the University of Chicago since Thornton Wilder and would become one of Roth's closest friends. He wrote a memoir of the department that captured its mix of camaraderie and competition, beginning with the daily 4:00 p.m. coffee and cookies organized by Walter Blair, the rotund Canadian-born chair who specialized in American humor and, more specifically, Mark Twain. Held in a former storage space in Wieboldt Hall, it mixed veterans with newcomers.

The departmental focus seemed to be on editing, with an emphasis on the eighteenth century: Goldsmith, Johnson, Addison and Steele. Ex-soldiers and sailors populated the faculty, including the department's only woman member, Catherine Hamm, who had been an officer in the WAVES. Among the students was the future poet-editor George Starbuck—in a few years to edit *Goodbye, Columbus*—and the European-educated intellectual George Steiner.[23] Accenting James Sledd's savage humor at these gatherings, Stern reports, was his ability to pop his glass eye into his palm "during heated colloquies," part of his "black comic repertoire."[24]

Dean of Humanities Napier Wilt, an ex-soldier who had been "gassed" in World War I, was a gruff-voiced, bald Americanist who would somehow persuade a new instructor like Stern that his $200 raise was a blessing. His patronage was genial. And the department was democratic. Politics and new books were the focus, and most kept up with the latest scholarship. Roth, as his character Zuckerman explains in *The Anatomy Lesson*, found that Chicago opened new doors for him, intellectually and socially. It was a world of "inspiring teachers, impenetrable texts, neurotic classmates, embattled causes, semantic hairsplitting," and he loved it (AL 175). A sentence in *The Anatomy Lesson* summarizes his career and its future shape: "Chicago had sprung him from Jewish New Jersey [but] then fiction took over and boomeranged him right back" (AL 180). By June 1955, he had completed his MA, but to avoid the draft he enlisted in the U.S. Army in September.

America 1955: the Korean War had ended two years earlier, in July 1953, and America was entering a prosperous period, with Eisenhower on the brink of a second-term victory over Adlai Stevenson. But America in 1955 was conservative and conformist, the simplest way, perhaps, to sustain a return to prosperity. It was the year "In God We Trust" was added to all U.S. paper currency, Disneyland opened, and Ray Kroc started his first McDonald's. But it was also the year Rosa Parks was arrested in Montgomery, Alabama, for refusing to give up her seat on a bus to a white person, putting the civil rights movement into motion, and the year the fourteen-year-old Emmett Till was murdered for not showing respect to a white woman in Mississippi. Internationally, America was settling into the Cold War against Communism and confronting the newly formed Warsaw Pact. West Germany joined NATO, while Illinois passed a Loyalty Oath Act, requiring all state employees to take an oath or be fired. General Motors became the first U.S. corporation to make a billion dollars.

The draft was still in effect, but rather than wait to be conscripted, Roth enlisted for two years, quickly becoming Private P. Roth, with uniform and helmet and knowledge of the bayonet and its ability to kill. Roth's army career was short lived, however. In Basic Training at Fort Dix, New Jersey, in August or September 1954, he suffered a spinal injury caused while serving on KP detail. He and another soldier were carrying a large kettle of potatoes when the other fellow suddenly slipped and dropped his end of the heavy pot. Roth instinctively tried to pull up his side to prevent the kettle from landing on the other's feet and damaged his back in the process. He continued with the remaining four or five weeks of infantry Basic Training despite his constant pain, an event alluded to in his 1962 short story in the *New Yorker*, "Novotny's Pain." It recounts the painful adventures of the Polish American draftee who, in the second sentence, "woke one morning with a pain on the right side of his body, directly above the buttock" (NP 261). Like Roth, he continued with Basic Training, all in preparation for the Korean War, which figures importantly in Roth's late novel *Indignation*.

In the short story, there are general features related to Roth's time in the military, but whereas Novotny's sense of patriotism and duty persevere, Roth seemed to focus on correcting his injury and seeking medical treatment. Novotny, who had marched fifteen miles with a full pack the previous day, which may have been the origin of his morning pain, did not. But like Roth, Novotny worked at KP scrubbing potato bins and then refilling them with dirty potatoes. Roth provides a description of what more or less happened to him and caused his back problem. As Novotny's aide Reynolds became upset over not calling his girl, he began to cry, threw his hands up to his eyes, and dropped his end of the bin: "Novotny's body stiffened; with a great effort he yanked up on the can so that it wouldn't come down on Reynolds' toes. Pain cut deep across the base of Novotny's spine" (NP 264, 279).

The remainder of the story deals directly with Novotny's pain and his evolving relationship with his girlfriend, the army's casual attitude toward his injury, and the likelihood of his being sent to Korea. But on his return from another leave, he is admitted to hospital. Further fear of going overseas and increased pain lead to a refusal to join his company and its deployment, which could be grounds for a court-martial. Traction and a slow recovery see Novotny return to duty (without charges), but he is eventually sent to a psychiatrist, where he admits his fear of death and is finally told to stop thinking about his back and admit that he is passive-aggressive (NP 277).

Roth is mixing here his own back problems and his recent involvement with psychoanalysis, which began in 1962, the year the story first appeared. And through the voice of the unsympathetic colonel, Roth conveys something of the army's reaction to his own suspicious back pain, as Novotny receives a dishonorable discharge for not convincing his superiors of the authenticity of his ailment, although the debilitating but intermittent pain continued (NP 278–80).

After his injury and basic training, Roth spent some time in the clerk-typist school at Fort Dix and received physical therapy. After eight weeks, he was assigned to the Public Information Office at the Walter Reed Army Hospital in Washington, D.C., where he drafted and distributed stories about the soldiers in the hospital and sent them to the men's hometown papers. It was there he briefly met President Eisenhower, who came to tour the facility. But the stationary work led to increased back pain, often so bad that his barracks mate Nelson Goldberg had to put on Roth's socks for him.

When the back pain kept him from performing his desk duties, he went to the army's nearby rehabilitation center, a wooded retreat in Forest Glen, Maryland, where many of the other patients were amputees and paraplegics. Their problems dwarfed his; he would listen to their cries throughout the night for over a month, beginning in June 1956, before he was finally discharged, still believing not that life was disorderly and irrational but that he could control his destiny. His body, however, began to control him, as it would do for a good deal of his mature life. He was gradually learning that things happened independently of one's efforts. During this time in Washington, Roth began to write at night; two results were the "The Conversion of the Jews" and "Epstein."

Roth's honorable discharge for medical reasons resulted in a disability pension but constant discomfort. He would use his army experience in his fiction; one of his earliest stories, sent to Saul Bellow, was about GIs stranded on an island at the end of the war. "Expect the Vandals" would eventually be published in *Esquire* in 1958 and become the first of Roth's works to be filmed. The peacetime army of 1955–56 was routine and unexciting, and Roth's injury kept him out of much physical activity and danger, unlike the hero of *Indignation*, who, after being expelled from college, is drafted and dies in Korea.

Earlier, a Cornell University literary magazine, *Epoch*, published "The Contest for Aaron Gold" (1955), soon reprinted in the *Best American Short Stories of 1956*. Before that, his first story to be published outside the Bucknell literary magazine, "The Day It Snowed," appeared in the *Chicago Review*.[25] It tells of the disappearance (a euphemism for death) of the young hero's stepfather, the loss and absence seemingly inexplicable. The searching of Sydney, the young protagonist, becomes a quest to locate the dead father figure and in the process learning that he had an actual father who had also disappeared. An old man in the park tells him such men do not "disappear" on purpose, a revelation to the young man who, after confessing this to his mother at the funeral for his stepfather, is himself unexpectedly killed when he runs in front of a hearse in his search for the old man who revealed to him that he had an actual father. The child, stepfather, and possibly his actual father die, Roth projecting some elements of his own, at times Kafkaesque relationship with his father and irrational feelings of the past on to the action, developing a kind of doppelgänger of fathers, possibly the father he loved and the father he had to reject. Roth was twenty-one when the story appeared.

Roth's original letter to the *Chicago Review* of 25 September 1954 reflects the formality and ambition of the young writer. To the editor he wrote that he was presently a student in English and working on his master's degree and that he was editor of the Bucknell literary magazine, where five of his own short stories appeared.[26] Cynically, one might think he used the Bucknell magazine as a vehicle for his own publications, aided by his position as editor-in-chief. His own critique of these works in *The Facts*, however, suggests their weakness. But in February 1956, while still in the army, he submitted two further stories to the *Chicago Review*: "The Patriarch" and "Emmett." Eager to know their fate, Roth followed up in May, giving as his return address 9901 TU, Walter Reed Army M.C., Washington 12, D.C. The stories were not accepted, and he later tried to place them with the *Paris Review*.

One of the interesting features of Roth's time in the army was his failure to encounter any anti-Semitism, as he told an interviewer. This is in contrast to what he describes in "Defender of the Faith," one of his early and controversial stories, but one based on the experiences of his friend Art Geffen, whom he met at the University of Chicago. The story, appearing in the 14 March 1959 issue of the the *New Yorker*, brought immediate condemnation for its seeming anti-Semitism. Rabbis and the Anti-Defamation League were quick to jump on him. "Writing About Jews" was his response, an essay derived from remarks he made in 1962 and 1963 at the University of Iowa's Hillel House, the Hartford, Connecticut, Jewish Community Center, and Yeshiva University in New York; it appears in *Reading Myself and Others* (193–211). Importantly, he learned early that controversy, if not outrage, could become a powerful stance, writing to offend because that alone showed that he was (1) being read and (2) taken seriously.

Chicago set an intellectual style if not outlook for Roth, echoed in certain ways by two others who attended the university before him: Susan Sontag and Robert Silvers. Sontag, born the same year as Roth, entered the University of Chicago at sixteen and had, among her instructors, Leo Strauss, Richard McKeon, and Kenneth Burke. She graduated at eighteen in 1951, having married a young University of Chicago sociologist, Philip Rieff, at seventeen. Mike Nichols was one of her classmates.[27] Like Roth, Sontag would discontinue her doctoral work (at the University of Paris, Sorbonne) and, like Roth, move to New York.

Silvers graduated from Chicago in 1947, began law school, but became a speechwriter for the governor of Connecticut and then senior officers of the U.S. Army before joining the *Paris Review* as managing editor under George Plimpton. In 1956, he became the Paris editor of the review, where Roth would have early success. After some time with *Harper's Magazine*, Silvers became a founding coeditor with Barbara Epstein of the *New York Review of Books* in 1963.[28] Roth appeared in the review the following year, critiquing plays by LeRoi Jones, James Baldwin, and Edward Albee.

After his army discharge in August 1956, Roth had options other than Chicago. First, he went to New York and interviewed with the *New Yorker*. Through the influence of the novelist Charles Jackson, who was writing advertising copy for the same firm where Sandy Roth worked, Roth also had an interview with Roger Straus, the publisher. A few days later, he was offered both jobs, one as a fact-checker at the *New Yorker*, the other a copyeditor at Farrar, Straus and Cudahy. But before he could decide, he had a telegram from Napier Wilt, now dean of humanities at the University of Chicago, offering him a last-minute position teaching freshman composition. He took the teaching job because it offered him the most freedom to write.

Roth had missed Chicago and felt closer to it than any other city he lived in. He enrolled in the PhD program in 1956, while teaching three sections of composition for an annual salary of $2,800, and soon made a series of new friends, including Ted Solotaroff, fighting the fourteenth round of his PhD, and Richard Stern, the novelist. Solotaroff recalled meeting Roth in the James seminar taught by Wilt, who, in contrast with the traditionalist Morton Zabel, was a relaxed instructor who encouraged debate and discussion. Wilt was heavy-set, congenial, and protective of deserving graduate students. Roth was one of them. His colleague Norman Maclean taught contemporary criticism with strict discipline, also taken by Solotaroff and Roth. Zabel taught Conrad, another seminar taken by Roth.

In a 1970 memoir entitled "Philip Roth: A Personal View," Solotaroff recalled how he and Roth met in 1957. They discovered a shared temperament ("aggressive, aloof, moody and as graduate students go, worldly") and similar backgrounds—they were both from neighboring cities in northern New Jersey (Elizabeth and Newark)—and shared a knowledge of the Jersey Shore, the Empire Burlesque House, and possessive Jewish mothers.[29] Solotaroff was five years older, married with two young children, and eking out a living teaching at Indiana University's Calumet Center while taking three graduate courses. Roth had quit graduate school by then but continued to teach, while getting several of his early stories published. Yet Solotaroff and Roth often socialized, and Jewish jokes and family anecdotes flowed, mostly from Roth, whose mimicry and wit enthralled everyone. They were both in school to learn how to be "civilized," not earn a living, although their paths diverged, Roth to be a creative writer, Solotaroff to be an editor and critic.

Even at this early stage, Roth recognized his own aggressive manner, recalling that he was "fanatically about seriousness" and that he was "High-strung. Volatile. Opinionated. Argumentative. Playful. Animated. Quarrelsome."[30] This late assessment of his early behavior remained consistent throughout his mature years.

Early on, Solotaroff recognized Roth's talent, a natural prose style and informal tone relaxed as conversation that showed the actualities of life, sourced in the "practical, coarse, emotionally extravagant life of the Jewish middle class."[31] Only Salinger came close in the late 1950s to writing that way, Solotaroff believed. But the youthful mix of idealism and cynicism and Roth's appetite for life, much heartier than Salinger's, gave him the edge. His ability to imitate gave him, as well, a terrific boost as a writer. Roth and Solotaroff at one point exchanged stories, Roth's about a refugee artist working as a pottery teacher in a summer camp who befriends a gifted misfit. This is "The Contest for Aaron Gold."

Returning for the PhD program after the army, Roth was considered debonair in a jacket and tie and kept everyone laughing despite looking like "he strayed into class from the business school."[32] You didn't have to be Jewish to be a graduate student at Chicago in the 1950s, Solotaroff adds, but it helped because of "our history of intellect and suffering and the sense of humor of a people chosen by God to maintain both." Incongruity was a way of life and "irony the local accent."[33]

Roth at the time had several girlfriends, one named Sally ("a Hyde Park siren," according to Solotaroff), who joined Roth and the Solotaroffs when invited by Wilt and his partner to a gourmet dinner they had prepared. It was spirited, elegant, and delightful.[34] Sally had shining blond hair and milkmaid features and "looked like a Clairol Girl with legs that meant business."[35] But a previous boyfriend, Jay Aronson, saw that beneath her fetching surface was trouble and had soon split. Roth did not and seemed attracted by her divorce and custody problems.[36] He saw her, in Solotaroff's words, "as a project," something Roth later acknowledged. She was not Jewish and not from Newark and likely could not spell Weequahic, but that was precisely what appealed to him. The relationship, however, blew up and Roth moved on to the daughter of a Chicago doctor-businessman who needed no looking after, Solotaroff likely referring to Susan Glassman.[37]

"I owe 'Goodbye, Columbus' to Dick Stern," Roth announced in 1983. One day over lunch at the University Tavern at 55th and Ellis, Roth was telling Stern about the New Jersey Jewish country club set into which he had *not* been born and his summer adventures. " 'Why don't you write them down?' " Stern asked. So, despite his absorption with James's *The Golden Bowl*, he did and saw that they qualified as fiction: "That's what I learned in Hyde Park: how to talk back to all those great books," he triumphantly said (CWPR 143). Talking back soon became his *modus operandi*, most gloriously achieved in his 1995 novel, which he claimed to be his favorite, *Sabbath's Theater*.

In 1957, Stern received a $2,000 grant from Dean Wilt to bring writers to his writing class for a week's visit. Four writers came that first year: Saul Bellow, Robert Lowell, Howard Nemerov, and Peter Taylor. Roth wanted to meet Bellow and asked Stern if his new story "Defender of the Faith" might be used by the class for discussion. It was, and Bellow admired it, beginning a long, complex friendship between the older and younger writer. (Bellow was eighteen years his senior.) Stern parlayed his class visitors into a list of important figures, and Roth recalled these encounters in Stern's *New York Times* obituary of 24 January 2013.[38]

Roth distinguished himself among his fellow graduate students by his confidence, ability, and decision to drop out of the doctoral program to write. His ideas and his style were orderly. He taught two sections of freshman composition, something that was onerous and a chore because of its rigid structure and narrow standards. He and his fellow fiction writer Tom Rogers called the course "Block That Punt"![39] The course was frustrating and distracting for Roth. Solotaroff, also an instructor, saw it as a mission.

Saturday nights with their friend Geffen (who went on to teach English at the University of Minnesota) and a few others became a round of one-liners, recalled anecdotes, and a chance to refine their wit, Jewish and otherwise. Roth mined not only the exchanges but his personal experiences.[40] It seemed to the others that Roth was able to make public the attitudes of those who were trying to liberate themselves from communal (i.e., Jewish) solidarity and moral authoritarianism, infected by hypocrisy. Both "Eli, the Fanatic" and "The Conversion of the Jews" did that. The choice between allegiance and resistance was the challenge. While the relationship with Solotaroff was at times competitive, it grew in later years into mutual admiration and help. Solotaroff was one of the first to publish excerpts from *Portnoy's Complaint*, while Roth included Solotaroff and his son in a scene at the end of *Operation Shylock* eating at Barney Greengrass's deli on Amsterdam Avenue in New York.

Solotaroff was critical, however, suggesting at one point that Roth was selling himself out when he had early success with *Esquire*. But he praised the intense vulgarity and obscenity appearing in Roth's writing, as strong as Lenny Bruce's, Solotaroff wrote. This would occur during their humorous exchanges and go beyond his mimicry, imagery, or timing. Solotaroff noted that it characterized a tense transgression between Roth's precision and excess. "Epstein," however, put off Solotaroff, who found the description of physical aging and ridicule of Jewish sex unappealing. "Why all the *schmutz* [dirt, filth]?" He asked. "The *schmutz* is the story," Roth replied.[41] Ironically, it would be Solotaroff's *New American Review* that published early excerpts of the libidinous *Portnoy's Complaint*, "The Jewish Blues" appearing in volume 1 (1967) and "Civilization and Its Discontents" published in volume 3 (1968).

In 1959 Solotaroff wrote a long review of *Goodbye, Columbus* for the *Chicago Review* entitled "Philip Roth and the Jewish Moralists." He placed the early Roth with Bellow and Malamud, uniting literary and Jewish experience, something new for writers and readers. The aesthetic and the moral are the same, Solotaroff proposed, drawing on the traditions of Yiddish writing as outlined by Irving Howe and Eliezer Greenberg. The review caught the eye of the editor of the *Times Literary Supplement,* who asked Solotaroff to contribute an essay on the Jewish voice in contemporary American writing.[42]

Roth's second piece for the *Chicago Review* did not appear until 1957, "Positive Thinking on Pennsylvania Avenue," a satiric critique of the Eisenhower White House, published in the same issue with an essay on Schiller by Thomas Mann and two poems by Donald Hall.[43] The "Positive Thinking" satire anticipates the presentation of Nixon that will form the basis of *Our Gang* in 1971. Exploiting the supposed obedience of Eisenhower's prayers each night and his reliance on God to make his decisions, Roth exploits the way Eisenhower blames his failures on God but credits the successes to himself. He also uses analogies to football, which Eisenhower played at West Point, again anticipating several comic scenes with Nixon in football gear in *Our Gang.* George Starbuck, a Chicago friend, was an editor at the *Review,* so it was only natural to give him the piece for consideration.

At the time, Roth was twenty-three and an instructor in the College of Humanities at Chicago ending his enrollment as a part-time graduate student. A few weeks after the Eisenhower piece appeared, the *New Republic* reprinted it. That led to his doing movie and TV reviews on and off for the magazine for a fee of $25 each, everything from *Funny Face* to *Pal Joey* and such TV shows as Sid Caesar's "Comedy Hour" and Edward R. Murrow's "Person to Person." In September 1957, he reviewed the Miss America pageant.

Roth was also getting more of his stories published: "You Can't Tell a Man by the Song He Sings," for example, appeared in *Commentary* in November 1957. Norman Podhoretz, then an assistant editor and only three years older than Roth, pulled the story from the slush pile. It was one of Roth's earliest publications in a national magazine. Roth had first come across the journal, founded by Elliot Cohen, as an undergraduate at Bucknell in the periodical room of the library. "I was stunned. So *this* is what it's like to be Jewish," he thought, the writing free of parochialism and apologetics. The magazine "furnished a whole education, a way of being Jewish and intelligent and American—all at once," he told the writer Benjamin Balint.[44] And with increasing confidence and a desire to write full time, he left the graduate English program, deciding, to the surprise if not bafflement of his fellow students, to strike out on his own, although he continued to teach. At this time, he also read Malamud's *The Assistant* and Bellow's *The Victim*, both works exploring the idea of duality which made connections between literature and neighborhoods. He also realized that he could transform the Newark Jews of his youth into literary characters.[45] It was during this second stint at Chicago that Roth followed up Stern's suggestion to write about his previous summer in New Jersey. The result became "Goodbye, Columbus," the satiric portrait of middle-class Jewish materialism offset by the attempts of Neil Klugman to find love and social acceptance. All this was happening in 1957–58.

And then he began to appear in the *Paris Review,* an association that laid the groundwork for a set of new literary connections, from George Plimpton to Irwin Shaw and William Styron. The *Paris Review* originated in 1952 when Peter Matthiessen met Harold Humes, who had just purchased a down-and-out literary magazine, the *Paris News Post,* and wanted Matthiessen to be fiction editor. With a first story by Terry Southern, Matthiessen thought they could do better and suggested a more ambitious magazine, calling his friend George Plimpton, then studying at Cambridge, to come to Paris and act as editor. He did.[46] William Styron acted as a kind of contributing editor; he was the only one among the group who had actually published a book (*Lie Down in Darkness*), a work entirely unknown in France or England.

Styron recounts the experience of the early *Paris Review* in a letter of 19 July 1952 reporting that friends of his, including Matthiessen, were starting a magazine. What distinguishes it from other similar enterprises, he explains, is that it will focus on creative writing and not criticism or theory. It is also well-funded, the principal backer Prince Aga Khan, brother of Aly Khan. Aga Khan was a classmate of Plimpton's at Harvard and socialized with the set of young American writers in Paris.

They started in a one-room office 8 rue Garancière, although most meetings were held at the Café de Tournon around the corner, well-known for its pinball machine out in front. Because the iron gates to their building swung closed early in the evening, the editors were often seen dropping down from the ledge of their second-story office window after working late, to the surprise of the *Garde républicaine* on horseback patrol. Another feature was the Common Book. Initiated by Plimpton from his days at the Harvard *Lampoon*, it was a ledger-like volume where anyone could enter messages, jokes, letters, or thoughts. It became a running commentary on the daily life of the *Review.*[47]

What particularly excited Styron, who would write the opening statement of purpose for the first issue, published in February 1953, was the
inclusion of a page or two of a fiction or poetry manuscript along with the
author's comments. This was the beginning of the well-known Paris Review
Interview series, which published Roth in 1984. E. M. Forster was to be in
issue 1, Styron, with a passage from *Lie Down in Darkness,* in issue 2.[48]

Matthiessen named the magazine the *Paris Review* in his Paris apartment
at 14 rue Perceval, behind the Gare Montparnasse, after much sharing of ab-
sinthe with the others, including Styron. The magazine began with a simple
but clear editorial mission. "Dear reader," Styron began the letter that served
as the manifesto for the inaugural issue, announcing that they would emphasize creative work, eliminating any emphasis on criticism. The magazine
would welcome the "good writers and good poets, the non-drumbeaters and
non-axe-grinders. So long as they're good."[49] A decade later, Roth's early girlfriend Maxine Groffsky would become the Paris editor, directing the magazine from 1965 to 1974.[50]

As a young writer, Roth was equally startled and thrilled when Rose Styron
pulled his "The Conversion of the Jews" from a pile of unsolicited works and
accepted it. This was only his third publication in a literary magazine, this one
clearly the most prestigious. On a visit to New York, Plimpton invited Roth
to lunch at his East 72nd Street apartment; Roth was impressed, not only
by Plimpton's worldliness but by his contacts, which included Hemingway,
whom he had interviewed in Key West, S. J. Perelman, E. B. White, James
Thurber, and William Styron. And he was interested in Roth's writing, tremendously flattering to the youthful composition instructor from Chicago.

At the luncheon, Roth also met Bob Silvers and Blair Fuller, two other
editors. The former had been an editor at *Harper's Magazine*; the latter
was a novelist who had spent time in West Africa.[51] When Roth moved to
New York in September 1958, he struck up friendships with all three. He
also became friendly with John P. Marquand Jr., whose father was an emi-
nent Pulitzer Prize–winning novelist in the mold of John O'Hara and John
Cheever. After the Plimpton lunch, a fired-up Roth returned to Chicago and
promptly wrote "Epstein," about a middle-aged Jewish adulterer drawn from
the situation of a next-door neighbor who had "misbehaved" when Roth
was a kid in Newark. Unlike "The Conversion of the Jews," sent to the *Paris
Review*'s general fiction pile, "Epstein" went right to the top, to Plimpton. It
was not only accepted for publication but won the Aga Khan Prize for Fiction
offered by the magazine. The story appeared in the summer 1958 issue.

That summer Roth booked third-class passage on the Holland America Line and sailed to Europe to receive the prize and travel around England and France. He arrived in London on Bloomsday, 16 June 1958, to rainy weather and a bus strike. He had work to do, trying to get a hundred pages in shape for the Houghton Mifflin novel fellowship. Bestowing the *Paris Review* prize on 8 July would be Aly Khan himself, diplomat, horseman, and ladies' man. The son of Aga Khan III had formerly been married to Rita Hayworth.

The award ceremony and reception were held at Aly Kahn's Bois du Boulogne villa. Roth was somewhat less than his usual ebullient self, recovering from stomach flu and restricted to drinking Perrier. The night before the event he met a slightly disheveled French student at the Café Odeon and invited her to the gathering. She arrived late in chic Left Bank leather on a noisy motorbike but was refused entry by the butler. Alerted to the scene, Roth left the party to negotiate her entrance; he then returned upstairs with her to receive his "first literary award from the hands of Rita Hayworth's third husband."[52]

At the ceremony, he met one of his early literary heroes, Irwin Shaw, then living in Paris (and who in 1952 showed Styron the *haute monde* of the Right Bank, often in his large, green Ford convertible). Shaw was a bestselling novelist, author of *The Young Lions*, one of Roth's favorite novels, published in 1949. They later sat next to each other at a Parisian restaurant, and in Brooklyn tones Shaw revealed himself to be anything but stuck up. This, wrote Roth, was a long way from correcting comma faults at the University of Chicago.

Roth also met Nelson Aldrich, a Paris editor of the *Review*, who took him around the city to meet friends and women. Reinforcing the success of his summer in Paris was acceptance of another work by the *Paris Review*, "Goodbye, Columbus," which would appear in issue 20 in 1959.

Writing from Florence on 25 July 1958 to Bob Silvers in New York, Roth mentions that a dear friend of his, Margaret Williams, "a totally charming woman" from Chicago, was then in New York and beginning work at *Esquire*. She has a good "editorial head" and might be suitable for the *Paris Review*. He mentioned her because in Paris he learned something of the history of the *Review* and all the "stately women" who surrounded it. "She's the only person alive for whom I change whole sentences in stories," he added.[53] This is Roth's first mention of Maggie, who a year later would become his wife, although he later referred to this period in New York as one in which he was trying to escape from "a hectic romance" in Chicago (CWPR 142).

He closes his letter to Silvers by mentioning that he will be back in New York on 21 August and expresses a willingness to amend "Goodbye, Columbus" if necessary. He had spoken to Plimpton on the phone, who suggested Roth might be "too windy in a few places. He may be right." Finally, he points out he was still owed $50 for "The Conversion of the Jews" but suggests it just be added to the fee for "Goodbye."[54] Money would quickly become one of his lasting concerns, and he never forgot an unpaid fee.

When Roth first spied her, Margaret Martinson Williams was twenty-eight; he was almost twenty-four. It was October 1956 and he was recently out of the army. She was divorced with two children, David and Holly, and involved in a custody battle. He approached the striking, well-built blonde with Nordic features in a doorway of Woodworth's used book store in Hyde Park, Chicago's oldest bookstore, partly known for its wooden medieval monk who sat at his own writing desk at the end of an aisle. Maggie's father was, in fact, Swedish, and his family had settled in Michigan, details Roth understood more clearly after he saw the film *The New Land* starring Liv Ullmann and Max von Sydow in 1974.

Through persistence, Roth convinced Maggie to have coffee with him at Steinway's drug store. Her blue eyes and blond hair and symmetrical face had a fascination for him—as did her American midwestern wholeness. Writing about her long after their relationship ended, he notes her early mistakes and need for bouts of "desperate deviousness" in order to survive because of a general distrust of others, especially men, originating in her childhood (FAC 81). Her difficult family background, with a father who had actually served time for petty theft in Florida and Indiana, left her without a sense of family pride. She was also anxious over her situation as a recently divorced woman with two young children and only a semester and a half of undergraduate education—or so she said.

Her father remained a constant shadow who even hovers over Roth's second novel, *When She Was Good*. In letters written to his ex-wife, Evelyn, from an Indiana jail in the early 1950s, kept by his daughter and then Roth, "Red" Martinson enigmatically refers to questionable behavior with his daughter, implying sexual abuse. Writing to Evelyn in 1954, Martinson tells her, "As far as Margaret is concerned, you don't know all of it. In fact, probably a very small half. So there is no need to go into that." Earlier letters reveal a self-pitying man who admits that his actions caused pain and suffering in the marriage. He knows she was afraid and disillusioned, while he was dissolute and beaten down by life. Cynical about the justice system, he nonetheless hopes that when he gets out, he will find a place as a mechanic, his trade.

Transferred to a Michigan prison, he writes in a later letter of his forth-coming release and his belief that he can make something out of the balance of his life. "It is still time to accomplish something and send you some of the things you have so long deserved," he tells her. But by December 1955, he is still in jail, although she does write and send him small amounts of money. But he acknowledges that, as she has written, "everything is so completely torn now that a solution is beyond the realm of my mentality." Their twenty-four-year marriage is clearly "a complete wreck."[55] Finally released, he lives in a rundown hotel in a small Michigan town working as a mechanic, unhappy and alone and without money.

Maggie appealed to Roth precisely because she was different in temper-ament and experience from any of the East Coast Jewish woman he had known. In his 1994 essay "Juice or Gravy," he explains that his attraction was to her "adventures in failure" and how she had fashioned into a legend a life that might educate him in how one cannot actually, independently, shape one's future. The idea that her father was in jail, rather than pickles or plumbing fixtures, thrilled him. She embodied everything about the unfair-ness of life and what his grandparents feared most in America: she was alien, a *shiksa*, a woman from an unstable background. But it was *because* of these things that she appealed to Roth, who was elated by the chance to distinguish between "American realities and *shtetl* legend" (FAC 84).

Maggie's childhood had been difficult, her early marriage no better, resulting in a custody battle over her son and daughter. But Roth found her life engrossing and desired to bring her into his personal and literary orbit. At the time he met her, she was a secretary in the Division of Social Sciences at the University of Chicago. Soon, he would excitedly rush off at the end of an academic day to a class in what he called "The Unfairness of Life" with his "school-of-hard-knocks inamorata."[56]

In his autobiography, Stern describes his thirtieth birthday party in 1958 and how he put Roth and Margaret together—again. She was a "small, solid, pretty blonde who baby-sat for and charmed us in the late fifties. At my thir-tieth birthday party, we invited her and Philip separately, playing a disastrous Cupid role (though like a river, Maggie would have found her way to Philip somehow or another)."[57] From this meeting, actually a remeeting since Roth had earlier picked her up at the bookstore entrance, a strong but turbulent relationship emerged, one with severe consequences for both. This was a period, Solotaroff writes, when "one of the principal occupations in Hyde Park seemed to be difficult marriages," some of this captured by Roth in his first novel, *Letting Go*.[58]

Maggie's outlook and past made it possible for Roth to experience a world other than his own, as well as extend his own rebellion from a seemingly restricted and conservative youth. Maggie was new social territory and another step toward his personal declaration of independence. As an older woman, she represented maturity and a set of life experiences unknown to him. He had not encountered her midwestern toughness before. But over time, he also learned that she was oppressed by an "inextinguishable resentment over the injustice of her origins." She was "raving within and stolidly blonde without" and presented him with a "bracingly American amorous adventure" (FAC 81, 84). He had yet to learn that she was manipulative, demanding, and deceptive.

3

An Education in Intensity

Shouting is how a Jew *thinks things through*!
—Philip Roth, *Sabbath's Theater*, 1995

Early in *My Life as a Man* (1974), Nathan Zuckerman writes, "I met the woman with whom I was to ruin my life only a few months after arriving back in Chicago in the fall of 1956, following a premature discharge from the army" (MLM 46). This ironic reference to Roth and his affair with Maggie Martinson Williams contains some truth. Their relationship was rocky at the start and the end, although they shared the early stages of Roth's success, from his life as a writer in New York to nearly five months in Italy, followed by teaching at Iowa and Princeton, roughly the years 1956 to 1962. But his "education in intensity" came at a high price.[1]

By May 1958, Roth had left Chicago and Maggie for New York and then Europe, following the turmoil of a relationship that generated only discord and conflict. He began to date the alluring Susan Glassman, a Radcliffe graduate and daughter of a wealthy doctor and real estate developer. Roth found her strikingly beautiful but admits that his interlude with Glassman was brief. At a Hillel talk, he introduced her to Saul Bellow, who would make her his third wife in November 1961. At the talk, Maggie turned up, leaving him a nasty note the next morning.[2]

The trip to Europe, his first, was a relief and an escape from the turbulence with Maggie. In addition to meeting the *Paris Review* crowd, at a dinner that evening Roth sat next to Irwin Shaw, an early literary hero for his novel *The Young Lions* about soldiers in World War II. Shaw had also written radio scripts for *Dick Tracy, The Gumps,* and *Studio One* and been profiled in the "Art of Fiction No. 4" series for the *Paris Review.* Shaw was not a literary lion as much as a Brooklynite who delighted in giving Roth encouragement. It was a memorable dinner.

Not only Maggie but a fellowship awaited him upon his return to New York: he successfully received a Houghton Mifflin Literary Fellowship, which allowed him to resign from the University of Chicago that September and remain in New York. Or to be more precise, to move in with his parents at 11 Greenvale Road, Moorestown, New Jersey, where he spent weekdays. Weekends he spent either in his own two-room East Village apartment on East 10th Street or with Maggie in her small apartment on West 13th Street between 6th and 7th avenues, before she moved in with him. Roth had settled into his basement apartment in the East Village at the beginning of November 1958. Rent was $80 a month. Washington Square Park was a ten-minute walk, but Tompkins Square Park, two blocks east, held more interest. After a day of writing, he would often go there to read and to observe the Puerto Rican and Ukrainian immigrants who loitered there.[3] There was always some action, as he outlined in *My Life as a Man*. Maggie, however, was having no luck in finding work. Roth wrote to Solotaroff in Chicago, hoping for everyone's health and sanity that she find something soon. She was doing only intermittent freelance reading for publishers and occasional public relations work.

As their relationship became more enmeshed and she found work on the periphery of publishing, he found it harder to shake her, or her children, David and Holly, who sometimes visited. At first they were a welcome diversion, but then a distraction, although he had grown fond of Holly and often tried to teach her about literature and culture. As Maggie began to cling more intensely to Roth, while orbiting around his developing career, she more aggressively pursued publishing. More arguments followed that were characterized as "venomous" by Roth, who took to wandering the streets alone, feeling as though his life had fallen apart. He thought he could turn to his brother, but they had grown apart, largely because of Sandy's developing career in advertising, while Roth was pulled to the more artistic, if less successful, life as a writer. By November 1958, Maggie was disconsolate and confronted him at dawn with her suitcase on the steps of his basement apartment (FAC 101). Roth was prepared to abandon his apartment and leave its contents for her, but his sense of duty prevailed: he had a two-year lease and a commitment to his parents to remain in the East. He refused to run.

The relationship remained fraught and tense, Roth admitting to Maggie on his return from Europe that he had not been faithful, which angered her. Maggie began to tell various literary acquaintances that she had actually edited several of Roth's stories that were beginning to be published. This was a half-truth because she did, in fact, offer editorial comments, title suggestions, and other ideas which Roth always denied despite letters that confirm her partial involvement.

Their life for the next three months (December 1958 to February 1959) on the Lower East Side mixed mayhem with anger. Maggie created an atmosphere in which he could not write or think. It was that February when she announced she was again pregnant, the first time being in Chicago the year before, which was handled by a D & C after drug-induced heavy bleeding (FAC 94–95). To Roth's surprise, he learned that she had listed her religion as "Jewish" on a hospital admission form. This occurred just after he returned from Boston to review the galleys of *Goodbye, Columbus* with Starbuck. Roth knew it was a lie the moment she said it, the result most likely of her desperate reaction to his Boston trip, which she thought would somehow solidify their relationship (FAC 103). Maggie feared his conscience would expand beyond the reach of her accusations and he would have the courage to leave her.

During her earlier pregnancy in Chicago, four months after beginning their affair, Roth was too naïve to question her honesty or her constant tales of victimization by her father and first husband. What distracted and appealed to him was his immersion in the disorders of gentile family life, the sordid realities that inspired the "goy hating legends" of his grandparents (FAC 102). But in New York, his basement apartment had become "a psychiatric ward with café curtains" (FAC 102).

Roth's rejection of Maggie's first claim of pregnancy led to more threats, recalling for him the summer of 1957, when he went alone to a rented room on Cape Cod and became involved with a senior from Boston University, who, like him, had relationship problems. Her boyfriend wanted to get married but she had doubts; for his part, Roth had a friend coming whom he did not want to see. Their common troubles united them, and when he picked up Maggie at the Boston airport, he felt the loss of the university senior and the resumption of old quarrels, including anger over Roth's having taken his Bucknell girlfriend (Betty Powell) to his parents, while Maggie had yet to meet them. Constant attacks on his character resumed, with the word "wicked" repeatedly thrown at him. Why, she kept asking, couldn't she meet his parents?

Roth knew his parents would not be happy with this divorced woman four years his senior with two children who had been taken from her by her ex. But on their return from Cape Cod, the two of them went to Moorestown. It was a disaster, epitomized by Maggie asking his mother to do her laundry.

Yet Roth hung on, feeling, like a good Jewish boy/man, somehow responsible for Maggie's well-being, having inherited his father's determination to save others when in need. Inexplicably, he was unable to say no to her and her demands. Her neediness matched his weakness, and the result was persistent unhappiness. But she possessed an allure he could not resist: she was blonde, midwestern, exotic, and different, an irresistible mix for a Jewish boy from Jersey. However, these attractions were also his vulnerabilities. Nevertheless, when he briefly returned to Chicago to get his things that fall, he pursued Susan Glassman again and then an editorial assistant for the *Bulletin of Atomic Scientists*. Neither was interested.

Roth initially supported Maggie's efforts to find work in the publishing world, suggesting her to friends like Silvers and editors like Starbuck at Houghton Mifflin. Later, it was to Joe Fox at Random House. He praised her supposed editorial skills and even promoted a book idea of hers to Starbuck. Maggie herself sought to find a foothold or at least a ledge in publishing, frequently proposing ideas for volumes. And she seemed to support Roth's literary goals as he worked on his first novel in Rome and then in his first full-time teaching job at Iowa. He dedicated *Letting Go* to her.

But the very idea of marriage was itself a difficult negotiation, recounted by Roth in *My Life as a Man* and again in *The Facts*. Maggie and marriage left an indelible stain of betrayal and distrust. Arriving in New York before Roth had returned from Europe, she attached herself to him, hoping to be settled in a career through his growing contacts. They quarreled, as they had in Chicago, and he wanted her gone. She would reluctantly agree, then call from a phone booth in a subway station, lost. He would "rescue" her, something of a habit with him. She then revealed she was pregnant; surprised, he demanded she be tested. The results were positive; he himself went to the pharmacist to retrieve them. A shocked but noble Roth, succumbing to moral blackmail, agreed to marry her, but only if she had an abortion. Maggie agreed, but with the $300 he gave her for the procedure she went instead to the movies and spent the rest.

Roth had introduced Maggie to his parents (after she nagged him) before the wedding. They tolerated her, accepting the fact that she was four years older than Roth and a divorced mother of two. If they had hesitations about their son marrying her, they did not reveal them, although they did want the couple to have a Jewish as well as a civil ceremony. Some months later, and against Roth's better judgment, Maggie converted to Judaism after study with a rabbi, Jack Cohen, at the Reconstructionist Synagogue in Manhattan.

Rabbi Cohen then performed a Jewish marriage with Roth's parents present. Roth, however, found this second ceremony unnecessary, ludicrous, and vulgar, partly because he felt it was a misguided attempt on Maggie's part to "manufacture a marital bond where the mismatch was blatant and already catastrophic" (FAC 126). For Roth, being a Jew had to do with the historical predicament you were born into, not an identity you selected after reading a few books (FAC 126).

Nevertheless, in a letter to Solotaroff in early March 1959, he thanks Solotaroff for his congratulations on the marriage, admitting that they have been having a rough time with his family. They need all the blessings they can collect, he writes, and comments that there is very little like the "kinds of destruction loved ones can pour upon other loved ones" and that no one else in the world except "the god damn Jews can kill each other so."[4] But the difficulties are either waning or just hiding, when his father tells him to move to a better apartment and buy Maggie a new coat. Roth's brother, who had earlier gotten married also interfered. The sister-in-law, in particular, constantly attacked Maggie and Roth, making him feel especially guilty for marrying a gentile and not being able to provide for her. And his parents were more upset than they showed. To Solotaroff he admits that the last two years with Maggie before their marriage had not been easy, and only a small amount of wind would knock them both over. Roth is doubly grateful, then, for Solotaroff's support. Nevertheless, he states in a much later letter, and possibly as a defensive gesture, that he did not enter the marriage because of any self-destructive tendency. He claims that its failure blindsided him, although he was quite conscious of their difficulties before they married, and his statement might be disingenuous. Maggie left deep marks on his work and his mind. The relationship encompassed a thousand arguments in thirty-three months, filtering into his early work as quarrels appearing throughout *Letting Go, When She Was Good,* and *My Life as a Man.*[5]

Roth's civil marriage took place on Sunday, 22 February 1959, in Yonkers, New York, performed by a justice of the peace with just two friends, Vernon and Diana Gibberd, as witnesses (Figure 3.1). Roth chose the date because thirty-two years earlier, his parents had married on 22 February 1927.[6]

Vernon Gibberd was an English architect Roth had met on the boat back to New York in September 1958. His wife, Diana, was to work at *Vogue.* Roth remained friends with the Gibberds, and when Roth, separated from Maggie, and visited England with Ann Mudge in 1968, they stayed part of the time with the Gibberds. Several snapshots from the wedding day show a

Figure 3.1 Roth with his arms around Maggie on their wedding day, 22 February 1959, Yonkers, New York. Credit: Vernon Gibberd. Philip Roth Papers, Library of Congress.

smiling Roth towering over Maggie, the happiness of the moment masking the conflicts he details in *The Facts* and the deal that he would marry her only after she had an abortion (FAC 110–11).[7] In one photo, standing on an elevated train platform, they enthusiastically embrace after the ceremony. Another shows the couple standing somewhat rigidly, almost at attention, on the platform as they face the camera, revealing a satisfied Roth but a slightly sullen Maggie. A further photo has Roth jubilantly smiling at the camera in front of a furniture store advertising tables for $7 (Figure 3.2), while one more photo has a self-assured, if not smug, Maggie standing alone before a window in a winter coat, staring at the camera.

Three years later, Roth learned the truth: in a drunken and semisuicidal state, Maggie confessed that she had deceived him about the pregnancy test, actually paying a pregnant Black woman in Tompkins Square Park in the

Figure 3.2 An exuberant Roth in front of a furniture store on his wedding day, 22 February 1959, Yonkers, New York. Credit: Vernon Gibberd. Philip Roth Papers, Library of Congress.

East Village for a urine sample which she had tested. Roth recounts the incident in *My Life as a Man,* where Maureen traps Peter Tarnopol. Maggie also admitted that earlier in Chicago she did not use a diaphragm, which led to her first pregnancy with Roth. In retrospect, the searing event was Maggie's greatest invention, Roth declares in *The Facts,* her only wholly original act (FAC 107). But for Roth, learning the truth created a lasting psychological "wound" that led to his distrust of women, especially those who might seek a permanent relationship. But he, too, was at fault. The reason Maggie nearly overdosed in January 1962 was that she learned of Roth's affair with a student. He had actually suggested they run off together, but the student wisely said no.

In New York, long before these revelations and the betrayal of Roth's trust in Maggie, the two socialized with a variety of literary figures, including Leslie Fiedler, who possessed a series of odd mannerisms. One of them, Roth noted, was scratching his head as if his brain itched. Originally from Newark, Fiedler had six children, prompting Maggie to ask if he was Catholic. "What a golden mouth she has," Roth sarcastically remarked, before she added that Protestants can have kids too.[8] Ralph Ellison was at the same party, but

Roth had nothing to say to him. A symposium at Columbia on the role of the writer in America followed; Wright Morris, Bellow, Dorothy Parker, and Fielder participated. Admitting he missed Chicago somewhat, what Roth really missed was his independence.

Roth in general seems to have edited his actual family life. His parents were dismayed at his marrying Maggie and unhappy with the life Roth and she were leading. Roth remained at odds with his father and his authoritarian, know-it-all attitude. Roth's brother was also meddling in his life, and Roth certainly was not happy with Sandy's wife, something of a Jewish princess who did not approve of Roth and his artistic, semibohemian ways. In his fiction, family life is nostalgically idealized; in reality, it was tense, emotionally distraught, and often argumentative.

In his earlier letter to Solotaroff, Roth soon turned from family to his year away from teaching, which renewed his love of writing and books; the academic approach to literature, with its symbols, theories, and criticism, unnerved him. Writing alone satisfied him. But he admits this is hypocritical because he will soon be applying for a teaching job: he needs the money and hates to depend upon writing for his living. However, he would accept no less than $5,200 a year, showing, even at this stage, his confidence in estimating his own worth and claiming its value. He was also waiting to hear about a Guggenheim Fellowship but was skeptical. If he could stay in New York, Maggie could continue with her job as production editor at Harper's Books.

At the beginning of this tumultuous period, Roth's constant concern was the fate of *Goodbye, Columbus*. On 16 June 1958, Starbuck told Roth in London he had no news yet on the story collection earlier submitted. Ten days later, Starbuck wrote to apologize for the delay and to say that a letter from a Ms. Donadio (Roth's agent at Herb Jaffe Associates; she would soon go out on her own) suggests that Roth will pull the collection, although his intent is not clear.[9] From Paris, Roth sends Starbuck the manuscript for another project which initially interested Houghton Mifflin more than a collection of short stories; this is *The Go Between*, his German-centered novel. He also sent an application for a Houghton Mifflin Literary Fellowship. Attending to detail, Roth writes that where the word "German" appears in the margin, he intends to have the English translated and printed in the text as German.[10]

From Florence a month later, Roth again writes to Starbuck: no word— I'm anxious. What of the stories, what of the $7,500 Houghton Mifflin fellowship? Since next year's plans rested on Starbuck's decisions, Roth would like to know what they are. Describing his trip as everything from stirring to aggravating and thrilling, he announces that he will return to the States on 21 August. He met a strange breed of American abroad but surprisingly likes them: "the vulgarer the better." And don't worry about Candida Donadio, he assures Starbuck. She was not handling Roth's stuff for Houghton Mifflin, but if Starbuck turned it down, Roth would likely give it over to her.[11]

On the same day as Roth's letter to Starbuck (25 July 1958), Paul Brooks of the Houghton Mifflin editorial board wrote to Lovell Thompson concerning the fellowship and the synopsis of the Frankfurt novel and said they had a problem. This twenty-five-year-old Jewish instructor at Chicago has published a series of short stories, and all who read him think he has talent and feels Houghton should secure him for their list. But "Goodbye, Columbus" poses a challenge at 37,000 words.[12] It's a story of first love, but the denouement hinges on a contraceptive device a topic rarely written about so clearly at the time, especially involving unmarried young couples. Roth believed that it was hard to see how the story could be changed without damaging the entire work. And the *Paris Review* has just taken the story, which is unusual, since they generally do not do long works. What are our choices, Brooks asks? Publish the novella with several short stories, as with Carson McCullers's *Ballad of the Sad Café*? But what of the fifty-seven pages and synopsis of the novel set in Frankfurt?

Roth planned to set his novel in Frankfurt dealing with the guilt the world inherited from the Holocaust, "symbolized here by an unattractive, neurotic American Jew who has come back to look for traces of his family."[13] Two Houghton editors responded enthusiastically to the synopsis, but Brooks and two others were skeptical. The difference between the proposed German story and Roth's American writing was the difference "between a story that starts with an intellectual idea and a story that embodies the life that the author has lived."[14] The second is preferable and more convincing. Brooks would option the novel but definitely publish the story collection. The novel seems to have been forgotten, partly because there were reservations about the authenticity of atmosphere and the national character of the Germans as presented—in contrast to the Jewish milieu of New Jersey, which Roth knew down "to the last cuff-link."[15] It would be Starbuck who, in selecting the stories to be in the collection, provided a Jewish focus for the volume. In a way, Starbuck fashioned Roth's writing future because Roth did not think Jewish life was his subject. At the time, he had no idea *what* his subject was.[16]

On 30 July, Starbuck wired Roth that Houghton Mifflin would publish "Goodbye, Columbus" with other stories. If he signed, he would receive a $1,000 advance and 10 percent royalty on the first five thousand copies sold, and HM would have first refusal on his next completed book. Questions about the proposed novel's atmospheric authenticity, however, remained, with one editor feeling that the novel was a little out of the blue given the quality of the short stories. Roth received the wire in Paris and was delighted, although he was still anxious to discuss whether "Goodbye, Columbus" could stand alone. He told Starbuck he had another story, "Defender of the Faith," which he had recently finished. Apologies if he seemed too pushy earlier, he added, but "now if I'm pushy it'll be about getting that book out: I'd love to see it printed tomorrow."[17] Again, Roth, the new but assertive author, is unafraid to direct his editor and even publisher, telling them to move fast. Self-confident, he has no hesitation in shaping his new book.

Writing to Solotaroff in July 1958 from Europe, Roth summarized his travels: London, Paris, then the south of France and Italy. He refers to a hundred pages of a novel he'd been working on as flashy but without sparkle or wit. He reports that it looks as if Houghton Mifflin will publish a book of his short stories and that the *Paris Review* will likely take "Goodbye, Columbus," although he has changed the original business enterprise of the Patimkins from glass to sinks. Solotaroff's father was in the glass business.

Roth also tells him that he's just finished a fifty-two-page story entitled "Eli, the Fanatic" but can't decide if it's good or bad. Initiating what will be a common practice for Roth, sharing late drafts of works with close friends, he asks if he can send it to Solotaroff for a solid opinion. He may have taken his cue from Virginia Woolf, who in her essay "Reviewing" (1939) comments that readings by professional reviewers in contrast to book journalists would benefit a novelist more than any other form of commentary. Roth himself adjusted this to asking close friends, more honest and open than book reviewers, to critique his work. He cites Woolf as an example. One of the important aspects of Roth's life and work is the reception of his work and the history of mistaken readings, inflammatory associations, changing perceptions, and even popular misconceptions.[18]

During this relatively short and early European trip, Roth asserted his "Americanness," as he would do again some thirty years later, telling Solotaroff that he missed the "hot aggravation of American summers" and the vulgarity of the beach and the traffic. On this trip, he felt his "Americanness" and he didn't mind it at all.[19] Later, during his regular visits to England with Claire Bloom, he would miss America even more and after every return feel more eager to understand the country than before. The result, in part, was his American Trilogy, written, he explained, to reclaim his knowledge of the country.

He added that he hadn't heard from Maggie, who, it seems, had also moved to New York, telling Solotaroff she's a rare person, "and if I were a little rarer I'd have not screwed things up so often."[20] The statement reveals a highly conflicted Roth, admiring Maggie when he wasn't, in the extreme, prepared to harm her. Their relationship was complex, one moment dedicating his first novel to her and the next distraught because she would not consent to a divorce. His role seemed to alternate between a martyr prepared to save her and a hostage imprisoned by her control over him and his finances. Why did he marry this needy and damaged woman? In 1958 he knew she was trouble, but he wanted trouble, rebelling against the placid and conventional lives led by his parents and his Newark friends. His savior complex kicked in, overlooking the difficulties of life with this divorced mother of two. He wanted the mess, not the cleansing experience of a stable, middle-class, college-educated woman from Short Hills or even West Orange. He became the escape artist he identified in this contradictory phrase: "I always seem to need to be emancipated from whatever has liberated me," while also craving order and domesticity. This is the Roth problem.[21]

While battling Maggie, he was making preparations for the publication of *Goodbye, Columbus*, underscoring Roth's early efforts to take control of the publishing process, displaying a youthful sense of self-confidence. These early attempts at literary control anticipate later disagreements about advances, print runs, marketing budgets, jacket copy, and editorial judgment with subsequent publishers. From the beginning, even as a young and inexperienced writer, Roth was sure about what he wanted. Although he realized that a collection of short stories from a "novel-less" writer was something of a gamble, he nonetheless believed that if pushed in certain ways, with proper publicity, advertising, and marketing, *Goodbye, Columbus* could have "a very wide appeal perhaps to that same group who buy Salinger by the thousands."[22]

Despite this self-confidence and determination, he was unable to respond with such self-assurance in his relationship with Maggie. The conflict between his Judaic sense of moral obligation and the almost willing self-destructiveness brought on by her jealousy and fear led to a paralysis of will. Regarding books and his writing, he could be decisive, but not so in his private life.

By September 1958, Roth was back in Chicago and preparing to visit Boston to review the contents of the collection. His preferred arrangement of the short stories was now the following:

Goodbye, Columbus
Conversion of the Jews
Epstein
Defender of the Faith
You Can't Tell a Man by the Song He Sings

This would be almost the final sequence, which would see "Defender of the Faith" switch with "Epstein" and the addition of "Eli, the Fanatic" (finished in October 1958) as the final story, forming a book of 298 pages.

In early October, he worked on some changes Starbuck suggested and reported that the *New Yorker* bought a funny piece entitled "The Kind of Person I Am." "Defender of the Faith" had gone all the way to William Shawn. Rachel MacKenzie, Roth's editor at the magazine, told Shawn they would be distressed if they didn't take it. Concerning an epigram for *Goodbye, Columbus*, Roth cites a statement from his character Ozzie Freedman in "The Conversion of the Jews," saying it applies to all his heroes in one way or another: "Is it me? It is me, Me ME ME ME! It has to be me—but is it!" (GBC 148). The statement reflects Roth's underlying narcissism and determination to promote his work and career at any cost. He would not let up, displaying an intensity of focus that would lead to a sustained presence in the public's eye. He did not live on hope but on action supported by ambition.

At the time, the *Paris Review* was running into problems with the printing and scheduling of "Goodbye, Columbus." Richard Seaver, who went on to become a publisher in New York but at the time was the editor of *Merlin* in Paris, wrote that while Paris may be their mistress, "the political realities of the time were our master."[23] The *Paris Review* never paid its editors or assistants a salary, banking on goodwill and literary excitement as proper currency. But Plimpton's return to the U.S. in 1956 ostensibly meant that the energy and social activity shifted from the Café de Tournon to 541 East 72nd Street, Plimpton's apartment.

Roth told Starbuck that the *Review* had only an illegible Thermofax of "Goodbye, Columbus"; was it possible to send him the HM copy, which will be used as setting copy for the journal? Of course, he'll return it, adding that he sold "Defender of the Faith" to the *New Yorker* for a "fine fine price"

($2,200). Starbuck wrote on Halloween 1958 that he and another editor liked "Eli, the Fanatic" very much and saw it as the final story in the collection, although he was not happy with the title—perhaps it keyed the story too much. How about "The Man in the Black Suit" or "The Diaspora of Eli Peck," he asked. Some changes to the ending of the story reached Starbuck in November, when Roth inquired about the jacket art, noting that he liked the work of Milton Glaser.

In December, Roth expressed upset to Starbuck with the New Yorker because they made some "rather abusive changes" in "Defender," to appear in April. He wanted things shifted back, but they paid well, which made him a weak bargainer, he wrote, but not that weak. He liked that "jazzy 25 year old crew neck sweatered photo" Houghton Mifflin would use on the jacket, taken by his brother. Candida Donadio would now deal with his advances and contracts, he told Starbuck. But he persisted in making changes, writing on 30 January 1959 that he wanted to provide additions to "Defender." They involved adding a couple of paragraphs and a sentence here and there that arose out of some unnecessary changes suggested by the New Yorker.[24]

But the jacket caused some controversy, solved by Roth getting his brother to do it. Apparently, Glaser wasn't quite right; the new jacket by Sandy Roth is conventional but appropriate, said Starbuck, and makes it look like a novel that may boost sales considerably, although the addition of a nude is sensational. No one at Houghton Mifflin can recall an HM novel jacket with a nude other than Raintree County by Ross Lockridge Jr., which had a woman's naked body worked into a landscape, low hills doubling as her breasts. But disagreement over the use of gray and orange then emerged, contrary to the mood of the original Goodbye cover, which was gay, youthful, and sensuous. The new jacket was too moody and melancholy and unoriginal, Roth declared: "Instead of a girl standing in front of a window in day light, summery day light, it's a brooding girl looking oh so wanly out the window (anything but the energetic Brenda Patimkin, the central female figure in "Goodbye Columbus!") in back of a blob of orange fruit, ridiculous finally . . . truly a waste."[25] Roth objected to the alterations and that the production department did not let Sandy see the changes. He preferred a yellow cover that had not been "blandized. Isn't there enough gray in the world?" (Portnoy's Complaint will later appear in a bright yellow jacket.) Starbuck agreed that Sandy's image attempted to avoid the potential of wistfulness in "Goodbye," but somehow that didn't happen.

When the book finally did appear, Roth took a hand in its promotion, suggesting to HM that they take out an ad in the *New Yorker* because of the reaction generated by his story "Defender of the Faith." Noting that he was now the center of a debate accusing him of anti-Semitism, perhaps it was time to "put a little gas on the fire." Although ads were planned for the *Paris Review* and the *Partisan Review*, those audiences are small. Let's push for the *New Yorker*, he tells Anne Ford at HM. He wants to sell this book: "The fact that I have made Scarsdale mothers irate is not to be disregarded. As I said to Anne [Hall], where there's a row there's an audience."[26]

Roth slightly underplayed the "Defender" controversy, the story focusing on a Jewish army sergeant showing no favor to a Jewish soldier seeking a noncombat assignment. It loomed large, as he describes in *The Facts* (115–18). The story's appearance in the 14 March 1959 issue of the *New Yorker*, his second piece to appear in a large-circulation magazine (the first had appeared in *Esquire*, for which he received $800), preceded by a month the publication in book form of *Goodbye, Columbus*. Had it appeared in *Commentary* or even the *Paris Review*, reaction would have been low key.[27] But the *New Yorker*—widely read by gentiles as well as Jews—that was too much. Jewish response to the story was vocal and persistent, from synagogue sermons to newspaper columns and household debates; he was repeatedly accused of anti-Semitism because his Jewish sergeant refuses to help a fellow Jew. It then exploded to his supposedly divulging Jewish secrets and falsifying Jewish lives.

Roth was especially offended by a letter from Rabbi Emanuel Rackman, then the dean of Orthodox rabbis, who, despite being a vocal civil libertarian (he spoke out against the death penalty for the Rosenbergs and the American Legion's opposition to Paul Robeson), was an unbending Orthodox leader.[28] At the time "Defender of the Faith" appeared, Rackman was the rabbi of the Fifth Avenue Synagogue, former president of the New York Board of Rabbis, and chair of the Rabbinical Council of America. In that capacity, he wrote a scathing letter to Roth, referred to in the opening paragraph of Roth's "Writing About Jews" (RMY 193–94).

An angered Roth replied to Rackman in a four-page single-spaced typed letter of 30 April 1959. He begins his response to Rackman's "outrage" by explaining that Sheldon Grossbart, who perverts his Jewishness into a conflict of loyalties for Sergeant Nathan Marx, no more stands for all Jews than Hamlet stands for all Danes. Nor does Marx stand for all Jews. Challenging Rackman, Roth explains that it is not an anti-Semitic story but one that calls for "responsible Semitism," a community of understanding, not deceit. The characters are individuals and are not meant to stand for others in the story.[29] It is as intellectually dishonest, he continues, to represent all Jews as good as it was for Hitler to say all Jews were bad. Why not celebrate Marx, who, despite the chicanery of Grossbart, remains a man of "stern moral conscience" and is sympathetic to Grossbart because of their Jewishness? "To represent a person who happens to be a Jew as a person who also happens to be deceitful and mean is not to say that *all* Jews are deceitful and mean," he adds. And it's odd that most who write to him say nothing about Marx—they only chastise him while displaying a fear of liberty and narrowness similar to that of the late Senator McCarthy. Roth then draws parallels between his critics who claim he was anti-Semitic and the labeling of those who criticized America in the 1950s as anti-American. Should all who criticize be silenced? That is the question that troubles the young author.

Roth goes on to connect the rabbi's charges with those of the Russian government against Pasternak. But in his clearest statement, Roth declares, "I am a writer of fiction and not a propagandist." His purpose is not to sell Judaism, nor to write fiction that avoids provocation. To write truthfully will always provoke some. Yes, he has some negative attitudes toward his heritage, and even his positive ones are not entirely uncritical. Even his view of American history is critical: "Blind faith is not for Americans and, I pray, not for Jews."[30]

The letter to Rackman shows a confident, assertive Roth opposing the claims of those intolerant rabbis and dogmatic individuals (Judge Wapter in *The Ghost Writer* is another) who instantly condemned his story and attitude. It also shows how Roth both instinctively and rationally considered these questions and formulated a sustained response. His promise is not to a falsified view of Jewish life and behavior but to a complex, contradictory, and truthful examination of its weaknesses as well as strengths. Years later, in a 2009 interview in Germany, Roth could not forget Rackman's "nasty attack" on the then twenty-six-year-old writer. He still wanted to retaliate.

Further correspondence shows Roth pushing Houghton Mifflin to promote and publicize more, especially when in late March the publisher suggested they wait for the book to appear first before they start advertising: "That's the way it's done in all publishing houses."[31] The next day Starbuck reported that $1,500 was committed to advertising, much above average, adding, on the topic of anti-Semitism, "Harry Golden, but also Malamud, should teach you a disheartening lesson: to be safely a Semite, be less the comic artist than the sentimental buffoon."[32] Roth, of course, would energetically disregard such advice and tell Starbuck that after Anne Hall's misunderstanding about his wanting to play up his readers' misunderstanding, "I don't trust anybody but you. Oh. And Maggie of course." The reference to Maggie crucially signals Roth's complex, at times self-contradictory relation with her. He had just received copies of the book and was happy except for the "m-f cover. Jesus! But enough of that."[33] The gray cover, dominated by a large, orange bowl of fruit with a nude sketched in the background looking out a window, misrepresented what he felt was the content of the stories.

When the book was finally published on 7 May 1959, Roth was ecstatic. On the 23rd he told Starbuck that he was creating demand for the work by calling up bookstores, asking for the book, and then quickly hanging up. He then referred to a positive lead review in the *New York Post,* though it made the book seem "a little like the Torah, a necessity for all Jews." On 25 May 1959, Starbuck told Roth that 4,312 copies have been sold, which means a third printing order soon. Starbuck also asked about the German novel: Will it be your *Felix Krull,* incubating while you pile up other work?

Positive reviews soon appeared, although Roth continued to push Starbuck for more ads and promotion, more so after Kazin, Bellow, Fiedler, and Howe wrote positively about the collection. But by early June, he was upset, writing a two-and-a-half-page single-spaced letter to the advertising person at Houghton Mifflin. Everything from failing to identify Kazin in a *New Yorker* ad to small font upsets him. There are also facts about the book that should be emphasized, namely that it is funny. Also, he's only twenty-six, and while he doesn't want to be seen as a boy genius, his youth should be highlighted. He then tells someone at Houghton Mifflin named Connie how the ad in the *Village Voice* should read, and that the real push should be in New Jersey, where there are "2000 women in the Jersey hills just waiting for a book like this." Why no ad, then, in the *Newark Evening News*?

> Unrestrained, Roth offers a sample of what should appear in the paper. It
>   begins:
> LOVE (young and comic) AND LIFE (opulent and comic)
>   In NEW JERSEY
> Nation-wide acclaim for GOODBYE, COLUMBUS by
> Philip Roth

After appropriate quotes from reviews, it should close with:

> Whoever knows New Jersey, Will Have Trouble
>> Putting Down One of the Most
>> Acclaimed Books of the Year—
>>> GOODBYE, COLUMBUS
>>> By Newarker, Philip Roth

He even suggests a photo, perhaps the one on the back jacket taken by his brother. Roth is now clearly the promoter, combining advertising with marketing, who does not want to overlook his special readership, but he also wants those New Jersey women readers to know that the book is being read all over the country. The collection turns into a product for him, telling Connie that the Jersey women don't believe the book until it's merchandise, something they can buy. Don't put the ad in the book section but somewhere else in the paper, he advises.[34]

Kazin began his review in *The Reporter* of 28 May 1959 by noting that "Defender of the Faith" startled him when it first appeared in the *New Yorker* and calling it a story with "guts." The idea of a Jewish sergeant punishing the ringleader of three Jewish soldiers was bold and shattering. The moral complexity of Sergeant Marx astonished Kazin, who admired the courage of the sergeant to make a painful decision. Sidestepping the more universal and collective themes of Jewish life and the Jew as an individual was admirable: the drama of personal integrity was the underlying value of the story. That Jewish organizations were offended was a sign of the story's honesty, not its offensiveness, he added. But the new collection shifted the focus to love defeated by a "brutally materialistic society."[35] The faceoff was now between Romantic infatuation and bourgeois materialism.

Roth's tone, Kazin continued, is particularly accomplished: "acidulous, unsparing, tender." Yet he sees life sympathetically even if he recognizes that the gap between poor Jewish boys and rich Jewish girls is final.[36] But brilliant as it is, Kazin writes, it does not match *The Great Gatsby*: it is too much in control and sharp-edged. He criticizes both the "Conversion of the Jews"—the theme is too clear—and "Eli, the Fanatic" as adding up only to its theme of Holocaust guilt and European Jewish identity. While admiring the fierceness of Roth's mind, he worries about Roth's future because he makes the conflict in each story too clear. He needs more of the creative writer's "delight in life for its own sake, figures that do not immediately signify a design."[37]

Bellow, writing in *Commentary*, gushed that it was a first book, "but not the book of a beginner. . . . At twenty-six he is skillful, witty and energetic and performs like a virtuoso."[38] Bellow's complaint, however, is that Roth is too sophisticated. His subject is the paradoxical life of Jews in prosperous, postwar America. Neil Klugman is something of an outsider, descendent on his Jewish side from the *Shlimazl* (a person born without luck), on the Russian from the clerk in Gogol's "The Cloak." But now possessions have a new glamour for the Jews, and Roth does a superb job in satirizing this desire. Burlap formally ruled the life of the Jewish hero; now it's furs.

Roth's interest is in the society of manners newly emergent in the Jewish middle or aspirational class. But Roth goes deeper, Bellow writes, especially in the scene of Neil entering St. Patrick's Cathedral on Fifth Avenue in New York while Brenda gets fitted for a diaphragm and admits he is carnal and acquisitive but uncertain of his direction. To sacrifice oneself or to acquire? The answer hit Neil when he stepped out: "gold dinnerware, sporting-goods, trees, nectarines" (GBC 100). Bellow ends by applauding Roth's decision not to write some form of public relation releases for Jews overlooking excess and wrongs.

The book itself, especially the novella, reinforced differences among Jews, most strikingly between Newark and Short Hills. To cross the borders of social class dividing Newark, with its crowded apartments in four-family homes, desperately honking traffic, and rumbling Lackawanna commuter trains, from suburban Short Hills, 180 feet higher in altitude, was to become "closer to heaven, for the sun itself became bigger, lower, and rounder" (GBC 8). Nevertheless, Neil reassures his Aunt Gladys that the Patimkins are "real Jews," even though they live in *goyishe* Short Hills. "I'll see it I'll believe it," she replies (GBC 58). But Brenda's humor is more Newark than Short Hills: asked at her brother's wedding by the nosy and condescending Gloria Feldman what she has been doing all summer, she replies, "Growing a penis" (GBC 110).

The theme of difference is nowhere more evident than in "Eli, the Fanatic," which appeared in *Commentary* in 1958. The story of the civic friction caused by a yeshiva run by displaced Orthodox European Jews emphasizes the disruption of postwar Jewish life when tradition intrudes, especially in assimilationist Westchester. The orthodoxy of the Holocaust survivors actually embarrasses the well-integrated Jews of the New York suburb. Critics focused on the doppelgänger element, the story's social commentary, and even its parody of psychoanalysis, but overlooked its origin, drawn from an actual episode of 1948 in Mount Kisco, New York. That year, a zoning controversy pitted the town against Holocaust survivors eager to open a yeshiva in an unused mansion they had purchased. A report of the so-called Nitra Yeshiva controversy appeared in *Commentary*, a journal Roth regularly read.

More specifically, Rabbi Chaim Weissmandel was the worldly leader of the yeshiva, which had originally flourished in Hungary before the war. Working to save Jews through various contacts did not prevent his own deportation to Auschwitz, but he escaped by jumping from a moving prisoner train. In 1947, with surviving students from the Nitra Yeshiva, he arrived in the U.S. and eventually acquired a building and land in Westchester County. Soon, public opposition—the yeshiva disrupted the harmony of the neighborhood—took over. Anti-Semitic objections, however, were masked in opposition to the use of land: it should remain a farm and that way ensure increased property values. Roth alters the events in his story, adding irony by suggesting that it was suburban Jews who opposed the new settlement; records from Mount Kisco indicate the opponents were non-Jews, although further research has revealed that successful local Jews were likely behind the opposition.[39]

Roth's intellectual affinity was with the *Partisan Review,* then edited by Philip Rahv. *Commentary* educated him to be unapologetic about the Jews of his past, becoming the magazine of "Jewish self-scrutiny." Noting in an essay from 1989 that two of his stories in his collection appeared in *Commentary* and one in the *New Yorker*, he nonetheless singles out the *Paris Review* for special notice, partly because its editors, from a privileged gentile background, encouraged his Jew-centric work. For the novice writer, this was exhilarating. And he thought he was absolutely moving upward from the world of "unsubtle locutions and coarse supplications" of the families of Weequahic, a "tiny provincial enclosure." His study of the language and ideals of the kind of literature Eliot praised and James demonstrated would be his escalator to an elevated cultural world. Seneca, instead of street talk, he thought, would be his way out in his search for a world of intellectual consequence.[40]

In a final paragraph of his essay, Roth offers an astute critique of his stories as portraying the dilemma of departure and return, perpetuating the contradictory feelings of a young man eager to rebel and yet remain. The stories enacted what he calls the ambivalence that stimulated the struggle his imagination would continue to encounter in his writing. As a writer, he could now reimagine the folk stories of what had previously been his everyday life under a sheen of satiric social comedy.

One result of the publicity for *Goodbye, Columbus* was invitations to speak to large congregations in the Newark suburban area, including one from a group of 750 women. Roth declined them all but told Starbuck, again, get an ad in the *Newark Evening News*: "The book the Nation is reading and all New Jersey is talking about" was his tag line, suggested earlier. He wrote Starbuck from Amagansett, Long Island, where he and Maggie were spending the summer, that he had turned down a chance to go to Hollywood in order to get back to a long story after he completed a TV script that took him away from his novel. *Playhouse 90* wanted an adaptation of "Defender of the Faith" for a large amount of money. But they were still in the talking stage, he writes on 6 June 1959. A mail-out piece appealed to his ego. "I could look at all that stuff about myself all on one page," he preened; it's fabulous. A note from Starbuck of 21 July 1959 reports that sales are now almost 8,400 copies with another hundred just ordered.

Amagansett in East Hampton in 1959 provided relief for Roth from bickering with Maggie, and he spent a good deal of time there with a new set of friends, mostly Canadians, notably the Irish Canadian writer Brian Moore, his wife, the French Canadian journalist Jackie Moore, and a young writer soon to become a name in Canadian letters for his own outrageous style, Mordecai Richler, whose *The Apprenticeship of Duddy Kravitz* appeared that year.[41] Wallace Markfield, later to publish *To an Early Grave,* was another. But the happiness of the summer was disrupted when Roth's mother, visiting for a weekend, abruptly left because of an intense argument between Maggie and Bruce Ruddick. Ruddick, from Montreal, was a psychiatrist and a poet who had founded the Canadian Psychoanalytic Society and had moved to New York in 1957. Mark Rothko was a friend who suffered from depression and consulted him, although Ruddick declined to treat him. By this time, Roth and Maggie had been married six months, but his mother, witness to the anger and intransigence of her daughter-in-law, had to leave.

And, of course, there were criticisms and attacks, especially on "Epstein"— Do Jews actually commit adultery?—as well as "Defender of the Faith." Roth summarizes these responses in his essay "Writing About Jews" (1963). He understood that his stories might offend, but the sustained public assault surprised him. Editorials, sermons, articles, and confrontations greeted *Goodbye, Columbus,* which, many claimed, ignored the accomplishments of Jewish life. The base charge was that he was a self-hating Jew and anti-Semitic. His exposure of Jewish materialism and distorted values only confirmed the views of the gentiles, he was told. It was unusual enough that the debut work for a fiction writer was a collection of short stories—traditionally those appear only after a first or second novel; Roth not only had an award-winning title but sustained, if controversial, publicity.

In "Writing About Jews," Roth emphasizes the value of fiction to free us from conventional attitudes and behavior, especially toward Judaism. This, he argues, is the very nature of his stories. He begins by stressing that we do not even know we have a range of complex feelings and responses "*until* we have come into contact with the work of fiction" (RMY 195). Fiction allows us to expand our moral consciousness. His stories are not so much about Jewish tradition or behavior as character: Epstein, not the Jews, is the subject. The test of a literary work is not the breadth but the depth of its representation (RMY 199).

Roth addresses, in particular, the controversy over "Defender of the Faith," which appeared in the 14 March 1959 issue of the *New Yorker*. He was so excited by its publication that he ran to the newsstand on 14th Street at least three times, a figure he inflated in Claudia Roth Pierpont's account to six. The story, by the twenty-six-year-old Roth, is about a conflict of loyalties. It deals with the Jewish sergeant Marx and the young recruit Grossbart who seeks special favors because of their shared religion. Grossbart is a "Jewish fact," not an anti-Semitic stereotype, Roth emphasizes as he did in a four-page letter to Rabbi Rackman dated 30 April 1959 (RMY 201). He is not to represent the Jews or Jewry. Marx is the central voice of the story but is only tentatively a Jew. But letters quoted by Roth indicate the harm to the Jews done by publication of "Defender" by making many readers believe that all Jews were cheats and connivers. Another letter sent to the Anti-Defamation League simply asked, "What is being done to silence this man?" (RMY 204). The threat Roth posed was that he "informed" on the Jews, telling the gentiles something they long ago suspected. In his essay, Roth confronts the timidity and paranoia that existed among narrow-minded Jews.

Roth actually downplays the controversy bordering on furor caused by the story and the collection, attacked in pulpits, community centers, papers, and magazines. That a greedy, conniving, manipulative Jewish soldier would be at the center of the story outraged and embarrassed many complacent Jews. With his single book, his first book, Roth gained immediate notoriety, yet his response was not contrition but aggression.

Roth was a pugilist, a counterpuncher schooled in the streets of Newark, seen in his controlled but aggravated public responses. He confronted opponents in synagogues and community centers. He deconstructed the opposition in a rational, although not necessarily conciliatory manner. In *The Facts*, he recalls a meeting with two representatives of the Anti-Defamation League at Ratner's kosher dairy restaurant on Delancey Street on the Lower East Side of New York. He found the meeting disorienting, partly because in high school he was thinking about studying law and occasionally imagined working on their staff to defend the civil and legal rights of Jews. But the intent of the current meeting was the opposite, although no chastisement or accusations came forward during their lunch, only a polite exchange of views, according to Roth (FAC 123–24).

But despite, or perhaps because of, the upheaval and controversy, sales grew and in 1960 the collection won the National Book Award and the Daroff Award of the Jewish Book Council of America. He learned from Bob Silvers, who accepted the Daroff Award in Roth's absence (he was in Italy on a Guggenheim—value $3,200—but did fly back for the National Book Award), that he was an unpopular choice among the sponsors as well as attendees. The previous year, the highly acclaimed, super pro-Semitic *Exodus* by Leon Uris had won.

Confrontations continued, one of the most publicized occurring at Yeshiva University's symposium on 29 March 1962, "A Study in Artistic Conscience: Conflict of Loyalties by Minority Writers of Fiction." Joining Roth in what would become a tribunal was Ralph Ellison, known to all as the author of *Invisible Man,* and the Italian American Marxist writer Pietro di Donato. David Fleisher, then chair of the Division of Language, Literature and Fine Arts (and a Roth fan) moderated (Figures 3.3–3.5).

The symposium was part of a yearlong set of events held in conjunction with the diamond jubilee anniversary of the university and was later broadcast on radio station WNYC in mid-July that year. Roth would cite the event in "Writing About Jews" and later in *The Facts*.

Roth, described as an "undiscouragable young man of letters" in a citation from the National Institute of Arts and Letters which accompanied a small grant, quickly became the center of controversy. Roth had come East for the event from Iowa, attending with Maggie and his New York editor, Joe Fox of Random House, who were about to publish his second book, the novel *Letting Go.* Roth was sensitive to the irony of his Nordic-looking recently converted Jewish wife watching what he later overdramatized as the "excommunication" of a young writer who had spent seventeen years in Semitic Weequahic.

Figure 3.3 Poster for Yeshiva University symposium, 29 March 1962, listing the three participants with the moderator. Credit: Yeshiva University Archives, Special Collections, Yeshiva University, New York.

But he anticipated the antagonism and spent at least half of his talk addressing his detractors *before* any questions. He presented prepared and logical remarks in an effort not to be misunderstood. But he was angry and ready to take on the crowd. Yet the first question from the moderator unsympathetically directed at Roth (who may have mistaken Fleisher for the more vitriolic Rabbi Emanuel Rackman, Roth's nemesis and in the audience) was "Would you write the same stories if you were living in Nazi Germany?" This is a question Roth would use when Judge Wapter confronts Zuckerman in *The Ghost Writer*. No response seemed to satisfy Roth's interlocutor, but the audience was on his side, as a recently discovered tape of the evening confirms. The tape, in fact, reveals that Roth was the one who first raised the Nazi analogy. But Rabbi Rackman began to chastise Roth from the floor,

Figure 3.4 Four Yeshiva University symposium speakers: (*left to right*) Pietro di Donato, Ralph Ellison, David Fleisher (moderator), Philip Roth. Credit: Yeshiva University Archives, Special Collections, Yeshiva University, New York.

as did Fleischer from the podium, and the event remained, in Roth's mind, traumatic.[42]

In response, Roth claimed that the position of Jews in America was secure enough that a writer could write anything he felt to be true, explaining that the experience of Epstein, in the eponymous story in *Goodbye, Columbus*, was typical of Jews and gentiles. Reading from a Detroit letter-writer—"Is it conceivable for a middle-aged man to neglect his business and spend all day with a middle-aged woman?," Roth paused and replied, "The answer is Yes." The hall echoed with laughter. But as his tenacity was fading, Ellison stepped in to defend Roth's position, stating that his own situation was identical: he had received hate mail from readers furious with him for depicting incest in a black family. At the end, a boisterous crowd surrounded Roth; a few shouted insults, until he was accused by someone of being brought up on anti-Semitic literature. "What's that?" an angry Roth shouted. "English literature" was the emotional cry of the accuser (FAC 129). But the tape contradicts Roth's

Figure 3.5 Roth at the lectern speaking at Yeshiva University symposium, 29 March 1962. Credit: Yeshiva University Archives, Special Collections, Yeshiva University, New York.

memory of the event. He was not the victim but the star, fully prepared to face his antagonists.

Roth's account in *The Facts* emphasizes the anger and bitterness of the exchanges, sensationally referring to the evening as a "trial" (FAC 127). Jason Rosenblat, who covered the symposium as features editor of the Yeshiva school paper, remembers a less rancorous debate.[43] Later, at the Stage Delicatessen in Midtown, an upset Roth told Maggie and Fox that he was finished with writing about Jews—although he did not abide by his declaration, of course (FAC 128–29). Nevertheless, Roth referred to the encounter as "the most bruising public exchange of my life" and asserted that it did not so much end his imagination's involvement with the Jews as mark its true beginning, displaying an emotional resilience and aggressiveness that turned a disturbing and even traumatic event into something provocative but positive (FAC 130). He realized that night that the roots of Jewish drama lay in fanatical insecurity (disputed by a Yeshiva professor of English literature in a 1989 review of *The Facts*).[44]

One issue related to "Goodbye, Columbus" was that of sources. Did Roth actually know anyone like the Patimkins or Brenda? Did he know anyone in Short Hills? The answer is not exact, although Plimpton in "The Paris Review Sketchbook" correctly states that Maxine Groffsky, later Paris editor of the *Paris Review*, was the prototype for Brenda Patimkin.[45] Groffsky, from Maplewood, New Jersey, and three years younger than Roth, dated the tall writer-to-be from Weequahic. This began at about the time she was to go off to Cornell in 1954, where she took, among other courses, a survey of English literature from M. H. Abrams on Saturday mornings, a course that no one ever missed.

At the end of the first semester of her second year, she transferred to Barnard College because of Roth and graduated as an English major in 1958. When she told Abrams of her decision, after a few characteristic puffs on his pipe, he thoughtfully said, with his characteristic smile, "Ah, love wins out." A photo from 1955—the year Roth received his MA from the University of Chicago and in September enlisted in the army—shows Roth and Groffsky visiting Bob and Holly Heyman at the home of Bob's parents in Weequahic. Just out of college, Groffsky worked in the editorial department of Random House, where she read Harry Mathews's eccentric novel, *The Conversions*, Mathews one of the early *Paris Review* gang. Groffsky said that reading *The Conversions* was like "seeing Merce Cunningham for the first time." Mathews became one of Groffsky's clients when she opened a literary agency years later. After she and Roth broke up, she began a relationship with the painter Larry Rivers, who claimed he stole her from Roth and declared that she was the model for Brenda Patimkin.[46]

Following *their* breakup, she went to Paris in 1962, where she eventually became the Paris editor of the *Paris Review,* working in the rue de Garancière office from 1965 until it closed in January 1974. She appeared on the masthead from 1966 to 1973. In fact, she became the only female editor of the magazine and brought, or restored, a more international perspective to the publication. This occurred visually when she and Silvers initiated a new graphic look for the *Review.* Plimpton was hesitant at first, but accepted the change, which reinforced the individuality of the journal.

In *George Being George*, an oral biography of Plimpton, a photo of the attractive, redheaded Groffsky appears at the *Paris Review* Paris office studiously examining a file labeled "POETRY." A 1972 photo of her in a Paris park by Lee Friedlander reveals a thoughtful figure on a bench, a figure of some mystery. In Paris, she lived with Mathews and raised the children he had with the artist Niki de Saint Phalle. She was also involved with the Paris Review Editions, a series of *Review*-sponsored publications, and oversaw the move of the *Review* to New York, largely for economic reasons. During these years, Roth had little contact with her. Soon she returned to New York and began a literary agency representing Kenneth Koch and poets of the so-called New York School plus leading art historians.[47]

But Groffsky was not thrilled to be the model for Brenda Patimkin, and after the short story appeared, she had her lawyer file a letter of complaint to Roth, dated 13 April 1959. She claimed that she and her family were "recognizably portrayed" by Roth, who "traduced and maligned her." She asked that to avoid postpublication complications the manuscript be submitted to her for "inspection" so that the offending matters can be "considered and removed." Roth did not comply, and the story appeared in the *Paris Review* and the book unchanged.[48]

Another piece of good news for Roth was that his story "Expect the Vandals," which appeared in *Esquire*, had been optioned by Columbia Pictures. The $2,000 was welcome. This would in fact become the low-budget film shot in Puerto Rico and released in 1961 entitled *Battle of Blood Island*, organized by the sexplitation producer Roger Corman and directed by Joel Rapp.[49] In the same letter to Solotaroff, Roth comments on Bellow's *Henderson the Rain King* (1959), complaining that its invention has run amuck. It tries to astound with the intensity of the author's imagination, but it's impossible to start with gags and then achieve profundity. It's really the other way around. The novel seemed too far from the concentrated style of *The Victim*, a novel Roth, at this early stage of his own writing, preferred.

Nineteen-fifty-nine was certainly an *annus mirabilus* for Roth and a year of change in America. Mailer published *Advertisements for Myself*, Lenny Bruce released *The Sick Humor of Lenny Bruce*, Miles Davis recorded *Kind of Blue*, the *Lady Chatterley* obscenity trial took place, the FDA gave approval for the birth control pill, Roth married in February and published *Goodbye, Columbus* on 7 May 1959, positively reviewed in the *New York Times* on 17 May 1959 by William Peden. Changes in his professional life equaled changes in his personal life.

In June that year, Roth tells Solotaroff that his year away from Chicago has allowed him to see it clearly enough to start to write about it. He hopes to "rescue academic fiction from stories of guys with no nuts and stacks of themes to grade laying girls in tight pedal pushers."[50] This partly anticipates the themes of *Letting Go*, although that was not his first impetus for a novel.

Later that July he writes from Long Island that he's been working on a novel in the isolation of Amagansett and loving it. He's making progress, although he's unsure exactly what the novel is to be. In August, he's asked to write a TV drama for NBC after a possible deal with *Playhouse 90* fell through. After discussion with Maggie, he agrees to try it; also, he's some two hundred pages into his novel and has written the first draft of a sixty-page story, he confidently tells Solotaroff. He's upset, however, because he finally got a chance to see the script for the film of "Expect the Vandals" and found it a travesty; among other things, they inverted the theme.

By October, he was finishing his TV play and learning a great deal about the craft and strangely enjoying what he calls the country life on Long Island. He and Maggie were constantly with each other, walking, talking, and "being bored and irritable and pleased almost side by side." They rarely saw people, although meeting a stranger on occasion was refreshing.[51]

Roth was working on a variety of projects, ostensibly his "German novel," dealing with an American Jewish businessman who travels to Germany to kill a German, possibly something on Anne Frank, and a series of other works, including a manuscript entitled "Distracted and Unblessed." [52] Alternate titles were "Shaking Loose," "Breaking Loose," "The Craving," and "Confessions of a Distracted Young Man." He worked on this between *Goodbye, Columbus* and *Letting Go*, roughly in 1958–59. The unfinished novel is about a girlfriend named Polly Barnes and a student at the University of Chicago in the late 1940s, with this telling sentence reflecting Roth's emerging attitude and action with women: "With other girls, as soon as I had begun to suspect that intensity had outdistanced pleasure—or what I surmised was pleasure—I would manage to precipitate an argument and leave."[53]

Such behavior became a pattern for Roth and one he would repeat throughout his life: needing to extricate himself from a relationship or difficult situation, he would manufacture circumstances to permit an exit. For Maggie, it was his 1962 move to New York (although she followed him). For Bloom, it was his depression in 1993 and time at Silver Hill Hospital. It happened professionally as well: ending his important association with his first editor, George Starbuck, he avoided directly telling him. Repeating the situation with his second, Joe Fox, at Random House, he sent him a letter rather than tell him personally. In many ways, Roth lacked the courage to end these relationships properly. He preferred to villainize the other, which then gave him cause to leave.

At this time, Roth also worked on a *Playhouse 90* script ("Coffin in Egypt" about Jacob Gens and the Vilna ghetto and Jews bartering other Jews) and turned down a chance to go to Hollywood and to do a piece on Stanley Kramer for *Esquire*. He and Maggie discussed it, but he finally said no. His commitment was to finish his novel, as well as a longish story he titled "Debts and Sorrows" about teaching in Chicago. This would become the first section with the same title for *Letting Go*. He noted that Maggie's kids were visiting, followed by his parents. In September, he learned from Starbuck that *Goodbye, Columbus* sold 10,000 copies with 11,500 printed.

By 1 December 1959, however, Roth had changed course. He had dropped the German novel and written almost two hundred pages of a comic novel set in Chicago during the 1948 Wallace campaign. Starbuck read part of yet another unfinished work when he visited Amagansett in late November, something more serious which he thought would be a better follow-up to *Goodbye, Columbus*. Roth hoped to leave a copy with him before he sailed for Europe on 23 December. Starbuck said it was the "expectable young autobiographical novel but Roth is making it into something funny." Its characters are young, confused, and between university and the artistic life, the steel mills and daddy's business: "The hero's flaw and saving grace is that he is always escaping from his own failures and problems by compassionately . . . and sometimes disastrously meddling in the problems of others."[54] The details, including its supposed comic end of the hero possibly kidnapping a baby ready for adoption, became *Letting Go*. Starbuck also noted that Roth and Maggie were organizing an anthology of modern American stories concerning marriage and divorce, originally an idea of Maggie's.[55]

In 1959, Roth and Maggie went to Italy for nearly six months, a trip made possible by a Guggenheim Fellowship. They went first to Florence for three weeks; at the end of January they settled in Rome at Via di S. Elgio 4, a four-room apartment formerly occupied by "a principessa" and around the corner from the busy Via Giulia, where Roth often had a daily shave from Guglielmo after a morning spent writing or arguing, often both. Roth and Maggie would stay until mid-July, stopping in London and then New York on their way to a teaching job at the Iowa Writers' Workshop at the University of Iowa. It was a period of cultural exposure for Maggie and a combination of culture and work for Roth. He wrote and rewrote what would become *Letting Go*, noting that he had made some "violent changes" between the previous draft and the current, changes in point of view and attitude. It was also getting funny, he told his new publisher, Random House. In Rome, Roth was productive and happy, or at least content enough to allow him to work, with Maggie supporting and encouraging his writing.

Roth and Maggie soon made new friends, notably William and Rose Styron, an important relationship that would continue for decades. Styron, eight years older than Roth, became a mentor. He, his wife, and their two young children were in Rome partly to escape the publicity surrounding the publication of Styron's third novel, *Set This House on Fire*. At 507 pages, it was large and the marketing widespread. Demonstrating a strategy Roth himself would later follow, especially during the release of *Portnoy's Complaint* in 1969, Styron removed himself from the publicity and the fray, insulating himself in Europe from what he thought would be negative reviews.

Styron was largely unhappy during his time in Rome, and meeting the young but eager Roth, who had already appeared in the *Paris Review* thanks to the editorial eye of Rose Styron, an upbeat change. Random House, however, was pleased with the sales of *Set This House on Fire*, including $35,000 for paperback rights and selling over twenty-one thousand hardback copies.[56] A visit from a representative of the French publisher Gallimard, eager to secure French rights for the book, was a further lift. Styron at the time was thirty-five, Roth twenty-seven.

Another important new connection was Wallace Stegner (age fifty-one), in Rome as a writer-in-residence at the American Academy. He quickly became part of the Styron-Roth circle, while he reworked his novel *A Shooting Star*. Anticipating a decision Roth would soon make, Stegner had recently changed publishers, from Houghton Mifflin to Viking. Stegner, who ran the creative writing program at Stanford and had published seven books, urged Roth to teach at Stanford the next year. In a letter to the chair of the department on 1 March 1960, he seemed confident that Roth would accept a position as the Jones Lecturer in writing. Roth, he wrote, wanted to come for two years, which would suit their purpose; he then listed his friend's accomplishments. Besides that, Stegner wrote, he's decent, pleasant, "most intelligent," and one of the nicest people Stegner and his wife had ever met. And he came cheap: only $3,000 for half time. Roth, he continued, was "one of the best young writers in America and we ought to get him while we can. He will write his way out of the job in a couple of years," but meanwhile, he would enrich the program.[57]

Stegner added that the night before, he had dinner at Roth's apartment in Rome and met Donald Hall (in Rome to interview Pound for the *Paris Review*), Robert Williams, whose novel Viking had just taken, plus other local writers and poets. (Roth had also met but disliked the *New Yorker* short story writer Harold Brodkey, in Rome on a Prix de Rome, a prize Roth thought *he* deserved.) In the end, however, Roth chose Iowa over Stanford. Stegner was still feeling the sting of disappointment in June, telling Malcolm Cowley that if they could only have "hung onto Phil Roth we'd have had a red hot infield combination" in the writing program.[58] Six years later, he would tempt Roth again by offering one or two writing courses at Stanford: "Name what you think you're worth and I'll do my damnedest to get it."[59]

Maggie was the reason for Roth's decision to accept the Iowa offer. She pressured him into taking it because her ex-husband had just been divorced from his second wife and was raising his and Maggie's children alone in Chicago. According to Roth, Maggie also forced him to give up the second year of his Rome fellowship for Iowa City because it was only four hours away from her children in Chicago. Reluctantly, he agreed.[60] Although he had a Guggenheim, Roth received an additional $1,500 from the National Institute of Arts and Letters, but not a Ford Foundation Grant, nor a Prix de Rome. However, in March 1960 he learned that he won the National Book Award for fiction, beating out Bellow's *Henderson the Rain King*, Faulkner's *The Mansion*, and Updike's *The Poorhouse Fair*. The citation marked *Goodbye, Columbus*'s assured writing style and "rare high spirits." He would fly back to New York to attend the awards dinner with Maggie, especially because costs (after various clarifications) would be covered by Houghton Mifflin.

They made a triumphant return for the awards ceremony, held on 23 March 1960 at the Astor Hotel: a photo shows a beaming Roth alongside Robert Lowell and Richard Ellmann, Joyce's biographer (Figure 3.6). A second photo, which appeared in the *New York Times*, shows a confident Roth who appears to be speaking with Ellmann while Lowell looks on.

During their visit, Roth did a thirty-minute TV interview with Mike Wallace on 28 March 1960. In addition, he and Maggie made a brief trip to the Newark Public Library (Figure 3.7).

On their return to Italy, he learned that he won the Daroff Memorial Fiction Award as well, $250, which Silvers would accept on his behalf in May at the Jewish Book Council of America meeting. Roth's career as an award winner was beginning.

In April, Maggie wrote a long letter to Paul Brooks at Houghton Mifflin outlining Roth's choice: Stanford or Iowa. She asked for a role for herself at HM as an intermediary reader-editor between undiscovered writers at Iowa or even Chicago and the publisher. She told Brooks that Wallace and

Figure 3.6 Roth (*right*) with a smiling Richard Ellmann (*center*), winner of the Biography prize for his biography of James Joyce, and Robert Lowell (*left*), poetry winner for *Life Studies*. National Book Award ceremony, 23 March 1960, at the Astor Hotel. AP File.

Mary Stegner had just such an arrangement for the West Coast. She mentioned her experience as an assistant fiction editor at *Esquire*, as an editor and reader for Criterion Books, and as a reader for Harper's and Macmillan, as well as editing college texts in the production department at Harper's. "I've also worked with a number of authors, before, most notably, I suppose my husband" she added.[61] She referred to her proposal for a love/marriage/divorce anthology, citing work by Updike and Herb Gold. She signed the letter "Margaret Roth." Brooks would reply positively in June and note that sales of *Goodbye, Columbus* had hit 12,682. But about this time the Grossbart incident emerged.

In late April, while in Italy, Roth received a concerned letter from Houghton Mifflin saying that a Mr. Sheldon Grossbart, through his lawyer, pointed out that he has the same name as a character in "Defender of the Faith" and that he had been in Basic Training with Roth. The use of the

Figure 3.7 Roth with his wife Maggie at the Newark Public Library, April 1960. She is holding a copy of the National Book Award winner, *Goodbye, Columbus.* Credit: Newark Public Library.

name in the story caused him "anguish," and now Grossbart claimed he was libeled and ridiculed. Do you know this Grossbart, Dorothy de Santillana of Houghton Mifflin asks?

Replying on 3 May 1960, Roth denied any association with or knowledge of Grossbart. He actually chose the name because he wanted the term "gross" to be hidden in the character's name, "the kind of playfulness even Henry James engaged in."[62] The name was entirely his invention, and the germ of the story was told to him five years earlier in Chicago by a friend (Art Geffen). He noted that his brother reminded him that there was a Grossbart at Weequahic High who might have been a friend of Sandy's in Scouts, but he (Roth) never personally knew a Grossbart. Furthermore, the story had appeared two and a half months earlier than in the book—so why was Grossbart or his lawyer contacting the publisher only now? And Roth had never been to either Germany or Missouri, where the story was set. The whole thing was suspicious and sounded like a "Grossbartian move—*my* Grossbart—and not a very crafty one," suggesting or anticipating the figure who actually impersonated Roth in Israel in *Operation Shylock*. This is also an early example of the playful self and questions of identity. The matter was dropped.

Shortly after this, Roth told Starbuck that he'd accepted the post at Iowa, against Starbuck's advice. One motive was the money, the other "simply to get a regular schedule and a secluded spot in which to finish the book." Iowa was Stegner's alma mater: he received an MA there in 1932, a PhD in 1935. Richard Stern at Chicago attended the Writers' Workshop from 1952 to 1954 and went on to do a PhD there. But before Roth's exodus to the Midwest, his parents "swooped into Europe armed with traveler's checks and confusion" for fourteen days. His father, Roth writes, couldn't decide if everyone in Europe was poor or rich, while his mother was busy buying gloves.[63] Roth told Starbuck that he and Maggie would be back in the U.S. on 6 September. Difficulties with Houghton Mifflin were brewing, largely because of perceived slights concerning the marketing of his book.

Rome would shortly and unexpectedly alter Roth's career. His friendship with the Styrons meant a professional change in direction because when Styron's publisher Donald Klopfer visited, he and Roth began to talk. Roth was unhappy with the promotion of *Goodbye, Columbus*. His second work, *Letting Go*, was nearing completion and he was anxious about its advertising and an advance. Klopfer promised him better marketing and money. Tempted by the Random House interest and offer, Roth seriously considered the firm, despite being under contract through an option to Houghton Mifflin. He soon began to negotiate with both Starbuck and HM, initially through his agent Candida Donadio and then with Klopfer and Bennett Cerf of Random House.

Later in November 1960, Brooks stated in a memo that Donadio was in favor of Roth staying with Houghton Mifflin as long as they matched the Random House offer, and so advised Roth, but he decided otherwise. Styron had gone to Random House from Bobbs Merrill when his favorite editor, Hiram Hayden, accepted the position of editor-in-chief there in 1955.

To Starbuck, Donadio reported on Roth's "prolonged and intense dissatisfaction" with the handling of *Goodbye, Columbus* as well as its shoddy production and mishandling of his brother's design for the jacket. After the National Book Award event, he felt there should have been a more aggressive advertising campaign, something similar to Sinclair Lewis writing to Max Perkins after he won the Nobel Prize that he didn't do a good job in promoting him in Europe. This was all in early July, likely a surprise to Starbuck. To Brooks, Starbuck reported that Roth was asking for a release of the option on his new book or a figure to match the supposed offers coming from other interested publishers, the best being a $20,000 advance. Three hundred pages of the manuscript would be sent to show the nearly completed work of the novel now called "Debts and Sorrows." Correspondence with Starbuck indicates the intensity of the exchanges, Starbuck emphasizing his role in promoting Roth's work and that in spite of the "aggravating foul-ups like the jacket-color decision," it was well produced and publicized.[64]

Starbuck believed Houghton Mifflin offered consistency and quality for Roth's work and that shifting to a new publisher would inevitably cause problems and adjustments. Interdepartment memos reveal that Roth, yes, has potential but also that he perhaps thinks too highly of himself in expecting a large promotion budget and advance. But writing for five members of the editorial committee, Brooks tells Roth in mid-July that they have enormous enthusiasm for the new manuscript and that they "intend to back it to the limit." To Donadio, however, Lowell Thompson, a director of HM, distinguished between the more stately style of Park Street (the location of Houghton Mifflin), where their advertising campaigns were organized, and the Madison Avenue touch, flashy and brassy.[65] In the fall of that year, Brooks, in something of a pique, explained the situation to Evan Thomas of Harper's, remarking that if *Goodbye, Columbus* had not been successful, Roth would likely not have thought of leaving Houghton Mifflin.[66]

Writing from London, where they went in mid-July, Maggie asked for a monthly retainer or fee for reporting on all potential manuscripts from undiscovered writers she would assess. From the Stegners she had learned that they more or less did the same on the West Coast, although Brooks made it clear that HM had thoughts of opening a West Coast branch and the Stegners would be their representatives.

Professional and personal factors influenced Roth's decision to switch publishers, despite threats from Houghton Mifflin—and exchanging publishers for better deals would characterize Roth's later career as well, sometimes returning to publishers he previously spurned. Following his favored editors was another reason. Furthermore, the money with Random House was simply better: $20,000. On 9 September Donadio asked for a formal release for "Debts and Sorrows" from Houghton Mifflin. On 13 September 1960, HM acquiesced, and Roth began his publishing career with Random House. Much later in their careers, Styron and Roth, walking along a beach in East Hampton, "loftily" classified people into three categories: the well-poisoners, the lawn-mowers (most of the people), and the life-enhancers. They agreed that Bennett Cerf of Random House clearly belonged in the last category, financially and morally replenishing the world of his authors.[67]

Italy, where he initiated his change of publishers, began to appear throughout Roth's fiction even before his early novels. In "You Can't Tell a Man by the Song He Sings," in *Goodbye, Columbus*, Alberto Pelagutti, a seventeen-year-old Sicilian-born ex-con, appears, as well as the reptilian Duke Scarpa, stereotypes fashioned before Roth had experienced the country. In *Letting Go*, John Spigliano is chair of the Humanities II program at Chicago and "publishes pathologically," an article a month (LG 63). In *Portnoy's Complaint*, Rome is where Portnoy and the Monkey entertain a prostitute and engage in a lively threesome and a fight. In *My Life as a Man*, Peter Tarnopol lives unblemished in Italy with sixteen-year-old Moonie after Lydia's suicide and offers to marry her there when she turns twenty-one (MLM 82–85). Kepesh and Claire spend time in Venice and the Italian countryside in *The Professor of Desire*. In *The Plot Against America*, the Roths' Italian neighbor, Mr. Cucuzza, provides them with a gun to use in a riot. Italy became an important locale for him; he visited often, and it was where he conducted a memorable visit and interview with Primo Levi in Turin in 1986.

After Rome and London, Roth and Maggie stopped in New York in early September to meet Bennett Cerf and Roth's potential editor, Robert Loomis, who came to Random House in 1957 and edited Styron (they were friends from Duke University days). The meeting went well and Roth joined Random House.

After New York and a stop in Chicago, Roth and Maggie settled in to Iowa City at 721 N. Linn Street, Roth looking ahead with excitement to a new editor and publisher. Both his teaching and his new novel had the promise of a potentially satisfying life, although Maggie's appeal was waning, especially because he was finding other women more attractive and monogamy restrictive. In early November, he wrote an upbeat letter to Starbuck making no reference to his recent break with Houghton Mifflin, choosing to focus on his teaching, work on his novel, and improved advertisements for *Goodbye, Columbus*. He comments on Lionel Trilling's admiration of his social accuracy, although it left him feeling a bit like an IBM machine, he says, and suggests that Starbuck should actually visit (an ironic request since Starbuck would be a director of the school from 1966 to 1969). "I am feeling pretty sporty," he writes, having just come in from 27 degree weather.[68] He clearly tries to maintain his friendship with Starbuck, despite their split. Surprisingly, he also wrote an endorsement for the Houghton Literary Fellowship in September, noting that its receipt in the late summer of 1958 freed him from returning to university teaching: "Occupation, and a sense of proportion, made me call myself a teacher, not a writer. The fellowship came along, however, and cut me loose from my Job. I was able to write and to live, and to have the pleasure of thinking of myself as a writer, and even better, a writer with a publisher."[69]

The Iowa Writers' Workshop in the 1960s was gaining national prominence: *Mademoiselle* magazine ran a laudatory profile of the program, noting that sixty novels by graduates had been published in the previous twenty-five years. *Writer's Digest* and *Look* ran articles on the program. Random House published *Midland: Twenty-five Years of Fiction and Poetry Selected from the Writer's Workshops*, edited by Paul Engle, the director from 1941 to 1965. The workshop began in 1936 as a group of poets and novelists. In the introduction, Engle repeated the case for creative writing programs in universities which at first seemed an anomaly.

Political battles between the University of Iowa English Department and the workshop seemed systemic. Members of the department were unashamedly condescending toward the program, believing that creative writing simply did not demand the effort and precision of scholarship. By the mid-1960s, however, the graduate program was developing prestige that could not be denied, largely the achievement of Engle, who persistently found financial support outside the university to keep the program going with fellowships and student aid.[70] Graduate workshop courses meet weekly, and a student would select either the workshop in fiction or poetry, which involved the circulation of work among fellow students to then be critiqued at the meeting, the seminar led by a recognized writer. In 1963, Rust Hills of *Esquire* wrote that one-third of the total number of writers who appeared on *Esquire*'s list of important writers were former Iowa students or faculty.

At the time Roth taught in the Writers' Workshop (officially the Program in Creative Writing), he was listed as a lecturer in the Department of English. He arrived in Iowa after the catalogue was printed so only appears in the publication for 1961–62, alongside Vance Bourjaily and R. V. Cassill (who also began in 1960). In 1960–61, his colleagues were Hortense Callisher and Curtis Harnack.[71] George P. Elliott was also on staff at that time, while Ray B. West Jr. was acting chair of the fiction writing program.

Roth used his new appointment not only to lead a fiction workshop but to further his own practice of fiction. He taught classes in novel writing while deeply immersed in an American triumvirate: Hawthorne, James, and Wolfe. *Letting Go*, the novel he was completing at the time, reflects the pull of the realist, which he would further in his second novel, the more Midwest-centered, Sinclair Lewis– and Willa Cather–like *When She Was Good*. He was yet to engage with the American drive or need for confession that would characterize his breakthrough work, *Portnoy's Complaint*.

The weekly three-hour classes were held in the supposedly temporary Quonset-style army barracks of corrugated metal arranged in camp-like rows near the Iowa River. Assessments of students' work was often savage, several instructors noted for their heartless, if not brutal, evaluations.[72] It would not be uncommon for fierce debates, and occasional violence, to erupt, like the time the poet Philip Levine punched John Berryman in the face in the winter of 1954 (although after the fight, they remained lifelong friends).[73] Paul Engle, competitive and critical of students' work—Mark McGurl in his study of creative writing programs claimed it bordered on sadism—was the feared but admired director.[74]

Each of Roth's predecessors leading the fiction workshop seemed to have had a theory, perhaps the most pertinent for Roth Bourjaily's belief that the composition of a self and of a text go hand in hand. To underscore this, he would come to class on occasion with a shotgun after a morning of duck hunting, lean it against a wall, and conduct the seminar.[75] Art was not an escape from personality, as T. S. Eliot commanded, but the reverse: the embodiment of a personality, something Roth absorbed fully by the time of *Portnoy*. Another principle was that in a tense dramatic scene the characters never talk about exactly what are the real issues between them. Yet moving away from censure was critical. Such ideas were part of what Iowa contributed to Roth, expanding his attention to the craft of fiction which has characterized his work from the beginning. He worked at writing and understood it was always a labor.

What Roth brought to Iowa was the eagerness of a newly published, award-winning young writer who was learning the ropes with mostly un-published students. What he carried away from Iowa was a stronger sense of technique and a determination to get it right, likely approaching but not fully absorbing Flaubert's adage "Beware of that intellectual overheating called inspiration." Objectivity and structure, measures of aesthetic distance, were gradually now shaping his writing (partly a Jamesian inheritance), although his current work in progress, *Letting Go,* contained many autobiographical elements from his Chicago graduate days. But writing for Roth was not a "sometime thing," in the words of one workshop graduate.[76] His dedication to the daily task of writing was genuine, confirmed by his dedication to writing throughout his career, with constant revisions, proofreading, and documenting details when necessary. He forged a compact with each book but needed disciplined concentration, as represented by E. I. Lonoff in *The Ghost Writer.* Roth was a literary laborer.

The Iowa classes were simple, although the seminars were not. The format followed tradition: a "senior" writer would lead a discussion about a work written by a member of the class, and others would share their advice, impressions, and sometimes insults. Students, after an introduction to three fiction instructors, selected one to "sign on with" for the term. Classes were often intense and bruising, especially to one's ego. Richard Yates, who succeeded Roth at the workshop in 1964, was especially opinionated and admired, equally blunt and enthusiastic over student writing.[77] The focus was always on the craft rather than a career.

Teaching, while writing on the side, was the common goal of the students.[78] Paul Engle's vision of the workshop was America's equivalent of the Parisian café where younger writers would meet older writers to discuss their work, although it was Iowa, not Paris. While few can actually be taught writing, the workshop established an environment where creative writing was the single, shared activity. Much of the teaching also took place out of the classroom, often at the poker table, Roth joining Bourjaily, Mark Strand, and others in instructing. Poker was the occasion, conversation the substance.

Enrollment at the time was nearly 150 students in the fiction, poetry, and drama program. "Forms and Theory of Fictions" and "Fiction Writing" were two of the graduate courses. Distinguished guests included Dylan Thomas, John Crowe Ransom, James T. Farrell, C. P. Snow, and in 1962, Roth's new publisher, Bennett Cerf. John Cheever would teach there in 1973. One of the students who completed the two-year program then was the poet Mark Strand. Raymond Carver enrolled the year Roth left, 1963.

Clark Blaise, the Canadian American author, was also there and recalled Roth spending a good deal of time playing tennis and leading a softball team the writer Nicky Goldstein called "Jews against the Whites." Roth liked to upset conventional attitudes, telling Blaise at a celebratory cookout in honor of the publication of Letting Go in June 1962 that he gleefully enjoyed slices from the roasting pig, a very un-Jewish act. In the fall of 1962 Roth ran a fiction workshop and taught a course on theory and form but was largely in-different to his students, being more involved with his own writing and life. Blaise later reported an unexpected encounter with Roth early one morning as Roth departed the bedroom of a female student in the same rooming house where Blaise lived. They silently greeted each other but said nothing about the meeting, one startled, the other surprised.[79]

Roth in fact was having an affair with one of his students. Maggie found out about it in January 1962, and after a fight, he told her he was leaving for good. She threatened suicide, but he had heard that before and left. Out on the street, however, he had second thoughts and returned. She just might do it to spite him, and he couldn't imagine her daughter returning from school to find her dead mother. In the apartment, he found that she had taken a mix-ture of whisky and pills and passed out. She threw up in the bathroom where Roth took her, and in that state, thinking she might die and wanting to clear her conscience, she revealed that she had not been pregnant in New York. She then explained the trick with the urine sample, bought in Tompkins Park from a pregnant woman. But all this might have been a lie as well, Roth thought. From that moment, he slept in a separate bedroom, rationalizing his staying on only to help Holly while he continued his affair with the twenty-two-year-old writing student. He was twenty-nine and infatuated with her. In the spring of 1962, Roth asked her to marry; she declined. She does reappear, however, in My Life as a Man as Karen Oakes seduced by Peter Tarnopol. Despite Tarnopol's pleas to her to remain in the creative writing program, she leaves; he did, however, give her an A+ on her paper.

Roth's affair was not that unusual: sexual encounters with female students were rampant, the young women looking up to the experienced male writers.[80] Nor was it unusual for Roth, who found monogamy an outmoded idea and realized that any marriage situation for him would be inhibiting. There is every reason to believe that Roth's philandering might have pushed

Maggie into her extreme reactions regarding their relationship. From the start, it was stormy and often reached hurricane force, especially by 1963, when she attempted to have him arrested just before he departed for Israel. He left three days before the announced trip and thereby got away.

Kurt Vonnegut, who followed Roth to the Writers' Workshop, was candid in the impact of the women who intrigued him: they had the "power to renew the ambition and wit of men adrift," often curing writer's block and priming one's creativity. This was how Bellow and Mailer renewed themselves, he quipped, "again and again, as though buying new cars."[81] Roth was no stranger to this action. Indeed, by the 1970s competition within the workshop was the keynote, what the writer Jane Smiley called the Mailer period, patterned on aggression, confrontation, and dispute. Boxing, a favorite Mailer sport, became the preferred form of exercise, expressing an ideal "hypermasculine authorial identity." Literature meant dominance.[82]

But if Iowa gave Roth time to write (and undertake various escapades), it gave Maggie time to become envious of Roth and his success. She found little to do, the Houghton Mifflin project ending before it began because Roth switched to Random House. She was preoccupied, however, with her ten-year-old daughter, Holly, who came to live with them, a well-intentioned but emotionally underprepared and abused young woman, according to Roth (FAC 108, 142). Maggie suddenly became distrustful of Roth and repeatedly threatened to kill him if he attempted to seduce the girl. He, in turn, tried to teach Holly how to tell time and read. He acted as her surrogate father and grew to enjoy her company, despite outbursts from Maggie that at one point became so intense he surreptitiously gathered the knives in the house and locked them in the trunk of his car.

Not long after settling in Iowa City, Rust Hills, fiction editor of *Esquire*, invited Roth to participate in a symposium entitled "Writing in America Today." In mid-October 1960, Roth reported to Cerf that he would be leaving on the 18th and that he would have to miss a party in New York for Bill and Rose Styron, as well as the episode of *Alfred Hitchcock Presents* that features Roth's early story, "The Contest for Aaron Gold." He told Cerf he was pleased to be with Random House from his first talk with Donald Klopfer at Doney's restaurant on the Via Veneto in August 1960 in Rome.[83] He was nearly done with his manuscript, although it was a large book. (Indeed, the first edition ran 630 pages.) Replying to Roth in Iowa City, Cerf told him the Styron gathering had been a "liquid success."[84]

Roth was to join John Cheever and James Baldwin in a tour of the San Francisco Bay area. It was thought that with a WASP, a Black, and a Jew, there might be fireworks. Cheever began the series by speaking on the topic "Some People, Places and Things That Will Not Appear in My Next Novel" at Berkeley on 20 October. A panel discussion that included the other two speakers followed. Roth spoke on 21 October at Stanford, his speech "Writing American Fiction" to be published in *Commentary* in March 1961. Baldwin spoke on the 22nd at San Francisco State University, his title "Notes for a Hypothetical Novel." And contrary to press expectations, all three got along well, Cheever actually a strong admirer of *Goodbye, Columbus*. In his journal for 1963, Cheever wrote of Roth, "[He] has the young man's air of regarding most things as if they generated an intolerable heat. . . . He holds his head back from his plate of roast beef as if it were a conflagration."[85]

"Writing American Fiction," in its published form, begins with an account of the horrific murder of the Grimes sisters, who went off to see an Elvis Presley movie on a December evening in Chicago and never returned. Their unclothed bodies were eventually found when the snow melted; they were in a ditch in a forest preserve west of the city. The media sensationalized every aspect of the life of the two teenagers. A skid-row character confessed but was then released and claimed police brutality. Then money started to flow to the girls' mother and she decided to remodel her house and buy two parakeets she named after the murdered girls. Roth's point? The writer in America can hardly make credible most of American reality: "The actuality is continually outdoing our talents" (RMY 168). It exceeds one's impoverished imagination.

Addressing the Nixon-Kennedy debates, Roth expresses exasperation at the attention to the superficial and neglect of the important. It was so weird he began to wish he had invented it. Astonishment at such later Nixon statements as "It isn't what the facts are but what they appear to be that counts when you are under fire" continued, anticipating the satire *Our Gang*.[86] Not surprisingly, the idiocy, piety, and lies create wonder and despair. But what does this mean for a writer of fiction, Roth asks? The need to incorporate such nightmares into the novel, although the results are not very good because such works—he cites *Cash McCall* and *Marjorie Morningstar*—do not confront the corruption and vulgarity of American public life *nor* the complexity of human character. Feeling alienated in America emerges as one of his strongest themes, "the result of the second post-immigrant generation coming into conflict with the first great eruption of postwar media garbage" (CWPR 177).

But lesser minds and talents do not entirely rule. He cites Mailer, an actor in the cultural drama of the moment—but to act takes time away from writing. It's the age of the slob, Roth quotes a character saying in Styron's novel *Set This House on Fire,* and if you're not careful, they will drag you under. But then you get *Advertisements for Myself,* published the same year as *Goodbye, Columbus,* a boisterous, indulgent book by Mailer, who substitutes his life for fiction.[87] Yet the issue that looms largest for Roth is the loss of a subject, leaving the serious writer without a genuine response to the cultural dilemma and decline. Only, it seems, does J. D. Salinger appear to keep to the wind and address the shattering issues of the day and the conflict between self and culture.

Roth, in this lengthy talk, published in *Reading Myself and Others,* then moves on to Malamud and Bellow, and not only their content but their style, noting the nervous, edgy, metropolitan prose often associated with Jewish writers. Taking a passage from *Augie March* and one by *Therefore Be Bold* by Herbert Gold, Roth shows Bellow's vitality and Gold's complexity but argues that the muscular prose relates to the unfriendly relations existing between the writer and the culture when the prose rejects the age (RMY 177). What he calls "the bouncy style" defines a new movement, presciently forecasting his own method in *Portnoy,* incorporating the nuances and emphases of urban speech, caging a language of new and rich emotional power with an irony all its own. Yet the affirmation of these works surprises him: even their moral is bouncy.

Importantly, Roth turns to his friend Styron as the concluding reference, rather than Bellow and *Henderson the Rain King.* The hero-critic of America in *Set This House on Fire,* largely set on the Amalfi coast and involving two murders and a rape, returns to the States in the end, although it is the America of his childhood, as Roth will return to the Newark of *his* childhood, rarely the Newark of the present. As Roth celebrates, Styron's hero chooses being, living, over where one lives or with whom one lives (RMY 181). To come through a serious personal struggle intact *is* an accomplishment, he believes. He ends with the image of Ralph Ellison's solitary man, who has rejected the world to live in the underground. In this essay-talk Roth displays a wide knowledge of contemporary American writing but, more forcefully, a strong sense of the dis-ease at the center of American culture and, in turn, literature. For a twenty-seven-year-old, it's a dazzling performance.

But dislocation, the principal theme of "Writing American Fiction," has an ironic twist in relation to Roth's career: he wrote his New Jersey collection *Goodbye, Columbus* in Chicago; his university novel focusing on Chicago and partly Iowa in Rome; his midwestern novel, *When She Was Good,* in New York; and a good portion of his New York novel, *Portnoy's Complaint,* at Yaddo in upstate's Saratoga Springs. Many of his later books were written not near or in their locales but at his Connecticut home near Litchfield, in the rural western part of the state, or in London.

Back in Iowa after San Francisco, Roth tells his editor Robert Loomis that "Debts and Sorrows" is progressing well, although he now has a new title, "The Presence of Choice," disliked by Maggie but favored by him. But the manuscript is expanding and he does not yet see the end. It will likely take a year to finish, including revisions, possibly until Thanksgiving or Christmas 1961 but ready for a 1962 publication.[88] Loomis replies that the timing is okay but the new title is flat and not provocative in a fresh way. Further exchanges in the new year (1961) show Loomis's guidance—keep a list of possible titles, but a good book makes almost any title good—and he'll send him what he requested: Paul Goodman's *Growing Up Absurd,* Isak Dinesen's African stories, and a Modern Library edition of Robert Lowell's *Life Studies.*

During the fall of 1960, Maggie went to court to "rescue" her children, sup- posedly living with her ex, newly remarried. In fact, the children were living with him alone in southern Illinois, his new wife apparently leaving him while Roth and Maggie were in Italy. Maggie sought to regain partial custody of her children, her son to board at a private school (for which Roth would bear part of the costs) and her daughter to join them in Iowa City. Roth threw himself into the court battle (this experience may have turned him away from the wish to have any children of his own), frequently contacting their Chicago lawyer to review progress. He also arranged for them to spend the summer with him and Maggie in Amagansett. Their father objected. But placing the son in school and the daughter with them, as well as a summer on Long island, would diminish the need for the children to witness yet another marital breakup, while assuaging Maggie's sense of desperation and no doubt guilt. The children were also falling behind in school. In his marriage, one "beyond reclamation before it had even begun," the needs of the unhappy children overtook his "unaccountable sense of personal obligation" gener- ated by Maggie's "wreckage of her chaotic emotional past" (FAC 54). This behavior Roth's psychiatrist will later highlight as entirely incorrect; children never repair a fractured relationship. Under these circumstances, it was a wonder Roth was able to either teach or write.

During these difficult times, Roth educated not only Holly but Maggie's son, David. Roth gave him books to read, starting with *The Red Badge of Courage*, to prep him for entrance to Morgan Park Academy in Chicago. He also taught him a smattering of European history, partly in response to some naïve remarks about the relation of the Nazis to the Jews in World War II (FAC 155). The young man was interested in social problems and later became a community organizer in the Midwest when not working at his job as a truck driver in St. Louis. Roth, the young man remembered in a 1975 newspaper article, was a positive and important influence on him.[89]

By April 1961, Roth wanted a change of editors. He suddenly felt that Loomis might not be the man to give him the help with the final editing of *Letting Go* he hoped for; he liked Loomis and recognized his abilities, but they lacked rapport. In a long letter to Klopfer of 21 April 1961, he asked to meet with other editors before any final assignment to work on his book. Cerf replied that Loomis was not officially assigned to *Letting Go*; a decision could wait until Roth had met other editors at the firm. Loomis, Styron's editor, had simply assumed he would be editing Roth. Klopfer, closer to Roth than Cerf since they had met in Rome, wrote in late April 1961 taking the blame for Loomis as Roth's temporary editor. Loomis told Roth he was not hurt; he was too professional to express upset. When you come East, he wrote, you can meet the editorial staff and make a choice without embarrassment. Those who have read the samples admire them. Our one desire is to get the best possible book from you. You can work with Joe Fox, Jason Epstein, or anyone else of your choosing.[90] Loomis was with Roth only because he was Styron's editor; when in Rome with Roth, Klopfer thought it might be a decent fit. But Loomis, a legend, and Roth did not see eye to eye, Roth perhaps sensing that the experienced Loomis would be unreceptive to his directions, admonitions, and input.

During a summer trip to the East and staying again in Amagansett after a stop in New York, Roth told Cerf that after two meetings with Fox, he'd like to work with him. Fox was intelligent and alert, and Roth sensed a rapport between the two of them. He was now in final revisions and cutting. Cerf confirmed Roth's choice of an editor on 21 June 1961.[91] In September, from 124 Grand Avenue Court, Iowa City, Roth told Cerf that Fox was working out well: he had a fine eye for "audacity and modesty" and didn't get too tenacious when a suggestion appeared to offend.[92]

The act of changing editors was another instance of Roth's seeking to control his publishing experience, co-opting the senior figure in the firm who, not wanting to lose the talented, if young, author, gave him leeway in a number of areas. In this first instance, it was Cerf and Klopfer. Later, it would be Roger Straus of Farrer, Straus & Giroux, and after he left them because of a new contract negotiated by his new agent, Andrew Wylie, it was Richard Snyder of Simon and Schuster. At Random House and other firms, Roth chose his editors carefully, beginning with Joe Fox and (after frustration with Fox) Jason Epstein; at Farrar, Straus, it would be David Rieff (Susan Sontag's son). At Simon and Schuster, Michael Korda was editor-in-chief. Late in his career and back to Houghton Mifflin, it would be Wendy Strothman, editor and executive vice president.

Further correspondence at this time with Fox and *Letting Go* deals with the ending (possibly too abrupt) and the title. Fox prefers "Debts and Sorrows" rather than "What They Want of Me" or "Letting Go," as well as name changes for certain characters. George P. Elliott and his wife and Bill Styron and Rose thought the intended "Teller" to be a Jewish name for Martha Teller when Roth intended the exact opposite. So he changed her name to one he had wanted to use for some time: Reganhart. It makes one think of Regan and Goneril, he thought, and possibly "Regal Heart." More important, he added on 20 July 1961, he liked the way it sounds.

Additional letters detail other changes, from italicizing the opening letter and all that follows to a new line about Gabe's loneliness without using that powerful word. And Reganhart should not be thought of as a Jewish name. Maggie, he writes, prefers that spelling. Important is his reliance on Maggie, both for the character's name and earlier title. In late August, he sent in the remainder of the fourth section and said that Maggie wouldn't have time to read it, explaining that the brackets containing the word "out" were for her, but now are for Fox. It is clear that Maggie had a vital part in the working details of the manuscript and its characters.

By September 1961, back in Iowa City, Roth was trying to finish up the manuscript while thinking of an idea for his next book. He thanks Fox for Ford Madox Ford's *Parade's End*, although he admits confusion over the time sequencing in the novel. By 9 October 1961, he has finished, having revised and provided a new ending for what will be *Letting Go*. He did not change the point of view at the end—it's still in the third person—but it begins differently, he reports.

Titles still bounce about, but it looks as if *Letting Go* will win by default, Roth writes.[93] Fox replies that he likes the changes and that the first half is sharper and more effective than in the first draft: you are your own best editor, he tells Roth, and have a sharp eye for what is excessive and unnecessary. Maggie still plays a role, writing to Fox about details on adoption as Roth represents them. Roth, in turn, suggests that Maggie try her hand at jacket copy—she's good at that. A month later, he notes that Maggie believes the scene in Gary, Indiana, isn't wild enough and that she may be right. Clearly, Roth listens to her views and she plays an important first-reader role in this early stage of his career, which he later, and somewhat maliciously, disregards. He overlooks her contribution, sharing decisions about the jacket art and copy for his first novel—and the price. It had to be reasonable: it sold for $5.95, retailing less than its pagination, Fox tells him.

Soon, jacket design and copy obsessed him. Maggie couldn't do it because she was involved in learning the cello and seeking work from publishing houses. He did make suggestions concerning the design: it should be just type, possibly tall type so that the letters take up most of the front cover. The end product was in fact a kind of starburst of straight lines with the words LETTING on the first line and to the right, GO. Under the starburst in smaller type, "by the author of Goodbye, Columbus winner / of the 1960 National Book Award for fiction." And below that in largish type, all caps, PHILIP ROTH. Offsetting the black background is the white lettering and the blue and pink starburst. For the author photo, he suggested the images taken at Amagansett by Nancy Sirkis for *Mademoiselle,* although they seem to be lost. Nevertheless, a photo from that shoot is the back jacket image, showing a relaxed Roth in a rocking chair on a porch holding a book and half-smiling at the camera. On publication day, tentatively 1 June 1962, he told Fox, he wants to be out of New York. No interviews, either; he's always misquoted.

Matters of style absorbed both Roth and Fox as they moved toward production, Roth emphasizing that punctuation is style and he'd rather keep even his misguided style rather than the copyeditor's. He doesn't want too much playing with the surface of the manuscript; too much polish creates slickness. The copyeditor is the young Nan Talese, who went on to have a distinguished career as an editor with her own imprint at Doubleday. In the midst of his production queries and revisions, Roth offered insight into the book, at one point remarking that the trouble with most of the characters is that they are "young enough to want to be happy, and old enough to want to be good. . . . Many of the problems in the book grow out of that very human dilemma." "I'm feeling mellower today, and more in control," he added.[94] He would take the nearly nine-hundred-page manuscript with him to New York when he visits his parents on 10 December and deliver it to Fox in person on the 11th. His time in the city was spent with Fox in his office and walking the streets, convinced that that was where he and Maggie should live. Although he was happy to be in Rome, London, and Iowa City to write the book, he was ready, as Maggie was, for life "in a big city where they speak our language."[95]

During one of his 1961 visits, Roth, ever alert to sexual adventure, met the versatile Alice Denham at a party. Denham was a free-spirited literary groupie who, according to a cheeky statement in *Publishers Weekly*, was "the only woman whose fiction and breasts have appeared in the same issue of *Playboy*."[96] She was the July 1956 Playmate in Hugh Hefner's magazine and made it her goal to populate her bedroom (or other rooms) with literary figures, from Joseph Heller and James Jones to William Gaddis, Evan S. Connell, and Philip Roth. She turned up at literary parties held by Plimpton (where Fox appeared; he once took her to lunch for literary and seductive reasons). Others, like Mailer, also appeared. "The worse sin," she believed, "was to be respectable."[97]

In her vivid, tell-all autobiography, *Sleeping with Bad Boys* (2006), she devotes a chapter to Roth, unimaginatively titled "Philip Pulls a Portnoy, 1961–1964" in which she narrates her encounter and conquest of Roth, opening with "Book parties were the gyms of the day where I worked out."[98] At six-foot-two and with "laser jet" eyes, Roth was irresistible; when his eyes landed on her, "those sexy black darts heated me up like acupuncture." He looked "hot as a pistola," she gushes. With him at the party where they met in 1961 was Maggie, a woman Denham describes as "long trunked and stubby-legged." His memorable first words to Denham were "Giving out your number?"[99]

He called and soon they were in bed, sex her great adventure: "Manhattan was a river of men flowing past my door, and when I was thirsty I drank." Roth, she writes, "was clearly a make out artist. It was in his actions, his movement, and was he ever cocksure. Philip expected. Philip got." A passage on his sexual prowess followed, Denham concluding that "Philip was on fire."[100] This was 1961.

Roth reconnected with Denham in 1964, pulling a Portnoy on her, suggesting a threesome with his wife, although they had by then separated.

He was joking, he said, but when he did visit Denham alone, she wanted to talk about her novel and literature. I don't "rap" about writing, he told her: "I do it." He only wanted sex, although the scene turned comic as she rejected his aggressive moves; when he pursued her about her apartment, she kicked him out, anticipating Portnoy's experience in Israel when he pursues a Sabra at the end of the novel.[101]

A friend of Roth's, the sociologist Ned Polsky, author of *Hustlers, Beats and Others* (1969), told Denham that Roth was afraid of women and felt he had to move before they did. He had to get the woman before she got him, like Maggie with men. Only writing kept him sane, Polsky said, and in many ways he never recovered from his possessive mother. Roth felt grabbed and trapped by women, said Polsky, although in *Portnoy*, he "turned guilt into high-rolling angst-ridden comedy."[102]

By the middle of January, back in Iowa City, Roth wrote to Fox that he was already into a new book, while fretting over *Letting Go*, like sending a child off to college: you've done all you could but you know he's still not ready. But if Roth found the landscape and social life of Iowa unstimulating and insular, the context of writers, teaching, and a university was not. He was struggling with *Letting Go* and its university world and actually used the Iowa setting in a portion of the novel, although the light and life of the Midwest most directly influenced his second novel, *When She Was Good*. One of the heroes of *Letting Go*, Paul Herz, is a struggling writer seeking to complete his first novel as part of his dissertation at Iowa, where he meets Gabe Wallach, who will complete his thesis on Henry James. Herz eventually lands a teaching job at the University of Chicago with the assistance of Wallach, who is already there. But if James was the controlling presence of his first novel, the Midwesterners—Dreiser, Cather, Anderson—took over his second.

The academic environment and context confirmed and extended many of Roth's experiences of university life for junior faculty and graduate students that he experienced at Chicago and Iowa. Although in his *Esquire* article of December 1962, "Iowa: A Very Far Country Indeed," he was critical of Iowa as something of a backwater, Iowa, nevertheless, contributed to the texture of *Letting Go*, supplanting the University of Chicago. The writing environment also encouraged revisions and rewriting when he felt the novel lacked the credibility he sought. To Cerf he reported in September 1961 that he was almost done with the novel, with possibly just another month's work. He was comfortable with Fox, but he had been working on the book for nearly two years and was eager to finish. He endorsed a possible May publication although still unsure of a title. He had discarded "Come and Go Away," which he'd suggested to Fox, and had been thinking of a title Maggie suggested while crossing the Irish Sea with the Styrons, "The Mad Crusader" (which became the title of the sixth section of the novel). Personally, however, he still preferred "Letting Go." And despite their persistent difficulties, he would dedicate the novel "To Maggie."

But Iowa was isolated from the active literary world Roth sought. Only the Paper Place, one of the first paperback bookstores in the country and certainly the first in Iowa, was a literary center, though noted more for its collection of folk records, which were always playing. Photos of famous writers, such as Thomas Mann and Jack Kerouac, were pinned to the wall. Upstairs in a loft-like space was once the Renaissance II Coffee House where student readings took place, but it had become a student art gallery. Kenney's Fine Beers, a hangout for workshop students, was across the street, making Clinton Street between College and Washington the city's limited Left Bank.

The Writers' Workshop was gaining prominence. The year before Roth arrived, the Second *Esquire* Writer's Symposium took place at the university (4–5 December 1959) and brought Ralph Ellison, Mark Harris, Dwight Macdonald, and Norman Mailer to town.[103] Moderating was Arnold Gingrich, publisher and editor of the magazine along with Paul Engle. The discussion was about the writer in a mass culture. Harris initiated the Iowa proceedings with a talk entitled "What About the Rigged Book Show?"

While teaching and revising the final draft of *Letting Go* absorbed Roth, Maggie found little to do. Tensions continued to develop. Early on, in fact, he had been concerned about her mental stability, noting in *The Facts* that before they married he worried about her possible breakdown (FAC 100). She began to make him feel guilty because his growing literary fame made her feel useless.

Iowa clearly did not satisfy Roth. In November 1960 he told Solotaroff that he was learning he didn't actually like teaching very much. It's an easy job in terms of time, but he doesn't have the constitution for conferences with people about "absolutely atrocious stories." It's bad enough to read them, but then having to think about them is too much. The workshops are like teaching a more pretentious freshman English. He does enjoy the company of George P. Elliott and Donald Justice, however, and he actually likes the socializing, especially in contrast to the "ambitiousness" of New York socializing and that of Rome.[104] He notes that he will give a talk at Princeton in February and that he's "sweating thru a rough part of the book—writing has never been such a ballbuster," and he doesn't want to take his attention off it again. If the book fails, it won't be for lack of anguish, he adds.[105] His latest title is "The Presence of Choice."

He explains that he did not switch publishers because of the money, although most people believed that. HM offered just as much as Random House, but he decided to leave them while he and Maggie were in England on their return journey from Rome. The editors at HM were not quite in the game, he felt; it was like being published by Ginn and Company or Funk and Wagnalls. He's upset at comments in the papers that misrepresent what he said at the *Esquire* symposium in San Francisco, and he objects to criticism of *Goodbye, Columbus*, although he admits the book is "little more than apprentice work, with plenty of mistakes."[106] He then adds that Maggie is "hot on Henry James." But new opportunities appeared: earlier sent Roth's remarks from the *Esquire* symposium, Solotaroff, now an associate editor of *Commentary*, tells him in November 1960 that he wants it turned into an essay: tighten the argument, remove points that show you're talking to an audience and find a Bellow quote. Revised, the essay appeared in *Commentary* in March 1961.

In his *Esquire* article on Iowa, Roth expanded his critique of the isolation and distance from cultural centers and its celebration only for its number-2-ranked football team. The vividness of the landscape appealed, but there was a "vacancy of imagination" concerning architecture. What does one do there, especially at night? The answer is to go to the movies or out for a beer or both. What did intrigue him was the establishment of a local chapter of the American Civil Liberties Union in 1958, plus the weekly newspaper, the *Iowa Defender*, an underground paper to counter the student daily. Thought by the administration to be run by "malcontents," they were convinced that Kenney's bar was populated only by effetes and intellectuals, "when and if that distinction is made."[107]

Blacks tended to hang out at Kenney's, with its jukebox full of jazz records, a further sign of its radical nature. The de-pledging of the first Black student to be asked to join an Iowa fraternity, about two years before Roth arrived, also takes up his interest in his *Esquire* essay. The prejudicial action and covert discrimination clearly exercised Roth. As a consequence of these issues, the Black students tend to stay together. Their place was really on the football field, not the streets of Iowa City. And the only thing that you can drink over the counter in Iowa is beer. Hard liquor could be bought in state-run stores but not in bars. In a city of thirty-four thousand with twelve thousand at the university, the single state-run store is always crowded, and no purchase is possible without your liquor booklet, which records your name and purchase.

Social life in Iowa City is not so much in the lines and administrative tangle at the liquor store but at dinner parties. There is no other place to go, with the best food home cooked. A decent restaurant can be found, but only in Chicago, a four- to five-hour drive away. The alternatives are the modest restaurants of the community of Amana, a German enclave from the nineteenth century, where food is served communally in common bowls. Rhubarb wine and Danish or German beer are the staples, as well as starch.

Roth's essay on the life of Iowa City succeeds through irony and detail, while conveying his disappointments and boredom. The highlight is his retelling of the centennial celebrations of the publication of Baudelaire's *Les Fleurs du Mal,* marked by an outdoor banquet in one of the Amana towns where a glee club sang and a blonde majorette demonstrated her skill at cartwheels and baton twirling at the inn of a former pitcher of the New York Yankees.[108] Only in America, he remarks, where Engle managed to finance the event through a Chicago ice-cream company.

Interestingly, in the piece Roth refers to Holly as "our daughter"; he relates that the principal called to insist Roth (not her mother) immediately come to her school and take her home because she was feeling ill for the second day in a row—"immediately," he repeated.

What astounded him about Iowa was the transformative power of sport as the community shifted from stable middle-class merchants and housewives into rabid fans. The supposed folksiness also disturbed him because it assumed "an intimacy in excess of the facts," breaking down either to obsequiousness or arrogance. Never had he been so talkative to strangers, he confesses. But by then, Roth had, in fact, decided to leave Iowa and accept a post at Princeton. He wrote to Fox on 15 February 1962 to tell him the news and that the time required would be no more than what he was expected to do in Iowa. After his year at Princeton, he hoped to return with Maggie to Europe. They planned to spend the summer at Wellfleet, on Cape Cod, before moving to Princeton.

With Roth's philandering, publishing opportunities, and realization that life with Maggie was uncontrollable and could not reasonably continue, he had much to anticipate, both good and bad. But while he sought escape, he also had difficulty giving up his relationship, telling Fox of future plans with Maggie. But her erratic behavior may have been as much Roth's as Maggie's: he was caught in a whirlwind of emotions, needing sympathy and love from others but still feeling oddly obliged to sustain his problematic marriage and care for vulnerable Maggie and her daughter. The contradictory impulses resulted in confusion, which he initially hoped to solve by running away to New York, where he will live and commute to Princeton. He was attempting to find his way, but Maggie wouldn't let him. To his despair, and in spite of her accusations that he was a cheater and possibly a sexual predator, she would soon follow him.

Roth later reflected on teaching at Iowa by saying (without irony) that a lot of students came to the Iowa Writers' Workshop for self-expression or therapy but the faculty tried to put an end to that. He saw the workshop serving three purposes: giving young writers an audience, a community, and an acceptable social category, that of "student." If a young man went to his father and said he was going to New York to be a writer, his father would be upset, but if he said I'm off to get a master's degree or even a PhD, who could quarrel with that? And part of the function of the writing faculty was to discourage those "without enough talent."[109]

Letting Go appeared while Roth was still in Iowa, at 124 Grand Avenue Court, to be precise. The 630-page work, the longest Roth ever published, emerged with great expectations. The front flap announces that the work justifies "the expectation aroused after the publication of his first book, *Goodbye, Columbus*."[110] In a letter of 19 April 1962 to Cerf, Roth characteristically offers critiques and suggestions for a second printing, disappointed in the appearance of the first few pages he's read. He dislikes the cluttered feeling one gets with the opening and objects to the breakup of the epigraphs without his permission, giving special emphasis to the Thomas Mann quotation where he did not want it. Three quotes precede the text: Mann from *A Sketch of My Life*, Simone Weil from *Gravity and Grace*, and nine lines from Wallace Stevens's "Esthétique du Mal."

Displaying, again, his desire to control the text, even though it has been published, Roth wants to change the ending. The hefty page of type (a long letter from Gabe to Libby) diminishes the impact of the conclusion, he says, followed by the unexpected introduction of the author's bio. Can that be published on the reverse side of the last page, he wonders? He ends by saying he's well into a new work that is he tentatively calling "Time Away." On a sheet entitled "Suggestions for a Second Printing," he jots down, "Is it necessary for the book to begin on the left hand page? Can it start on the right?"[111]

On 23 April, Cerf replied that, following a phone call, he, Fox, and the manufacturing department reviewed Roth's requests and will try to achieve them in the next edition.

Two of the things Roth does not complain about is the jacket copy, which he and Maggie tried to write, and the material under the author's photo on the back. This is a rather lengthy, three-paragraph description of his education, with such details as his Bucknell election to Phi Beta Kappa; time spent traveling, writing, and teaching following his MA from Chicago; and that he and his wife have lived in a variety of cities. Next is a summary of where his stories have appeared and the awards for *Goodbye, Columbus* plus his Guggenheim Fellowship and grant from the National Institute of Arts and Letters. A quote from his citation completes the second paragraph. The short third paragraph simply states that he will be at Princeton in 1962–63. What's emphasized is his academic pedigree but also that he is a well-traveled writer. Little is made of Newark, but the material greatly expands the back copy from *Goodbye, Columbus,* which emphasized where the stories in that collection had previously appeared.

During production, Roth was a constant bother, as letters to Fox confirm. Detailed notes on the page proofs were common, as well as remarks on the catalogue copy: he disliked the word "selfish" for Gabe and preferred "prudent," as the character tries to understand the difference between sympathy and love, between rescuing others and interfering in their lives. He'll come up with his own jacket copy after he sees what Random House offers, he writes. He adds that the book investigates what one intends to do in life and what one actually does, one's idea of oneself and what ideas others have of one. Much of this relates to Roth's involvement with Maggie, especially the remarks on rescuing a life and balancing a life of good fortune with one that is not so lucky.

Jacket photos were for Roth semiotic signs indicating the author at different stages of his career. The back jacket photo of *Letting Go,* selected by Roth and taken by Nancy Sirkis, possibly at Amagansett, shows him in a short-sleeve shirt, casual pants, and shoes sitting forward but relaxed in a rocking chair, a closed book held in his right hand and a slight smile. To his left are a series of books on a low shelf. The image is of a relaxed but serious author, tilted head looking at the viewer. This expands the gaze in the photo taken by his brother, directed outward to the reader, used on *Goodbye, Columbus.* There, the author, in a crew-neck sweater, turns slightly to the right, his hands in his back pocket. He's outside near a stream, no books in sight.

For *When She Was Good*, the author photo is more artistic and abstract, a headshot taken by Naomi Savage, emphasizing his intense dark eyes and surrounded by yellow with purple lettering. The background of the photo is black, and Roth, again staring intently at the reader, captures our gaze. Alongside his image is his biography, emphasizing prizes. *Portnoy's Complaint* has no author photo on the back jacket, but on the inside back flap there is a candid photo by Ann Mudge of a nearly smiling Roth, sitting on a bridge, gesticulating with his left hand (Roth was left-handed) and holding a pair of glasses. He seems to be speaking, appropriate for the monologue-driven text.

In a harsh letter to Fox, Roth restates his shock at the division of the epigraphs (it looks like hell, he writes), the sudden appearance of the "About the Author" section too soon after the last page of the text destroying the final effect of the work, and that the failure of any book club to take copies will harm sales. Furthermore, the competition from Nabokov, Faulkner, Baldwin, and O'Hara, all with books coming out at the same time, definitely hurts his chances for popular attention. What will you do, he aggressively asks, and then wants to know where advertisements will appear. As an addendum, he reports that his next work, now titled "Time Away," progresses, adding that a woman's point of view now controls the story, which he finds satisfying.[112]

An early review of *Letting Go* in *Publisher's Weekly* struck him as prickly; to counter, he tells Fox that he wrote a lovely sentence in "Time Away" which *does* live up to the promise of *Goodbye, Columbus*. He then provides a list of critics who should review "Letting Go," beginning with Alfred Kazin and Leslie Fiedler, followed by Edmund Wilson, Malcolm Cowley, and Irving Howe, in that order. Others include Lionel Trilling, George Steiner, John Updike, Bernard Malamud, and Saul Bellow. He crossed out Jacqueline Kennedy but not Kirk Douglas as recipients of free copies. He then added the names of Robert Penn Warren and William Styron, with additional copies to be sent to Ralph Ellison, Richard Stern, F. R. Leavis, and Elaine May.[113]

In a Woody-Allenesque letter to Fox on 30 April 1962, after receiving his author's copies, he starts with his dreams of Edmund Wilson, someone he never met. In the dreams, he reports, they got on well, probably because "I'm something of an apple polisher." Wilson is shorter than he imagined, but in his dreams, even he himself is even shorter than he imagined. Maggie, he then writes, is bearing up, but it is her daughter who is the anchor in the house and the most comic eleven-year-old around. He complains about Paul Engle's review and the jacket copy, which fails to note that Roth teaches at Iowa. He adds that excerpts were to appear in *Mademoiselle* and *Harper's* soon and that

Fox should send one hundred copies to Iowa City bookstores. Keep everyone at Random House on their toes, he writes, "I am on mine here."[114]

Compounding the isolation he felt with midwestern life was the increasing antagonism between him and Maggie, although as late as May 1962, he was still making plans with her to join him on a trip to Israel, stopping in France and England on the return. (The trip did not occur.) But he felt he had to move on, back to the East Coast and freedom from his erstwhile wife, which meant a New York apartment and teaching as writer-in-residence at Princeton.

4

"Walked Out on the Platinum!,"

or New York, New York

DON'T RUN FIRST THING TO A BLONDIE, *PLEASE*! BECAUSE SHE'LL
TAKE YOU FOR ALL YOU'RE WORTH AND THEN LEAVE YOU BLEEDING
IN THE GUTTER! A BRILLIANT INNOCENT BABY BOY LIKE YOU, SHE'LL
EAT YOU UP ALIVE!

—Sophie Portnoy, in *Portnoy's Complaint*, 1969

Reactions to *Letting Go* began to appear in the summer of 1962, just as
Roth departed Iowa. They were mixed. Critics generally found the book
dour and depressing, lacking in development and drama. How exciting can
the drudgery and penury of graduate school be? Flaubert's *A Sentimental
Education*, a work on boredom, failure, and waste, came to the minds of several readers, the dual heroes almost matching each other: Frederic Moreau
is a romantic counterpart to Gabe Wallach, while Paul Herz is a kind of
"mole of duty" in contrast to Flaubert's man of action, Deslauriers. The class
backgrounds of the two pairs are also of note. Disillusionment characterizes
both works, especially seen in Roth's focus on the period from the end of the
Korean War to the recession of 1957, with the Eisenhower era as backdrop.

In the novel the man of feeling (Gabe) is half-hearted and the man of duty
(Paul) tormented. Paul is "diligent at unhappiness," but like Gabe a man of
goodwill who ironically acts in bad faith.[1] They are set against the actions
of Mordecai Wallach, Gabe's father and a dentist, and the slangy *spieling* of
Uncle Asher, Paul's uncle, a kind of older Augie March. Limitations attach
themselves to everyone. No ambition or career emerges, although Herz is to
be the writer, Wallach the scholar. In Flaubert, when Moreau awakens from a
night with a courtesan, it is to go down into the streets to meet the Revolution
of 1848; in *Letting Go*, when Gabe awakens after feverish sex, it is only to
listen to and remember soap operas on the radio.

Ted Solotaroff found the work reflective of graduate student life at the time and especially at the University of Chicago (he, of course, had lived and become a model for Roth of that life), adding that one of the principal occupations of Hyde Park (adjacent to the university and where most faculty and graduate students lived) was marital bickering. Amid the conflicting views of the book, Roth watched the novel modestly climb the bestseller charts, satisfied more or less.

In July, the second printing of *Letting Go* arrived, and that month, writing from Styron's home in Roxbury, Connecticut, Roth tells Bennett Cerf that he's delighted with sales but anxious that all of the attention is fading, noting that his debut on the *New York Times* bestseller list for 8 July at number 12 has now, a week later, dropped to 13. He would resent Baldwin, rising to number 10 that week, were it not for Nabokov with *Pale Fire* lagging behind him at number 14. *Letting Go* hovered around 13 until 12 August, when it moved up to 11, just behind Irving Stone's *The Agony and the Ecstasy* but below *Franny and Zooey* by Salinger at number 9. By 26 August, he had moved up to 10 and the following week even higher, to 9, ahead of both Stone and Salinger but well behind Faulkner's *The Reivers* at 5 and Herman Wouk's *Youngblood Hawke*. Number 1 was *Ship of Fools* by Katherine Anne Porter. By 16 September, Roth had fallen to 13, and the following week he was gone.

But he was also deep into his next novel, "Time Away," with 150 pages written over the summer. He tells Fox that he wants it to be shorter and a different type of book than *Letting Go* in technique and feeling. He doesn't want to solve the problems it presents by letting it run on. The proposed Jerusalem trip is off because he couldn't and wouldn't take Maggie; she had become a burden he sought to escape. He needed some peace and quiet. The Yeshiva University experience also soured him in ways he was just learning, but he had expanded the talk for an article in *Commentary* that would become "Writing About Jews," published in December 1963.

Roth now had an apartment in New York and a new position at Princeton. And he thought he was free from Maggie, a relationship that survived, he admitted, largely by antagonism and anger. When he left Chicago in June 1958 to travel to Europe and then live in New York, he thought he was leaving her for good; he thought he had done so three or four times earlier in Chicago and was dating other women. They were still friendly, but he was not free: she followed him to New York, and no matter how much he sought to leave her, she found him, turning up at 128 East 10th Street in February 1959.

Princeton, however, kept him busy, although it was an unlikely place for a Jewish writer beginning to rediscover his roots in Newark. But Bellow had preceded him ten years earlier, the result a caustic portrait of the university in *Humboldt's Gift*. Humboldt, the poet, wangles a job at Princeton analogous to Bellow's. R. P. Blackmur, a notable drinker, ran the creative writing program and needed a stand-in for the 1952–53 academic year. Delmore Schwartz, the chosen temporary chair, proposed Bellow as his assistant, and after a bibulous interview and lunch, Blackmur offered Bellow the job. That summer Bellow went to Yaddo to finish *Augie March*. Sewell, the critic in *Humboldt's Gift*, is an unpleasant portrait of Blackmur. Princeton continued to attract writers, and through the 1950s Theodore Roethke, Ralph Ellison, John Berryman, and Edmund Wilson taught there, often in the Christian Gauss seminars. Parties were *de rigueur*, events where drinking exceeded writing as a literary pursuit.

Staffing the department in 1962–63, with Roth listed in the English section of the General Catalogue as "Resident Fellow in Creative Writing," were a set of distinguished academics: Carlos Baker (biographer of Hemingway), Blackmur (poetics and criticism), E. D. H. Johnson (Victorianist), G. E. Bentley (drama), L. R. Thompson (biographer of Frost), and Willard Thorp (distinguished Americanist and chair). Others included A. Walton Litz (Joycean), Robert B. Martin (Victorianist), Julian Moynahan (Lawrence specialist), and Robert Fagles (poet and translator of the classics). In the listing for the Creative Arts Program, Roth joined Blackmur, Alan Downer, and Moynahan, teaching a course entitled "Creative Writing." The program, established by the Carnegie Foundation in 1939, was to provide opportunities for undergraduates with an interest in painting, sculpture, music, and writing. The goal was not to form professional artists as much as it was to allow students to develop their creative faculties in connection with a broad program for "humanistic education."

Roth clearly made an impression, as he was nominated by the *Daily Princetonian* of 23 December 1962 as "Princeton Man of the Week." A long, enthusiastic double-column editorial on his selection became the front page. Roth was a presence on the campus, a week before his nomination giving a student interview stressing the surprising lack of interest in the arts; Iowa was "thick," unlike Princeton, with its bright students but noticeable absence of women. The story reported that Roth would instruct sixteen undergraduates and knew six faculty well. The preceding week, the novelist John Dos Passos cited him in a talk for his youthful accomplishment in winning the National Book Award in 1960. From the paper's interview, we learn his campus habits:

> On campus, the 29 year old Roth sticks to his regime, working on his current novel before lunch, with office hours at 1879 Hall in the afternoon. He meets with his creative writing section in the evenings. You don't teach creative writing, he emphasized. What you do is teach the writer's point of view. He has no hobbies, he claims, but does keep up with politics and declares that he's always been against the Republicans. There seems to be no reason to be for them, he adds. Until 21 he had an incomplete idea of a private school which he thought was only for kids from broken homes. Then he met some girls who went to one and he concluded that it was for kids from broken homes and girls. College, he continued, is terrific because you don't have to identify yourself with a class or cultural background; it's a period of disconnection and of putting to the test everything you arrived with.[2]

The following March, Roth gave what became a controversial lecture on 12 March 1963, the Farnum Lecture, attacking the "highfalutin" approach to literary study that emphasized symbolism and archetypes. By contrast, the writer-in-residence can work to reestablish the connection between literature and life. The problem is that students become critics rather than readers, eager to explicate rather than understand. This is the result of courses focusing on style and structure, concentrating on abstraction, not content. Objects found in a work of art are remade into symbols unrelated to the meaning of the story, which extends to student creative writing. He cited a story submitted to him where the character seemed to be taking a shower when he was actually being baptized. All of this, he claims, shows disinterest in the matter of life. "You cannot look at the ripples in the pond without first looking at the pebble." A writer cannot teach writing but can help the student see the importance of matter found in poems and stories. He can keep the student from "letting what he knows conceal what he feels." Literature connects first with life, he concluded.[3]

The talk made front-page news in the *Daily Princetonian* a day or so later, when reactions from faculty colleagues ranged from agreement to denial. Carlos Baker endorsed Roth's criticism that there was too much emphasis on symbolism, although he defended the department's approach as balanced. He did admit, however, that symbols were often worked hard as shortcuts to relieve students of the obligation to "penetrate deeper into the meaning." Chairman Willard Thorpe was more reserved: "There could very well be too much emphasis on structure and form as a result of modern criticism." But the business of the department *was* to train critics, not readers. Richard M. Ludwig flatly rejected Roth's criticism as not fitting the Princeton department. Alan Downer also criticized Roth: ten years ago the emphasis on technique was extreme: now there was an equal division between technique, historical context, and ideas. Everyone agreed on the value of a creative writer in the department, but also that creative writing cannot be taught.[4]

A month later, Roth participated in a three-day "Response" conference on campus headlined by Yevgeny Yevtushenko with a panoply of distinguished writers and artists: Edward Albee, James Baldwin, Cheever, Styron, Malamud, Ellison, and Robert Penn Warren. The Dave Brubeck Quartet performed. Philip Johnson, I. M. Pei, and Arnold Gingrich of *Esquire* participated, as well as Muriel Rukeyser and Howard Nemerov, plus Barnett Newman and Harold Rosenberg. In such a circle of writers and artists, he felt at home.

A mark of Roth's popularity with the students is a story about Skip Downing, a center on the 150-pound football squad and newly elected captain. His interest in creative writing led him to submit a four-thousand-word story on small men's football to *Sports Illustrated*. At first rejected and told to make it more personal, he consulted Roth, who suggested revisions to a second draft; it was accepted.[5] But as late as 1993, Roth's presence at Princeton still seemed to upset some. That year, in the process of digitizing the library catalogue, it was discovered that someone had systematically and repeatedly removed all the cards relating to the novels of Philip Roth. Technically, or rather bibliographically, he did not exist.

Despite the WASPish, conservative English Department of 1962 when Roth arrived, he found a lively Jewish comrade-in-arms in the Newark-born sociologist Melvin Tumin, who specialized in educational reform, desegregation, and race relations. Tumin was a buddy of Bellow's from the University of Chicago; letters between them date back to 1942, and Bellow loaned Tumin $2 to buy a marriage license and a necktie to wear at his wedding. Bellow may have facilitated Tumin's meeting Roth in Princeton, which would lead to a lasting friendship, Tumin at one point supposedly storing Roth manuscripts in the basement of his home.[6] A 1968 faculty profile of Tumin presented him as brainy, energetic, and direct, critical of education's attachment to grades and competitive testing. He criticized an educational system more concerned with the skills needed to pass exams than curriculums focusing on what the young might become. He was also a strong civil rights advocate. Of Rumanian descent, his father's father and great-grandfather were rabbis. At Princeton, he taught courses in deviant behavior, social stratification, and education.[7]

At Princeton, Tumin was one of the first in the 1950s to speak up strongly against what Roth, quoted in Tumin's obituary, called "blatant patterns of discrimination against Jews" in the university's student clubs. Such discrimination took years to overcome. Roth would reveal, years later, that an incident in Tumin's class became the initial motive of *The Human Stain* (2000).[8] Tumin is one of the two dedicatees of *Sabbath's Theater*.[9]

In early November 1962, Roth declined Solotaroff's invitation to review a work by James Baldwin, claiming that he was simply too busy. He noted that the quarterlies were getting at *Letting Go*: the *Hudson Review* treated him with disdain, but he was "hot stuff" at the *Kenyon*.

Sales continue to concern him, as well as royalties. He asked Joe Fox in February 1963 for details on the paperback sale to Bantam and whether the remaining $17,500 owed him would be in the form of royalties, noting that he had received only $5,000. He also referred to a movie option. A royalty statement ending 31 March 1963 indicates nearly 2,500 copies returned and only modest sales except for the sale to Bantam, resulting, after deductions, in a total of $6,386.52.

To earn extra money, Roth began to publish in popular magazines such as *Seventeen*, which in its April 1963 issue had a short essay entitled "Philip Roth Talks to Teens," subtitled "They Won't Make You Normal." Essentially an explanation of why reading novels should make you uncomfortable—they encourage you to be dissatisfied or skeptical—he goes against the grain of received, schoolroom views. Novels are good for you precisely because they disorient you. We often deceive ourselves into thinking something is right or justified when it is not. Novels provide ways for understanding that and admitting that sometimes in life we cannot distinguish right from wrong. To live is to take chances. But writers do not write to transmit information. The *feel* of life, not just the facts of life, matter and concern the writer. The job of the writer is to "liberate the imagination of the reader."[10]

Figure 4.1 Roth with Maggie in Central Park, 1962. Credit: Carl Mydans, Getty Images.

Roth ends by listing ten novels that show novelists doing their job. These books are not good for you and will not make you normal, but they are works that deal with individuals seeking to discover what it is to be a human being. His list:

> Anderson, Sherwood. *Winesburg, Ohio*
> Connell, Evan. *Mrs. Bridge*
> Fitzgerald, F. Scott. *The Great Gatsby*

Flaubert, Gustave. *Madame Bovary*
Golding, William, *The Lord of the Flies*
Malamud, Bernard. *The Assistant*
Moore, Brian. *The Lonely Passion of Judith Herne*
Styron, William. *Lie Down in Darkness*
Tolstoy, Leo. *Anna Karenina*
Wolfe, Thomas. *Look Homeward, Angel.*

Not every teenager will understand every page of these books, he admits, but if you want to move ahead in your life, read two of them, or better yet, all of them. Prescriptive Roth, assuming a teacherly voice. The author's note for the essay emphasizes his "authority": he's won the National Book Award for *Goodbye, Columbus,* his first novel appeared last year from Random House, and he is currently writer-in residence at Princeton, all of these details offering an *imprimatur* for his views.

In the midst of advising teenagers, he was also dealing with Maggie, their toxic relationship defined by tension and disagreement. The strain was palpable: at one point in June 1962, traveling from Iowa to his brother's apartment in Stuyvesant Town, New York, he became physically ill, nauseated, with diarrhea and the chills. His collapse reinforced his need for help, and the next day he went to see a psychiatrist for the first time in his life. He glosses the event in *My Life as a Man,* giving the correct date but not the intensity of the experience (MLM 202). Maggie, as he recognized, was "destructive," a term used by her son, David Williams, years later in a 1975 interview.[11] It was in 1962, following her suicide attempt, that Roth learned of Maggie's tricking him into marriage with the false pregnancy claim.

One who did recognize the danger of Maggie was Bob Baker, a friend from graduate school who was teaching in Oregon. In July 1963, Baker wrote to tell Roth it was great to find him sounding, for once, upbeat. Roth had by then separated from Maggie and returned from a sponsored trip to Israel. Baker could not refrain from agreeing with Roth that Maggie seemed "self-doomed" and that there was always an inner tension which had turned into a "raging unassuageable self-pity that will swiftly corrode the best elements in her and leave her harsh and brassy." He predicted that she would require more and more money to maintain her supposed "status." "I am glad you are going to fight," he told Roth but added, "The more she gets the longer and more costly the delay of her ultimate . . . encounter with reality. Tough it through. Or better, let the lawyers tough it through."[12] The comment was prescient.

An example of the financial difficulty Roth was facing is a note from the comptroller of Random House dated 31 January 1964. It states that they sent Roth a check for $71.93 for *Letting Go* but that it should not go to him because in July 1963 they were served with a copy of a State of New York Supreme Court Order sequestering his funds. All future royalty payments had to go to a court-appointed sequestrator. In short, Roth was broke because of his 1962 separation from Maggie, who claimed support. The separation occurred when he took the Princeton job, and became legal, after much battling, in 1963.

While Roth commuted weekly from New York to Princeton, his main occupation remained dealing with Maggie and her lawyers, and writing what was eventually his second novel, *When She Was Good*. The events were inextricably linked. As a diversion, he had his first trip to Israel, sponsored by the American Jewish Congress, but shortly before he departed on 15 June 1963, he told Cerf that he and Maggie had separated again and had been for some time.[13] What he didn't reveal was that she tried to have him arrested so he could not leave the country, but this "cunning Jew" left three days before his announced date and saved his life. I might have killed her if I stayed, he tells Solotaroff.[14]

Roth went to Israel to participate in an American Jewish Congress symposium in Tel Aviv and other cities. Joachim Prinz, an early admirer of Roth and the dean of Newark rabbis (who will appear near the end of *The Plot Against America*), organized the trip as a director of the American Jewish Congress and accompanied the group as part of the "Encounters" conferences he organized as president of the American Jewish Congress.

In Israel, Roth, Leslie Fiedler, and others in the delegation had a meeting with Israel's first prime minister, David Ben-Gurion; photos from the gathering in Ben-Gurion's office show an enthusiastic prime minister pointing out the window. Roth's caption for the photo, prepared for the Roth @80 conference in March 2013 in Newark, declares that Ben-Gurion was passionately telling everyone, "See that tree, that's a Jewish tree. See that bird, that's a Jewish bird. See up there? A Jewish cloud." Roth didn't look; in one photo he impassively takes a glass of water just below Ben-Gurion's outstretched and pointing left arm. In another photo, with Ben-Gurion seated at the head of the table, Roth appears skeptical as he listens to the prime minister telling them they must all move to Israel and stop living in the diaspora (Figure 4.2).[15]

The Congress Bi-Weekly for 16 September 1963 contains a full report of the events, formally titled "Second Dialogue in Israel," and lists Roth as speaking

Figure 4.2 Roth listening to David Ben-Gurion in Israel with other members of the 1963 delegation sponsored by the American Jewish Congress. To Roth's left, Margaret and Leslie Fiedler. Credit: Newark Public Library.

on 18 June in Jerusalem. The program title was "The Jewish Intellectual and Jewish Identity," and the American panelists were David Boroff of NYU, Leslie Fiedler of the University of Montana, Max Lerner of Brandeis University, and Philip Roth, "Novelist, Winner of the 1960 National Book Award." The Israeli panelists included Shalom Kahn of Hebrew University and Yehuda Yaari, novelist and diplomat, plus two others. This was an all-day affair. The next evening, in Tel Aviv, with the title "The Creative Writer as a Jew," Moshe Shamir, novelist and playwright, debated Fiedler. Finally, on Thursday morning, was "Jewishness and the Creative Process" with Boroff, Fiedler, Lerner, and Roth in discussion with Aharon Megged, novelist, and Yaakov Malkin, critic.

The purpose of the dialogues was to close the gulf between American Jewry and Israel and overcome any persistent cultural misunderstandings. Prinz provided a rationale in "The Meaning of the Dialogue" in the September *Congress Bi-Weekly*. Ben-Gurion spoke at the first dialogue, but because of his sudden resignation on 16 June 1963, Abba Eban, deputy prime minister, gave the opening address. Four days of "uninhibited conversation" was the goal of the second dialogue. Discussion revealed unanimity among the writers and intellectuals, who agreed that Jewish literature should not be confused with Jewish public relations. The politicians differed, however, the Israelis believing that only living in Israel confirmed one's support for Judaism. The dialogues were widely covered in Israel and, Prinz suggested, found similar, if not equal, interest in Jewish America.

In the transcript from the dialogue of 18 June 1963, Roth began by citing his visit with others to the prime minister's office, where, in answer to the group's question "What is Jewish?," Ben-Gurion got up, went to the window, and proudly proclaimed, "Jewish trees, Jewish roads, and Jewish fields." To be able to say "That is mine" is to be able to be a Jew, Roth added. He then elaborated that he, and many American Jews, had inherited not a body of law and not a body of learning. Ironically, it was this very absence of codified knowledge that defined Judaism, although there were constant reminders that one was Jewish. What one received, Roth explained, was a psychology, not a culture or a history in its totality. And the psychology could be reduced to three words, "Jews are better," a point of psychology, not fact.[16] In America, one had to create a moral character for oneself: "one had to invent [being] a Jew." There was a sense of specialness, but you had to create it, he repeated.

This condition bound together a large number of Jewish writers and books, two of his favorites Bellow's *The Victim* and Malamud's *The Assistant*. In both, the central characters had to find out what it means to be a Jew and then invent a character for himself. Happily, not everyone invented the same character or moral response: the striving and yearning to be special was the common bond. Even in his short time in Israel, it seemed to him that all conversation returned to the question of Jewish specialness. Where is it Jewish, where is it special? Ironically, the blessing and burden of growing up Jewish in America was to have been given "a psychology with a content" and not having to invent it, although one still had to learn it.[17]

In discussion and in response to Fiedler's remarks that to be a Jew might mean being a victim, Roth replied that he understood the remarks to emphasize dissent: that is the essential quality of Jewishness (an idea, of course, appealing to Roth, who had been attacked as being anti-Semitic for his stories in *Goodbye, Columbus*). But if dissent means being victimized, so be it. Yet not to dissent because of the threat of being a victim is intolerable.[18] Bearing witness, however, often means dissent, to confront the whitewashing, politicking, and deception of governments, if not history.

But Roth remained puzzled, asking the physicist on the panel, W. Z. Low, just what values of a moral nature are Jewish? Low's answer was ambiguous, that you need a concrete framework before you can address conceptual matters. In a later exchange, Roth identified himself as "a writer of fiction who is a Jew"; "I am not a Jewish writer; I am a writer who is a Jew," he repeated. His biggest concern and the passion "in [his] life is to write fiction, not to be a Jew."[19] Roth found that the debates and presentations forced him to assess his own ideas about what it meant to be a Jewish writer, a topic he could not escape.

In answer to an anticipated question—Why don't you come to Israel for a year and learn what it means to be a Jew?—Roth offers his most extended comment on being a writer. He includes a reference to James Michener, who was in Israel at that time researching what would become his massive bestseller, *The Source* (1965), and points out that such writing is different from what Roth does. The serious writer "does not seem to pursue subjects or places, but is pursued by them."[20] What interests him is the mysterious connection between events and character: Who causes what, and how did it happen? Yes, at certain times he was pulled to write about the American Jewish scene, especially when he was close to it, and his first stories reflect that; they were stories he had been carrying around with him for a long time. But he moved on, not only geographically but in other ways, and the subject of the fiction changed, although the same moral and psychological obsessions continued.

Importantly, it is Roth who focuses on the psychological as an aspect of identity, Jewish or otherwise. Being born a Jew in America confirmed a certain specialness, but it was obscure. Hence, one had to "invent being a Jew." "If I can make any sense about my Jewishness and of my desire to continue to call myself a Jew, it is in terms of my outsideness in the general assumptions of American culture." The Jew in America and elsewhere is always an outsider surviving with only a psychological shell that is empty inside. Through assimilation, which is not a dirty word to him, he was able to "discover American and English literature and also the American language. I do not regret that at all."[21] The tension between commitment and disengagement is at the heart of the situation for the Jew in America.

On 20 June 1963, in Tel Aviv with the topic "Jewishness and the Creative Process," Roth begins by countering the view that you have to love Jewish life to write about it. Instead, you have to love writing. We do not protect Jews by giving them an image of themselves that satisfies them. What is ironic, he says, is that Jews can be so intolerant of dissent. Because "the Jew is to the Gentile world what the writer is to the world itself." What the writer says to the world is "Don't kid yourself, that's not the way it is." The very existence of Jews makes this claim to the gentiles. Ever provocative, Roth says Jews cannot swallow the central fantasy of Catholicism, the Virgin Birth, which is to him "highly comic" and which he finds "hysterical." But it is possible. And in response to a speaker the previous night who discussed a list of bestselling writers, Uris, Wouk, and Roth, he adds, "It should only happen"![22]

Reacting to Fiedler and his thinking like a critic, Roth says that he writes from a much narrower point of view. He does not think archetypally or in terms of myths but in terms that are closer to him: American Jewish life and the lives some Jews have led in America. Lately he has become discontent with the use of Jewish characters in his fiction. He reveals he's working on two projects, one with no Jews at all (*When She Was Good*). Any Jew appearing in it would clearly be out of place. But he is also writing something which he says is more Jewish than anything that he has written before: a comic fantasy about an orphan who gets farmed out to lots of different Jewish families and is brought up by a Jewish gangster and a Jewish milkman and at least six different Jewish mothers.[23] And he came all the way to Israel to find that writers think alike and that he has an allegiance to no single community.

In the final session, Roth mentions that he wrote a special preface to the German edition to *Goodbye, Columbus* in which he tried to differentiate the situation of the Jewish reality in America from that in Germany. Published by Rowohlt, his preface expressed anger at what had happened in Germany and that, yes, his stories would likely be misread but that he still possessed confidence in America as a Jew. But his Jewishness was different from that of a Jew born in Germany, and he would not let ignorance or cruelty in any country limit his freedom to write about any subject or group.[24]

But moral concerns remain primary in his work—interrupting himself to ask if that is a Jewish feature—and the very focus of two writers he believes influenced him the most: Tolstoy and James, neither Jewish. It is difficult for a writer to speak of his sources: one winds up either being wrong or sounding pretentious. He also responds to Gogol and Dostoevsky with strong feelings and thinks of them as Jewish in a way. In a contrarian statement, he says that the greatest burden of a Jew is to have the courage to deny his or her Jewishness. Is there a moral act or some way of being, he asks, "in which a man can deny being a Jew?"[25] What really counts for the writer is not the reality around us but the one we invent.

From London on his return after three and a half weeks in Israel, Roth told Solotaroff (somewhat disingenuously) that the symposium was unexciting but that he was hardly the bad boy the *New York Times* made him out to be. The country surprised him: the police are Jews, the gays are Jews, and so are the truck drivers and dishwashers. He generally said little in Jerusalem but spoke frequently in Tel Aviv, making anybody's mother proud, to an audience of older people, most of whom came in to sit down and get out of the sun. Fiedler was Fiedler (brash, outspoken) and entirely new to the Israelis. He doubts the heroic nature of literary criticism that Fiedler always promotes. It's really not work for heroes, Roth believes.

Most important, Roth tells Solotaroff, he seems to be healing from the bitterness of his ongoing fight with Maggie. Why, he asks, is he happy? Perhaps it is "just the narcissist having his day," alone in terrific surroundings. In a telling and comic sentence commenting on his well-being, he writes, "I'm willing to give up irony if it cuts down anxiety."[26] But on Maggie he's tough, telling Solotaroff that she's being as outrageous as possible, equaled only by her self-righteousness, and he recounts how she tried to have him arrested to prevent his departure for Israel. He says he's unable to meet a deadline for Solotaroff, partly justifying this by explaining that in any case, any penny earned is a "penny more that can be cut up for alimony."[27]

Also from London he tells Fox that he's enjoying his personal time without Maggie, that he's slowly at work, and that like Henry James he is invited out to dinner so often that his days are "round and pleasant." But the marital problems continue: Maggie's lawyers attached his Random House money and stopped his accounts in New York, but he took measures beforehand so all is not dire. *His* lawyer is even making an offer to her lawyer, although he won't know the result for a while. He hopes they do not have to go to court. He apologizes for his behavior of the last few months. He is chagrined that no one in London knows his name or work, even though one of the "burdens" of going to New York the previous fall, he writes, was discovering the extent and notoriety of his reputation.

Roth stayed in London for the remainder of the summer and reports that Maggie turned down an offer he made of 23 percent of his income with a minimum of $4,000 and maximum of $47,500. She wants 33 percent of his income with $6,500 minimum and no maximum, plus all the furniture and books and two years of psychoanalysis at $100 a week, in addition to being named the beneficiary of his life insurance and will, recalling Margaret in Bellow's *Seize the Day*: "She lived in order to punish him."[28] Apparently and ironically, while pursuing Roth and his assets, Maggie also wrote to Fox about a job. But he cannot think of a way to get a divorce, short of catching her in bed with someone else. He ends the note by saying he has no intention of becoming the "Jewish George Plimpton, though it might be something George might want to try." Plimpton was known for temporarily assuming different roles, from boxer to NFL football player. Fox replies, "You sound manic. I agree with you that it's unnatural for you to be so happy."[29] Fox adds that Maggie did not formally ask for a job, only casually mentioned interest in publishing work.

Roth was beginning to write about psychoanalysis, first in *Letting Go* (1962) and then in his short story "The Psychoanalytic Special," published in the November 1963 issue of *Esquire*. In the same issue as Tom Wolfe's "There Goes (VAROOM! VAROOM!) That Kandy Kolored Tangerine-Flake Baby," Roth's prose seemed tame as he dramatized psychoanalysis but not its content.

Importantly, his early treatment of the subject revolves around women in unhappy marriages, anticipated by Miriam, who leaves "Eli, the Fanatic" in the final pages, remarking on an Oedipal experience with her baby. Libby Herz in *Letting Go* visits a Dr. Lumen, while "The Psychoanalytic Special" introduces for the first time Dr. Otto Spielvogel as the therapist for Ella Wittig (in her third marriage), who regularly travels to New York to see him.[30] Caught between triviality and desire (her current husband wants her to repeatedly ensure that the buttons on his topcoat and shirts are not loose), only clandestine affairs activate her passion. She seeks a kind of salvation or at least self-understanding through her analysis, but it does not happen. She remains unhappily stuck in her dependent life. Subsequent psychoanalytical patients in Roth are male, highlighted by Alex Portnoy (*Portnoy's Complaint*) and Peter Tarnopol (*My Life as a Man*).

Roth's frequent appearance in *Esquire* was in no small part the result of support from the fiction editor Rust Hills, with whom Roth began to correspond as early as 1957. Fiction at *Esquire* in 1957, when Hills was hired, had turned away from its original aspirations: once the home of Hemingway and Fitzgerald, by the late 1950s it had shifted toward adventure stories for adventure's sake. Hills set out to make the fiction serious again, soliciting stories like "Nude Croquet" by Leslie Fiedler, a poisonous depiction of New York intellectuals, and Arthur Miller's decline-of-the-old-West parable, "The Misfits."

Energetic and quick to spot good work, Hills forged literary friendships easily: Dorothy Parker once remarked to him that his name made her forget all the other New Jersey suburbs. Eager to identify new talent and restore some literary luster to *Esquire*, Hills offered encouragement, opportunity, and money to the young Roth, whose earliest work for the magazine, "Heard Melodies Are Sweeter," appeared in August 1958, followed by "Expect the Vandals" in December that year. The first piece of fiction Roth published in three years, "Heard Melodies Are Sweeter" is only a single page and takes the form of a short play set in the production office of a TV studio. Writers plan a show for a singer, Timmy Thrush. They decide he needs a gimmick and come up with a wink as a kind of motif. His partner and their children will also appear, all winking, as well as Frank Sinatra, Bing Crosby, Perry Como, and Dinah Washington and their children—all winking.

The absurd dominates "Heard Melodies," although not in the telling. An epigraph, "Art or kitsch: only a wink could tell," suggests that, indeed, heard melodies are sweeter than those unheard, the title taken from Keats's "Ode on a Grecian Urn." Here, the "heard" is the seen. The aptly named Thrush is a singer, but his voice is not enough to carry the show. The popularity of musical variety shows in 1958 partly explains Roth's interest in the story, plus the unusual sense of humor and treatment of entertainment which he would later exploit in "On the Air" in the *New American Review* of 1970. The presentation of "Heard Melodies" as a play foreshadows his attempt at playwriting a few years later.

"Expect the Vandals" is a more elaborate war story of two stranded soldiers on an island in the Pacific, the remaining troops of a failed landing attempt. The two, a Christian named Ken Moyer and a Jew called Moe Malamud, dislike each other but must band together to survive. Moe is a thirty-five-year-old accountant who scampers about to find ways to survive, while his buddy Ken is paralyzed by a bullet and hides in a cave. They survive in isolation, but Moe, exploring the wilderness, witnesses a small contingent of Japanese soldiers commit suicide. The two Americans remain for eleven months on the island until unexpectedly rescued just before the island is to be used as a nuclear test site. *Battle of Blood Island* was the 1960 movie of the story, a mix of survivalism and religious friction filmed in Puerto Rico.

Rust Hills initiated the *Esquire* symposiums entitled "The Writer in America," the second held in Iowa on 4–5 December 1959. This was likely the first time Hills and Roth met. One result was Roth's participation in the third symposium, held in San Francisco with John Cheever and James Baldwin. One of Hills's great skills was to identify sections of a longer work and present it as a short story. "Very Happy Poems," appearing in *Esquire* in 1962, is actually pages 322–42 of *Letting Go*, where Libby attempts to write poetry. Excerpting, he would say, was the true editor's art, later demonstrated when, for example, he turned sections of Styron's *Sophie's Choice* into what appeared to be discrete short stories.[31]

During this period, Roth was toying with drama, largely to secure additional money, and in 1963 received a Ford Foundation Grant for playwriting in connection with the American Place Theater. In his archive at the Library of Congress are titles of unproduced works, like the TV play "A Coffin in Egypt" (1959), as well as "Greed or the Egomaniacs" (undated), "Buried Again" (1964), and "The Fishwife" (1964). "The Nice Jewish Boy" (1963) received a reading in 1964 at a workshop of the American Place Theater with a then unknown actor, Dustin Hoffman, taking the lead.

Roth's playwriting grew out of an early interest in social justice and the stage going back to primary school, where he wrote and performed in a play on freedom in eighth grade. At Bucknell, he also acted. He would review drama for the *New York Review of Books* in 1964 while lecturing at Stony Brook and begin writing his essays on drama in late May 1964. The 28 May issue of *The New York Review of Books* had as its cover headline "Philip Roth on the New Plays by James Baldwin and LeRoi Jones." The actual title of the review was "Channel X: Two Plays on the Race Conflict." The plays were Baldwin's *Blues for Mr. Charlie* and Jones's *The Dutchman*. Whatever he reviewed (later it was Albee's *Tiny Alice*) brought a response, Jones writing on 9 July 1964 to say Roth was feebleminded in his refusal "to see any Negro as a man." The "rot" in the minds of academic liberals like him is to take his own "distortion of the world to be somehow more profound than the cracker's. There is little difference, except you guys have hipper cover stories." The error of those like Roth is to abstract human beings.[32]

Roth assertively replied that Jones misunderstood his point and that tension within the character Clay is not properly dramatized. His views originate in Jones's failure to render into action the complexity of character because of the other character he had to "fry." The failure to follow through with the tension was because it did not serve Jones's moral purpose, which was essentially to destroy the moral purpose of the play, written, as Roth stated in his review, so that a white audience would be moved not to pity or fear but to humiliation and self-hatred.

His review of the Baldwin play, referred to by one writer as "incisive and penetrating," concludes that the characters do not seem real because they are not adults but juvenile delinquents,[33] and these alienated youth strike out blindly at society. Roth should have noted, wrote Walter R. Dean Jr., a leader in the 1950s civil rights movement and then a Maryland legislator, that Negro characters have a point but that before "a Negro can really *be* an American" he must "attack senselessly" and "break down the walls which existentially bind him" so that he can "coolly commit suicide in order to be born again." Roth replied that Baldwin's characters are not delinquents and that the writer's view is unjustifiably pessimistic *and* cavalier.[34]

His review of Albee's *Tiny Alice* the following year (25 February 1965) led again to complaints because Roth presents Albee as having a dirty secret in the play he cannot reveal.[35] The title of the work itself is homosexual slang for a masculine *derrière,* as Morris Belsnick explains. Does Roth point to the play's homosexuality as its meaning or just to identify its commonplace Freudian structure?[36]

A confident Roth responds to the series of letter writers by stating that what one academic thinks is symbolism, Roth thinks is decoration. And what the writer believes is a metaphysical theme is no more than a banal cliché. What Roth is asking from homosexual playwrights in America is not a cover-up but "*less* defensiveness." Only that way does one begin to embrace or defy what is unusual in his nature, a point Professor John V. Hagopian (author of the first letter) would understand immediately if Roth had been more obscure, he sarcastically concludes. And of the third writer, who pointed out the pun in the title, Roth asserts that if it is intentional, the play "is even worse than I thought it was."[37]

These exchanges show a witty, self-possessed Roth, unafraid to state his views and justify them, which would soon be evident in sections of *Portnoy* that began to appear first with "A Jewish Patient Begins His Analysis" in *Esquire* (April 1967), fully and dramatically rendered in the questioning but self-assured voice of self-discovery that sustains the entire novel.

As Roth began to publish his short stories, he was asked to adapt some of his work for TV, such as "Defender of the Faith" for *Playhouse 90.* When he learned that the Ford Foundation had grants for young playwrights, he set about drafting a work. In 1965, in fact, he tells an interviewer that in the preceding year he took time off working on his new novel (*When She Was Good*) to write a long play and two one-acts that combined fantasy and form (CWPR 11). This is likely the unproduced work "The Nice Jewish Boy," drafted in 1963.

The play is about a young woman who unexpectedly visits her actor-apprentice boyfriend in New York after a five-week absence and her conflict with his parents. Lucy, angry at her boyfriend, at one point claims, "You never say what you feel, Mendy—you're so busy standing guard over your little ego-maniacal life!" She claims she is pregnant, but the boyfriend doesn't believe her, even after a pregnancy test (shades of Maggie's deception of Roth). He wants her to leave, while his father, visiting from L.A., tries to buy her off. At the end, however, the guilt of Lawrence Mendelson overwhelms him, and he falls to his knees and begs her to tell his father they're getting married: "Tell me I'm good, I'm good." Lucy: "Oh you are. You are. You are very very very very good." The need for approval and the goodness of the nice Jewish boy overwhelm his knowledge that their future is desperate. This is an essential Rothian situation: he acts badly but wants to be thought of as good and makes the wrong decisions thinking they will result in good. It is an extension of Roth's savior complex. He actually canceled a staged reading because he was uncertain how to use the story of Lucy's betrayal.[38] Roth kept the name Lucy, however: she becomes the protagonist of *When She Was Good* (RMY 26).

With his Ford Foundation grant, Roth was able to have "The Nice Jewish Boy" read at the American Place Theater, but hearing it thoroughly confused him, he said. Theatrical dialogue, he admitted, is narratively challenging. But in the summer of 1966, his Vineyard friend Robert Brustein, then director of the Yale School of Drama, noted that Roth was halfway through a comic play he called "The Lone Ranger," which he wanted to produce. It remained unfinished.[39]

In 1964, his short story "An Actor's Life for Me," dealing with a similar situation of a weak male, although this time not Jewish, appeared in the January issue of *Playboy*. In it, Roth uses the theater world as the context for the story of the disintegrating marriage of Walter Appel, fledgling playwright, and his wife, Juliet, who is seeking an acting career. In New York, they find themselves outclassed. Walter has an affair when he temporarily leaves his wife and then begins a job on the business side of the theater. His wife begins to work as an assistant to a producer, giving up any wish to be an actor. On a trip to London, Walter falls for the voluptuous Tarsila Brown, wife of the successful if profligate British playwright Foxie Brown.

Feeling remorse for his actions, he questions Tarsila's behavior as nothing more than theatrics, what she felt for him only an act—much of this anticipating what Roth will show with Eva Frame in *I Married a Communist*. The story combines sexuality with broad, if indefinite references to psychiatry with behavior that is more performative than genuine. Walter's future will be acting, even in loving his wife. Roth, confronting his own situation in his own psychoanalytic sessions, here works around the subject of psychiatry rather than integrates it into his story. The psychological remains outside the characters, the narrator only reporting what they feel rather than letting us feel it. But the story is a step toward the inner life he will develop with Alex Portnoy.

Another work from this period before he began *When She Was Good* was similarly titled "The Nice Jewish Boy" but subtitled "A Masochistic Extravaganza." It would become part of the first draft of *Portnoy's Complaint.* This may also be the two-hundred-page manuscript titled "The Jewboy," loosely based on growing up in Newark and discussed in *Reading Myself and Others* (RMY 29–30). Although unfocused, Roth continued to write, attempting stories in different genres, balancing his effort to maintain his contrived Willa-Catherish, midwestern tone (to dominate *When She Was Good*) with a freewheeling, wisecracking energy in a set of unpublished pieces, a tone he consciously worked to curtail, believing he had an obligation to a greater American literary tradition defined by Hawthorne and James. He outlined the back-and-forth process between styles of fantasy and reality as typical of how his work evolved, while serving as a means to alternately check and indulge his inspiration: "The idea, in part, is to keep alive fictions that draw their energy from different sources" (RMY 31).

Importantly, it took Roth five years to convert Maggie's history into his second novel, which would be the longest time he would take between published works, with money a constant issue: alimony and court costs drained every dollar he could earn from teaching and writing. He had to borrow from Joe Fox to pay for his analysis. But he knew he had to write himself free of Maggie, a difficult task which laboring on *When She Was Good* partly permitted, although it would take *My Life as a Man* (published seven years later) to achieve actual liberation. In March 1967, he told his London friend Vernon Gibberd that it took close to four years to complete *When She Was Good,* "much of the time spent howling with pain—but I'm pleased with it."[40]

Yet the issues with Maggie persisted, Roth telling Fox about his "divorce horror" in September 1964. In the theater one evening with Holly, then twelve, he was handed a subpoena as he sat in his seat; unsure what it was for, he knew only that Maggie's lawyers had issued it because he had previously been served by the same polite man at the dentist's. In the men's room, he opened the order to reappear in court. He could have been served at his apartment, but, he believed, Maggie wanted to expose her daughter to another scene of conflict and humiliation (FAC 142). Incensed, he told Fox, "Murder is often on my mind and maybe in the end I will take a swing at somebody. I wouldn't mind it."[41]

Correspondence throughout 1964 with his lawyer Shirley Fingerhood, later Solotaroff's wife, shows the financial and psychological strain of his breakup with Maggie.[42] It even made the papers: the New York Daily News headline for a 14 April 1964 story read "Walked Out on the Platinum!" The reporter, Alfred Albelli, was a specialist in divorce trials. Appearing on the same page as Roy M. Cohn resting his case in federal court on charges of perjury and conspiracy, the Daily News story, with a photo of Maggie, reports that Roth walked out "on his platinum blonde wife, Margaret, just as she charged." The allusion was to Jean Harlow's hair color and her starring in the 1931 film Platinum Blonde, which had a Newark connection. Longy Zwillman had spotted Harlow backstage at a publicity event at the Adams Theater in Newark for a 1930s war movie, Hell's Angels; within weeks he began to pay for her schooling in acting and fashion. She soon became his mistress, and he pressured Howard Hughes into giving her bigger roles and better scripts, getting her a two-picture deal with Columbia facilitated by making a large cash loan to the studio head, Harry Cohn. Platinum Blonde, directed by Frank Capra, was a modest hit but greatly contributed to her legend.

In court, Roth had no objection to a separation decree, but he could not afford the proposed $1,500-a-month alimony. Maggie, countering, presented what she believed to be the income of the thirty-one-year-old writer. Noting their marriage on 22 February 1959, the reporter writes, "After a delayed European honeymoon the following winter, [they] settled down to the good life in Princeton—but not for long. Roth packed up and left on 1 March 1963." This is slightly distorted factually; to Justice Samuel C. Coleman, Roth explained that he was not doing well financially and had just started two one-act plays. The judge reserved his decision "on the whole business."[43]

In My Life as a Man, Roth recalls the presence of Albelli, transformed into "the stout, black-coated Mr. Valducci of the Daily News" (MLM 263). In the novel, Tarnopol verbally attacks him, the next day's headline reading, "Prize-winning Author Turns Courtroom Prizefighter," since Tarnopol also took a swing at Maureen's lawyer. He also refers to photos that in fact appeared in the actual Daily News story. Tarnopol's reaction is pure anger, telling Spielvogel that to be done with it, he should have killed the reporter as well as the judge, plus Maureen and her lawyer (MLM 264).[44]

Earlier, on 12 November 1963, temporary alimony was awarded to Maggie, although the judgment did not determine liability for her debts incurred before that date. The 13 April 1964 trial was to formalize grounds for separation, the action claiming that the reason was the defendant's supposed abandonment of Mrs. Roth and nonsupport on 1 March 1963. By 1 September 1964, a formal separation agreement had been signed, all matters handled by Shirley Fingerhood.[45]

But Maggie continued to be difficult: in July 1964, she refused to sign a joint tax return unless it was "worth her while," and in September Roth received a summons, Fingerhood telling him not to worry—why would they litigate when things can be settled? But Roth tried to get the alimony payments ($150 a week) reduced. His lawyer told him to wait, pointing out that his 1964 income was pretty good. Postpone any action until early in 1965 so you can show your income is small, Fingerhood advised. And don't spend too much on an apartment because it will not look good "if, with your analyst's bills and your legal obligations to Maggie, you are extravagant."[46]

In July 1965, a court-appointed referee recommended a reduction of weekly alimony to $110, partly because of Roth's uncertain income. That year he had a Ford Foundation grant of $700 a month and lecture fees and copyright payments for use of his work that totaled $3,000. His expenses included amounts shared with or dispensed for the benefit of Maggie's two children, including paying for a hosteling trip for David, although Roth was under no legal obligation to support them. Roth also reported that he received $1,430 from *Esquire* for "The Psychoanalytical Special."

In May 1966, Roth provided a full accounting of his income, confirming that he had few resources. From his writing, $3,183; teaching at University of Pennsylvania and Stony Brook, $4,600; nine months of a year's $8,000 grant = $6,000. The total for the year: $13,783. A month later, he worried about his increased income and the court's reaction if *When She Was Good* were accepted and he received an anticipated advance of $7,650.[47]

Increasingly desperate, in August 1966 he was prepared to take a teaching job at the University of Arkansas in Fayetteville offered to him by Bill Harrison, a former Iowa writing student. He would live there for two years, which would allow him to file for divorce without Maggie's consent. His attachment to a new woman, Ann Mudge, however, prevented him from following through.

In September 1966, a revised formal separation agreement was finalized, noting that they were married on 22 February 1959 in Yonkers, New York, that Roth would pay Maggie $5,000 as a lump sum and then $110 weekly until September 1969 so long as she did not remarry. But all of this became null and void when Maggie died in a car crash in Central Park in May 1968. Roth admitted relief that the arrangement was over.

Fingerhood continued to act for Roth throughout 1968 and 1969, advising him on how to deal with his sizable payments as *Portnoy's Complaint* was being negotiated. The question became tax deferral. He considered literary fellowships at Yaddo and a series of units (an asset package of preferred and ordinary shares with the possible addition of a warrant to acquire or sell additional units) from Prudential Oil which cost $10,000 each but were 80 percent tax deductible. He even considered real estate investments, but of the three choices, he chose the oil units. One additional matter that disturbed him were remarks made by Truman Capote on the Johnny Carson show. As reported to Roth, they sounded defamatory, and he asked Fingerhood to get a transcript and investigate. Even Fox wrote to Roth in April 1969 to say Capote's comments were outrageous. They likely had to do with his view of a "Jewish Mafia in American letters," which Capote elaborated in a 1968 *Playboy* magazine interview.[48] Roth decided to take no action, possibly because of the expense and difficulty in proving defamation.

During this distracting time, Roth managed to support the anti-Vietnam movement. In 1967, in response to the Gulf of Tonkin Resolution, he joined a group on Martha's Vineyard, where he would often vacation with Ann Mudge, in signing a petition published in the *Vineyard Gazette* of 23 August 1967 protesting the testimony of Undersecretary of State Nicholas de B. Katzenbach, and asking him to speak out against President Johnson and his "diplomacy of violence."[49] Other signatories included Robert Brustein, William Styron, Lillian Hellmann, John Hersey, Jules Feiffer, and John Marquand Jr. In February 1968, he donated the manuscript of "Novotny's Pain" to the 5th Avenue Peace Parade auction. In a letter to the committee, he wrote that Solotaroff had the manuscript of "The Jewish Blues" if they wanted another sale item. In turn, the committee told Roth that the "Novotny" manuscript had been acquired by the book dealer Robert Wilson (Phoenix Books) for $80.

In 1970, in response to the My Lai massacre in Vietnam, Brustein organized *The War Show* with his company, with proceeds going to Vietnamese children. At a performance, he read Roth's "The President Addresses the Nation," which became an addendum to *Our Gang*. It consists of Nixon addressing the country from the Oval Office, acknowledging the right of

Congress to impeach him but his refusal to leave. The hypocrisy was rampant in Brustein's portrayal of Nixon, with the added terror of a group of actors in National Guard uniforms who suddenly appeared in the aisles to protect the victorious but disgraced president.

After the success of *Goodbye, Columbus*, expectations were high for another hit, and *Letting Go*, published in June 1962 with a fourth printing in September, seemed to be that book. A Book Find Club edition appeared in August 1962; a Bantam paperback edition appeared in June 1963, with a third printing in April 1967. But overall sales slumped. Many found the book depressing, with its set of failed relationships and unsuccessful ending. The anger and distress of the couples likely reflected Roth's own situation with Maggie, who was the ironic dedicatee of the book. He moved on to *When She Was Good*, a period documented by Albert Goldman in a *Life* magazine profile of 1969.

The novel became, Goldman says, Roth's "primary obsession," writing and rewriting it for years.[50] His apartment had four large cartons stuffed with the manuscript, but he was so invested in it he could not tell what was good or bad. One day he put the latest draft in his briefcase and went to the expansive Rose Reading Room of the New York Public Library at 42nd Street and Fifth Avenue. In the quiet, he read through what he had done and found it unpublishable. Walking into Bryant Park behind the Carrère and Hastings–designed Beaux-Arts structure, the largest marble building in the United States at its opening, he thought of teaching as his salvation, but went instead to Yaddo.

Yaddo, the four-hundred-acre writer's colony in Saratoga Springs, New York, would become his retreat and sanctuary where, in semi-isolation, he was able to work on, and nearly complete, *When She Was Good*, called at this time "Time Away." In many ways, this was a working out of his attraction and repulsion toward Maggie and what she and the Midwest represented. Yaddo became a home without family for him, allowing him the security to write; its routine was a comfort. He would make annual five- to eight-week visits to Yaddo until 1972. He first visited in 1963, the year after he legally separated from Maggie and the year he began his intense psychoanalysis, initially funded by Fox. A promissory note indicates that he borrowed $2,000 from Fox at 5.5 percent interest per year; it was dated 15 November 1965.

Founded in 1926, over the years the artists' retreat hosted Langston Hughes, Aaron Copland, Truman Capote, and Saul Bellow. Spencer Trask (a financier) and his wife Katrina (a poet), had bought the property in 1881.

The current mansion of fifty-five rooms plus surrounding studios was built in 1893 in the Queen Anne Revival style following an 1891 fire that destroyed the Trasks' original home. Their small daughter suggested the name "Yaddo," partly because it rhymed with "shadow." All four of their children were lost to illness at early ages.

The reputation of Yaddo over the years grew; among the books that were written there (or supposedly were written there) were Roth's *When She Was Good* and most of *Portnoy's Complaint*, part of Alfred Kazin's *A Walker in the City*, most of Rick Moody's *Purple America*, and Alan Lelchuk's *American Mischief*.[51] Other writers who stayed at varying times included James Baldwin, Dorothy Parker, William Carlos Williams, Ted Hughes, Sylvia Plath, Elizabeth Bishop, John Cheever, newlywed Delmore Schwartz (who snuck his wife in), Anne Carson, and David Foster Wallace. Philip Guston, the artist and later a friend of Roth's, was also a guest.

Sex, as well as sophistication, characterized Yaddo time, cut off from publicity, publishers, and the public. Roth cherished the independence. In *The Ghost Writer*, Yaddo appears as the Quahsay Colony, where Nathan Zuckerman retreats to write. Later, Roth would become a director of its foundation. Brustein remembered a visit to the retreat in 1968 to find Roth phonetically teaching four-letter words to a somewhat decorous woman writer from New Zealand. Laughter could be the only response.[52]

More important, perhaps, Yaddo initiated Roth's love of the country, possibly first experienced by excursions as a child to the South Orange Mountains outside of Newark. The rural, the pastoral, took him to a virgin land, and his life in Iowa, Yaddo, and then Woodstock before his home at Cornwall Bridge reconnected him to a certain natural tranquility. It not only connected him with America's natural history but allowed him escape from the pressure of success and public expectations. He could remain the writer he wanted to be, separated from the publicity whose attention soon became overwhelming.

Roth's connection to the land, initially the need to escape from Maggie, his editor, and the distractions of New York in order to complete his second novel (and later the necessity of escaping the publicity surrounding *Portnoy's Complaint* and the urban entrapment of New York), underscores his success in locating an alternate America, partially attained by Swede Levov when he settles in Rimrock, New Jersey, or Zuckerman in the Berkshires in *The Human Stain*. Avoiding the urban in favor of the country, he discovered a space in which to write, think, and gain distance on his own life, although he still maintained a *pied-à-terre* in New York. But his rustic Cornwall Bridge home (bought in 1972), with its barn and writing studio and surrounding acreage (expanded over the years to almost 150 acres), provided solace. Nevertheless, the urban settings of his fiction continued, excepting only *The Ghost Writer* and *The Human Stain*. Again, a Rothian contradiction: loving the land and life there but still unable to give up the city, a kind of Newark hangover. The land became one of a series of metaphors for American beginnings, evoking the trope of the American Adam.[53]

To write America for Roth was initially to inherit the world of Cather, Dreiser, Sinclair Lewis, and Bellow, but Cather in particular. A work like *O Pioneer* is entirely about the land and the movement west, buttressed by the irony that from 1906 virtually until her death in 1947, Cather lived mostly in Greenwich Village. Roth, while he wrote frequently of Newark, did not live there after he turned nineteen and went off to Bucknell in 1951.

By August 1966, Roth was revising and worried about the reception of *When She Was Good*, telling Klopfer on 26 August that he was surprised to hear of a debate at Random House about the salability of the book. Why, then, the big advance, he asks? He believes it's the best work he's done and cites praise from the critic Philip Rahv. By October, Roth was in the final preparations for publication, expressing to Fox characteristic concern over its promotion. He was in New York, moving to 300 East 33rd Street at the end of the month, and had developed a curious habit of not answering his phone; Fox had to send him telegrams asking that Roth call him. The dedication to the novel, as he outlined earlier in July, was to include a long list of those who helped him transition from his difficult relationship with Maggie to a more stable relationship with his new love. The dedication included his brother, Alison Bishop, Robert Brustein, George P. Elliott and his wife, Howard Stein, Mel Tumin, and last but separately, Ann Mudge, "For words spoken and deeds done."

While *When She Was Good* was in production, jacket copy suddenly became an issue. Roth wrote most of it.[54] Some, however, thought it too abstract. The first paragraph emphasizes Lucy Nelson's belief in her moral superiority and the lengths she goes to prove herself right and the destruction it brings. He then emphasizes how Lucy's crusade is to get men to live up to their responsibilities, beginning with her alcoholic father and then her "boyish young husband," Roy Bassart, "one of the author's most brilliant portrayals." James and Dreiser are mentioned and the possibility that Lucy may take her place with their heroines. For Lucy, men are to be strong and yet obedient, an impossible situation. To quote the jacket, she is both "ordinary and pathological" in her pursuit of "moral perfection." The author photo by Naomi Savage is a close-up of a dark Roth romantically staring at the reader.

The first printing of *When She Was Good*, Fox reported, was 25,000, with a break-even figure of 15,087. Fox told the head of sales that Roth would not speak at their sales conference: he is so sensitive about the book that he "can't stand hearing any criticism about it, no matter how rational."[55] A shorter work than *Letting Go*, at 306 pages, with a dramatic pink cover of a woman's face and white and yellow lettering, *When She Was Good* would meet with widespread critical attention, although most of it negative.

In early November, bound review copies went out to Alfred Kazin, Paul Engle of the Iowa Writers' Workshop, George Steiner, and others; earlier Roth had given a copy of the manuscript to Philip Rahv. Fox soon received a letter from Roth stating his unhappiness with the production: the author, Fox told the production manager, had "very fixed and stubborn convictions about almost everything to do with his book and he is not happy about the front matter of *When She Was Good*."[56] One early reader reported that the appeal of the book was that there are no Jewish characters. The price, which he did not criticize, was $5.95.

When finished copies reached Roth in late January 1967, he was incensed, and in a letter to Fox, provided a list of errors. On page 232, ten lines up from bottom, for example, the sentence should end with a period, not an ellipsis. He wanted a blank page before the biographical note, especially given the effects he hopes to produce with the final paragraph of the novel. The official publication date was 6 March 1967. When he sees a copy of the advertisement to appear in *Harper's*, the *Atlantic*, and the *New Yorker*, he corrects it. The word "satiric" should not appear—that is what my "*next* novel is going to be," he tells Fox.[57]

A long letter of 5 August 1967 from Roth to Fox harshly criticizes the low advertising budget, claiming it should have been explained to him earlier. He reminds Fox that the two of them have had grievances large and small since he handed in the manuscript, and while he welcomed Fox's opposition in the past—indeed, Fox's strong-mindedness and will appealed to him when deciding on a new editor—for the past ten months such opposition has struck him as "pointless negativism of a kind I couldn't make any sense of or any use of."[58] Too often he has been cast as the "pushy" writer, and he's had enough. The problem is that he believes he is no longer proving himself as a writer. And publishers must support and invest in their writers: that's what an advance is for. He also resents being thought touchy or oversensitive. Importantly, Roth writes that he feels he has earned what he wants in terms of an advance, advertising, and promotion. It's simple: either you and Cerf agree or you do not. This bitter and aggressive letter ends with a P.S. to add that he has nothing to say about Fox's decision to call Roth's analyst for his own therapy.

The disagreement grew until abusive sentences appeared in each other's notes, such as this question from Fox in January 1968: "Why the fuck should I justify myself to you?"[59] The next month, Roth encloses a check for $3,554 in payment for monies borrowed in November 1965 at 5 percent interest. It was for his Kleinschmidt therapy bills. Their deteriorating relationship clouded the appearance and reception of *When She Was Good*, which was not warm.

An early reader was Solotaroff. Writing to Roth in December 1966, he describes staying up to 4:00 a.m. to finish the novel, which he calls "very unfashionable, brave and true," the last fifty pages particularly powerful. He's especially taken with Roth's decision to be dull with the dull, citing Auden's phrase to be "faithful to the truth of the life you're describing." He's impressed, too, by the authority with which Roth invented his world, plus the narrative skill to keep it moving to its inexorable end.[60] The writer and journalist Josephine Herbst also wrote a letter of praise, highlighting the book's concreteness as the source of what makes the "the whole thing breathe." You powerfully convey the ordinary world, she wrote, giving it a dramatic stature. Even when they are warped, your women are human beings. Lucy is "kind of like our official national face; so self-righteous, so sure everyone else is wrong. She has meanings beyond her own individual one."[61]

The press, however, was less understanding, the *New York Times* particularly harsh. The novelist Wilfrid Sheed criticized Roth for thinking he could write a novel about white Anglo-Saxon life, not realizing that the "highstrung, socially impacted novel" no longer exists, that it takes an outsider to invent it. All Roth has done is superimpose his own sense "of social textures onto his Lutheran characters, making them just like Jews only duller."[62] The novel is nothing more than an old-fashioned family melodrama. These are linear people in a linear novel. What Roth has achieved with *When She Was Good*, Sheed concludes, is a nineteenth-century novel out of step with the mid-twentieth.

Robert Alter in *Commentary* opened his review with this memorable indictment: "The kindest thing one can say about Philip Roth's new novel is that it is a brave mistake." Trapped by his initial success, Roth clearly hoped *When She Was Good* would be his way out of the "narrow precincts of Jewish urban and suburban life."[63]

Roth himself maintained a positive view of the work, stressing its formal properties and traditions. While writing Maggie and the Midwest out of his system and offering his version of a "Midwestern Medea," he believed he captured something of the American Midwest's landscape and character.[64] In a 1984 interview, he defended his portrait of Lucy Nelson as an unhappy adolescent who only wants a decent life, confronted by men who prevent it, resulting in a kind of rage—not unlike his perception of what brought Maggie to her deceptive behavior to control men. The work deals with Lucy's struggle to free herself from disappointment with an irresponsible father and ineffectual husband. Loss and contempt define her response to her alcoholic father, compounded by her contempt for the feckless man she marries. It is a novel about a "wounded daughter" driven by hatred and rage, not unlike Maggie at her worst (CWPR 172–73).

At thirty-four and after two books (*Goodbye, Columbus* and *Letting Go*), Roth "seems to have seen, felt and thought everything crucial to an under-standing of American family life. We repeat our errors as if by rote. . . . We hunger for love and consume our loved ones. We extract from others the price we paid for our lives. We carry expectations beyond fulfillment." And Roth doesn't tell us this; he shows it. He also has the secret of fiction: the "gift of characters."[65]

Critics soon noted parallels between Maggie and Lucy, especially the alco-holic father, early marriage, and disappointment in love. Lucy and Martha of *Letting Go* also share features, notably their dissolute fathers, college pregnan-cies, marriage to weak men, and financially strained, failed marriages. Both seem to conflate Maggie. Like the two characters, she was a Midwesterner who managed to jump class barriers by taking a few college courses before leaving to have children. All three women also work as waitresses when their future husbands meet them.

In *The Facts*, Josie (the renamed Maggie) is the angry daughter of a drunkard, oppressed by resentment over the injustices of her origins and driven to bouts of "desperate deviousness" (FAC 81). Maggie and Lucy never rise above their origins: Martha Reganhart does. Roth created Lucy during his separation from Maggie, but anger, resentment, and desperation over-whelm both Lucy and Maggie. Yet despite Roth's aggravation with Maggie, he had, in fact, relied on her, counting on her editorial judgment for his early works, while seeking to get her settled in publishing (likely a move to get rid of her) when he wrote his first novel.

It wasn't until *Portnoy's Complaint*, however, that he could praise Maggie in a backhanded, grudging way. Only when writing *Portnoy* could he "cut loose with anything approaching her gift for flabbergasting boldness. Without doubt she was my worst enemy ever, but, alas, she was also nothing less than the greatest creative-writing teacher of them all, specialist par excellence in the aesthetics of extremist fiction" (FAC 112). At the end of *The Facts*, Zuckerman raises several critical questions about Roth's marriage, particularly that he supposedly conspired to make happen to him what happened, becoming "the victim of the victim of a victim" (FAC 177). You were not that openly angry before marrying her, Zuckerman tells Roth, but now you have become an "angry angry man" (FAC 177). You aim that explosion of anger, which required psychotherapy, at her and the explosion of Portnoy at her, not at Lyndon Johnson.

But can everything about Maggie be so vengeful? She was likely both worse and better than you've portrayed her, Zuckerman suggests. She was likely an alcoholic, and you actually owe everything "you are today" to "an alcoholic shiksa" (FAC 178). And the other women? They are interchangeable, transparent, partners and pals. You shield them from your ability to see through them, which you probably do in life.

In this remarkable close to his autobiography, Roth allows his other, analytic voice to criticize his creation, sharply and frankly, something he himself cannot do in the text proper. Only by impersonating another voice can he become objective. Ross Miller, in conversation, suggested that he might have been the source for this criticism of Roth, who had given him a draft of *The Facts* to read. Miller's response, a lengthy letter, likely formulated a part of Zuckerman's.[66] Zuckerman looks in on his creator and describes honestly what Roth cannot or chooses not to see: you hold back too much and fail to see that Maggie (poorly disguised as Josie) is the heroine of the book, your "true counterself." Harshly he says that she is the one who called the shots; honor her with her real name because it is through her that you achieved your freedom from being a "lovingly manipulative good boy who would never have been much of a writer" (FAC 179–80). Her destructive force, along with that of the angry suburban Jews, threw you into the struggle with repression, inhibition, humiliation, and fear.

In an insightful passage, Zuckerman suggests that through the duality of "fanatical security" and "fanatical insecurity" Roth sees embodied in the

Jews, Josie "unearthed in her Jew and beautifully exploited." And that is not just where "the drama is rooted [but] where the madness begins" (FAC 180). Roth owes his career as a writer to her. *Goodbye, Columbus* was his; everything after, at least through *My Life as a Man* and beyond, was hers.

Roth recalls in *The Facts* the story of how he and Maggie came to be married, a story too astonishing and unbelievable to give up. In any other profession, he would have been angry and forgotten it, but as a novelist it was gold. The trick of the urine test was to have appeared in *When She Was Good* (a sign of how he linked the characters of the story with his situation), but it didn't fit; focusing on Maggie's upbringing, adolescence, and first marriage did. Visits to her hometown in northern Michigan introduced him to the saga of a gentile family with a less than wholesome past. It fascinated him (FAC 144). Her mother proved to be more capable than Maggie made out, less a defenseless victim and more able to handle life. In the novel, however, Roth chose not to present the actual woman's character but the narrative Maggie presented of a defenseless mother, making everything more vivid and dramatic.

Roth attempted to discover the origins of Maggie's life in order to understand the destructive force of her "hypermorality," a reaction to what she perceived to be the immorality of her father, mother, and first husband. (FAC 145). Liberty Corners, a stand-in for Maggie's hometown, had its mix of betrayers, enemies, and cowards. Writing the novel, he admits, was an exorcism of Maggie's narrative spell accomplished by taking her story as gospel and then enlarging it until it led to her self-destruction (FAC 145). Lucy's death at the end of *When She Was Good* was not retribution against Maggie but the result of Lucy's complete disintegration.

While the critics reacted to *When She Was Good*, Roth had begun psychoanalysis, although he had little money because of his alimony payments. He needed to borrow from his editor Joe Fox for his sessions, money he would quickly repay. He required the sessions to prevent him from what he later believed to be the possibility of committing violence: the strain of the alimony and court costs was unrelenting. The image, he said in a 1984 interview, was of a train speeding on to its destination suddenly shunted to the wrong track and speeding off into the wilds (CWPR 172). But by 23 December 1967, Roth had repaid Fox with a check for $710, of which $210 was the 5.5 percent interest on the $4,000 loan. Five hundred dollars, he pointed out, was payment toward the debt itself, now reduced to $3,500. The formality of the note and formal signature ("Philip Roth") indicates the increasing separation between Roth and his editor.

On 29 February 1968, Roth sent Fox a check for $3,554, the balance of the monies originally borrowed on 15 November 1965, the formal start of his psychoanalysis. Within five months (in June 1968), Roth would formally end his relationship with Fox, caused by disagreements over *When She Was Good*. He began his letter to Fox, "It turns out that my confidence in our relationship hasn't survived the difficulties we two had with *When She Was Good*." Fox replied to further letters from Roth with a handwritten note complaining that Roth did "not feel able to tell me [about their divided views] yourself" but relied on a third party, implying a certain cowardice on Roth's part.[67]

Roth's psychoanalysis continued throughout the period preceding the appearance of *When She Was Good* in October 1967. In fact, in April 1967, Roth's short story "A Jewish Patient Begins His Analysis" appeared in *Esquire*. Although Roth remained ambivalent toward the psychoanalytic process, his use of the therapeutic setting allowed him the freedom to create Portnoy's high-intensity voice and allowed Roth to overcome his self-destructive obsessions.

Dr. Hans J. Kleinschmidt (1913–1997) was Roth's psychiatrist. Born in East Prussia in 1913 and educated in Berlin, he began his medical training at Freiburg, but in 1933 fled to Italy, completing his medical studies at Padua. In 1939 he escaped to Jerusalem and then emigrated to the U.S. in 1946, joining Mt. Sinai Hospital in 1952 as an associate clinical professor of psychiatry. He began a practice at East 67th Street but soon had an office on Park Avenue and 79th Street (903 Park Avenue, Suite 2E).

Because of his European background and immersion in artistic culture— he was a serious collector of abstract paintings (especially Kandinsky) and understood Dada—Kleinschmidt attracted photographers, composers, artists, and writers. Richard Avedon, Leonard Bernstein, and Adam Gopnik were among his patients.[68] He edited the memoirs of Richard Huelsenbeck, a psychoanalyst who founded the Berlin Dada group and later emigrated to the U.S. to escape Nazi authorities. *Dada Drummer* was the title of Kleinschmidt's book.

An essay by Gopnik details his six years of analysis (1990–96) with Kleinschmidt, whom Gopnik calls Dr. Grosskurth, outlining his method, from silence as the patient spoke to details of his office furnishings: an Eames couch and Robert Motherwell prints. He was tall, commanding, and humorless, preferring dark suits and heavy handmade shoes.[69] He boasted about his "creative people" and spoke freely about their work and habits. His bookshelves contained volumes of a psychoanalytic journal "rising to the ceiling."

Since Gopnik saw him in the early evening, the room was only half-lit, the sitting room possessing a "European melancholia, as though directed by Pabst." What Gopnik learned during these sessions were essential words, especially "banter" and "genre studies," the former the actual import of criticism, the latter a code word for journalese.

Gopnik also summarizes Kleinschmidt's view of artists: they all suffer from a rage originating in a disappointed narcissism, which could "take a negative, paranoid form or a positive, defiant arrogant form." The psychiatrist's job was not to cure the narcissism but to fortify it, protect it. He used the analogy of a fort, suggesting that the major figures in New York literary life were similar to a chain of forts surrounding Lake George in upstate New York. Fort Mailer, Fort Sontag, Fort Frankenthaler, all defended the writer or artist. This is a metaphor with application to Roth, who seems to have surrounded himself with a cadre of devoted, protective defenders, including himself; when those supporters question their role, they are dismissed, a pattern followed by many of his friendships over the years.[70]

Another habit of Kleinschmidt's, in Gopnik's account, was his preference for monologues, often on the touchstones of twentieth-century European intellectual history, with a preference for Freud and Thomas Mann. Roth appears to have transposed that to Portnoy, although some elements of it appear in Spielvogel, the psychiatrist in *My Life as a Man*. And Kleinschmidt seemed to enjoy bringing in the scandalous or off-color, telling Gopnik that the great theologian Martin Buber kept pornographic images on the lectern, mixed in with his lecture notes. The pictures would excite him to "a greater performance as a lecture."

Although not an orthodox Freudian, he was, nevertheless, wedded to psychoanalytic dogma and the Freudian idea that shaping human life is a series of "selfish, ineradicable urges, particularly sexual ones"; everything else in life works to tone down these urges to make them acceptable. Another habit unnerved Gopnik: Kleinschmidt often fell asleep, awakened only when he heard or partially heard gossip. Gopnik's example was idle talk about Roth's divorce from Claire Bloom. Instantly, Kleinschmidt would jerk up and listen.

According to Gopnik, Kleinschmidt's practice blended a turn toward, but never exclusive attention to, Freud united with a sense of the practical. His central approach was that "you don't want to overcome your narcissism, or self-attention, but you want to use it to build an impregnable fortress that will defend you from the world." The idea of a fortress resonated with Roth, who kept his intimate feelings private, expressed only through not so hidden

transpositions in his fiction. The relationship between narcissism and creative anger is built-in; an artist has to use it, but productively, not neurotic-
ally.[71] A further element of Kleinschmidt's therapy was that he was against
using children or fathering as a means of psychic healing (ironic, since he
was the father of four). Parenting, he thought, was only "a kind of sentimental
displaced narcissism."[72] Roth avoided that trap: he never had children of his
own, although he became quite attached to Holly Williams and later to the
twins of Julia Golier.

In Roth's sessions with Kleinschmidt, he discovered the method and substance of *Portnoy*. Kleinschmidt may have misunderstood Roth's relationship with his parents or thought of it too simply (his father was not weak,
but tenacious), but Kleinschmidt pointed a way for Roth to write out of or
from his own anxieties. The Portnoy family of the weak father and dominant mother was not his family but a kind of folk family reconfirmed through
the stories the Jewish students at Iowa wrote for him.[73] Combined with
the almost parodic presentation of Freudian issues by Kleinschmidt, Roth
projected Freudian thought to extremes, making unceasing lust natural and
Jewish mothers universal.

In 1967, the same year *When She Was Good* appeared and portions of
Portnoy's Complaint were published in *Esquire* and the *New American Review*,
Kleinschmidt published a thirty-page essay in *American Imago* entitled "The
Angry Act: The Role of Aggression in Creativity."[74] The essay was part of an
issue devoted to "Genius, Psychopathology and Creativity," and the general
editor confidently concluded his introduction by stating that "psychoanalysis rarely, if ever, plucks out the inner-most core of a patient's neurosis."[75]
The titles of other essays in the issue include "Clinical Aspects of Creativity"
and "Psychopathology and Creativity."

Kleinschmidt's essay explores family dynamics, narcissism, and creativity,
emphasizing that creativity, in particular, represents "a temporal triumph
over human conflict." The making of symbols is the primary focus of art; the
primary focus of psychoanalysis is understanding "the conditions underlying the emotions that are being symbolized." Narcissism emerges as a defense for the artist for being different, which causes alienation or separation
from normal society. It also protects artists from emotional vulnerability or
attachment, a working out of anger against the dominant love of the mother
and rage against an ineffectual or weak father. The unique identity achieved
through a creative act justifies aggression toward the mother, for if the artist
is unique his dissatisfaction in that relationship "is warranted," Kleinschmidt

posits. But guilt over such aggression results in feelings of unworthiness, which can be offset only by "a further push toward narcissism."[76]

Narcissism restores balance in the ego threatened by anger at the parents, Kleinschmidt writes and cites Roth's favorite European writer, Kafka, both in his letter to his father and *The Trial*. The narcissist, he adds, has almost total disregard for other people's needs, a safety valve against the possibly dangerous implications of involvement in object relations. But, he adds, the "narcissistic world is an emotional vacuum" and precludes compromise.[77] Kleinschmidt then moves to a detailed discussion of Kandinsky and Mann, reiterating his controversial view that the artist "*is the irresponsible brother of the criminal and the outcast.*"[78] He then adds that it is likely that "a man has to be at home in some kind of jail in order to become a poet."[79]

Kleinschmidt moves on to two case studies, noting again that in performing the angry act—making art—the artist is capable of confronting "emotional reality without involving himself in it." Establishing such a unique identity and the artistic object means "to have committed the crime, the angry act."[80] Kleinschmidt then discusses his patient, an artist who has been preoccupied with death, whose primary defense is narcissistic detachment, including the denial of his "emotional history," a useful Kleinschmidtian term. For him and for the playwright Kleinschmidt discusses next (a disguised Roth), "to accept love means loss of identity through the breakdown of [a] major defense, the narcissistic detachment."[81] The remark has direct application to Roth and his resistance to sustained female relationships.

Details of Kleinschmidt's next patient, a southern playwright, broadly parallel Roth's history, from ambivalence at leaving his wife several years his senior to a prolonged custody battle over her son, although for Roth it was Maggie's daughter and son. The patient felt very much the hero for the victory of joint custody, echoed by Gabe Wallace's securing the adopted baby for Paul and Libby Herz in *Letting Go*. But dependency of the children on Roth as a surrogate father might have created further hesitation about leaving the mother.[82]

Particularly galling to Roth was an incident he disclosed to Kleinschmidt which appeared in "The Jewish Blues" and which was repeated in "The Angry Act." In Roth's story in the *New American Review* volume 1, Alex recounts his humiliation at eleven when he wants a bathing suit with a jock strap. "You don't need one. You have such a little one that it makes no difference," says his mother (JB 145). He's devastated. In *Portnoy's Complaint* the event appears on page 51. The identical episode appears on page 125 of "The Angry Act," although in the disguised experience of the southern playwright. The suggestion is that the castrating mother creates the rage of creativity in the child's response to the threat of normal love. Narcissism becomes a defense against anxiety. What the incident reveals, echoed by its presentation in "The Jewish Blues," is, first, betrayal and, second, the construction of a family saga that validates the theory of narcissistic aggression.

Such aggression dominates the pages of *Portnoy*, at one point Alex admonishing Dr. Spielvogel, "PUT THE ID BACK IN YID! Liberate this nice Jewish boy's libido, will you please? Raise the prices if you have to—I'll pay anything!" (PC 124). Of his mother he asks, "Where did you get the idea that the most wonderful thing I could be in life was *obedient*? . . . Of all the aspirations for a creature of lusts and desires!" (PC 125). Yet he also realizes that all he does is complain. Is he delivering up truth or just *kvetching*, or is *kvetching* just a form of truth for people like him (PC 94)? In Israel, where he cannot get it up, he admits to Naomi, the redhead he cannot bed, that he says "fuck" in anger because he is "rich with rage . . . with contempt" (PC 270). Here, Roth's history of his discontent is most nakedly and immediately displayed. A last lunge at Naomi's leg results in a swift kick to his chest and defeat. He has become "impaled again upon the long ago" (PC 271).

Roth's later workup of Dr. Spielvogel in *My Life as a Man*, even including an article by him about creative artists focusing on the castration anxiety, is an oblique literary insult. Loosely based on Kleinschmidt, who actually admired Spielvogel, Roth did acknowledge that the character was "nasty." This form of literary revenge will later take shape through the Milton Appel–Irving Howe figure in *The Anatomy Lesson* and shape Eve Frame in *I Married a Communist*, inspired by Claire Bloom.

In Kleinschmidt's article, the playwright's way of avoiding a confrontation with his "feelings of anger and his dependency needs toward his wife was to act out sexually with other women."[83] Roth did this frequently before and during his marriage to Maggie in 1959 and his marriage to Bloom in 1990. When he went off to Cape Cod in the late 1950s, he had an affair with an undergraduate, opposite in temperament to his soon-to-be wife. At Iowa he spent various nights with coeds; when married to Bloom, he was repeatedly unfaithful, both in London and in the States. Of such behavior Kleinschmidt writes, "He felt castrated by his wife and restituted by his mistress." His way of avoiding painful feelings and avoiding "any true confrontation with emotional reality has always been to libidinize both anger and anxiety."[84] This sentence, more than any other in the essay, pinpoints Roth's behavior in his life and in *Portnoy's Complaint*.

Reading the essay some time after it had been published, Roth found himself easily identifiable and was livid, retaliating via the attack by Peter Tarnopol on Dr. Spielvogel in *My Life as a Man*. In the novel, Roth reveals the identity of the writer in Spielvogel's fictional essay, "Creativity: The Narcissism of the Artist," closely based on Kleinschmidt's "The Angry Act."[85]

Narcissism and aggression become the fixed poles of not only Tarnopol but Roth. Both Roth as patient and Tarnopol as character act out repressed sexual anger as a means of avoiding any confrontation with their own feelings of resentment or dependency toward their wives or other women.[86] Such hostility against women is the performance of anger by reducing them to "masturbatory sexual objects" and then using these hostile fantasies in one's "literary output," according to Kleinschmidt.[87]

Interestingly, in the excerpt from what would be a portion of the novel, the protagonist speaks of his adolescence as an "extended period of rage" against his father, a further step in "the history of my discontent" (JB 138).[88] More disturbing is that every incident described by Spielvogel in *My Life as a Man* corresponds to a similar incident in the discussion of the southern playwright in "The Angry Act." But whereas *Portnoy's Complaint* confirms the analyst's clinical interpretation in "The Angry Act," *My Life as a Man* attempts to refute the charge of artistic narcissism.

Roth's anger at discovering that an incident he included in "The Jewish Blues" contained material his analyst used in "The Angry Act" led to worry that anyone reading both would quickly identify Roth as the patient. The result was the end of Roth's sessions with Kleinschmidt and the birth of *My Life of a Man*, an extended commentary on the relationship between the creative and therapeutic processes. But *My Life as a Man* and not *Portnoy's Complaint* opens up connections most closely between Roth and "The Angry Act." In *My Life*, Tarnopol accuses Spielvogel of exposing his life to biographical scrutiny, although in some ways Roth had been asking for it.[89] The introduction of the term "narcissism" is also significant, for in Roth narcissism increasingly dominates the behavior of his characters.

Psychoanalysis not only liberated Roth's imagination to create *Portnoy's Complaint* but created a fear that what appeared in "The Angry Act" might be true. He responded in kind, aggressively confronting Kleinschmidt via his representation as Spielvogel and sustaining an anger articulated throughout the remainder of his writing career. Stung by life *and* his psychoanalyst, Roth stung back.

After writing *When She Was Good,* with its concentration on gentile dysfunction, while combating the deteriorating relationship with Maggie, Roth turned inward to unleash his Jewish inhibitions, while outwardly and personally turning to an alternate representative of non-Jewish American life, the stable Ann Mudge, a thirty-four-year-old from Pennsylvania he met one evening at Bennett Cerf's, a companion whose calmness and confidence and financial independence allowed him to concentrate on stabilizing his life and his writing.

In his fiction, Roth broke free of linear realism and narrative form for the frantic, manic, emotional, unleashed self, but in his life he sought and found in Ann the refinement and orderliness of everyday existence. The disorder now took place on the page, his overall situation expressed by a quotation by Flaubert stuck above Tarnopol's desk in *My Life as a Man* but first seen on the doorframe of William Styron's study: "Be regular and orderly in your life like a bourgeois, so that you may be violent and original in your work" (MLM 174).[90]

Ann was a socialite who occasionally modeled, appearing in *Look* in June 1962 as one of a series of international trendsetters from Paris, London, Rome, and New York "modeling the latest hair styles." More important, she represented natural beauty, *Look* calling it "a kind of beauty that is typically American yet can hold its own anywhere in the world."[91] She was twenty-nine at that time and identified as an assistant to the producers of the National Repertory Theater. Two years later (24 January 1964), the *News Courier* of Charleston, South Carolina, printed a glamorous photograph of her with swept-up hair. The caption reported that she would be attending the Diamond Ball in New York on 29 January wearing a white damask gown from Pauline Trigère. She also appeared in the 25 August 1968 Sunday *New York Times* "Fashion Report." Her taste, education, and background made her the direct opposite of Maggie.

In *The Facts,* Ann appears as May, and in appreciation of her steadying his life, Roth dedicated *When She Was Good* to her, (in addition to others) a sign of her support and importance while he completed the book. Her photo of Roth—casual, outdoors, and apparently speaking—became the author photo for the back flap of *Portnoy's Complaint.* She may have also been the prototype for "the Pilgrim" (Sarah Maulsby) in *Portnoy* and Susan McCall in *My Life as a Man,* both refined and well-educated women without anger or resentment but also without the intensity of the Jewish experience or know-ledge of the Jewish libido.

During his romance with Ann, Roth began to encounter several medical problems. At the publication party for Styron's *Confessions of Nat Turner*, a pulsing pain emerged on his right side. As his fever rose, he went to the hospital. A surgeon dressed in a tuxedo (he was heading to a formal dinner) came in and pressed down on his abdomen: Roth was in pain. When they operated, they found that his appendix had already burst and there was pus throughout his stomach cavity. It needed to be drained; he was heavily drugged, and when he woke up he found Ann—they had been together three years—at the foot of his bed. But instead of warmly greeting her, he suddenly shrieked that she should change her clothes. Put on a short skirt, he ordered, "you look like you're dressed for my funeral!"[92]

A family predisposition toward appendicitis was the genetic cause. It killed two of his uncles and nearly killed his father in 1944, becoming the opening episode of *The Facts*. Surprisingly, and perhaps disappointedly, Roth could not attribute the danger to Maggie, though she often threatened him with "murder" for his behavior, or lack thereof. A few days after the emergency operation, Ann phoned Fox from Doctors Hospital at East End Avenue and 87th that Roth was improving: intravenous feeding had stopped and he could walk with her briefly.

Ann, at Hunter and working as a volunteer counselor with a Quaker group advising young men about alternatives to the draft, came to see Roth every evening. Her own self-discovery was taking place, her strength to oppose the war marked by a decision to divest her trust of so-called war stocks. She was developing an independence that contradicted her earlier, socially bred conservatism. But Roth's recovery was slow: he was released after a month, only to return to deal with an infection, and then another month went by before he was finally discharged from the hospital. When able, he and Ann vacationed in Captiva, Florida, in February 1968 to recuperate, after a brief visit with his parents, who had rented an apartment in Miami. He gradually felt stronger and grateful to have survived.

But he was impatient and eager to get back to writing his new work, a sec-tion of which, "Whacking Off," had appeared in the *Partisan Review*. Joe Fox and Jason Epstein at Random House were eager to see more after reading a rough first draft. Most eager for him to return to work was Maggie because her alimony would again flow (FAC 141).

But five years after his separation from Maggie, he still did not have a divorce and she planned to go back to court a second time to have her alimony increased to $125 a week. New York State law at the time prevented a divorce if one party opposed the alimony amount; she did. Meanwhile, her two children were in boarding school in Chicago supported by an aunt and uncle of her first husband.

Even the intervention of Senator Robert F. Kennedy could not help. At the Vineyard in the summer of 1967, Roth and Ann had dinner with Kennedy at the home of his speechwriter, Dick Goodwin. One of ten at the table, Kennedy enjoyed Ann's presence. Asked if he intended to marry her, Roth replied that it depended if he could get a divorce in New York from his current wife. Kennedy, beaming, said he would look into it, but nothing happened (FAC 147). His assassination on 6 June 1968 shook both Roth and Ann, as had the death of Martin Luther King Jr. only a few months before, on 4 April.

But seven months after the dinner with Kennedy, Roth had hope. Writing to Gibberd in London in December 1967, he enthusiastically tells him that he may have a divorce next fall: a new state divorce law will not require the consent of the unwilling partner. He's also just finished two long sections of what would be *Portnoy* and he finds himself very different than what he was ten years ago "and just the same." Writing *When She Was Good* exorcised the devil and he "feels better for it."[93]

But ironically and unexpectedly, between the violent deaths of King and Kennedy was that of Maggie, in a car crash in Central Park in New York on 11 May 1968. She was being driven home from a party between 4:00 and 5:00 a.m.; the car went out of control and hit a tree and she died instantly, while the driver was unhurt. At the time, she was suing Roth for alimony of $300 a week. Had she lived, he writes to Gibberd, she would have fought him until he died. Holly and David seemed more baffled by these events than anything else, he adds.[94] In the same letter, he reports Holly's forthcoming marriage and refers to her as "bewitching," although she had seen much too much, referring most likely to the arguments and fights he had had with Maggie. He also notes that David flunked out of his first year of university and may be drafted.

In a 1975 interview, David recalled receiving the news of his mother's death from his sister: "She was with this black dude and [I] understand they were stoned and she was killed when he crashed his XKE into a tree at 4.30 a.m." He and his father, Dan Williams, flew to New York for the funeral.[95] The driver was her former employer, a black editor at a publishing company, who had recently fired her. Her obituary notice in the *New York Times* read:

> **Roth—Margaret M., on May 11, 1968.** Wife of Philip Roth, mother of David Williams and Holly Williams Roth. Service at Frank E. Campbell, Madison Ave. at 81st on Mon. at 1 pm.[96]

The notice is incorrect, as Roth never adopted David or Holly; their correct last name was Williams.

Roth's reaction to her death was surprise mixed with relief, telling Gibberd that he was actually a little "giddy about the immediate future." The editor survived and appeared at her funeral, as did a number of people from her therapy group, who no doubt held Roth responsible for her death. No, he did not divine Maggie's death through the fate of Lucy who freezes to death in *When She Was Good,* but a year after the publication of the novel, he was absorbed by the overlap between the novel's end and Maggie's fate. He also recalled in *The Facts* that her will might have figured in her accidental death, remembering how in an intense argument with her in the spring of 1960, driving from Italy to France, she tried to grab the wheel of their small Renault and drive off the mountain road. Her "defiant extremism" (FAC 149) would remain a mystery.[97]

Holly, now seventeen and an outspoken critic of the Vietnam War to such an extent that at school she was called "Hanoi Helen" (Holly being her nickname), had been living with Maggie in New York, and it was she who called Roth on a Saturday morning to say her mother was dead, similar to what Tarnopol in *My Life as a Man* would experience (FAC 149). Both Roth and his character expressed disbelief. Surely, it was a trick, a deception like others in their life together, he believed. Could it be true, could she have died in the very park where Roth and Ann had been participants in antiwar demonstrations? Roth went to console Holly, and while in the apartment she shared with her mother spotted his library of secondhand books. A judge deemed that half belonged to Maggie. Again, he imagined a trick and that she was actually there behind a door in the next room. "How could she be dead if I didn't do it?" he thought (FAC 151).

A Jewish funeral was what Maggie wanted and what she got on 13 May 1968 at the Frank E. Campbell Funeral Home at Madison and 81st Street, funeral home to the stars: services for no less than Rita Hayworth, Greta Garbo, Judy Garland, Mae West, Jackie Kennedy Onassis, John Lennon, and

Norman Mailer took place there.[98] Roth taxied from downtown to make the arrangements, realizing that he no longer had to economize because his alimony responsibilities were over. When he was getting out of the cab, his driver looked at him and asked, "Get the good news early?" He must have said that, Roth later wrote to Bloom, because he was likely whistling in the back of the cab as they headed north, or else the cabbie "was an angel of God's."[99]

Ironically, the rabbi who officiated at the funeral was the one who was on the record as thinking Roth a menace to the Jews for his writings. Sitting in front of the casket, Roth said to Maggie, "You're dead and I didn't have to do it." He imagined her replying, "Mazel tov!" (FAC 152). He answered for her because she could never speak back to him again. She was cremated as per her wishes but against Jewish practice.

Years later, Roth's friend Nina Schneider corrected him. In a September 1988 letter, concerning Roth's reaction to Maggie's death in *The Facts*, Schneider writes:

> You could be a bit kinder to yourself, and still not twist the facts. In fact, you and I were standing at your parlor window looking toward Campbell's funeral home when you said something like "I didn't wish her to die, I only wanted her to go away." I remember how painfully you tried to be civilized— Provincetown and the unlived season at Wellfleet (Truro) and the peculiar relationships of her job with us; a memorable walk of Commercial Street . . . and I have photos of her with Elise Asher Knit and the Rothkos. She *was* pretty and naïve looking. You weren't altogether blind. Who knew that she was no more innocent than Elise the venom-tongued, the great face[?][100]

Bob Baker wrote at the time of her death that he was shocked but not surprised: she seemed "spinning inevitably toward some such end." He and his wife, Ida, felt great pity for the pain she gave Roth and herself, as well as her children—it seemed so unnecessary. Ironically, she could have chosen otherwise. She was intelligent and possessed a "certain fey charm," but she smothered both. It seemed, he writes, that she was "deeply split; for *herself* on the one hand, she appeared to think that because a thing could be imagined that was sufficient reason to do it, while at the same time she was absolutely ruthless in the standards against which she judged others." Her "outraged presence, surfacing in legal hassles," must have conditioned nearly every one of Roth's moves.

If you were more Italian than Jewish, he tells Roth, "you'd not carve your-self so deeply, but view her as a horrid, long-term but transient *accident* that you merely happened to encounter along your pathway." But of course, Baker also knows these are only moments in a difficult and complex stage in Roth's life, although he is now able to recover his freedom.[101] But Roth's letter to Gibberd of 22 June 1968 indicates that his recovery was well underway; he announces that he'll be appearing in London "with a pal named Ann Mudge" and that he's "just made a pot of money, and the trip is designed to spend some of it."[102] A photo from their crossing on the *Île de France* shows Roth in a tuxedo and Ann in a sleeveless gown at an elegant first-class dinner.

Roth admits that it would take years for him to "decontaminate" himself of his rage. *My Life as a Man*, he would come to understand, would become less his revenge on Maggie than hers on him. Writing it became a chore with nu-merous false starts (FAC 152). Indeed, if he hadn't felt some responsibility to her children, he likely would not have attended the funeral. And if his heart was flint, as she told him as early as their first breakup in Chicago in 1956, her need for a compassionless monster as a mate was met by his need to be with someone who was not only a victim he had to "rescue" but someone who represented the American other: midwestern, non-Jewish, small-town, divorced. Marrying her was marrying an America he sought to understand. Yet her death at thirty-nine was a release.

But he may have overplayed Maggie's negative dimension. She had a much greater supportive role than he admitted; he portrayed only the bad, not the good of her. In letters to his editors, he repeatedly praised her critical sensi-bility and even reinforced her efforts to work in publishing, including sev-eral projects she proposed, although they were not fulfilled. She was also an important part of his five months in Italy, where he met Styron, Stegner, and Donald Klopfer of Random House.

Following the funeral, Roth escaped again to Yaddo, traveling by bus to the Adirondacks and rereading the first draft of the last two chapters of *Portnoy*. Virtually alone, he worked steadily in a cabin until the book was done. The hyped-up monologue of hyperbole and invention marked his new freedom via his "comical counteranalysis" (FAC 156). The work liberated him from a restricted literary past overshadowed by James and Flaubert. Replacing de-tachment and narrative poise was Jewish lightning and verbal energy. Both struck in unexpected places. No more *Portrait of a Lady* or *Madame Bovary*. Instead, it was the discharge of Jewish repression, inverting Freud as well as Kafka.

During the completion and publication of the *Portnoy's Complaint*, Roth remained with Ann. While the book worked out issues with the "ball-buster" Maggie, who until her death would not free him from his impossible marriage, Ann provided constancy and well-being. In June 1967, they rented a house on Martha's Vineyard. She was accommodating and obliging, representing to Roth yet another America, the opposite of the desperate situation with Maggie.

Ann came from a privileged family and background which she tried to evaluate and readjust. Roth describes her beauty as "delicate," fair, and green-eyed. And he offers comparisons: where Maggie, the daughter of a "working class loser," was scrappy and blunt, resentful and opportunistic, May (as he calls Ann in *The Facts*) "camouflaged her uncertainties" behind an almost self-suffocating decorum. What attracted him to both women was that they were "estranged from the very strata of American society of which they were each such distinctively emblazoned offspring" (FAC 132–33). Ann and Roth were together for five years, roughly 1964 to 1969. The positive inclusion of her in *The Facts* is testament to her important role in his post-Maggie world. But when her mother came to town, he would retreat to his small apartment in Kips Bay, while Ann entertained on East 78th Street. He was then teaching part time at the University of Pennsylvania and Stony Brook on Long Island.

But while Ann's parents did not meet Roth, Roth's met Ann because he wanted them to see how his life had been made anew. His mother, in particular, valued Ann's graciousness and good manners. This in contrast to Maggie who, when she and Roth separated, actually visited his father at his office in South Jersey and, in lieu of alimony payments she claimed had stopped, demanded money from him. When he correctly told her Roth was in fact making the payments, she then berated him for his irresponsibility (FAC 134).

Ann often tried to downplay her privileged past and adjust to Roth's New York friends. But she soon found her own friends, for whom she did occasional decorating but soon quit to enroll in Hunter College and complete an undergraduate degree that had been interrupted in 1952 during an emotional crisis at Smith College. She returned at that time to her home in Pennsylvania (in *The Facts*, he disguises it as Cleveland). Like his relationship with Maggie, however, what interested them in each other was their unlikeness.

Sexually tender, Ann was sweet-tempered and would never feign pregnancy or turn herself into a pathologically addicted female victim. Her integrity and strategy-less desire encouraged Roth's emotional and psychological regeneration, although when they did break up, the split had a devastating effect on her. And just as he had a need to release his libido in *Portnoy's Complaint*, he had a need to reveal his new self-esteem, ego, and stable sense of self, outlined in *The Facts* and aided by Ann, whose sensitivity and his own need for affection established a mutual convalescence.

Her undisguised, "unequivocal gentleness" made her as "unimpeachably Aryan as I was Jewish," Roth wrote, which she would never hide; it provided a dimension to their relationship that identified just the sort of differences "that would empower Portnoy's manic self-presentation" (FAC 137). Ann's calmness was especially important when, in the autumn of 1967, Roth's appendix burst, nearly ending his life, though he understood it as the denouement of nearly a decade that posed tests of strength.

Ann was polished and arrived without the marital baggage or sexual abuse of Maggie. Six months older than Roth, she brought a maturity of outlook that he had not experienced with Maggie. He insisted she have the first copy of *Portnoy's Complaint* when it was published on 12 January 1969. "I received your letter after I called last weekend," she writes. "Otherwise I would certainly have told you that I am very touched that you want me to have the first copy of Portnoy because I am. For different reasons I, too, am anxious to see it."[103]

Martha's Vineyard became their summer retreat largely because of Roth's New York friend, Robert Brustein, then teaching drama at Columbia and writing reviews for the *New Republic*. At the Brusteins' Upper East Side apartment, Roth often found an audience for his noisy comedy of Jewish life, the opposite of what was in *When She Was Good*, which he was completing at the time. *Portnoy's Complaint* began to materialize as entertainment for the Brusteins and their friends, who had a taste for "farcical improvisation" that he had lost touch with since leaving Chicago and living with Maggie (FAC 136). This was an audience who could sense where "reportage ended and Dada began" and enjoyed the overlap (FAC 136).

Not embarrassed by their "unrefined Jewish origins," confident of their equal American status, his new audience of "city Jews . . . felt American *through* their families' immigrant experiences," not in spite of them (FAC 136). When Roth and his listeners and readers connected, America was the point of intersection. They felt at the center of a city and a culture defined by an abrasive, hypercritical atmosphere evolving out of a response to the Vietnam War. Lyndon Johnson became the boisterous inspiration for "the extremes of theatrical combat" dividing the society, Roth writes (FAC 137). It was this presence that initially activated "the fantastical style of obscene satire" that challenged the prevailing mores (FAC 137).

These sociopolitical ingredients, Roth writes, inspired the voice and material of *Portnoy's Complaint*. Witnessing the barrage of verbal invective against Johnson gave him the energy to unleash his own verbal tsunami and inflated libido in *Portnoy*. Ironically, while in New York finishing his midwestern novel without Jews, he was in the middle of American Jewish intellectual life as measured by his receptive New York audience, rediscovering a childhood talent for comedy that would explode in *Portnoy*, which united satire and psychoanalysis. Between his appreciative audience and intense psychoanalysis, undertaken to restore "the confidence shredded to bits in my marriage," he discovered a model for the "reckless narrative disclosure" he hadn't seen in Henry James (FAC 137).

With his newfound wealth in advance of the publication of *Portnoy*, Roth paid his agent Candida Donadio her 10 percent, gave a tidy sum to his accountant for quarterly tax payments, and paid all his debts, which totaled $8,000 (FAC 157). One day he was in debt; the next he had a check for $250,000. He also bought two first-class tickets on the *Île de France* for passage to England for himself and Ann. The trip was luxurious, including a stay at the Ritz. All this in the summer of 1968, before the novel appeared. But a sudden restiveness emerged in England, and he tried to seduce a young English journalist who interviewed him; she politely declined, but not a Chinese prostitute he solicited. And even in London, he was concerned with money, sending Epstein a royalty statement from Houghton Mifflin and telling him they were doing a terrible job with the reprint rights to *Goodbye, Columbus*. They don't know what they've got—buy the rights from them, he urges his editor.

In the spring of 1968, however, Roth refers to "oceanic" personal changes in a note to Epstein and feels odd about himself, alluding to a possible separation from Ann—despite her seeing him through his life-threatening appendicitis attack and marital wars. His preference was for what he calls the hermit life, reinforced by time at Yaddo.[104] A fundamental anxiety and fear of a long-term commitment likely leading to marriage created unrest or, as Kleinschmidt might argue, a threat to his artistic anger, originating in narcissism, which sustained his art.

Roth's break with Ann after nearly five years was unquestionably traumatic. He had found her needy. She, too, was seeing a psychiatrist when he finally decided to end their relationship in mid-March through April 1969.[105] He drafted a letter to her doctor warning him of her possible reaction to the news; he begins by saying that he had written her a letter making clear to her that their affair was over. (This was typical of Roth's handling of such matters: rather than personally convey the news, he would resort to a letter or a third party, as he had done when he decided he no longer wanted Joe Fox as his editor. The letter, rather than a face-to-face meeting, hurt Fox more than their breakup.)

Paradoxically, precisely because he was free to marry Ann after Maggie died, he found the idea frightening and threatening. He did not want to be emotionally or financially "enslaved" by another marriage now that he was free (FAC 159). He could not tolerate the idea of handing over to the state control over his freedom. Neither could he become a father as defined by the state (FAC 160). His attitude is clear and his need to end his affair with Ann indisputable; it began to unravel during the early spring of 1969. The state's control of his life, finances, travel, and freedom was unacceptable. It was marriage and its legalities he rejected, not Ann. But he could not separate one from the other. Yet he was determined to be a completely "self-sufficient man" (FAC 160).

"I've tried to be firm and truthful with Ann," Roth tells her doctor, but he knows she will be "badly shaken" by his letter. He planned to mail it on 15 March 1969 (he wrote the note to the doctor on the 13th), to be received on Monday the 17th, likely after her therapy session. He wants her protected from her own "desperation," so he thought it would be better to notify the doctor first. He made no mention of the letter to her, anticipating her response would range from irritation to humiliation. A further note in Roth's hand indicates that he did not send the letter to her.[106]

Roth was right: Ann reacted strongly to the news of their breakup when he finally told her, although he did not anticipate the extent of her response. On the night of 19 April, after returning from a date with the painter Jules Olitski, whom she had been seeing as she and Roth became more distanced, she attempted to overdose with sleeping pills and bourbon, although she hadn't had a drink for some fifteen years. Olitski was apparently with her when she washed down the pills with the bourbon but then left her, according to Roth. She was unconscious for two days before her friends Barbara and John Jakobson discovered her, anxious because she did not turn up for her psychiatrist's appointment. Fortunately, she had thrown up most of the pills; the bourbon had made her sick.

Rushed to St. Luke's Hospital in New York, she survived. Roth, who was at Yaddo at the time, hurried to be with her when he learned of it on 22 April. "Why did you do this?" he asked when he entered her room. "Well, it got you here, didn't it?" she supposedly replied. He then said something like "Don't think by doing this I'm going to marry you."[107] She later wrote to friends that she hadn't yet realized the "full shock of what she did" but seemed relieved that her attempt failed. She remained in psychic pain and unhappy and went to Philadelphia to recover.[108]

In a lengthy letter dated only four days before Ann's attempted suicide, Roth wrote a detailed account to *his* psychiatrist about his doubts, anxieties, and worries. I've been in the grip of anxiety and melancholy for days, he says. But he has also been with someone new: Barbara Sproul. He has looked with her at places in Woodstock, New York, to rent for the summer. He finds her youth exciting (she was twenty-three and he thirty-six), and he tells her he loves her, admitting that he can't take the isolation he's imposed on himself over the past few months much longer. Solitude yes, isolation, no. His melancholy and anxiety have a lot to do with Ann, he admits. He misses her but he also realizes that Barbara, whom he met in December 1968 at a dinner party, is a very special young woman but "I feel on the brink of a largish unhappy emotion much of the time now."[109]

In a later letter of July 1969, Roth explains to Gibberd that his new notoriety thanks to *Portnoy* drove him out the city to Woodstock; that his new novel is for once not about narcissism but art, "that is life-and-art" (this will become *My Life as a Man*, 1974); and that Ann is a woman of quality and intelligence and his decision not to marry her was not taken casually. He still has strong feelings for her, but they were at an age where they had to "go on, and separately." Yet he accepts Al Alvarez's remark in his review of *Portnoy* that Portnoy is a "closet husband." Why, "it may even describe me," Roth acknowledging, if momentarily, his conventional side.[110] And by then, he had met a new woman.

Barbara Sproul was an attractive graduate student pursuing a PhD in religious studies when Roth encountered her at a dinner party in December 1968. They soon spent time in Woodstock, until Roth purchased his home in Cornwall Bridge. In Woodstock, where Roth went to escape the tumult over *Portnoy*, he rented a modest home tucked halfway up a hillside meadow; Sproul, who had previously rented a small cabin in the area, found it. He described the move in "Pictures by Guston" in *Shop Talk*, a collection of interviews and short profiles of writers. His isolation allowed him to write three works: *Our Gang* (1971), *The Breast* (1972), and the beginning of *The Great American Novel* (1973). He subsequently moved further west to Cornwall Bridge, near Warren, Connecticut, unafraid of "the utopia of isolation . . . the oasis defense against rage and grief." There, he located "an impregnable solitude," as Murray Ringold explains to Zuckerman in *I Married a Communist* (IMC 315). It was also the beginning of a satisfying, six-year relationship with Sproul, preceded by a familiar pattern between Roth and his publishers.

Roth was unhappy with the promotion, advertising, and print run of *When She Was Good* and blamed Random House. First to his agent Donadio, Roth repeatedly made it clear that he was disappointed. A two-and-half-page letter of 28 July 1967 outlines eleven points of unhappiness, ranging from the jacket (he asked for no illustration, but a ghastly one appeared) and the size of the first printing (only lobbying Klopfer and Cerf ensured a run of twenty-five thousand) to vulgar advertising copy, missed advertising opportunities (no ad in the *New York Times* on publication day), and reasons for not wanting a publication party: the money for it would come out of the advertising budget. The only thing that matters to him is that the book be promoted as the major work that it is, the way John Barth's *Giles Goat-Boy* (1966) was treated. Is this the way you will advertise Styron's book, Ellison's or Capote's, he asks? In a threatening tone, he says tell Cerf that he is going to watch carefully the advertising of Styron's book (*The Confessions of Nat Turner*, 1967). And he informs Donadio that he's quite fed up with Random House and Fox.[111] He feels they are not paying enough attention to him.

Donadio conveyed the complaints to Cerf and Fox in late July 1967. Fox responded with a personal letter to Roth apologizing if any of his remarks or attitude had interfered with the good work he believed they could do together. Fox had taken it all personally. Initially he was hurt, then horrified, and now he was just numb. He then, somewhat ironically, tells Roth that the situation has pushed him into therapy, reasoning that if he is so insensitive to the anguishes of someone he thought of as a close friend, he thinks he's in trouble. He called the very psychiatrist Roth was seeing, Hans J. Kleinschmidt, and spoke to him for a moment; he was departing for a vacation so was unable to see him until he returned.

By 9 August 1967, however, Fox is defending himself to Roth: if I have been negative to you and your work, everything you say is justified. He adds that such an attitude is the worst an editor can have toward a writer; he will never take that approach again. He doesn't think Roth is a prima donna, or touchy or overly sensitive, clearly feeling he must address those charges Roth has specified to him.[112] A reference to a "subtle conflict" between the two of them confuses Fox, however. Explain, he asks. He then gives information about the *New York Times* bestseller list, knowing they were knocked off it but are now back on. *When She Was Good* debuted at number 8 on 30 July 1967 competing against *The Chosen* by Chaim Potok, *Rosemary's Baby* by Ira Levin, and *Washington, D.C.* by Gore Vidal. The book disappeared the following week but came back at number 10 on 13 August. It reached 9 the following week, fell to 10 on 27 August, and then disappeared. Fox shows patience with the mercurial Roth, despite the insults and claims of insensitivity.

A month later (8 September 1967), Fox tells Cerf that *When She Was Good* had another big week and to date has sold 27,589 copies. For three or four weeks in a row they have gone over a thousand copies a week. No need to spend more on advertising—they've already spent over $14,000, although Roth is making a fuss over a seeming lack of advertisements. He had dinner with Roth the preceding night, but they did not discuss business.

The relationship between author and editor was clearly fraying. Ten months later, in a letter of 28 July 1968, Roth expressed his lack of confidence in Fox. The difficulties over *When She Was Good* led to their deteriorating association, hastened by Fox's caution against Roth's asking for a $250,000 advance for *Portnoy*. Roth did not listen to him and received the amount from Random House. Roth went on in his letter: It makes little sense to go on struggling against one another. You were a great help when I first joined Random House, but now our ideas diverge as they relate to my work and career. What he feels is best for him differs from what Fox believes. Fox's curt reply, sent the same day, is "I'm sorry, for both our sakes, that you did not feel able to tell me yourself"—in person.[113] Roth, despite his upset, avoided a person-to-person meeting, unable to face Fox directly with his complaints.

As a gesture of truce and support for Roth, on 21 August Fox wrote enthusiastically about "Whacking Off," one of the early sections of *Portnoy*, reporting that at a dinner with Jason Epstein, his wife, and others, Epstein read aloud portions of the section. He had to stop because he was giggling so uncontrollably; Fox took over. The passage floored everyone. Nine days later, he tells Roth that sales figures for *When She Was Good* totaled 26,931 with 1,331 sold in the past week alone. But Roth remained dissatisfied with Fox, while action on *Portnoy* was beginning.

Fox that month soon reported to Epstein that film rights for *Portnoy's Complaint* were sold to Columbia for $250,000 with Sidney Beckerman producing. But Roth and Fox were about to break up. A letter of late August 1968 begins with Fox writing, "Yes, that meeting at Plimpton's was awful and I hope that future encounters will be less stiff." But there seems to be little point in having lunch—what is there to say, after all, a disappointed Fox asks. He criticizes Roth for his failure to tell him directly that he wanted to change editors. Obviously, you couldn't do it, indicating our relationship meant less to you than to me. What Fox really objects to is the way Roth carried out his decision, not the decision itself—through an impersonal letter, not even a phone call. He ends by sending his love to Ann and that his wife Jill is keen to keep in contact with her. In a revision to this letter dated 28 August 1968, Fox added, "I considered you one of my closest friends."[114]

Roth's new editor would be the enterprising Jason Epstein, who joined Random House to run the Vintage paperback division in 1958. He had previously initiated the quality trade paperback at Anchor Books for Doubleday in 1952, which revolutionized paperback sales. In 1963, he backed the effort of his wife, Barbara Epstein, and Robert B. Silvers to establish the *New York Review of Books*, assisted by Elizabeth Hardwick and her husband Robert Lowell. Roth clearly did not want to leave Random House, which, if they did not succeed in meeting all his postpublication demands with his second novel, at least met his new financial demands. The money, the advance plus the sale of movie rights, gave him new confidence. They were rightly anticipating and planning great success for *Portnoy*. But why did Roth switch editors? Was it merely pique at Fox's seemingly lack of response to Roth, or a genuine distrust of his commitment to previous, as well as new, projects?

There is no single cause, but Roth felt a lack of commitment from Fox to *When She Was Good*. Roth's temperament, even though he was a young writer, was sensitive to criticism and certainly insult. Fox's less than full support, measured in limited advertising and promotion monies, implied less than full support of Roth as a Random House author and a critique of his ability as a writer. His ego was at stake. From the beginning, Roth was supremely confident of the value of his work and how it should be presented to the public, as seen in his earlier exchanges with George Starbuck and the promotion of *Goodbye, Columbus*. Everyone at Random House agreed that Roth was a first-rate writer with an "enormous natural talent" who required virtually no editing, according to Epstein.[115] Anticipation of a bestseller was high, despite Roth's limited commercial appeal (earning back his advances on only two of his titles throughout his career), although Random House believed that it had a winner in 1968–69.[116] Expectations were sky high.

5

Portnoy: "Let It Rip"

> Where did you get the idea that the most wonderful thing I could be
> in life was *obedient*?
>
> —Alexander Portnoy, in *Portnoy's Complaint*, 1969

Sex in America; sex and America. The two cohabit in *Portnoy's Complaint*, Roth's breakout novel which de-iced Jewish inhibitions and thawed Jewish and other hang-ups with humor, verve, and pizazz. By the time Roth began to publish portions of *Portnoy's Complaint*, inhibitions were already fading. Sexual repression, family neuroses, masturbation, Jewish behavior, all came undone or, at the very least, unstuck. The turbulent 1960s repositioned sex, beginning, perhaps, with William Burroughs's *Naked Lunch* (1959) and climaxing (as it were) with Jacqueline Susann's *The Love Machine* (1969). It included *City of Nights* (1963) by John Rechy, *Candy* (1964) by Terry Southern, *Valley of the Dolls* (1966) by Jacqueline Susann, and *Myra Breckinridge* (1968) by Gore Vidal. *Couples* (1968) by Updike had unprecedented popularity as it represented the intersecting sex lives of ten couples in a small Massachusetts town. Preceding this was Henry Miller's *Tropic of Cancer* (1934) and *Tropic of Capricorn* (1939), which introduced the sexually explicit novel to America anticipated by Erskine Caldwell's *God's Little Acre* (1933).

Suddenly, masturbation, fellatio, and threesomes all made their aggressive way to the American page and screen. In 1969, the year of *Portnoy*, Denmark legalized pornography, the first country in the world to do so. That year also introduced the so-called Golden Age of Porn, beginning with Warhol's *Blue Movie* and followed in 1970 by *Mona* and then in 1972 by *Deep Throat* and *Behind the Green Door*. Viva, the star of *Blue Movie*, explained that the film was about sexual disappointment and frustration, "the way nine-tenths of the population sees it, yet pretends they don't."[1] "Porno chic" was suddenly in, discussed on talk shows and the tabloids. The U.S. Supreme Court seemed to agree with the new standards, in *Stanley v. Georgia* allowing the private possession of materials formerly deemed obscene. Prior to this, the prevailing precedent was *Roth v. United States* (1957), whereby obscene material was determined to be unprotected by the First Amendment right to free speech. This Roth was Samuel, known for selling *American Aphrodite* and publishing pirated passages of Joyce's *Ulysses*.

But *Portnoy* was unique: it was indecent, salacious, arousing neo-porn, focusing on an educated *Jewish* man bursting out from the repression of family, society, and culture, with the fourth section of the novel appropriately (if ironically) titled "Civilization and Its Discontents."[2] Civilization imposed not only discontent but sexual dissatisfaction, which became the condition of the age. But now *Portnoy's Complaint* liberated not only Jewish men and women but readers of every type. Libraries banned the book; Australia prevented its importation for a period. But it became a phenomenal best-seller and transformed Roth's life and career. His psychoanalytic sessions, manic mimicry, and unexpected personal freedom from the death of Maggie encouraged him to let loose and destroy any set of Jewish complexes that might have earlier restricted him or his generation. The combination of his therapy, comic performances, and permissive times made the writing and reception of the text perfect. Jews may not have been prepared, but society at large was eager for such a no-holds-barred display of sexual liberation. The act of breaking free, like Huck Finn lighting out for the Territory, was equally threatening, ennobling, and, for American fiction, liberating.

Roth "let it rip," as he told Scott Raab in a 2010 *Esquire* interview. His previous three books were carefully constructed in terms of their language, structure, and even story. There was nothing libidinous or outrageous and certainly not scandalous, although the diaphragm in "Goodbye, Columbus," the affair in "Epstein," and the mistreatment of Jews by other Jews in "Defender of the Faith" shocked Jewish readers expecting Leo Rosten, Harry Golden, or Herman Wouk.[3] To Raab, Roth explained that in reaction to the tempered prose and modulated voices of *Letting Go* and *When She Was Good*, he veered in another direction: the theatrics of the 1960s, his own psychoanalysis, and the times gave him the internal permission to "let it rip."[4] The mixture gave him confidence to write wildly, unleashing a high-velocity nozzle of style where the *spritz,* not the paragraph, becomes the signature form. Sublimation was no longer in control or even in view.

The tail end of the 1960s in New York was a time of performance, impersonation, exploration. Roth witnessed this change as a kind of Dante guided by a number of Virgils. He was both a participant and an observer, and it came gushing out in the frantic, nonstop, Lenny Bruce–like narrative of *Portnoy's Complaint*.[5] Roth was actually to write a piece for the *New York Review of Books* on Bruce about his lengthy 1964 trial. But Bruce got sick, a segment of the trial was postponed, and Roth left for Yaddo to work on what would become *Portnoy*.

The opening pages of Bruce's *How to Talk Dirty and Influence People* (1965) are not unlike *Portnoy* in terms of stringing together moments and material. Talking about his vocabulary, Bruce describes it as flavored with the "jargon of the hipster, the argot of the underworld, and Yiddish." He then adds this definition of what it means to be Jewish:

> To me, if you live in New York or any other big city, you are Jewish. It doesn't matter even if you're Catholic; if you live in New York you're Jewish. If you live in Butte, Montana, you're going to be goyish even if you're Jewish.
>
> Evaporated milk is goyish, even if the Jews invented it. Chocolate is Jewish and fudge is goyish. Spam is goyish and rye bread is Jewish.
>
> Negroes are all Jews. Italians are all Jews. Irishmen who have rejected their religion are Jews. Mouths are very Jewish and bosoms.... Gentiles love their children as much as Jews love theirs; they just don't wear their hearts on their sleeves.... Celebrate is a goyish word. Observe is a Jewish word.[6]

Ending Chapter 1 in his autobiography is a scene of masturbation, but where Portnoy finds enjoyment in his secret act, Bruce finds punishment: he's caught by his father.

At this time, the counterculture was big, and one of its guides and one of Roth's Virgils was Albert Goldman, author of *Freakshow, therocksoulbluesjaz zsickjewblackhumorsexpoppsych gig and other scenes from the counterculture* which appeared in 1971, to be followed by Roth's account of Bruce in 1974. With Goldman, Roth went to meet B. B. King, Jimi Hendrix, James Brown, and Albert King, attended a Janis Joplin concert and then one by The Doors. In an *Esquire* interview of 2010, Roth remembered Goldman as "a terrific live wire." He taught at Columbia, wrote a classical-music column, and then became rock critic for *Life* magazine.[7]

Living on the twenty-first floor of a Manhattan apartment building, Roth greeted Goldman with a song when he visited in the summer of 1968, most of *Portnoy* written. Summarizing his year of personal obstacles, from his appendicitis attack to his recovery, the death of Maggie and the forthcoming release and celebration of *Portnoy*, he told Goldman he's on to a new book, one that will stand Kafka on his head, alluding to *The Trial* and its opening sentence: "A terrible mistake has been made." Released suddenly from jail, the protagonist has his life restored and is a celebrity, no doubt a projection of Roth's state of mind at the time, released from his state of penury with Maggie and facing new riches (Goldman in CWPR 34). Interestingly, the lead image for Goldman's article in *Life* of 7 February 1969, titled "A Comedian of Guilt: 'Portnoy's Complaint,'" is a haunting full-page composite photo of Kafka made shortly before his death in 1924 next to a brooding, thirty-five-year-old Roth in a turtleneck. The caption reads, "Kafka is the great comedian of guilt; a writer who finds self-persecution funny obviously owes him plenty."[8]

Robert Brustein, drama critic and professor of theater, confirmed the raucous Roth on raucous evenings with New York friends plus what Roth called the "uncensored shamelessness in my psychoanalytic sessions" (CWPR 177). Such a *shtick* also displayed a manic intensity aimed at being the center of attention, once he found his style. This became not only Roth's intense, almost nonstop jokes and sense of humor but, later, a remarkable productivity, year after year, that even age would not discourage. He began his American Trilogy at sixty-four and continued publishing novels until he was seventy-seven.

In the lengthy profile of Roth for *Life* of 7 February 1969, Goldman presented a candid view of Roth's comedic style and even fantasy plays, "The Terrace" (a satiric version of Jean Genet's *The Balcony*) and "The Blue Network." "The Terrace" was a brothel for nice Jewish boys where they would go to be tucked into bed listening to a radio with a bright orange dial. "The Blue Network" was his comic riff on a radio network filled with Jewish jokes and off-color remarks. Goldman conveys the frantic comic style of Roth in person, the imitator, the performer that *every page* of *Portnoy* would confirm and that Roth would later display at full "volume" in his short story "On the Air" in the *New American Review* 10 (August 1970). Roth became a comedian of the Jewish living room and luncheonette and likely learned this technique amusing his boys as they walked from the Chancellor Avenue School to the Schley Street Synagogue's Hebrew School and certainly on the playground. Roth knew how to entertain and work an audience, whether at Syd's having hotdogs or heading to the movies. He did not join the Bucknell Drama Club out of modesty. Goldman suggests that being bad and being funny were the same in Roth's mind: they both involved transgression, the cornerstone of *Portnoy's Complaint* (CWPR 31). Be bad, not good, in your writing, Goldman urged.

But the volatile 1960s—*Portnoy* is set in 1966—while influencing the author and the writing of the book, made few inroads in the text. The neuroses of an angry Jewish man in his mid-thirties is his singular concern: dominating the text is the family and Freud's Family Romance, while combining "the dramatic, stagey atmosphere of the city" and his uncensored psychoanalytic sessions. They inspired him to try a new voice, "a fourth voice, a less page-bound voice" than that of his earlier books, as he explained to Hermione Lee in 1984. So did the opposition to the Vietnam War, when "rage and rebelliousness" was in the air; defiance and "hysterical opposition" seemed everywhere. He felt the consciousness of New York, suddenly replacing that of Newark and childhood (CWPR 177).

The actual gestation of the novel, however, was complicated, as Roth partly explained to David Remnick in 2000. After finishing *When She Was Good* in mid-1966, Roth wrote a monologue significantly more scatological than anything said by Portnoy. It involved a monologist delivering a slide-show lecture on sex with color images of the genitalia of the famous, including Jean Genet's anus and Mickey Mantle's penis. It remained unpublished but included several thousand words on adolescent masturbation which Roth felt had interest (RMY 32). Another manuscript, "Portrait of an Artist," marking the debut of the Portnoy family, was followed by an autobiographical fiction about growing up Jewish in New Jersey with another family living upstairs in their two-family house (RMY 33). Roth drew themes partly from the writing of his Jewish students at Iowa, notably parental smothering and obsessive worrying. He named the upstairs family the Portnoys and described their evolution in a later essay, "How Did You Come to Write That Book, Anyway?" (RMY 29–36).

Other writings from that period seem to contain the seeds of *Portnoy's Complaint*. "The Jewboy," a two-hundred-page experiment, was its first incarnation using a Newark childhood, which may have also been titled "The Nice Jewish Boy: A Masochistic Extravaganza." A play with the same title, "The Nice Jewish Boy," was next. But the breakthrough work was a story entitled "A Jewish Patient Begins His Analysis," set in a psychiatrist's office; it appeared in *Esquire* in April 1967. Roth drew this story from the "odds and ends" of his "Portrait of the Artist" he liked best (RMY 36). Narrated by the Portnoys' son, it is supposedly his introductory remarks to his psychiatrist, who originally appeared in the stories written by those Jewish graduate students at Iowa who created the watched-over son who has sexual dreams of "The Other" (RMY 36).

In this early excerpt of *Portnoy's Complaint* (sans sex, sans masturbation), Alex Portnoy describes his family: his overweight sister, his meticulous, all-powerful mother, and his feckless but hard-working insurance salesman father. Supporting this is his idolized mother, who could accomplish anything, "including Jell-O with sliced peaches. . . . She sews, she knits, she darns—she irons better than the *shvartze* (black)."[9] Carefully watched by his father, the young boy leads a controlled life of neatness, study, good grades, and no fun. The father, in particular, is presented as self-sacrificing in his service to his family and suffering intensely from constipation. But he wants his son to succeed and to do so through learning. At university, when the son tries to educate his father via a gift subscription to the *Kenyon Review*, it's dumped unopened into the trash.

But his mother, vying with twenty other Jewish mothers in their apartment house to be "the patron saint of self-sacrifice," reigns not only where health and cleanliness are concerned but in sewing, shopping, and, like her husband, self-sacrifice. The son never seems to satisfy her high standards, and when "bad" he is locked out of the apartment until he assures everyone that he will do better—even when he shines his shoes every night on a sheet of yesterday's *Jersey Journal*. On the nights when he will not eat, she threatens him with a bread knife with a silver blade and he does not know why. In a brilliant ending, Roth writes:

> Oh, how, how can she spend such glorious afternoons in that kitchen, polishing silver, chopping liver, threading new elastic into the waistband of my little jockey shorts—and feeding me all the while my cues from the mimeographed script, playing Queen Isabella to my Columbus, Betsy Ross to my Washington. . . . How can she rise with me on the crest of my art during those dusky, beautiful hours after school, and then at night, because I will not eat some string beans and a baked potato, point a bread knife at my heart?
>
> And why doesn't my father stop her?[10]

Roth may actually have switched genders here: it was his father who was insufferable.

The overall narrative is not quite *Portnoy's Complaint*—they live in Jersey City, not Newark, for example, and masturbation has not yet been introduced—but there are countless similarities, including bursts of energetic style. Roth said of the story that there was nothing obscene or novel about it except for the form: the psychoanalytic monologue. Putting the narrator on the couch frees him from social niceties and proprieties. It wasn't a question of overcoming inhibitions as much as finding a new technique, "of finding in the form the *justification* for saying the unsayable" (CWPR 116). The short story "A Jewish Patient" is incorporated in *Portnoy's Complaint* as the end of the first section, "The Most Unforgettable Character I've Met" (PC 11–17). The sequel to "A Jewish Patient" was "Whacking Off," the title of the next part of the novel.

The discovery of Portnoy began with the discovery of his mouth, his voice, in contrast to the near silent Dr. Spielvogel. Through the psychoanalytic monologue, Roth drew together the fantasy of "The Jewboy" and documentary elements of "Portrait of an Artist" and "The Nice Jewish Boy" which legitimized the obscenities of the slide show on sexual parts. Instead of a projection screen, there was the couch. Interspersed was "The Nice Jewish Boy: A Masochistic Extravaganza," a novel begun after *When She Was Good* and never completed. One chapter became part of the first

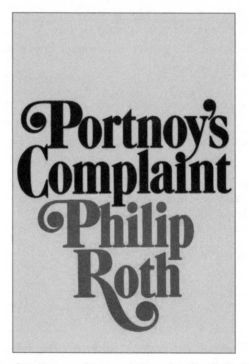

Figure 5.1 First-edition cover of *Portnoy's Complaint* by Philip Roth.
Credit: Designed by Paul Bacon; published by Random House, January 1969.

draft of *Portnoy*. In essence, Roth had been working on a series of separate, discrete stories, some of them quite salacious. He managed to publish them and then stitch the texts together when he settled on the narrative frame of the psychoanalytic session.[11] That gave him both the narrative freedom and boundaries of his character's voice. The sessions have a frame, although not a structure. Portnoy could free-associate and riff without fear of violating any preestablished form, something Roth could not do with his two earlier novels. This freedom would soon govern later works, like his short story "On the Air," his unproduced play "National Pastime" (sex on TV!), and satires like *Our Gang*.

Preparations for the appearance of *Portnoy*, which Epstein and Random House expected to be a hit, meant substantial, record-setting presales: a large advance of $250,000, sale of paperback rights to Bantam for $360,000, and sale of movie rights for $250,000. The Literary Guild paid $35,000 for book club rights, all *before* publication. In anticipation of sales and the need to cover more extensive printing costs, Random House increased the price of the book from $5.95 to $6.95 (FAC 157).[12] In 1959 Random House had gone public, becoming the first major American trade publisher to issue stock and pay profits to shareholders. In 1966, it was taken over by RCA, forming part of a large communications conglomerate. This gave them access to greater capital than previously available, resulting in larger advances. Suddenly, there was a more commercial approach to the book trade which the orchestration of *The Confessions of Nat Turner*, published in 1967 and winner of the Pulitzer Prize, reflected, followed by *Portnoy's Complaint*.[13]

One of the last issues remaining with the novel was the choice of an epigraph. Roth had originally used a passage from the popular psychiatrist R. D. Laing, author of the widely read *The Divided Self*; he then came up with a definition of "Portnoy's Complaint," telling Epstein from the Ritz Hotel in London, where he had gone with Ann Mudge, to drop the Laing and substitute the enclosed. He wanted it set like a dictionary definition and described exactly how it should appear: "Portnoy's Complaint" in bold type (cf. the *Psychiatric Dictionary*) with the rest in a narrow, dictionary-style column. The definition begins, "A disorder in which strongly-felt ethical and altruistic impulses are perpetually warring with extreme sexual longings, often of a perverse nature" (PC iii). The definition frames the book, matched by Spielvogel's single utterance, his punch line, at the end.[14] In a subsequent note from an underfurnished studio flat at 60 Globe Place, London, Roth tells Epstein that he sent a copy of his definition to Kleinschmidt and received a prickly reply; he may have felt himself mocked. He doesn't like it, but too bad. News of the movie sale and another $250,000 surprises him. What does it mean—that he'll have to buy a house and a car and a dog? He's making notes for a new book, called "ZUCK."

In a letter of 13 July 1968 to Epstein from the Connaught, Roth writes, "Ann flourishes; I am as mercurial as ever." Admiring London's miniskirts, he says the girls have "big milky buns and pussy is but an inch from the fingertip." (Twelve days later he would write, "The pussy on the King's Road is now only *half* an inch from the fingertips. I'm going to get arrested here, I know it, but thank God for my New York Review press card.")[15] Indeed, he propositioned an English journalist and hired a call girl one afternoon, met on Curzon Street while Ann was out. He addresses the objections to the last line of *Portnoy's Complaint*: George P. Elliott, Solotaroff, and others disliked it. Only he and Epstein liked it.

A later letter of 27 July to Epstein emphasizes that he does not want to write a statement about the book for the Literary Guild until he's read the galleys and recalls what the book is about. If the movie sale goes through, and Random House gets the proposed $10,000, will it be used to expand the promotion budget? He doesn't want to beg for such money as he did for *When She Was Good*. His concern, as with his previous and future books, was always with marketing: spend more, let the public know about the book, for only that way will you get readers and sales. He mentions that he's written to his lawyer, Shirley Fingerhood, that all decisions on contracts and methods of payment be put off until he returns. Sarcastically, he writes that he likes to be privy "to all discussions relating to my dough and my future."[16] Roth is not kidding: he was constantly alert to his financial well-being, which he felt he could improve by telling his publishers how to promote his books.

On 31 July 1968, Epstein tells him that enthusiasm for *Portnoy* in New York "would dazzle you more than the money you are making." Everyone agrees it will be the biggest book in history: "You will have an effect on the current generation like Byron's on his so that every man of fashion will have to model himself hereafter on A.P."[17]

In London with Ann, he had suits custom-made and from their rented flat watched on TV the battles in Chicago between the police and demonstrators at the Democratic Convention in August 1968, wondering why he was in England when all America was boiling over. With his new wealth, he was experiencing an inner turbulence that was upsetting and quick. The upheaval of his "rebirth" was profound, but its outward manifestation, he realized, with or without the experience of a call girl, was superficial, although symptomatic.

The "annihilation" of his "nemesis" (Maggie) and the imminent publication of his book were only beginning to infiltrate his psyche. The fundamental elements of his life, he realized, had changed. On their return to New York on the *Queen Elizabeth,* departing 28 August, he decided to live alone and end his relationship with Ann, although he certainly did not tell her and did not break up with her as precipitously as he suggests in *The Facts.* His hope was to work on the galleys and "cross the sea with Portnoy," although that did not happen.[18] He mentions meeting his U.K. publisher, Tom Maschler, and spending time with Jonathan Miller and an American architect living in London named Nathan Silver who published a photo book entitled *Lost New York* (1967) with a half-dismantled Pennsylvania Station on the cover. He and Ann also visited Vernon Gibberd and his wife, Diana (Figure 5.2).

Anticipating negative reactions to *Portnoy,* Roth tried to prepare his parents for embarrassment after returning to New York. He took them to

Figure 5.2 Philip Roth and Ann Mudge at the country home of Vernon Gibberd in the U.K., 1968. Credit: Vernon Gibberd, Philip Roth Papers, Library of Congress, Washington, D.C.

lunch and explained that they would soon be subject to gossip and press attention. But you don't have to speak to reporters or answer the phone: just disregard the hullabaloo. Some years later, he learned from his father that on the cab ride home, his mother broke down in tears, telling her husband that she was deeply upset—not because of the book but because her son seemed to be suffering from delusions of grandeur. Such success would never happen: her son would be deeply disappointed and hurt.[19]

As publication neared, Roth postponed his breakup with Ann. *Portnoy* took precedence, and he looked forward to the publicity, believing he could still control reaction. He told Epstein that a small launch party, possibly on 21 February—the official release date was 29 February—should include Epstein and his wife, Barbara, Jules Feiffer and his wife, the Brusteins, New York friends the Jakobsons, the Howard Steins, Ann and himself. Even after publication, he persisted in telling Epstein the kind of ad Random House should run: for example, use material from a review by Isa Kapp in the *New Leader*; she's intelligent. To counter the focus on masturbation and obscenity, he wanted something intellectual in an ad whose purpose was *not* to sell the book: the goal was to educate readers, not sensationalize the text. He then outlines the order of the advertising copy and arrangement of typefaces. The appeal of the thing is its seriousness and completeness to counter the carnival air surrounding the novel. Roth clearly wanted the book to be treated seriously, as a work of literature, not entertainment or scandal.

Excitement over the serial publication and prepublication sales of *Portnoy* convinced Random House they had a winner. They were right, and so, in addition to the trade edition, they prepared a signed limited edition of six hundred copies. When the novel appeared on 29 February 1969, it sold a reported 275,000 copies within two days of publication and 420,000 copies within the first ten weeks.[20] Roth, thirty-six, had never sold more than 25,000 copies of a book before.

In an interview in the *New York Times* just days before its publication, George Plimpton asked Roth about the genesis and style of the novel. Roth explained that he tried to use "blocks of consciousness," emphasizing story by association, not logic or chronology.[21] He then stressed the tone and vibration of spoken language he attempted to get onto the page. But delivery is everything, since the topic of Jewish men and gentile women was hardly new. His goal was to become the writer Jewish critics had all along told him he was: irresponsible, unserious, perverse, and, finally, unsympathetic to

Jews (RMY 76). A monologue on sex, the Jewish family, and psychotherapy seemed precisely the ingredients to exacerbate everyone.

More important, Roth outlines that while Portnoy refuses to be bound by current taboos, he is also in a battle with his conscience. The novel is an investigation of his passion, but the joke is that breaking taboos for him turns out in the end to be as unmanning as honoring them. He loses on both sides of the coin, or perhaps bed, something of a Kafkaesque situation.[22] Roth wanted to raise obscenity to the level of a subject, he tells Plimpton, something of a high-minded goal that may have occurred to him as a late defense. But, as the Sabra at the end of the novel asks, why must he use "fuck" all the time? The "why" is what the book is all about, Roth replies. And it's not Lenny Bruce or Mort Sahl who influenced him, not those stand-up comics, but the "sit-down comic" Franz Kafka and "The Metamorphosis."[23] Again, this may be more wish fulfillment rather than practice. Kafka is hard to spot among the moments of cunnilingus and sexual acrobatics. What he *did* like about Bruce, however, was his precise social observation and dreamlike sense of fantasy—and convincing display of exhibitionism which he transferred to Portnoy.

He explains that when he was thinking about Portnoy, he was teaching a good deal of Kafka at the University of Pennsylvania, where he taught once a week. Readings for the course, he joked, might justify renaming it "Studies in Guilt and Persecution," the essential sense of Kafka in the novel, but obliquely, not directly.[24] The morbid preoccupation with guilt and punishment he actually found funny. Only when he realized that guilt could be comic did he free himself from his previous book and discover the liberation necessary to write the new one.

Others, however, found the new humor uncomfortable. A secretary at Stony Brook, where Roth was teaching part time in 1968, threatened to quit rather than type up sections of the book. She overcame her objection to the obscenities, however, and continued with the job, possibly discovering some new pleasures. As Roth predicted, response to the book was sharply divided. They ranged from celebration to insult: Geoffrey Wolff in the *Washington Post* called *Portnoy* "the most important book of my generation"; Bruno Bettelheim analyzed Roth in "Portnoy Psychoanalyzed"; all America seemed to be fixated on masturbation and Jewish mothers. Roth's own mother was in his mind idealized as a generous and warm woman, although underneath he had reservations, as his psychiatrist (and Roth) discovered. Nonetheless, Barbara Sproul, his new partner, confirmed his view of the caring mother.

In a letter to Roth dated 31 May 1982, Sproul refers to photos of Bess Roth and the fun she and Bess had "flattering each other about the economics of the home. . . . She was like a great general creating pleasant order in the ranks of house and family. And her softness was always so subtle, in the eyes like yours and Sandy's."[25] Roth admitted that his brother had a different view; he found their mother distant and unloving, making him, in turn, closed and careful, especially as an artist. Claudia Roth Pierpont, not related to Roth but a *New Yorker* writer of long standing, in her study *Roth Unbound* believes that "it was Sandy's relationship with their mother that Roth used as a model for *Portnoy*."[26]

Even the *New York Times* editorial board would chime in on the negative effect of *Portnoy*. An editorial of 1 April 1969 entitled "Beyond the (Garbage) Pale" expressed contempt for the novel. Among editorials concerned with federal budget cuts in welfare spending and shifts in New York hospital re-organization was one denouncing the exposure of sex on stage, film, and the page. A notable offender was a current bestseller that "drowns its literary merits in revolting sex excesses." This is not "cultural emancipation" but a descent into "degeneracy," the *Times* argued. There should be no "exemption from the laws of common decency." It did agree, however, that it was "prepos-terous" to banish topless waitresses when there is no "bottom to voyeurism." Ironically, the preceding page contained a half-page ad for "An American masterwork," *Portnoy's Compliant,* noting 450,000 copies in print. The first quote in the ad is from the front page of the *New York Times Book Review* by Josh Greenfeld: "a bullseye hit in the ever-darkening field of humor . . . a work certainly catholic in appeal, potentially monumental in effect." The ad and the editorial intensified curiosity, if not eagerness to read the book.[27]

The most negative critic was the esteemed Judaic scholar Gershom Scholem, who, writing in Hebrew in *Haaretz*, declared that *Portnoy* was the "the book for which all anti-Semites have been praying." It confirmed the anti-Semite's belief that Jews were degenerate and corrupt, while at the center of Roth's "revolting book" is Portnoy's singular quest for "*shikse* cunt."[28] Marie Syrkin was equally vitriolic, claiming that Roth's novel was one with "Julius Streicher's satanic Jewboy lusting after Aryan maidens." Diana Trilling was no more receptive: in a lengthy essay in *Harper's* that criticized Roth's treatment of guilt and the Jewish mother, she reprimanded him.[29] Roth responded with a long letter he never mailed but published in *Reading Myself and Others* im-personally titled "Document Dated July 27, 1969." In it, he berates Trilling for failing to understand that the novel is not a farce with a thesis but a complex work embedded in "parody, burlesque, slapstick, ridicule, insult, invective, lampoon, wisecrack, in nonsense, in levity, in play." In short, "Comedy with a capital C" (RMY 28).

Goldman, in a later essay, understood this strategy, writing that the Jewish comic is an "adolescent urban funny boy—hysterically intense. The key to his comedy and the ironic clue to his tragedy—is that he is intellectually and verbally overdeveloped at the same time that he is emotionally and sexually underdeveloped." The paradox is that Jewish comics were "as much in love with their imperfections as they were enraged by them." Heine, not Kafka, might be a closer model because his wit rests on a sense of caricature, "his fusion of sentiment with irony and also his penchant for self-satire."[30] This, in a word, is Roth.

Bettelheim's hostile reading of *Portnoy*, which he later claimed was itself a satire, likely stemmed from a reaction to the negative portrayal of psychoanalysis in literature at the time. Bettelheim was determined to reduce the book to a case study, suggesting that uncontrolled sexual acting-out is not sexual freedom but bondage to sex that destroys it and turns the hero impotent.[31] In Bettelheim's opinion, Spielvogel's patient hides his "intellectual arrogance behind ironic self-deprecation," his empathy buried in a Jewish boyhood suffocated by an overprotective mother and ineffectual father.[32] But it is Portnoy's disgust with himself, Bettelheim's doctor explains, that forces him to defeat all who love him, his promiscuity an effort to keep satisfaction from his parents, while punishing himself because he gets nothing meaningful from these relations.[33] Only at the end of his essay, after six sessions with Portnoy, does Spielvogel consider the work as a literary text and not a clinical file.

Alfred Kazin in an early review initially complained that *Portnoy* reduced his experience to psychology and the redefinition of a role notable in Jews who have been born not to a faith but a neurosis. It is psychoanalysis, Kazin writes, that willed the Jew to a new consciousness, if not creativity. In the hands of the talented mimic Roth, who writes of Jews as hysterics, we witness partial liberation, yet, as Kazin carefully notes, Bellow's Herzog suffered twice as much as Portnoy, but he also lived in history, while Portnoy lives only through his mother. Roth reduces Jewish history to a Jewish voice. But Roth sustains the defiant voice of Portnoy, creating a humor that lasts in his "manic aria" where sex remains his favorite form of protest. A seemingly less generous response was that of the writer Richard Yates, who was unforgiving in his hostility to Roth, believing he was condescending to his characters, until *Portnoy*. Yates thought Roth terrifically overrated until *Portnoy*: "Then I forgave him everything including his millions of dollars."[34]

Another response was an article in the *New York Times* headlined "Some Mothers Wonder What Portnoy Had to Complain About." Jewish mothers—of Norman Mailer, Leonard Bernstein, and Mark Rudd, a founder of the Weathermen—struck back with comments. These women were supporters of Sophie Portnoy. Roth's own mother, quoted first, inclusively said, "I think all mothers are Jewish mothers." A therapist explains that the basic problem with the overbearing if caricatured mother is that she is unable to let her children go, while reminding them of the debt they owe to her. The wife of Senator Jacob Javits, mother of three, points out that this may originate in the European ghetto attitude of "wanting to protect." But don't pester, says Bernstein's mother, while Bess Meyerson, at the time New York's commissioner of consumer affairs and who in 1945 became the first Jewish Miss America, predicts a Jewish mother's backlash: they are going to stop calling their sons to find out how they feel, and stop asking them to visit. Why, she adds, they might even write books about their children.[35]

Countering the negative reactions was the proud response of Roth's parents. Herman Roth reported to his son on 15 March 1969 that friends had just returned from Acapulco, where everyone was talking about and reading *Portnoy*. Many relatives now proudly called, including cousins on his mother's side they had not heard from in years. Even a Dr. Brodkin, whom Herman saw at the Y every day and who just turned sixty-eight, got a copy, which he was sending to his son in Vietnam, an intelligence officer. "To make the story complete," Herman writes, "I gave the Doc a rub down in the steam room. This he will relate to his great great grandchildren. Portnoy's father gave him a rub." In addition, "people who don't even know us insist you have a sister."[36]

Roth, worried over how his parents would react to the attention, learned that they were thrilled to be the center of attention: "So you ask how we are bearing up? Nothing but *Nachas* (pride). Mostly good and bad little. We remain aloof and accept the plaudits." When CBS called and wanted Jack Paar to interview them for TV in their Elizabeth home, Herman proudly reported that Roth's mother was confident and clear: "No-Dice."[37] A week later, Herman enthusiastically writes, "The bomb is still bursting. I am a Celebrity," so much so that when Roth sent them to Israel on a cruise, Herman took copies of the novel with him and kept asking people if they wanted an autograph copy, which he signed himself: "From Philip Roth's father, Herman Roth."[38] They thoroughly enjoyed the country, staying first at the King David Hotel in Jerusalem and reporting that on a tour of the Dead Sea they met a young American girl reading *Letting Go*. She told them that *Portnoy* "was the best written [book] in the last century!"[39]

The film of *Goodbye, Columbus* opened that spring, capitalizing on Roth's astonishing renown after *Portnoy*. And, of course, his parents went to see it. Herman, however, was more impressed by the marquee, which, instead of the actors' names, had just the title and a facsimile of a book and Roth's name. Throughout the lobby there were large signs advertising your previous and newest book, he tells his son. In the same letter, he notes that three rabbis are reviewing *Portnoy* and that in general the "under 40 love it. Over 40 mixed emotions, over 50—Eh!"[40]

The director of the film, Larry Peerce, son of the well-known cantor and opera singer Jan Peerce, recalled that Roth did not want to have much to do with the screenplay prepared by Arnold Schulman. The release of *Portnoy* no doubt distracted him. But there was constant worry over Roth's reaction to the film. Seeing it the day after it opened, Roth called Peerce to congratulate him. The box office was similarly content, the film earning $10.5 million, making it one of the most popular films of the year. It also introduced Ali McGraw to the screen and made her a star. Originally planned to be shot in Newark, the film had to relocate; the mayor thought a Hollywood crew in a city recently devastated by riots would not be wise. Similarly with the opening swim club sequence: it had to be moved from New Jersey to New Rochelle, New York.[41]

Peerce had a challenge in locating an actor to play Brenda's jock brother, Ron Patimkin, who listens relentlessly to the song "Goodbye, Columbus." At the Plaza Hotel in New York on a June evening, a mere two weeks before shooting was to start, Peerce noticed a tall young man at a wedding rehearsal who physically looked the part of a basketball player. He had his location manager approach the six-foot-four Michael Meyers, then a recently graduated college student preparing to start medical school that fall.

After a meeting the next day, followed by an audition with Richard Benjamin and Ali McGraw, Meyers was hired for $4,000 to play Ron, who had the third largest number of scenes in the film. In his 1976 memoir, *Goodbye Columbus, Hello Medicine*, Meyers recounts the challenges of a first-time actor on the set.[42] He also discusses *Mad Magazine*'s parody of the movie, "Hoo-Boy, Columbus," where he appears in several panels.[43]

Twenty-five years after the novel appeared, Roth included an afterword, an inventive, semi-autobiographical essay/short story intriguingly called "Juice or Gravy? How I Met My Fate in a Cafeteria" (1994). In his mid-twenties, teaching freshman composition at Chicago and involved with Maggie, whose father was in jail, he summarizes his literary outlook and struggle to write dazzling stories, while attending "unfairness of life" classes with her. Occasionally, he went to Valois (known as "the Valoys" by the locals), a cafeteria on East 53rd Street that opened in 1921, not far from the lake in Hyde Park, for a rare dinner of roast beef with a counter man asking every diner, "Juice or gravy?" (Juice, Roth's preference, was the blood the meat secreted while being cooked; WR? 317).

Cheered by the singsong delivery of that phrase in the mouth of the Sicilian who ladled the liquid, one stormy night Roth finds a sheet of paper a previous diner had forgotten or left on his chair. It was a single-spaced paragraph with nineteen sentences making little sense. He reproduces the page, which he calls a gift, a burden, and a prank, which comes to him some thirty years before his father developed his brain tumor, the center of *Patrimony*. We, of course, recognize the nineteen first lines of his first nineteen books. Roth says they are mere chance, that perhaps a different author wrote each sentence. After contemplation, debate, and discussion with an older Roth, the younger accepts that these were the first lines of the books he had written, and the reader smiles or smirks in response to Roth's jibe at literary creativity and fate. Roth is here laughing at himself, satirizing the idea of literary composition and a literary career that he believes is suitable to restate for the twenty-fifth-anniversary edition of *Portnoy*.[44]

Forty-five years after publication, Roth offered further thoughts, realizing, as Updike colorfully said, that becoming a celebrity is a burden: "Being a famous writer is a little like being a tall dwarf. You're on the edge of normality."[45] Written for the *New York Times* in advance of an auction in December 2014 of seventy-five first editions annotated by their authors to benefit the PEN American Center, Roth expresses shock, pleasure, and then shock again that he could have been so "reckless" as to have written *Portnoy's Complaint*, but, he repeats, he was seeking to jettison any "prose decorum" in presenting a figure "who is the repository of every unacceptable thought." And in a characteristically pungent sentence, Roth writes, "Portnoy is as rich with ire as with lust," adding, "Who isn't?" He then cites the first word of Robert Fagles's translation of *The Iliad*: "Rage." For Roth, Portnoy is a book for which "one need censor nothing."[46]

The annotations to the auctioned edition are themselves fascinating and begin on the title page: "An early book driven by high spirits, happiness, & the liberating spirit of the times." On the half-title page and the blank facing it, Roth has written four short paragraphs and a quote from Mark Twain. Underneath the first phrase, "the man who is the repository of every socially unacceptable thought," Roth writes "improvisational chaos." Next, he says, "Without quite knowing it, I had stumbled upon my theme—impurity, impurity of the human compound," followed by "Psychoanalysis provided its vessel for everything. Hatred, pettiness, aggression, nonsense, exaggeration, farce—everything allowed in, except decorum. Let the repellant in!"

Facing the half-title page is Twain's remark, "The Jews are members of the human race. Worse than that I cannot say about them," and then in a separate paragraph: "To write a repellant book not so as to shock but so as to represent what is repellant (albeit at the local level). The Heshie scene. The crucial scene in the book. Because it reveals *the* secret which is not masturbation but *brutality.* The raw brutality of family relatives, the raw intensity, the raw emotionality."[47] Roth refers here to Portnoy's older cousin Heshie, an athlete who stars in the javelin throw (as Bucky Cantor will do in *Nemesis*) and who, just before he is drafted in 1943, becomes engaged to Alice Dembosky, a blond Polish *shiksa* and the head drum majorette of the high school band, known as "Legs Dembosky" (PC 54). Families destroying families is what troubles Roth.

Rabbi Warshaw, called to intervene, insists the relationship end; Heshie retreats to the backyard in agony and then anger, with aunts and uncles and cousins swarming between father (Uncle Hymie) and son, preventing their attack on each another. A few days later, when he excitedly calls Alice to report his coming in third in the state in the javelin throw, she tells him she can never see him again. Enraged, Heshie confronts his father—What did you *do?*—and runs to the cellar, ripping the door off and throwing seltzer bottles at the wall. His father cautiously enters and they fight until Heshie, in tears, succumbs. Only later do we learn that Hymie told Alice of a supposed incurable blood disease of Heshie's. Doctor's orders: he should not marry. When he offers Alice $100 to ease her pain, she takes it.[48] The engagement ends, and the family basks in what they (but not Heshie or Alex) imagine: Alice went after Heshie only for money. Heshie goes off to fight and dies in the war. All the family could say to Heshie's parents, and here Roth is devastating, is that at least he didn't leave them with "a *shikse* wife . . . with *goyische* children" (PC 60).

The "goodnik" Ronald Nimkin displays behavior the opposite of Heshie's and his failure to pursue his rage. Just before he commits suicide, he pins a note on his shirt for his mother about a Mahjong game she has later that day. Both are paradigms for what Alex will *never* do: submit. Heshie's surrender builds Alex's strength: ironically, at the end of the novel and in Israel, Alex attributes his ability to pin down Naomi in a hotel room to his working out with Heshie's weights, although to little avail. He simply can't "get it up," and after Naomi kicks him in the chest, she stomps out. Anger is Alex's weapon, not his compulsive masturbation, which is fundamentally a way of countering his mother's control rather than the intense drive to become "the Raskolnikov of jerking off" (PC 20). In these annotations, Roth has adjusted his own reading of the novel from his personal encounter with psychoanalysis and what it released concerning a Freudian Family Romance.

But in the novel, even Portnoy is aware of his indulgent voice, asking at one point, "Is this truth I'm delivering up, or is it just plain *kvetching*? Or is *kvetching* for people like me a *form* of truth?" (PC 94). Irving Howe called this "literary narcissism" and indicted the book as an outright failure in an agitated 1972 attack on Roth that appeared in *Commentary*. The novel confirmed that Roth could not live up to his potential, Howe claimed, and no work of his since *Goodbye, Columbus* has any literary interest. Furthermore, even *Goodbye, Columbus* seemed programmed: his narratives seem to drive only toward "cognitive ends fixed in advance"; the stories and stereotypes are "prefabricated."[49] Where he originally celebrated *Goodbye*, the stories now seemed to Howe tiresome.

Howe does, however, neatly summarize the Roth technique: he begins with a "spectacular array" of representative social details, the speech mannerisms and milieu of his subjects, but then interjects substitutions not necessarily from the logic of the narrative but because they emphasize the point Roth seeks to make. But Howe objects to Roth's reliance on the first-person point of view, the limits of the narrator's perception becoming the limits of the work itself. This is mere literary indulgence. Only "Defender of the Faith" exhibits Roth's true talent, his moral seriousness, and work in the tradition of Jewish self-criticism and satire as seen in Singer, Malamud, or Bellow. But the American Jewish tradition does not nourish him, nor does mainstream American culture with its democratic idealism or romanticism, Howe concludes.[50]

Before addressing *Portnoy*, Howe suggests that Roth suffers from an "unexamined depression" manifested in his "unfocused hostility," a defensive

strategy perhaps reflecting more of Howe than of Roth. Roth displays irrita-
bility in excess of the literary situations he creates, becoming an "exceedingly
joyless writer; even when being funny." Then comes his memorable opening
sentence on *Portnoy*: "The cruelest thing anyone can do with *Portnoy's
Complaint* is to read it twice." The book is no more than a set of gags, a skit
without a coherent form, displaying brashness and crudity. Can Portnoy ever
sever his sexuality from his moral sensibilities? He tries, but Howe knows
he cannot. Yet the book is not anti-Semitic; according to Howe, the work
attempts to "undo the fate of birth," not to harm the Jews. The burlesque
of a case history even questions the power and truthfulness of kvetching,
questioning its functionality in transmitting any truth, and here Howe cites
Bettelheim's review as a source. Howe objects to the value of vulgarity: for
him, it has no value.[51]

The hypocrisy of Howe's attack became evident some years later, when he
approached Roth for an op-ed in support of Israel and later complained that
he was slow in being paid for his introduction to one of the volumes in Roth's
"Writers from the Other Europe" series. Roth, of course, would not forget (or
forgive) this attack, as he made clear in *The Anatomy Lesson*, transforming
Howe into Milton Appel, pornographer.

By contrast, the bestseller lists reflected no doubts or rejection of
Portnoy: it remained on the charts for forty weeks, its main competition ad-
venture/spy novels like John le Carré's *A Small Town in Germany* and *The
Salzburg Connection* by Helen MacInnes. On 16 March 1969, less than one
month after being published, Roth beat them both to become number 1,
after hitting the list at number 9 on 23 February. Throughout the spring,
he retained the first position, although competition mounted with Mario
Puzo's *The Godfather*. By June the top three—and it would remain that way
throughout the summer—were Roth with *Portnoy*, Puzo with *The Godfather*,
and Susann with *The Love Machine*. By 20 June, however, Susann trumped
Roth as number 1. Number 4 was Nabokov with *Ada or Ardor: A Family
Chronicle*. Roth remained on the list until 23 November.

Portnoy was the breakout novel that placed Roth's name everywhere in
America and beyond and made him rich, receiving nearly a million dollars
in prepublication royalties and rights sales. But his notoriety was not necessarily for literary reasons. Pornographer, anti-Semite, masturbator, destroyer
of the Jews, and the "Castro of cock" (AL 225) were only some of the epithets
used against him, causing outrage from pulpits and synagogues and causing
Australia to ban the book.

Even a comic strip appeared, the quasi-pornographic *Little Annie Fanny* (a parody of *Little Orphan Annie*), which regularly appeared in *Playboy*. Often a parody of contemporary figures engaged with, or rather in pursuit of, a buxom blonde, the Little Annie Fanny episode on Roth and *Portnoy's Complaint* deals with the liberating effect of an aphrodisiac, taken by the Roth-like author, to conquer his "bulbous little blonde inspiration."[52] Fannie is to have Portnoy Alexander (the hero-author) over for dinner, although she knows he thinks only of sex, and despite a transparent attempt by Annie to cover up her sexuality by wearing a minidress, Portnoy, having taken the aphrodisiac, goes after her, her roommate Ruthie, a Mahjong club on the floor below, *and* the janitor. The rampant, unbridled sex of "Roth," who pursues everyone and everything in sight in the comic book, parodies the supposed unleashed sexuality promoted by the book itself. Raquel Welch and Ursula Andress appeared in the same issue.

But despite (or because of) the controversy, *Portnoy* sold phenomenally well: on 26 March 1969, Epstein told Roth, then at Yaddo, that cumulative sales for that week topped 325,000 with almost 500,000 copies in print or on order. A five-column quote ad will appear in Monday's *New York Times*, he adds. Within a year, more than 420,000 hardback copies had sold, outselling *The Godfather*. In paperback, it would sell 4 million copies, becoming at the time Random House's biggest bestseller.[53]

But the publicity caused Roth to recoil, telling Epstein earlier that month not to let people bother him at Yaddo, where he had gone for three months: Tell them I've gone to Europe. I'm back at work, he says, and I think it's "good stuff."[54] *Portnoy's Complaint*, in fact, drove Roth out of New York and was a traumatizing experience. He could not escape being identified with Portnoy. Even when walking down a country road with Sproul, a car slowed and someone recognizing him shouted, "Hey, Portnoy!" He felt vulnerable, the book turning him into a joke. After Yaddo, he sought to hide from the public by moving to Woodstock, New York, and then, in 1972, bought a colonial farmhouse built in 1790 in Cornwall Bridge, Connecticut. He later hinted that he regretted publishing the book because of the notoriety it stirred and the gnawing sense that any follow-up had to match its success.

As he explained in the 1984 *Paris Review* interview, *Portnoy* set a pattern previously enacted by Styron, who also was not around when his early works appeared. Roth purposefully avoided the hoopla at the publication of his novel: "It was too big, on a larger and much crazier scale than I could begin to deal with, so I took off."[55]

His new wealth and future prospects meant he had to write a will. It's a revealing document, specifying a bequest of $5,000 to Holly Williams Weiss, "daughter of my late wife, living in Rochester, NY"; $10,000 to his friend Howard Stein in New Haven; similar amounts to Robert Baker, Julius Goldstein, Alan Lelchuk, and Vernon Gibberd; a lifetime annuity of $12,000 to his parents; and a trust income to go to his two nephews, Sandy's sons. The executor was his lawyer, Shirley Fingerhood, to be succeeded, if necessary, by Jason Epstein. George P. Elliott was a substitute co-trustee and, if he became unavailable, Alan Lelchuk. The will is dated 4 November 1969.[56]

To look beyond the sex in the book is to see *Portnoy* as an American novel. Throughout the work, Portnoy uses America and American traditions to measure his success. Not only are American documents like the Declaration of Independence (PC 224) and the Emancipation Proclamation (PC 228) cited, but his quest is to be the sexual Columbus of America. As Portnoy gleefully announces, "Through fucking I will discover America" (PC 235). In grade three, Portnoy played Christopher Columbus and, continuing his American mandate, insisted on returning from a Sunday in New York with his family only across the George Washington Bridge—it's educational, his mother would explain to others (PC 28). Later, he spent Thanksgiving in Davenport, Iowa, not only to experience the Midwest but to be with his latest girlfriend and her very American family. His reading list for the Monkey (Mary Jane Reed from West Virginia) is solid, with titles ranging from Dos Passos's *U.S.A.* to Steinbeck's *Grapes of Wrath* (PC 208–9).

As he vividly declares to Dr. Spielvogel, his pursuit of *shiksas* is a quest for America epitomized by Kay Campbell from Iowa and Sarah Maulsby from Connecticut, aka "The Pilgrim." To his psychiatrist, Portnoy explains, "I don't seem to stick my dick up these girls, as much as I stick it up their backgrounds" and "*My* G.I. bill—[is] real American ass!" (PC 235, 236). And his manifest destiny is to screw a girl from every American state, then forty-eight in number, joining the ranks of such conquerors as "Columbus, Captain Smith, Governor Winthrop, General Washington—now Portnoy" (PC 235). And be sure, he adds, "any guilt on my part is *comical!*" (PC 249).

Ironically, at the end, the Jewish American Portnoy fails most dramatically in Israel, unable to maintain his erection with a female army lieutenant or sustain his sexual advances with Naomi, who challenges his American views and values. In America's landscape, Portnoy had no trouble making love, whether in Iowa, Washington, or New York. But in Israel, in the Jewish home-land with Naomi, a Kibbutznik and Sabra, he cannot. American freedom means sexual freedom expressed on Lexington Avenue; freedom in Israel means impotence. In the novel, Roth, or at least Portnoy, has reaffirmed his Americanness, not his Jewishness—"I am a patriot too," he desperately cries out to Naomi in Israel, but it is a lame and unconvincing lament (PC 271).

Adding to the book's American notoriety was its becoming the subject of one of the Nixon tapes. On 3 November 1971, Nixon and his assistant H. R. Haldeman discussed Roth and *Portnoy*, Haldeman telling the president that the novel is "the most obscene, pornographic book of all time." Haldeman then admits he never actually read the book but understands that despite being well-written, it is "just sickeningly filthy." Nixon responds with "Roth is of course a Jew." "He's brilliant in a sick way," says Haldeman.[57] As Portnoy confirms, "Doctor, maybe other patients dream—with me, *everything happens*. I have a life *without* latent content" (PC 257).

Kleinschmidt is again relevant, Roth having shown the psychiatrist portions of the novel and, just before publication, his proposed definition of *Portnoy's Complaint*. Kleinschmidt was not amused. Suggesting to Epstein that they cite an actual international psychiatric journal as the source of the definition, Roth wonders if that might create a problem. If so, let's ask Kleinschmidt to make up a new name, signaling the involvement, if minor, of Kleinschmidt in the shaping of the novel.[58] Kleinschmidt chose not to participate.

But letters between Kleinschmidt and Roth suggest a much closer relationship than psychiatrist and patient, the doctor, at one point in August 1966, suggesting titles for Roth's work.[59] In 1968, Kleinschmidt criticizes several ideas attributed to Dr. Spielvogel, beginning one letter to Roth with "Spielvogel does not like to be misquoted." He then criticizes a number of ideas in "The Puzzled Penis," correcting certain statements by Roth and the misstatement about mother-sibling relationships, which should be mother-child, and then sibling. Two weeks later, he comically comments on the psychiatric dictionary Roth was likely consulting. Don't be too disillusioned by it: "What probably happened is that the author had one brother too many." And although there is no actual Dr. Spielvogel, there is a Dr. David Portnoy who was apparently to speak at the Karen Horney Clinic.[60] From at least 1964 through the early 1990s, Kleinschmidt and Roth keep up a correspondence, Roth continually sending him signed and inscribed copies of his work, Kleinschmidt continually praising him. In particular, Kleinschmidt complimented the way Dr. Spielvogel in *My Life as a Man*, came alive and improved his English.[61] Roth even kept a copy of Kleinschmidt's February 1997 obituary from the *New York Times* in his files.

"To be bad—and enjoy it!" Roth wrote. "That is what makes men of us boys.... I am marked like a roadmap from head to toe with my repressions."[62] But ultimately, this is precisely what Portnoy cannot do; he cannot enjoy his newly won sexual or psychological freedom. At the end of the novel, his psychoanalysis is just beginning. Interestingly, some astute readers thought Roth might have taken the name Portnoy from Joyce. In *Finnegans Wake* (323.7–10), Joyce writes of a character who, "voyaging after maidens, belly Jonah hunting the polly joans, and the hurss of all portnoysers befuddle him, he sazd till I split in his flags ... [the] Reefer was a wenchman." Roth, however, explained that except for the Anna Livia section, he had never read *Finnegans Wake* and that Portnoy was a name he knew from childhood in Newark, although he never met anyone with that name. He just liked the odd sound of it.[63]

Ever alert to reviews of the book, he celebrated Saul Maloff's comments in *Commonweal* as the best thing written on the book so far.[64] But he doesn't want to return to New York yet: "I MUST STAY WITH THIS NOVEL" as "our poor pal Portnoy might put it," he writes in a letter referring to his new project. He notes that Brustein and Lelchuk are both with him at Yaddo, adding in a final comment that his new work "will establish me as a failure again, which may do wonders for my peace of mind, and my tax problems."[65] Here, Roth is comically responding to the pressure to write another success. The book he is writing, although it will not appear until 1974, is *My Life as A Man*, a work he would later describe as something he had been writing "on and off since 1964" (RMY 137).

But Roth was unable to escape the public's perception that he was Portnoy. So he decided that if everyone thought he was Portnoy, he would be Portnoy—but in disguise. He invented an alter ego, Nathan Zuckerman, who grows from a budding novelist to the notorious author of *Carnovsky*, a lewd, scandalous, sexually energized, and thoroughly enjoyable book. David Kepesh, another invention, succeeded Zuckerman in works like *The Professor of Desire*. For the next decade or so, Roth created characters and pseudo-selves that satisfied the public's prurient desire to believe in his personal misbehavior. He even invented another "Philip Roth" in *Operation Shylock*.

Crime, anti-Communism, and race gradually replaced lasciviousness as story-making itself became his new addiction, not oversexed, overeducated young Jewish men. A change was slowly occurring, as a character in *Deception* notes: For you, she declares, listening has become more interesting than sex. Most men talk to women to get them in bed, but "*you* get them in bed to talk" (DE 87, 86). However, this is not entirely correct. For as Roth's characters understand, erotomania has no age limit.

With a new literary authority, he tells Epstein in April 1969, in response to a piece by Solotaroff in *The Atlantic*, that although *When She Was Good* was a struggle to write, it is "the best sustained piece of writing I've ever done."[66] It should be reissued in a Modern Library format with an introduction by Solotaroff. Later that month, he complains that the book was ignored, misunderstood, misread, and "*un*read. Re-issue."[67] Roth is on a quest for self-promotion, returning to his second novel and seeking to promote a work that most felt was second rate and definitely unlike *Portnoy*.

Roth explains in a 15 April 1969 letter to Kleinschmidt that the loss of Ann—he had finally broke up with her—"makes me ache."[68] The stress and changes of the recent past, while giving him experience, nevertheless led to mistakes. His small errors of judgment have been piling up and have robbed him of "serenity and stability," the two elements he now seeks in his life. It is a letter remarkably open and filled with undisguised feelings. He would sacrifice a good deal to give himself to Barbara Sproul (age twenty-three; Roth is thirty-six) and wants her "for good"—as perhaps he should have done with Ann. "But how could I? Everything in my life combined against her interests. I don't know that I've ever been so sad about anyone as I am about her [Ann] right now. . . . This is in part why I can't take Barbara."[69] The sting of life has again stung.

Roth admits that he's afraid of his new position with Barbara, embarrassed and perspiring when the conversation turns to him, feeling much like Uncle Vanya, who is defined by his failed hopes. The small social life at Yaddo is easily upset by intrusions and strangers, as is the social circle in Chekhov's play with the arrival of Serebryakov and his young second wife, Yelena. But what bothers Roth the most is attention: in Vermont he was instantly recognized in a restaurant and asked to autograph a copy of his book by a waitress, but no one recognized him in a motel when he registered under a Nabokovian pseudonym as Milton Ross, a play on Milton Roth, his middle and last names, and an allusion to *Lolita*'s "Vivian Darkbloom," an anagram of the author's name. Thought of the National Book Award eleven months away and a possible prize caused Roth further anxiety, worry, and terror. "I really do want to retreat—for good," he tells Kleinschmidt.[70]

He had shared some of his painful past with Barbara, expressing his unhappiness from such a negative experience, adding to Kleinschmidt that he often feels like a convalescing patient. His new book, however, goes along well. Presently titled "My Life in Art; or, Zuckerman Delivered," he feels he is on top of it, with a strong sense of where it's going. But he goes through mood swings "like a chimp, or chump, through the trees and vines of the crazy jungle."[71]

What he wants, he tells Kleinschmidt, is a woman he can trust and love, sweet and passionate, and his own home to allow him to write the best he can. But how can he find the fearlessness, the steadiness and bravery? He may ache only with vanity, but he would give it up along with social aspirations and that "ghastly, stinking bastard" shame—but how? "I'll never be able to hook myself up to that confident kid I was when I first got out of Chicago." Over the past twelve years, ever since he set eyes on his "own worst enemy [Maggie] and wrestled her to the ground . . . there's not one of those PR's [Philip Roths] I can even think of as anything but some *visitor*."[72] Self-performance has been exposed, but nothing has filled the void. This is an important personal admission contrary to the public persona of the successful writer. Here, one sees his painful, contradictory inner life looking at loss and the inability to recover a self-confidence that gave him the drive to write with assurance. The security of self-identity is absent. Too many places, too many people, he adds.

Roth knows he has to come back to New York, but he dreads "the gaping people" and his own red face and fears seeing Ann "for the love I still feel for her." There's only you and Barbara on the roll call of his New York friends, he concludes.[73] The letter offers a rare, unvarnished glimpse of Roth's feelings at a troubling time, supported by Sproul, who tells him that New York will be "bad, but not as destructive as you fear (and not as destructive as your own anxiety in any case)." She is there to help and love him.[74]

His friend, the young novelist Alan Lelchuk, whom he met at Yaddo, warns him not to be too hard on Barbara: "She's slaved and slaved to get that house [in Woodstock] in condition for you, etc. compassion, compassion." The next day he writes to Roth, "What you can't have in life you take in fiction, or what's great for fiction is upsetting for life."[75]

Sproul's warning that New York will be bad was accurate. And another problem soon presented itself: a lengthy legal battle over the film rights for *Letting Go*. As far back as 1964, a production team sought to make the film and acquired the rights, led by the actor-producer (Peter) Mark Richman and Harvey Hart. Richman would write the script and star, capitalizing on his profile as a TV and minor film star. He and Hart would coproduce. In 1969, they renewed their option, as reported in the *New York Times* of 15

July. But Roth was now unhappy with the proposed production company, believing they were not capable of fulfilling an assumption agreement concerning proper backstop financing (the new production company was not even named in the legal financing documents) and took action to halt the project and retrieve the rights. He also believed that with his new notoriety and the release of the film of *Goodbye, Columbus*, the property was worth more financially. And with his new financial clout, he felt he could successfully challenge the company. What followed was a ten-year legal fight with the intransigent Roth and his lawyers battling American International Pictures while Richman painfully struggled to write and place the script.

Richman, in particular, longed for a fight after the time and money he had invested in the project, but soon bitterness intervened. The *New York Times* reported that the book would head toward the screen with shooting starting in Toronto and then New York in September, but its follow-up story on the legal battle led to rancor.[76] In print, Richman called Roth "a man with the inner life of a roach," the phrase appearing in his autobiography *I Saw a Molten White Light* (2018) in a chapter titled "The Nightmare of *Letting Go*."[77]

Richman's lawyer renegotiated the contract and finagled another extension in 1969, giving Roth more option money. The script made the rounds of production companies, but reaction was only lukewarm. And once the *Times* and *Variety* reported on the new plans, everything changed. Roth and his lawyers attacked again, claiming that AIP was incapable of assuming the financial responsibilities of doing the film. Richman's lawyer had not included AIP in his example of viable entities; Roth used it as an escape clause. In addition, he questioned the quality of the screenplay, the first written by Richman. Hostile negotiations followed, with a countersuit by AIP and then Sam Arkoff, studio head, offering to put up personal assets of $25 million as a guarantee. But that wasn't enough for Roth, who for years had taken option fees and now wanted out: "A more despicable sonofabitch was never born" Richman said of Roth.

Roth would not consent to the project, and the production had to shut down. Writing his account of the debacle some fifty-four years after it happened did not lessen Richman's anger, itself a Rothian quality. The financial loss and pain following the investment of time and energy still rankled. He had invested $510,000 and came out only with resentment. Depositions and examinations continued for years, but when this "illustrious parasite of an author" realized that things might not go his way, a settlement was rumored but the excised Richman emphatically said no, as did Arkoff, although Harvey Hart thought yes, so that he could still make the film he wanted to direct.

The details of this incident illustrate the lengths to which Roth and others would go to protect his property and the legal machinations involved. Richman had become too old to play the part of the graduate student Gabe. But despite the disagreement, in January 1974, Richman and Hart tried again and agreed to a new, two-year deal with Roth while paying him more option money. Revisions and submissions followed, but the studios, including AIP, turned it down, fearful of further Rothian litigation. By 1976 the project was dead, but not Richman's anger, an ironic Rothian twist. Resentment, it seems, never disappears.

Despite his breakup with Ann and her attempted suicide in April 1969, she and Roth were still in contact. An undated letter from her to Roth headed only "Sunday 1969" begins with a sad reminder that when he stopped relationships, they stopped: "Dear Philip: I guess I'll give up phoning you since you don't return my calls anymore." She lists several items of his he stored at her apartment, available if he wants them.[78]

In subsequent years, Ann would write to report of her marriages and of her response to meeting him. In 1973, she wrote:

Dear Philip:

I realized—almost at once, in fact, that I was awfully prickly when we were talking at the Styrons Saturday. For a variety of reasons, I seem to feel I must defend myself against you. Anyway, these are *my* reasons and feelings and not really related to the present circumstances, so I'm sorry that I was unpleasant or sarcastic. I'm going to try not to do it again.

A.[79]

Even later, Roth told Pierpont that Ann was "one of the loves of his life," being a remarkable antidote to Maggie.[80]

This situation outlines a pattern for Roth: he would desire but reject the companionship of women who increasingly sought to be close to him and solidify a long-term commitment or marriage. But despite their being dumped, they would remain in touch. Women, Roth understood, were necessary but also distracting and, from his Maggie experience, perhaps even untrustworthy. As he repeated to Kleinschmidt, he needed stability and solitude. His obligation was exclusively to his work, not to his intimate psychological life. To get perspective on his work, he must withdraw; to write, he needed seclusion—from the public, the press, his publishers, and especially his women. The Rothian paradox. Yaddo, Woodstock, and then Cornwall Bridge were his refuges.

A letter from Roth to Kleinschmidt dated 20 July 1969, the day of the first moonwalk, refers to Barbara's maturity, a friend telling him that she was a woman before she was a girl. He prefaces his comment by comically noting that it seems "irrelevant trying to be honest about fucking a girl in the ass while Neil Armstrong is on his way."[81] This was part of a new but aborted fiction about Abner Abravanel. (Later, the flashy novelist Felix Abravanel will appear in *The Ghost Writer,* a tongue-in-cheek portrait of Bellow.) In his first draft, he writes that the female character used to resemble Ann Mudge. The pages are an early version of Zuckerman in *The Ghost Writer.*

Sproul went to Sarah Lawrence before receiving a PhD in religious studies from Columbia in 1972. (Ann, by contrast, did not finish university, although at Roth's urging, she began courses at Hunter.) In the same letter, he offers a glimpse of his state of mind, noting that he succeeds nicely with younger, innocent girls, prompting Kleinschmidt to reply, "A mature woman wouldn't take your shit." "Some mature woman," Roth answered. He also admits a "nearly overwhelming nostalgia for Ann, a good deal of it inspired by this section I'm writing." He jokes that he met a couple at brunch the past week and that it was good "to be with people who know me only rich and famous and so aren't bothered by it; and who don't know Ann, or even that I was ever married." Remarking on his loneliness, he acknowledges that it was good to be "with a couple of Hebes. Those goyim. They don't know about hate, that's their trouble."[82] This may be Roth saying internally that they can't relate to him because they don't understand the anger within. A return, again, to anger, his defense against being stung by life.

He tells Lelchuk that he's teaching Barbara how to cook some terrific meals. "If I train one more girl I get to retire or so Kleinschmidt says . . . but I may really be working a gem into shape for the next guy. When will I be the next guy?"[83] But Barbara was already ultra-competent, efficient, and well-organized. In 1970, when they went virtually around the world, he let her make all the arrangements. Only his mother, a pro at neatness, cleanliness, and orderliness of the home, matched her in organizational skills. Barbara was also passionate and intelligent but suffered from migraines. What Roth does not reveal is that his breakup with her, after their travels to Thailand and Cambodia and then to Czechoslovakia, where they met Vaclav Havel, will be over his misunderstanding that she wanted a child and his resistance to the idea. She would eventually go on to a distinguished career as a professor of religious studies at Hunter College and marry.

Roth's attraction to needy, unhappy women—Maggie, Ann, and even Barbara—is paradoxical. As they became more dependent on him, perhaps their initial appeal to him and his desire to "rescue" shared with his father, he felt compelled to pull back, if not reject them. Above anything else, he prized privacy and stability, necessary to write. The paradox is that he was drawn to needy women, but over time their needs repelled him—needs he may have seen in himself, leading to his own self-contradictions that he wanted to dismiss and which he does dismiss in his writing. Interruptions on any level were not to be tolerated. Such desire would even characterize his later relationship with Claire Bloom, who grew to find an isolated life in the country intolerable.[84]

In mid-April 1969, Roth summarized his progress with his Zuckerman project, now some four hundred pages with four composition books of notes. He's at it six months with easily another two years' work, he explains, and what he needs to do is keep going. He requires serenity and solitude, obtainable only with a degree of loneliness. New York, he believes, is only distraction and silliness. All he does well is fiction, he tells Epstein: "The gap between writing and the rest of my life is awesome, and ridiculous and makes my heart sink."[85] This is an astute self-commentary. To Jean Ennis of Random House, he asks that she hold all fan mail and that he will not do a *Playboy* interview—it's not the moment for him to take advantage of the chance to talk out loud, the success of *Portnoy* providing for Roth literary freedom but also the freedom to disappear.

During his time in Woodstock, Roth befriended the New York Abstract painter Philip Guston. The Montreal-born, California-raised artist, who moved to New York in 1936, became a friend of Roth's in 1969, when Roth settled in the tiny community known for being an artists' colony that held the Maverick Art Festival and drew artists, musicians, and writers. Guston (formerly Goldstein) had a studio in Woodstock and moved permanently to the area after a severely criticized show (similar to the later experience of R. B. Kitaj in London in 1994) of his work at the Marlborough Gallery in 1970. In the late 1960s, Guston had become frustrated with abstraction and returned to representational painting, but in a cartoonish manner. He sought, according to Roth in his essay "Pictures by Guston" in *Shop Talk*, to overturn his own history as a painter. He wanted a new medium to show himself to himself and break out of the restraints of elegance or formal coherence. He wanted to get back into life, as Zuckerman does in *The Anatomy Lesson*. Guston's aesthetic of "the unknown of doing" appealed to Roth's sense of getting to the work regardless of what it demanded. What Roth truly admired in Guston was his sense of, and enactment of, the subversive.

Guston's shift in the last decade of his life from the purity of abstraction to figurative painting validated Roth's own counterlife, assumed in midcareer. It is the determination not to be "tamed by inhibition" as he writes in *The Anatomy Lesson* (AL 195). In Guston's abandonment to the corporeal, he found new energy and purpose. Unburdened by purity, he was left to his own stimulating perversity, sounding much like Mickey Sabbath from Roth's midcareer novel. Excess becomes a source of energy, a true letting go, but also a kind of immaturity that Sabbath or Milton Appel might exhibit. To Roth, Guston became an example of fecundity unleashed when one rejects the formal and abstract. The "thereness of every day life" was what Guston sought, declaring, "I wanted stronger contact with the thickness of things."[86] Physically, Guston was a large, bulky figure of immense presence, embodying Zuckerman's declaration in *The Anatomy Lesson* "I want an active connection to life and I want it now. . . . I want the real thing, the thing *in the raw* and not for the writing but for itself" (AL 204).

In 1978, Guston recalled the late 1960s and how he was torn between what he thought and felt. Furious at the political and social events around him, he found it impossible to go into the studio to adjust a red to a blue. A burned-out Zuckerman five years later echoed a similar division: "I can't take any more of my inner life. . . . I've had it" (AL 204). Guston reaffirmed Roth's decision to resist and not to bend to external pressure, even when it exacts a price. What Roth learned, as Guston understood, was that art is a boundary that must be broken. As Zuckerman and Roth and Guston realized, "it's impossible just to suffer the pain, you have to suffer its meaning" (AL 200).

"Pictures by Guston" in Roth's *Shop Talk* narrates their friendship. Roth was thirty-six and trying to escape his "overnight notoriety as a sexual freak" linked to the success of *Portnoy's Complaint*; Guston was fifty-six and experiencing middle-age doubt about his work.[87] He struggled to discover a new style through the exaggeration of the everyday, the crap of the everyday that surrounded him. Roth shared this viewpoint, which became a tool in providing access "to a style of representation free of . . . complexity" and creating a kind of "self-subversion" (ST 135). This shapes a new counterlife, one of freedom that disregards convention and expectations. It also parallels another artist Roth admired: R. B. Kitaj, the American-born London painter.

Roth began to work on four uncharacteristic books in the first four years or so of his rural life: the first, *Our Gang* (1971), is a fierce satire of Richard Nixon, followed by the Kafkaesque satire, *The Breast* (1972), which so intrigued Guston that he did eight drawings inspired by incidents in the novella. He then published his satiric and comic baseball novel, *The Great American Novel* (1973), while also working on the more troubling *My Life as a Man* (1974). Both Guston and Roth found liberation through the destruction of respectability.

Another rekindled relationship at this time was with Holly Williams, Maggie's daughter. Married in November 1968 in Little Meadows, Pennsylvania, to a Jimmy Weiss, a graduate student in biophysics, she began to reconnect with Roth, who still thought her "bewitching."[88] In a handwritten note on yellow paper, she begins by acknowledging how her family brought him pain but that also "one time we—you had a lot of love for me, enough to help me out of something at a time I had no idea even existed." She asks for the opportunity to see him in an effort to break the bonds with her family's past.[89] Her marriage had fallen apart, and she was broke. He sent her $500 when he finally received her letter, which had been sent to Random House and not forwarded for some time.[90]

Hatch Williams, the wife of Roth's friend Bob Williams (he became a creative writer who had met Roth at Iowa), had become friendly with Holly and believed that her marriage to Weiss would work, although Hatch told Roth that she hoped Holly was not getting married just to get out from under life with him and Maggie. She said, "Maggie was a resourceful, if destructive, fighter for herself. This lousy outside fate [her death] seems so unfair and terrible. I hope after being stunned, you'll not treat yourself to a siege of guilt."[91] Bob Williams wrote that Holly visited him in California with her husband and that he offered to put her through college, but she was not interested. Instead, they fished.

Roth's affection for Holly, attempting to educate her as a young girl, was in a certain fashion problematic, raising the specter of incest. This particularly troubling theme runs throughout his work and to a limited degree in his life. Claire Bloom suggests a similar interest by Roth in her daughter, Anna Steiger, and certainly in her surrogate daughter, Rachel Hallawell, a friend of Anna's. Bloom refers to this as "perpetrating a virtually incestuous betrayal" (LDH 225). More than once Maggie had suggested, or Roth inferred, sexual abuse by her father, which Roth advances in *The Facts*, writing of her experience of a "half realized attempt at childhood seduction" endured at the hands of a family member (FAC 83; also see 81–82). There are hints of this and general abuse in *When She Was Good*, where the actions of the unemployed, alcoholic, and sometimes violent (and later convicted felon) "Whitey" Duane Nelson suggest Maggie's father, "Red" Martinson.[92]

In *Portnoy's Complaint*, even the pliant twenty-nine-year-old Monkey was supposedly abused by her father, while at the end of the novel Alex extends the incest theme, admitting that he associates Naomi, "the Jewish Pumpkin" and kibbutznik, with his mother and even his sister—"another big girl with high ideals." But ironically, he is impotent and cannot consummate a relationship with her, even when he suggests love and marriage (PC 259–61). They fight, and his "mother-substitute" defeats him with a kick in his chest, the final humiliating blow before she leaves (PC 266). Where other Jews flourish, Portnoy perishes.

Incest haunts Roth's writing, seen most directly in *My Life as a Man*, in which Zuckerman marries Lydia Ketterer, a victim of child abuse (and five years Zuckerman's senior, as Maggie was four years older than Roth).[93] Discovering Zuckerman's affair with her stepdaughter, Monica, begun "under the guise of father and daughter" (MLM 82), Lydia commits suicide, but not before she screams at Zuckerman, echoing Maggie, "If you ever lay a finger on my daughter, I'll drive a knife into your heart!" (MLM, 34, 40, 82). But this does not halt his incestuous actions with the sixteen-year-old "with already budding breasts more enticing than her [Lydia's] own" (MLM 63).

Echoing *Lolita* and Humbert Humbert's travels around the country with the twelve-year-old Dolores Haze, Zuckerman takes Monica off to Italy, where they live together. When she turns twenty-one, he proposes marriage. Wisely, she refuses, but they remain together. Published in 1974, the novel may be the transference of Roth's own unconscious desires for Holly. In that same novel, we learn that Maureen, Tarnopol's first wife, was sexually abused by her first husband and his friend and that she was herself perhaps "forced" by her father (MLM 115).

By implication, incest appears in *The Ghost Writer* (1979) when Amy Bellette, in a conversation overheard by Zuckerman, asks to sit on Lonoff's lap and calls him "Dad-da" (GW 199–20). She tells him that in Florence, "we could make each other so happy. I wouldn't be your little girl over there. I would when we played but otherwise I'd be your wife." She then disrobes (GW 119). Sexual desire may be at the root of self-invention, a desire Freud traced to unconscious incestuous fantasies.[94]

In *American Pastoral*, Swede's lingering kiss, which he sensuously recounts, possesses sexual dimensions for both himself and his eleven-year-old daughter Merry. Swede, Roth writes, "lost his vaunted sense of proportion, drew her to him with one arm, and kissed her stammering mouth with the passion that she had been asking him for all month long while knowing only obscurely what she was asking for" (AP 91). Swede believes, in fact, that this transgression led to Merry's becoming a radical and to her bombing the Rimrock post office (AP 89). Incest seemingly causes the fall of the House of Levov.

In *The Facts*, "Roth" refers to Holly, Maggie's daughter, as Hanoi Helen because of her outspoken views about the Vietnam War; there may be a connection between Holly/Helen and Merry in *American Pastoral* and a curious resistance but also the same attraction to Holly that Swede displays for his daughter (FAC 149).

One critic has even suggested that Roth may have twice "used Maggie's daughter as inspiration for a character subjected to incest (Monica aka Moonie in *My Life as a Man* and Merry of *American Pastoral*)."[95] Another has analyzed the significance of incest and its relation to paternal narcissism and family destruction, echoing Milton's representation of incest as an apocryphal genesis story but showing it narratively related to Zuckerman, rather than Swede, functioning as a collective fantasy.[96]

But it doesn't stop there. In *Exit Ghost* (2007) incest appears more explicitly, the biographer Kliman suggesting that *the* secret of Lonoff, exposed in his unfinished and unpublished final novel (and why he could never publish or finish it), is that he had an incestuous affair with his half-sister (EG 118–20, 185). Zuckerman cannot believe this, but Amy Bellette confirms it. Roth draws this in part from the experience of the novelist Henry Roth, who actually had an affair with his sister Ruth which began when he was twelve and she ten, suggested in *Call It Sleep* and his later work.[97]

In his foreword to *Playing House* by Fredrica Wagman, a former student of Roth's at Penn, he comments on the protagonist's confession to incestuous desires that are simultaneously her downfall and escape. Roth notes the importance of the "traumatized child; the institutionalized wife; the haunting desire," while praising the sustained "voice of longing in which the heroine shamelessly confesses to the incestuous need that is at once her undoing and her only hope."[98] Roth knew "Ricki" Wagman and her husband Howard from Philadelphia. In fact, he heavily edited her first two novels and introduced her to the editor Aaron Asher. The Wagmans, in turn, presented Roth with a valuable

Kafka manuscript in the 1970s, a speech Kafka made at a celebration for his boss at his insurance company.[99] Wagman went on to publish five novels, including *The Lie*, dealing with Rita Hayworth, who was herself the victim of incest.

Incest in Roth is a troubling and persistent subject, originating most likely in Maggie's own sexual abuse. It is obliquely referred to in *The Facts* when the narrator refers to Josie's experience "as a young woman already haunted by grim sexual memories" and an alleged, "half realized attempt at childhood seduction," generating a view that men had been abusing her all her life (FAC 81, 82, 83, 102). Roth added that he was enslaved "to her sense of victimization," caused partly by a drunken father (FAC 106).

The backdrop to Roth's treatment of incest reflects the shift away from sibling incest (Portnoy has a sister, but she is of no interest to him) to that of father-daughter. Swede cannot forget what he did, and worries that it might have changed his daughter: "What did he do to her that was so wrong? The kiss? That kiss? So beastly. How could a kiss make someone into a criminal?" But "the torment of self-examination never ended" (AP 92). She had asked, "Daddy, kiss me the way you would k-k-kiss umumumother," as the shoulder strap of her bathing suit slipped over her arm, exposing her nipple (AP 89–90). This is the Electra Complex in full play, a girl's psychosexual competition with her mother for possession of her father. This moment of father-daughter incestuous desire shapes the novel, incest shown as a universal and not a particular force; inbreeding remains the great crime resisted by the Jewish enforcement of the separation of the sexes, especially in Orthodox Judaism, unless for procreation.

Exit Ghost foregrounds the issue of incest when Zuckerman asks his mother in a dream, "Can we have incest?" The dead mother seeks to please but knows she cannot, being "in the grave." Zuckerman discounts that fact and persists: "Still, I'd like to commit incest with you. You're my mother. My only mother." "Whatever you want," she answers, satisfying the deeply felt Oedipal desire of the son for the mother (EG 241–42).[100] Roth's macabre and unnerving scene epitomizes his long if unacknowledged absorption with incest, returning us to his essay on Wagman. There, he admits, "Her moral outlook is so much a matter of personality that there is really no valid argument possible between her sense of things and anyone else's" (RMY 250). Or as a character remarks in *My Life as a Man*, "Fiction does different things to different people, much like matrimony" (MLM 116).

Incest in Roth extends his obsession with transgression and betrayal. In many ways, it is the ultimate betrayal, destroying parent-child restrictions in favor of something unorthodox and forbidden, driven by sexual desire. Roth's interest in young women may be the social expression of incestuous wishes.[101] Expressed in his fiction, this absorption propels the trip Kepesh and Birgitta take to the Continent in *The Professor of Desire*. Museums during the day, hunting for young girls at night (PD 46). Meeting with success, Kepesh also fantasizes Birgitta with a series of older men, including her roommate Elizabeth's father. Throughout *I Married a Communist*, there are hints of projected incest between Ira Ringold and his stepdaughter, Sylphid, the daughter of Eve Frame; parallels to Bloom and her daughter are clear.

Roth gravitated to trauma and suffering in areas of his life beyond romance and fiction. When he saw suffering in family or friends, he sought to remedy its effects. He was witness to it growing up with the near death of his father from appendicitis when ten, and the death from cancer of an aunt with whom he shared a room as a teenager. His back injury in the army caused lifelong physical trauma. In his friendships with men as well as women, he sensed their traumas and difficulties, as when he detected James Atlas's depression and Ross Miller's with his varied love life. Throughout his own romances, Roth was drawn to women who experienced trauma, often sexual abuse or alcoholism. In his nonfiction, he was similarly drawn to writers who had experienced trauma directly, not only the writers from Eastern Europe who experienced political repression, but those writers who survived the Holocaust. *Shop Talk* contains a large number of such survivors. His friendship with Primo Levi, in particular, intensified his absorption with traumatic experience; Levi's death in 1987 deeply affected Roth. The writers he admired—Kafka, Appelfeld, Levi—had all suffered. An explanation for this attraction may be his concern with the imponderable question "How did they survive? What was their secret?" This was his own worry: how could he survive, a traumatized figure, a suffering artist?

Kafka may offer an answer, the story with the greatest resonance for Roth not "The Metamorphosis" or *The Trial* but "A Hunger Artist." The traumatic experience of the artist—his suffering, victimhood, and self-deprivation—displaying his asceticism for public viewing, alternating between fasting and recuperation, demonstrated a rhythm of survival analogous to Roth's isolation when needing to write but then return to society when required. "Look at my fasting and what it produced," he seems to be saying each time he released a new work. His purity of solitude and devotion to his craft were unassailable, as was the Hunger Artist's to his cause. Roth's powerful, idealized self as a writer ruled, even if "the fantasy of purity is appalling" (HS 242).

Roth actually refers to a "fastidious hunger artist" in the narrator's reference to Lonoff from *The Ghost Writer* in *Deception* and his "self-imprisoning scrupulosity" (DE 96).

The Hunger Artist, like Roth, gains fame but is dissatisfied and feels misunderstood, becoming irritable. Fasting was performance, although few recognized why the Artist repeated his trauma, and some wondered if he was merely a showman, seeking attention through the conscious act of a traumatic experience. But when experienced in others, Roth could identify and often act. One reading of the story is the late realization that we survive not by food but by the gaze of others.[102] Roth's "gaze" of others and others of him allowed him to survive his own traumas. His response to his father's illness (he constantly "gazes" on his father's decline, recorded in *Patrimony*) is his most extended record of such a response.

The impact of a series of traumatic incidents, including his despairing marriages, followed by heart problems influenced Roth's narrative conception of his own life and that of his characters, in which he tries to reclaim, if not replay, these difficult moments from the past. Repetition of the traumatic event (often a delayed experience) is one of the characteristics of its effect, the temporal impact occasionally imposing itself upon the entire lifetime of the victim or witness.[103] There is not a major text of Roth's that does not confront trauma, his writing a constant self-examination of the traumatic event and its meaning. But for Roth the meaning is in the reaction to rather than the identification of a trauma. His enactment of a performative style of comedy and wit aided in adjusting to these moments, while simultaneously eliding the discord they generated.

A secondary focus related to trauma in Roth is adultery, evident as early as "Epstein" from *Goodbye, Columbus* and cited early in *The Facts,* when Roth's uncle divorces his wife of twenty years to marry another woman (FAC 14). *Deception* is likely the epitome of the theme for him; he may have known this troubling, crossover line from John Marston's *The Malcontent* (1603): "Adultery is often the mother of incest" (Act I, Sc. 2, l. 132). Roth himself committed adultery: still married to Maggie, he had relationships with a number of students and a lengthy relationship with Ann Mudge. When married to Bloom, both during his treatment at Silver Hill Hospital in Connecticut and earlier in London, he had several affairs, one captured in *Deception*.

Affairs run throughout Roth's works. The opening of *The Counterlife,* with Zuckerman's thirty-nine-year-old brother Henry and his twenty-two-year-old dental assistant, Wendy, focuses on their affair, which follows an earlier affair with a former patient, Marie. In *Everyman*, the deceased narrator recounts his affair with the youthful Phoebe for whom he leaves his first wife, Cindy. But then he betrays Phoebe for the model Merete. And as he recovers from a heart operation, he longs for the buxom red-headed nurse, Maureen.[104] Even the vaunted Lonoff may have had an affair with Amy Bellette in *The Ghost Writer*, or so his wife believes. As Roth laments in *The Human Stain*, "The fantasy of purity is appalling. It's insane" (HS 242).

Portnoy's Complaint allowed Roth to explode into a comic voice of his own, discovering the freedom to express the id, ego, and superego, sometimes all at once. He rebels against his parents, "the two outstanding producers and packagers of guilt in our time" (PC 36). Not only did he find the permission within himself to do so, but he found an audience responsive to his discovery. The satire of *Goodbye, Columbus* becomes the frenetic comedy of *Portnoy*, soon to take form in the energetic if lewd "On the Air" and the satires of the 1970s: *Our Gang, The Breast, The Great American Novel*. Two streams emerged in his writing: the psychological and the playful. Both expressed the contest of lingering inner issues, notably his disastrous marriage with Maggie (*My Life as a Man*) and the liberating element of farce, satire, and comedy (*Our Gang, The Breast, The Great American Novel*).

The voices in "On the Air" and subsequent satires gave energy and momentum to works that would blend introspection and politics, self and society. The purging of his personal past (although not childhood) occurring in *My Life as a Man* gave birth to a new innocent, a modern American Adam, Nathan Zuckerman. But with comedy, seriousness was undone; *My Life as a Man* was his "war novel" after failing to receive the Distinguished Service Cross for putting up with Maggie (CWPR 171).

"On the Air," published in *New American Review* 10 (August 1970), sustained Roth's quest for freedom; he turned to outlandish, fantasy-directed prose, pushing the content of *Portnoy* further. It also reconfirmed Roth's belief in radio as *the* medium and entertainment as the new purpose of life. "Hearing is believing," says Milton Lippman shoe store owner and incipient talent agent *extraordinaire*, searching for a new Answer Man (ONA 12). (Milton was Roth's middle name, later used in *The Anatomy Lesson* for the pornographer Appel). His answer? Albert Einstein, not only the smartest man in the world but a Jew! Deferentially writing to him (I can "understand how busy [you] must be thinking"), he nonetheless pursues him for a new radio show (ONA 10). In his attack on the *goyishe* bullshit he hears, Lippman wants to pit the smartest man in the world against others on a radio quiz show and possibly start a separate Jewish radio network; let the Goys have theirs.

What he realizes, extending the exuberance of Portnoy, is that all the world *is* some kind of show: "We are all only talent assembled by the great Talent Scout Up Above" (ONA 20). The narrator, a comic alter ego for Roth, exclaims that he's only a talent scout who has an eye out "for the gimmick, for the strange! People don't notice the unusual things that happen in life until somebody that does comes along. . . . And that is all I do, and is nothing I will 'be ashamed of.' A talent scout is only a person who happens to see what the other person doesn't" (ONA 19).

The plot of the story is how Lippman with his wife and child (named Ira, used later in *I Married a Communist*) travel to Princeton to see Einstein, who has yet to reply to the letters from Lippman. Stopping on the way, they encounter various forms of anti-Semitism, walking mistakenly into a bar and then a Howard Johnson's with a one-arm ice-cream attendant with a silver scoop attached to his arm (whose aunt is supposedly the ever popular singer of the 1940s, Kate Smith). The manager offers them only woolen- or paper-flavored ice cream. Tasting the newsprint cone causes the young boy to keel over. The final episode, "Gangbusters," after the popular radio show, has a manic police chief threaten Lippman while his wife and child lie ill on the floor.

This out-of-control, nihilistic story, splitting off into farce, religious persecution, and social injustice, with an abusive law officer part of the onslaught, was never reprinted, Roth possibly heeding Updike's remark that it was simply too offensive (RMY 134). The mockery of the story knows no limits, mocking even the mocker, starting each section with the name of a popular radio show or radio world. Replacing nostalgia is antagonism, especially in the world of the goyim, kikes, colored, chinks, and even homos. Everyone is prejudiced. Mainstream America is exposed in *its* prejudices, lurking not so far under the surface, as the plot dissolves into a series of scenes that intensify recriminations, making the reader uneasy through the irreverent surrealism.

The dangerous and the hilarious mix, while a Rothian aesthetic emerges: "What you could imagine could also be so. What was not could become" (ONA 16). But the imagination is no competition for reality: "The things you could make in this world! The things that were already *made*! The acts they were just *giving* away! For Nothing!" Lippman exclaims (ONA 17). This corroborates Roth's earlier statements that the imagination cannot keep up with reality and that the writer's job is to make "*credible* much of American reality" (RMY 168).

In a 1984 interview, Roth said that in "On the Air" he was trying to blow up more of himself in the wake of *Portnoy*, exploding old loyalties and inhibitions, the very thing he had started with *Portnoy* and the reason so many Jews were incensed with the book (CWPR 175). If someone with Roth's seriousness of purpose and credentials couldn't be controlled, then something was definitely wrong. But he soon realized that not to be serious about seriousness was essential to survive in terms of his writing and life (RMY 134). It's not to give up being serious but to approach it in a different way. And with this newly liberated self, he entered the next phase of his writing life without sacrificing the polemical or antagonistic. In fact, it began to expand. Instead of the Jewish writer of poise and refinement, perhaps Malamud or even Bellow, there was the raucous voice of an outsider marinated in anger.

6

Jewish Wheaties

Oh, to be a center fielder, a center fielder—and nothing more!
—Alex Portnoy in *Portnoy's Complaint*, 1969

Just as the late 1960s would culminate with the blockbuster *Portnoy*, the 1970s would be a period of high productivity culminating in *The Ghost Writer* and reestablishing Roth's claim as a literary writer, not just a satirical Kafka. He began the decade focused on American excess but ended with a Jamesian novella uniting writing practices and the Holocaust. Partly anticipating this was his "Writers from the Other Europe" series. In 1970, *Our Gang* appeared, and he began to write *The Breast*, a satirical take on "The Metamorphosis," and then the energetic, encyclopedic baseball saga, *The Great American Novel*. In the midst of this, Irving Howe offered a surprising attack on Roth and *Portnoy's Complaint*, despite his earlier celebration of Roth's writing. But the year his exuberant baseball novel appeared, 1973, a kind of *envoi* to things American and the Newark years, Roth became enmeshed with the suppressed and blacklisted writers from Eastern Europe, which would absorb him for almost a decade.

Marking the apogee of this period is *My Life as a Man* (1974), the purging of his troubled life with Maggie and introduction of the innocent Nathan Zuckerman (from Camden, not Newark) in a work that set off further new directions for his writing. During the 1970s, Roth expanded his palette to include Europe, replacing life in Newark with that of Mitteleuropa, underscored by *The Professor of Desire* (1977) and *The Ghost Writer* (1979). Contributing to this would be a new life with Claire Bloom, met in 1975, followed by a move to London in 1976 to be with her, regularly spending six months in Britain and six in the U.S. until 1988.

But difficult, problematic women during the post-Portnoy period were still circulating in his life, and with the same pattern: as they became more needy, he retreated. Psychologically, he may have been drawn to such women because, like his father, he possessed a deep urge to help, and they were the opposite of his mother, who seemingly hid her inner needs in her pursuit of a stable family and domestic security, acting as the glue for her two sons and husband. Roth's father, by contrast, always made his needs, his demands, known, which in part drove the young Roth to leave for Bucknell after his first year at Rutgers Newark. But for Roth, stability and solitude were never enough to trump romance.[1]

In April 1969, Barbara Sproul wrote to restate her love for Roth and that she was there to help him feel loved and happy. "Write brilliant and feel better and write me a letter if you get the time," she told him. And a few years later, she would admit that she wanted a child with him.[2] Throughout 1969, her letters buoyed Roth's depression as well as anxiety. Sometimes, she remarks, you seem "very distant and foreign to me, unknown really, while at other times you seem close and near."[3] She often offered advice, telling him not to feel sad over the misrepresentations of *Portnoy* in the press and that his inability to tell the Zuckerman story (he was beginning to grapple with the character) would soon be overcome. When she visits him, it is always joyous. Of watching the movie *Shane* together she wrote, "You did all the parts plus a critique at the same time." "I want to make love with you . . . softly and roughly, quietly and loudly," she wrote in an earlier letter.[4] Eager to be with him, she teases that he will probably remain at Yaddo until he falls to number 2 on the bestseller list.

The 1970s began with a trip to Asia with Sproul, beginning in Greece and then on to Bangkok and Rangoon. She was finishing her PhD in religious studies, focusing on creation myths, and suggested the adventure to Roth. Bangkok fascinated him, especially the behavior of the prostitutes who would gather at the airport to welcome American troops arriving for R & R, who often spent a week with a girl. The same women would see the men off at the airport and then wait for a new shipment to arrive to repeat the process. He observed kickboxing and met a group of GIs who had gone AWOL. In Cambodia in March 1970, he and Sproul visited Angkor Wat only weeks before America bombed the country. (It had secretly been doing so since 1965.) On his return home, Roth published an essay in *Look* magazine entitled "Cambodia: A Modest Proposal" (RMY 224–28), suggesting that dropping appliances and shoes rather than bombs would be more effective for the Cambodians. Imitating Swift, it was a gesture toward satire that he would expand with his indictment of Nixon in *Our Gang*.

His relationship with Sproul was unraveling, partly because she wanted it to be more serious and he did not. Children again became an issue. But their breakup in 1974, after six years together, seemed sudden and unexpected to Roth. It brought on the first of what would be three serious bouts of depression, his emotional pain leading to physical pain. And although they loosely kept in touch, as he often did with other women in his life, he later turned against her for what she said was his weakness for "sycophants."[5] But despite the anger and feelings of betrayal, he modeled the figure of Claire in *The Professor of Desire*, published in 1977, on her.[6]

The Vietnam War, which Roth opposed, had been going on for some fifteen years, and by the mid-1960s, like other writers and artists, Roth took action. In February 1967, he wrote an editorial following a story on a bulldozed Vietnam village in *New York Times* of 11 January 1967 headlined "Vietcong Village to Be Bulldozed." A typed headnote, appearing in *Authors Take Sides on Vietnam*, possibly by Roth, reads, "The following article, describing the final solution of the Bensuc problem, appeared on page four of the *New York Times*, January 11, 1967." After the article, Roth wrote, "*The Allies also believe that they will be able to win the allegiance of the people once they have been removed from the Viet Cong sphere.* After leveling their homes, their shops and the graves of their ancestors with a bulldozer. Who can be 'for' such a war as we are fighting?"[7]

Roth argued often that the war in Vietnam was criminal and unwarranted, even challenging Updike when Updike defended the fighting. One of their arguments supposedly appeared in *Rabbit Redux*, Updike's conservative views expressed by Rabbit, Roth's by a black revolutionary named Skeeter. Updike also supposedly carried a slip with the slogan of the Weathermen, a radical group, in his wallet (likely the phrase attributed to John Jacobs, "Bring the war home"), to remind himself how outrageous was their extremism. With slight changes, Merry Levov puts such a statement up on her wall in *American Pastoral*.[8] Vietnam in Roth's fiction becomes a central pivot in *American Pastoral* with Merry's act resulting in a death that sends the Levov family spiraling downward. In *The Human Stain*, the depressed and angry Vietnam vet and ex-husband of Faunia Farley, Les Farley, is a threating force. Roth actually went to a VA hospital to talk to Vietnam vets to understand the character of Les Farley more clearly.

In an Amazon.com interview, Roth cited three postwar moments that had the greatest impact on him: the McCarthy era, Vietnam, and the impeachment of President Clinton in 1998.[9] Concerning *American Pastoral*, he remarked that he had "begun the book some twenty years earlier, near the end of the Vietnam war." But he never knew how to proceed after the first seventy pages, titled "The Hero of Our Time," an ironic allusion to Lermontov's 1840 novel *A Hero of Our Time*. In the preface to that novel, the author explains that it is not the portrait of one man but "a portrait built up of all our generation's vices in full bloom."[10] The five stories that make up the historical novel with its military focus employed fragments and incompleteness, reflecting the actual experience of life Roth may have incorporated in *My Life*. But Roth at this time never knew how to proceed with *American Pastoral* after Merry blew up a building to protest the war.

What Roth discovered from *Portnoy's Complaint* was that undermining seriousness through a set of comic devices was his *métier*, uniting voice and style refined in his satires of the 1970s. He learned that seriousness is best approached comically, so he became a virtual "pornographer of seriousness." Not the modernist's "Make it new" for Roth, but "Make it serious in the least likely way" (CWPR 250). This transition partly resulted from his discovery of the value of the exuberant comedy woven through *Portnoy's Complaint* and partly from a renewed social and literary conscience—recall his grammar school play on American democracy and protest against the exclusion of the singer Hazel Scott—and from his exposure to Eastern European repression in countries like Czechoslovakia and Hungary, an awareness partly generated by his understanding of Kafka. It is not coincidental that "Looking at Kafka" (1973) appeared after his first trip to Eastern Europe (May 1972). Replacing baseball's center field is the decimated medieval Jewish cemetery of the Pinkas Synagogue in Prague.

Any engagement with Mitteleuropa could not begin, however, until he dealt with America, and the only way to do that was through satire. Roth needed to remake America even if it was dysfunctional (*Our Gang*), adjusting to a new sexuality (*The Breast*), or reaffirming its natural heritage, baseball (*The Great American Novel*). Such concerns were efforts to redeem the country, just as his celebration of sexual liberty was his effort to redeem himself. This is the very obscenity of the novel—the search for liberation—Roth told Plimpton in a *New York Times* prerelease interview of 1969. "Maybe other patients dream," Portnoy tells Spielvogel, but "with me, *everything happens*. I have a life *without* latent content" (PC 257).

Paradoxically sustaining Roth's turn to satire at this time was his inability to go further with *My Life as a Man*: he was blocked and lacked an adequate structure to tell the story. He wrote numerous drafts until he eventually realized that the answer lay in the problem: he needed to find a setting and method to approach the sordid event of Maureen's falsely obtained urine sample from a Black woman in Tompkins Park in New York. He thought at first it might have been a scene in *When She Was Good* or perhaps a scene in *Portnoy's Complaint,* but he felt it was too malevolent for that type of book. Meanwhile, he wrote drafts and drafts of *My Life as a Man,* realizing at last that the sordid event was the heart of the novel.

The structural problem remained intractable, so he turned to Nixon and Watergate, a more overt and political form of corruption. He tried again but still could not find the form to tell his story of Maggie through Maureen, so he wrote his baseball book as relief, and while finishing that he also wrote *The Breast,* a diverting *jeu d'esprit.* It seemed as if he were blasting through a tunnel to reach a book he couldn't write. Each of the preceding books was a blast to clear the way to get to *My Life as a Man,* he explained in his *Paris Review* interview (CWPR 172; RMY 138).

What Roth's summary does not address is his persistent absorption with satire as the genre that permitted him to "write America," using satire to correct, modify, and alter the wrongs brought on by government or society. "On the Air" of 1970 is one example; "Looking at Kafka" (1973), much in the fantasy/satiric style of Bruno Schulz, another. Satire masks aggression and challenges abuse, immoral conduct, or exploitation. Acknowledging that it is always a literary not political act, Roth explains, "satire is moral rage transformed into comic art—as an elegy is grief transformed into poetic art."[11]

Our Gang, which first appeared in the *New York Review of Books* and the journal *Modern Occasions,* allowed Roth to offer his criticism of governmental abuse, personal greed, and the shifting compass of the country, while extending his early concern over social injustice and political abuse. As one might expect in 1971, however, initial reaction by Random House to *Our Gang* was hesitant at best, negative at worst. They thought it was in bad taste and might be politically counterproductive. To counter this response, Roth invited Lelchuk to interview him so that he could reconstruct his early ideas of the work and counter the objections of his publisher.

The discussion, published as "On Our Gang" in the *Atlantic Monthly* in December 1971 and reprinted in *Reading Myself and Others* (RMY 37–50), begins with Roth commenting on a tradition of American political satire but emphasizing that its topicality causes its short shelf life and that it's hardly being written, let alone being published. H. L. Mencken comes to mind and earlier James Russell Lowell, but few others, he notes. Yet he sees his purpose as other than the obvious exposure of Nixon's abuses: his aim is to critique American public rhetoric, although he does so through exaggeration and parody. He then cites a certain tradition of American comedy, especially the Marx Brothers, the Three Stooges, and Abbott and Costello, whose slapstick seemed suited to the shenanigans of Nixon and friends.

The book naturally received immense attention, both good and bad. Roth's impersonation of Nixon's style was flawless, while some considered his exposure of abuses in bad taste. Roth explained that it was not the "regal" Nixon he wanted to portray but a baggy-pants burlesque player.

Roth had written satire at Bucknell that was published in the college literary magazine, *Et Cetera,* and one of his early published pieces, appearing in the *New Republic* (along with his movie reviews), was a parody of Eisenhower's religious beliefs and prose style, "Positive Thinking on Pennsylvania Avenue," inspired by a sermon by Norman Vincent Peale. Even *Goodbye, Columbus* had a satiric intent. Satire and Roth was hardly new.

But the more specific catalyst for *Our Gang* was Nixon's response to Second Lieutenant William Calley's conviction of April 1971 for the My Lai massacre. Nixon announced that Calley would not have to await his appeal in the post stockade for his conviction of murdering twenty-two civilians but would be restricted to quarters until Nixon reviewed the decision. Given a life sentence, Calley would serve only three and half years of house arrest, although he had murdered four times the number of those killed by Charles Manson. The tricky behavior of the president confirmed for Roth his moral turpitude and low-handed manner. And it required a response. Even his trip to China was pure opportunism, Roth believed. So why satire to confront Nixon? Because, Roth explained, it conveyed moral rage through the lens of comedy (CWPR 51). The murder of Trick E. Dixon in *Our Gang* is only just desserts. But in the next chapter, he's alive in Hell debating Satan. To Epstein, Roth wrote, "I don't think I've hated anybody so much since Maggie."[12]

In ending his interview, Roth, again protesting social injustice and political abuse and anticipating some of the moral character he will soon display in his support of the repressed Eastern European writers, cites the courageous Russian writers Yuli Daniel and Andrei Sinyavsky, sentenced to hard labor for their satires of Soviet life. And in the assassination chapter of *Our Gang*, Roth seeks to exploit the discrepancy between official pieties and unpleasant truths, exposing the banal mentality of the media in particular. The art of government lying might be the quick summary of Roth's farcical satire of a president devoid of morals.

Random House was, nonetheless, nervous and sought blurbs. In letters to Epstein, Jules Feiffer called *Our Gang* a "paradigm of unparalleled portentous perception. . . . Roth has Nixon down Pat"; Anthony Burgess praised its Swiftian manner, suggesting that it was "worth suffering from such a Duce to be able to produce such a vigorous pasquinade"; and Dwight Macdonald wrote that he "laughed out loud sixteen times and giggled internally a statistically unverifiable amount."[13] Reviews, however, were mixed, divided between praise and condemnation. *Time* magazine editorialized that the work was a "manically scurrilous satire" and accused Roth of being "extravagantly hostile." The *New Republic* felt Roth was too bold and did little to hide his target.

Dwight Macdonald in the *New York Times* summed up the general critical reaction when he wrote that the work was "far-fetched, unfair, tasteless, disturbing, logical, coarse and very funny." A "lunatic logic" triumphs, making a kind of comic sense.[14] Twenty months after *Our Gang*, Roth published "The President Addresses the Nation" at the height of the Watergate hearings in the spring of 1973. Reprinted in *Reading Myself and Others*, the parody displays Nixon's defense of his actions following his removal from office. Arguing that he should follow the law, he twists his logic to say he must stay in office to protect the welfare and security of the nation. He doesn't go. Those who praised both works celebrated Roth's skill at mimicry as he captured the rhythms and cadences, as well as the clichés and repetitions, of Nixon. Roth also wrote two new prefaces, the first a preface to the Watergate Edition, the second to the "Pre-Impeachment Edition."[15]

Between *Our Gang* and *The Breast* there was an important change: Roth switched publishers, finding Holt, Rinehart and Winston more receptive to his demands for larger advances than Random House, which, frankly, found him too expensive. After *Portnoy*, in fact, Roth never earned back his advances and did not have a bestseller again until *The Plot Against America* in 2004.[16]

But Roth had a fan in Aaron Asher, who was then an editor at Holt. They had both been at the University of Chicago and likely crossed paths several times in the world of New York publishing, and when Roth began to question his relationship with Random House, initiated by his disappointment with their response to his financial demands as he was completing *Our Gang*, he began to consider alternatives. A story in the *Book of the Month Club*

Newsletter entitled "The Letting Go of Random House by Philip Roth," reported the break, although the major players disputed the narrative.[17]

What essentially precipitated the shift was Roth's disappointment with his agent Candida Donadio. A note dated 7 February 1972 from his lawyer Arthur J. Klein to Epstein announces that Roth's agency representation is over. Either Klein or his partner, Martin Garbus, will now negotiate and/or advise Roth. Initiating the break with Random House was a disagreement over a new paperback contract with Bantam in October 1971. Garbus was particularly worried that Roth would lose money in the event that a paperback came out prior to six months after the date of a hardback publication. On 14 April 1972, Roth, now representing himself, detailed submission and royalty requirements for two new books to Epstein and Random House following *Our Gang*: *The Breast* and *The Great American Novel*. If their best offer was acceptable, he would instruct Klein to draw up a contract. Importantly, he wanted each title dealt with separately. If the terms were not acceptable, he would go elsewhere. For *The Breast*, he seeks an advance of $225,000; for *The Great American Novel*, $236,250. And for both, he wants to retain all paperback rights. An offer in response on 24 April from Epstein caused Roth to reconsider slightly reduced figures, but for hardback rights only. He was pressured to make a decision in two days.

Roth declined the counteroffer. To Bennett Cerf of Random House he would explain that despite the failure to reach an agreement, his time with the publishing company had been successful and in almost all respects happy. He admitted that he would miss Epstein's editorial acumen but believed he would do better financially elsewhere. An exchange with Donald Klopfer was more pointed and personal: he had known Klopfer since meeting him through Styron in Rome in 1960. On 20 May 1972 from Cornwall Bridge, Roth wrote Klopfer:

> Your generosity and charm won me over back in Doney's on the Via Veneta back in 1960, and . . . each time we were together you seemed to me the same kind gentleman one could rely upon and trust. . . . Your presence at Random House was always a comfort to me.

Yours
Philip[18]

Klopfer's response of 27 June, after Roth's break with Random House, expresses unhappiness with the decision:

> Obviously, I was terribly disappointed that we couldn't come to an understanding with you about your two new books. I received three copies of the Book of the Month Club Report while I was in Rome. I must say that I think Aaron handled it in a dignified and honest way, but I was really irritated by your lawyer's statement. It showed a complete lack of knowledge of the publishing business, which I am sure is the case. . . . I believe that the offer we made was a generous one, and I am sorry you decided to split yourself up as you did—but I do wish you luck. I hope you will sit down and write many more good books, and not become too bewitched by the money.

> My best to you.
> As always,
> [Donald Klopfer][19]

Roth, slightly offended by the story in the *Book of the Month Club Newsletter* and Klopfer's closing phrase, replied on 29 June that he was upset by Garbus's quoted comments about negotiations and explained to Klopfer that he did not turn to lawyers for advice concerning his two books, nor was he driven entirely by money. Klopfer's response of 10 July tried to defuse the comment on money and gesture toward a friendship of some sort.

Asher's own statement about the affair, which preoccupied New York publishing gossip for several weeks (anticipating much later gossip, when Roth signed with Simon and Schuster for hefty fees negotiated by his new agent, Andrew Wylie, in 1989), was professional. Attempting to end rumors that Roth left Random House for Holt only for the money, Asher explained that negotiations with Random House broke down after they could not agree on certain demands from Roth. He would have liked to have stayed, but they couldn't agree. He and Roth had known each other for a dozen years (he, too, graduated the University of Chicago, with a BA in 1949 and an MA in 1952), so it was almost natural that Roth thought of Holt, which quickly met his demands. But he would have gone elsewhere if necessary. He did not auction his work, Asher emphasized.

Garbus, as quoted in the *Book of the Month Club Newsletter*, said the new publisher had only the hardcover rights; Roth had complete control over the paperback rights and all other rights, which is what he wanted in the first instance (although no mention of the higher advance was cited). The money is in the paperback business, Garbus went on to say, "so why shouldn't the writer get his fair share?" These are likely the remarks Roth was uncomfortable with.[20] Ironically, perhaps, *My Life as a Man* was dedicated to both Aaron Asher and Jason Epstein, in that order, which is itself telling.

An incident from this period confirms Roth's growing pleasure with what his friend, the novelist Alan Lelchuk, called "American mischief," the title of his 1973 novel. It also shows how he defended young writers when bullied or abused. The incident occurred in late September 1972, brought about by a scene in Lelchuk's forthcoming novel concerning the fictional murder of Norman Mailer—shot in the ass with his pants down in his hotel room . The title of the draft account of the encounter is "The Godfather of the Literary World & a Young Offender."

It began with Roger Straus, Lelchuk's publisher at Farrar, Straus and Giroux, receiving a telegram from Mailer asking to meet to discuss a reported scene in Lelchuk's forthcoming novel where he is assassinated. Straus contacted Cy Rembar, Mailer's lawyer, to negotiate, but Mailer persisted with his complaint, although FSG's lawyers felt it was "Ok" to use Mailer's name since he was a public figure. Lelchuk removed the names of other intellectual figures but wanted to keep the high-profile Mailer. Indeed, he felt betrayed by FSG for even acknowledging Mailer's request. In the novel, the protagonist, Lenny Pincus, reading Nietzsche at Widener Library at Harvard—Mailer was to lecture at the school the next day—follows the argument of Mailer's *White Negro*, that he must knock off the arrogant, pushy writer, which is also knocking off the institution of literature. In questions after his fictional lecture, Mailer exclaims, "Show me a red-blooded American boy who reads books and I'll show you a potential murderer."[21] Lenny Pincus fulfills that claim.

A meeting was scheduled, where Mailer's lawyer, Rembar (who had successfully won a case for Grove Press suing the U.S. Post Office for confiscating copies of *Lady Chatterley's Lover*) suggested that Lelchuk bring Roth as a second. Roth was invited partly because he wrote a critical preview of the novel in *Esquire* from which Mailer supposedly learned of the scene, although a professor at the University of Pennsylvania, Robert Lucid, who was planning an anthology of fictional portraits of real authors, had also written to reveal the scene to Mailer.[22] Roth was an artful ally not only of Lelchuk but of Roger Straus: he knew of Straus's anger in 1970 over the slight to *Portnoy's Complaint* when it failed to win the National Book Award. Within a year

Roth would join Farrar, Straus and Giroux. In a parallel incident at the time, Roth contradicted a false report of his death.[23]

One fear and reason for the Lelchuk-Mailer meeting, and hoped-for removal of the murder scene, was that it might encourage real assassins to attack Mailer. Lelchuk's own lawyer would accompany him since his interest was literary, "not pugilistic and I wanted the referee to be a legal one."[24] Lelchuk had prepared for the meeting by reading Mailer on censorship in his *Presidential Papers* and *Advertisements for Myself*. Rembar had even written an introduction to a book on obscenity and censorship, so Lelchuk was convinced that ethically and legally he was right in his literary murder of Mailer, shot by a radical in the buttocks with his pants down.

The meeting occurred on 29 September 1972 on the thirty-sixth floor of the New York law office of Lelchuk's lawyer, Martin Garbus. Roth, Lelchuk, Mailer, Robert Giroux (an FSG editor), Georges Borchardt (Lelchuk's agent), and others were present. Mailer was in a suit but with no tie and his shirt open and "wild hair." Lelchuk, defending his first book, wore a sport coat and tie and carried a briefcase. An account of the gathering published in the *New York Times* of 18 October reversed the dress, with Mailer in a pinstriped suit and Lelchuk the bohemian and "bearded bachelor." (The thirty-four-year-old Lelchuk, then teaching at Brandeis, was, in fact, bearded at the time.)[25] At Roth's suggestion, Lelchuk would treat the encounter as if he were teaching a class.

Mailer attacked the moment Lelchuk and Roth were seated: "I'd like to beat you two guys to death," he shouted. "Understand me?" Roth angrily responded, according to Lelchuk's account, with "Don't you pull that stuff! You're not going to bully me or Alan with that violent talk! Got that?"[26] Garbus tried to establish some order. (Pete Hamill, the journalist, was to be Mailer's second, but he didn't show.)

Mailer then went after Roth as if he, not Lelchuk, had written the scene. It turned out later that Mailer had not read Roth's *Esquire* piece, nor the book in galleys. Rembar, Mailer's cousin, they later learned, then tried a different tack: just remove the scene. Garbus cried censorship, supported by Roth. Mailer backed down, but for the next two hours there was a mixture of "Hemingwayesque profundities and Hollywood poses, and all the way through a stream of physical threats." Mailer was convinced that either Roth or Philip Rahv put Lelchuk up to writing the offensive scene, encouraging would-be assassins and holding him up to ridicule. Lelchuk responded by claiming that Mailer always provoked people to an adversarial, combative, and even murderous stance toward himself and referred to him as the "Muhammad Ali of novelists." But Mailer could not separate criticism from ridicule, offering new antagonisms toward Styron, Bellow, and, of course, Roth, who had suggested using Mailer's own words against him. Mailer responded by stating that the depiction of his death was more fitting for Roth than for Mailer. Taking his pants down in order to survive was the way Mailer would depict Roth behaving if Mailer were writing the scene. "Obviously," Lelchuk wrote, "I didn't know the first thing about Mailer himself." Lelchuk again argued that it was his protagonist, Lenny Pincus, who acted with dishonor in the scene, not Mailer. Twice Mailer said he wasn't interested in pursuing any legal action. In fact, Lelchuk felt he met not Mailer the defender of freedom but a fake, an imposter: "Beneath the studied rage, the venal bullying . . . was an ordinary man whose feelings were hurt." The meeting ended as it had started, with threats, Mailer in a Godfather-like tone whispering, "Revenge is a dish tasted best when cold."[27]

Roth's role in all this was as a strategist, directing Lelchuk to statements by Mailer on freedom of expression, using Mailer himself to expose his hypocrisy. The greatest irony of the encounter is that Mailer, acting cowardly and cheaply in his role as demagogue and godfather, seemed to come off better as Lelchuk's creation than in the flesh. The fictional Mailer acted like the Mailer of his own prefaces and talks as a figure of originality and bold force, even if the act brought with it the element of "demonic danger."[28] The episode showed that Mailer was less than Lelchuk's imagination and less than his own rhetorical creation.

At the end of Lelchuk's account, he cites a string of real figures in fiction under assumed names: Sherwood Anderson burlesqued as Scripps O'Neill in Hemingway's *Torrents of Spring*, J. Middleton Murry as Gerald Crich in *Women in Love*, Turgenev as Karmasonov in *The Possessed,* and even Jack Kennedy in Mailer's *An American Dream*. By exposing these figures, real people in texts, Lelchuk anticipated what Roth did with Nixon in *Our Gang* and what he will do with himself in works like *The Counterlife, The Facts, Zuckerman Bound,* and *Operation Shylock*, placing Roth the character in a contest with Roth the man, where he both protects and reveals himself obliquely. "Tell all the truth but tell it slant," Emily Dickinson wrote.[29] The scene with Mailer in *American Mischief* remained, running for a full five pages.[30]

The Mailer-Lelchuk encounter made the Johnny Carson show. On the 26 October 1972 broadcast, Carson asked Mailer if what he said to Lelchuk was true. Mailer reported that he told the neophyte writer that if he ever met him in an alley, all that would "be left of [him] would be a hank of hair and some fillings."[31] As Lelchuk recalled, Mailer had difficulty understanding that Lelchuk was not interested in fighting but in literature.

Another incident of the early 1970s clarified Roth's attitude toward women, especially needy women he felt he could help. In late December 1972, a former student from Penn wrote to him complementing him on his course on Kafka and Bellow. Roth responded, and their exchange reveals his interest in her future, intensified when she refers to herself as "silently complicated" and fascinated by her mind as a result of Roth's course and a conversation they had earlier on a park bench. He seeks to boost her lack of self-confidence, something he repeatedly did with women, drawn to those who needed such support, likely the case with Maggie. The former student ends her letter with "Very glad you liked my paper—can you make anything more out of me now?"[32]

The correspondence continued through the spring of 1973. She sends him a paper on chronic "wrist-cutting." He doesn't immediately reply, and in July she pursues him: "Why haven't I heard from you? . . . Did you find my paper too upsetting?"[33] Her lengthy letter soon parallels her situation to that of K in *The Trial*. She keeps in touch and even asks him about his trip to Prague. She is in California but without a plan or a purpose. She awaits a letter of recommendation from him, but it does not appear. Roth finally replies in late July, telling her to make her wrist-cutting essay more mundane and bloody but dismissing the link to Kafka. She becomes more upset and depressed but apologizes for her defensiveness which, she admits, is a need to be understood. She will likely go to graduate school in psychology, she then writes.

The final letter, of August 1974, is her comment on *My Life as a Man*, in which she admits she is captivated by Peter Tarnopol and Dr. Spielvogel. The exchange illustrates Roth's attraction to vulnerable women and his effort to help them, which, in turn, creates their dependency on him and which he, of course, resists. The wrist-cutting will reappear in his late novel *Indignation* (2008): Olivia Hutton, the attractive coed Marcus Messner meets at his college, has scars on her wrists from an attempted suicide at Bryn Mawr. Marcus thinks of pursuing her, but she drops out of college and goes to Cleveland, partly because of a rumored pregnancy.

Following *Our Gang* and sustaining his satiric drive was *The Breast*, a work of absurd sexuality and role reversal, his first title for his new publisher, Holt, Rinehart and Winston. It comically addresses the dangers of literature: "*Did* fiction do this to me?" David Kepesh asks in the novella (BR 81). Did teaching Gogol and Kafka transform him from a student to a subject of literary study? Dedicated to Elizabeth Ames, executive director of Yaddo, *The Breast* playfully addresses sexual politics and literature, Kepesh transformed into a 155-pound breast with sexual desires. Exaggerating Freud's transference theory, the book farcically and comically explores the dangers of reading.

One nonliterary inspiration for *The Breast* was musical. Reading about a specially outfitted van used by the harpsichordist Igor Kipnis to transport his instrument, Roth got the idea for the special, foam-fitted van with giant seatbelts and foam-rubber cushioning to safely transport Kepesh as a breast to the countryside.

He enjoyed writing the book so much, Roth told an interviewer, that in 1974, he started a sequel and completed eighty pages before abandoning it.[34] In an earlier interview, Roth explained that writing *The Breast* continued his interest in writing about "extreme behavior in ordinary situations"; living beyond one's moral and psychological means fascinated him. He enigmatically added that Kepesh as a breast may be his first heroic character (CWPR 55, 56).

Citing Kafka and Gogol, Roth highlights the comic tradition of his story and his hope that it succeeds not because it is heavy with meaning but because of the quality of the overall invention and that there is no way out through literary interpretation (CWPR 58). But Kepesh is lost, akin to Descartes at the opening of his *Meditations*: "I am certain that I am, but what am I?" (quoted in CWPR 59). Taking a potentially hilarious situation seriously was how Roth took the joke and stood it on is head.

But his publisher was hesitant about its reception and sought assurances and blurbs from a set of distinguished writers. They turned on their own comic powers in response. Cynthia Ozick told Asher that the book "equalizes sanity and madness," summarizing it as "Hegelian *meshugas* [madness]!" "Reading it [I] was noisy with pleasure," she says. In a second letter, she provides a unique analysis of Roth as a talented Freud. Both have "dazzling strokes of craziness," but, she advises Asher, *The Breast* should be kept out of the hands of every writer in America

> because reading it is just too damn discouraging: with *that* sort of brain around, why bother? I predict that after its publication there will be a great desert of non-novel-writing; watch and see; everyone will dry up. . . . The middle-aged will sit home and sulk, sucking their breast-shaped thumbs

for a decade or so. All this is maundering. If I write a third time, I'll keep it to the following three words: what an idea![35]

Rosalyn Drexler, a New York artist, screenwriter, and novelist, wrote to Asher to say that she just "saw *Claire's Knee* [Éric Rohmer's 1970 film] and now I've read Philip's Breast . . . just like the supermarket chicken in parts. You buy what you like best." The book shows that even "when a man becomes a breast, he still thinks like a prick."[36]

Roth's second title for Holt was *The Great American Novel*, Asher again his editor. In many ways, the story of Roth is the story of his editors.[37] But this linguistic extravaganza was a financial and popular disappointment. Sales were modest at best and reviewers hesitant to endorse the non-Portnoy universe of fable and myth in his overwritten sports novel. Still, it provided a diversion from his struggle with *My Life as a Man*.

What this activity largely shows is Roth's habit of bouncing from publisher to publisher during his career, often going where he got the best price for his work. And once Andrew Wylie entered the picture in 1989, precipitating Roth's departure from Farrar, Straus and Giroux after they published nine of his books, for Simon and Schuster, Roth's price skyrocketed as he continued to shuttle from one publisher to another. Rarely would he return to his original publisher, although his last four novels, *Everyman, Indignation, The Humbling,* and *Nemesis,* saw him go back to where he started: Houghton Mifflin. He initiated the pattern when he left Houghton Mifflin to go with Random House in 1960. Loyalty even to editors did not prevent him from moving in the marketplace to either follow them or obtain top dollar or both.[38] The catalyst for these changes was his belief that he deserved higher advances for his work, while familiarity with his new editor could ensure the kind of editorial, marketing, and distribution treatment he believed he deserved. From Joe Fox to Jason Epstein, Aaron Asher, David Rieff, and John Sterling, Roth developed strong relationships with his editors, but he also broke with them when economics led to a better opportunity.

Aaron Asher is a case in point, himself something of a journeyman in publishing. After five years at Viking as senior editor (where he worked with Bellow, Arthur Miller, and Frank Conroy), the thirty-nine-year-old editor went to Holt as general books editor in July 1969. CBS had taken over Holt in 1967, and Asher able to meet Roth's financial demands partly because the president of Holt was prepared to invest more funds in its general books list.[39] After Holt, Asher moved on to Harper & Row (1981) and then

Macmillan, FSG, Harper & Row again, and finally Grove Press, where he was the publisher. He later edited Milan Kundera and in 1990 set up his own imprint at HarperCollins before he retired in 1993. Among key Roth titles he edited were *My Life as a Man* (Holt, 1974) and *Zuckerman Unbound* (FSG, 1981).

Roth continued to maintain a close relationship with him as Asher moved about, understanding that by industry practice he was expected to follow. He did not, preferring to stay at FSG, despite the offer of a sizable figure from Asher at Harper & Row for the last of the Zuckerman books. Asher did, however, edit Bloom's *Limelight and After* (Harper & Row, 1982), largely because of his relationship with Roth (although Roth typically expressed unhappiness over its promotion and distribution). To Epstein, before he left Random House, he expressed similar concerns: *Our Gang* had sold only 80,000 copies when the number should have been 150,000. More ads, he suggests. Such intrusive efforts to promote and market his books, starting with *Goodbye, Columbus*, continued throughout his career.

Once the contractual matters were settled with Holt, Roth returned to writing his lengthy satiric novel, what he called "the Moby Dick of funny books" dedicated to Sproul, the underappreciated *Great American Novel.* The work displayed his resilient, exuberant prose style, drawing as much from Mark Twain in his meandering, energetic, comic sentences as from an off-beat, Lenny Bruce–style of comedy. His emphasis on grotesque figures of semi-athletic prowess—midgets, mental patients, and more—created a work of intense, fascinating humor, drawing from his deep-seated love of baseball. The public, however, didn't find it funny.

The audaciously titled work focused on the most American of games and is perhaps Roth's most American novel, despite the American Trilogy and *The Plot Against America*. Baseball defined Roth's young life; he described a ball, a bat, and a glove as his totems at age ten and eleven (FAC 32). And for Roth, the story of the Patriot League blended sports with politics, as well as literary figures like Shakespeare and even Chaucer, whose new pilgrims travel "from every shires ende / OF AMERICA to COOPERSTOWN they wend / The holy BASEBALL HEROES for to seke" (GAN 14). Parody, satire, irony, and burlesque define the work, a paean to good writing, bad speaking, and the unrelenting geography of the baseball diamond as the story of the Ruppert Mundys unfolds in their contest to win the title of the Patriot League with their irregularly shaped and irregular players. The initial inspiration may have been the Newark Bears farm team, Ruppert Stadium their home.

Figure 6.1 Roth in New York, March 1973. Credit: Copyright Nancy Crampton.

Naming the novel's team the Ruppert Mundys pays tribute to many hours he and his brother and father spent at Ruppert Stadium.

A forty-five-page prologue by the eighty-seven-year-old Word Smith, aka Smitty, an ex-sportswriter, begins the tale. Expressed in unrelenting alliteration, the prologue is a tour de force of comic writing, which is actually harmful to Smitty's health, his doctor tells him. These "unrestrained excursions into alliteration" will only accelerate your death, his physician advises; continuing to write in this way is "tantamount to suicide." Even reading alliterative texts should stop, "or you'll be a goner" (GAN 10–11).

Hemingway suddenly appears, and he and Smitty take a manly fishing trip in Florida in 1936. Soon the macho author unabashedly offers punchy critiques of American fiction, mostly to correct the naïve views of a twenty-year-old female Vassar student working in a restaurant:

> Moby Dick: "A book about blubber, with a madman thrown in for excitement."
>
> Henry James: "Polychromatic crap, honey! Five hundred words where one would do!"
>
> Faulkner: "Unreadable unless you're some God damn professor!" (GAN 27–30).

With characters like Gil Gamesh, Luke Gofannon, Mike the Mouth, Seymour Clops (shortened to Cy Clops), and Base Baal, there can only be high jinks, as when the dispossessed team—they've been kicked out of their home field because the government needs their stadium for departing troops—finds its roster filled with a one-armed outfielder, a one-eyed pitcher, and an infielder who stops line drives with his teeth while another player rushes over, removes the ball, and throws it to first, backed up by a midget pinch hitter.

Roth opens with an imitative eighteenth-century style found in Fielding and Swift, with introductory headnotes on the leading characters and their fate. The remainder of the novel is essentially a flashback of the team's travails and trials, all conveyed in a sustained comic tone. The team is on a perpetual road trip, dogged by a political plot involving possible Communists seeking to destroy the Patriot League, the last chapter prophetically titled "The Return of Gil Gamesh; or, Mission from Moscow," which includes a "Secret Spring Training Report on Communist Infiltration of Patriot League" (GAN 347). Late in the novel, defining the most homeless team in baseball, is their inexplicable winning streak.

This is the result of a secret recipe to create champions out of losers: one Isaac Ellis has reformulated "Wheaties, the Breakfast of Champions" and it turns the players into "a team of red-blooded American Boys" now given over to only one thing: winning (GAN 287). As Smitty poeticizes, "You really can't say enough good things about it. There is nothing quite like it. Win hands down, win going away, win by a landslide, win by accident, win by a nose, win without deserving to win—you just can't beat it, however you slice it. Winning is the tops" (GAN 287). And the secret is Jewish Wheaties, "manufactured by a seventeen-year-old Jewish genius" (GAN 286). With their special ingredient, the Breakfast of Champions will make champions of a team as uneven as the Ruppert Mundys (GAN 286).

In the winsomely titled *The Great American Novel*, Roth has fun, stylistically, thematically, and narratively, as baseball details abound: there are 108 stitches on every baseball, and the number of sections of the book equals the number of innings in a ballgame. In what other novel would villagers parade a contest winner by shouting the title of a Melville novel, "*Typee! Typee! Typee!*" (GAN 301)? The novel is a triumphant, if occasionally strident, celebration of baseball, winning, America, and even religion: "'So there is a God on high, and He does love baseball.' 'It would appear so, Billy,'" a character remarks (GAN 308). The presence of the Communists in the league, however, means its quick demise at the start of the 1944 season with an investigation by HUAC, the same committee that would reappear in Roth's *I Married a Communist* marring the life of the beloved English teacher Murray Ringold (GAN 367). Anticipating Murray, Word Smith refuses to answer the committee's questions, expressing himself in uncontrollable alliteration.

In the "Epilogue" to *The Great American Novel*, a celebratory Smitty shares with the reader his rejection letters from a set of New York publishers about his book (such self-criticism will also appear in *The Facts* with Zuckerman's late comments on the text), but Smitty ends the novel with a memorable epistle to Chairman Mao that draws comic parallels between his situation and that of Solzhenitsyn, who could not find a publisher for his work in Russia. He is facing a similar crisis in America because he has written "a historical novel that does not accord with the American history" as taught in the schools (GAN 380). Of Chairman Mao he asks, Won't you publish this work in China? Surely you will consider a work of art that exists "for the sake of the record," a work that is not false but true (GAN 381).

Roth's appeal here is to fiction as history, reality as truth, plus the renovation of American values, claims he will similarly make in his American Trilogy and *The Plot Against America*. *The Great American Novel* is more than a burlesque or a parody of *Moby Dick* or any other work that might aspire to such a title; it is the first shot of a long fusillade prepared by Roth on the weak and the corrupt in America in an effort to correct. Athletic competition is a model for both self-realization and assimilation, a point Roth reminds us of in the final scene of his final novel, *Nemesis*, when the athletic coach Bucky Cantor re-creates for his students his glorious, heroic javelin-throwing days.

Critics were less than pleased with the playful, complaining that the book was too joyous and convoluted. Get serious, they cried. The farcical differed from the comical, while the humor lacked any of the redeeming elements seen in *Our Gang* or *The Breast*. In his attempt to renew the mythic elements of an America attacked by forces such as HUAC, the threat became the effort to undo the very elements that defined the strength of the country, notably freedom of thought and independence. How could a writer who venerated Henry James and Kafka find meaning in center field? The multilayered novel filled with bravado was his answer, a world where the underdog can triumph on a diet of Jewish Wheaties.

One other event from late 1973 reinforced Roth's new satiric confidence. His nemesis Irving Howe wrote to Lelchuk asking if Roth would write an op-ed in support of Israel. The request, passed on to Roth, brought out a mix of anger, sarcasm, and comedy, noting that he chose not to respond to Howe's earlier attack in *Commentary* in 1972 because it was wrongheaded and perpetuated a view of Roth as "disliking the Jews" and being anti-Semitic. That Howe would now ask him to write for Israel showed Howe's complete hypocrisy that he could not let go unanswered. He typed a three-and-a-half-page, singled-spaced letter in response. "You want to have your Jewish author who doesn't like Jews" exploit his audience so you can say even a writer like Roth who dislikes Jews supports Israel?[40] Not a chance. Mixing a tone of *How dare you* with *You must be kidding*, Roth lambasts Howe while also attacking Norman Podhoretz and Marie Syrkin for their hostile reaction to his work. He then satirizes Howe's critique of his work by suggesting that he would even find his reaction to UFOs twisted. Will I be accused of being antigalactic when the first UFO lands, as I am accused of being antiwomen and anti-Jewish, he asks? There is a difference, he writes, between being antigalactic and just not liking the galaxy. The letter also exposes Howe's misreading of *Portnoy* and his failure to distinguish between character and author.

If *Portnoy's Complaint* was the forerunner of a cluster of works wherein psychoanalysis was fundamental for writing and understanding the fiction, its impact continued, notably in *My Life as a Man, Zuckerman Unbound, The Anatomy Lesson,* and *The Counterlife.* Writer doubles appeared often in many of these texts, centered on the re/discovery of self, transposing Freudian psychoanalytic practice.[41] His major work dealing with psychoanalysis at this stage of his career is *My Life as a Man.*

Psychoanalysis liberated the artist's imagination in *Portnoy's Complaint* but provoked a countertattack in *My Life as a Man.* The war in the novel is less with the self than with theories of the self and its obsessions, beginning with the war between narcissism and aggression which he outlined in a passage from the text:

> "Spare me that word 'narcissism,' will you? You use it on me like a club."
> "The word is purely descriptive and carries no valuation," said the doctor.
> "Oh, is that so? Well, you be on the receiving end and see how little 'valuation' it carries!"(MLM 252–53)

Peter Tarnopol knows Dr. Spielvogel is wrong and realizes that the surest way to provoke a narcissistic reaction is to call a person a narcissist, but Roth and his characters persist in confronting and exploiting the term redefined in *Operation Shylock* as "Me-itis. Microcosmosis. Drowning in the tiny tub of yourself" (OPS 55). In *The Facts*, the narrator explains, "The person I've intended to make myself visible to is myself" (FAC 4). Self-love playfully counters self-doubt.

Perhaps no term is more loaded in analyzing Roth than "narcissism," exacerbated by his anger at betrayal, reignited when he wrote *My Life as a Man*.[42] Most important is the anger directed at his psychiatrist, Dr. Hans J. Kleinschmidt, and his thirty-page article about creativity and psychopathology, "The Angry Act: The Role of Aggression in Creativity."

' Roth began working on the novel as early as 1964, and drafts of the work exist from 1968. But the issue became the correct way to tell the story: two stories by Tarnopol followed by his "autobiography" was the final, workable form. During the 1970s, he was also deeply involved in teaching Kafka, which came to influence the text. Transgression and punishment become the themes not only of the novel but of Tarnopol's senior literature course at Hofstra (MLM 233). In a deleted passage, he names this course "Studies in Guilt and Persecution."[43] Finally completing and publishing the book for Roth was cathartic.

Part I of the novel, "Useful Fictions," sets up the dilemma for Tarnopol via the first of two stories, shifting in Part II, the second story, into a dual narrative of betrayal resulting in anger at Maureen and resentment at Spielvogel, who published details of Tarnopol's life in his article, now titled "The Riddle of Creativity" (MLM 231).

All of this, of course, is another engagement with personal injustice, which Roth angrily and repeatedly confronts personally and fictionally, combining to further the history of his discontent. Such moments simply piled up, beginning with his mother ridiculing the size of his penis when at eleven he wanted a bathing suit with a jockstrap, followed by intense arguments with his father concerning his freedom as a college student, then his army injury preventing him from being a manly soldier, succeeded by Maggie's deceiving him into marriage. Collectively, these events led to persistent misgivings concerning his editors and their support for his work. Next, it was Bloom's declamatory dependency, compelling him to marry her and then her seemingly outlandish claims in her autobiography published after their divorce.[44]

The untrustworthiness of his Library of America editor (he did an inadequate job with volume 3 of the series and was superseded by in-house editors) and then his ineptitude after being appointed his first biographer furthered Roth's upset. The final betrayal was of his body, undone by illness. These problems compound the irony in *My Life as a Man*: Zuckerman writes his fiction nightly while in an army hospital, which frequently brings on migraines. Writing becomes a literal headache. Could it be, he asks, that "for me illness was not a necessary catalyst to activate the imagination" (MLM 56)? For Roth and his lifetime of ailments this signifies.

One of Roth's early readers at this time was Cynthia Ozick. In April 1974, she wrote to Roth with her thoughts after reading a prepublication copy of *My Life as a Man*. Offering sharp commentary—she titles one section the "Jewish Writer's Social Responsibility"—she expresses displeasure with the fixation of the popular press only on *Portnoy*. She also parodies Roth's own style, calling one section of her four-page, single-spaced letter "My Life as Someone Who Thinks a Lot about the Work of Philip Roth."

Ironically, she reports that whenever she presents a talk, someone always, always brings up the topic of Philip Roth and the Jews. "You are an obsession," she writes. She responds to her audiences by explaining that a writer writes not to show the world as a single subject complete, such as the Jews, but only to "seize on a speck here, a tendril there, and that by doing this he, nevertheless, includes everything that is omitted, because each speck suggests another, and the whole is implicit in every tendril."[45] This is also Roth's aesthetic: to stress the particular, the detailed. If a text shows something vulgar or coarse, it is the reader's problem, not the writer's: "Philip Roth documents. He documents what's there. And it *is* there," she declares.[46]

She offers a set of suggestive comments about Roth and satire, his "metaphysical clowning." She believes it is all about "falling short": "If Philip Roth (or Voltaire or Swift, or any of these guys) didn't know about the falling short, he couldn't write what he writes! The insight into the falling short *is the very same thing* as the insight into the kingdom of priests and the holy nation! One is implicit in the other!"[47]

The issue of the Jewish writer's social responsibility takes over, and she responds strongly by saying a writer can't be "saddled with the notion of 'responsibility.' It's a strangulation, a bit in the mouth, an early twitch toward Soviet socialist Realism and self-censorship," and she won't have it. This emanates partly from *Portnoy*, but she suddenly interjects that she wishes there would be more talk about *Letting Go*: "Oh, how I envied you Letting Go!" She repeats, "Those necessary fragments that are novels get written by novelists, not by politicals." She concludes the first part of her letter with a testament, Rothian in tone and nature: "Jewish Freedom Now! And no masks, or waiting or hiding out, or withdrawing or restraining, 'only until' the ripe and perfect moment. . . . I'm a Jew, and take the world as given, and Now."[48]

Following this vigorous defense of Roth's goals and her own feelings, she addresses *My Life as a Man*, stating that she read it turned inside out "as if it were all written on the underside of my belly: the hand writing on the wall of your novel turning out to be my own." Tarnopol's life isn't mine, she writes, "only it is. You've made it mine," including the Bildungsroman-writer part, the fights, the sex, the turmoil, everything. The passages on craft are especially cogent, and she values his use of quotation marks and their function as signs of irony, adding layers of meaning to the words on the page: "Tone! Snot! Gravity! Seriousness!" The way Tarnopol slips into the future is astonishing, especially because he has not yet told it: "It drove me crazy with joy and expectation."[49] Especially powerful but low key is Tarnopol's brother, Morris, who above all is kind. Kindness: no one can bring that off anymore, but you have, she tells Roth. And he's not flat but has shadows and is even a kind of conventional Jew![50]

At the end, Roth seems to take over from Tarnopol. The reporter from the *Daily News* was bugging Roth, not Tarnopol; similarly with the court stuff, she writes. Cleverly, she saw that Tarnopol became not Philip Roth the writer but Philip Roth the public phenomenon who is talked about at congregations and seminars. But it's only a tiny flaw in a terrific book. It affects little. Putting aside *The Breast*, a minor but perfect work, *My Life as a Man* is "your best book. So far." Closing with a wish to devote herself exclusively to his talk at a forthcoming dinner at the home of the Vienna-born refugee novelist and translator Lore Segal, she comically complains about those "subtle people from Vienna! Everybody from Vienna is a natural-born psychoanalyst who [always] says it's *your* fault."[51]

In *My Life as a Man*, as Jeffery Berman insightfully remarks, literature and therapy symbiotically react with one another. If *Portnoy's Complaint* confirms the analyst's "clinical interpretation" in "The Angry Act," the later novel ingeniously attempts to refute the charge of the artist's narcissistic personality. The two novels [*Portnoy* and *My Life*] represent, "transferentially, the loving idealization and harsh devaluation of the analyst respectively."[52] Psychoanalysis liberated the artist's imagination in *Portnoy* but provoked a counterattack in *My Life as a Man*. The interaction with Kleinschmidt is crucial, and "the psychoanalytic descriptions of Spielvogel's analysis of Tarnopol and Kleinschmidt's analysis of the Southern playwright in 'The Angry Act' could not be coincidental," Paul Mosher and Berman argue.[53] But for Roth or Tarnopol, all that is learned is that there is no forgetting the past and all the writer can do with his story is "tell it. And tell it. And tell it. And *that's* the truth" (MLM 231). "No forgetting" is the Roth mantra.

Spielvogel's breach of confidence in *My Life as a Man* duplicates Kleinschmidt's breach of confidence in "The Angry Act," while Tarnopol's five-year psychoanalysis with Spielvogel parallels Roth's almost six years with Kleinschmidt. Psychoanalysts in Roth form a long line: Dr. Lumin in *Letting Go,* Dr. Klinger in *The Breast* and *The Professor of Desire,* preceded by Spielvogel in *Portnoy's Complaint* and then in *My Life as a Man.* Interestingly, when Bloom wrote to Roth following their meeting in New York in 1975 and after she read a copy of *My Life as a Man* that he gave her, she wrote that underneath his observations was a "deep and irrepressible rage: anger at being trapped in marriage, fear of giving up autonomy," paralleling a number of ideas Kleinschmidt had identified and ironically foretelling the nature of her own life with Roth (LDH 145–46).

For Kleinschmidt and Roth, aggression "may be the prime mover or the unconscious motivating force for a creative push."[54] A narcissistic character also provides some "semblance of balance within the ego, constantly threatened by the tremendous anger at parental figures, and, subsequently, all authority. A person with such enormous narcissism is always saying to himself: 'How dare they?' the stance of never forgiving the parents and thus never really allowing anyone to get close is the primitive defense against the fear of ego disruption."[55]

The paragraph is rich with Rothian elements, not the least of which being Roth's self-protection and resistance to letting anyone get the better of him, expressed in the "How dare they?" To confirm this view, Kleinschmidt cites one of Roth's heroes, Kafka, who, in a letter to his father, wrote, "Ever since I can remember[,] a deep anxiety about safeguarding my mental existence has made me indifferent to everything else."[56] The narcissistic posture is a device preventing all "dangerous implications of involvement in object relations." The search, instead, is for an "oceanic blending with the *idealized* mother, the unattainable infantile love which must elude the adult ego."[57] Roth's anger at the women in his life and in his fiction may be because they shattered the ideal vision of his own mother, seemingly protective, nurturing, and always loving.

The narcissist's world "is an emotional vacuum" in which he feels an excessive "reliance on the intellectual endowment in the creative person and justifies his feelings of omnipotence or, in any case, of being different." The relationship with the parents is intellectualized, evident in Roth with the exception of *Patrimony.* While the artist "creates his own emotional history through his personal myth," which Kleinschmidt develops in a discussion of

Kandinsky and then Mann, his focus is on what Kandinsky expressed: "Art is very jealous and permits no rivals." Another way of expressing this is that the artist "confronts emotional reality without involving himself in it."[58]

According to Kleinschmidt, the rebellion of the writer against his mother "was sexualized, leading to compulsive masturbation which provided an outlet for a myriad of hostile fantasies. . . . The sexual acting out of a polymorphous nature occurred simultaneously with his creative writing." Finally, while the artist gives form and hence meaning to his emotional experience, art signifies the triumph of Eros over Thanatos, "the triumph of libido over aggression."[59] Neurotic conflict provides the energy and passion channeled into art. "Unease and dis-ease are essential conditions for creativity," the editor of this issue of *American Imago* writes.[60] Roth's representation of his mother or mother figures, as in *The Anatomy Lesson* and *Sabbath's Theater*, contains the seeds of these views.[61]

The Kleinschmidt essay is useful in understanding the ethos of *My Life as a Man*, the novel that lingered in Roth's imagination for so many years. Its appearance in 1974 was a release as much of anger as of literary freedom. Also making it possible was his recognition that comedy was an essential part of his *métier*, which was absent in his first two novels. An early passage in *My Life as a Man* confirms what Roth had discovered with *Portnoy*: the necessity of comedy to confront dismay. Tarnopol suggests that if Zuckerman would narrate "with fidelity" his youthful misfortunes, it would require "a darker sense of irony, a grave and pensive voice," or perhaps what the story needs is "neither gravity nor complexity, but just another author, someone who would see it too for the simple five-thousand-word comedy that it very well may have been" (MLM 31). "Just another author" suggests the multiple authors and selves that would soon and persistently appear in Roth's fiction.

Roth explained in 1988 that comedy did not come overnight: it "required time to work up confidence, to take my instinct for comedy seriously, to let it contend with my earnest sobriety and finally take charge" (CWPR 250). But incorporating comedy as a form of self-knowledge and literary expression masked both self-betrayal and self-deception. It allowed for masks, irony, and satire to hide, or at least distract, from the more deep-seated issue of self-exposure. Competing with the "sit down comic" Kafka was an innate exhibitionism, a carryover from *Portnoy* through *The Great American Novel*. Roth knew that what gave his fiction its vitality was not the accurate but animate detail.

7

Travels with Kafka

Narrative is the form that his knowledge takes.
—Philip Roth, *The Facts*, 1988

Politics soon expanded Roth's creative focus—not American malfeasance but European repression. His first trip to Czechoslovakia, in May 1972, introduced him to a world of political suppression. In his important essay "In Search of Kafka and Other Answers," he explains that it was Kafka who got him to Prague, where the combination of a Jewish past and repressive present coalesced in his efforts not only to publish restricted Czech writers in English but to write "Country Report" on suppression in Czechoslovakia for PEN in 1973.

But in the early 1970s he was facing his own critical clouds, initiated by Irving Howe, who complained in 1972 that Roth lacked Jewish street cred and failed to render a proper portrait of his Jewish subjects. His personal culture was thin, Howe argued: that is, it was insufficiently Jewish. Roth did not grow up in a *shtetl* environment or even with the odor of such a past. He was not Polish or Russian born; he lost no one in the Holocaust. He knew nothing of Mitteleuropa culture. He knew the heartache of Ashkenazi life in Europe only secondhand, if at all. In Mark Shechner's words, "He grew up knowing neither Beethoven nor Sholem Aleichem, neither Scarlatti nor Isaac Babel . . . neither Rashi nor Trotsky . . . neither Zionism nor Yiddishism, Talmud nor Torah."[1]

Roth grew up largely or directly untouched by the European Jewish tragedy, the opposite of Isaac Bashevis Singer and even Bellow, who spoke Yiddish at home, likely before English.[2] Roth was vulnerable on the score of a historical Jewish culture.

But Roth's innate defiance, a kind of Stephen Daedalus *non servium*, armed him with what would soon shape itself into a kind of Eastern European resistance, opening a new phase of his writing, manifested by replacing America with Czechoslovakia and its constant threats to writers and restraints on literary and personal freedoms. His target was initially Czechoslovakia, but it soon widened to include Hungary and Poland, transformed into the series he edited from 1974 until 1989 entitled "Writers from the Other Europe." It contained works formerly unobtainable in the U.S. and England by writers prevented from publishing in their own countries and subject to oppression in various forms. The project might be understood as his reaching back to the culture he supposedly lacked. In typical style, in the face of criticism he took action. The experience transformed Roth for more than a decade into America's most Eurocentric, politically conscious writer, anticipating his later engagement with America's social and political problems addressed in the American Trilogy. Eastern Europe educated him to understand America. It also encouraged new narrative strategies.

For some fifteen years, his focus on Eastern Europe dominated his thinking and writing, as *The Professor of Desire, The Ghost Writer*, and *The Prague Orgy* confirmed. This is a surprising turnabout from a writer immersed in Jewish misbehavior and the American pastimes of baseball and political satire. Or perhaps not. The same year he published his baseball novel, 1973, his essay-fiction "Looking at Kafka" appeared in the *New American Review*.

I

Broadly speaking, the 1970s was a period of cultural repression and shattering political texts: Solzhenitsyn's *Gulag Archipelago* appeared in 1973 and the memoirs of Nadezhda Mandelstam, *Hope Against Hope* and *Hope Abandoned*, in 1970 and 1974. Systematic cultural repression was evident in Latin America as well as Communist Europe.[3] Artistic freedom was impossible. Roth's journeys to Eastern Europe and his series were in response to these developments, actions that took place while *The Great American Novel* was in press and months before the attacks by Howe and then Norman Podhoretz in *Commentary* of December 1972. In reaction to such uninformed criticism, in 1977 he quipped, "I find the best place to be when a book comes out—at least for a Western writer—is behind the Iron Curtain" (CWPR 105).

Much of his work took inspiration from his exposure to the texts and writers of Eastern Europe, including reaction to the politics of the Cold War. It is no accident that the earliest drafts of *American Pastoral* began in 1972, immediately after his first trip to Czechoslovakia. It was called "How the Other Half Lives." This early draft involved Swede Levov traveling through the Iron Curtain as a narrative device, although the final text dropped the adventure. Roth's engagement with the "Other Europe" shaped formal elements of his historical fiction, especially the American Trilogy, where he draws directly from Czesław Miłosz and Bruno Schulz for *The Plot Against America*.[4] The collision between the fictional and the historical was becoming real, but a solution appeared in the writings of the "Other Europe" which propelled the increasing political complexity of his own fiction. Hungarian, Yugoslav, Polish, and Czech writers composed the series.

Roth was actually thinking about Prague as early as 1968, according to a manuscript in the Library of Congress.[5] That year, Warsaw Pact troops ended the "Prague Spring," enforcing a period of suppression that lasted until the fall of the Soviet Union in 1989. "Normalization" was the euphemistic term for the period. Restrictions on freedom of speech and the imposition of censorship became standard, whether one was a writer, filmmaker, journalist, or dramatist. Czech writing fell into one of three groups: official, illegal (including samizdat), and exiled. Many pre-1968 writers, such as Václav Havel, Ludvík Vaculík, and Ivan Klíma, were banned from publishing. Others, such as Milan Kundera, Josef Škvorecký, and Pavel Kohout, chose exile.[6]

In New York after his first visit to Prague in 1972, Roth explained that his life was now "lived in the Czech exile community. . . . I ate every night in Czech restaurants in Yorkville, talked to whoever wanted to talk to me and left all this *Portnoy* crap behind. . . . I didn't want the New York gossip and the exiles could tell me something." Out of the city, he had his friend the artist Philip Guston, but "[I] had my East European world in New York, and those were the things that saved me."[7]

In his important 1973 PEN "Country Report," the result of his early visit, Roth explains that in his early thirties it was Kafka who renewed his goals as a writer: Kafka's tales of "spiritual disorientation and obstructed energies" matched his own difficulties at the time, while the obsessions outlined in his stories matched, with a "strange grave comedy," his own, providing clues to Roth's own efforts at imaginative expression.[8]

While teaching at the University of Pennsylvania one semester a year, Roth began to study and read Kafka intensively with his students. Citing Kafka's painful letter to his father as a model, he refers to his own letter beginning "Dear Mother," an obsession expressed in *Portnoy*. Portnoy was, indeed, somewhat shaped by his detailed reading of Kafka, he claimed. His four days in Prague were essentially a tour of Kafka sites and an attempt to see what Kafka might have seen, ending at Kafka's grave. As he outlines in "In Search of Kafka," he toured his gymnasium, synagogue, and back streets, returning each day through the fifteenth-century Jewish cemetery behind the Pinkas Synagogue (the third oldest in Europe) and then through the building itself, which had become a memorial to the children and adults murdered in the Terezin concentration camp, numbering almost seventy-eight thousand.

In Prague Roth clearly felt a deep connection to a place that in the past "must have been not too unlike those neighborhoods in Austro-Hungarian Lemberg and Czarist Kiev where the two branches of my own family had lived. . . . Looking for Kafka's landmarks I had to my surprise, come upon some landmarks that felt to me like my own."[9] On previous trips to England and Europe, he never sensed more than being an American passing through; this time, he felt rooted in the Jewish past of European persecution and specifically that of Prague. It reminded him of his own sets of grandparents uprooted from Mitteleuropa when they emigrated to the United States.

He describes his own experience with censorship. Contacting his Czech publisher of *Goodbye, Columbus* and *Letting Go*, he was surprised to learn that they would not do the same for *Portnoy's Complaint* or *Our Gang*. Both were considered unsuitable by the authorities, although a translation of *Portnoy's Complaint* had been commissioned and completed in 1969 but not published. Part of the reason may be that the Russians replaced the entire editorial board in 1968 after crushing the Prague Spring. They were unsympathetic to "radical" writing. Roth learned that the U.S. Information Agency actually deemed the books inappropriate for distribution in American libraries attached to U.S. embassies. The sex in *Portnoy* made it improper, and the satire of *Our Gang* was too anti-Nixon. Three years later, during another trip to Prague, he discovered how widespread this "censorship" had become, the USIA excluding books by numerous American writers thought to be too erotic or sensual. Upon his return to the U.S., Roth wrote to the director of the USIA for an explanation and received an appropriately bureaucratic reply. Ironically, the USIA gave the impression that literature in the U.S. is controllable by the government, a truly Kafkaesque situation, despite the freedom of the press and the right to free speech unavailable in Czechoslovakia.

Following his May 1972 trip and meeting with his Czech translators Luba and Rudolph Pilar, who outlined the repressive situation for writers in the country, Roth returned to New York and met the exiled Czech journalist, film critic, and editor Anton (Tony) Liehm and attended his weekly classes on Czech history, literature, and film at the College of Staten Island, part of the City University of New York. Through Liehm, Roth met other Czech exiles, including the directors Ivan Passer and Jiří Weiss.

Roth did not believe totalitarian governments were required to produce great literature, but he did acknowledge that in Czechoslovakia "nothing goes and everything matters; here, everything goes and nothing matters."[10] Roth would be profoundly marked by his Czech and Hungarian visits of 1972 and 1973, followed by annual spring trips until he was denied entry in 1977. Clearly, he felt an affinity between "his own imagination of entrapment and a world in which entrapment was everybody's daily fare."[11] But he had to invent his connection to Mitteleuropa. "Looking at Kafka" was the first step; his later novels, starting with *The Professor of Desire* and ending with *The Prague Orgy*, the second. Epitomizing the new vision and cementing his credentials as a student and supporter of Mitteleuropa may be his November 1976 interview with Isaac Bashevis Singer about Bruno Schulz, which appeared on page 20 of the *New York Times Book Review* for 13 February 1977 and was reprinted in his 2001 collection *Shop Talk*. The interview coincided with the appearance of Schulz's *The Street of Crocodiles* in the "Writers from the Other Europe" series.[12] In terms of intersections, Roth told Singer that Schulz translated Kafka's *The Trial* into Polish in 1936; Singer was not surprised.

To aid the oppressed writers whose foreign royalties were taxed at about 90 percent, Roth wrote a letter he sent to literary reviews and magazines to court attention to the plight of the dissident writers. Next, he set up the Ad Hoc Czech Fund, a bank account in New York. Fourteen literary friends each contributed a hundred dollars a month, with single contributors linked to a corresponding author in Prague. Arthur Schlesinger was matched with a historian, Arthur Miller a playwright. Other participants included John Updike, John Cheever, William Styron, and John Hersey. Roth worked with a travel agent in Yorkville to get the money to Eastern Europe via coupons. Klíma in Prague made sure the money was received and distributed.[13]

"Looking at Kafka" is an unusual, challenging work resulting from Roth's early encounter with Eastern Europe. Dedicated to his students at Penn and dated fall 1972, the work, half–literary history and half–short story, reflects his thinking about Kafka and other Eastern European writers, their impact measured by the amorphous form of the text: essay, lecture, short story, autobiography, the work crisscrosses genres and times, like the experiments of Klíma, Tadeusz Borowski, Kundera, Danilo Kiš. No single form could contain the history he encountered. In the story, Kafka, having escaped tuberculosis and the Nazis, is now teaching at Roth's old Hebrew School at the Schley Street Synagogue. The time is 1942, when the young character in the story (and Roth) were nine. But this is Part II of the work; Part I is an essay on Kafka written by Roth when he is forty, which opens with him staring at a photo of Kafka taken in 1924 when *he* was forty. It is also the year of Kafka's death.

As he describes the portrait, Roth links the image of Kafka to those of the many Jews killed at Auschwitz, although he, but not his three younger sisters, died too soon for the Holocaust. Could he, if he had lived, escaped? The question leads Roth to imagine Kafka's future. If he had lived, would his books have been published? If he had come to America in 1938, would he have been a bookish fifty-five-year-old bachelor with the unpublished manuscripts of *The Trial, Amerika, The Castle,* and several more fragments in his trunk?

Roth then continues with Kafka's actual narrative, beginning in 1923, eleven months before his death in a Vienna sanatorium. He had met Dora Dymant and, although she is half his age, they fall in love. Two early engagements had failed, one with Milena Jesenká Pollak, who wrote the only obituary of him of consequence. But Kafka broke off their affair (Milena was unhappily married); she later died in a concentration camp. With Dora, however, he goes off to live in a Berlin suburb, freeing himself at last from his family and Prague. But how could this author of "counterdreams" that mocked ideas of salvation and justice escape? And quickly? Was it Dora or death or both, Roth asks? In his quest to marry Dora, another father blocks the way (first his own father loomed over any personal decision Kafka wanted to take): Dora's father refuses their request to marry (and behind him stood yet another father figure, who advised him: the Gerer Rebbe). Kafka was lost, as was the Hunger Artist, the background for Part I of the essay-fantasy.

Kafka lived with Dora for nine months, contravening her father's wishes. With her, Kafka seemed free from the self-loathing and doubt and guilt that plagued him. He studied Hebrew with Dora, attended lectures on the Talmud at the Berlin Academy for Jewish Studies, and gave permission for four of his stories to appear. Here, Roth reveals the transformation that he imagines for Kafka: he awoke one morning to find himself "transformed in his bed into a father, a writer and a Jew" (RMY 289). This is not Gregor Samsa but a renewed Kafka. Nevertheless, a story he wrote at the time, "The Burrow," continues the themes of entrapment and obsession. The critique of self in the story becomes a fable of how art is made through this "portrait of a magical thinker" at the end of his rope (RMY 290). Part I ends with a passage from

"The Burrow" and the report of Kafka's death from tuberculosis a month before his forty-first birthday.

Part II is a fantasy, in some ways anticipating *The Ghost Writer* and Nathan Zuckerman's belief that Amy Bellette is Anne Frank.[14] Dr. Kafka, aka Dr. Kishka, is fifty-nine and teaching Hebrew to the nine-year-old "Roth." In Newark, the skillful Roth has no problem mimicking Kafka to his buddies. But alone, the narrator sympathizes with the refugee teacher and his threadbare suit; his guilt shadows his studies and he suddenly decides to save Kafka, his personal attempt to save the Jews of Europe. Sharing his embarrassment with his parents at Kafka's condition and life in a single room, they invite him to dinner—along with Aunt Rhoda, long single, in an effort at matchmaking. Kafka comes; Aunt Rhoda comes; they hit it off, despite his father's overbearing praise of family (RMY 294–95). But Rhoda initially thinks Kafka acts superior, sneering at the Newark family; not so, says the father: he's just a quiet gentleman.

After a movie and a play, Kafka encourages Rhoda's return to the amateur stage, visiting Philip's parents to celebrate her new part in *The Three Sisters*.[15] One weekend they go to Atlantic City—but something happens that the narrator is not permitted to know and the relationship quickly ends, his brother explaining to Philip that it was probably sex, or the lack thereof, that ended everything. But the cause remains a mystery.

In college years later, the narrator receives Dr. Kafka's obituary from the *Jewish News*. He is at the school in the summer to write short stories and because he cannot face his own interfering father, whose love for him is actually oppressive, duplicating the condition of Kafka's own father and Roth's (RMY 301). In his need for independence, the narrator contests the power of love. In the obituary we read that the seventy-year-old Kafka died at a New Jersey heart and lung center, leaving no survivors and no books. His papers do not exist, except four letters to Aunt Rhoda after the Atlantic City debacle. Dr. Kafka disappears. In a final paragraph, Roth mixes the fate of the imagined Kafka of New Jersey with his imagined but inconclusive heroes: Does the Land Surveyor from *The Castle* reach the castle? Does K. in *The Trial* ever learn the charges against him? Does Georg Bendemann ever escape his father's judgment in "The Judgment"? Kafka, the narrator admits, can never become *the* Kafka—that would be too strange; no one would believe it, not even Kafka himself (RMY 302).

The story confronts fable, fathers, and fame. To transform the alienated and unhappy Prague Jewish writer into a Hebrew teacher in New Jersey is inspired because the situation projects the burden of European Jewry upon the young, American-born Jewish child-narrator, while also representing in its two parts Roth's engagement and evaluation of Mitteleuropa and its sufferings. Ironically, to free Kafka meant the replacement of the writer by the Hebrew school teacher. Yet even if he was, or became, the teacher, the confinement he resisted (perhaps transposed to marriage with Aunt Rhoda) duplicated the need of the narrator to free himself from *his* family. For Roth, the story is a commentary on his own relationship with his father and his need to be free of Newark and the family, forcing him to depart for Bucknell, which became his salvation. The story is also the means for the Newark writer to link himself with Prague: Kafka not only teaches at his synagogue but through marriage might have become his uncle. Prague becomes a staging ground for a new myth, a substitute for the psychiatrist's couch or Weequahic High.

On his Czechoslovakian trips, Roth learned how writers managed to survive under government repression. Before a two-week trip in the spring of 1973, for example, Roth read what he could in translation (novels, poems, plays, essays) by contemporary Czech writers. He met with dissident writers and expanded his connections on two subsequent visits. The unnamed writers (unnamed because of fear over their safety) took him about the country and established friendships. He was encouraged to read other writers from Eastern Europe, and in 1975, after visits to Budapest and again Prague, he was able to interest Penguin Books in a reprint series, "Writers from the Other Europe." The Penguin European Poets series, edited by Roth's friend, the late British poet and critic A. Alvarez, was a model: Alvarez had recently published a volume of poems by the Czech poet Miroslav Holub. In a summary statement about his proposed series, Roth describes it as an attempt to publish influential works of fiction by Eastern European writers, many of the writers acknowledged as "powerful forces in their own cultures" but unknown in the West. Reprinting them with contextual introductions should make their work "more accessible to a new readership."[16]

Roth's "Country Report" for PEN's American Center (founded in 1921, PEN originally stood for "poets, essayists, and novelists") was a result of his second trip and an example of how Roth put into action his ideas and responses against suppression. The report was the first of a series of accounts by PEN on countries where repression prevented the freedom to write and publish. The overall concern was the writer's relation to his government and the restrictive regulations preventing writers from working freely. Opposition to control over the free expression of literature, the PEN mandate propelled Roth to produce the first "Country Report," published in August 1973.

Roth begins his report with "A Visitor's Notes on Kafka's City," opening with an anecdote about a student who, when asked why he doesn't pack up and go, answered "Why don't *they* go?," referring to the Russian troops in his country. The self-irony and suppressed despair convey, Roth suggests, the tone and tenor of the country and state of writers, academics, and intellectuals who face suppression and subjugation. Serious writers have no voice and no future in the country. To back this claim, Roth cites the dire situation of Miroslav Holub, Ivan Klíma, and Milan Kundera. Helena Klíma, wife of Ivan and a political journalist, is allowed to work only as a typist. The political journalist Ludvík Vaculík has been made a nonperson, disgraced and without income. Roth's interview with Vaculík appears in the report. The regime, Roth writes, seeks to commit no less than "cultural genocide upon its own people."[17] No one in Prague is optimistic about the future.

Roth next summarizes the impetus for the Prague Spring of 1968, giving the history of the 1967 Fourth Congress of the Union of Czechoslovak Writers, held that June. Well-informed and clear, Roth documents the abuse of writers who spoke, all of them ejected from the Communist Party. The Ministry of Culture took over the publication of *Literary News*, a weekly paper from the Union, which normally printed 300,000 copies. By February 1968, however, the Prague Spring occurred and censorship of press, radio, and TV was abolished. Vaculík published "Prague 2000 Word Manifesto." As Roth notes, it was the intellectual community that not only consistently supplied the leadership of the political movement but made the Prague Spring possible.

Roth continues to provide a detailed narrative of the struggle for liberalization in Czechoslovakia led by artists in theater, film, and literature. But this also made the intelligentsia prime targets for repression. Regarding the armed occupation from August 1968 onward, Roth describes the tensions between the government and the liberals and the process of so-called normalization. The Union of Writers was dissolved, the Academy of Science under attack. A blacklist of writers appeared; a purge of volumes by dissident writers in public libraries occurred. Writers of conscience were either exiled, imprisoned, or lived a precarious life under threat and had only the most menial of jobs. By 1972, the Russian-appointed government of Gustáv Husák began show trials of activists in the reform movement. The repression created in essence "a cultural cemetery," to quote Heinrich Böll in 1972 when he received the Nobel Prize for Literature.[18]

Authors who did not join the Union of Writers were considered nonpersons. Yet blacklisted writers continued to publish, although without access to their foreign royalties; Roth details the mechanism by which this happened and lists the ten most prominent writers prevented from accessing their funds. Initially dropped when the abuse was made public, the government then instituted secret regulations and decrees, which Roth lists. Again, he emphasizes the ongoing prevention of writers and artists from publishing or exhibiting their work, deprived of their right to work and incomes. He concludes his report by reprinting speeches made by Czech writers at their Fourth Congress in June 1967. He includes remarks by Kundera, Laco Novomeský (editor and poet), and Vaculík. Books of interest follow, and then an abridged interview with Vaculík which originally appeared in *The Nation* on 21 May 1973. Illustrating the despair is Vaculík's citing a friend who once had a prominent position in a publishing house: he is now a proofreader and, beginning in 1974, will be unemployed. All of this commentary from the author of *Portnoy's Complaint* revealed a dimension of Roth publicly unknown up to this point.

Roth's reaction to the social injustice and political repression he witnessed not only in 1972–73 but up to 1977, when he was finally prevented from entering Czechoslovakia, was the "Writers from the Other Europe" series, concentrating on prose fiction in paperback reprints. For the most part, they were books from Eastern Europe already translated and occasionally published in either the U.S. or England but newly edited and with original, contextual introductions. Intermittently, he would commission a new translation, such as *The City Builder* by György Konrád, translated by Ivan Sanders. Roth was general editor of the series, which would see three or four English reprints a year. The first two titles were Kundera's *Laughable Loves* and Vaculík's *The Guinea Pigs*. Two Polish novels followed, Borowski's *This Way for the Gas, Ladies and Gentlemen* and Tadeusz Konwicki's *A Dreambook for Our Time*.

Roth himself occasionally offered introductions or afterwords; two notable introductions appeared in the *American Poetry Review*: the first for Kundera's "Edward and God," the second for two stories about Nazis and Jews by Jiří Weil.[19] Roth calls "Edward and God" his favorite Kundera story, one that concentrates on a libidinous teacher offering false pieties as he seduces a beautiful student and is then censored by the directress of the school board who is herself sexually aroused by the young teacher. Farce balances satire in what Roth in his introduction claims is typical of so many stories in Prague, where the powerless become adept at narrating their lives, taking aesthetic pleasure from the absurdities and paradoxes that define their hardships.

In his longer introduction to the Weil stories, one entitled "Shanghai," Roth describes his meeting with Weil's translator in New York and discovery of Weil's work and his hatred of the Nazis.[20] His writing reminds him of Isaac Babel, although Weil's style is colloquial rather than minimal. He writes about savagery with a brevity that is in itself a severe commentary. Roth adduces further parallels with Babel, including their mutual victimization by socialist realism and Stalin. Roth then celebrates Weil's novel *Life with a Star*, about the Jewish star worn by Jews under Nazi occupation, and *Mendelssohn Is on the Roof*, about an SS officer charged with removing a statue of Mendelssohn from the roof of the Prague Academy of Music. Unable to recognize Mendelssohn, he chooses the statue with the largest nose: Wagner.

Reaction to *Life with a Star* was positive, the novelist Anne Tyler praising Roth's determination to see the book in an English translation and quoting Roth's original letter to FSG on its importance. But the volume in Roth's series did not appear until 1989, thirty years after Weil's death. The story focuses on a former bank clerk now leading a restrictive and punishing life; his only occupation is raking leaves in a cemetery, and he soon witnesses many people sent off in transports to the camps. But Tyler disagrees with the two translators' reading of the novel, explaining connections in their prefatory note, replacing Weil's spare and abstract language with obvious references in an effort to be particular. Where Weil uses "they," the translators make clear it should read "Nazi." But the word never appears in the text, nor the word "Jew." The abstract maintains the universal dimension of the narrative; the particulars limit it.[21]

One of the instrumental figures in the establishment of Roth's Czech contacts was Rita Klimová, who introduced Roth to Kundera and Klíma. Escaping Hitler, she and her family lived for a number of years in the Bronx, but she returned to Communist Czechoslovakia after the war. By the early 1960s, however, while teaching economic history at Charles University, her commitment to the Party had waned. Expelled from the university because of her support of the reforms of the Prague Spring initiated by Alexander Dubček beginning in January 1968 (to end in August), she became a full-time translator, although her past as a Communist and present as a Jew caused skepticism in the new reformist government. Working as a translator and, later, as part of the Velvet Revolution, a member of Havel's new government, she became ambassador to the U.S.

Present with Roth at his first meeting with Kundera at Klimová's apartment was Barbara Sproul, Roth's companion. In 1990 she recalled the importance of Klimová's father, Stanislav Budín, a journalist and editor of what at one time was the most important Communist paper in Czechoslovakia, important in the intellectual life of the country. At the first meeting between Roth and Kundera, Sproul remembered, the language became more and more racy, with Klimová translating and occasionally turning red.[22]

Moved by the plight of the Czech, Hungarian, and Polish writers, and aware of a similar series in the U.K., Roth proposed his new series to Penguin U.S. Katherine Court, an editor, liked the idea and recognized the cultural importance of the undertaking. Roth's name and contacts were clearly a draw. But surprisingly, one critic of the project was Kundera. In several letters, he objected to the political implications of the series title, arguing in 1976 that the regional context for "the other Europe" was wrong. Yugoslavia, Poland, Czechoslovakia, and Romania are not a culture unity, he asserted; the Other Europe is a bastard born from Yalta and Stalin. Some ideas I take seriously, he wrote, and one of them is this view about the nonexistence of the other Europe. He asks that his text not be published in the series.

In 1988, Kundera again wrote to Roth to excuse himself from the series and the publication of *Life Is Elsewhere*. Of course, the series helped writers in the repressive Eastern Europe, but his reservations over the title continued. Even the phrase "eastern Europe" is a "monstrous mystification. . . . Gombrowicz is Europe as Mozart or Broch or Chopin or Kafka are Europe and not eastern Europe. Eastern Europe exists only in political, post-Yalta sense. Not in [a] cultural sense."[23] Nevertheless, when Kundera suggests he may give a lecture series in Paris entitled "The Culture of Middle Europe," he tells Roth, "Your series will be for me the single reference, the single enterprise based on this concept."[24]

Ten years earlier Kundera warned Roth, who was no longer permitted to visit Czechoslovakia, that he must be careful concerning further contact. The police interrogated Věra Saudková, and they only wanted to know about Roth. Individuals could be accused of sedition if he were in contact with them, or worse, be accused of sedition even though he had no contact with them. Partly out of concern and partly out of admiration for Kundera's courage, Roth asks if he may dedicate *The Ghost Writer* to him. Kundera is flattered; later he tells Roth that *The Prague Orgy* is "absolutely one of the *six* or *seven* books of my life."[25] By that time, Kundera and Roth were close, the exiled Czech writer having visited Roth in Connecticut in 1978, meeting Roth's friend, the editor Veronica Geng of the *New Yorker,* who would soon become Kundera's editor at the magazine. *Shop Talk* reprints Roth's conversations with Kundera in London and Connecticut, originally published in the *New York Times Book Review.*

Bruno Schulz, along with Kundera, is the only other writer with two or more titles in the series: *The Street of Crocodiles* (1977) and *Sanatorium Under the Sign of the Hourglass* (1979), the second with an introduction by Updike.[26] Updike emphasizes how Schulz's gaze upon "local particulars turns objects into signs." He creates a "fluid confusion of the graphic and the actual" in his work.[27] Schulz is able to launch heavy objects "into flight," although always with a sense of menace behind the beauty. Updike alludes to Singer, Proust, Borges, and Kafka in introducing Schulz's work. He articulates the position of father in both Kafka and Schulz, adding that from mothers, men derive "their sense of their bodies; from the father, their sense of the world." Schulz presents an "antic . . . picturesque cosmos, lavish in its inventions but feeble in its authority." He spends more attention on boredom than Beckett does. His surrender to the distortions of "obsessed reflection" is purer than Proust's or Kafka's, Updike argues. A hidden man whose end was tragic (shot on the street by an SS officer), Schulz was, nevertheless, a witness to "the paradoxical richness and poverty of . . . our inner lives."[28]

Schulz was a writer with particular significance for Roth, who used his life and death as a trope in *The Prague Orgy* and the search by Zuckerman for the lost manuscripts of a Jewish writer. Part of the Schulz legend remains the search for a legendary novel, *The Messiah,* which appears in one form or another in David Grossman's *See Under: Love,* Cynthia Ozick's *The Messiah of Stockholm,* and Roth's *Prague Orgy.* In Ozick's novel, a Swedish book reviewer believes he is the lost son of Schulz and searches for the lost novel of his supposed father. The dedicatee of the novel is Roth, who introduced Schulz's work to Ozick. In Grossman's novel, a character named Bruno carries a manuscript called *The Messiah.* Elements of the real Bruno Schulz blend with Grossman's fictional figure. Obsessed with Schulz, Grossman published an interview in the *New Yorker* in June 2009 with a survivor of the Nazi "Black Thursday" action in which Schulz was killed, although his account raises questions about whether Schulz was shot by the Gestapo officer Günther or common soldiers.[29]

Despite Kundera's objections, his *Laughable Loves* and Vaculík's *The Guinea Pigs* began the "Writers from the Other Europe" series in 1974, Roth providing an introduction to the Kundera text and the series. Beginning with the work that made Kundera famous and infamous in Czechoslovakia, *The Joke*, Roth summarizes its focus on the life of a Czech Communist Party intellectual during the postwar, Stalinist years. Offering a brief political history of the Prague Spring and the 1968 Soviet invasion, Roth emphasized the condition of the demoralized Czechs and the removal of their prime minister, Dubček, to the post of inspector in a trolley factory. Kundera suffers from similar "exile," fired from his position at the Prague Film School and forbidden travel to the West, his works removed from bookstores and libraries. High taxes aimed at ten dissident writers effectively ban their writings.

Displaying a wide knowledge of the repressive conditions in Czechoslovakia and citing comments by Vaculík and Holub, Roth emphasizes the importance of focusing on the writing, not the political situation of these and other dissident authors. They need a readership in the West not because of their political oppression but because of their work. He again discusses *The Joke* and how three lines on a postcard destroy the life of the young student, Ludvik Jahn, locked in a Kafkaesque situation. Misunderstood by the authorities, Roth explains, *The Joke*, indeed, expresses "socialist content in national form," Stalin's definition of socialist realism. The joke upon the loyal citizen Ludvik seems in keeping with the spirit of Stalin's command, although the consequences of a joke in the socialist universe are devastating. After Ludvik's release, he attempts revenge by seducing the wife of the political friend who exposed him, but that, too, has ironic results.

Turning to *Laughable Loves*, Roth stresses Kundera's focus on erotic play and power and the presence of Don Juan characters who see women only as sexual objects. Reviewing the individual stories, Roth ties Kundera's work to Mailer, Mishima, and even Chekhov, emphasizing how Kundera's jokes begin in whimsy but end in trouble. Insightfully, Roth notes that in Kundera's Czechoslovakia, no matter the comedy, everything turns out "grimly serious."[30] Roth also mentions his own favorite, "Edward and God."

Later, Roth wrote the Afterword for Kundera's *Book of Laughter and Forgetting*. Others who wrote introductions or afterwords include a stellar list of international writers: Czesław Miłosz, Carlos Fuentes, Angela Carter, Jan Kott, John Updike, Joseph Brodsky, Heinrich Böll, and Josef Škvorecký. Irving Howe provided an introduction to Konrád's *The Case Worker*. In all, eighteen titles appeared in the series, running from 1974 to 1987 with one or two straggling titles appearing up to 1989.[31] After the series ended, Roth's project continued to gain acclaim among contemporary writers. In 2001, for example, William T. Vollmann praised Roth for bringing forward the work of Schulz, Jerzy Andrzejewski, Bohumil Hrabal, and Konwicki, as well as Kundera. Vollmann understood that the merit of these writers was literary and not their repression.[32] Nicole Krauss, in her preface to *Best European Fiction 2012*, would credit Roth's series for introducing her and other American readers to writers previously appearing only in clandestine *samizdat* publications.[33]

Epitomizing Roth's engagement with Eastern Europe is *The Prague Orgy*, first drafted in 1968, before the *Zuckerman Bound* stories but not published until 1985 (but set in 1976). In the story, the dead writer Sisovsky, protected in the war by a Nazi, is murdered in a revenge killing by a rival Gestapo officer, just as Schulz was. Roth uses the apocryphal line supposedly enunciated in the actual shooting of Schulz: "He shot my Jew; so I shot his." It is later revealed that Sisovsky's father died in a bus accident; the murdered writer was one who did not even write in Yiddish, as Sisovsky's father did.

Roth's work with the translators in the series alternated from hands on to hands off. Ivan Sanders, who translated the Hungarian György Konrád's *The City Builder*, had minimal exchanges with Roth. In an early note, Roth tells Sanders, who had written in appreciation of Konrád's work in June 1977, that he would be interested in anything exceptional in Hungarian literature, especially in contemporary fiction. In various exchanges, Sanders suggested that Roth include a second Konrád novel in the series, *The Case Worker*. Replying in February 1978, Roth is firm: no, the second Konrád text is not very good, but he did try to get *The Case Worker* but lost out to Bantam Books. He included Sanders's translation of *The City Builder* but had reservations about it, finding the book "hard going and overblown."[34]

Later, Roth would ask Sanders for an evaluation of the Hungarian translation of *The Humbling*; he was worried because a friend had pointed out grave mistakes in a translation of some other texts. Sanders replied that the translation *Humbling* is fluent and polished and challenging. Citing specific passages in English and Hungarian, Sanders explains that in each Hungarian sentence, an "ordinary but expressive figure of speech is used; the meaning sinks in quickly." Dialogue is especially effective: even when they are highly charged with emotion, the language remains "natural, colloquial."[35] The title, however, was changed to the equivalent of "A Burnout," as the Hungarian equivalents to *The Humbling* were too moralistic.

Roth would ask for a similar evaluation of *Nemesis* from Sanders, who thought well of the translation because the language both soared and was elevated with colloquialisms and street talk sprinkled throughout. At times, in fact, the translator's usages are more informal than the original expressions. However, the translator is also mindful of the subject's gravity and chooses adequate diction to convey that gravity. In this period from roughly 1972 and his Kafka parody, *The Breast*, to 1985, *The Prague Orgy*, Roth had substituted Mitteleuropa for center field.

Prague became Roth's political unconscious, offering a more complex Jewish history than he could have ever known in Newark. Prague and Central Europe also made it possible for Roth to confront Israel, as he does in *The Counterlife* and *Operation Shylock*, following its introduction in *Portnoy*. Involuted and ironic, Prague offered new possibilities, united in *The Prague Orgy* where repression and lost Yiddish manuscripts contend with each other. Central Europe replaces center field as the position or place Roth most wants to be. *The Breast* was his satiric take on "The Metamorphosis," followed more seriously by his experience of Eastern Europe penetratingly expressed in his guidance of the "Writers from the Other Europe" series. This, with the follow-up of *The Ghost Writer* and then the *Zuckerman Bound* series, may mark not only a major self-transformation but Roth's most heroic years.

Roth's immersion in the writers of Eastern Europe both extended and surpassed his engagement with Kafka. They stylistically and thematically provided material for texts like *The Professor of Desire*, *The Ghost Writer*, and *The Prague Orgy*. His contacts anticipated later friendships with Primo Levi, Norman Manea, Aharon Appelfeld, and I. B. Singer, lengthening his European roots and identity, documented for the most part in his published interviews with these writers. His involvement with them is part of his effort to reconstruct a European past he never had. His American-born parents did not carry with them Jewish Europe. He had to learn that, as he had to learn the power of the comic.

Roth skirts those critics who impugned his Judaism, for in firming up his European credentials, he firms up his Jewish identity. Through his friendships with Appelfeld, Levi, Kundera, and Klíma and his intense reading of Kafka, Babel, Anne Frank, and Schulz, he established his credentials, extended by attachments with artists like Guston, dedicatee of *Zuckerman Unbound*, and later R. B. Kitaj. In *Shop Talk*, interviews with many of these writers, Roth reads himself through the guise of reading others. At this time, he also befriends surviving members of Kafka's family, including two nieces.

He thickened his culture through the world of cosmopolitan European Jewishness. Roth became, in fact, "a model diasporic artist" who carried out what a Jew may consider to be his birthright, as Shechner suggests: rescue books, exactly what the "Writers from the Other Europe" achieves.[36]

In the midst of this new focus, Roth completed and published *My Life as a Man* (1974), a book necessary to free him from the struggle of his first marriage, which then gave him permission to turn his attention away from Newark, the Midwest, and New York analysts to confront twentieth-century Eastern Europe. The 1970s are a momentous decade for Roth, marked by personal freedom and a new relationship (with Claire Bloom) and an expanding sense of his role as a writer through new experiences and friendships. The *Professor of Desire* (1977) and *The Ghost Writer* (1979) sustain this shift, summarized later by *Zuckerman Unbound* in 1981 and then *Zuckerman Bound*, containing the important story, "The Prague Orgy" (1985). Indeed, short of the intense period in which he would write the American Trilogy in the late 1980s, this is the most important decade of Roth's work: in it, he discovers his European, Jewish roots which propel his writing forward and outward. It was also the period of perhaps his greatest education.

The exposure and involvement with Eastern Europe expanded Roth's writerly universe, an exposure that had significant impact on the breadth of his writing. If Hawthorne (morality and romance) along with James (form and consciousness) had an early effect on his work, and Kafka (dark comedy and bureaucratic confusion) a later effect, the Eastern European writers confirmed a bleak stream of self-exposure and recovery through irony and history, taking Roth out of his Newark narcissism. What affected Roth early in his meeting with Czech writers was the realization that he worked in a society where repression ruled. Tom Stoppard, born in Czechoslovakia in 1937, felt a similar difference between England and Russia, which he dramatizes in *The Coast of Utopia* (2002) when Bakunin realizes his need to return to Russia from exile, for only there will he be valued as a writer, even though he knows he will be censored. The enemy, Roth and Stoppard realize, is authoritarianism that both suppresses and yet encourages free speech.

Blended with exposure to writers like Singer, Levi, and Appelfeld, Roth's Eastern European encounters made him more aware of the obligations of an author to the culture and events of the recent past. Instead of Newark, Prague; instead of Brenda Patimkin, Anne Frank; instead of Consuela, Kafka's whore. This expansion laid the groundwork for *Operation Shylock* and *Sabbath's Theater* and the remaking of America in the American Trilogy.

Critical recognition of this episode in his life and its importance has been late. Only in May 2013 did he receive a PEN/Allen Foundation Literary Service Award for his support of the persecuted writers of Eastern Europe. In his remarks, Roth described being under constant surveillance during his visits of 1972–77 and being detained on his last visit by the police as he left an art museum and a show of Soviet realistic art. He departed the country the next day, unable to return until 1989. Critiquing the harmful elements of totalitarianism in his speech, Roth notes that it cranks out "the worst of everything." He ends by repeating the story of how, on the evening of the day he decided to leave, the police picked up and interrogated Ivan Klíma, the Czech Jew and survivor of the Terezin concentration camp. They did not badger him over his seditious activities but wanted to know about Roth's annual visits. "Don't you read his books?" Klíma asked the police. They were surprised by the question until he provided the answer, which explained Roth's multiple visits: "He comes for the girls."[37]

Turning this experience into fiction, Roth devotes three pages in *Deception* to his run-in with the police and his detention in 1975. He escaped by hopping on a trolley while the police were distracted, and he repeats the story told by Klíma about Roth going to Czechoslovakia only for the girls, although in the novel he alters it to say he went for the jokes, adding, "I come to England for the girls" (DE 134).

Ironically, one of those "girls" was Věra Saudková, Kafka's niece met in 1974, arranged through Professor Zdenk Strybyrny. The niece showed Roth Kafka family photographs and family items; in London, Roth became friendly with Marianne Steiner, the daughter of Kafka's sister Valli. He also met the widow of Jiří Weil and in New York arranged for the publication of Weil's novel *Life with a Star* and several short stories in the *American Poetry Review* for which he supplied the introduction. At Princeton, he met Joanna Clark, the Polish wife of his friend Blair Clark, and soon, a series of Polish writers. His London proximity to Eastern Europe (he spent half the year in London after he and Bloom began their relationship) made trips easier, and after Kundera moved to Paris in 1975 to live as an émigré, they met frequently.

Soon, however, Roth's new focus would be Israel, instead of Czechoslovakia, a character in *The Counterlife* comically transferring Roth's early sports passion when he cries to Zuckerman near the Wailing Wall, "Not until there is baseball in Israel will [the] Messiah come!" (CL 94). The character, one hyper Jimmy Ben-Joseph, formerly Lustig, of West Orange, New Jersey, announces that he wants to "play centerfield for the Jerusalem Giants" and then rushes from Nathan as if "to follow the flight of a ball struck off a Louisville Slugger from somewhere up in the old Jewish quarter" (CL 94). Gaining speed, he runs toward the Wall chasing his imaginary fly ball, leaping into the air while screaming "'Ben-Joseph catches it!' The game is over. The season is over! 'The Jerusalem Giants win the pennant! Messiah is on his way!'" (CL 93). Baseball, Judaism, and Israel are one.

II

> All the time I thought you loved me for my body when in fact it was only for my sentences.
>
> —Philip Roth, *Deception*, 1990

Instrumental in this development and facilitating his visits to Czechoslovakia was Claire Bloom.

Born Patricia Claire Blume in February 1931 in Finchley, North London, the eldest child and only daughter of Edward Blume and his wife, the former Elizabeth Grew (originally Griewski), she moved frequently with her family before World War II. The change in spelling to Bloom occurred in the 1930s. Bloom's maternal grandmother was the daughter of the chief rabbi of Frankfurt, although her parents were born in England. In 1941, to escape the Blitz, her father's brother invited Claire, her mother, and her siblings to live in Florida. There, she attended dancing school, sang on the radio, and performed regularly at a Miami Beach hotel. After a year, they moved to Forest Hills, New York.

The family returned to London via Lisbon in 1943, her father's fortunes having improved. They lived on Curzon Street in Mayfair. Claire began drama school at the age of thirteen and soon was acting in repertory theater. Her father had moved to South Africa and asked her mother for a divorce. By 1952, after various auditions, Bloom won the part of the ballerina in Charlie Chaplin's *Limelight*, which made her an overnight star; it opened the same week she debuted as Juliet opposite Alan Badel as Romeo in the Old Vic. At twenty-one she was celebrated. Dramatic successes followed, working with Laurence Olivier in *Richard III* in 1955 and with Richard Burton in *Look Back in Anger* in 1958; she had originally met Burton almost a decade earlier when they were both in Christopher Fry's *The Lady's Not for Burning*. She had an early affair with Burton, before one with Yul Brynner, her costar in *The Brothers Karamazov*. In 1958 she played Broadway in *Rashomon* (1959) with Rod Steiger, whom she married; at the time, she was four months pregnant. Their daughter, Anna Justine, was born in 1960.

After ten years of marriage, she and Steiger divorced in 1969; she then married the theater producer Hillard Elkins, who convinced her to return to the stage—throughout the 1960s she had concentrated on film, including *The Chapman Report* (1962), *The Spy Who Came In from the Cold* (1965), and *The Illustrated Man* (1969). Elkins produced *A Doll's House* staring Bloom as Nora, an exceptional performance. She later played Hedda in *Hedda Gabler* and Blanche DuBois in *A Streetcar Named Desire*. Collectively, these roles consolidated her reputation as one of the most successful actors of her generation, which she described in her 1982 memoir, *Limelight and After: The Education of an Actress*, a work dedicated to her mother, brother, daughter Anna, and Roth. Roth, in fact, played a major role in organizing the book, interviewing Bloom, who used her answers in the acting portion of the memoir as notes. Roth also helped her with corrections to the text.[38]

They had first met informally in 1966 in East Hampton, where she and Steiger had rented a summer home. At the time, Roth was with Ann Mudge. In 1974, her marriage to Elkins was over and she moved with her daughter back to London. On a stopover in New York on her way to Hawaii to make Hemingway's *Islands in the Stream* with George C. Scott in 1975, she and Roth met again, as Roth was walking down Madison Avenue on his way to a session with his psychoanalyst; she was to meet her yoga teacher for tea. She was forty-four, he was forty-two. Woody Allen did not set the scene.

In her memoir *Limelight and After*, Bloom observes that only on the stage was she "wholly alive and wholly at ease." Revealingly, she remarks that those who feel unsure about themselves were very sure of themselves "when they were being someone else." What is rewarding is the disappearance of self as the actor becomes someone else, celebrating "egolessness" and demonstrating on stage what a playwright—Ibsen, Shakespeare, Chekhov, Tennessee Williams—imagined. The key is performance, performing someone else's character. Actors allow themselves to be taken "into the play" rather than superimpose themselves "onto a play."

"A limitless capacity to pretend" is what an actor must possess, a strength and perhaps a downfall, most pointedly revealed in her private relationships, including that with Roth. In notes to her second autobiographical volume, *Leaving a Doll's House*, she believed that with Roth it would be "brutally difficult but totally fulfilling" to make a life together. Part of the problem, she quickly realized—he had planned a two-week vacation to Saint Martin before they met and would not change his plans—was his pattern of approach and withdrawal, "drawing up close and then violently pulling apart," which would characterize their association.[39]

But the couple soon worked out a plan: he would spend six or seven months of the year in London with her and then retreat to his farmhouse in Cornwall Bridge, surrounded by forty acres. Roth's Connecticut home and cabin on Melius Road was a late eighteenth-century farmhouse bought in 1972, ascetic and functional in nature; the writing studio, separated by some hundred yards from the main house, contained filing cabinets, a photograph of Kafka, a drawing of Roth by Philip Guston, and a large desk for the left-handed writer, plus a standup desk allowing him to write when his back did not cooperate. In the main house, lithographs by Bruno Schulz, framed jackets of Roth's books blown up to poster size, books, and typewriters populated every room; translations of his works resided in the guest closet. A swimming pool, dubbed the Franklin Library Memorial Swimming Pool because of the publishing house that paid him well to sign tip-in sheets of a limited edition of *Goodbye, Columbus*, was adjacent to the home.[40] There was also a barn. At one point, Roth and Bloom created an outdoor gazebo with screens to enjoy summer evenings and entertain guests.

In London, Roth would join Bloom at her Chelsea townhouse, bought in 1974; they would keep this routine for the next twelve years (Figure 7.1). But witnessing an argument between Bloom and her daughter the first night he arrived to take up residence should have been a warning. The mother and daughter actually engaged in a fistfight. He should have left either for a hotel or America, he later wrote; he knew he didn't belong but thought he could make things work. And he was in love with Bloom. But her battles with her seventeen-year-old daughter were legendary, Bloom acting the supplicant and Anna the tyrant. Bloom became scornful, resentful, and yet dependent on her daughter, and over time Roth fell out of love. In the end, only one of the three was unbroken by the relentless conflict: Anna.

Bloom, persistently dependent on her daughter to such an extent that she would begin to cry over missing her and would call her daily from the U.S., sought numerous ways to return to London. It became so dominating a need that Roth set up a special travel fund for Bloom with an initial deposit of $10,000, but it didn't help. She often broken down and sobbed when she arrived at Roth's home, distraught over being separated from Anna.

Figure 7.1 Roth and Bloom walking down a Chelsea Street, London, 10 March 1990. Credit: Ian Cook, Getty Images.

In the early years of their relationship the feelings were intense. In a letter to Roth of 21 July 1978, Bloom ends with "This letter factual and dull contains not my full feeling, of love and passion beyond end." A letter the next day begins, "My sweetest love." In 1984 she writes, "You are my sweet and darling boy," and in a letter from 1986 she tells him, "I am so ideally happy with you. . . . You are always so kind and wonderful." In a vivid letter from Jaipur in January 1987, she playfully tells him the wife of her producer proudly told her she bought "COUNTERTOP when she was in N.Y. Remember our endless discussions about the title The Counterlife, A Counterlife, A Counter Life. Well, this [is] how much it all means. Countertop."[41] Roth in a set of parallel letters reveals an equally relaxed and happy demeanor, although underneath he was harboring issues, mainly about Bloom's dependency on her daughter, her feelings of financial insecurity, and her increasing anxiety over her career.

From the beginning, Roth was an amalgam of the two types of partners Bloom outlined in the final pages of Limelight and After: the servant who comes with you wherever you must go for a play or film, and the one who demands a lot for himself, and you either live apart or you get together "getting ready to depart" (LA 175). Roth was physically living with Bloom in London but psychologically and sexually living alone in the same city. He sought to become part of her life, accompanying her to rehearsals and productions and working with her on scripts. A translation of Chekhov's The Cherry Orchard for her performance at the 1981 Chichester Festival contains annotations by Roth and Bloom. Roth often helped to shape her performance. She, in turn, would help him improvise dialogue for his books, joining in role-playing games with him, and coming up with lines that would appear in his fiction. She accompanied him when he received honors and awards, such as an honorary degree from Bucknell in 1979 (Figure 7.2). He at this time expressed admiration for her poise and presence.

In April 1982, Foyles bookshop in London gave a literary luncheon for Bloom on the publication of Limelight and After. To Roger Straus Roth wrote proudly, "She was terrific, far better at being an author than I am. She's a better actress, and a better author and better looking. And she has more hair." But she can't hit the ball out of the infield, he adds, "so there, I'm still ahead." He ends by describing his work on the script of The Ghost Writer and says that James Mason seems to have signed on to play Lonoff with Bloom as Hope, his wife.[42]

At other times, he would distance himself from her activities and remain at home, although when she filmed Brideshead Revisited (playing a memorable Lady Marchmain), he often visited her on weekends, joking about becoming a Jewish couple in the castle and warning her not to touch the curtain fabric or ask how much per yard. He also comically requested no Yiddish before breakfast (LDH 161). Their rhythm of unity and separation seemed to work with the relationship in phase 1, a blend of romantic, cultural, and certainly artistic interests and socializing in London. But in phase 2, as her dependency on her daughter grew, Roth found himself trapped between a desire to leave and her greater need for him to stay.

Figure 7.2 Roth and Bloom at Bucknell University in 1979, when Roth received an honorary degree. Credit: Special Collections/University Archives, Bucknell University.

Part of Roth's behavior with Bloom, Maggie, Ann, and Barbara may originate in a "savior complex," his desire to salvage the lives of women he perceives to be, who or actually are, damaged in one way or another. (Recall his father's unconditional willingness to help others, especially in the family.) Only in this role can he allow himself to be loved, believing that helping people in need will result in their approval *and* love of him. But acting this way does not allow the other individual to take responsibility for their own actions, which came to annoy him, creating a dilemma. This goes beyond the lack of fathers among his women to a contested desire to alleviate their suffering psychologically or sexually but then growing increasingly frustrated because they seem not to be able to become independent and act on their own. As one psychologist has noted, people are addicted to suffering and "we frequently support each other in maintaining these addictions."[43] Roth's comments on Bloom and on Maggie indicate his sense of how hurt these women were and how he would, or could, correct that, but he had little success.

Roth repeated this pattern frequently, finding himself often attracted to women of low self-esteem who felt inadequate. The women who don't feel or act this way are strong-willed and often a threat to men and, with few exceptions, appear only in his fiction, not in his life. Three of them are Naomi, the Sabra Portnoy encounters in Israel at the end of his novel, Drenka in *Sabbath's Theater,* and Olga Sisovsky of "The Prague Orgy," who pursues Zuckerman. A fourth is the sexually aggressive Birgitta Svanstrom in *The Professor of Desire,* who lingers in Kepesh's mind even after he has accommodated himself to the passive Claire Ovington.

Strangely, Roth's male protagonists can enjoy the aggressive women only when they are physically incapacitated, as when Zuckerman, in *The Anatomy Lesson,* must lie on his back while various women visitors dally with him. Diana, a twenty-year-old, is the most physical, exceeded only by the experienced Jaga from Warsaw. But once erect (that is, able to stand plus sexually capable), he lacks the confidence to pursue them. Incapacitated heroes are attracted to aggressive women, as with the unnamed narrator of *Everyman,* who desires the buxom, red-headed day nurse Maureen who accompanies him home after one of his heart operations. He thinks of pursuing her only because he is unable to. Physical pursuits for Roth's late heroes bring only discomfort, dissatisfaction, and even fear, marked by Simon Axler in *The Humbling.* Without the assistance of the bisexual Pegeen and certain sex toys or new arrangements (a threesome), he would likely never have sought new sexual adventures. The ironic response to these confident women is the undoing or paralysis of the male, who often becomes impotent or passive (or in Axler's case, suicidal). Interestingly, all of these types reflect real women Roth knew.

In his fiction, Roth shows the consequences of misreading women; in his life, he protects himself by avoiding independent, combative women and runs from those who pursue him. Combined with his sense of anger (identified in Dr. Kleinschmidt's paper), this explains both the caring and the volatility of Roth's relationships. On one hand, he helps, as he did with the academic career of the London-based American writer David Plante, and in arranging for Kundera to be published in the *New Yorker*, bringing exiled writers such as Norman Manea to America, quietly providing a high school scholarship and offering financial assistance to Holly Williams. But when he cannot control others depending on him, the relationship blows up.

Quickly and decisively, Roth ends any association that threatens him or gets away from his control. They conclude coldly without him ever feeling defensive or guilty. Although his early editor at Random House, Joe Fox, worked at his friendship with Roth, even loaning him money for visits to his analyst, Roth ended their relationship when he and Fox disagreed over the promotion and marketing of *When She Was Good*. Similarly with Ross Miller, his first official biographer: when Miller's editorial weaknesses and failure to conduct the interviews Roth suggested created distrust of Miller's ability and how he would actually present his Roth's life, Roth fired him.[44] Miller's emphasis on Roth's salacious relationships with certain women rather than trying to understand Roth's character finally torpedoed their association. James Atlas, a longtime friend, received similar treatment when his biography of Bellow appeared, written at Roth's encouragement. Roth disliked the portrait of his friend and ended his connection with Atlas almost immediately. He also began a search for a new biographer of Bellow. Many felt hurt by Roth. As the writer Janet Malcolm wrote, "The man gives nothing (Yes, except to literature). He is completely selfish and manipulative. How taken in I was."[45]

In his books, Roth rarely allows his characters (especially the men) to give way to helpless feelings, feelings that make them vulnerable to more than what the author allows them to be, although certain female characters, such as Libby Herz in *Letting Go* and Faunia Farley in *The Human Stain*, contradict this. The theme of the savior begins with Neal Klugman in "Goodbye, Columbus," expanded by Gabe Wallach in *Letting Go*. In both these early examples, however, such action backfires, expressing something of Roth's own slow recognition that his role as a savior was tenuous and often greeted with uncertainty.

But his characters are always under his control. That control, Plante believes, is why so many critics say all Roth can write about is himself. The driving force of his novels is how often he can convince his protagonists to act decisively, breaking out of his authorial control, as seen in Portnoy, Peter Tarnopol, and Mickey Sabbath. Ironically, they never quite achieve total freedom despite their desire for independence. Similarly, when friends didn't meet his standards or appear committed to his ideas, Roth would end their friendship, as happened with Fox, Atlas, Francine du Plessix Gray, and Miller.

One particularly difficult break was with Herman and Nina Schneider, whom Roth had met on Martha's Vineyard and who remained friends for over twenty years. During that time, they grew close to Ann Mudge. Indeed, Ann asked that Roth write to them to tell them of her crisis, that she had nearly overdosed. His letter is detailed and precise but not emotional. The Schneiders were also warm and receptive to Barbara Sproul.

Retired science teachers, Herman was at one point supervisor of science programs for the New York City school system and the author, with his wife, of over eighty books in their Schneider Science Series designed for children, with titles like *Everyday Weather and How It Works*. In one letter, Nina wrote to Roth that they had "run out of numbers . . . and it's hard to figure what's a book" any more at their age (they were in their eighties). After giving up their West 11th Street Greenwich Village brownstone, they moved to Look's Pond in West Tisbury on Martha's Vineyard and collected arcane, antique science instruments. Belgium-born Nina published a novel to critical acclaim in 1980. Entitled *The Woman Who Lived in a Prologue*, it narrated the story of a Jewish matriarch surviving the war and working through a life in the New World.

Sometime in 1979, the friendship between Roth and the Schneiders abruptly ended. Bothered, Herman wrote Roth, "I'm sure you didn't do it lightly and on our side we have felt it heavily," generously adding, "Relationships have been known to outwear themselves." Given their friendship throughout the late 1960s and 1970s, the break is still a mystery.

In 1985, Nina recalled Roth visiting them and their walks, "on which you shared with me your searing inner conflicts about B[arbara]." In a later letter, she reminds Roth that he should be less hard on himself concerning Maggie's death and "not twist the facts. . . . She *was* pretty and naïve looking. You weren't altogether blind. Who knew that she was no more innocent than Elise the venom-tongued, the great face?"[46] But Roth, it seems, had little time for the couple at that point, even when Nina wrote a consoling letter on the death of his mother in 1981.

Roth claimed that Bloom's role of supplicant to her daughter damaged his physical and emotional health. Their life in London was completely counter to Roth's ideal, which, as he writes in "Notes for My Biographer," was to be free and to write what he wanted, to take on his enemies in any way he chose and to sleep with anyone he wanted to. He also wanted the freedom to leave a relationship that no longer satisfied.

At this time, the mid-1980s, Roth did not relax his textual vigilance as various titles and reprints began to appear. Galleys he received from Fawcett in New York highlighted countless typos, dropped lines, and awkward typefaces, particularly in the paperback edition of *The Anatomy Lesson*. In an aggressive letter to the editorial assistant of Leona Nevler, a Fawcett executive who earlier in her career spotted and edited *Peyton Place* by Grace Metalious, he lists the errors and demands to review the corrected page proofs. In a separate letter to David Rieff, he summarizes the problems, sarcastically writing that such problems are "very cheering for a perfectionist maniac" like himself. But then, for distraction, he tells Rieff he must see the film *Swann in Love*, especially the young actress who plays Odette (Ornella Muti) and who looks like "she sells jeans at the Gap." But she has "a delicious pair of tits. Worth waiting to see. Should have been called Remembrance of Paired Tits." Jeremy Irons, her costar, is a porn star "who doesn't know it. Even his name is right for a porn star."[47]

During this period, one of Roth's closest London friends was David Plante, an American writer who had lived abroad since 1966. He met Roth in 1975 and collaborated with him on a screenplay on the Jean Rhys section of Plante's *Difficult Women*, a memoir of Sonia Orwell, Rhys, and Germaine Greer. Plante elaborates on their friendship in two engaging autobiographical volumes, *Becoming a Londoner* (2013) and *Worlds Apart* (2015). He earlier published the presciently titled memoir, *American Ghosts* (2005), an account of his Catholic and gay adolescence. Plante asked if he could dedicate it to Roth, who agreed.

London and literature enamored Plante, who writes in his first autobiographical volume that once, while traveling on the London Tube, he mesmerized himself by carrying a two-volume first edition of *Du côté de chez Swann* from the Baroness de Rothschild to Stephen Spender: "That I was carrying Proust, as if he himself were contained in a little coffin on my lap and his ghost hovered around it, seemed to me to expand the world outwardly into a world of literature that would be my world when I wrote it all down in my diary"—which of course he did.[48] Roth expresses similar feelings about literature through Kepesh in *The Professor of Desire* and Zuckerman, notably in *The Ghost Writer*.

Plante and Roth first met after Roth praised *Difficult Women*. He told Plante that he recently had had a blow-up with Harold Pinter over the book.[49]

It may have ended their relationship, he said, something fairly common for Roth. Among the few friends who did remain close were Theodore Solotaroff (although there were periods of friction), Hermione Lee, Judith Thurman, David Rieff, and Benjamin Taylor. Al Alvarez and the painter R. B. Kitaj were two long-standing London friends, as well as Plante.

Monsieur Thompson's restaurant in Notting Hill became a regular haunt for Roth and Plante, with its white tablecloths and white peaked napkins on white plates. There, Plante heard Roth praise his recently published *New Yorker* story "Paris, 1959," somewhat chagrined that a writer like Roth would care to comment on his work. Plante also recalls Roth telling him why he would never leave a then demoralized Bloom, even if their meals were held in silence: "If I left her, she would kill herself." I do everything possible to support her, he explains, but it's difficult "because as I'm holding up one wall, another wall is collapsing. If I left her, and she collapsed, I wouldn't recover. Also, I love her." But her distractedness separated her from Roth. Asked what initially attracted her to him, he thought hard and then said, "Her aura." He had seen her in *Limelight* "and fallen in love with her years before." And she was, after all, connected to the interesting world of the theater.[50]

Plante offers three insightful comments: (1) Roth has a "compassionate sense for helplessness in people," which surprisingly does not always come through in his books; (2) he is relentlessly honest and will admit to anything about himself, even "perhaps as he's doing it, however crude he is in the self-exposure"; and (3) his therapy kept him from killing his first wife. He then adds that the important women in Roth's life were all without fathers, including Bloom.[51] Roth recounted his depression following the end of a long affair (likely with Sproul), so severe that he crawled to the bathroom in the morning and mistakenly put on his shoes while forgetting his socks. This was likely in 1974 when, he explained to James Atlas in September 1987, he was, in fact, on antidepressants for several months and couldn't stand living alone. And then he met Bloom and his life changed.

As Roth began to spend more and more time in London, he confided in Plante that he felt deeply uncomfortable about the British attitude toward Jews and that the English were embarrassed when he said "Jews" instead of "Jewish." He confessed that his family and relatives were not as intelligent or sensitive as he made them out to be; in fact, they were uneducated, bigoted, and close-minded. In his writing, he had to elevate them.[52] The paradox of Roth, as Plante understood it, was that he could only write about people in extreme situations—nothing else interested him—but in person, he gave way to feelings of helplessness, telling Plante at one point that he had no subject, that he was lost.[53]

While in London, Roth often rented a studio in Notting Hill, a simple room in a white stucco townhouse, according to Plante. A large electric type-writer on a desk and a large wastebasket filled with discarded pages were the only furnishings. Sometimes he would rent a room at the Royal Automobile Club off Paul Mall, outfitted, at least in the summer of 1983, as a purposeful writer's studio with an IBM typewriter, file holders, dictionaries, aspirin, and felt-tip pens for correcting. The bookshelf, according to Hermione Lee, who visited him there, held copies of Howe's autobiography, Erik Erickson's *Young Man Luther*, Leonard Woolf's autobiography, Cheever's *Oh, What a Paradise It Seems*, and Claire's *Limelight*. He liked the RAC because of their swimming pool, which he visited regularly.[54]

Roth formed new friendships in London: with the American painter Kitaj, who would do a charcoal portrait of him in 1985 (Figure 7.3), Pinter (dram-atist), Lee (professor), Michael Kustow (arts producer and gallery director), David Hare (playwright), and the Vietnam War correspondent Michael Herr. Ava Gardner was another. According to Robert McCrum, when Roth attended a seventieth birthday party for conductor Leonard Bernstein, "he

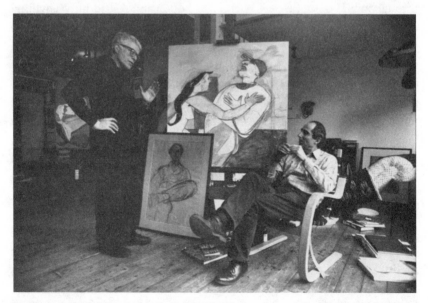

Figure 7.3 Roth listening to R. B. Kitaj in his London studio, 1985. Credit: Ian Cook/Getty Images.

was seated next to Ava Gardner, who had been living in seclusion in London for several years. Gardner, who had been married to Frank Sinatra, joked to Roth, 'I used to go out with a boy from Hoboken.' " The pair spent the evening in intense conversation. Roth, a "cocktail of vanity, optimism and defiance," likely dominated.[55]

Roth's early years in London were electric with ideas, gossip, and energy, even if he felt unwelcomed or at least marginalized as an American and a Jew. Inventive talk flourished, whether the guests were from Greece, Amsterdam, Paris, or even New York. Editors, publishers, writers, painters, actors, directors, and musicians tripped over each other, creating a *bouillabaisse* of creativity that differed in variety if not intensity from New York. The excitement inspired, highlighted by his work with its European focus. During Roth's Anglo period, he wrote *The Professor of Desire, The Ghost Writer, Zuckerman Unbound, The Counterlife, Deception,* and *Operation Shylock.* From London he was able to visit France regularly to meet Kundera and the French philosopher Alain Finkielkraut, then Israel, where he would see Aharon Appelfeld. But where others integrated into their new society, Roth was constantly aware of being an American and a Jew in England. Kitaj, for instance, told Plante that although England was an alien culture, he and his wife oddly felt a part of it.[56]

In England, however, Roth felt uncomfortable because he was generally comfortable: "Nothing drives me crazy here, and a writer *has* to be driven crazy to help him to *see.* A writer needs his poisons, the antidote to his poisons is often a book." He observed, "Here Claire is English in spite of being Jewish, but I'm American because I'm Jewish."[57] He missed the vulgarity of New York: London offered only "hypocritical politeness." He needed someone to shout "Asshole" at him in a traffic jam. This, he said, "would make him relax," something he would share with his character Mickey Sabbath. Only shouting would make him feel at home. He was proud that he taught Bloom to use the word "fuck" and once printed a headline in a fake paper, something like "SHE HAS USED THE WORD!" She was amused when he gave it to her.[58]

Roth would go on to critique England and its anti-Semitism in *The Counterlife* (1986) and *Deception* (1990). In the former, Zuckerman confronts a pseudo-aristocratic couple dining while he is celebrating Maria's birthday in a posh London hotel restaurant. Challenging the insulting comments of the elderly woman nearby, he stands up for his Jewishness while identifying English anti-Semitism despite Maria's denial of such behavior. "What exactly do they smell when they smell a Jew?" he asks out loud (CL 294). In *Deception*, there are various discussions about Jews having to try harder in England and a pronounced English disdain toward Jewish success. The English, the protagonist/writer notes, resist education about Jewish life and behavior (DC 31–32, 35, 77–82). Being Jewish *and* an American in England makes the unnamed protagonist "a very contentious fellow" (DC 82). No one in England screamed at each other, a daily occurrence in New York. "England made a Jew of me in only eight weeks," Roth told BBC's Alan Yentob.[59] Yet he would not leave, at least not until his social discomfort, compounded by his deteriorating relationship with Bloom, was complete.

8

Supercarnal Productions

The Jersey boy with the dirty mouth who writes the books Jews love to hate.

—Philip Roth, *The Counterlife*, 1986

The title of this chapter is the name Nathan Zuckerman, impersonating the critic Milton Appel, gives to his pornographic film and magazine empire in *The Anatomy Lesson* (AL 192). And the epigraph is a critique of Zuckerman's work by his Israeli journalist-historian friend Shuki, parodically summarizing the legacy of *Portnoy* at the same time it points to Roth's European orientation accentuated by 1977's *The Professor of Desire* followed by *The Ghost Writer* (1979) to be trailed by the Zuckerman novels, culminating in the *Counterlife* (1986), a blend of New Jersey, London, and Israel—and a counterweight to *My Life as a Man* published twelve years earlier.

Europe still loomed large during this period, which preceded Roth's return to America. In the late 1970s, he began to consolidate his writing, having distilled his engagement with Kafka. On a return visit to the U.S., he widened his Eastern European connections via Joanna Rostropowicz Clark, who introduced Roth to contemporary Polish writing. During this period, he also published "Imagining Jews" in the *New York Review of Books,* and in 1975 he published his first collection of essays and interviews, *Reading Myself and Others*. It appeared with Farrar, Straus and Giroux where his former editor Aaron Asher had moved after leaving Holt, Rinehart & Winston.

But in London, where he continued to spend a good deal of time, Roth expanded his circle of friends, one of the most important being Al Alvarez (1929–2019), author of the classic 1972 study of suicide, *The Savage God*. Alvarez became poetry editor of *The Observer* (associating with Ted Hughes, W. H. Auden, Sylvia Plath, and John Berryman) in addition to writing fiction, poetry, and nonfiction. Roth first met Alvarez in London as early as 1959 when Roth was passing through on his Guggenheim Fellowship on his way to Rome. They became immediate friends because, in Alvarez's words, they were both "edgy young men with failing marriages and a nose for trouble" and believed that literature was "the most honorable of all callings and were baffled when life didn't work out as books had led us to expect."[1]

Four years older than Roth, Alvarez was also a friend of Plath's, which added resonance to his well-received study *The Savage God*. Divorce was another of his subjects, studied in *Life after Marriage* (1982), having ended his relationship with Ursula Barr (m. 1956–60), the granddaughter of Frieda Lawrence, D. H. Lawrence's widow. Parallels with Roth are clear, although not the suicide attempt.[2]

Poker and mountain climbing were two enthusiasms, as well as swimming, a passion shared with Roth.[3] Alvarez's *Pondlife* (2013) is a narrative of his almost daily swims in the four ponds of Hampstead Heath, exercise but also a form of protest against old age. Alvarez began his passion for swimming with his first plunge in the Finchley Road Baths at eleven during the Blitz.

Roth renewed his friendship with Alvarez in the mid-1970s when he began to spend time in London with Bloom and quickly found himself in the company of Alvarez's Hampstead neighbors, especially David Cornwell (aka John le Carré) and the pianist Alfred Brendel. Roth would maintain a correspondence with Cornwell from 1984 to 1992. At dinner at Brendel's, he would often encounter the likes of Noel Annan or Isaiah Berlin. Socializing in London became his new style. Reading in the evening, he remarked, was for the country.[4]

In a 2004 interview, Alvarez celebrated Roth's late flourish, noting that from roughly 1994 until 2004 there was an unprecedented set of books. Alvarez also admired Roth's determination to write despite severe back pain, age, and distractions, which he always tried to limit. He, like Alvarez, was athletic and commented that he paced often when writing and quipped that "he walks half a mile for every page he writes."[5] Much later, Roth analogized his writing to that of a stonemason repairing a wall stone by stone after seeing his Connecticut stonemason at work on his property. The next day, he inscribed a book of his to him, "To Russ, another wall of words."[6]

At the time, Roth separated life and work, living with Bloom near Fulham Road but writing in a small flat in adjacent Kensington. A separate writing studio and apartment was a Roth pattern: in Connecticut, he used his separate writing cottage, a short walking distance from the main house; in New York, for a while, he had an apartment on the Upper West Side for living and a smaller one, a studio, on the twelfth floor of the apartment building for writing. Furnishings in the large, one-room studio in New York included a drawing by Philip Guston of an open book with a text that might be in Hebrew. A lectern at which he wrote, an easy chair, a lamp, and a bed were the only other items.[7]

Alvarez also profiled Roth as a meticulous writer who wrote carefully and preferred an isolated if not austere existence, attributing this partly to growing up in an age of normative 1950s goals. He grew up more or less "doing what he was told"; "he couldn't help being a good boy, however much he yearned to be bad," Alvarez wrote. Portnoy allowed him to unleash that underside. His Newark upbringing was in an orderly, commercially centered city at the time, the largest in the state with half a million people but small enough for many workers—in breweries, leather goods, small manufacturing, and department stores—to walk to work.[8]

Visiting Roth's London studio apartment, his working place, Alvarez noticed a manuscript page near the typewriter dense with corrections. Who will notice the difference, he asked? "'You are,' he answered. 'I am.'" Alvarez drew parallels between the two of them, being "angry young men with bad marriages" and a "yearning for *shiksas* and literature." But Alvarez lacked the genuine novelist's temperament that Roth possesses: to be "an invigilator, constantly on the watch, listening," and weaving it into story. Roth lived like a hermit because all he needed was in his head. By comparison, Cornwell needed to be on the move, checking locations and finding odd characters.[9] But like Cornwell, Roth was a great mimic who turned anecdotes into mini-dramas.

Alvarez was in certain ways an outsider, giving up the security of an academic life and literary journalist to be a freelancer. Like Kafka, Bruno Schulz, Guston, or Kitaj, he was at the margin, and Roth was attracted to those who went against the grain, rule breakers who preferred the unconventional, and found in their marginalized status a spur to creativity likely expressing what he himself had become since the publication of *Portnoy*. This implicit identification with those who were outsiders may have provided part of his courage and determination to publish his "Writers from the Other Europe" series, focusing on outcast and repressed writers who had no visible voice, echoing his early grade school support for Hazel Scott. This youthful moral outrage was translated into texts that proclaimed the importance of outside, transgressive voices that refused to be silenced. He continued to stand up for the unrepresented, in later life helping the Romanian Norman Manea and the Congolese writer Emmanuel Dongala find their way to America and an American life.[10]

Another literary figure, recognized for his outspokenness and who become a friend of Roth's during this period, was Harold Pinter. The go-between was Bloom, who was working on Pinter's adaptation of Henry James's *The Turn of the Screw*, retitled *The Innocents* and directed by Pinter. Roth came to London during rehearsals in 1976, also attending tryouts in Boston and Philadelphia and offering notes to Claire. The Broadway opening was a disappointment, however, and the play closed in ten days (LDH, 149–51). Nonetheless, it created a friendship that became so playful that Antonia Fraser, Pinter's wife, used to guess who would be first—Roth or Pinter?—to use the word "Jew" in conversation. Roth, when told of this, asked David Plante, "How long do *you* give me?" When we meet, it's usually your first word, Plante replied. Roth laughed.[11]

Pinter, a Jew from Hackney in the East End of London, had on the surface certain similarities with Roth, beginning with lower-middle-class origins, a Jewish background, and literary ambitions. Pinter began as an actor on stage, Roth as an actor in his works. Pinter worked in a separate house in the garden of his Holland Park home where he lived with Fraser, as Roth worked in his cottage some yards from his house in Connecticut (CWR 206). Pinter, like Roth, was an outspoken defender of liberty, focusing on Latin America, Eastern Europe, and Turkey; he also regularly assaulted the Bush-Blair foreign interventions, as Roth "attacked" Nixon and Vietnam. They differed, however, in Pinter's "savage melancholy," outlined in Fraser's *Must You Go? My Life with Harold Pinter* (2010).

Roth began to see a great deal of Pinter during the South Kensington rehearsals of *The Innocents*, often walking Bloom to and from the theater space. When he rented a studio in Notting Hill in 1977, it was not far from the home of Pinter and Fraser, and he often met one or both of them for lunch. He admired the "social edge" of Pinter's work, and their friendship became important for Roth in his early London years.[12] Pinter, in fact, recorded some thirty-eight meetings with Roth and often Bloom from the fall of 1976 until February 1987 in his appointment diaries. In her memoir of life with Pinter, Fraser observed that Roth was always funny but that he was never "very far from the works of Roth," referring to his repeated allusions and references to how he incorporated his life into his writing.[13]

Occasionally, Roth would comment on Pinter's work. After seeing a production of *One for the Road* (1984), about a woman raped by an authoritarian male who then kills her child and likely her husband, Roth told him he should write a sequel. What happened when Gila later meets up with the man who destroyed her life, Roth asked? Pinter later told Roth that after reading *Death and the Maiden* (1991), he didn't have to produce a sequel; Ariel Dorfman did it for him.[14] That same year, 1984, Roth and Pinter attended the Dramatist Club dinner, the year Pinter and Fraser visited Roth and Bloom at Roth's Connecticut home. After Roth and Bloom separated, Pinter occasionally saw Bloom.

Other London friends and acquaintances included Marianne Steiner, Kafka's niece, who had inherited several Kafka manuscripts, notably of *The Castle, The Metamorphosis,* and *Amerika.*[15] Ian McEwan, Simon Gray, Ian Hamilton, Stephen Spender, and Emma Tennant were friends and acquaintances, as well as important conduits into London literary life, which Roth was happy to explore. Between these contacts and those of Bloom, Roth found himself in the maelstrom of London cultural life.

One of his most lasting and intriguing friends was R. B. Kitaj (1932–2007), the American painter who made London his home beginning in 1958. Kitaj, at seventeen, became a merchant seaman on a Norwegian freighter, visiting Havana, Mexico, and South America. A stint in the U.S. Army followed. He attended art school at Cooper Union in New York and then the Akademie in Vienna in 1951 before the Ruskin School at Oxford in 1958. By the autumn of 1959, he was at the Royal College of Art in London. In the early 1960s, he began to attach texts to his images, commenting in a 1964 essay, "Some books have pictures and some pictures have books."[16] Images were for him visual writing.

Kitaj became part of the so-called London School, a group of artists that included Lucien Freud, Francis Bacon, Frank Auerbach, and David Hockney (met at the Royal College of Art in 1959). In 1963, he had his first one-man exhibition at the Marlborough Fine Art gallery; it was an immediate success, with one painting purchased by the Tate. He was thirty. His style presented expressive, figurative works incorporating identifiable cultural and often Jewish figures like Freud or Walter Benjamin. Jewish themes increasingly dominated his painting, notably, *London WC2 (The Refugees), The Autumn of Central Paris (after Walter Benjamin), The Jew Etc.* He titled his 1988 charcoal drawing of Roth *A Jew in Love (Philip Roth)*: it shows a mature Roth holding his head in his left hand.[17]

Kitaj taught at Berkeley and UCLA in 1967–71, retuning to London in 1972. His work continued to receive notice, and in 1985 he was elected to the Royal Academy, the first American since John Singer Sargent to be so honored. But critics derided his major Tate retrospective in 1994, claiming his intellectualism was a sham, and made personal attacks, despite the popularity of the show, which moved to the Met in New York and then to the Los Angeles County Museum. Approximately two weeks after the show closed, his second wife, the beloved American painter Sandra Fisher, suddenly died on 19 September 1994 of a brain hemorrhage.

In shock, Kitaj was convinced that the critics caused her death. What should have been his triumph from a lifetime as an artist in England turned tragic; anger and disillusionment followed. "London died for me when Sandra died," he wrote in a letter.[18] The situation confirmed earlier feelings of alienation matched by Roth.[19] But despite the 1994 debacle, he still had admirers, including Joyce Carol Oates, Brian Eno, and Paul McCartney.[20] Much earlier, in 1962, when teaching in Ealing, a student recalled that Kitaj entered the classroom upset and declaring to the entire class, "This is what being an artist is about. Pain."[21] Kitaj returned to America in 1997 and lived in Los Angeles, where he thematized individual rooms in his home: the two most prominent were the Cezanne and Jewish rooms.[22]

The subjects of Kitaj's work resonated with Roth: exile, isolation, and the Holocaust, summarized in the concept of the diaspora, the very subject of Kitaj's *First Diasporist Manifesto* (1989), which Roth incorporates but alters in *Operation Shylock*. The work is enigmatic, with statements like "I've always been a Diasporist Jew, but as a young man I was not sure what a Jew was."[23] The frontispiece to the "Prologue" of the manifesto is a 1985 close-up from a drawing of Roth with the quote, "The poor bastard had Jew on the brain" taken from *The Counterlife*. The art critic John Russell referred to the manifesto as a work of "self-excavation," broadening the term "diaspora" to include anyone who has survived dispersal, actual or imaginary.

For Kitaj, and even Roth, diasporism was a question of moving from place to place, nowhere quite feeling like home. Roth in London would understand this clearly, as well as Kitaj's pointed writing style: he held back little when stating his ideas. Art for Kitaj was something taken in a "refugee's suitcase, a portable Ark of the Covenant."[24] The artist was what Abraham once called himself: "a stranger and a sojourner" (Genesis 23:4). For Kitaj and Roth, who himself has been a wanderer, diasporism was dispersal, or as Russell explained, "The Diasporist painter [or writer] is rooted not in any given place, but in the shared experience of the Diaspora." Such shared feelings are to such artists similar to but opposite from what rootedness meant to a Faulkner or a Grant Wood.[25] But Kitaj stressed that "you don't have to be a Jew to be a Diasporist." But such a diasporist life is "often inconsistent and intense; schismatic contradiction animates each day," according to Kitaj. Many complained that the meanings of his paintings "refuse to be fixed, to be settled, to be stable: *that's* Diasporism, which welcomes interesting, creative misreading. The Zohar says that the meaning of the book changes from year to year!"[26] The text of the *First Diasporist Manifesto* is itself fragmentary, embodying the idea of dispersal.[27]

Kitaj's art was vivid, colorful, tactile, and detailed, his figures, like Roth's, always caught in action. Marco Livingstone, in a late edition of his comprehensive study of Kitaj, points to a more specific connection, claiming that *Sabbath's Theater* "grew directly out of Kitaj's experiences, specifically the loss of Sandra and even incorporated almost verbatim transcripts of the conversations Roth and Kitaj held over the telephone." Citing a letter to him by Kitaj of 6 April 1999, Livingstone writes that Roth used some of what he said about his time at sea for Mickey Sabbath and some of what he said about Sandra's death. Livingstone also claims that Mickey Sabbath is a "thinly disguised transformation of the artist."[28] Roth published *Sabbath's Theater* in 1995 (Figure 8.1), the year after Kitaj's Tate show and Sandra's death. An advanced reader's copy has this inscription to Kitaj from Roth on the title page: "For my hero— / Philip / May 1995." Kitaj's holograph signature appears on the top right corner.[29]

Parallels persist in *The Human Stain,* where the sudden death of Coleman Silk's wife comes very close to Kitaj's situation. Silk blames her death on his college and the adverse publicity he received for his supposed racism. Roth writes that Silk's "enemies . . . in striking out at him, had instead felled her . . . they had not merely misrepresented a professional career . . . they had also killed his wife" (HS 11). The link to Kitaj and the death of Sandra are obvious.

Kitaj and Roth shared a love of exactness and structure, evident in Livingstone's description of Kitaj's practice for interviews: "Written correspondence suited [Kitaj] much better. As with his carefully planned paintings, the ability to consider his replies in his own time allowed him to be more precise in expressing his meaning. When, in the early 1980s, he first offered to revise the written transcript of our first encounter, he said to me, 'Even if you wrote down exactly the words that I said, they might not have been exactly what I meant.' "[30] This could describe Roth, who similarly preferred written questions and knowing exactly what he would say and, more important, how it would be reported. Roth also edited his interviews before approving their publication.

Figure 8.1 Cover, *Sabbath's Theater*, 1995. Credit: Houghton Mifflin Publishers.

Kitaj's multilayered paintings absorbed intellectual history and ideas, often from texts. *The Autumn of Central Paris (after Walter Benjamin), 1972–3* is one example. The autumn is 1940, shortly before Benjamin left Paris in advance of its Nazi occupation and the beginning of his unsuccessful escape from France. *The Jew Etc.* and *Jewish Rider* are other examples of Kitaj's new Jewish awareness, supposedly sparked in the 1970s after he read Hannah Arendt's *Eichmann in Jerusalem*.[31] Kitaj often tried to explain the works attached to his paintings to his audience, something critics disliked partly because it seemed to show up their shortcomings. Hence, they turned on him in 1994. But if currently overlooked, "Kitaj offers a running commentary on the 20th century in all its fragmentation and randomness, its displacement and essential strangeness," as one critic recently noted.[32] And John Ashbery's comment on Kitaj applies equally well to Roth: "A certain kind of American sensibility had to extricate itself from America in order to realize itself."[33]

Living in England with Bloom for half a year from roughly 1976 to 1988 prepared Roth to write his American Trilogy: his absence from America primed him to report on its social and political decline. What Ashbery wrote of Kitaj could easily be applied to Roth: "a spirit of genuine contradiction, fertile in its implications, thrives in the work," creating the contrast between a "stable world of change . . . where threats of disorder are contained to be exhibited."[34] This, of course, is what Mickey Sabbath, but also Alex Portnoy, Nathan Zuckerman, and Ira Ringold disrupt. In Roth, little is contained.

Roth's friendship with Kitaj and grasp of his writing may have conversely influenced and inspired much of Kitaj's thinking, particularly on the question of Jewish identity. As Kitaj wrote in his *First Diasporist Manifesto*, published in 1989,

> One outcome of my study of this strange people of mine is that painting, Diasporist painting in my own life, begins to assume some of the Jewish attributes or characteristics assigned to that troubled people. The listing of traits would be endless and funny. For the moment I will leave all that to my buddy Philip Roth (b. 1933) and his great book *The Counterlife*, which is quite encyclopedic on these questions. I think that what the Jews promise, paintings may be made to promise.[35]

The *First Diasporist Manifesto* reflects Roth, just as Roth may have been in-spired by Kitaj in creating not only Sabbath but Moishe Pipik, who advocates a doctrine of reverse diasporism—send the Ashkenazi Jews in Israel back to their homelands!—in *Operation Shylock*.

Kitaj included his 1985 drawing of Roth sitting, his leg crossed, in the 1994 retrospective exhibition at the Tate Gallery, and it was singled out for praise by several critics. The artist retained the later portrait of Roth until his death; *A Jew in Love (Philip Roth)* remains in the collection of the Kitaj estate.[36]

One of the last books Roth supposedly read was Kitaj's *Confessions of an Old Jewish Painter*, with a preface by David Hockney.[37] In the work, Kitaj ex-tensively comments (again) on the 1994 Tate show and the pain it inflicted, suggesting that this is what happens when "a neurasthenic American

Jew-Exegete . . . overstays his welcome in London by about 30 years."[38] Like Roth, Kitaj could not let insults or criticisms of his work be forgotten.

One other vital figure from Roth's London period was the American writer Michael Herr, best known for *Dispatches* (1977), his vivid memoir of nearly a year in Vietnam as *Esquire*'s war correspondent. Herr traveled with patrols, carried a rifle, witnessed death firsthand, and filed only one report during his entire time in Asia. *Dispatches* appeared some ten years after his experience in Vietnam, where, unlike other journalists, he avoided daily press conferences offered by the U.S. forces, preferring to embed himself with the soldiers to document their exhaustion, fear, and drug use. The war was too overwhelming to file neat, monthly dispatches, he later explained.

Herr became a friend and resource for Roth, not the least of which because Herr was Jewish and had married an Englishwoman and made London his home (much the way Zuckerman would do in the final section of *The Counterlife*). In a prescient sentence for Roth and his evolving relationship with America from the perspective of England, Herr wrote, "A lot of things had to be unlearned before you could learn anything at all."[39] Subtracting rather than adding to one's mental habits might be the means, freeing oneself from the myths and protocols of America to freshly reengage with them. Roth did his "unlearning" in England and in his trips to Eastern Europe; from encountering repression and persecution he rediscovered the values of America that had been subverted. *Dispatches* famously begins with Herr commenting on a tattered map of Vietnam hanging on his apartment wall in Saigon, offering an illusion of order, the map substituting for the territory. Roth, too, returns with a map marginally greater than Newark, one he learned to redraw, made possible by his absence and return to America.[40]

Dispatches was a particular favorite of Roth's, who occasionally taught the book, a blend of autobiography, journalism, and fiction written in a visceral style. It was also labeled "a non-fiction novel," a *mélange* of genres that appealed to Roth, who developed it in *The Facts*. Creative nonfiction appealed to both men, although for Roth the factual always crisscrossed with the fictional, whether in his ostensible autobiographical efforts or in thinly disguised fiction like *My Life as a Man*. But both *Dispatches* and *The Facts* were liberated from facts, the former with its observer-participant a possible model for what Roth would do.

The writing of *Dispatches* took a toll, however: after eighteen months consumed by the book while living in Greenwich Village, Herr suffered a breakdown and split from his wife for a year. Like Roth after *Portnoy*, Herr sought to escape the spotlight once *Dispatches* appeared in 1977 and then the publicity surrounding the 1979 release of *Apocalypse Now,* for which he wrote the voice-over. Herr moved to England in 1979, where he met Roth, possibly facilitated by Sonny Mehta, who was then running Picador Books, publisher of the U.K. edition of *Dispatches.* Herr returned to the U.S. in 1991, paralleling his lengthy British stay with that of Kitaj and even Roth, who would return in 1988. Herr married Valerie Elliott in 1977 (as Roth would marry his Englishwoman, Claire Bloom, although many years later).[41]

Herr, like Roth, felt that Americans were not introspective people: "We're ignorant of our history. We're great perverters of our tradition." We are not "great at telling the truth about certain kinds of national behavior. . . . We haven't felt the same about ourselves since Vietnam. We're haunted by it, but we won't name the shape of the ghost; we won't say what it is."[42] Ghosts and America. Roth would confront these hauntings in his American Trilogy, especially in *American Pastoral.* Roth may have gone to England for personal reasons, to be with Bloom, but there was also an undercurrent of disillusionment with American political and social attitudes. The chance to not only see America from afar but to experience the opposite of its tolerance in his trips to Eastern Europe almost forced him to reengage with the country. His eight or nine years away, although he regularly returned for limited periods, provided a foil for his own encounter with not simply his past but America's.[43]

Another person important in Roth's life at this time was the Irish writer Edna O'Brien; she and Roth were friends for over forty years. They met in 1969 but did not become close until the late 1970s. O'Brien's first Roth text was *Goodbye, Columbus* (1959); Roth's first reading of O'Brien was her experimental novel, *Night* (1972).[44] The two began to see and admire each other's work during Roth's frequent stays in London after 1976, and Roth interviewed her for the *New York Times* in 1984, the year he provided a preface for her short story collection, *A Fanatic Heart,* where one senses his affection toward her. As O'Brien later admitted, it was his displeasure at the negative criticism she had been receiving that led to his convincing an editor at the *New York Times Book Review* that an interview with her would be timely.[45]

In his interview, Roth opens with the standard description: where O'Brien lives, how her study is furnished, and her view of a large green lawn in her new London neighborhood of Maida Vale. He mentions the books that surround her, from a volume of Flaubert's correspondence to a collection of J. M. Synge's plays. He cannot resist commenting on her white skin, green eyes, and auburn hair. He begins the interview with a strongly negative quote from Beckett and asks why she used it as the epigraph of *Mother Ireland*.[46] The remainder of the interview focuses on how writers are "dogged by the past—pain, sensations, rejections, all of it," but that clinging to the past is "a zealous, albeit hopeless, desire to reinvent it so that one could change it" (SHP 103). The comment applies equally to Roth and his constant re-creation of his Newark.

Parallels between the careers of O'Brien and Roth begin with condemnation. Just as Roth was condemned by Jews for his depiction of materialistic, middle-class, anti-Jewish Jews, O'Brien was criticized soundly for her breaking sexual codes and allowing women independence. What made her work especially threatening was that it was from a woman's point of view. The priest in her County Clare village burned her novels in the churchyard.[47] Her debut novel, *The Country Girls* (1960), was banned in 1961 and her books remained proscribed until a change in Irish censorship legislation in 1972. Ruling over the Irish Censorship Board of the early 1960s was the anti-Semitic Archbishop of Dublin, John McQuaid. The Board also resented the portrait of Catholic and Jewish intermarriage in *Letting Go* (1962).[48] A number of Roth's early novels were also banned, notably *Portnoy's Complaint*.[49] And some argued that even *Goodbye, Columbus* should be forbidden for its treatment of sex, contraception, and blasphemy. Just as O'Brien wrote against the myth of Irish racial and moral purity, so, too, did Roth write against the ideal of assimilated, nonthreatening, morally stable Jews, beginning with "Epstein" and "Eli, the Fanatic" and reaching a fever pitch with *Portnoy*.

In his "Foreword" to *A Fanatic Heart* (1985), Roth counters views of O'Brien as a writer only interested in sex or who wrote only love stories. Quite the opposite, he argues: she has "an acute, sometimes searing, social awareness."[50] The stories shuttle between "the innocence of Childhood" and the "scars of maturity," giving her work a remarkably "wounded vigor." And he cites the English writer Frank Tuohy, who said that while Joyce was the first "Irish Catholic to make his experience and surroundings recognizable, 'the world of Nora Barnacle' had to wait for the fiction of Edna O'Brien."[51]

Roth soon provided blurbs for *The Country Girls Trilogy and Epilogue*, *The Little Red Chairs*, and a reprint of O'Brien's memoir, *Country Girl*. The last reads, "Only Colette is her equal as a student of the ardors of an independent woman who is also on her own as a writer." The blurb appears on the cover, just below the title.[52] Ghosts, so crucial to Roth, is the title of the first chapter of the memoir. Roth, in turn, used as the epigraph to his 2001 novel *The Dying Animal* a sentence from O'Brien that appears in his 1984 interview with her: "The body contains the life story just as much as the brain" (SHP 105). She dedicated her anthology *The Love Object* (2013) to Roth and introduced him at his eightieth birthday party on 19 March 2013 at the Newark Museum as "feared and revered, plagiarized, envied . . . [a] lover and hater . . . [and] undoubtedly, one of Yeats's Olympians."[53] She publicly (but not privately) confirmed that they were not lovers. They did see each other frequently, however, in both London and New York.

In her memoir *Country Girl*, O'Brien speaks of a wonderfully funny and entertaining Roth, who, when in a jocular mood, can spin a story "to such a dizzying height that it is like witnessing a mind in excess of itself."[54] She reports his admiration for the boxer Jake La Motta, who reenacted his epic fights for Roth at a December 2009 birthday party for O'Brien in New York. It was, Roth told her, "like a page out of fiction, to meet his boyhood hero."[55]

O'Brien's Irish charm and attractiveness parallels that of the movie star Caesara O'Shea in *Zuckerman Unbound*. The character and O'Brien have much else, too, in common, from their births in rural Ireland into difficult families to the experience of being marginalized by their communities because of their professions. Caesara reports an encounter with Fidel Castro; O'Brien actually attended one of Castro's marathon lectures/speeches/ diatribes. Caesara offers a counterlife for Zuckerman, as O'Brien might have done for Roth on the similarities between the challenges of Irish and Jewish cultural identity. Bloom, of course, also figures in the Caesara figure, since the Irish star in the novel is reading *The Crisis in the Life of an Actress* by Kierkegaard, a book Bloom introduced to Roth.[56]

In another O'Brien-Roth intersection, she was a friend of Jackie Kennedy's for ten years, detailed in her memoir *Country Girl*.[57] Roth befriended Kennedy in 1964 when he briefly dated her after they met at a party. But Roth felt intimidated and "lacked the proper wardrobe" to keep up the relationship. He was her escort at a second dinner party and returned with her to her apartment. Invited upstairs, he felt conflicted. "Am I supposed to kiss her? What about the Cuban missile crisis?" They did kiss, but it was unemotional.[58]

During the 1970s while dividing his time between London and Connecticut, Roth continued to write prose, partly in response to the politics of *Our Gang* (1973), his Nixon satire, and partly because he felt the need to comment, if not defend, his work. "How Did You Come to Write That Book

Anyway?,'" appearing in 1974, addressed the issue of *Portnoy's Complaint,* as he detailed its inception and how finding a voice opened the door to self-expression. Using the "psychoanalytic monologue" permitted the linking of the fantastic element of his early effort "The Jewboy" with the "realistic documentation of *Portrait of the Artist* and *The Nice Jewish Boy.*" It also legitimized "the obscene preoccupations" with sex (RMY 36).

He also wrote about his past, discussing the Newark Public Library, baseball, writing American fiction, and his recent publications *The Great American Novel* and *My Life as a Man,* and three new writers for American audiences: Alan Lelchuk, Fredrica Wagman, and Milan Kundera. "After Eight Books" (1974) is a example of Roth "taking stock," in which he explained, "Sheer Playfulness and Deadly Seriousness are my closest friends; it is with them I take those walks in the country" (RMY 96). He published this collection of prose in 1975 as *Reading Myself and Others* (reprinted and expanded in 1985) as a way of reminding the public of his ideas and attitudes regarding contemporary issues.[59]

At this time, Roth also published *The Professor of Desire* (1977) with Farrar, Straus and Giroux, the second book in the Kepesh trilogy. Kepesh, the cerebral but sexually alert academic, first appeared in *The Breast* (1972) and will make his final appearance in *The Dying Animal* (2001). Semifixated on Chekhov and Kafka, Kepesh, professor of comparative literature, will confront the lingering presence and impact of Kafka when he and his twenty-five-year-old companion Claire (likely based on Barbara Sproul) visit Prague. He recently completed a Kafka seminar and republishes one of his final exam questions in preparation for his visit. In the company of a Czech professor, the protagonist sits in the square facing Kafka's house and then explores Kafka's neighborhood. Later, Kepesh, who actually owns three pages of a Kafka manuscript (Roth would own one page), will visit Kafka's supposed whore.

Kepesh soon learns that the spiritually and morally starved Czechs survive because of Kafka, his Czech professor-guide demoted from his university post to that of a typist in a meat-packing plant. Only Kafka makes it possible for such people to keep up their morale. For survival, the disgraced professor, "retired" at age thirty-nine, translates *Moby Dick* into Czech, even though a perfectly fine translation already exists (PD 170).[60]

The Professor of Desire solidifies Roth's Mitteleuropean credentials, drawing from his own recent experiences in Czechoslovakia. For Kepesh, this European trip with Claire balances his earlier trip in the novel, where he meets Elizabeth and Birgitta, two young Swedish women with whom he has sex. Birgitta proves to be the more adventurous, and she and Kepesh make a sexual pilgrimage across Europe looking for a series of sexual partners. Elizabeth returns home, partly because of unhappiness over her failed love of Kepesh. The sexual elements of the story, fantasy as much as fact, extend Roth's imaginative eroticism but may also express the underlying desire of an older man for younger women, even though he was still attached to Bloom, the dedicatee of the novel. Roth was forty-four when the novel appeared, Bloom forty-six.

One other dimension of the novel is its critique of Jewish writing, expressed in Kepesh's friendship with the poet Ralph Baumgarten, an expert at disarming women with his candor. Kepesh encourages the poet to write about his fragmented family, but he refuses. Baumgarten castigates those Jewish works on the family, "with their rituals of rebellion and atonements" (PD 139). He is impatient with suffering "Jewish culture bearers": they "*need* a fallen Jewish ass to atone for their sins in public—so why not mine?" he asks (PD 139). To him, virtue is anathema, anticipating the behavior and attitude of Mickey Sabbath in *Sabbath's Theater*. One comic moment for Baumgarten is when he ties up a willing woman with dental floss on her bed, retreats to his place for sex-enhancing drugs, and then forgets the woman's address. Anticipating Zuckerman's role in *The Anatomy Lesson* as a pornographic publisher, Kepesh and Baumgarten pick up a young woman in a bookstore and tell her, back at the poet's apartment, that they are starting a new erotic picture magazine and would like her involvement.

Throughout the story, Kepesh thinks of his psychiatrist Dr. Klinger who hovers throughout as a voice to stabilize the fluctuating libido of Kepesh, who longs for the sexual Birgitta with an intensity denied to his feelings for Claire (PD 162). Klinger is a parody therapist, smoking cigars and taking calls during his consultations, although his practical point of view helps Kepesh after his divorce from the attractive but unstable Helen, who was the mistress of a Hong Kong tycoon before marrying Kepesh. Claire's conventionality and sense of order depresses Kepesh: her lists, snapshots, and proper behavior unnerve him. What he fears is being "sealed up into something wonderful" (PD 164). This rebellion against happiness, often linked to a conventional existence, is a thread throughout Roth's life and writing, explaining his preference for the enigmatic and divorced Maggie (rather than any Brenda Patimkin type from South Orange) or challenging Maureen in *My Life as a Man* (in contrast to the stable Sharon Shatzky in the novel). To be drawn to the unorthodox is to be energized rather than demoralized.

The final section of *The Professor of Desire* attempts to duplicate the idyllic life of Roth and Bloom, as the novel describes an ideal summer existence for Kepesh and Claire: he writes, she gardens, they discuss *Young Törless* by Robert Musil. Disrupting the calm is a visit from Helen and her new husband. And she is pregnant. After she leaves, tension between Claire and Kepesh is high until his father arrives, as Herman Roth would regularly visit Roth and Bloom at Roth's Connecticut farmhouse. Kepesh suddenly worries that the blandness of his life with Claire may cloy at and destroy him. But there is also a new element: the Holocaust. Late in the novel, Kepesh's father becomes friendly with a Mr. Barbatnik, a survivor, who has seemingly transcended his suffering. Visiting Kepesh and Claire in the country, the father and Mr. Barbatnik mix nostalgia (the father) with a narrative of escape and survival (Mr. Barbatnik) whose goal was to be "a human being" (PD 257). Two years before *The Ghost Writer*, the Holocaust intrudes.

Outwardly, Claire and Kepesh seem content, the book ending with a pseudo-idyllic moment between the two (offset by his fear that death could quickly take the two elderly visitors) only to be further undermined by Kepesh's admission that he knows his desire for her is already beginning to fade. Contradiction rules: he robs himself of the life he desires, no longer a sympathetic sufferer as in Chekhov but a frantic, emotionally amputated figure from Gogol in search of his nose (PD 261). His passion is dying; no happy ending is permitted (PD 261).

At the time, cracks were beginning to appear in the Bloom-Roth marriage, which took place in New York on 29 April 1990, generated largely by her continued dependency on her daughter and increasing anxiety over growing old without money. Roth tried to mitigate her anxiety with a gift of $100,000 in 1978. Then, in 1980, he established a trust for her whereby for twelve years she could collect interest from the trust, which amounted to almost $28,850 yearly. He also offered to pay $1,000 a month for the upkeep of her London house during the months that he lived there. There was no reciprocal arrangement when she lived with him in a New York apartment he purchased at 6 West 77th Street in 1988. But her persistent loneliness for her daughter increased, and she would often begin crying hysterically the first thing in the morning when they were in New York and often in Connecticut. Reconsidering his unraveling relationship, Roth believed that it wasn't her relationship with him, or his with Anna, that was the problem but Bloom's "servile, anxiety-laden hysterical relation with Anna and Anna's antagonistic relationship" with her. Oddly, counterbalancing Bloom's fear of

Anna was Anna's contempt for Bloom (NOT 230). Compounding the issue was Bloom's manner of overly dramatizing Roth's emotions toward her and everyone else. He described her behavior becoming nothing like that of the adult he had first fallen in love with in America. At the end, he lost emotional respect for her, although he may have had some sense of what involvement with an actress of her range and experience might mean in terms of stability. After the romance stage of their relationship, as he witnessed more of her insecurities and behavior, especially with her daughter, his concerns no doubt increased.

In an assessment of his two marriages, Roth explains that he was no match for Maggie's deviousness or Bloom's hysteria: he could not compete with "someone who was an expert at screaming anywhere and crying everywhere and falling to her knees in public," admitting that he was sucked "into that pathetic neediness, weak-willed uncertainty and outright panic." He was incapable of extricating himself, until he himself was in a dire condition, leading to his own collapse and becoming a patient in a psychiatric hospital (MM 4–5). Angrily, he writes in 2014, "I married them because of circumstances growing out of the emotional volatility of the second wife and out of the criminality of the first" (MM 6). The actions of the frantic Eve Frame in *I Married a Communist* portray Bloom just as Maureen in *My Life as a Man* exposes Maggie. Roth may be reacting angrily to both women, taking it out on his two self-dramatizing and deceptive characters. The actual situation in both instances was more complex, more interdependent that Roth would admit.

The uneven *Professor of Desire*, shifting between the comic and the serious, from being a "visiting fellow in erotic daredevilry" to anxiety over a disappearing love, while encompassing psychological features of Roth's life, expanded to include Roth's enlarged European and even Asian experiences. But it also questioned the satisfactions of literature: Is being an expert on Kafka and Chekhov enough? Drawing in part from his March 1970 trip to Asia with Sproul, with a stop in Hong Kong, he writes (uncomfortably) about Helen and her life in Hong Kong, the gay investment banker Donald G., and the tycoon Jimmy Metcalf.[61]

The stereotypical view of Hong Kong shows that Roth has difficulty writing about a world he does not know. This is not the problem when he writes about the Jewish family, especially his Aunt Sylvia in *The Professor of Desire*, labeling her "the Benvenuto Cellini of strudel" (PD 103). Roth emphasized that the work was a prequel to *The Breast*, which developed after an unpublished 1974 piece that was, in fact, to be a sequel that did not work.

Written in the present tense, *The Professor of Desire* actualizes some of the issues in *The Breast*. The comic verve of *Portnoy*, however, is missing, literature partly to blame: the incessant references to figures as diverse as Colette, Kafka, Chekhov, Melville, James, and Musil, not to say Mann, Flaubert, and Hemingway, interfere with the story. But boredom with innocence undoes the happiness of Kepesh, and possibly Roth, since convention and stability are alternately desired and rejected. The first printing of *The Professor of Desire* for the Literary Guild brought Roth $362,000. The first offer for the paperback was $250,000, but his publisher Robert Straus wanted to wait for more.[62] But the book did not do well in a year with new titles by John le Carré, Irwin Shaw, Leon Uris, John Fowles, Anaïs Nin, and Toni Morrison. The *Kirkus Reviews* modestly praised the novel but complained that Roth was writing "from the waist down": "the same old story, sans laughs; but, in head and heart—a subdued and seductive journey."[63] It did not make the *New York Times* bestseller list until 20 November 1977, when it appeared as number fifteen, below Robin Cook's *Coma*, where it stayed for two weeks and then disappeared.[64]

In 1977, Roth began to concentrate on adaptations, one of the first a short story by Chekhov, "The Name-Day Party," and then *Journey into the Whirlwind*, the Gulag autobiography of Eugenia Ginzburg. He also worked on a modernized version of David Margarshack's translation of *The Cherry Orchard*. The choice of the Russians is revealing since in the 1970s the so-called refuseniks, Jewish citizens of the Soviet Union refused permission to emigrate to Israel or the West, suffered punishment and imprisonment. This awareness supplemented Roth's involvement with Eastern Europe, especially Czechoslovakia. Unconsciously, he may have felt affinities: his paternal grandparents came from Polish Galicia; his maternal grandparents, who met on the Lower East Side, came from the region near Kiev in Ukraine.[65]

It was Bloom who prompted his efforts at adaptation. She, with Roth's assistance, was continually looking for strong stage material and he frequently proposed texts that would include a part for her. The Ginzburg autobiography is an interesting example, sustaining his commitment to social justice and exposing the abuses of authoritarian regimes. Originally published in English in 1967, the memoir is a detailed account of Ginzburg's eighteen-year imprisonment during the Stalinist period of the 1930s. Before her expulsion from the Communist Party and arrest in 1937, she was head of the Department of the History of Leninism at Kazan State University. She denied all accusations of being a part of a counterrevolutionary Trotskyite organization but, after a seven-minute trial, was found guilty on 1 August 1937 and sentenced to ten years' imprisonment with deprivation of political rights for five. Nonetheless, she was thrilled that she was not sentenced to death.

After a period in the infamous gulag Magadan, Ginzburg was released in February 1949 but had to remain in Magadan for an additional five years. But in October 1949, she was rearrested and sent to the Kolyma gulag. She had begun to write her memoir in secret, and in June 1955, two years after the death of Stalin, she was released from exile and allowed to return to Moscow and work as a reporter. Her manuscript was smuggled out of the country since she could not get it published in Russia until 1990. Mondadori in Milan and Possev in Frankfurt were the first to publish the work in 1967. The gulag is its principal setting; Ginzburg died in Moscow in 1977.

For Roth, the text critically outlined the oppression of the writer-intellectual. He thought to dramatize a part of the memoir for TV, with Bloom playing the principal role. Ginzburg's story appealed because it dealt with a woman's false arrest, interrogation, and eighteen-year imprisonment in Soviet penal camps. "'She is to the Russian terror what Anne Frank was to the Holocaust, as a witness and writer,'" Roth stated.[66] This would have been Roth's second TV adaptation. Later, in January 1984, his version of *The Ghost Writer* would be broadcast.

Roth began and completed a partial draft of an adaptation and then called Ginzburg's son Vasily Aksyonov, a dissident Soviet novelist living in Washington. Roth's agent at the time, the Berlin-born Robert Lantz, whose clients included Leonard Bernstein, Lillian Hellman, James Baldwin, Elizabeth Taylor, Richard Burton, Yul Brynner, and Montgomery Clift, contacted Aksyonov, who approved of the project but explained that the publisher Mondadori had sole rights. What ensued was a complicated and frustrating effort to secure permission.

During negotiations, Roth lined up Michael Kustow of BBC's Channel 4 as producer, and he, in turn, brought in Christopher Morahan to direct. Another offer to adapt was rejected by Aksyonov, but Mondadori chose the competing offer, by a Hollywood screenwriter, Will Lorin, because he had been negotiating for rights longer. The tangled issue of *droit moral,* or author's rights, left the publisher superseding the son and heir's decision. Roth's nine-month quest failed but not his commitment to Ginzburg.

During this period, Roth also worked with David Plante on an adaptation of the Jean Rhys section of Plante's *Difficult Women,* but it, too, did not succeed. Additional works remained unproduced, such as his television script of "The Prague Orgy," abandoned before production began. The manuscript is a creative adaptation with new characters, rearranged events, and added background information on Zuckerman. Roth enjoyed the freedom of such work, allowing new ideas and even scenes but often displeasing producers who felt the changes strayed too far from the original. Ironically for "The Prague Orgy," he created several scenes he wished he could have put into the original book; he thought the reformulated text was in several ways more appealing than the original.[67] And in some ways more exposed. For instance, Zuckerman explains that it's not his job "to try to raise the prestige of Jews in the eyes of the non-Jewish world any more than it's my intention to disparage or denigrate Jews so as to confirm vicious anti-Semitic stereotypes. I'm not a polemicist, a publicist, a propagandist, an apologist. I'm a novelist."[68]

Another figure from this period, who may or may not have been the model for Maria in *The Counterlife*, is Janet Hobhouse, an American-born writer with a British father. She moved to Britain at sixteen and read English at Oxford, receiving a B.A. in 1969. The darkly attractive Hobhouse, with large eyes and curly black hair and a slightly turned-up nose, lived in London, New York, and Paris between 1970 and 1975 and married the journalist Nicholas Fraser, from whom she eventually separated. In London, she became a book editor and art critic, publishing in *Art in America* and *Art News*. After 1975, she lived in New York and published her first book, a well-received biography of Gertrude Stein (1975) that was nominated for a Pulitzer Prize. She went on to publish three novels, often concerned with the conflict between freedom and security embodied in marriage. In 1988 she wrote *The Bride Stripped Bare: The Artist and the Female Nude in the Twentieth Century*, dealing with thirteen male artists who painted or sculpted the female nude. She died in 1991 from ovarian cancer while working on an autobiographical novel, posthumously published in 1993 as *The Furies*. Both her grandmother and stepmother had died from cancer.

In *The Counterlife*, Zuckerman meets Maria in New York when she and her estranged husband move into the duplex above his apartment. Hobhouse, in fact, lived upstairs from Roth in 1974 at 18 East 81st, although the exact date is unclear; according to a chronology prepared by archivists, she lived in New York only from 1976 to 1980.[69] Apparently Hobhouse and Roth met during this time and soon began a relationship, although he was also involved with Bloom. They clearly stayed in touch; a 6 March 1986 entry in her appointment diary reads "dinner w Philip Roth," and six days later, in red pen, "Philip/8pm. Orso W. 46th Street." On 19 March 1986, her diary records, with a line through it, "Philip Roth's bdy" (birthday). For 1986 and 1987 she refers several times to Roth; the entry for 12 September 1987, for example, reads "Call P. Roth Essex House Hotel."

In *The Counterlife* (1986), four months after Maria divorces her husband, she and Zuckerman marry and move to England (CL 65). Roth, to protect an English lover (a former BBC journalist) at the time he was writing *The Counterlife*, shifts the model of Maria to Hobhouse, according to Pierpont.[70] Complicating the situation was his decade-old relationship with Bloom at the same time. Later, in *Deception* (1990), a kind of notebook for *The Counterlife*, a close female friend appears, suffering from cancer, with whom the protagonist had an affair in New York: Hobhouse, by implication. In *Deception* she candidly writes of her chemotherapy. In *Leaving a Doll's House*, Bloom corroborates Roth's use of Hobhouse, fifteen years his junior, as the prototype for Maria (LDH 168). She was another woman who described her reaction to Roth, as Bloom would, as combining "a sense of danger and . . . bravado."[71]

The Furies (1993), her posthumous novel, touches on their affair as recounted by Helen Lowell, the Jewish narrator, who also spends a great deal of time on her intricate relationship with her mother. But Roth, appearing in Chapter 8, is the centerpiece, more biographical than fictional. The habits of Roth—in the novel called Jack—are equally detailed and analyzed. He was, to begin, "unnervingly scrutinizing"; "what he noticed about people was unnervingly sharp, etc." In a later passage, Hobhouse writes, "It seemed pointless trying to defend yourself against it [his attraction], or to object when the play got rough." There is great secrecy about their affair, although Roth/Jack is a conversationalist: "He liked talk to be like Ping-Pong, but he also liked to take the stage himself and perform." But "all this sexual brainpower made for a kind of nerve-racking exhilaration." In speaking of his seemingly austere lifestyle, Hobhouse cannot resist writing the Kafkaesque "I admired his fasting. I admired his stony separateness and self-sufficiency."[72] "The Hunger Artist," noted much earlier, is the quintessential Rothian metaphor.

But how much of this is true? Compared to other descriptions of Roth and his life, a great deal of it, as Roth admitted in a letter to Janet Malcolm of 6 August 1994. Although fictionalized, Hobhouse, some twenty years after her affair with Roth, still remembered precisely its intensity and his appeal. Her notes for the book even include a sketch of Jack's apartment, incorporating the layout of the furniture from the living room to the bedroom. With the drawing is a note on a small white sheet of paper: "Work is prayer."[73] Her only criticism of Jack is that his transposition of her into Maria neglected what she believed to be her most unique quality: "the struggle to be free in the world." Instead, he made her into "some kind of English lady/saint. It was that entirely fabricated 'poise' of mine he celebrated, that and the damned English accent."[74] Yet it is the "brutality of the infatuation" that ruled both of them, softened by the laudatory, if not romantic, ten pages on Roth. Roth told Malcolm that missing from the account were his recent suicidal depressive episodes and his time at Silver Hill. That's why he "couldn't take on a married woman taking lithium" and so his affair with Hobhouse was brief.[75]

Throughout the text, the narrator senses his contradictions, his ability to dare in his work but in his life to be restrained, calling this an "old-maidish Prufrockery." She notes his "cultivation of dullness" to allow him to be free in his work, but also his "depression and melancholy" because the narrator herself had experienced it. The narrator lacks the courage to leave her husband and pulls back from the writer, who himself disengages and is then relieved: "love was trouble," he admits, and in his view "more trouble than it was worth."[76] Part of this view may be that Hobhouse, like so many of the women Roth found attractive, experienced an unhappy past and often suffered from depression.

Hobhouse's affair with Roth resonated throughout her life, even in her final six or seven years. Her papers include photographs of Roth attending a book launch, possibly for her biography of Gertrude Stein. And it is evident that she listened to him: on page 21 of her unpublished novel "The Ex-Husband," she refers to "Jewish Lightning," the habit of landlords burning down their own buildings for the insurance money. This would come from Roth.

Roth enjoyed his six-month romance with Hobhouse and later helped her during her illnesses, first when she and her husband were Connecticut neighbors. Bloom was furious. When Hobhouse developed cancer, Roth would take her to chemotherapy sessions and once had lunch with her while she awaited news from the doctor about her tumor. If it had shrunk, she would have more radiation; if not, nothing could be done. She called the doctor hourly only to learn it had not shrunk. They walked together silently in Central Park.

But if she did not forget Roth, neither did he forget her. They saw each other in the mid-1980s, as confirmed by her appointment books. He would write a blurb for the paperback reprint of *The Furies* published in 1993. But self-protective Roth limited their relationship, somewhat restrained by her dependence on lithium and an innate fear on his part of entanglement with another unbalanced woman.

After she died on 2 February 1991, Roth buried her in the Revolutionary Cemetery in West Cornwall, Connecticut, near his home, as she had wished. Roth also acquired the gravestone.[77]

In a 1987 interview, she elaborated on what she found important in Roth's writing, essentially his moral intensity and urgency, the idea that issues like manhood, Jewishness, and fatherhood mattered. She also offered a comment on transforming experience into fiction which applied to Roth: life is chaotic, but writing gives it form, reduced to certain "significant shapes and forces." The order, she explained, "comes out of it [the chaos] when you realize fictionally what it felt like to experience it.... Writing has things to tell me more than I have things to tell it."[78]

In *A Sistermony,* Richard Stern reports that Roth told him that he would often visit Hobhouse's grave and "tell her things I don't tell anyone. I ask her advice."[79] Importantly, he told Janet Malcolm that visiting her grave gave him the inspiration for *Sabbath's Theater,* which he dedicated to her (and to the Princeton sociologist Melvin Tumin). He explained to Malcolm that Hobhouse would have enjoyed the fact that his "mischief was aroused by her corpse."[80] Although Roth's involvement with Hobhouse was reasonably short, he remained attached to her throughout her illness and death. The reason may be illness itself, something that continued to link him to her even after her death. He understood its devastation; it was always in his backpack, analogous to Bunyan's Pilgrim, although Roth seems unable to leave the "City of Destruction" and arrive at any "Celestial City" with his burden released. His last novel, *Nemesis,* confirms its hold on him. But comedy keeps him out of the "Slough of Despond" and leads him to the "Hill of Difficulty," from which he is able to move forward after battle with his personal Apollyons.

In his blurb for the 1993 edition of *The Furies* (the book was reissued in paperback in 2004), he wrote that it was "a grim, tough powerful and beautiful book, the memoir of a genuine heroine." Citing the coldhearted father and helpless mother, and a wrecked marriage, a mother's suicide, and the author's own fatal illness, Roth states that the core of the book is the "tortuous bond of love between mother and daughter. Suffering TRANSFORMED into confession is its accomplishment with verve and honesty;" it "strikes me as a considerable moral as well as literary achievement."[81]

Following *The Professor of Desire* and his direct engagement with Eastern Europe (or perhaps because of it), Roth turned to the survival of an isolated but respected writer in the countryside who unexpectedly agrees to meet with the young Nathan Zuckerman, who is keen to learn from the venerable author. Also visiting would be the writer's young assistant, who may or may not be Anne Frank. The shadow of Hawthorne, who had lived in the area, plus Henry Roth the novelist, who, after his important *Call It Sleep* (1934), could not complete any of his later fiction until very late in his life and retired to the country, are additional presences. Appropriately, the title is *The Ghost Writer* (1979).

In *Leaving a Doll's House*, Bloom writes that she was frequently "instrumental in the conception and development of a character" of Roth's and that one evening Roth had asked her what it was like to live with a writer in the country (LDH 168). Her response was a mini-diatribe, anticipating the views of Hope Lonoff in *The Ghost Writer*: "We don't go anywhere! We don't do anything! We don't see anyone!," she yelled, which appears almost verbatim in Roth's book (LDH 168). Ironically, some years after the book's publication, Bloom would be cast as Hope in a TV production of the novel. She was not the origin of the character, however, since in the novel Hope is a New England WASP and the mother of several of the hero's children. But Bloom does claim she was the youthful model, at least physically, of Amy Bellette/Anne Frank, born a year and a half earlier than Bloom. Roth kept a photo of Frank and Bloom, each as children, on his studio desk in Connecticut (LDH 169).

In the Roth Papers at the Library of Congress, among the notes for his 1973 essay story "I Always Wanted You to Admire My Fasting, or Looking at Kafka," is a note page headed "Jewish Ghosts." Listed are six aspects of Kafka's life Roth dealt with in the story, and beneath a dividing line are two words: "Anne Frank." She, along with Kafka, would become two Jewish ghosts that would haunt him the most. Bruno Schulz would be a third. Roth would address Kafka in his 1973 story and Frank in *The Ghost Writer* of 1979; Schulz would emerge in "The Prague Orgy" of 1985.

The ghosts in *The Ghost Writer* are many, with Zuckerman perhaps a ghost of Roth, Amy Bellette the ghost of Anne Frank, Lonoff the ghost of both Hawthorne and Henry Roth. Some have even suggested Bernard Malamud as another figure. Zuckerman becomes a ghost of himself in *The Anatomy Lesson*, anticipating the ghostly, nameless Czech Jewish writer who left behind an unpublished and unlocatable manuscript of Yiddish stories in *The Prague Orgy*. *Everyman* might be said to be narrated by a ghost, the deceased protagonist.

In *The Ghost Writer*, there is also what might be called the disappearing narrative voice, evident in Zuckerman's inadequately imagining what actually happened during his eavesdropping on the conversation of Lonoff and Amy while he stood on a Webster's Dictionary and Henry James's *The Middle Years*.[82] "Oh, if only I could have imagined the scene I'd overheard! If only I could invent as presumptuously as real life," he laments (GW 78). But for Roth, thematically and technically, absence is greater than presence. The former allows for play and interplay; the latter is an obligation to exactness. Yet it is Zuckerman who ghostwrites Bellette's story, working through a doubly imagined history that is more "as if" or alternately reimagined than articulated into a realistic retrospection.

Roth explained this process in an interview with Hermione Lee, telling her that he decided not only that Amy was Zuckerman's creation but that "she might possibly be her own creation too, a young woman inventing herself *within* Zuckerman's invention. . . . To be ambiguous *and* clear—. . . that was my writing problem through one whole summer and fall" (CWPR 165). The result is a kind of disappearing presence, characters creating voices that renounce any authority because they repeatedly correct "their ever-unfinished fictions."[83] Creating a work immediately implies its erasure, although his own "Higher Education," the twenty-three-year-old Zuckerman's controversial short story that brings him public disapprobation, also brings him to Lonoff.

"The hatred for me I had inspired by telling the whole truth had me particularly confused. If only I had lied" is Nathan's response to the reaction of others, which ironically expresses the condition of the narrator and even Roth's (GW 28). Had he been less direct in his satire of the Jews in *Goodbye, Columbus* or *Portnoy's Complaint*, Roth's life would have been simpler but artistically dishonest. In the preface to a limited edition of the novel, Roth admits that *The Ghost Writer* is "about the unreckoned consequences of art" previously presented in *The Breast* and *My Life as a Man*. It's about the uses "to which books are put by their readers"—and the use put to books by their authors, addressing how Zuckerman appropriates the use of Lonoff's work to defend his own when so many see it as "conscienceless" and a repudiation of his Jewish identity.[84]

Set in 1956, *The Ghost Writer*'s engagement with Anne Frank proved both absorbing and controversial, partly because 1956 was only a decade after the end of World War II and Frank was still sacrosanct in the Jewish American imagination. At one point, Roth thought that Bellette might actually be Frank, but resisted. He had thought of bringing her story into his fiction ten or fifteen years earlier, he told an interviewer in 2014. But more important, he wanted to bring the function she seemed to perform for his generation into the story, especially for the young Zuckerman, who had to confront Judge Wapter, moral watchdog for the Jews of Newark, and his mother, who wonders if her own son is an anti-Semite.[85] What he allows Zuckerman to do is desanctify Amy/Anne through his ability to fully imagine her.

Roth worked with the young but astute assistant fiction editor and satirist Veronica Geng at the *New Yorker* to polish the text. Born in Atlanta but raised in Philadelphia, she went to the University of Pennsylvania. She had had a difficult childhood, her career army father constantly bullying and berating both Veronica and her brother, Steve, who became a drug addict.[86] She came to New York in the mid-1960s (after writing an honors thesis on Salinger's Seymour Glass), beginning her writing career under the pen name Phillis Penn, offering advice to single girls for *Cosmopolitan*. She was a parodist and essayist as well as a film critic and book reviewer whose parody of the esteemed film critic Pauline Kael caught the eye of Roger Angell of the *New Yorker*, who offered her a job. Like Roth, she was a natural mimic who wrote penetrating satires of contemporary cultural icons. But she was also known as a harsh critic, euphemistically described as "uncompromising."

Aaron Asher, Roth's editor at Farrar, Straus and Giroux, likely sent an advance copy of *The Ghost Writer* to Geng at the *New Yorker*. She read it and told the editor William Shawn that he must publish the whole thing. He listened. She and Roth edited the book long distance in 1979. Roth admired her sense of detail, from revising the first paragraph (too much information in a sentence that is too long, she told him) to why Lonoff is wearing a suit to greet Zuckerman and that commas needed to be added.[87] Your writing has "the natural rhythm of a human voice [so] commas shouldn't be put in where they create jerky, unnatural pauses," she told him. But they do have a role.[88] Roth, in London, responded with concern but delight when he learned that he was going to receive an extra $10,000 for the story, now a payment of $30,000 because accounting miscalculated the word length. Geng in New York even cleared up Bloom's problem with her foreign subscription to the magazine.[89]

By May, Roth was back at Cornwall Bridge and following proofreading instructions sent by Geng. Concerning Judge Wapter's letter and the questionnaire, she writes, "I've left it to you to decide how illiterate you want him to be."[90] The most fascinating correction and detail is from the legal department, afraid that some Zuckerman in Newark might want to sue. And they want assurances that the park Nathan and his father approach from

Elizabeth Avenue can also be approached from other streets. This will make it impossible for a Zuckerman family on Elizabeth Avenue to claim they are the Zuckermans here.[91] The story appeared in the 2 July 1979 issue to great acclaim.

One of the ironies associated with *The Ghost Writer* is that despite the Pulitzer Prize Committee selecting it in book form for their prize in 1980, the Pulitzer board, which had the final say, rejected it in favor of Mailer's *The Executioner's Song*. Nevertheless, the critical reception of *The Ghost Writer* was strongly positive. Mike Nichols thought of filming it. He and Roth had lunch in London in February 1981. He was enthusiastic about the book and planned to go to a studio seeking money. Roth, writing to Roger Straus, said that he thought Nichols was actually serious.[92]

Geng and Roth kept up their friendship through the following years until her death in 1997. She constantly displayed a wonderful sense of humor in her letters. On April Fool's Day 1980, for example, she told him, in response to his apparent comic request to work at the *New Yorker*, that the magazine already had "a messenger named Philip Roth (in fact, he sometimes passes himself off for you at parties), but when he retires there will probably be a slot for you."[93] She even became a Connecticut house sitter for Roth and Bloom, writing a personal letter of thanks and outlining what happened to the laundry and a so-called Zuckerman pudding made by Miss Ruby of Miss Ruby's Café in West Stockbridge.

She complimented Bloom on her book *Limelight and After*, especially the sections on childhood. She praised the writing for being "harmonious and strong, with a terrific sense of proportion." Contributing to that style was Roth, who assisted in the editing of the manuscript. Roth, in turn, wrote a blurb for Geng's first collection, *Partners* (1984). It reads, "Geng's subject is the barbaric trivialization of American rhetoric under the avalanche of popular, media and political rubbish."[94] In 1987, when Roth admits that he has missed her, she tells him, as he is recovering from his knee surgery, that until now she has rarely seen his "heartfelt side." In 1989, she published *Love Trouble Is My Business*. By 1992, however, she had resigned from the *New Yorker* because of disagreements with the new editor, Tina Brown. Life as a freelance writer and reviewer followed.

In a memorial statement on Geng, who died of brain cancer in December 1997, Roth praised her ability as a comic writer and as an "independently-minded fiction writer who possessed, along with all the aversions and hatreds necessary for American survival, the most finely attuned ear for American

English of anyone I've ever known."[95] She could not "just spot the haywire sentence in a paragraph where a writer's vigilance had faltered," he continued, "she could spot the syllable." He praised her "grasp of prose aesthetics—and an intuitive understanding of its moral significance." Roth said that he always gave her his novels to read and she acted as a kind of unofficial editor.[96] He dedicated *I Married a Communist* to her. Janet Hobhouse had also died of a brain tumor, the affliction of Amy Bellette in *Exit Ghost*, published ten years after the death of Geng.

The dedicatee of *The Ghost Writer* is Milan Kundera, whom Roth first met in 1972. They sustained a close and important friendship, Roth troubled by the freedom of America, and the suppression of art in Eastern Europe. Roth brought Kundera to the attention of Geng at *The New Yorker*, where he soon appeared. Pictures of the three in Connecticut taken during a 1978 visit reflect their camaraderie which trickled down into their work. Not only did Roth and Kundera write on each other's work, but one influenced the other in terms of their fictional worlds.[97] The first title in Roth's series "Writers from the Other Europe" was Kundera's *Laughable Loves*, introduced by Roth (1974).

Other matters of the late 1970s involved contracts, money, reprint rights, and paperback editions. By February 1978, Roth was again in London with Bloom, where he received a note from Asher on the 16th in response to Roth telling him he'd had a note from a dwarf: "How many other such suffering, isolated, silent, a little crazed but intelligent people there must be out there? I'm happy I don't have to answer his letter and would like to see a copy of yours." "Still another enclosure is perhaps most notable," Asher comically adds, "for being Roth's first appearance in the pages of Midstream not dressed in his SS uniform. I don't know how it got by Marie Syrkin's censorship office." Syrkin, wife of the Objectivist poet Charles Reznikoff, consistently harbored antipathy toward Roth and his critique of the Jews.

Asher says he will visit in April: "[This] quarrel with you about preferring to live there comes not from wanting to give you the pain of being here but us the pleasure of your company." He adds, "I know hardly anyone else whose conversation is so sane. For example, your 'I'm sorry, Mr. Mailer, then you'll just have to get cancer' plus the Hitler cold routine which I just tried to reproduce for Susan, who was immensely amused. Well, at least you're writing, and there's always the summer hard as it is right now to believe that such a season exists."[98]

At this time Asher began to act as Roth's agent, writing to Marc Jaffe of Bantam Books on 20 November 1979 with details on renegotiating Roth's contract to allow reprinting *The Breast* and other titles in the *Philip Roth Reader*. He also asked for a $1,000 advance against a flat 7.5 percent royalty for reprinting *The Great American Novel*.

What Ted Solotaroff was to Roth in his early career, Aaron Asher became in Roth's midcareer. The role of these editors, however, will be supplanted not by another editor Roth became attached to but, after 1989, a literary agent, Andrew Wylie, who partly wooed him by approaching at a cocktail party and whispering, "I'd give the last hair on my head to be your agent."[99] At the time, Wylie had little hair to offer. But money was more convincing, and ten years after *The Ghost Writer*, Roth would join Wylie's agency.

The 1970s ended and the 1980s began with work, completing *Zuckerman Unbound* for a 1981 publication and a visit from Kundera. The sudden, unexpected death of his mother in the spring of 1981 from a heart attack in a restaurant in Elizabeth shook Roth. He had spoken to her that very Sunday morning from London.

Surprisingly, Roth writes little directly about his mother—almost to protect her. She appears in a fictionalized portrait as the obsessive homemaker Aunt Gladys in "Goodbye, Columbus," fixated on domestic bliss, where canned and fresh fruit were jammed together in her refrigerator "like stolen diamonds" (GBC 6). In *The Facts*, her behavior is on display, not in the home with the threatening incident of the bread knife recounted in *Portnoy*, but poised, in her best outfit, when the family travels to Bucknell for Roth's interview. There, his well-dressed mother is attentive and supportive of her son's academic wishes. Her dignified and respectful demeanor remained throughout her life, Roth at one point proud of the way she stood up to Maggie when she expected Bess to do her laundry. Both Ann Mudge and Claire Bloom maintained their respect for her, shared among her friends, as well as those who admired her orderliness and attention to detail. Barbara Sproul praised her resilience. It seems odd to think she died, she wrote to Roth in May 1982: "she seemed so indestructible, not because of outward strength but because of rootedness in the everyday business of life. . . . She was like a great general creating a pleasant order in the ranks of house and family." Sproul adds, "You gave her deep and lasting pleasure."[100]

Her recipe cards best reflected this gift for organization, recipes shared with other mothers in their Newark neighborhood. When a childhood friend of Roth's writes to him in October 2004, reminding him of their Weequahic youth, she includes several of his mother's recipe cards with her name neatly typed on the right-hand corner.[101] After reading the marble pound cake recipe (referred to in *The Plot Against America*), he replies that his mother kept her recipes in a small metal box in the pantry just off the kitchen, all of them handwritten in blue ink. Also recorded, at the top right of the card, was the name of the friend who had passed on the recipe. But he confesses that cream, eggs, and butter were no longer part of his diet and that it is unlikely that he will "plunge ahead to eat one of my mother's pound cakes again. But there's pleasure enough in just reading the recipe, and being reminded of some of the terrific things we all had as kids."[102]

Sophie Portnoy is not a portrait of his mother but a caricature, an exaggeration of qualities Bess Roth possessed but hardly unleashed. Sophie's overbearing and hovering manner—don't let her son eat a hamburger, and definitely not French Fries—morphs into the interfering Jewish mother. Roth had great affection for his mother and her support of Sandy with his art and Roth with his writing. It was at his mother's typewriter in the kitchen, in fact, where Roth wrote perhaps his earliest work, a story entitled "Storm off Hatteras" using the pseudonym Eric Duncan. His reticence about her in his writing may be a way of protecting her memory, which he did not want altered by any conflicting reality.

Surprisingly, Roth offers a limited description of his mother's May 1981 funeral in *Patrimony* and of a later, somewhat accidental, visit to her grave (because of a wrong turn off a highway) on his way to see his father in Elizabeth. The treatment is more objective than emotional: no sense of Bess as an individual emerges. Rather, it is Roth and his response to cemeteries that matter, and they only remind him that the dead have departed and cannot return (PAT 19–21). He also suggests that his father might have felt guilty for prompting his wife to overlook her angina, encouraging her to go on a lengthy walk which might have led to her fatal heart attack (PAT 34).

The "destructive struggle" that Roth portrays in family life is often between father and son, not mother and son (IND 8). This may be the pull of Kafka: Roth gravitated to Kafka because he saw himself in that complicated dialogue Kafka represented, the constant struggle with a powerful, unrelenting father. In Roth's late fiction, the fathers partially take on the role of the mothers, Marcus Messner in *Indignation* writing that he needs to be free of a "strong, stolid father suddenly stricken with uncontrollable fear for a grown-up son's well-being," a quality mostly found in mothers (IND 34–35). When Marcus's mother does appear, visiting Marcus in a campus hospital room as he recovers from appendicitis, she cleans his hospital bathroom rather than question the depressed Olivia, with a scar on her wrist, also present at the bedside. She tells her son that she may leave his unmanageable father, but in the end, she lacks the courage to do so, making a deal with her son: she will stay with his father if he agrees to give up Olivia, "a girl full of tears." "Other people's weaknesses," she states, "can destroy you just as much as their strength can. Weak people are not harmless" (IND 174). It is a sentence Roth likely wrote out of his experiences with Maggie and Bloom.

Roth did not idealize his mother, but neither is she the relentless Sophie Portnoy. In fact, to counter what Roth perceived to be malice toward his mother by Ross Miller in particular, he prepared a nine-page document with examples from numerous friends of her positive qualities, confirmed by Bloom in *Leaving a Doll's House*. In *Patrimony*, however, Roth's mother receives only one direct sentence; it's on the second page of the text.

By the mid-1980s illness and ill health began to dominate Roth's writing. Illness had plagued his family before his birth: appendicitis had killed two uncles, and his own father nearly died from it when Roth was ten (FAC 11–13). A lengthy document in the Princeton papers painfully lists his hospitalizations for coronary artery disease, back surgery, cataract removals, and an appendectomy. The log begins with a hernia repair (left side) in 1943. His numerous stents were legendary and at times comic. Relatively pain free between 2002 and 2003, he suddenly began to grow short of breath in September 2003 while walking and ended up at Lenox Hill Hospital in Manhattan for another stent to relieve a blockage.

It is no surprise that one result of his earlier bouts of pain is *The Anatomy Lesson*, his more recent encounters creating the depressed Simon Axler of *The Humbling*. Illness on a community scale—the crippling polio of *Nemesis*—shapes his final novel. "Between my vascular system, my cardiovascular system, and my musculo-skeletal system, I've been busy," he wrote (PIH 29).

Misdiagnosis, inadequate drugs, and painful recovery characterize Roth's medical history, which he detailed in a document of some thirty leaves, recording his experience with aches and illnesses, recognizing how much pain had dominated his life. From his early hospitalization for a hernia to the extreme effect of painkillers taken after a knee operation, detailed by Bloom in *Leaving a Doll's House*, Roth suffered. His back injury in the army did not heal properly, and for some years after he needed a steel brace; back problems plagued him throughout his life, shifting partially to his neck and outlined in detail in *The Anatomy Lesson*. From 1989 onward, he lived with serious heart problems.[103]

His account of his father's death in *Patrimony* furthered the illness narrative that runs throughout his career, from *Goodbye, Columbus* to *Nemesis*. His sense of death from disease mixed worry with anxiety and rarely left him. As Ben Taylor notes in his recent memoir, ever since learning of his heart disease in 1982, Roth ended each writing day organizing his papers, not knowing if he'd return: "I was more afraid for the work in progress than for myself," he claimed.[104] Impotence, a side effect of the drug he was given, was only one of several embarrassments. Reports of his own final days, dying of heart failure (as did his brother) on 22 May 2018, recount his sense of the end, telling hospital visitors that in relation to dying, "he had work to do." Dying, like writing, was labor, echoing what he wrote of his own father's death in *Patrimony*: "Dying is work and he was a worker" (PAT 233). The text, in fact, begins and ends with death, starting with his paternal grandfather, watched over by his father, and then Roth's own father, watched over by Roth (PAT 11, 233).

The Anatomy Lesson is the clearest example of Roth's relation to pain. Writing despite his own back problems, a constant burden, he studied textbooks and interviewed doctors to get the story right. Roth always researched his novels, providing them with authentic detail.[105]

Depression was another condition affecting him physically as well as psychologically. He explained that he did not really understand it until 1974, when he ended his affair with Barbara Sproul. He had been unhappy before, but intense emotional pain had so far escaped him. Afterward depressive episodes were always accompanied by severe and chronic physical pain and often the breakup of a relationship, no matter how genuine or satisfying. He admitted that the relationship was not clear: Did the pain lead to depression or depression to the pain? And was the result always a breakup? In his medical account, he says he can deal with each independently but not when they occur together.[106] The combination is devastating.

9

Thinking in Straight Lines

What do I know, other than what I can imagine?
—Nathan Zuckerman, in *The Ghost Writer*, 1979

Throughout the 1980s, Roth battled himself, beginning with unavoidable health problems, from back pain to an unsuccessful arthroscopy on his left knee, which led to physical discomfort and depression, largely from a sleeping pill, Halcion.[1] His relationship with Claire Bloom was wearing thin, leading to conflicts that precipitated his return to America, followed by unexpected bypass surgery and then the death of father. Life suddenly interrupted literature and, try as he might, "thinking in straight lines"—a phrase used by the critic Alfred Kazin—was impossible.

While experience knocked such behavior aside, he instinctively reacted through performance: "I am a theater and nothing more than a theater" (CL 321). But he knew this was, itself, an act. "Being Zuckerman," he adds, is "one long performance and the very opposite of what is thought of as being oneself" (CL 319). Locating that self, if it exists, was Roth's constant challenge. He pursued that challenge through performances on the page and in person. Performance became both an escape from self and the means to find it.

Roth had been dividing his time between London and New York/ Connecticut, a tiring if not unsettling reshuffling of time and place. And although London brought him friends and contacts and his writing pivoted to more European concerns, he was becoming both personally and intellectually restless. Pain now pursued him as much as the drive to create. Whether in the U.K. or the U.S., his back, knee, and then his heart began to disrupt his writing and life. Furthermore, death bookended the decade, with the unexpected death of his mother in 1981 and then his father in 1989.

Zuckerman, the Rothian alter ego of the 1980s, appeared at an auspicious time in Roth's career, having written out his anger at Maggie in *My Life as a Man* (1974) and experimented with new forms in *The Counterlife* (1986).

Roth was also extending contacts with Eastern European writers. His 1976 interview with Isaac Bashevis Singer about Bruno Schulz, whose *Street of Crocodiles* would appear in his "Writers from the Other Europe" series, was instrumental in, again, widening his perspective beyond Newark toward Eastern European Jewish writings and twentieth-century Jewish history. In his Connecticut home, Roth had fifteen framed reproductions by Schulz.

Zuckerman, appearing first in *The Ghost Writer*, is the product of Peter Tarnopol's efforts to find the right narrative space from which to view and transform material provided by his own biography. The act of impersonation is key, as Tarnopol unveils how his story came to be written, something Zuckerman would do repeatedly in *The Prague Orgy* and *American Pastoral*. Roth expanded on this when he explained to Hermione Lee the importance of being a ventriloquist: art "consists of being present *and* absent." The author is most himself when he is "simultaneously being someone else." You distort or parody your own biography "to give the biography that dimension that will excite your verbal life" (CWPR 166–67).

Zuckerman offered that freedom for Roth in his nearly nine-book narrative presence, ending with *Exit Ghost* (2007). It is a geographical whirlwind: between *The Ghost Writer* and *Exit Ghost*, Zuckerman appears in the U.S. in *Zuckerman Unbound* and *The Anatomy Lesson*, then Czechoslovakia in *The Prague Orgy*, followed by the U.K. and Israel in *The Counterlife*, and, finally, with the American Trilogy, back in the U.S.A.

Zuckerman first appeared in *My Life as a Man* (1974) but is not fully drawn until *The Ghost Writer*, his life uncannily parallel to Roth's, beginning with his birth in Newark in 1933. The exuberance of the youthful Zuckerman in the "Salad Days" section of *My Life as a Man* will be offset by "Courting Disaster," the narrator prefacing that section with references to the "story of Zuckerman's suffering," beginning with his being drafted into the army, marriage to Lydia, her suicide, and then life with his stepdaughter, Monica, partially outlining some of Roth's own adventures (MLM 31). In a later passage, we learn that after a set of short stories, he hits fame with *Carnovsky*, his fourth book (as *Portnoy* was Roth's), the confessions of a young Jewish man sharing his exploits with his psychiatrist. Even Zuckerman's writing habits parallel Roth's, especially an absorption with masks: "I can only exhibit myself in disguise. All my audacity derives from masks" (CL 258). The creation of Zuckerman allows Roth greater distance and freedom from his own life at the same time he can incorporate its details into his literary fictions. Authorship and authority as narrative form become performative, as readers witness the aging of Zuckerman until he becomes not only the mature voice of the American Trilogy but the experienced eye and "I" of *Exit Ghost*.[2]

Zuckerman provides Roth with the confidence and freedom to experiment, intervene, and participate, even if at times only at the edge of his narratives (as an observer), while giving him license to transform biography into fiction. And voices. As the older Zuckerman comments in *I Married a Communist*, "The book of my life is a book of voices. When I ask myself how I arrived at where I am, the answer surprises me: 'Listening'" (IMC 222). Underlying this is the desire of both Roth and Zuckerman to create the convincing illusion of experience, facts, and life.

Throughout the Zuckerman years and beyond, Roth, like Zuckerman, carried "his books from one life into the next" (ZUB 49). Incidents, characters, settings, and situations may change, but Roth's themes remain constant, whether in a Chicago hospital (*The Anatomy Lesson*) or the Berkshires (*The Human Stain*). This is evident throughout Zuckerman's moral and literary education. The aggressive pursuit of the recognizable Zuckerman is nowhere stronger than when Alvin Pepler accosts him on a 5th Avenue bus heading south in *Zuckerman Unbound*. Now financially secure, he was still vulnerable to a public more concerned with publicizing his identity than reading his books. In this, Roth offers a comment on his own resistance to celebrity and its dangers.

In *Zuckerman Unbound*, it is 1969, in the midst of the Vietnam War protests and a year after the assassinations of Martin Luther King Jr. and Robert Kennedy. Wherever he goes in the city, Zuckerman's "made," and it makes him uncomfortable. Called out as "Carnovsky," as Roth was labeled "Portnoy," Zuckerman realizes that his public had "mistaken impersonation for confession and were calling out to a character who lived in a book," the very situation created by the readers of *Portnoy* (ZUB 10). And then a Newarker interrupts him as he is about to order in a New York deli, yelling to everyone that here is Newark's own Marcel Proust (ZUB 13).

References to Newark run like a river in the book, from the new interloper, Alvin Pepler, would-be writer and one-time game show winner, to Rochelle, manager of his answering service dealing with calls from Newark's Rollmops King (pickled herring rolled around a filling). The source of comedy is not the satire of fame but how Zuckerman's subjectivity permeates the overall narrative perspective. In this fashion, the reader experiences the intensity of Zuckerman's celebrity status as detail enables identity, whether it is the location of a restaurant, Zuckerman's new East Side apartment, or the actions of his father.

Of course, Roth is satirizing such attention with Zuckerman replacing Roth, who was often subject to similar intrusions. But with the appearance of Pepler, the short novel is off and running, Pepler and the reader in "hot pursuit" of Zuckerman, who works to hide, divert, and obstruct others, especially if they seek help in placing their own work, including the retired Harry Nelson, who has a fifty-thousand-word romance with "college characters and explicit sex" (ZUB 106). Later, the comedy turns to kidnapping as a crook tries to extort $50,000 from Zuckerman, claiming he has seized his mother (ZUB 109). Additional details anticipate the "Basel" chapter of *The Counterlife*, dealing with Zuckerman's brother, Henry (ZUB 188).

But fame can have its price, as Zuckerman's father rebukes his son with his final word uttered from his hospital bed. Thought to be "Better" or possibly "Batter" or "Vaster," it turns out to be "Bastard" (ZUB 199, 208, 217). Resentment replaces reputation, underscored by his brother's exclamation, "To you everything is disposable! Everything is *exposable*!" (ZUB 217). In the ultimate accusation, the brother shouts, "You killed him, Nathan . . . with that book. *Of course* he said 'Bastard'": he saw what you did to him and mother and that book (ZUB 217). The apostasy of the son is undeniable.

While composing the book, Roth shared its gestation with James Atlas, whose biography of Delmore Schwartz had intrigued Roth. Atlas and Roth grew close, Roth encouraging Atlas to undertake a series of new projects (he was working at the *New York Times Magazine* and *Book Review* at the time), such as a life of Edmund Wilson or Bernard Malamud or a study of literary fame for which Roth prepared ten questions to consider. At one point, he even offhandedly suggested a life of Bellow, which Atlas would do, publishing his biography in 2000. However, Atlas's critical, even unflattering, account of Bellow's life precipitated a break with Roth. Before that, in correspondence with Atlas, Roth shared insightful remarks on Malamud, Updike, Styron, and Singer, finding in him, especially Singer's *Enemies*, that he "doesn't seem to worry for a second about story *telling*. Which I worry about all the time."[3]

Atlas, part of the small group often asked to comment on drafts of Roth's writing, offered comments on both *The Ghost Writer* and *Zuckerman Unbound*. In a 14 September 1981 note on *Zuckerman Unbound*, Roth thanks him for his remarks, "maniacal though you were while making them. I've practically rewritten the whole first half of the book and it is much much improved."[4] Atlas also wrote an introduction to *Letting Go* for a 1982 reprint of the novel for which Roth, in his wonderfully self-deprecating humor, predicted, "They'll be lining up outside Books & Co [a popular New York bookstore] to get their hands on it, and putting up with all that Roth just for Atlas."[5] Roth then tells Atlas he went to Florida to see his father and had lunch with Singer. In the lobby of the Singapore Hotel in Miami, he saw the last of the old Jewish men from Newark he remembered as young men when he was growing up. "Strange to think of the anger it once took to free myself from their embrace," he writes, adding that Bloom was also learning about the literary life. Her autobiography, *Limelight and After* (1982), in which he had a strong editorial hand, had been reviewed nowhere and she was stunned.[6]

Another event from this period was a mock trial Roth conducted for the writer Janet Malcolm, a close friend, who was about to go to court to defend herself in a $10 million libel action against her for an article in the *New Yorker* on the battle over, and in, the Freud Papers published in two issues of the magazine (5 and 12 December 1983). It essentially narrated the succession of the directorship of the Papers to be transferred from the dean of Freud studies, Kurt Eissler, to the upstart Jeffrey Masson (a professor of Sanskrit and nonpracticing analyst from Toronto) who was "unmasked" in two articles by Ralph Blumenthal, which caused Eissler and the Papers board to reverse their decision appointing Masson. Masson argued that Malcolm had fabricated quotations attributed to him and that these passages brought him into disrepute.

Concerned that she might lose in court, Roth held a "rehearsal" in his New York apartment with himself, Ross Miller, David Rieff, and one other to quiz her rigorously as if she were on the stand. Initially, a court held against Malcolm; the case would go forward for trial by a jury. After a decade of proceedings, a jury finally decided in Malcolm's favor on 2 November 1994, claiming that more evidence would be needed to rule against her. In 1984 she published her *New Yorker* account in a short book, *In the Freud Papers* (1984), with a new afterword. In August 1995, Malcolm claimed that she discovered a misplaced notebook containing three of the disputed quotes.[7]

Malcolm and Roth maintained a lively correspondence partly because he was unafraid to criticize her writing and she could take it. At one point, he told her that her account of Sylvia Plath, *The Silent Woman*, could drastically improve. Write with more playfulness, he suggested, more freely. His astringent comments derive from his own self-scrutiny: "I gave you the kind of reading I give myself," he told her, writing in the margin in caps, "THINK THIS THROUGH." But even she became irritated with his admonitions.

"Why are you yelling at me?" she asked in response to another outburst, this time related to an attack on the writer Edward Hoagland for his supposed homophobia. Later she penned a note to herself in response to one of his letters that expressed her frustration with Roth: he is constantly selfish and manipulative. Nevertheless, the two had a brief relationship. He does admit, at one point, that he fixates on the past, wondering, "What must it be like to let things go?" Clearly, he cannot.[8]

During this period, the public persona of Roth and Bloom was upbeat, if not idyllic. A 1983 *Vogue* profile implied Roth's obsession with control, but the article presented an ideal country life of the celebrity couple surrounded by nature. But Roth made his role as a writer clear: in contrast to an actor, who must listen to the director, perhaps the producer, and often other actors, "the point about being a novelist," he emphasizes, "is that you're absolutely in charge. You're the director, and you're the casting director, and you're the cast. I think I prefer that. . . . I don't need anyone else."[9] The characters must listen to me, he's saying. But crossing over into life for them can be torture, as Hope Lonoff reveals in *The Ghost Writer*. "Let me out of the prison of your decency," she screams at her husband, whose honor traps both of them. "I cannot take any more moral fiber in the face of life's disappointments" (GW 42). She means his rectitude refusing to give in to his desire for Amy instead of giving in to the monotony and boredom—all this controlled by Roth.

With color photos of their pastoral life, the *Vogue* profile artificially radiates pleasure. But the adulatory interview of the celebrities could not avoid a remark on Roth's "fealty" to his work, having just published *The Anatomy Lesson* and underway on a new book. Like Lonoff, he works constantly. A tour of the home features the photographs: a reproduced photo of Kafka, an image of Tolstoy, and a picture of Bloom as the queen in *Richard III*, the easily seduced Lady Anne prompting Richard's cynical comment foretelling her future and possibly that of Bloom: "I'll have her, but I will not keep her long" (I.2.231). Shadows surround the images in the *Vogue* interview.

Roth's writing at this time, *The Anatomy Lesson* (1983) and *The Prague Orgy* (1985), soon pursued Zuckerman in two different directions, the first on his back, where he essentially tries to conduct a sexual and literary life before mustering the energy to go to a Chicago Hospital to learn more about his troubles, and then on his feet in Prague in pursuit of lost Yiddish manuscripts. In the former, Zuckerman skillfully plays Milton Appel, pornographic publisher, a parody of Roth's early nemesis, Irving Howe. In the latter, there is an allusion to Henry James, the entire story a Jewish "Aspern Papers," a quest for a set of lost documents of immense importance.

The Anatomy Lesson, which doesn't end with death, concludes in a cemetery where Zuckerman falls and breaks his jaw; for a Jew this is akin to death.[10] Just as Ivan, the hero of Tolstoy's "The Death of Ivan Ilyich," about a provincial judge who suffers from an incurable illness, realizes that life means more than status or reputation, Zuckerman realizes that "not everything has to be a book" and that he no longer has to live "as a man apart" (AL 281, 291). As Alfred Kazin noted, throughout *The Anatomy Lesson* "wisecracks pop like champagne corks in an emergency room." Kazin further wrote that in pre-Hitler Europe, "the Jewish problem meant: 'what shall we do about the Jews?' In America the question seems to be: 'what can the sensationally successful American Jew do about himself?' "[11] Roth sees the double side of everything but always asks, is it life or story?

By the time of *Exit Ghost*, Zuckerman is seventy-one and looking back on his encounter with Lonoff and the aged and ill Bellette. But as a sustaining voice in Roth's writing, his role remains significant and satisfying for Roth's purposes. Most interesting is Zuckerman's obituary, prepared by a Christopher Tayler for the *Guardian* in September 2007, coinciding with the release of *Exit Ghost* and citing the importance of Felix Abravanel (based on Bellow) and E. I. Lonoff (supposedly, but not only, Bernard Malamud). In the obit, Zuckerman's details emerge: he was divorced from his first wife, Betsy, in 1960 and his second, Virginia, in 1965. Laura, a lawyer, was his third; he left her. His fourth, Maria, left him. He also began to work on his celebrated monologist, Carnovsky, at this time, and the epic masturbator brought Zuckerman instant notoriety. Age and isolation in rural New England brought his demise, an artist hiding out in "the *goyish* wilderness of birds and trees where America began and long ago had ended" (GW 4).

The irony of Zuckerman's career is that except for *The Ghost Writer* and *Exit Ghost*, he has been an observer, a narrator, a listener. In *Exit Ghost*, he becomes a principal and somewhat unsuccessful major character—all of this perhaps something Roth sought: as he aged, not to be a player but a fan watching from the stands. But Zuckerman served Roth well, taking the flak, earning the praise, and standing just off stage when Swede Levov, Coleman Silk, or Ira Ringold took over. He also allowed Roth to "go around in disguise. To act a character. To *pretend*. The sly and cunning masquerade" in which he found great pleasure (CWPR 167). What interested Roth in Zuckerman is that everybody has split, but Zuckerman can't hide or heal it.

What determines his life "are the lines of fracture in what is by no means a clean break. I was interested in following those lines" because they were his (CWPR 166).

In the midst of working on the Zuckerman texts, and specifically *The Anatomy Lesson*, Roth asked for reaction from David Plante. He was supportive but candid, his diary providing insights into Roth's thinking during his London years. At one point, Roth told Plante, "Updike and Bellow hold their flashlights out into the world. . . . I dig a hole and shine my flashlight into the hole. You do the same."[12]

Plante also accompanied Roth to Israel in 1986, summarized in a chapter from volume 2 of his diary, *Worlds Apart: A Memoir*. The trip began with Roth worrying about his brother in Chicago, who just had open-heart surgery, mentioning that when Sandy became sick, Roth himself would often come down with the same sickness. Ironically, three years later, Roth would have his heart surgery.[13] He invited Plante to Israel because he wanted to see how a non-Jew would react to a Jewish country. He had already started work on what would become *Operation Shylock*, but he was stuck and so wanted his character to visit Israel and meet the fanatics, the aggressive, narrow-minded right-wingers. Semicomically, he tells Plante he will turn him into an anti-Semite.

Roth took the Catholic Plante first to the Tomb of the Holy Sepulcher and then the Wailing Wall before venturing to Ofra on the West Bank, where they toured the settlement and met many Americans. Roth then made a second trip to the West Bank but without Plante, and much of the material from the excursion found its way into *Operation Shylock*. After his second visit, spending time with an extraordinary right-wing partisan, he was elated, remarking that for once he was not thinking about himself: "Fifty-one years I've spent thinking about myself. Not thinking about myself is what I've always wanted." Euphoric, he shouted, "It's shit, it's shit, literature! I'm going to kick writing novels. . . . I don't want to deal with nice people any more. They bore me."[14] Of course, this wouldn't happen until 2010.

Following Jerusalem and the West Bank, it was Tel Aviv and the Museum of the Diaspora, but a sentimental lecture about Jewish virtues appalled him, so he and Plante explored by themselves. Roth commented that he lived the life of the virtuous Jew and found satisfaction only in being the bad Jew, encouraging Plante and joking that he might actually be Jewish after scanning computer names at the museum, and that he could now enjoy the double status of being both a Jew and an anti-Semite.[15]

Roth met with another right-wing ex-politician but told Plante that the man was too reasonable: "I want the mad fanaticism of the man I saw yesterday on the West Bank."[16] After each encounter, Roth would go into his bedroom and write notes about his experiences before rejoining Plante for the evening. The trip ended with a lunch for Aharon Appelfeld, Holocaust survivor and writer. Soon, Roth would transform his Israeli extremists into the composite character of George Zaid, thirty years earlier a graduate student with Roth in Chicago, who has been radicalized. Living in Ramallah and asked what he did there, Zaid incisively answers, "Hate" (OPS 121). He also taught and wrote for a newspaper.

On his return to London, Roth found that life with Bloom was progressively more demoralizing. He increasingly felt dislocated. Plante noted that Roth's characters rarely give way to helpless feelings: "The feelings of his characters are in Philip's control," perhaps the reason so many say all he can write about is himself. He alone shapes the actions of his characters. Yet ironically, as Plante astutely observes, the driving force "he impels in them is to break out of the control he imposes on them, so he makes the driving force extreme." A deliberate tension and resistance, projecting his own life-long battle against restraints and his own inner conflicts between being good and bad, dominate. The irony is that no matter how intense the situation, he governs the characters, who fail to break free. As he admitted to Plante, only people in extreme situations interested him.[17]

Throughout this uncertain period, with its conflicting forces of creativity and confusion, especially with Bloom, Roth's productivity remained high, his commitment to literature unwavering, although it created a dilemma he had outlined earlier in *My Life as a Man*: "It seems either that literature too strongly influences my ideas about life or that I am able to make no connection at all between its wisdom and my existence" (MLM 86).

But despite his illnesses and despite the challenges of life with Bloom, he wrote, although the constant travel between London and Cornwall Bridge did not help. Not only was he promoting his Zuckerman series, working with Bloom on a number of TV adaptations, overseeing publication of *A Philip Roth Reader*, edited by Martin Green, but he was also hosting the Kunderas in Connecticut, working with Aaron Asher now at Farrar, Straus and Giroux, and writing his Zuckerman tales, while encouraging the exiled Romanian writer Norman Manea, in Berlin, to emigrate to the U.S.

During this period he was also receiving reassurance of his importance from another writer. Cynthia Ozick wrote to him in June 1986 thanking him

Figure 9.1 Roth and Bloom in their London home, March 1990. Credit: Ian Cook/Getty Images.

for alerting her to the value of Bruno Schulz and sending on two prints, one a self-portrait of Schulz and the other one of his drawings. They hung in her living room. More important, she tells Roth she owes her new work *The Messiah of Stockholm* to him. The novel concerns a reclusive and obsessed book critic who believes he is the son of the legendary Polish author Schulz and begins a quest for the lost manuscript of his last novel, *The Messiah*. She hesitatingly asks if she can dedicate her new novel to Roth. She makes this request not because she wants to ride on the back of his fame but because, she says, "you *gave* me this book" and I want to acknowledge it. "If not for you, I would never have come to Bruno Schulz: never."[18] She also thanks him for introducing her to Witold Gombrowicz: she and Roth had recently met at a screening of *Shoah* and he sent her some examples of Gombrowicz's writing.

The following year, 1987, Roth expresses his longing for America in a letter to the critic Alfred Kazin:

England's made a Jew of me, England's made an American of me, and I miss what I'm rooted in terribly. I'll be glad to be home, limping or not. Somebody should write a book on the way we self-examining, current-event addicted, mixed breed Americans talk to each other; there's nothing like it. David Rieff says I've become a "nostalgic American" and it may all just be no more than that. It nonetheless feels like much more.[19]

Roth and Kazin became acquainted in 1962 in Wellfleet and later at Yaddo but did not become friends until Roth purchased his farmhouse in Cornwall Bridge. Kazin lived only thirty miles away in Roxbury, home also to William Styron. They visited each other and met from time to time in the city. Kazin thought Roth's sensibility was sharp and uncompromising, possessing a "pointy instrumentalist personality."[20] Roth thought Kazin was intelligent and liked his pugnacity, referring to him as a "fellow pugilist."[21]

Kazin, who had written one of the first reviews of *Portnoy's Complaint*, referred to the novel in his journal for 29 June 1968 as a "savage, endlessly inventive satire of the Jewish son against his parents. Very funny, dirty, impressively clever, but not easy to be fond of . . . all genitals, mother hatred and mother fucking."[22] Kazin's review of *Portnoy* appeared as "Up Against the Wall, Mama!" in the *New York Review of Books* of 27 February 1969. In the review, he developed some of the ideas he outlined in a journal entry of 14 December 1968, notably that "there is no firm *language* for the adult male embarked on a career of voluptuous enjoyment." He pursues a destiny of gratification because the idea of being loved for himself alone heals the breaks and fills in the blanks of his beset existence. "The negative *politics* of [the] everyday drives Portnoy and even Roth onward." He later remarked in his journal, "The Jew 'analysand' is still better than the Jew as ideologist of current American power. Power works on different ways in us Jews!"[23]

A further journal comment on Roth after having dinner with him and Bloom in October 1987, where Roth dismembered Arthur Miller and *Timebends*, shows Kazin's insight:

Philip always thinks in straight lines, fancies himself a specialist in common sense, but when he goes bang, bang, bang like this (and I have been through the performance before) I realize why I see him only for short or formal dinners . . . and despite the edge he fosters, am always glad to see him depart in all his prosperity and self-satisfaction. The cleverness, the sharpness, the continual *edge* somehow turn even an evening, to say nothing of his fiction, into *performance*. There are no purely meditative, unexpected moments, no reflection outside professional ones. The competition is keen![24]

Earlier, Kazin commented that Roth is a "sharp, logical analyst of character and motivation in whatever he sees and reads." In discussing Bellow's *Herzog*, he spotted "all sorts of illogicalities." He has an antennae for moral confusions and implausibility, Kazin added.[25]

Measuring the closeness of the two was Roth's presence as the only non-family member at the private funeral for Kazin shortly after his death on 5 June 1998. There was no rabbi: family members simply read favorite pieces they felt appropriate and passages from his works. His daughter, however, read the Kaddish in Hebrew. Afterward, Roth told Judith, Kazin's widow, it was the finest funeral he had ever attended.[26]

As discontent with Bloom increased, he was rupturing relationships with various London friends. David Hare found in him a new "and frightening ferocity." Roth, he noted, "might have been overly in love with a writer's necessary ruthlessness." Roth claimed he was driven away from England because of upper-class anti-Semitism, but Hare believed the reason was simpler: an "American passion for newness" which was the source of his inspiration.[27]

Compounding his difficult situation were taxes. As early as April 1979, Roth wrote to Roger Straus about the tax implications of his partial residence in the U.K., where he might be liable for U.K. tax. Roth discussed a plan with a U.K. lawyer whereby FSG would hire Roth to work in England for six months a year on a nonfiction project on twentieth-century English and Continental literature. Compensation from his royalties would take the form of a salary for the assignment. In this way, he would be taxed only on income from an American company, working for them in England, not his world-wide income. Any paid U.K. tax could then be deducted from his U.S. tax.

The scheme, however, was not necessary since Roth kept careful tabs on the days he spent in the U.K. and returned to the U.S. before he needed to pay any U.K. tax. But his income was substantial: the figure from FSG in August 1979 was $185,774. The advance from Bantam for the paperback of *The Professor of Desire* was $192,500, still due. Aaron Asher, at the time his FSG editor, also acted in the late 1970s as Roth's agent, confirmed by Straus in a letter of 31 May 1977. This lasted until 1989, when Andrew Wylie took over as agent for all trade and mass market paperbacks not published by FSG.[28]

Wylie innovated a new scheme for Roth: instead of selling the reprint rights to the original publisher of a work, his agency retained and resold them. Wylie used the leverage of his backlist to extract a higher price and established oversight on his translations, avoiding such confusions as when Roth noted that the Italian translation of *Goodbye, Columbus* changed the name of the hero from Neil to Tony and retitled the book *La Ragazza de Tony* (Tony's Girlfriend) and left out five stories.[29] The end of the 1980s were a period of important changes, professionally and personally.

An event in the late 1980s had a strong effect on Roth: the apparent suicide of Primo Levi on 11 April 1987 in Turin. It was a complete shock. Many of his friends thought of Levi as composed, serene, at ease with himself, while others felt his recent writing about the Holocaust in *The Drowned and the Saved* had altered his outlook to be even more positive. But Levi's son believed that the end of *The Truce* (1962) foretold why he might take his own life: "A dream full of horror has still not ceased to visit me. . . . I am in the Lager once more, and nothing is true outside the Lager. All the rest was a brief pause." Lager means the storeroom or warehouse, often holding items of those murdered in the concentration camps. Elie Wiesel remarked, "Primo Levi died at Auschwitz forty years later."[30] Writing of Auschwitz renewed an ever-present despair.

The death of Levi, whom Roth had interviewed only seven months before (he had also been teaching him in a course on Holocaust writing at Hunter College and believed *If This Is a Man* one of the essential texts of the time), was devastating. In London, where he heard the news, Roth spent the day with the Italian journalist Gaia Servadio, who had introduced him to Levi when the writer visited London in April 1986 to participate in a conference on literature and chemistry at the Italian Institute of Culture at 39 Belgrave Square. Servadio had met Levi several times in Turin when she worked as a reporter for *La Stampa*.

Servadio had been in London since 1956 and became a writer, journalist, broadcaster, and historian; she was herself the daughter of a chemist whom Levi knew. She had met Roth at a luncheon in Chester Square with Martin Amis and Mick Jagger. When she told Roth, in answer to his question "What do you think of Woody Allen?" that nothing came to mind, he became interested. They became close friends, and when he learned that Levi was coming, he asked to meet him. She also soon sensed his disillusionment with London: "I think he hated that fair play under which the worst garbage hides." He felt upset when her daughter Allegra was to marry Boris Johnson. The two had met earlier at Oxford. Roth tried to intervene, telling Servadio he would speak to a friend of his, a Democratic senator looking for an assistant for an upcoming election campaign (most likely Frank Lautenberg from New Jersey). Arrangements were made, but at the last moment, the daughter turned down the offer and married Johnson in 1987. They divorced in 1993.[31]

Having met Levi through Servadio, in September 1986 Roth and Bloom flew to Turin for a weekend to interview him for the *New York Times* on the American release of *The Monkey's Wrench* (published as *The Wrench* in Italian in 1978). Their first stop with Levi was Siva, the paint factory where he had worked as a research chemist and then manager, followed by a return to Levi's apartment (where he was born) and his large study just off the entrance. It is here where the often reprinted photos of the two were taken (Figure 9.2).

Unusually, Roth did not record the interview, nor did he take notes during their conversations.[32] After the weekend, Roth sent Levi a series of questions to which Levi responded. The interview appeared on 12 October 1986 in the *New York Times Book Review*, little more than a month after their meeting. It avoids any discussion of Levi's apparent depression, sensed by Bloom as they departed, nor the bonding of the two writers.[33]

Levi was sixty-seven. His depression may have increased the following April not only because of the continuing shadows of Auschwitz but because of recent prostate surgery (three weeks before his death) and his domestic

Figure 9.2 Roth and Primo Levi in Levi's study in Turin, April(?) 1986.
Credit: Primo Levi Center, Turin; La Stampa.

situation: retired, he was virtually confined to his apartment. Depression may have also been caused by his feeling he had depleted his writing capital and that his cancer-ridden mother, also living in the apartment, evoked the horrible state of men in Auschwitz. He had also recently finished what Roth believed to be his masterpiece of grief, *The Drowned and the Saved*.[34] Signifying the importance of his meeting with Levi is that the interview is the first in Roth's 2001 collection, *Shop Talk*.

To Kazin on 21 April 1987 Roth wrote that Levi's suicide horrified and haunted him every day, despite trying not to think of it: "I can't even look at his books right now. I'll have to do that later."[35] Some have questioned whether Levi's death *was* a suicide. A cardiologist friend of Levi's suggested that he may have died from the side effects of antidepressant drugs.[36] For Roth, this was telling since a few years later he, too, would experience extreme depression and suicidal thoughts sending him to Silver Hill Hospital. Levi might have fainted walking up the stairs, grabbed the low banisters of the stairwell, and in doing so fell over. Or he may have opened his door again after receiving letters from his concierge, stepped forward, and fell over the low railing. Depression and drugs were likely the cause, as even William Styron suggested in his short study of depression, *Darkness Visible* (1989).

Levi's death introduced a long period of the deaths of friends of Roth, from Bernard Malamud (1986), to Primo Levi (1987), to his father (1989) and Janet Hobhouse (1991), preceded by Philip Guston (1980) and his mother in 1981. Later, it would be Veronica Geng (1997), George Plimpton (2003), Bellow (2005), Aaron Asher (2008), and that same year his close friend Ted Solotaroff. From Levi to Bellow marks a period of intense unhappiness that saw Roth himself battle death at the same time he tried to appraise it in works like *The Counterlife, Sabbath's Theater, The Dying Animal*, and *Everyman* until it overwhelmed his late works: *Indignation, The Humbling*, and *Nemesis*. As he explained in a 2006 interview, the plan is that first your grandparents die, then your parents, and then "the truly startling thing": your friends begin to die. "That's not in the plan."[37]

Death suddenly, but not surprisingly, appeared in his texts as well as his life: *Patrimony* of 1991 was a triumphant challenge to death through the empathetic narrative of his father's last years, followed by the energetic but grief-stricken Mickey Sabbath, who fought death through anger at the loss of his brother Morty in the war and then the licentious Drenka. Next was the American Trilogy, which begins with the accidental death of Dr. Conlon in *American Pastoral*, followed in *I Married a Communist* with the murder of

Murray Ringold's wife and a haunting murder committed years earlier by Ira Ringold. Death even surrounds Coleman Silk in *The Human Stain*, from that of his wife to Les Fairley and his Vietnam experiences. As Roth summarized in *Everyman*, "Old age isn't a battle; old age is a massacre"—but so, it seems, is life (EV 156).

Shadowing this view were his own illnesses, but he tried to hold his ground as best he could, as Zuckerman's father advises in *Everyman* (4–5). To do this meant ceding control over life, giving it up to fate, something Roth found difficult if not impossible to do. As he told Kazin in July 1987, his medical problem then—his knee—led to depression: "The whole thing came out of nowhere with what was to have been minor surgery and has turned into a fiasco and semi-nightmare in which Claire has suffered terribly too, largely because of my emotional upset with being immobilized and in pain. A mess." "Much has exploded while I've been reeling," he adds. "This ain't the way it's s'posed to be."[38]

As his own health became more difficult, he witnessed three friends struck down, which he transposed into his writing in *Everyman* with Phoebe's stroke, then a suicide, and finally a heart attack. For Roth, stoicism seemed the only response to the end of a productive and vibrant life. One original title for *Everyman* was *The Medical History,* Roth commenting, "As people advance in age, their biography narrows down to their medical biography. They spend time in the care of doctors and hospitals and pharmacies, and eventually, as happens here, they become almost identical to their medical biography."[39] Roth was months away from seventy-three when he wrote this comment. In the fifteenth-century morality play from which *Everyman* derives its title, often performed in cemeteries, a young man meets Death on the road, and exclaims in surprise, in a line Roth cherished, "Oh, Death, thou comest when I had thee least in mind." The very opening scene of the novel alludes to the funeral of Saul Bellow, an event that had a major impact on Roth. Death had haunted him since childhood: as a young boy, Roth would often study actuarial booklets with their morbidity tables that were lying about the home, reading material of his father the insurance salesman.[40]

The black cover of the first edition of *Everyman*, he pointed out to an inquisitive reporter, suggested a tombstone. Was the publisher worried about the impact on sales? "I don't care, I just want it my way," Roth stated, exerting his control again.[41] In preparation for writing *Everyman*, he spent two full days in a cemetery to watch how they dug graves, the process forcing him to think of death:

For years I had decided never to think about death. I have seen people die, of course, my parents, but it wasn't until a good friend of mine died in April that I experienced it as completely devastating. He was a contemporary. It doesn't say so in the agreement I signed, I didn't see that page in the contract, you know. As Henry James said on his deathbed: "Ah, here it comes, the big thing."[42]

The reference is to Bellow, who died on 5 April 2005, a loss that dispirited Roth. Bellow was implicitly a mentor, and even if, in their long relationship, there were periods of disagreement, toward the last decade of his life Bellow and Roth reunited. And he could not forget the death of his good friend George Plimpton two years earlier, his memorial service re-created in *Exit Ghost*.

Roth, continuing in his 2005 interview, recounted how eight years earlier at a memorial service for an author who worked at a magazine, all his girlfriends and mistresses appeared, women of all ages. They cried and left because they couldn't stand it: "That was the greatest tribute." "What will the women do at your funeral?" the reporter asked. "If they even show up . . . they will probably be screaming at the casket" was Roth's answer. "Passion doesn't change with age," he added, "but you change—you become older. The thirst for women becomes more poignant. And there is a power in the pathos of sex that it didn't have before. The pathos of the female body becomes more insistent. The sexual passion is always deep, but it becomes deeper."[43]

His attitude toward death had become that of "resignation towards reality. It no longer feels like a great injustice that I have to die." But why continue to write? He replies with a valuable self-assessment:

It's a horrible existence being a writer filled with deprivation. I don't miss specific people, but I miss life. I didn't discover that during the first 20 years, because I was fighting—in the ring with the literature. That fight was life, but then I discovered that I was in the ring all by myself. . . . It was the interests in life and the attempt to get life down on the pages which made me a writer—and then I discovered that, in many ways, I am standing on the outside of life.[44]

But with friends dying, life with Bloom resetting, and his experiences with medication leading to psychotic episodes, his outlook was bleak. Darkness now defined his life, which in many ways he needed to assess. Personal experiences, illness, and writing triangulated in a powerful "geometry of unhappiness."[45] The coalescence of these elements required the reevaluation of his life and work, which he did in three critical, transitional texts: *The Facts, Deception,* and *Patrimony,* preludes to *Operation Shylock* and his wild, breakout novel, *Sabbath's Theater,* all a prologue to the remarkable American Trilogy.

In a 31 March 1987 letter to Farrar, Straus and Giroux, Roth expressed his unhappiness with yet another publisher, telling his editor David Rieff that he was back at last in his London studio but that his nerves had been shattered for the past six months for reasons he did not fully understand. He refers to his loss of physical confidence, the knee operation and its consequences, and something worse: his realization that his relationship with Bloom was unraveling. He has come back to discover her in a terrible mess over British taxes, the result of nearly eight years of incompetency by her London accountants. Their London home has been undergoing renovation, and that, too, is a "fuck up." Even the baggies he bought to ice his knee leak. "Imagine the condoms," he writes. "This is truly the most wretched of civilized places."[46]

Bloom still asks him why he couldn't have waited to have his knee surgery there—surgery that still makes it painful for him to walk, although he has started an exercise program. Yes, he continues to Rieff, you were right when you said I was nostalgic for America. And I've fallen in love with my eighty-five-year-old father. But he also sees that the life he built in Connecticut is falling to pieces after all the work he did there and "all the feeling I sunk into that place." He confesses that he "feels stupid at being childless, besides, I am nostalgic [for] *everything.* There is a lesson in all this. There had better be."[47]

His discomfort with England actually began earlier, writing in February 1979 to James Atlas, having just sent off a final revision of *The Ghost Writer,* that here in London, "it's all garbage and rain. No bubonic as yet, but I'll keep you posted. And I won't be offended if you wash your hands after destroying this letter. There are rats in Leicester Square, which is now a garbage dump, as you may know, and some have even been spotted shopping in Sloane Square. It's not the great empire you knew and loved, Jim."[48]

Nearly ten years later, he tells Atlas when they met in New York that "he doesn't want to live in London, because there are no Jews there, no vitality." Modernism, he argues in his brilliant way, was a Jewish phenomenon, and "it never arrived in London as it did in other European capitals. London is a city of philistines. 'So I made a mistake, falling in love with an English woman. It happens. Life is up and down.'" He was bored with writing and the country.

"I don't want to be Lonoff. I walk down the road one way, then the other. There's no one to talk to. I've had to move my study into the house to be near Claire. And there's no one to talk to in London. The loneliness is unbearable, especially when I'm not working."[49] This view, of course, contrasts with his attitude in 1968 when he visited London with Ann Mudge and found it almost impossible to resist the women. Kings Road in Chelsea was especially tempting, as he had told Ted Solotaroff.

In their 1988 meeting, Roth talks about others who have suffered, recognizing that Atlas is depressed because he gave up writing a biography of Edmund Wilson and left his job at the New York Times. Claire has suffered because she married the wrong people and had no money at forty-three. Judith Thurman's husband left her and she had to move into a tiny studio apartment and was unmarried without children at forty. Bernard Avishai, Roth's age, did not get tenure at MIT and was turned down for a Guggenheim, but he recovered with a new job and a grant.

Two years later, when he and Atlas meet by chance on the street in New York, he took a card out of his wallet "with a drawing of a heart on it, and five arteries; an illustration of a quintuple bypass. 'I'm going to put this on the cover of my next book. It would have been great on The Counterlife.'" "This will happen to you," he gloomily forecasted, adding that he married Claire to take care of him in old age and after the current book he would retire. "I hate writing," he added, saying he lost all the notes for his last book. Atlas praised his article on Klíma and Roth praised journalism: "You don't have to make anything up. The story's there."[50]

Having just published The Counterlife, a story cycle told in five movements (possibly alluding to the five books of Moses), FSG thought that it would make the top ten on the bestseller list.[51] It didn't. The complicated narrative structure and confrontation with the issue of Israel and the Palestinians may have limited its appeal. Roth knew it would be a challenging book and praised Rieff, whose influence was important on his execution of the work. It helped to know I was talking to you, he writes in a letter of 28 January 1987.[52] He felt so disenchanted with the American literary scene that, according to David Hare, he supposedly paid the local store near Cornwall Bridge 25 cents extra to deliver his Sunday New York Times with the culture section ripped out. The critics who formerly charged him with obscenity were now accusing him of misogyny. Anything now goes, but this was intolerable to him.[53]

Despite winning the 1987 National Book Critics Circle Award for Fiction and the National Jewish Book Award for Fiction, sales of The Counterlife were disappointing and he thought FSG did a mediocre job of promoting the book. Some readers, like Susan Sontag, did praise the work; he had begun to correspond with her as early as January 1969, apologizing for a story about him in *New York Magazine* that began with a joke at her expense. Their friendship continued, intensified when her son David Rieff became his editor.

In 1977, Sontag had written to celebrate *The Professor of Desire*: "I laughed and sighed. And sighed." And then in 1986, she praised *The Counterlife*: "I devoured it, and I'm beaming," she begins, celebrating his ability with dialogue outshining that of any of his contemporaries, beginning with Updike. In *The Counterlife*, the dialogue is "beautifully judged [and] so propulsive," and she refers to the work as a "brave book." She loves the "screwing around with the plot," admitting that she has a weakness for metanarrative. In the novel, it creates a more intense relation to the characters. She especially likes the way the dice are loaded against Zuckerman, and she praises Henry's tirade at the end of "Judae" and Maria's letter at the conclusion of "Christendom." This is a comic epic of the highest order, she concludes. Zuckerman will always be "bested, though indomitable. Like Chichikov," referring to Gogol's wandering hero in *Dead Souls*.[54]

Mary McCarthy was another fan, although she raised several concerns. Writing from Paris she felt the facts were not always clear and found the work uneven and inconsistent, although she praised the Hebron section as the most outspoken and honest on the Israeli-Palestinian question she had ever read. She admired the independent existence and integrity of each section, but that seems to have evaporated in the last two episodes, especially in the representation of the gentiles, which she found irritating and offensive. There is more to Christmas, she writes, than "Jew hatred."[55] And why the big deal over circumcision? "The men of my generation were all circumcised." But, she adds, the novel "forcibly" reminded her that she was a Christian (SHP 115).

Roth replied within a week, generously offering a long defense of his work, beginning with whether or not all gentiles are anti-Semitic, which is what Zuckerman also hears in disbelief at the Jewish settlement on the West Bank (SHP 116). Zuckerman's engagement with the topic, overtly and covertly, keeps him off balance. Next, he explains why Zuckerman feels alienated by Christmas and finds Christianity liturgically overbearing but objects more to the aesthetics of Christianity and its services than its beliefs. The circumcision comment was a response to Maria's mother to confront her belief that the baby should be christened. But what was really behind it, Roth explains, was a response to Zuckerman's father's final word to his seemingly Jewish self-hating son, "Bastard." Having his new son circumcised is an act that contradicts his father's insult and accusation. Roth ends by confessing that uncircumcised men still fascinate him (SHP 119). He thought the exchange with McCarthy so valuable that he included it in his 2001 collection, *Shop Talk*.

Particularly striking in the text is the scene late in the novel where Zuckerman, dining with pregnant Maria in a French restaurant, overhears several anti-Semitic slurs from an older British woman, her shrunken husband hardly visible on the banquette. Roth is scathing in presenting her remarks, but more so is Zuckerman's response. In the novel, the woman is offended that the older and Jewish-looking Zuckerman has as his wife a young, beautiful English woman. The old woman claims there is a terrible smell in the room, Zuckerman knowing instantly that it's a "racial insult" (CL 291). Then, in typical Rothian, confrontational style, Zuckerman challenges the woman and her insults, threatening her that if she continues in such a manner, he will have her and her skeletal husband thrown out (CL 292–93). She is shocked into momentary silence. Maria then tries to defend the behavior of the woman, claiming she is either drunk or mad or both and is only a mindless prejudicial Englishwoman. No, Zuckerman says: she sees "a Jew defiling an English rose" and he won't stand for it (CL 294).

The moment is precise, but a final ironic note undercuts Zuckerman's victory, marked by a brandy and dessert. As he and Maria leave, he manages to overhear the elderly matron announce to the dining room, "What a disgusting couple!" (CL 295). The incident precipitating the scene actually occurred, which Bloom recounts in *Leaving a Doll's House* (LDH 180). There, in a moment underscoring Roth's displacement in London, she recalls that in a restaurant on their last visit to London together, they overheard a woman telling her companion that she bought a ring from a "little Jew" who "naturally" cheated her. Roth immediately got up, went over to the woman, called her a "scumbag," and marched out. Bloom was left at the table "convicted of guilt-by-nationality." When she returned home alone, he accused her of "criminal indifference" for not supporting him and his act (LDH 181). The scene in the novel expanded the incident.

Against this background, and encouraging this output, Roth found financial recovery through his new literary agent. When he returned from London in 1988 his finances were depleted and he had to sell both his Kafka manuscript and an oriental rug. But his situation would soon change once he met the ambitious Andrew Wylie, who often poached authors from other agents or even publishers. With his aggressive tactics, Wylie always managed to turn well-regarded literary authors into front-list successes. He showed them that they were worth more than they were currently earning, often through multivolume deals.[56] The sequence of Wylie's trophies began long before Roth, but at this time, the late 1980s, it restarted with Rieff, who stopped editing to write. Sontag followed: she was anxious about money, voicing disappointment with the way Straus had underpaid her, and was looking for a new home. In Wylie she found a personality that suited her own: chameleon-like and willing to see the world from the writer's perspective.[57] A hard-won, four-book contract worth $800,000 negotiated by Wylie in 1989 convinced her to stay with FSG.[58]

Roth was a more complicated catch, and there are apocryphal stories about Wylie's maneuvers competing with one another. One story tells of Wylie going up to Roth in Straus's living room and, in pursuit of his literary quarry, proceeding to recite scenes and dialogue from Roth's works. Another is that Wylie asked Rieff to arrange an introduction and, over lunch, again quoting passages to Roth, outlined what was possible by reshaping the structure of his publishing arrangements. At the time, Roth was working on *Deception* and thinking of *Patrimony*. He had done poorly with the paperback rights of *The Counterlife*, earning a quick $200,000 but giving up copyright. Wylie pointed out what he was missing and told Roth he could get $2 million for his next three books. FSG had just spent millions to keep Tom Wolfe, so why not Roth? An epic and public battle with Roger Straus of FSG began over Roth's future, now backed by Wylie, with money at the root of it.

Straus, countering Wylie, argued that Wolfe had written five bestsellers; Roth was lucky to sell on average little more than thirty thousand copies—and he didn't always earn back his advances. But Wylie also wanted foreign rights. Wylie and Roth did not want to leave FSG, according to Wylie, but they also wanted more money. FSG offered $700,000. They rejected it, and a tempestuous Straus called Roth and told him to "fuck off."[59] That summer, when Straus essentially fired Roth, Roth had his quintuple heart bypass and his father was seriously ill. Money was a necessity, and when Dick Snyder of Simon and Schuster offered $1.8 million (partly financed by S&S's new owners, Gulf + Western), Wylie and Roth had a deal. The failed FSG negotiations made the press, and Wylie sent Straus a letter correcting certain misinformation.[60] In a pique, Straus sent Wylie Roth's sales figures: no title broke forty thousand copies. And Straus was right: the appearance of *Deception*,

Roth's first title for Simon and Schuster, despite a splashy advertising campaign, sold less than *The Counterlife*, which peaked at thirty-six thousand hardback copies.

The news of the publishers' feud led to a long story by Roger Cohen in the *New York Times* of 9 April 1990 with the headline "Roth's Publishers: The Spurned and the Spender." It began with Simon and Schuster's poster for *Deception*: a man's hand grasping the naked flank of a shapely woman. His new publisher favored the sensational image to get Roth out of the dull rut dug by FSG, according to Wylie. Cohen goes on to analyze the commercial value of Roth's writing, noting that FSG had published nine titles by Roth since 1977 and paid him nearly $180,000 for more recent titles, with only moderate sales. When asked about the *contretemps*, a deadpan and ironic Roth replied, "This is not a subject that interests me."[61]

Wylie made an important visual point: the covers of Roth's books published by FSG suggested they were difficult and literary; reading them you joined a special, almost elite FSG readership. By contrast, the new *Deception* poster and cover strike a widely different note: a book for any adult reader, preferably one who mixes Danielle Steel with Judith Krantz, Scott Turow, or James Michener, all of whom had bestsellers in 1990. Simon and Schuster hopes for large sales, printing nearly 100,000 copies of the novel, twice the FSG number for any of his works, but, Dick Snyder suggested, aggressive marketing might make the difference, especially with a visual if suggestive link to *Portnoy's Complaint*, which had no image on the cover, just striking lettering over a bright yellow jacket. But concern at Simon and Schuster grew high when, after entering the bestseller list at number fifteen, *Deception* fell off a week later.

An earlier article, also in the *Times*, headlined "Roth Changes Houses," summarized the shift to S&S and quoted Wylie as saying the purported figure of $1.2 million was "too low, by a substantial margin."[62] He may have been including the presale of paperback rights to Pocket Books when suggesting there was a higher figure, or just taunting Roger Straus. A report of a lunch between the two publishers floated even higher figures, Wylie telling Straus he could get $3 million to $5 million for three books, but that he would let Straus have them for $1.5. "Ridiculous," Straus replied. Roth gets paid around $160,000 for world rights and they break just about even, he said. But he wanted to keep Roth, so he offered between $500,000 and $700,000. Declining to give his version of the story, Wylie wittily said, "I think one of the reasons Roger is such a skilled publisher is that he's such a marvelous inventor of stories." Simon and Schuster was happy with what they paid because, among other factors, Roth sold well overseas.[63]

Despite the groundbreaking three-book deal with Simon and Schuster, which gained as much notoriety as praise, Roth struck out with his first title for them. Kazin called *Deception* clever but forgettable. Roth, he continued, lives mentally in a tunnel packed in on all sides by only two subjects:

> Roth as novelist, Roth vis-à-vis women. His intensity gets more and more subterranean. . . . His intense, afflicted, sometimes screaming sense of his own Jewishness comes down, ritually, to a kind of shell game. Things are never what they seem; he likes to work on the reader, even to show him up. . . . And what I hadn't expected in our insignificant relationship is how easily aggrieved he gets. . . .
>
> Jewish intensity—to get so over-involved in the smallest details of living. In Roth the kitchen has been replaced by the bedroom. . . . Of course, this intensity turned out to be irrelevant to the most frightful details of living. Like getting killed just for being a Jew.[64]

But if the first work disappointed, the second (*Patrimony*) was a critical success, but again only with modest sales despite Roth's going on an uncommon book tour. *Operation Shylock* was also a commercial and critical disappointment. Reviews were tepid, ranging from Updike in the *New Yorker* to *Publishers Weekly*, which criticized the entangled "Philip Roths" and unnerving plot. All of this disappointed Roth and Simon and Schuster.[65] The text seemed improvisational, with even Roth at one point seeking to escape from his own absurdist plot. Straus may have gotten his revenge. After fulfilling his three-book deal, Roth jumped back to Houghton Mifflin (and more money), where *Sabbath's Theater*, at 451 pages one of his longest works, did hit a home run, winning the National Book Award for Fiction, although again sales were modest. Wylie had set the new rules, and they were the ones that Roth now played by, but Straus may have gotten his payback and saved some money in the process.

At this time, Roth felt an increasing need to turn to American subjects, a confirmation of his resettlement. Coinciding with his return was a period of self-assessment: he had been writing *The Facts* and confronting his own mortality through the illness of his father, to whom he devoted himself, and then his unexpected quintuple bypass surgery, an event hidden from his father to avoid excessive worry. Roth told him that he would not hear from him for several days because he was at a Yale literary conference as a last minute stand-in (PAT 227). But in the process of describing his father's plight, Roth also came to understand what his father taught him: not the conventional American dad stuff, nor sports, but "something coarser" that came natural to an undereducated father with whom he united in facing up to anti-Semitism. What he learned was "the vernacular. He *was* the vernacular, unpoetic and expressive and point-blank, with all the vernacular's glaring limitations and all its durable force" (PAT 181). He was, Roth candidly writes, "*the* father, with everything there is to hate in a father and everything there is to love" (PAT 180). Hate and love joined.

The death of Herman Roth led his son to perform two contradictory acts the same year: marrying Claire Bloom on 29 April 1990 after fifteen years together and publishing *Deception*, a novel of marital betrayal. *Patrimony* appeared the year after. The death of his father allowed him to drop some of the masks and write more directly of his life, although contradictions persisted, a mix of the negative and positive: events in London, his Halcion episode, events at Silver Hill, anger at Bloom, the death of his father, and marriage. Life inescapable, underscored by a simple Jane Eyre–like statement by Bloom in her summary of the period: "I was Philip's wife at last" (LDH 190).

On the marriage—Bloom had asked Roth if it wasn't time—Gore Vidal, who knew them both, summed up the likelihood of its success: "He's tense; she's tense. . . . Each is neurotic. . . . It's always best to stay out of other people's divorces. And their civil wars." Earlier, Vidal had warned her not to get involved with "Portnoy."[66] When Bloom published *Leaving a Doll's House*, she ensured maximum publicity, obtaining a sizable advance from *Vanity Fair* for an excerpt before the release of the book in October 1996. Bloom was forty-seven when she began her romance with Roth, but at sixty-five, she, too, needed financial security.

When they began their relationship in 1975, Roth was suffering from severe shoulder pain, and many of his early letters described his problems and his impatience and distress with his ailment and eagerness to be with her. For relief, he had a toughminded physiotherapist who saw him three times a week, only five feet tall but she was strong enough to dig into his trapezius muscle and as a bonus offered literary analysis. "Do you know your best book she asked one morning? *Letting Go*. . . . So I get literary criticism too for my 40 bucks a shot."[67] He was also reading a great deal of Colette and Chekhov, telling Bloom to read Chekhov's "A Boring Story" and "Lady with a Lapdog." But he struggled, not only with a new electric typewriter, his physiotherapist, and his aches; asked if life got better, he answered, "Read Anton Chekhov, pal, dead at 44. We are lucky it doesn't get disastrous daily—that's the blessing."[68]

Further comments from this early period of their romance stress his longing for her, his sexual drive, his ailments, his teaching—he was at Penn for a term—and his pleasure in just thinking of her and her expected arrival at his country home, always with a sense of humor. Should she bring boots for walking in the forest when she visits in early spring, she asks? "Depends how much whipping you want to do or have done, but it won't snow," he replies.[69] He casually refers to his writing (comically calling it "my High Art") as always a struggle and what he does on his trips to New York.[70]

He often drove to the city when Bloom wasn't there, and one of his more intriguing urban episodes was viewing a pornographic film between errands. The title was *Candy's Candy* or *Candice Candy*. "Christ, the sperm was really flying in that theater. I thought I was in an air raid," he tells Bloom, but "miraculously, I came out without even a shrapnel wound." In its way, the film was remarkable, full of "startling erotic imagery and rather engaging acting. . . . You may think I'm waxing Roth but I am just seeing what was there."[71] The stars were Béatrice Harnois (Candy) and Sylvia Bourdon (Candice), whom Roth found particularly appealing for her Brigitte Bardot good looks.

Bloom's absence and anticipated arrival only accelerated Roth's erotic desire. In his letters, he writes frequently of their love-making, one letter opening, "I just have bodies on my mind this morning. I should be working, and I will, but felt you might want to know that I am pining in all ways and will gladly do it in the road, in the garden, in the salad dressing, in the tub, in the basement, the attic, the woods, the car, the *trunk* of the car, even . . . in the glove compartment. I'm yours."[72]

But he also enjoyed his country property and nature, taking great pride in the apple, ash, lilac, and maple trees that surrounded the house, the studio, and the barn. The flowers were key, and spring meant replanting; he would head to the village of Washington in Litchfield County to buy begonias and some myrtle, as well as peonies and irises. Later, he and a friend would traipse through the woods with *Peterson's Field Guide* to identify wildflowers: pasture thistle, wild pinks, joe-pye-weed. Merry Levov in *American Pastoral* would learn these very names at her 4-H club in Old Rimrock. Many of these details would appear in *American Pastoral* and *The Human Stain,* where the countryside receives proper but not overt attention.

In January 1990, after fifteen years together and despite Roth's decision to return permanently to America in 1988, Bloom asked Roth to marry her. On

2 February, after proper consideration, he sent her a letter while she was in a London revival of Ibsen's *When We Dead Awaken* at the Almeida Theater in Islington (her first performance on the London stage since 1977), asking her to marry, but impersonally signed with only "an Admirer" (LDH 188).

The marriage took place on 29 April 1990 in New York in the apartment of Barbara Epstein, coeditor of the *New York Review of Books.* Attending were Aaron Asher and his wife, Melvin Tumin and his wife, Norman Manea and his wife, Ross Miller, Maletta Pfeiffer and her husband, and Roth's brother Sandy. The best man was Bernard Avashi. Conducting the ceremony was his former lawyer Shirley Fingerhood, by then a New York Supreme Court justice. Dominque Nabokov, a close friend of Epstein, took photographs. She had photographed Roth on several occasions for French magazines. Shadowing the event was a prenuptial agreement Roth had drawn up by his lawyer Hélèn Kaplan that allowed him, should he decide to terminate the marriage, to be free of any financial or moral obligations to Bloom. She was upset, recognizing her limited rights, but two days before the wedding she signed (LDH 189).

From almost the beginning of their relationship, Roth faced challenges from Bloom, who demonstrated increasing demoralization: separation from her grown daughter caused depression, competition for acting roles was fierce, and life in rural Connecticut was dull. Roth sensed this and tried to satisfy her needs but found it more and more frustrating and distressing. His own increasing health problems added to the strain, although he found new energy when he met the married Minette Marrin (age thirty) in London and began an affair with her in 1982. He was forty-nine.

Minette worked for the BBC and was later a columnist and reviewer for the *Daily Telegraph* and the *Sunday Telegraph.* She was born in California but moved to England and renounced her U.S. citizenship. She attended Cambridge, where she won a *Granta* short story competition. Following five years in Hong Kong as a journalist, she returned to London in 1978 and began work with BBC TV documentaries, later becoming co-presenter of the BBC2 arts program, *Saturday Review.* She often met Roth in his Notting Hill studio, where he worked daily. He was stunned by her staggeringly fluent language and intelligence, qualities he gave to the unidentified lover in *Deception* and Maria Freshfield in *The Counterlife.* After she would depart from her frequent visits, he would often attempt to re-create their conversation and her intoxicating voice in his notebook. Her diction, syntax, and locutions startled.

The irony of *Deception* is that later, when he left a copy of the typescript in a binder in their New York apartment, Roth's latent wish was that Bloom would read it, which she did. She was appalled at the portrait of the whining middle-aged Jewish actress named Claire, whose husband, Philip, seduces younger women. Bloom blew up and insisted he change the character's name. If he didn't, she would sue. Reluctantly, he agreed. As a peace offering (or was it a bribe?), he offered her a Bulgari gold snake ring with an emerald head, as detailed in *Leaving a Doll's House* (183–84), purchased with the assistance of Judith Thurman.

But the stress between them was constant: at the beginning of their living together in London, it meant living with her daughter in the same home at 55 Fawcett Street, Chelsea. At one point, Roth gave Bloom a letter: he hated disturbances while working and insisted that the sixteen-year-old Anna had to leave the home or he would. A dormitory room at the Guild Hall was the answer; he had already inquired. Torn between Roth and her daughter, Bloom painfully chose Roth (LDH 157–58).

Ten years later, in July 1986, partly to ease his continued rupture with Anna, he bought her a bed, but he made it clear that it was only for her: if he learned that a "goy is sleeping on the other half," he'd jump out the window. Then you'd have to live with that, he wrote, and you'll hate the bed and wish it was never made. Half in jest and half in anger, he ended his note, "If you have any feelings for me at all, KEEP ALL GOYIM OUT OF THE BED!"[73]

Bloom's choice of Roth over Anna did not interfere with his affair with Minette, which lasted three years, and, following that, a longer relationship with Maletta Pfeiffer, from roughly 1978 to 1994. The Swedish-born physiotherapist originally lived in a house a half-mile from Roth and was thirty-eight when she met him. The intermittent affair initially began through her work as a physiotherapist aiding him with his back pain in her increasingly successful practice, which soon became the leading physical therapist group in the region.[74] Through the 1980s, especially during his difficult time after his knee operation and then hospitalization for depression in 1993, Maletta played a critical role in his recovery. She also became an instrumental figure in the writing of *Sabbath's Theater* as the origin and source of the exuberant Drenka.

Importantly, Maletta provided support during Claire's neglect. In June 1993, for example, after receiving an honorary degree from Amherst, Roth's pain was so great that on the way back to Cornwall Bridge, he had to stop the car every twenty or thirty minutes to get out and stretch. During one of his stops, he called Maletta to meet him at his home. Claire was in London and he was emotionally sinking under the weight of his protracted and prolonged discomfort. Emotional upset set it off, he believed, exactly what happened when Claire returned and began crying because her daughter wasn't there. She hated the Connecticut isolation and was oblivious to his suffering. Even his brother, Sandy, who flew out to help him, quickly realized that it was Claire who was harming him psychologically. Maletta is likely the "Erda" (the name of the Earth goddess) Bloom refers to in *Leaving a Doll's House* (233–34).

In 1993, in pain and depressed and finding no solace from Bloom, he had his psychiatrist approve a stay at Silver Hill. Visitors included Wylie, Thurman, Howard Stein, and Aaron Asher, but the only one who regularly came was Maletta. She brought a certain "brightness" and calm; she could handle a crisis. Bloom could not and, in fact, had gone back to London to be with her daughter. At the end of two stays at Silver Hill, each of approximately eighteen days, he knew he was finished with Bloom.

However, Roth could turn against even Maletta. Despite their intimacy and his drawing from her life for the behavior of Drenka and the powerful deathbed scene in the hospital where they both candidly recall their prurient actions together, nothing stopped him from undermining her and their relationship. Though he found her sexually irresistible, he could angrily call her "sinful" and her actions "slanderous" for telling Bloom and Francine du Plessix Gray that she only began to sleep with Roth when he was a psychiatric patient. It was a lie, he writes, promoting herself as a sort of "erotic Florence Nightingale," when in fact they had been carrying on since the late 1970s. Betrayed again by a woman.[75]

Another challenge bringing forward the angry Roth was an attack on his friend Edward (Ted) Hoagland, a recognized nature and travel writer who, as an adjunct professor at Bennington, was disqualified from his position because he had criticized anal intercourse as unhealthy. Reports of the incident appeared in the local newspaper the *Bennington Banner*. Roth, in a letter to the college of 17 June 1991, attacked the action and put a series of questions to the administration, beginning with what is it about anal sex that places it beyond all criticism and judgment? Was heterosexual anal sex as sacred as homosexual anal sex? If there are women on the faculty who disapprove of heterosexual anal sex, are they considered qualified to teach literature?

Roth continued: "Is vaginal sex as sacred as anal sex?" "Is it beyond criticism, discussion, satire, or parody at Bennington? If it isn't, why isn't it?"

Next is fellatio—is that considered sacred at Bennington? If not, why not? And what if he questioned the "sanctity of masturbation—would that have disqualified him from teaching at your college?" Or the Ten Commandments or capitalism or the American flag? What of circumcision? He concludes his outburst by asking if Bennington provides all applicants a list of acceptable sexual and social behavior that are considered beyond criticism?[76] The letter is a late Portnovian explosion attacking the conservative, distorted idea of sex at Bennington, while standing up for his friend.

At more or less the same time, literary matters were taking on a competitive tone, notably with John Updike. Roth and Updike maintained a friendly rivalry up to 1993, followed by a breakup and then a partial resumption at the end of their lives. Each published their first books in 1959: Roth's *Goodbye, Columbus* and Updike's *Poorhouse Fair*. *Rabbit Run* appeared in 1960, *Letting Go* in 1962, the year of Updike's *Pigeon Feathers* (short stories). Nineteen-sixty-eight saw the appearance of Updike's scandalous *Couples*; the following year was *Portnoy*. The in-tandem publishing continued with *Rabbit Redux* in 1971, the same year as Roth's satire *Our Gang*; in 1976 it was Updike's *Marry Me*; the following year it was Roth's *The Professor of Desire*. In 1981, *Rabbit Is Rich*, Updike having sent Roth prepublication proof and Roth heaping praise, telling David Plante (and Herman Roth) that Updike "knows so much, about golf, about porn, about kids, about America. I don't know anything about anything.... Here I live in the country and I don't even know the names of trees. I'm going to give up writing" (CWPR 151).

The two also had playful exchanges at lunch and socializing. Updike had his publisher send Roth a copy of his poems, *Midpoint*, but retitled *Poor Goy's Complaint*. Roth comically addressed an early letter to Updike at "50 Labor-in-Vain Road, Ipswich, Massachusetts 01938."[77] They sent each other teasing notes, Roth warning Updike to stay away from Newark: "Haven't I stayed away from the Amish in order not to tread on your toes?"[78]

The same year *Rabbit Is Rich* came out (1981), Roth published *Zuckerman Unbound*, and the following year Updike's *Bech Is Back* appeared, a set of short stories about the Jewish writer Henry Bech. The competition continued: in 1987 Updike's *Trust Me* (short stories) and Roth's *The Counterlife*; 1990 *Rabbit at Rest* and *Deception*.

Socially, they first met with their wives in 1959 at the home of Roth's Houghton Mifflin editor Jack Leggett outside of Boston, and they continued to meet intermittently during the 1960s, when Roth spent two summers on Martha's Vineyard with Ann Mudge. A long argument over the Vietnam

War, which Updike supported and Roth opposed, at the home of *New Yorker* writer Bernard Taper led to a sustained disagreement but inspired a similar scene in *Rabbit Redux*. Again, informal lunches and dinners followed when Roth was in Boston or Updike in New York.

Updike reviewed almost all of Roth's books in the *New Yorker*, and both read each other's books carefully. Roth sometimes wrote with praise to Updike and once called him from the Wyndham Hotel in New York after he had just finished *Roger's Version* to tell him how wonderful it was. In the late 1980s, another connection emerged: Roth's friend R. B. Kitaj provided six illustrations for Updike's *In Memoriam Felis Felis* (1989). But there was often friction. Despite Roth's believing he was in competition only with himself, there was an implicit race for recognition, at least in the eyes of others, Updike pulling ahead.

Updike's unsympathetic review (Roth called it "mean spirited") of *Operation Shylock* in the *New Yorker* in March 1993 created a split, Updike bristling at Roth's relentless self-centeredness and criticizing the novel as "an orgy of argumentation."[79] Roth had invested a great deal of his literary capital in the novel, Bloom noting that he was wildly optimistic about its success when he finished it in the winter of 1992; he talked about it incessantly (LDH 191). It was the second book dedicated to Bloom; the first was *The Professor of Desire*.

Angry over Updike's comments, Roth threw the magazine across the room—he and Bloom were at 6 West 77th Street—and refused to see Updike again (NOT 126). He did not, however, cry because of the review, as Bloom claimed in her autobiography, where she also misleadingly wrote that it was the Updike review and negative criticism of *Shylock* that sent Roth to Silver Hill in 1993. In 2008, however, in a *Daily Telegraph* interview, Updike modified his views of Roth, generously giving him the edge, but not before he said Roth wrote about people who want to be nice but can't. Updike emphasized parallels but when asked if they were still friends, despite not speaking to each other for nearly ten years, Updike answered, "Guardedly." But he did admire his work, although more the early rather than later books. And he granted him the "upper hand" in their rivalry, adding as a kind of dig, "There's no reason to be unhappy, except in art, perhaps, where it's an irritant that produces art."[80]

But Roth persisted in keeping score. In a letter to the *New York Times* dated 9 April 2014, the day after Dwight Garner reviewed Adam Begley's new biography of Updike, Roth wrote an impatient letter contradicting the statement that he checked into Silver Hill in response to Updike's review. Garner had, in fact, surmised that Roth denied that his depression was "Updikian in nature," but it might not be correct. Roth pointedly refuted any such claim, writing that for weeks and months after Updike's 15 March 1993 piece in the *New Yorker*, he was teaching, giving readings from *Patrimony*, and completing the first chapters of *Sabbath's Theater*. And on 19 March 1993, just after Updike's review appeared, he enjoyed his sixtieth birthday party with friends in Connecticut and in early June received an honorary degree from Amherst. Hardly the actions of a depressive. But "enjoy" is not the right word for the party, held at the home of his doctor and close friend C. H. Huvelle with fourteen guests; Roth was in excruciating back pain despite the entertainment: a magician he had met at the Hotel Windermere in Chicago. He hired a photographer, and the pictures document not only his discomfort but Bloom's detachment from Roth and the event.

He was anything but incapacitated, and his 2014 letter to the *Times* shows again his aggressiveness in clarifying what he felt was a wrong. Characteristically, and twenty-one years after the fact, Roth was unwilling to let errors from the past remain errors. Of course, the reasons for checking in to Silver Hill were quite other, although Updike had not held his criticism in check. The review opens, "Some readers may feel there has been too much Philip Roth in the writer's recent books," which exhibit his "narrowing, magnifying fascination with himself."[81]

However, they did fall out completely when Updike mentioned Bloom's autobiography in a *New York Review of Books* essay on literary biography in 1999. Updike appeared to take Bloom's side, referring to her as "the wronged ex-wife of Philip Roth" who shows him to be, "as their marriage rapidly unraveled, neurasthenic to the point of hospitalization, adulterous, callously selfish, and financially vindictive."[82] Roth wrote another letter of correction, but Updike responded by saying that the corrections were unnecessary. Roth again denied that the *Operation Shylock* review had any connection with his depression. And he was right, as his medical history confirms. They never met or spoke again. But when he reprinted his essay-review, Updike did make the correction Roth requested and notified Roth, who believed that a lawyer had advised Updike to do so. Despite everything, Roth still believed that Updike was "our greatest man of letters" and the writer closest to him in stature; he reluctantly attended his memorial service at the New York Public Library in March 2009.

In the late 1980s, Roth attempted to summarize his life, but with a cautionary sign. His seventeenth title was *The Facts*, its subtitle *A Novelist's*

Autobiography. It begins with a warning: "The facts are never just coming at you but are incorporated by an imagination that is formed by your previous experience. Memories of the past are not memories of facts but memories of your imaginings of the facts" (FAC 8). The writing and effort of the book is a modestly disguised attempt to clarify if not document (or pseudo-document) his life up until Bloom. Framing the central autobiographical narrative is an opening address to Zuckerman and a closing rebuttal by Zuckerman. The text itself is an incomplete account of Roth's life, a survey of his early education, marriage, illnesses, and recovery in the face of Zuckerman's insults, criticisms, and overly determined point of view, which emphasizes Roth's pull toward "broken women" and his affection for May (Ann Mudge) because she was placid and lacked Josie's (Maggie's) "working-class harshness" (FAC 182).

The uncertainty of facts was something Roth long questioned: for him, an "American fact" was always a disputed truth and he labored to evade them, cover them up, or mislead those in search of them. His various narrative voices, in both his fiction and nonfiction, plus the introduction of characters with his name, created a series of neo-facts that have taken readers and critics down dead ends and false starts. And Roth reveled in the deception, castigating readers for wanting to read his fiction as fact and fact as fiction, failing to see their fundamental misconceptions and general error in believing in the truth of facts.[83] Zuckerman's position is Roth's, seeing facts as decoys, believing that getting people right is "not what living is about anyway. It's getting them wrong that is living." Only by "getting them wrong" do we know "we're alive" (AP 35). Ironically, it's writing that "turns you into somebody who's always wrong" (AP 63). Knowing this, he still felt that some form of autobiography was justified.

Roth distrusted facts, which, of course, makes the title of his 1988 autobiography ironic. To him, they were always distorted and untrustworthy, hence his discomfort with the idea of biography. Experience he did not question, but the fact and meaning of an experience was always questionable. In his presentation of life based so strongly on his personal details, he offered enough adjustment to make the facts look like fiction and the reverse, often hiding or disguising the actual event.

A corresponding representation of his play with facts at this time is a 1993 essay from the *New York Times Book Review* entitled "A Bit of Jewish Mischief." In it he asserts that in January 1989 he was "caught up in a Middle East crisis all my own, a personal upheaval" when someone his age bearing a resemblance to him and calling himself "Philip Roth" turned up in Jerusalem shortly before he did.[84] Was this true or false? Presented as fiction (or factual fiction) in *Operation Shylock*, the work so confused booksellers that many contacted Roth's editor Michael Korda at Simon and Schuster for guidance on how to promote and place the book.[85]

In the novel, Israel became the backdrop for not one but two "Philip Roths," an imitator (the so-called Moishe Pipik, Yiddish for "Moses Bellybutton") and a fictitious figure named "Philip Roth" who goes off to confront the imitator. Through the act of naming, Roth has possessed the other Philip Roth, aka Moishe Pipik, and assimilated him into his own family history. Pipik was actually a treasured figure in the Roth family folklore when Roth was a child. He would appear after periodic weekend visits to Meema Gitcha's, his great-aunt (paternal grandmother's sister) and a widow, in Danbury, Connecticut. The visits were like a return to the Old Country, a five-hour car ride to the folk land of Galicia, with aunts and uncles, cousins and his grandmother, the most "Jewishy-Yiddishy event of my childhood," he told Ben Taylor. In order to assure Meema that the Roths returned safely to Newark, Bess Roth would place a collect call to Meema under the name "Moishe Pipik." Comedy came from the non-Jewish operator mispronouncing the name. There was an element of ritual in the act, while tricking the phone company and asserting their Jewish identity through Yiddish, not English.[86]

After a mock preface where "Philip Roth" the writer reports that his novel is drawn from his notebooks of an Israeli trip, he begins with an arrival in Israel, where he meets his most vigorous reader, himself, but in the form of an imposter. The dueling Roths echo the narrative Roth in *The Facts* and his own self-created commentator, Zuckerman. But in *Operation Shylock*, history is the mediator, whether it is of Israel and the Palestinians or of the trial of the accused Nazi camp guard John Demjanjuk which Roth, both in person and as a character in the novel, attended as he pursued the facts of his fiction which only indirectly arrive at the truth. What does triumph here, and in other Rothian fictions, is the truth of subjectivity under the contradictory and often opposing elements of the self. In *Operation Shylock*, Israel poses an identity crisis for diasporic Jews because of its symbolic power as a Jewish homeland.

Roth's constant play with the facts, narratively and historically, and creation of his double are signs of his ability to rejuvenate himself, a necessary stage as he freed himself mentally, sexually, and imaginatively from the constrictions of England and Bloom. There is a reason for calling the male

protagonist of *Deception* "Philip," although he bowed to pressure and eliminated the name "Claire" for the dowdy actress in the novel. Counterfictions
are necessary to understand the truthfulness of his life. Zuckerman becomes
a filter: writing is, and is not, deception. But Roth argues that it's all fiction
and only fools would see it as fact. Yet beneath it all is fact—of a sort.

Complicating the nature of *Operation Shylock* and its irregular reception
was the subtitle, *A Confession*. That immediately raised questions of reliability, which the end itself comically addresses: the Roth character takes up
the offer to work as a spy for Israel, traveling to foreign countries. But the
twelve-thousand-word account of his adventures, we learn, is deemed too
sensitive to Israeli security and had to be deleted from the book. The ending
becomes a deflationary epilogue set five years later, with the protagonist
meeting his handler Smilesburger over chopped herring at the unnamed
Barney Greengrass's in New York, where he even fits in a cameo by Ted
Solotaroff and his son. But now, Roth is paid off for canceling the original
ending. Has John le Carré met Groucho Marx amid the onion bagels and
whitefish?[87]

Even the narrator questions the veracity of his own story. As the work
becomes increasingly critical of itself and its own "improbable reality," it also
plays with its own internal references, as when the narrator, mentioning the
Berkshires, cites Lonoff and *The Ghost Writer* (OPS 360–61, 370). Further
twists include Roth's letter to Jinx about Pipik, aka "Philp Roth," stating that
he couldn't understand the excesses "he was driven to by me—or his mys-
tique of me," but that he, Roth, offers to ghostwrite what Pipik couldn't complete, ultimately becoming "his imposter's creature" or imposter's imposter
(OPS 374, 376). Here, Roth is parodying and reacting again to fame, showing
through comedy his own ability to understand how it so powerfully affects
others. Near the end of the book, Smilesburger offers an incisive remark
about Roth: "Name a raw nerve and you recruit it," adding that his book
is not a quiet book but "a *suicidal* book, even within the extremely Jewish
stance you assume" (OPS 397). Smilesburger then pronounces the Rothian
manifesto: "There is no verbal excess, no angry word, no evil speech that is
unutterable to a Jew with an unguarded tongue" (OPS 397). But this warning
of *loshon hora* (derogatory speech) means little to Roth in or out of the book.

A final "Note to the Reader" reminds us that "this book is a work of fiction,"
highlighted by the confusing last sentence of the entire text: "This confession
is false" (OPS 399). Roth wants it every which way, even when he purports to
tell the truth.

10

"Psychoanalysis and Laxatives," or Democracy in America

> I met Philip Roth. He has a novel coming out and another done.
> I looked at him. "Psychoanalysis and laxatives" he said.
> —Bernard Malamud in Philip Davis,
> *Bernard Malamud: A Writer's Life*, 2007

Roth's comic reply to Malamud was not entirely in jest. Nor his remark "I write fiction and I'm told it's autobiography, I write autobiography and I'm told it's fiction, so since I'm so dim and they're so smart, let *them* decide what it is or it isn't" (DE 184). But before he reengaged with America in the late 1980s, he faced charges of misogyny and bipolarity. He took offense to both, securing letters from two of his psychiatrists—he continued intermittently with therapy for twenty-five years after leaving Kleinschmidt—affirming that he was never diagnosed with bipolar disorder, as his first biographer suggested (NOT 87).[1]

The misogyny charge was more widespread and inflammatory. This long-lasting claim resurfaced in 2011 when Carmen Callil, literary critic and founder of the feminist publisher Virago (which published Bloom's memoir in 1996), asserted Roth's misogynist writing (as well as repetitiousness and general unreadability) should have disqualified him from receiving the Man Booker International Prize. When he did in May 2011, she resigned.

But many believed Roth was undoubtedly a misogynist, confirmed by Bloom in *Leaving a Doll's House* and inflamed by Vivian Gornick, who later wrote, "If in Bellow misogyny was like bile emanating from a festering wound, in Roth it was lava pouring out of an active volcano."[2] Animosity toward women took time to develop in his work, but when it hit, she argued, it hit big, with "fucking" replacing "tenderness." Portnoy was proof, as Roth happily showed: "chasing cunt" was his goal, "and *shiske* cunt to boot!

Chasing it, sniffing it, lapping it, *shtupping* it, but above all, *thinking about it*. . . . I want what's coming to me. *My* G.I. bill—real American ass!" (PC 101, 236). Gornick's assault in the *Village Voice* of 6 December 1976, "Why Do These Men Hate Women?," contained this jab: "So much influential prose, so little empathy."[3] And anger is again part of the mix: "For the first time in Jewish-American literature, woman-hating is openly equated with a consuming anger at what it means to be pushed to the margin." The argument became reduced to an "impassioned equation of woman-hating with being Jewish-in-America." Her attack culminated with the provocative claim "Not only are women monstrous in *Portnoy* but in all the books that followed for the next thirty years." She concludes, "The women are monstrous because for Philip Roth women are monstrous."[4]

As Gornick had it, Roth's women are only sexual objects, further vilified as they become the victims of older men, as Kepesh treats Consuela in *The Dying Animal* or Coleman Silk with Faunia Farley in *The Human Stain*. Few women can stand up to men: two exceptions are the Israeli Sabra at the end of *Portnoy's Complaint*, and the Czech actress Eva Kalinova from *The Prague Orgy*. But Roth's one-dimensional women constantly attract, as seen in the Monkey from *Portnoy's Complaint*, Birgitta and her roommate in *The Professor of Desire*, or Pegeen in *The Humbling*. This is Gornick's estimate; others felt each of these women displayed complex identities.

Roth did not take these charges "lying down" but responded in a series of private documents, detailing his respectful and admiring treatment of the women with whom he had relationships and the many professional associations he maintained with women, beginning with his first agent, Candida Donadio, and continuing with Shirley Fingerhood, the lawyer who represented him in his separation from Maggie, and Roslyn Schloss, a freelance copyeditor who worked with Roth for over thirty years. Other important female friendships included Lillian Hellman, Cynthia Ozick, Susan Sontag, Edna O'Brien, Hermione Lee, Veronica Geng, Janet Malcolm, Judith Thurman, Claudia Roth Pierpont, Wendy Strothman (editor), and, more recently, the writers Louise Erdrich, Nicole Krauss, and Zadie Smith. While he may have portrayed women unsympathetically—the Maggie period and then Bloom curdled his empathy for them—he did argue that the women he loved he treated respectfully and with warmth. In personal documents, he outlines how he contributed to their financial and material well-being, from replacing old cars to paying off student debts and, in one instance, making it possible to acquire a small home. Documents support his claims.

Roth's list is long with appreciative remarks on all with the exception of Maggie and Bloom. In addition to the list, he kept an extensive photo album of his girlfriends.[5] Why he never settled with one woman as a partner had more to do with his need for independence than dislike. Independence, freedom, and "intensity of experience" are what he always sought. Once the women began to make demands and he started to feel vulnerable, he drew back and found more to dislike than like. Yet a deep-seated ambivalence persisted: half the time he sought stability and love, but that played against his innate determination to be free. Independence battled domesticity. These irreconcilable elements brought havoc. His goal to be "strong in the magic," the magic of writing, was constantly at odds with his need to be loved and attached to someone he could trust (NOT 210). Ironically, it was a man at this time who received his most intense attention: his father.

Of writing *Patrimony*, his account of his father's death, Roth told Kazin that almost to the end his father managed to be obstinately himself. His loss was so powerful for Roth that after his death, he told Bloom that he would take an ad in the *New York Review of Books* that read "Unemployed son, 56 years of experience, excellent credentials, seeks new position."[6] Roth lost not only his father but himself, his self-identity as a son. His precarious identity gone, he lost his footing. Overshadowing his grief was the loss of a stable identity, and the aim of *Patrimony* to reassert that identity. Philip Roth, not Herman Roth, is the actual subject of the book; what he hopes for, stated in the final two pages of the work, is confirmation that he will remain the "little son" forever (PAT 237–38).

Kazin, ensnared by his own difficult father, wrote in a journal entry, "One looks for one's father—one looks—one looks and then one realizes: I *am* my father."[7] In an honest review of Roth's book, Kazin noted how Roth loved and resisted his father, that as Roth witnesses his father's "hard edged resistance to death, futile but wonderful," he "makes himself a duplicate of his father." Scenes with a "forceful attention to object, people and the dead" provide resilience in the text. And in a comment applicable to all of Roth's writing, Kazin notes that Roth has a "remarkable sense of *fact*. And in this book death is the supreme fact hanging over human existence."[8] Herman Roth died in the hospital in Elizabeth, New Jersey, in 1989.

Writing a straightforward account of his father's illness and death was for Roth the only way to deal with its reality, which for him became real *only* when written down. As he explained in a 1993 interview for the BBC, every day he would write notes about his father and the illness. That was how a writer confronted experiences when the "going got rough. It's what a writer does."[9] Writing became his means of confronting the actuality of his father's inevitable death. He had no conscious intention of publishing a book about the transition from illness to death, but it was a way of coping with the loss of a loved one, even if his father was, in Kazin's words, "a tyrant," a "nudge," a shrew but also a "loving shrew," always probing.[10] Not long after father's funeral, Roth returned home and wrote the last chapter of *Patrimony*.

Written language was for Roth the way to engage the real, both physically and psychologically. "What, you're taking notes?" the father asks the son at the end of the book. Writing, telling a story, was the only way for Roth to address the loss, even if it meant a rebuke (PAT 237). His commitment, "in keeping with the unseemliness of my profession," was to write everything down (PAT 237). Literature was salvation, with the arabesques of narrative still at play but in a more minor key. The fictionalizing was still at play, as in the taxi ride when the cabbie believed Roth was a psychiatrist and confessed that he was insecure and hated his parents *and* punched his father, knocking out his four front teeth. Could this be mythologizing as well as projecting? "He actually did it . . . annihilated the father," Roth says, but immediately backtracks, offering a defense: "We're the sons appalled by violence." But it seems artificial (PAT 159, 155–59).

Patrimony is in many ways the appearance of actual facts countering, in title and meaning, any form of deception, but not entirely. Dramatic invention persists. The book may be a process of discovery wherein Roth learns the meaning of the term "patrimony" and his inheritance, but without sacrificing the imagination, as with the fate of his grandfather's shaving cup that Herman Roth kept from his father as a kind of talisman of and from the past. The work, like Herman Roth, is a struggle between realism without sentiment—one cannot forget Herman's humiliation when he loses control of his bowels and Roth cleans up and then protect his father's shame from others—but also invention (PAT 172–73).

What Roth often emphasizes in his account is medicine itself and the effort to curb and at times refuse such interventions as a respirator, a feeding tube, an IV, and even an operation to remove his father's brain tumor. He is determined that his father will die with dignity, a cliché, but here vividly presented and emotionally meaningful even when attending to the departure of ritual, as when he discovers that his father had abandoned his little-used *tefillin* in a locker at the Y rather than pass them on to one of his sons, part of the father's relinquishing the past by renouncing its objects (PAT 94–99).

Definite, objective facts compose the carefully constructed narrative. Roth, in this work, is an unrepentant realist with only a tinge of imagination in a contest with emotional honesty.

But Roth is not uncritical, recalling his father's stubbornness, bossiness, and, after his retirement at sixty-three, loss of purpose. This unromantic account actually transcends the actual, as in the well-known cleanup scene in his Connecticut bathroom (PAT 172–73). But the prosaic was the man, Roth writing that his father "*was* the vernacular, unpoetic and expressive and point-blank, with all the vernacular's glaring limitations and all its durable force" (PAT 181). This carried over to his death, which was in a real sense labor: "Dying is work and he was a worker" (PAT 233).

To Roth, his father meant strength and a head-on approach to life. Roth told the poet Robert Pinsky, "He reacted quickly to things that upset him but had the stamina to endure the truly upsetting things," much like Roth himself.[11] When *Patrimony* appeared, Roth was teaching a course at Hunter College called "The Literature of Extreme Situations" with texts ranging from *Crime and Punishment* to Michael Herr's *Dispatches*. Marking his commitment to *Patrimony* (and in an effort to boost sales) were a series of readings to support its publication but at the same time displaying a public, moral commitment to the text and its value. Temporarily, he accepted factual truth, contradicting his literary belief, as Kazin phrased it, that "truth is truth only in fiction."[12]

Patrimony (1991) initiated one of Roth's triumphant decades, publishing five works of energetic imagination: *Operation Shylock, Sabbath's Theater,* and the American Trilogy: *American Pastoral, I Married a Communist,* and *The Human Stain.* But such productivity came at a price, principally the effort, so he argued with himself, to seek release from the debilitating, diverting, and destructive relationship with Claire Bloom. Or he might have just been fed up: she was a distraction from his work. Having turned sixty in March 1993, he anticipated new success with *Operation Shylock,* but it was a critical and commercial disappointment. Then his back pains returned with new force, having started in December 1992. Without relief from the pain, he became depressed and even had to stop working on a new project. In the summer of 1993, he contemplated suicide, his pain as serious as when he suffered from the drug Halcion five years earlier.

Living in Connecticut, he began to resent Bloom, who offered little help. His brother, Sandy, stayed with him for a few weeks and Roth returned with Sandy to Chicago. The depression continued and, after a call to his doctor, he was admitted to Silver Hill Hospital in New Canaan, Connecticut, in early August 1993. After an approximately eighteen-day stay, he returned to Cornwall Bridge.

Bloom was absent, as Roth had asked, although he later accused her of abandonment, a characteristic borderline personality ploy, such behavior often characterized by a pattern of unstable interpersonal relations supported by "inappropriate or intense anger" with "frequent displays of temper." This was likely Roth's actual condition as explained to Maletta on one of her visits to Silver Hill by a doctor, who added another diagnosis: "Histrionic/Narcissistic Personality Disorder" (often known as HPD, Histrionic Personality Disorder) as outlined in the *DSM–III*, (*Diagnostic and Statistical Manual of Mental Disorders*, third edition, revised, published by the American Psychiatric Association). Among the features of HPD are a pattern of excessive emotionality and seductive behavior in an effort to gain attention and desire for control, partly achieved by creating a dependent relationship of the other on the controlling subject. The quality of emotion and sexual desire may actually be quite immature. And when things go badly, blame is always placed on the other.[13]

By September, Roth felt the return of his depression and readmitted himself for another stay. Upon his late September release, he felt energized, the depression having caused him to evaluate his mental and creative life and concluding that he had to have a Bloom-free life. From Silver Hill he went to New York to begin working again on his new novel, which would become a celebration of freedom from the restrictive, inhibiting, and destructive bounds of marriage, convention, and society, an antidote to Bloom: the title was *Sabbath's Theater*. It was an obscene, all "hell let loose" novel. The domestic was still present but sullied. Sabbath's former coproducer Norman Cowan, living in New York, for example, exhibits a seemingly on-the-surface stable marriage, although his wife makes advances to Sabbath when he visits. Their nineteen-year-old daughter becomes the object of Sabbath's sexual lust, and in her absence, he rifles through her underwear drawer. Nothing is quite what it appears to be.

Among the ironies of his separation and divorce from Bloom is Roth's seeming devotion to her, calling her "Dearest, dearest pal" in letters from 1976 and later, while constantly telling her how much he misses her and that he finds himself enormously pleased "when out of nowhere I am recollecting something you said or did." But by August 1993 he had planned his break while professing devotion, telling her via fax, "I dearly want to help in any way I can." She replied the next day, beginning "My dearest friend of seventeen years." "I will continue to love you whatever you decide," she promises, but "I am in a terrible situation and must have some protection," referring to finances.[14] He acknowledges the sacrifice in her leaving their New York apartment, which he claims will make him more appreciative of her, adding that he wants to help her recover in any way he can. Bloom then tells him that she always wanted to help him recover and adds, "I believe and I always will, that my place is with you."[15]

These exchanges illustrate the games both played: Roth's perceived manipulation confronting Bloom's apparent selfishness. Neither could win, despite their surface expressions of support and endearment. It is unclear: does she genuinely want to comfort him, and does he genuinely love her? Or does she, too, want to leave him, matching his wish to abandon her? There is no single answer other than a confrontation operating at two different levels: his strategy to get rid of her, even if means temporarily professing love, and her fear of abandonment necessitating outcries of needy support, even though she realizes it might bring further abuse. Each indulges the weaknesses of the other.

Roth, answering in September, asks for time to get over his "suicidal depression" and find a way back to his former life. He needs the New York apartment for six months, partly for easy access to his psychiatrist, but resuming their domestic life is now out of the question. Yes, you need protection, that's why I made my offer, he writes, but I want to get to New York in October. And speaking on the phone is too difficult now, yet he opens his request echoing Bloom's words: "*My* dearest friend of seventeen years."[16]

Roth's erratic behavior seemed to exploit Bloom, masking his intentions to rid himself of her. One moment he was concerned for her well-being and eager to help, but the next he was cold and calculating. The "emotional swings," as Bloom calls them in *Leaving a Doll's House*, created constant imbalance (LDH 195). In July 1993, for example, after Ross Miller, who had been staying at the house, left, Roth tells Bloom his good friend Norman Manea would be arriving, suggesting he could not be alone with Bloom. But Manea was also melancholic and would not be an aid. Roth reluctantly agreed but decided instead to invite his brother, who arrived the next day. Bloom felt pushed aside, and more so when Roth asked if he could have their bedroom to himself (LDH 196). Bloom felt trapped and believed Roth was engineering their separation (LDH 197–99). He was, although Bloom's psychiatrist at the time assured her he would not file for a divorce. He did.

By 26 September, he is giving her advice on finding a therapist, reminding her, unflatteringly, that she's sixty-two "and in a crisis." You need a different sort of doctor, he says. He recommends a Dr. Sheehy, who knows of their situation and is astute. Janet Malcolm, our close friend, refers mostly intellectual types. You need someone practical. By November, however, the communications became hostile, Roth telling Malcolm that his attempt to write a simple letter of separation and negotiate directly with Bloom met with a vituperative reaction. The letter summarized terms he believed they had already worked out, largely when she came to see him at Silver Hill the night before he was to be released. The simple agreement, drafted by a lawyer, confirmed their six-month separation, that he would give her $5,000 a month, that he had exclusive possession of their apartment at 6 West 77th Street, apartment 16B, for a six-month period, but after that period, she was entitled to live there until they settled matters. He referred to this as a "temporary separation period." But knowing Bloom constantly changed her mind about such matters (according to Roth), he felt it wiser to have this written agreement.[17]

Her reaction did not surprise him. It began with a set of angry messages on his answering machine, and when he called, she was even angrier, telling him that she would be humiliated and degraded by signing such a document. The next day she sent him a letter confirming her opposition, but for Roth she had changed her mind too many times, verbally abused him too often, and was irrational and hysterical once too often. He called his lawyer and said he could not go any further with her and wanted a divorce. The day after, he got another letter from Bloom, recanting what she had said and that she would sign the informal separation letter. It was too late, he told Malcolm: she was just repeating a pattern of reaction that had nearly made him crazy during the marriage: "defiant, irrational opposition followed two or three days later by inexplicable submission (with tears in the middle)."[18] Roth had certainly experienced this before, so it could not have been new, but his tolerance for such behavior had lessened. And he had found other (female) interests, forgetting the past seventeen years together and his frequent claims of love. Not everyday together would have been irrational, nor would he have been so negative.

Money was the next issue: she was certainly not penniless, as she claimed, and certainly not a blameless victim. Roth contended that she actually had half a million dollars in securities with a New York investment bank and almost that much again in London, the result of selling her house plus savings from her professional income. She had recently made $60,000 for one week's work in Dublin in August, he reports. During their affair and marriage, Roth claims he gave her close to $400,000 in cash with no strings. And she did not cover any of their expenses in America, while in London he contributed $1,000 a month for the upkeep of her house. To claim she is penniless and then expect they can sit down and negotiate together seemed ludicrous to him: "I don't need another coronary bypass operation." Overstatement mixes with financial worry, both qualities Bloom long exhibited. But with the uncertain career of an actor, she was always unsure of an income. What especially incenses him is that Bloom has maligned him repeatedly. Losing Francine du Plessix Gray and her husband as friends is "the only good thing to come of this mess."[19]

Throughout this period, his friendship with the Grays deteriorated. Once part of a close group of Cornwall and Litchfield friends that also included Arthur and Inge Miller, the Grausmans, William Styron, and even Kazin, he turned against them because, as he tells Bloom, they have been "outspokenly malicious in slandering" him since he first got out of the hospital. He will not be able to control his contempt in front of them and thus will skip a reception at the West Street Grill, one of his favorite Litchfield bistros, because they will be there.[20] He will in fact later insist that "Francine Duplicitous Gray" be barred from any memorial service that might be held for him after his death.

On 12 March 1994, Roth signed formal separation papers at his lawyer's (LDH 230). During their separation, Bloom began a battle over their prenuptial agreement, calling it "unconscionable" and demanding certain assets, including his studio at 130 West 79th Street, where he was then living. He refused, even when his close friend and former editor Aaron Asher supported her, which precipitated an estrangement between the editor and author.

That summer events were more complicated than most people knew. By late July 1993, Roth had become involved again with the much more sympathetic Maletta, a relationship that had been on and off since the late 1970s. Once a neighbor but, more important, his Swedish physiotherapist, she was the woman who provided both emotional and physical support for him during and after his depression at Silver Hill. Her steadiness countered the hysterical reaction of Bloom to Roth's depression and recovery following his knee operation and suffering from Halcion. They became involved as early as 1978, when she began an outpatient physical therapy practice, after her move to Litchfield County following work in New York. She began with only $3,000 and little space. (In 2007, she had sixteen employees and sold the business to an associate.) Roth and Maletta's affair flourished in the 1980s and lasted until 1994. Her pleasure in sex and sexual encounters inspired aspects of the energetic Drenka in *Sabbath's Theater*. In many ways, Roth's writing Drenka is a celebration of Maletta, who did not die of cancer (or any other disease), as Drenka does in the novel. Nevertheless, their affair ended the year he completed the novel.

While Maletta nurtured, Bloom fantasized and was frequently hysterical in response to Roth's uneven behavior during her limited visits to Silver Hill, caused as much by Roth as her own emotional confusions. According to Roth, her preference was for unreality as she had earlier dealt with the death of her mother. For three days, she sat next to the body and refused to let it be removed to a funeral home. Only Roth's intervention permitted the transport of the slowly decomposing remains (LDH 172). Roth duplicates the scene in *Sabbath's Theater* where Nikki, Sabbath's first wife, sat with her mother's body for several days (ST 107–108). However, Roth's on-again–off-again feelings for her contributed to her ambiguity concerning him: does he love me or hate me, is this condition temporary or permanent?

Roth then turned nasty toward Bloom. A set of faxes sent in mid-December 1993 listed his demands for items to be returned—starting with stereo equipment for the London house, a white heater, 40 percent of the money he paid for her Saab 900, the mirror over the fireplace at Fawcett Street in London which he bought, various records and books, and the ring from Bulgari (cost: $7,500)—or the cash equivalent. He also offered an accounting of his time for writing the Chekhov one-act TV play, the Jean Rhys script, and for adapting the *Cherry Orchard*. He bills her at $150 an hour for five or six hundred hours. He also wants back the $28,500 he gave her for twelve years, and $100,000 he gave her to buy bonds with the Wertheim investment bank in New York. In return, he will give her $104 a week that went to the maid in New York, which he describes as her sole contribution to their living costs in New York and Connecticut. At the end of one fax (14 December 1993), he adds that for refusing to honor their prenuptial agreement, which she voluntarily signed, "I fine you $62 billion." And concerning Anna's outrage when you signed the prenup, he writes, "Ah, feminism! But then you never intended to honor it anyway, so that must have calmed her down, at least a little."[21]

He concludes his diatribe by telling her that he's assembling the bills from their various trips, including the restaurants, and she should pay half. But then there are the taxi rides they took together—hard to estimate, but "does around $4000 seem fair? That seems about half." Displaying a moment of generosity mixed with sarcasm, he tells her she owes him nothing for getting her a job at Hunter College (she needed some extra income) or teaching her how to teach, or for his attendance at her plays and recitals: "I believe I saw [Ibsen's] Rosmersholm some 15 times. That's on me."[22] And he makes it clear in that he wants absolutely no contact from her, not by fax, phone, or in person, although he does want his CDs back and the SONY stereo he bought her when she moved to the Cosmopolitan Club on East 66th Street in New York.[23]

What truly supported him at this time, Roth explained—Bloom was either too panic-stricken ("panicky" is her term) or ill equipped to handle his irregular behavior—was not only Maletta but another woman he said he fell in love with at Silver Hill, a woman who possessed a "battered soulfulness."[24] This was Roth's usual habit: constantly falling in and out of love with numerous female companions. He was always proposing, sometimes seriously and sometimes not. Yet if the other party thought he was serious and considered the offer, Roth reacted negatively. His paradoxical action was simultaneously the pursuit of companionship and rejection of marriage. According to Ben Taylor, Roth told him his most interesting proposal was to Věra Saudková, Kafka's niece, whom he met in Prague. No longer permitted to work in publishing, she warmly responded to Roth's curiosity about Kafka, even allowing him to sit at the writer's desk. Roth proposed to her as a way to get her out of Czechoslovakia. She declined: "Turned me down flat. Who the hell was she waiting for?"[25]

Roth later claimed that Bloom was destroying his creativity, while incapable of providing any emotional or physical comfort during and after his illness. The idea of a writer not writing haunted him. Maletta provided what was missing. It was Maletta, in fact, who contacted Bloom, on Roth's behalf, asking if he could have their New York apartment for six months to recuperate after his stay at Silver Hill (LDH 207). He did not want to be alone in the Connecticut home, Maletta suggesting that he might become suicidal if he stayed there. In an effort to convince resistant Bloom to move, Maletta and Judith Thurman visited Gray to repeat Roth's request to ask Bloom to temporarily move out.

Under such pressure, Bloom relented, and even departed a few days earlier after Malcolm called her again on Roth's behalf (LDH 209). Bloom moved to the Cosmopolitan Club. But Roth's behavior toward Bloom continued to be erratic, loving one moment, vengeful the next, which in an odd way matched Bloom's: hateful one moment and then eager to reconcile the next.

In certain ways, this echoes the behavior of the ballerina in her breakout movie *Limelight* with Chaplin from 1952. She played a suicidal dancer who suffered from a hysterical paralysis and was rescued by Chaplin. But in actuality, Roth was not going to rescue her.

At this time, Maletta herself became incensed at Bloom's treatment of Roth and sought to defend him. But for Roth, Maletta was another woman in need of saving, even helping her overcome the trauma of the loss of her father, a situation experienced by several of his other women. She also had a serious drinking problem which came and went during their relationship, gradually coming under control in 1994, when their affair was ending. At that time, her own marriage of twenty-five years was ending, despite her husband's support through her lapses and recoveries from alcoholism and sexual escapades.

In a letter of 30 October 1993 to Roth (nicknamed Schwarzie), Maletta tells him how hurt she felt by Bloom because "she let the man down, whom I love, when he was sick." She disliked the way it was only Bloom's selfish emotions that seemed to matter, no one else's. She ends by telling Roth again how much she loves him and how strong he is and able to pull through this difficult period. One day, she hopes, their love can be "out in the open," necessary for her own recovery. "I don't want my soul to cry silently."[26] Roth seems to be stringing Maletta along: as she seeks a public relationship after so many years together in secret, Roth denies her. He refuses to give her the acknowledgment she deserves. Manipulation or denial?

In 1994, Roth sued Bloom for divorce, claiming cruel and inhuman treatment. Bloom considered filing for divorce in Connecticut, where on rare occasions a prenuptial agreement had been overturned. In New York, where Roth had filed papers, they were almost never questioned (LDH 223–24).

By May 1994, Bloom had removed her possessions from Cornwall Bridge to her new New York apartment, resigned to Roth's "kindness and cruelty" (LDH 154). The divorce was finalized in June 1995, ending nearly three years as husband and wife preceded by fifteen years as a couple (LDH 237). The anti-inflammatory drugs and antidepressants accelerated his difficult mental state, resulting, he falsely believed, in clarity and uplift. He understood what he needed to do to regain some balance in his life, and that was to write and to live an emotionally stable existence, possible only without Bloom—or so he convinced himself. Ironically, he *was* able to write a set of powerful novels while attached to Bloom. He seems to forget that, or he wants it both ways: it was terrible, it was good. One outlet for his anger and new energy was in the highly charged prose of *Sabbath's Theater,* released on 12 September 1995, a blend of nastiness, sexual energy, and dark comedy.

But earlier, in March 1995, after their formal separation agreement had been signed and proceedings were underway, Roth asked Bloom, "Can we be friends?" A week later, in an effort to meet for coffee, he vowed not "to speak of old wounds if you won't. A deal?" By May he tries to sympathize with her over finalizing the divorce, telling her it's not a matter of Roth versus Bloom but "a necessary step so that each of us can continue to rebuild our lives."[27] What really interests him are plans for a new house, planting pine trees to obscure the old building, and hiring a contractor. A new road will even be constructed, and he plans to sell the old house but keep his swimming pool, the new house being smaller and modern. But these active plans, working with a former New York architect, Tim Prentice, came to a halt when his then companion, Julia Golier, visiting for a weekend, objected. Reconsider, she told him after taking him from room to room and reminding him of the potential and history of the building. The house, even if it was associated with Bloom, had its own integral past and should be preserved. Surprisingly, but reluctantly, he canceled the plans to rebuild.[28]

After his divorce from Bloom, Roth spent most of his time at Cornwall Bridge and the 79th Street *pied-à-terre* during trips to the city. He was occupied with writing his American Trilogy at the time. After its success, he moved back to the city and bought the apartment adjacent to his studio and combined the two units, turning the second kitchen into a walk-in closet and installing a second pair of doors near the front to decrease noise. On the kitchen wall was a pencil sketch of a floor plan of his childhood apartment on the second floor of 81 Summit Avenue. In the living room was a framed map of Newark. The Upper West Side quickly became his *milieu,* not least because of its large Jewish population. He became a regular at Nice Matin at 79th and Amsterdam and often stopped in at Zabar's on Broadway and 80th. Barney Greengrass, the famous headquarters for lox and whitefish, was just six blocks up Amsterdam at the corner of 86th, passing Sarabeth's and Jacob's Pickles on the way.

During this year (1995), he also changed publishers—again. In a 15 May 1995 letter to Bloom, he tells her how good it is to be back with "a real publisher," Houghton Mifflin, who were about to release *Sabbath's Theater.* Without much detail, he says things were awful at Simon and Schuster. But he won't be around to do any publicity or read any insulting reviews. He'll remain in the country. Six days later, he thanks Bloom for blessing his new house project and tells her he only wants happiness for her, ambiguously writing in an undated note, "YOU ARE A GREAT ACTRESS BUT I LOVED YOU BEFORE THAT."[29]

During Maletta's marital breakup, Roth was subject to malicious gossip emanating from Gray and her husband. Gray had told Bloom that Roth was responsible for the breakup of Maletta's marriage and (incorrectly) that Janet Malcolm was responsible for her own lengthy libel trial involving Jeffrey Masson. Gray also accused Updike of being a "collaborator" who would stoop to writing for Tina Brown. Roth, present when Gray made that insulting remark, objected loudly. Bloom then suggested that Malcolm, not Gray, had told her that the Pfeiffers were divorcing and that Roth had broken up their marriage. Such deceit infuriated Bloom, who called many friends to say such dishonesty by Roth illustrated the way he treated her and also explained his breakdown and bad back and their separation.

Additionally, Gray had earlier claimed without evidence that Roth was having an affair with Thurman. He actually received an unsigned letter that read, "Everyone Knows you're seeing Judith Thurman," written either by Gray or her husband, although Gray always denied it. He took quick action by having his lawyer Martin Garbus write her a letter accusing her as the author and making harassing and denigrating statements. Witnesses confirm that you are also making false and libelous statements about Roth, Garbus wrote, including that Roth's "secret plan" was to steal and sell Bloom's car. This must stop. You are violating Mr. Roth's legal rights, the lawyer adds, and "are subject to a suit."[30] Roth also hired a private detective to track down the sender; no luck, but a few years after he had a handwriting expert examine the note. The conclusion pointed to Gray. Not one to forget, Roth included the anonymous but harmful "Everyone Knows" letter in *The Human Stain*, received by Coleman Silk and later identified as written by Delphine Roux (HS 37–38, 173–74).

Francine and Cleve Gray seemed to be on a campaign to ground Roth's divorce in his being "a housewrecking adulterer." As revenge, Roth named the sycophantic supporters of Eve Frame the Grants in *I Married a Communist*. It is they who write the scurrilous book supposedly by Frame also titled *I Married a Communist* exposing Ira Ringold (IMC 242). According to Roth, one of the things that *did* contribute to the end of his marriage to Bloom was her "enslavement" to Gray, a woman he grew to hate, although early in their friendship, he seduced her, which he later admitted was not his "finest hour."[31]

However, Maletta was not unblemished. She, too, may have inadvertently contributed to what Roth in 2015 refers to as "false and slanderous testimony" about him that went in to Bloom's autobiography. But many were being betrayed. When Maletta later confided to a third party, a poet, details of her lengthy relationship with Roth, the poet, in turn, revealed the information to one of Roth's biographers without her knowledge or consent. No longer his central love, Roth turned against Maletta as he turned against so many close to him. But again, he overstates and exaggerates, claiming that her act of complicity with Bloom was the cruelest that has "ever been publically been perpetrated on me." He was particularly upset at her supposed "self-sanitation," presenting herself in several documents as a savior when she was actually a wanton seductress according to him.[32]

To gain further sympathy and further vilify Roth, Bloom digresses in her memoir to report his attempted seduction of a close friend of her daughter, the dark-haired Rachael Hallawell, who temporarily lived with them on Fawcett Street. This supposedly happened in 1981 and again in 1988 (LDH 224–27). However, a letter from Roth to Rachael dated 18 January 1988 indicates the ludicrousness of the accusation. It opens with "You tell Claire why you moved. It'll be much more hilarious from your mouth than from mine." Rachael had apparently left Roth a voicemail expressing a certain "sexual hysteria. How righteous! How affronted!" he claimed.[33] Bloom dropped the matter, although Roth did at one point express interest in the young woman, but nothing happened. Bloom's account might not be so ludicrous.

And Bloom? Despite threats from her lawyer to Roth questioning the legality of the prenuptial agreement, she settled for $100,000 and some furniture. Roth was too distant from her any longer to sympathize. He was eager to get out, hardly the portrait of their positive relationship featured ten years earlier in the whimsically titled *Vogue* profile, "A Meeting of Arts & Minds."

Both Bloom and Roth rewrote history, their letters revealing a closeness and mutual support that their postdivorce writings contradicted. Battles and bitterness replaced any mutuality. For Bloom, there was genuine hurt and not knowing what Roth wanted or how he would behave. For Roth, it was his pattern of villainizing devoted women and abandoning them when he wanted freedom or their needs impinged on his. His response was always negative. He repeatedly abandoned his loyal companions or found reasons for getting rid of them. Without cause, his conscience wouldn't allow their dismissal. Somehow, he fashioned their desires as his excuses, always blaming the other for wanting children, marriage, or domesticity. He always needed to believe he was the decent person acting out of need or survival. He always needed to be the good Jewish boy, but he also needed to be independent. He knew good Jewish boys don't leave their wives or partners unless they want to invite scandal. The women must be to blame or commit a wrong of some sort. Roth believed he was rarely the cause, constantly rewriting history via fact or fiction.

Bloom was sixty-five when she published her "revenge memoir," *Leaving a Doll's House*.[34] When she first met Roth, she was forty-four and he was forty-two. But by the end, she acknowledged that there was a sense of coequal misery: she felt deserted, while he felt drowned by her neediness (LDH 236). She also reports Roth's comment that his strongest relationships were with fatherless women who gravitated "toward emotionally unavailable men," commenting that he played that "elusive role" perfectly (LDH 236).

Soon, a series of dead or disappeared wives began to appear or reappear in Roth's work: Mickey Sabbath's first wife, the actress Nikki, has disappeared and is presumed dead; his second has given him up for the bottle and for all intents and purposes has vanished. In *I Married a Communist*, Eve Frame figuratively dies when she is revealed as an impostor, actually Chava Fromkin from the Bronx. And she actually dies alone in a drunken stupor in a New York hotel room in 1962, while Murray Ringold's wife Doris has been murdered on a Newark street. Then there is the dead wife of Coleman Silk in *The Human Stain,* and the incapacitated former wife of the narrator of *Everyman*, the stroke victim, Phoebe. Other dead wives include Lydia Ketterer who commits suicide in *My Life as a Man* and Maureen Tarnopol who survives an attempt at an overdose only to die in a car crash, as did Maggie. In *When She Was Good*, the married Lucy Nelson freezes to death. Dead wives may be retribution for his own unhappy marital experiences.

During the mid-1980s, Roth renewed his friendship with Saul Bellow, partly because of Janis Freedman Bellow, the writer's fifth wife, whom he married in 1989. The two writers had grown estranged, partly because of Bellow's sense of competition and Roth's continued busyness: within five years, from 1985 to 1990, Roth had released three novels, one, *The Counterlife*, a striking, narratively inventive text. But Roth, with Bloom, attended Bellow's surprise seventy-fifth birthday party in June 1990 at Le Petite Chef in Wilmington, Vermont. Over seventy attended: nieces, nephews, sons, and a Russian Jewish relative from Riga, plus the marvelous *New Yorker* cartoonist Saul Steinberg (who arrived by helicopter) and Alan Lelchuk. "It was very Chekhovian,"

Roth wrote. "People got up and burst into tears and sat down. The event was melancholy. . . . at the end, one of Bellow's Russian relatives got up and announced, 'I chav a song' and sang a song in Yiddish" before it seemed everyone again burst into tears.[35]

It was only in the early 1990s that Bellow dropped his guard with Roth, which Roth attributed to Bellow's happy marriage with a new wife (who provided a supportive review of *Operation Shylock* in the Winter 1993 issue of *Bostonia* magazine). She and Bellow felt the book had been poorly treated by the press. She encouraged Bellow to reread Roth seriously, although she denied such a critical role, suggesting that she and her husband had long discussed Roth's work positively.

There was some tension, however, because of Bellow's sense of rivalry. Roth, in turn, felt like an amateur in comparison to Bellow.[36] But Bellow was not afraid of speaking his mind and did so in a critical letter concerning *I Married a Communist*, complaining that Ira Ringold is the least attractive of all Roth's characters and that the pitiful Eve Frame and her pampered daughter, Sylphid, are thinly disguised images of Bloom and her daughter. Roth answered on 10 January 1999, explaining his multiple-narrative technique and that the effort to escape from violent rage is the theme, not its promotion. Bellow had asked that Roth accept his openness and not cast him off. Roth offered a similar truce.[37]

Years later, Roth began to work with Bellow on an extensive written interview on his life's work; it was never finished, but the letters to Roth appeared as Saul Bellow's "I Got a Scheme!" in *The New Yorker*.[38] The project began in 1998, when Bellow was eighty-three, but lost traction as the aged Bellow seemed to have lost interest (and mental clarity).

Free from Bloom, Roth found his own free expression for the themes of rage and discontent in his 1995 novel, *Sabbath's Theater*, a text driven by anger. The satire in the book masked moral outrage, transforming such anger "into comic art."[39] Riven with anger and surrounded by death, intensified by the loss of his father in 1989 and Janet Hobhouse in 1991, Roth discovered relief only in creating his temperamental and aggressive hero. At the same time, he faced questions of mortality addressed in *Operation Shylock* and then *Sabbath's Theater*, the playful narrative actions of the former preparation for the uncontrollable behavior of the hero in the latter. The novel charts the unsubtle priapic life of a Rabelaisian puppeteer who after years with an uninhibited sexually driven mistress who has just died must adjust to a world unaccustomed to his behavior.

In *Shylock*, death shapes the Israeli-Palestinian conflict and hovers throughout the text via the Demjanjuk trial (which Roth attended); in *Sabbath*, it steals Sabbath's first wife and his orgasmic, vital, insatiable lover, Drenka, a woman who wants to be paid to make her feel more like a prostitute when Sabbath arranges a *ménage à trois* with a former *au pair*, to be duplicated in *The Humbling*. Ironically (if not comically), such actual and imagined deaths became the stimulus for Roth's own search for a grave site. Thinking that he might want to be buried near his parents in Gomel Chesed Cemetery on the Newark-Elizabeth border, he surveyed the possibilities with a cemetery warden who discouraged him from a likely site by telling him he wouldn't have enough legroom.[40]

But the abrasive Mickey Sabbath never stops challenging death or rejoicing in his lust for life, love, and fucking, his relentless character unstoppable. A former seaman with a delight in prostitutes, Sabbath was largely derived from afternoons Roth spent in Kitaj's London studio as he narrated his sea adventures. The voice and behavior of Sabbath enlarged Kitaj's tales, Sabbath's Indecent Theater of Manhattan on Avenue C epitomizing the miniaturized expression of his mature and scandalous actions—which contributed to his removal from a New York theater company for lewd and obscene behavior with his street puppets and then dismissal from a rural college. The reason? The discovery of a phone sex tape with the red-headed Kathy Goolsbee, an undergraduate, broadcast on campus-wide radio. The tape was not invented. Roth actually had recorded a sex tape with a Hunter College student. In *Sabbath's Theater* it runs for twenty pages (pp. 215–35). He also often had one or two of his lovers listen to his sex calls and shared with them his own transgressions with other women, an act of either confession or pride.

In the novel, Sabbath had been in New England since leaving New York following the disappearance of his first wife, Nikki, an actress and the closure of his puppet theater for supposedly indecent performances. Sabbath, the puppeteer, could not pull enough strings to keep any of his jobs. Roth actually had an aunt (Aunt Rhoda in his fictional story of Kafka) who worked for a WPA puppet theater and kept two collapsed marionettes in the closet of the room Roth shared with his brother.

Sixty-four at the beginning of the novel (Roth was sixty-two when it appeared), Sabbath remains a "dirty old man" despite the undergraduate scandal and erotic involvement with Drenka (twelve years younger), his Croatian mistress who runs the local inn (modelled on the Hopkins Inn in

Warren, CT) with her husband. Vulgar, sensual, and outspoken, she is end-lessly attractive to Sabbath. But when the novel opens, she has recently died of ovarian cancer, leaving him bereft. He is also haunted by his mother's voice, which revisits him at the most inconvenient times. The dead surround him, not only from above (the mother often hovers overhead like a helicopter) but from below. Roth began the novel in April 1993, writing steadily, although interrupted by bouts of depression. But upon his release from the hospital and fired up by the story, he wrote rapidly. By March 1995, he was reviewing first proofs, completing third proofs by April 12.[41]

The death of a former friend who once backed his puppet theater prompts Sabbath to drive to New York to attend the funeral and possibly arrange for his own demise. But he lacks the courage to do so, especially when tempted by the sexual aura he discovers in the bedroom of his friend Norman Cowan's nineteen-year-old daughter, Debby. The emotional and sexual temperature of the novel is always on high, as when Sabbath compares the orgasms of his three lovers (Nikki, wife #1; Roseanna, wife #2; and Drenka, mistress extra-ordinaire [ST 131–32]). Michelle, Norman's wife, who has visited Sabbath in his bedroom dressed only in her kimono, declares, "Unbridled excess knows no limit in you" as Sabbath stands, robe undone, fully exposed before her (ST 333). All he can think of is that "beneath the kimono there appeared to be only her biography," his wit temporarily overcoming his desire (ST 328).

Reflecting Sabbath's undisciplined, careening thoughts is Roth's constantly shifting narrative structure relying mostly on flashbacks and fantasy. The structure reflects his own uncertain attitude at the time concerning the di-rection of his life post-Bloom. On one hand, depression, but on the other, freedom for new relationships and life. Bordered by death—he did indeed begin a pursuit for a suitable grave site some years earlier—he now found energy to live by writing a novel about loss but with emotional shockwaves on almost every page. And for once, a nonacademic hero: a sailor, puppeteer, philanderer. While writing the book, Roth spent time with puppeteers, learning how a wooden world could emulate emotional and sexual feelings.

Third-person, first-person, and narrative stops in between, including the reportorial and confessional, keep the reader awake and seated in Sabbath's theater, where the atmosphere is always "insinuatingly anti-moral, vaguely menacing and at the same time, rascally fun" (ST 97). Like the daily raising of the flag at the Rimrock post office in *American Pastoral*, every morning Sabbath must deal with his erection. But where he previously allowed his puppets to perform indecent acts, *he* now performs them. And in his world, the scandalous always triumphs: at one point contemplating his suicide in New York while overlooking Central Park, he exclaims, "Fuck the laudable ideologies." Enough of Virginia Woolf's *A Room of One's Own*—"get yourself *The Collected Works of Ava Gardner*," dead at sixty-two, a brilliant mix of "elegance and filth" (ST 157).

There is strong comedy here, as in the list of malapropisms spoken by Drenka and delivered with force: "bear and grin it . . . his days are counted . . . a roof under my head . . . the boy who cried 'Woof!' . . . alive and cooking" (ST 71). But women are no more than sexual objects, which appropriately offended numerous readers, while others could not stop laughing. As Sabbath sermonizes, he expresses Roth's overall philosophy: "For a pure sense of being tumultuously alive, you can't beat the nasty side of existence" (ST 247). This is Roth in a nutshell, his anger turned inside out.

Sabbath must retire from puppetry because of arthritic hands, but he remains enthusiastically unburdened by proper social behavior or moral constraints. His social, financial, and personal losses mount so high that nothing restrains him. He fights for life against the loss of Drenka, his own disabilities, and the tragic death of his older brother, Morty, in World War II. He spends a good deal of time visiting cemeteries and talking to the ghost of his mother, but also masturbating on Drenka's grave. One recalls Roth's frequent visits to the grave of Janet Hobhouse, near his home where he would occasionally perform a similar act.[42]

But even Sabbath can lose, this time his burial plot, which he thought he would have next to his mother. To his chagrin, when he goes to view it, it's occupied by his mother's older sister who died two years earlier. He ironically laments his bad timing: "Why does life refuse me even the *grave* I want! Had I only marshaled my abhorrence in a good cause and killed myself two years ago, that spot next to Ma's would be mine" (ST 359). The black comedy is real: commit suicide two years earlier and gain the plot you coveted. But he refuses to give up on life, protesting its loss while begging for more: "More defeat! More disappointment! . . . More disastrous entanglement in everything," he cries (ST 247). And most mightily, more sex, a jabbing, feinting, and even punching move against death itself. The text possesses the madcap energy of Roth at his most exuberant but always battling the undertow of death. His world at this time could not turn from death, but neither could he renounce desire, especially sexual desire. Roth's preoccupation with sex as a protest against death ignited the book and its style. Battling physical decline and emotional paralysis, Roth found in writing the novel release and protest against decay. Cousin Fish at one hundred stands as a symbol of living, even if his memory is fading. Anarchy may be the answer, embodying the anger and betrayal Roth had so long encountered. Written in overdrive, the novel becomes *the* Roth encyclopedia, the widest ranging novel containing his most consistent themes: aging, death, the body, sex, and family history. The ultimate irony which Roth realized through the writing of *Sabbath's Theater* was that his "life was never to be solved" (ST 108). The lesson Sabbath and Roth repeat is that revved-up emotions never change: "Everything passes! *Nothing* passes. . . . They're the same, fresh and raw" (ST 298).

The novel, as anticipated, created its own furor: critics were deeply divided. Kazin thought the character an improvement over "the schizophrenic wretch in Op Shylock," but he could not fully accept the "rebel hero" presented as an artist, possibly the last "independent Jew up against so much *dreck* in contemporary American life." The problem for Kazin was that Sabbath's fascination is not so much with sexual life as "with his own penis." And the theme was too repetitive, knocking off the scale of the book because of his penile obsession with the sex that becomes nothing more than symbolic.[43] An aggrieved Roth replied by asking what the words "rebel hero" have to do with anything and suggesting that the sex is anything *but* symbolic.

Harold Bloom offered a contrasting view: the novel was Roth's richest, if not a "masterwork," outshining everything that preceded it. William Pritchard in the *New York Times* agreed. Even Roth agreed, choosing to read the long scene of Sabbath's cemetery visit at his eightieth birthday party in Newark, repeated at his final public talk at the 92nd Street Y in New York in May 2014.[44] Many greeted the transgressive novel as "the final explosive discharge" of the author's obsessions—sex and death—and anticipated new themes, once past the affirmation of sexual practice as an existential defiance of death. I could have called the book "Death and the Art of Dying," he said in a 2014 interview, adding that Sabbath is pursued by death but "followed everywhere by laughter."[45]

At the time *Sabbath's Theater* appeared, August 1995, anger was "in." Bellow made this clear in a 1994 *New York Times* op-ed, a response to his supposed quip "Where is the Tolstoy of the Zulus? The Proust of the Papuans?" The implied racism of the remark created a controversy to which Bellow responded with an ironic celebration of rage: "Rage is now brilliantly prestigious. Rage, the reverse of bourgeois prudence, is a luxury. Rage is distinguished, it is a patrician passion. The rage of rappers and rioters takes as its premise the majority's admission of guilt for past and present injustices. . . .

Rage can also be manipulative; it can be an instrument of censorship and despotism."[46] But Bellow had anticipated the rage of Sabbath and Roth's use of it in his novel. Almost from the first page, rage, anger, blasphemy, indignation, and fury dominate the text, an outburst against loss, death, and time. If no one was offended or outraged, Roth felt his strategy failed. As he often repeated, it was his favorite book.

Roth conveys his outrage with consummate skill, expanding Prince Hal's comment in *Henry IV, Part One*, "I'll so offend to make offence a skill" (I.ii.211–12), into an entire novel. Shakespeare was very much in mind, appearing throughout Roth's work, most notably in *Exit Ghost*. To offend is everything. The "licentious abandon" of Sabbath and Drenka brought them unbounded pleasure, but to many readers, discomfort and unease (ST 9). But where the mistress of *Deception* spoke fluidly, with every syllable an expression of style, Drenka relies on misstatements and boasting, which Sabbath relishes, language itself becoming a form of "estrangement from the ordinary" (ST 27). Matching the libertine Drenka is the renegade Sabbath, whose actions embody the maxim "You can only be young once, but you can be immature forever" (ST 286). The "toxic masculinity" and even "dominating narcissism" of the novel is done with wit and emotional acuity, to cite a comment from the *New York Times*.[47] The upsetting, bitter, flawed, and lust-dominated puppeteer is also the most forthright and engaging figure of Roth's since Alex Portnoy. What actually impelled Roth to write as he did was an expansion of the Portnoy principle: no rules, no inhibitions, no restraint, no decorum after a period of restraint, disagreement, and unhappiness with Bloom, which affected his mental state. As Sabbath proudly announces, "I am the disorder" (ST 203). When asked by David Remnick in a 2000 interview when he was the happiest, without hesitation Roth said it was when writing *Sabbath's Theater*. Why? Remnick queried. "Because I felt free. I feel like I am *in charge* now."[48] Clarity, control, freedom: these are the driving forces of Roth's writing and personal life which come into relief when facing personal crises and their consequences. They are also the catalysts of his powerful, imaginative literature.[49]

But Roth had little relief following the controversial reception of *Sabbath's Theater* and its winning the National Book Award for Fiction. The following October, Bloom's *Leaving a Doll's House* appeared, a work he believed was largely written by Gray.[50] Angered at her likely participation, Roth fired back with her satirical portrait in *Sabbath's Theater* as Countess de Plissitas, the supposed author who attacks Sabbath and defends his first wife in her work

Nikki: The Destruction of an Actress by a Pig (ST 192–93). Nikki, by the way, refused to give up her dead mother's body, just as Bloom did. Roth could also not resist striking back at the *New York Times* book reviewer Michiko Kakutani, who, according to Roth, long harbored a grudge against him. Her reviewing him over the years was actually a mix of positive and negative comments. She was tough but not unreasonable, but again, Roth never forgot an insult, real or imagined. In *Sabbath's Theater* she variously appears as Dean Kuziduzi, Kakizaki, or the Japanese viperina (ST 243, 214, 221). For Roth, every affront, no matter how long ago, demanded retaliation.[51]

Roth quickly discerned the lies, falsehoods, and distortions contained in Bloom's summary of their life together, a life of reported quarreling, mental cruelty, financial penury, and general dislike. An element of theatricality runs throughout her account: "Philip made character assessments the way surgeons make incisions" (LDH 158). She describes her shock when learning of Roth's affair with an "Erda," a mutual friend, discovered after their marriage ended. But a good deal of the book might substitute for the actual text Bloom read during a break in filming *The Brothers Karamazov* with Yul Brynner in Hollywood: Dostoevsky's *The Insulted and the Injured* (LDH 96).

When Bloom's book appeared, Roth took off for the Jersey Shore, taking refuge at a bed and breakfast in Spring Lake, New Jersey, where he spent four days walking the beach and riding the waves, all anonymously. But the publicity was unavoidable; largely sympathetic to Bloom, reviews and commentary appeared in all the major media, preceded by an excerpt (for which she was well paid) in *Vanity Fair*.

The reviews generally asked how she could have put up with such an ogre. Roth's accusers outnumbered his defenders, although his close circle of friends offered defenses. The public details of their private life mixed embarrassment with anger, stressing her mistreatment with little self-blame. The exposure of his medical problems and need for painkillers as a result of his unsuccessful knee operation leading to an extreme drug reaction were equally frank, eliminating privacy on every level. Bloom elides the real reasons for Roth's turn against London and her daughter, skips her own hysterical overreaction to his depression and her own emotional needs, and neglects to comment on her reaction after reading a draft of *Deception*. She attempts to become the hero of her own story, although her self-portrait is not always kind.

Roth felt compelled to offer a number of aggressive defenses even after publishing his remade Bloom as Eve Frame in *I Married a Communist*. In

March 1999, three years after Bloom's memoir appeared, he wrote to the *New York Review of Books* to criticize Updike's seeming acceptance of her position. In an essay review from 4 February 1999 entitled "One Cheer for Literary Biography," Updike sided with Bloom, renouncing the neutral tone of his overall essay. In the same letter, Roth criticizes a review of *American Pastoral* that digresses to insult him and his behavior with Bloom. Updike offered a one-sentence reply: "Mr. Roth's imagined revisions [to a sentence of his] sound fine to me, but my own wording conveys, I think, the same sense of one-sided allegations."[52] Roth also sought to take revenge by hiring Ross Miller as his biographer to replace fiction with facts and correct Bloom's distortions with his own.

Later, Roth contradicted an account of a fight that he reportedly witnessed between Bloom and her daughter shortly after he arrived to live with them in 1976. Upon his arrival, Anna disappeared for several days; when she returned and they sat down to dinner, he reported that she began to argue with Bloom and then each hit the other, as re-created in *I Married a Communist* (172–75). Bloom denied anything like that happened; her daughter also repudiated the event. And then Roth denied their denials.[53]

Some saw *Leaving a Doll's House* as a transparent account by a woman lacking any self-awareness, while others thought it wasn't a strong enough indictment. Marion Winik in the *Los Angeles Times* wrote that finally Portnoy was "getting his": "The only shame of it is that it's not a better writer than Claire Bloom giving it to him." There is a heavy-handed pathos and "plodding pacing that mark this account." But Winik can distinguish between the man and the work—and the work still appeals. Nonetheless, Winik finds some value in Bloom's excessive account of Roth's sins. But Bloom seems unusually open to forgiving, perhaps because she desperately wanted to remain married (and wanted the financial security).[54]

Other views were less generous toward Bloom. Zoë Heller's review in the *London Review of Books* was titled "An Emerald Ring, a Portable Heater, and $150 an Hour"; she called the book a "calculated manoeuvre in a long psychosexual war of attrition." Heller notes that when Roth enters the story, Bloom's prose loses its "benign vagueness and takes on a shrill, Ancient Mariner urgency." Sentences grow feverish and even "baroque in construction."[55]

Throughout her account, Heller writes, there is a "princessy tone." Bloom admits that during a visit to Roth at Silver Hill she herself became hysterical, dramatically threatening suicide. She was promptly admitted overnight. But the tone is matter of fact. All Heller can cattily say is "Ho Hum." Harpy or angel? That's the dilemma in assessing Bloom's memoir.

Roth did not hold back in expressing his private, emotional response to Bloom's account. To Kazin he wrote:

> It's shit. . . . The deranged malevolence that nearly drove me to suicide three and half years ago has been joined to the deranged malevolence of the media to nail my personal and professional reputation to the cross of malevolent gossip.

Roth's anger is genuine and he adds that

> I tried half a dozen times to leave Claire and each time she ran to wherever I was and threw herself on the floor—and begged "I implore you! Don't leave me!" And I couldn't do it, couldn't leave her. That's what I should be shot for.[56]

The crescendo of such moments can be seen in the scene in Ira Ringold's shack in Zinc Town in *I Married a Communist* where a hysterical Eve bursts in at 3:00 a.m. in a melodramatic scene from Hollywood, throwing herself on her knees before Ira in the middle of the floor and crying out "Don't leave me!" with "two arms upthrust in [her] mink coat. The hands trembling in the air. And tears, as though it weren't a marriage at stake but the redemption of mankind" (IMC 180).

Roth ends his letter to Kazin of 28 October 1996 by saying that the best he can do is say nothing and write his books: "That's all I ever wanted to do, you know—I never wanted to marry anyone, I never wanted to father anyone, I just wanted to write books. And now that's what I'm fucking doing. This is my home, this house, these trees, etc. and New York can go fuck itself, and all the people in it."[57]

In *I Married a Communist*, Roth took his own revenge, Zuckerman at one point explaining, "How delicious to belittle people—and to watch them being belittled" (IMC 131). Roth then attacked Sylphid (a poorly disguised Anna Steiger), writing that she was young "yet so richly antagonistic," eager to antagonize everyone, and it was clear that she harbored an insurmountable grudge against her mother (IMC 131, 86). Zuckerman later realizes that the only way Sylphid can feel "at ease in her skin was by hating her mother and playing the harp" (IMC 138). And she succeeds in browbeating her mother into getting an abortion when she is pregnant with Ira's child, which he desperately wants.

The novel builds to a set of lies that parallel the lies, or at least misrepresentations, Bloom presents in *Leaving a Doll's House*. Novelistically, Roth enjoyed the creation of the opening pages of Eve Frame's book *I Married a Communist* (with an American flag printed on its cover) with such statements as Ira being a card-carrying Communist and "ringleader of the underground Communist espionage unit committed to controlling American radio" and taking orders from Moscow. I married him out of love, she states, but he married me because the Party ordered him to. Iron Rinn married her to "better . . . infiltrate his way into the world of American entertainment. Yes, I married a Machiavellian Communist, a vicious man of enormous cunning." This does not sound very far, especially in tone, from certain passages in *Leaving a Doll's House* (IMC 244–45).[58] The fact that the book was ghostwritten by the Grants parodies Roth's belief that *Leaving a Doll's House* was ghostwritten by Gray with possible assistance from her husband.

Anger runs throughout *I Married a Communist*, not simply the increasing anger of Ira toward Eve and the Grants but an anger in America epitomized by Ira who had to fight for survival on all fronts all the time. In his early years, there were always a lot of "angry Jewish guys around like Ira. Angry Jews all over America, fighting something or other," his brother Murray explains. But this is an American right:

> One of the privileges of being American and Jewish was that you could be angry in the world in Ira's way, aggressive about your beliefs and leaving no insult unavenged. You didn't have to shrug and resign yourself. . . . Just get out in the open and argue your point. That's one of the biggest things that America gave to the Jews—gave them their anger. . . . America was paradise for angry Jews. (IMC 163–64)

"Angry Jewish guys" appeared in Hollywood, the garment business, the courtroom, the ballfield, politics, and the bedroom. Murray Ringold tells Zuckerman that his union wasn't a teacher's union but actually the "Union of Angry Jews" with the motto of "Angrier than thou" (IMC 164). The passage on anger is one of the clearest self-reflexive declarations by Roth of his own complex makeup.

Impersonation becomes the currency of the book, Ira impersonating Abraham Lincoln as he gains fame, Eve impersonating the various characters she plays and even herself, exposed at the end as Chava Fromkin from the Bronx. She is no more than a Jewish actress with an English accent until she gets caught up "in her own impersonation" (IMC 157), her life a series of roles that ultimately fail. Ira's life begins as a series of roles that he constantly seeks to escape until his life becomes a parody of itself because of Eve's book at the end of the novel, accelerated because with Ira "everything emotional had to be superabundant" (IMC 167).

Roth had already moved into his American Trilogy, which began with *American Pastoral* in 1997. But that novel, and *I Married a Communist* and *The Human Stain*, which followed, completing the trilogy, emphasize an America unraveling, on the brink of dissolution whether as a result of the Vietnam War (AP), the McCarthy hearings and the Communist fear (IMC), or Political Correctness and the Clinton impeachment (HS). Zuckerman is minimally present in all three works, the on-the-margin observer of the stories of Swede Levov, Ira Ringold, and Coleman Silk. In the first, we see him as a mature writer eager to tell the story of the all-American Levov, athlete, Marine Corps veteran, and husband to the former Miss New Jersey; in the second, Zuckerman begins as a fifteen-year-old would-be playwright finding a new father figure in the politically radical Ira Ringold; in the third, he is a mature author settled in the countryside relating to the dismissed academic Coleman Silk. All three works stress the excesses of postwar America, subject to political and social storms. Interestingly, it is Eve Frame's daughter Sylphid, and earlier Swede's daughter Merry, who dismantle male fantasies of more virtuous times.[59]

Of course, fiction as revenge for Roth is not new: it includes the Maggie-like Maureen in *My Life as a Man* and Irving Howe–Milton Appel in *The Anatomy Lesson*. Even his revered Lonoff comes in for criticism. Modeled partly on Malamud (possibly with a touch of I. B. Singer) in *The Ghost Writer*, Lonoff, isolated in the woods, is also capable of having a secret affair, as Malamud did. In her 2006 memoir, *My Father Is a Book*, Malamud's daughter reports on her father's extramarital affair with a Bennington student in the 1960s named Arlene, which continued for some twenty years.[60] Lonoff's hidden feelings for Amy Bellette may be a reprisal of the reticent Malamud's activities. Even the revered Bellow (of whom it was said he wrote a novel about each ex-wife) comes in for criticism as the overly successful, pompous Felix Abravanel in *The Ghost Writer*.[61]

But for Roth, the function of writing was to correct wrongs, which simultaneously unmasks his anger and discontent and confronts shame. Anne

Frank in *The Ghost Writer* strives to reject shame. Don't be ashamed of your past, she is told by various foster families when she arrives in England: "I'm not ashamed. That's the point" is her reply (GW132). She would be exceptional not because of Auschwitz or Belsen but "because of what she had made of herself since" (GW 132).

Beyond Bloom, *I Married a Communist* shows American idealism and innocence betrayed, the destruction of what Murray Ringold calls the "myth of your own goodness" or "the fantasy of purity" (IMC 317–18; HS 242). The novel reconstructs a troubling American past (the 1940s and 1950s) but also the troubling relationship between Roth and Bloom, with other people from Roth's life transposed to fiction, notably his high school homeroom teacher, Robert Lowenstein, at the Hawthorne Avenue Annex in February 1946 when Roth was twelve. Lowenstein was the model for Murray Ringold and, like the character, had to testify because of union activities before the anti-Communist U.S. House panel when it came to Newark in the 1940s and 1950s.[62]

The masseuse Helgi Pärn, with whom Ira has an affair, is a partial recreation of Maletta, earlier represented in *Sabbath's Theater*. In response to Ira's harangues about the bourgeoisie stealing from the poor, she steals Eve's cigarette lighter. Eve finds out and in the crisis brings Katrina Van Tassell into her home. She, in turn, steals Ira's diaries and letters with information about Communist associates, an act Roth would not put past Gray. This becomes the source material for the ghostwritten *I Married a Communist*, published under Eve's name. Betrayal of a petty nature results in character assassination.

One of the critical themes of the novel is teaching, not only that of Murray Ringold or Leo Glucksman, teaching assistant at the University of Chicago, but John O'Day, a labor activist who educates the young Zuckerman, as well as Ira, instructing audiences in social politics. In his speeches, Ira enlightens his audiences on Communist values, political choices, and protest action. Other teachers and professors in Roth are David Kepesh, Coleman Silk, and Pegeen Stapleford, the forty-year-old who accepts a job teaching at a Vermont college and soon develops a relationship with Simon Axler, retired actor.

Roth cannot escape the classroom, where he himself felt most at home, whether at Chicago, Iowa, Princeton, Penn, Stony Brook, or Hunter. "Almost the whole of my life in public takes place in a classroom," he wrote in "After Eight Books," a 1974 essay reprinted in *Reading Myself and Others*. His reputation sometimes followed him, he wrote, but a few weeks after class began, when the students realized he would not be exposing himself or trying to sell his books, they allowed him to be a literature teacher "instead of Famous."[63] Roth himself was influenced by a set of key teachers: Robert Lowenstein in high school, Mildred Martin at Bucknell, Richard Stern and Bellow at Chicago, Kitaj as well as Al Alvarez in London.

Reminiscences by several of his students, mostly from Penn, emphasize Roth's humor, generosity, and high standards. Robert Brown, who took Roth's course in world literature in the spring of 1965, recalled how Roth imitated Groucho Marx when he walked into his class.[64] He used Groucho's duck walk to show that Kafka's *The Castle* was a comic text and that the novel was actually a Marx Brothers script. His teaching was text-specific, asking students about a scene, character, or line of dialogue. Never was he condescending, although they were warned not to bring up his own work or his personal life.

Dostoevsky, Tolstoy, Gogol, Mann, Nabokov were the key authors in the world literature course. Roth dissected Tolstoy's literary strategy in handling the scenes of sexual consummation between Vronsky and Anna Karenina. A comparison between *Death in Venice* and *Lolita* followed, with Roth asking if there was any difference between von Aschenbach's lust for a young boy and Humbert Humbert's for the young Lolita.

Another Penn student, one of seven in a creative writing class, felt part of an elect group as Roth talked about Kafka, his contempt for Nixon the trickster, and even, indirectly, problems with his first wife.[65] Lunch with Roth and another student at La Terrasse became a feast of comedy, and he continued to correspond with a few students and advise on their applications for different programs. In one letter, he shared his attachment to the South Side of Chicago, saying it was the only neighborhood he still felt connected to outside of his square mile in Newark.

When this student suffered a breakdown and returned from Stanford to Penn, Roth visited her in the hospital. When she recovered, he invited her to his comparative literature class. Even after graduate school, when the student "fell in love with self-destruction," Roth was there to help, writing encouragingly to her from London. And when she later wrote lengthy and often repetitive letters, he wrote that it was good she did not run of out words and that "talking is living too."[66] Throughout, Roth showed patience and empathy. He suggested a kind of "underground university" for her and books on which she would write him her thoughts and impressions. The first title was *Cancer Ward* by Solzhenitsyn; she read the book in two days and sent him pages. He replied that her handwriting was microscopic, hence illegible.

Roth, however, did pursue his students and not always Platonically. Throughout his teaching, he found the classroom an almost unending source of young and often willing females, as Kepesh and later Mickey Sabbath also noted. Roth's exploits with students began at the University of Iowa and accelerated at Penn with a student in 1971 when he was thirty-eight and she was nineteen. Thirty-five years later, they met again and she thought they might resume. When that original encounter ended, another student took her place. He fell in love with her, but she broke it off when she went to graduate school. This was in the early 1970s. They, too, remet years later and began again, but her work as an executive in New York interfered, although they regularly saw each other in Connecticut until they supposedly argued over an article on Bellow in the *New York Times Magazine* and it ended. Then he began a relationship with another former student living at the time in Litchfield, after he and Barbara Sproul broke up in the mid-1970s. In the late 1990s a relationship with one more student began, a graduate student in creative writing from Australia, Chloe Hooper, met at Columbia.[67] Their age difference was forty-two years, but he was quite taken with her and not only because of her figure, part of which he transposed to Consuela in *The Dying Animal.* She had written a first novel which Roth thought quite good, and so did Andrew Wylie, who sold it.

But during their relationship, Roth's friend, the Australian comedian Barry Humphreys of Dame Edna fame, once took her to a play (Roth and Chloe had met him after seeing one of his shows) and Roth thought something might be up. In fact, the night after seeing the "Dame Edna Show," seated at the Redeye Diner and Grill in Manhattan, Roth half-jokingly suggested that they elope and get married in Maryland. Hooper laughed and he dropped it. But for the first time that he could remember, Roth felt jealous over a woman, convinced Humphries was making a play for her. Humphries denied it, but Roth remained skeptical.

In a later document, Roth described his method of confronting such moments: "When something new and awful happens to me, I begin to make notes in a composition book," a process followed throughout his father's illness, which eventually led to *Patrimony* (NOT 221). The affair with Hooper ended rather suddenly when she unexpectedly decided *not* to visit Roth for the weekend in Connecticut. She was actually on the bus but impulsively got off. He was miserable. But months later, after she returned to Melbourne, they reconnected and stayed in touch.

Roth later wrote that he felt miserable over the Humphries incident but that the episode became an emotional model for what happens to Kepesh in *The Dying Animal* as he grows jealous of Consuela and likely competition from younger men. But Roth repeated the situation in other relationships of similarly notable age differences. With an Italian lawyer, the difference was thirty-eight years; with the next romance, forty-one years; after that, forty-six years. Following that association, there was a difference of thirty-two years. Among his women, only Maggie (four years) and Bloom (two years) were older. Mudge was only a few months older than Roth. Sproul was thirteen years younger, Hobhouse fifteen years, Maletta only eight.

With the London journalist there was a nineteen-year difference in age; with Julia Golier, met later in New York, it was thirty-one. Between Roth and Nicole Prevatt from Cornwall Bridge there was approximately a thirty-six-year difference, akin to the difference in age between Coleman and Faunia in *The Human Stain*.[68] The difference between Susan Rogers and Roth was also notable, Roth sixty-eight at the time. *Exit Ghost* acknowledges these differences when the seventy-one-year-old Zuckerman becomes infatuated with the thirty-year-old Jaimie, echoing the gap between Roth (seventy-two) and Catherine Steindler (twenty-nine).[69] Much of this may have been Roth proving to himself that as he aged, he was still attractive to younger and beautiful women, who were no doubt flattered to be of interest to such a renowned figure. He, in turn, was proud to show them off at awards ceremonies and dinner parties and even the White House. Two of them, Janet Hobhouse and Lisa Halliday, flattered him more by writing novels about him.

Halliday fictionalized Roth in her novel *Asymmetry* (2018), covering the years roughly from 2004 to 2011, where the age difference is also significant: in her account, the noted author Ezra Blazer is seventyish, but Alice, an editorial assistant, is twenty-five. They meet in the park; in actuality, Halliday and Roth met in the elevator at Wylie's agency, where she worked. (She in fact timed her departure that day to wind up in the same elevator as Roth.) He had noticed her in the office and asked her to lunch. They stopped at the Bagel Baron on West 57th, where her golden-reddish hair stood out in the sunlight, almost overshadowing her fluent speech, producing, Roth wrote, almost perfect paragraphs when describing herself. She was twenty-three but looked sixteen. Roth was sixty-nine. They kept their affair a secret.

"Are you game?" Roth asked Halliday as they left, precisely what the author in her novel asks, parroting exactly what the narrator in *Everyman* asks the buxom jogger he meets on the boardwalk.[70] But where the narrator failed,

Roth succeeded. In a notebook, Roth wrote that he was in fact thinking of Halliday when he wrote the scene.[71] Halliday said yes and shortly after an affair began. And soon, he gave her a wallet, a winter coat, and money to pay off her student loan. The Lewis Carroll references (Alice struggling through the surreal world of *Asymmetry*) are intentional and Ezra (Roth) has to educate Alice away from certain childish mannerisms. "Don't continually say 'I'm sorry,'" he tells her. "Next time you feel like saying 'I'm sorry,' instead say 'Fuck you.'"[72] But of course, their asymmetrical relationship leads to clashes and ends, although not bitterly.

Throughout his work, Roth's male characters repeatedly engage with younger women, nowhere more evident than in *Exit Ghost*. But earlier there is Kepesh and two Swedish students in *The Professor of Desire*, Kepesh again with Consuela in *The Dying Animal*, Lonoff and Amy Bellette in *The Ghost Writer*, Henry Zuckerman and his dental assistant Wendy Casselman in *The Counterlife*, the narrator of *Everyman* and his various mistresses and wives, Coleman Silk and Faunia and Simon Axler and Pegeen.[73] Roth and female youth is a constant, although occasionally there is an exception: Lydia Ketterer, a student in Zuckerman's creative writing course in *My Life as a Man*, is five years older but he still marries her, partly to gain joint custody of her teenage daughter, Monica, with whom he will flee to Italy after Lydia dies. When she turns twenty-one, he asks Monica to marry him. She refuses.

Children in Roth is a collateral theme, ranging from the young black boy who regularly comes to the Newark Public Library to study Gaugin in "Goodbye, Columbus," to the Newark buddies of Alex Portnoy and the insufferable Sylphid Pennington in *I Married a Communist*. The children of *Nemesis* further populate his fiction, anticipated by *Letting Go*, where children both dead and alive appear on almost every page, from Libby Herz's abortion to adoption. Martha has two children, one of whom dies; Henry and Theresa Bigoness have three. The affection Gabe feels for children throughout the novel duplicates Roth's affection for Maggie's two children. In *The Facts*, Roth recounts how he tried to not only teach her children but took them to various Chicago museums, as Gabe does with Martha's two when they visit the aquarium. And, of course, there is the issue of infanticide, implied in *The Human Stain* through the suggestion that Les Farley, Faunia's husband, may have set their house on fire, killing their two children (HS 235, 53, 66–67, 73). And there is Maureen Tarnopol's phantom child that she supposedly aborted in *My Life as a Man*.

What the 1990s culminated in for Roth was not marriage or individual children—he recounted how he was once given a gift of kittens but had to get rid of them because they were too delightful and interfered with his writing (EG 8–12)—but American children: Merry Levov in *American Pastoral*, the children taught by Murray Ringold and by extension Ira in *I Married a Communist*, the lost children of Faunia Farley in *The Human Stain*, the college students in *Indignation*, and the Newark students in *Nemesis*. In a letter from late March 1987 to David Rieff, when life in London and with Bloom was exceedingly stressful, Roth confessed that life seemed empty.[74] Ironically, from his early experiences with Holly and David to later encounters with the twins of Julia Golier, Roth enjoyed children. But responsibility for them and the realization that marriage would often be the conventional passport to fatherhood prevented him from pursuing. With one late liaison, however, he did in fact seek medical advice if he could legitimately father a healthy child. At the time he was in his mid-seventies.

During this period in and out of romance, Roth worked constantly and the books came out rapidly: 1997, 1998, and 2000 through to 2010, his productivity recalling the output of Henry James, who published three important novels in three successive years: *The Wings of the Dove* (1902), *The Ambassadors* (1903), and *The Golden Bowl* (1904).

But a divide emerged in the 1990s between the Roth with gusto and the Roth with nostalgia in his shaping a new guide to reclaim America. Some argued that his remarkable productivity in the late 1990s, creating his American Trilogy, exhausted his sense of imaginative play, marked by the mellower *The Dying Animal* of 2001. Supplanting that was an idealized nostalgia presented in his second bestseller, *The Plot Against America* in 2004, while his late works struggled against death and disappearance: *Everyman*, *Exit Ghost*, and then *Indignation*, *The Humbling*, and *Nemesis*. The replacement of the frenetic, outrageous narrator-heroes of *Operation Shylock* and *Sabbath's Theater* with an older Zuckerman or mature, if young, narrators, as in *Nemesis*, reflects Roth's own senescence matched by the aging of his protagonists as they look at the past from a bewildering adulthood. This shift found physical expression in increasingly shorter books.

Additionally, Roth's world seems in conflict with itself. His characters seem out of step with their times, Roth falling back on historical placement and contrasts. Swede Levov acts like an eighteenth-century landowner with his farm at Rimrock, Ira Ringold impersonates Lincoln, and Coleman Silk passes for a white Jewish academic at a rural college, all evoking a world of performance set in the past. Instead of the outrage, the anger, the explosive energy that took Roth into Sabbath's theater, there is a recessive, quasi-resistance but little fight or anger in any of his late protagonists. Resignation or reluctant acceptance is the new norm, or if you do resist, as Marcus Messner does, death.

Roth's identity as an American Adam remains full of expectation, seen most clearly *not* in Portnoy's sexual conquest of the country but in Swede Levov, former athlete and U.S. Marine and now married to a beauty queen. But preceding Swede's fall and the irony of his American dream is Zuckerman's celebration of Swede's innocent nation: "Hate America? Why, he lived in America the way he lived inside his own skin. All the pleasure of his younger years were American pleasures, all that success and happiness had been American. . . . Everything that gave meaning to his accomplishments had been American. Everything he loved was here" (AP 213).

By contrast, his daughter, Merry, hates everything American. The character is based on Kathy Boudin, the cofounder of the Weather Underground who spent twenty-two years in prison for her role in a 1981 robbery in Nanuet, New York, that left three dead. Roth had been friendly with her parents, Leonard and Jean Boudin, Leonard a civil liberties attorney and activist who represented Daniel Ellsberg in the Pentagon Papers scandal and Dr. Benjamin Spock who advocated draft resistance. Swede's life is the American Adam in reverse: filled with hope and a desire to erase his past, he seeks a new innocence, but his experience of America in the 1960s does not allow it. Rural Rimrock provides no salvation.

The American landscape becomes not just disillusioning but destroyed: a bomb ends Rimrock's potential as a place of unscarred American life for Swede and his family. In *Nemesis,* rural Pennsylvania, home to the Indian Hill summer camp promoting Native American traditions, becomes a literal source of disease when polio strikes, affecting even the swim instructor and athlete Bucky Cantor. Few, if any, traditional pioneers endure in Roth's work. An exception is Murray Ringold, former high school teacher maligned by the McCarthy hearings. But the murder of his wife damages him so severely that even he gives up and leaves Newark for Phoenix (which proves more isolating than comforting). Roth's America no longer allows for discoverers, but the ideal still appeals with its suggestion of individuality, grit, and hope.

Democracy in America might be the title for Roth's entire body of work given his continued encounter with American morality, injustice, and repression, creating an underlying anger more ferocious for its restraint than release—but then set free in Portnoy, Mickey Sabbath, and (partially) Swede. In this way, his heroes try unsuccessfully to unburden themselves from history in the style of the American Adam. But the moral paradox of Americans, according to de Tocqueville, is that they talk in a noble language while committing ignoble (but for Roth inspiring) deeds.

For Roth heroics do not make a hero, only antiheroics. Ozzie Freedman, standing on a roof in "The Conversion of the Jews," must become an apostate to express his faith as he orders his Hebrew school students gathered below him to acknowledge the Immaculate Conception. He then fulfills his threat to jump, but into a net held by kneeling firemen. Eli Peck, in "Eli, the Fanatic," loses his mental balance in his sudden turn to Orthodoxy, another sign of corrupted innocence. The late novels accelerate the situation: Marcus Messner dies fighting in Korea, Simon Axler in his attic. Bucky Cantor succumbs to that most American of diseases, polio, given national profile through the illness of FDR. Heroes in Roth have only tragic ends. Ironically, only antiheroes like Alex Portnoy and Mickey Sabbath survive.

Importantly, what emerges most clearly in the American Trilogy is an American aesthetic, the need to record everything, as Roth explained to the journalist Charles McGrath: "At the heart of the task to which every American novelist has been enjoined [is] to discover the most arresting evocative verbal depiction for every last American thing." The last four words offer a keynote to Roth's work and combine with his other themes: the divided self, sex, Jewishness, death, deception and betrayal, all keys to his work. The "American thing" combines with a "passion for specificity, for the hypnotic materiality of the world one is in."[75]

Roth constantly framed his work with American concerns, American issues, and American problems, from sex to success. He repeatedly asserted, "I don't write Jewish. I write American."[76]

He later explained, "I flow or I don't flow in American English. I get it right or I get it wrong in American English. Even if I wrote in Hebrew or Yiddish, I would not be a Jewish writer. I would be a Hebrew writer or a Yiddish writer."[77] This may be a late justification, but the situation is complex: in his early letters he welcomed being identified with Jewish writers such as Kafka, Bruno Schulz, I. B. Singer, and Bellow. But as he foregrounded American life, especially in the American Trilogy, he replaced an earlier Jewish identity with one purely American.

Throughout his work, Roth also constantly revised the idea of "the American hero" expressed through his problematic relationship with the

Figure 10.1 Roth at his standing desk in his Cornwall Bridge studio, 2004.
Credit: James Nachtwey/James Nachtwey Archive, Hood Museum of Art,
Dartmouth College, Hanover, New Hampshire.

figure of the American Adam. His preoccupation with sex, for example, is
not a restless, seemingly uncontrollable Jewish sex drive but a response to the
Puritanism of America originally challenged by Hawthorne and others. For
Roth, America's repression of sex became a source of constant social critique
and one that often defined, if not identified, American writing. He also quickly
recognized the conflict between the myth of success and sexuality: achievement in America was no guarantee of performing well in bed, especially in
a marriage. How Roth engaged with that struggle is part of his narrative revision of the complex paradigm of the American Adam: "All my poisons are
American poisons," he admitted in a 1997 French TV documentary.[78]

The statement, mixing Mickey Sabbath's "poisons" with the Declaration
of Independence, is one of Roth's most direct acknowledgments of his per-
vasive and troubled American character, an acknowledgment of his birth
into a disturbing national myth renewed when he returned from England in
1988. His work interrogates the conflict between possessing a nationalist and
an "other" identity, which Abe Ravelstein, Bellow's six-foot-six philosopher-
king of Chicago, understands clearly: "As a Jew you are also an American, but
somehow you are also not," he tells the narrator.[79]

One of Roth's readers at this time, who was actually an inspiration for the American Trilogy, was the South African writer Nadine Gordimer. (In 1991 she became a Nobel laureate.) Sent a copy of *The Human Stain*, she wrote a praiseworthy letter to Roth, calling the work the best he had done. (*American Pastoral* did not satisfy in the same way, she remarked.) *The Human Stain* incorporates everything he has absorbed about American beliefs, social practices, and prejudices, and the originality of creating a figure who is both Jewish and Black is remarkable. In any society, whether in South Africa or North America, there will always be stains that will offend, which come through the work of any writer who "says the unsayable, speaks the unspeakable." She ends by citing Coetzee's *Disgrace* and its shamed academic who retreats to his daughter's farm, although she finds it only a "fiery autumn leaf, dried between your pages" in relation to what Roth accomplished within the "leap-tides of human reaction and feeling."[80]

In response, Roth tells her that her novel *July's People* did much to stimulate the writing of his American Trilogy and specifically *American Pastoral*. He recalls that when teaching at Hunter College in the early 1990s, he put *July's People* at the center of his course on the novel, referring to it as a powerhouse and a masterpiece. The 1981 novel is set in a South Africa where a civil war is occurring to end apartheid. The banned novel appeared before the end of apartheid. Roth criticizes the decline of culture, referring to "a philistine vandalism" present in both the media and university life, "endlessly obsessed with the writer's biography and the horrid transgression of the writer's imagination feeding on life for fiction." And book publishing now occurs only to make a living. The public has no idea what a serious novel is, what it does or how it does it. Learning to get to "the heart of a novel is now a mystery to virtually everyone but the writers themselves."[81] In response, Gordimer tells Roth that she wrote *July's People* "with a scalpel rather than a pen in hand," and that she "avoided nothing, while fearing everything" she was writing about.[82]

One of the most controversial elements of *The Human Stain* was the source for Coleman Silk. In a lengthy letter to Wikipedia, Roth strenuously denied any connection with the writer and critic Anatole Broyard, emphasizing that the entire incident inciting the action where Coleman Silk refers to a number of absent black students as "Spooks," originated in a class by his friend Melvin Tumin at Princeton. Two letters to Updike, however, seem to contradict Roth's supposed ignorance or neglect of Broyard and his "passing." Roth tells Updike he knew Broyard back in the 1950s when Roth was at Amagansett and even thought then he might be "one-eighth" Jewish. He was talented, but his genius was "for elaborate mischief and deception." In a later letter, Roth's animosity toward Broyard becomes clear; he calls him a "fake white man and a fake writer." He had many appealing qualities, like his "seductive char-latanism," but he couldn't write after his interesting beginning.[83] The complexity of his identity, however, may be the very thing that appealed to Roth, which infiltrates Silk's character.

The title of Chapter 17 in volume 2 of de Tocqueville's *Democracy in America* suggests Roth's starting point and predicament in relation to America: "How Society in the United States Seems Both Agitated and Monotonous." Roth's engagement with sex, politics, and history in his work is an inquiry into American life—both its disruptive and conservative aspects. As Drenka tells Mickey Sabbath, "You *are* America. Yes, you are, my wicked boy," an identity defined by contradictions and confusions (ST 419). Such recognition blends the American self with sexual transgression, as Sabbath is shown visiting and even masturbating on Drenka's grave in the Colonial American cemetery near their town, the first burial in 1745, the last (Drenka) in 1993 (ST 51).

Renata Adler identifies Roth's solution to the problem of American identity and innocence when a character in her 1983 novel, *Pitch Dark*, explains that "under the American Constitution . . . everything is required to be, at heart, a story."[84] To be American is to be a storyteller in many ways, best embodied by the contradictions of the renegade Mickey Sabbath.

At the end of *Sabbath's Theater*, accused of desecrating the American flag and Judaism by Drenka's son (a state police officer), Sabbath displays a curious courage while wrapped in the U.S. flag from the box of his brother's mementos:

> Never take it off—why should he? On his head the red, white, and blue V for Victory, God Bless America yarmulke. Dressing like this made not a scrap of difference to anything . . . abated nothing, neither merged him with what was gone nor separated him from what was here, and yet he was determined never again to dress otherwise. A man of mirth must always dress in the priestly garb of his sect. (ST 413)

Triumphantly, he claims that his brother, Morty, did not die in the Philippines because he was Jewish. He died "because he was an American. They killed him because he was born in America" (ST 405).

Roth is an American romantic, but he constantly challenges the country's past, putting Puritanism on trial in *Portnoy's Complaint*, political repression in *I Married a Communist*, racial tensions in *The Human Stain,* and authoritarianism in *The Plot Against America*. He objected to the Vietnam War and objected to President Trump.[85] Mickey Sabbath may wrap himself in an American flag and stand on the seashore near the end of *Sabbath's Theater,* but he is a mournful patriot, conscious of both a dark past and an uncertain future.[86] An American flag may fly over the U.S. postal station in Old Rimrock, but it is quickly ripped apart by a bomb in *American Pastoral.* Years after that book's publication, as a sign of atonement as well as solidarity, Roth hung a large American flag in the window of his New York apartment after the attacks of 9/11.[87]

Epitomizing Roth's American condition and the difficulty of sustaining innocence in the face of experience is Nathan Zuckerman. His combination of naïveté and observation gradually disabuses him of his innocence, but he can still enjoy dancing under the stars with Silk to 1940s American music in the wilderness of the Berkshires in *The Human Stain.*[88] Roth himself alternated between optimism and worry, Murray Ringold warning Zuckerman to "beware the utopia of isolation" (IMC 315). "What innocence?" Roth rhetorically asked in response to the idea that America lost its virtue after 9/11. His own, overall sense of American history since the mid-1990s was dark: "From 1668 to 1865 this country had slavery; and from 1865 to 1955 was a society existing under brutal segregation. I don't really know what these people (who refer to American innocence) are talking about," he explained in 2002.[89]

Roth persisted in searching for an American identity that transcended politics and bias. As an American, he gestured toward an earlier, nostalgic time; in *The Plot Against America* the Roth family seeks the cherished myth of America during their trip to Washington only to meet a new, authoritarian horror. But even with such knowledge, Roth does not renounce his American identity. The obsession of a novelist is "finding the right next word," but for Roth that is an American word. America, and an American vocabulary, give his language currency.[90] There is no irony in the title of Adam Gopnik's 2017 survey of Roth's nonfiction writing, published as his tenth volume in the Library of America series: it is "The Patriot."[91]

11

Quintet, or The Jersey Style

Let's speak further of death and of the desire . . . to resist it . . . to see death with anything, anything, *anything* but clarity.

—Philip Roth, *American Pastoral*, 1997

Beyond Roth's romance with American history and storytelling came a late longing to re-create his personal past, reaching back to the 1940s and 1950s in his five late works: *Everyman, Exit Ghost, Indignation, The Humbling*, and *Nemesis*. Whether it is an older Zuckerman reencountering Amy Bellette and learning more of Lonoff in the post-9/11 world, or the narrator of *Everyman* turning back to review his life, in going forward with his work Roth looked back. The medieval title of *Everyman* (2006) signaled the shift to a retrospective narrative enacted by the ghostly voice of the narrator as he brings together cemeteries, funerals, and elegies initiated in *The Counterlife, The Anatomy Lesson*, and *Sabbath's Theater*. The final three novels all courted death, the first on the battlefield, the second in an attic, and the third in an iron lung. Ironically, the death of Newark may itself be Roth's final theme, initiated by his American Trilogy but culminating in his final works.

Zuckerman, incontinent and impotent in *Exit Ghost*, signals this late decay: he never reads a paper and doesn't own a television, let alone a cell phone, yet attempts to discover the truth of his early encounter with Lonoff and Bellette in *The Ghost Writer*. *Indignation* re-creates the world of the early 1950s and the Korean War, while *The Humbling* narrates the decline of an aging actor as his career ends and his sex life disappears (with only a temporary rejuvenation). In his final novel, *Nemesis*, Roth re-creates a Newark in double-time: the deterioration of its youth from polio and then, years later, its aftermath. Death by war, suicide, and disease dominates these last three books, proving, as his early favorite novelist Thomas Wolfe wrote, you can't go home again.[1] Roth's past had been decimated, projecting a prolonged discontent with personal and public history.

One expression of this change is the creation of what one might call a "Jersey style," identified by George Plimpton as a direct, unembellished, modulated, reportorial language.[2] The sentences are clipped and the rhetoric scaled down. The origin of this style was partly the world of Roth's father, who offered "something coarser" than literary talk, teaching his son "the vernacular." He was, Roth writes, *the* "vernacular, unpoetic and expressive and point-blank, with all the vernacular's glaring limitations and all its durable force" (PAT 181). This "point-blank" style was the language of the street, the apartment, the schoolyard, the hangouts, the office, the garage, and the store, straight language that nevertheless incorporated Jersey symbols: the working class, the industrial skyline, the shore.

The Jersey style, as one New Jersey book on usage suggests, is a technique where you "write as if you were speaking or giving directions aloud; avoid jargon, ambiguous wording." Its cropped style may seem easy to achieve but it requires "consistent attention to organization, format and grammar." Active voice is preferable because it "leaves no doubt who is responsible for the action described" and used correctly it adds clarity and "lessens a reader's burden by simplifying sentence structures and eliminating words," all habits of Roth's late style. Finally, one must be specific and prefer the indicative mood, "using the imperative sparingly." Language should be transparent and avoid calling attention to itself.[3] Or, as Roth remarked in *Exit Ghost* about death, "The end is so immense, it is its own poetry. It requires little rhetoric. Just state it plainly" (EG 152). This is the style of his last four titles and coincides with his increasingly poor health, thoughts of death, and onset of the infirmities of old age. A stylistic weakening matched his physical decline.

To write the world of his late fiction, Roth applies to the Jersey style a peculiar blend of old-school Jersey street talk matched against left-over Jamesian phrases with a touch of Conrad. *The Shadow Line*, Conrad's novella of 1916, was also a late influence, Zuckerman carrying a copy in *Exit Ghost*. The title alone might be a metaphor of Roth's transition from his early and mid-career style to that of his late. In crossing his shadow line (old age, a renewed sense of mortality), a new idiolect emerges which actually reverts back to his earliest methods of expression relying on unadulterated prose, as seen in such stories as "The Day It Snowed"(1954) and "Novotny's Pain" (1962). Characterizing this is his reliance on hard, clear nouns and unescorted verbs with syntax that is direct and not ornate. It is low-voltage writing to underscore writing with conviction. Several late examples: "Passing the time was excruciating without painting" (EV 124); "There's nobody less salvageable than a ruined good boy" (NEM 272).

In one scene in *Nemesis*, the Jersey style becomes its own subject through an act of writing when years later Bucky Cantor shows Arnold Mesnikoff, of the Chancellor Avenue playground gang and a polio victim, a letter addressed to him postmarked July 2, 1944, by his love, Marcia. Written in perfect Palmer Method cursive, it simply repeated two words over and over again: "My man" (NEM 251). Here, the boiled-down Jersey style speaks for and calls attention to itself. It was signed with only the initial "M" (NEM 251).

Through its emphasis on the colloquial (not the rhetorical) and reliance on a no-nonsense, straightforward, and unpretentious tone, the Jersey style becomes a democratizing move, life in a minor key played out in simple, honest, nonliterary, everyday language understood by all.[4] The technique de-emphasizes vitality for directness and access and may, in fact, explain why critics and readers found his late works disappointing, the simplicity of the expression understood not as a Jersey style but as a lessening of verbal energy, a clear decline. For Roth, also a weakening of his own vitality as he approached eighty. But this shift was itself a struggle, since his natural bent was to amplify, to enlarge. Now it was the reverse: the adaptation of a method that marked the origin of his earliest writing, a simpler style seen in the first sentence of "Goodbye, Columbus": "The first time I saw Brenda she asked me to hold her glasses" (GBC 3). Names themselves take on a simpler shade: no longer do we meet Knuckles Kimmelman or Niggy Apfelbaum or Shepsie Tirschwell (*The Plot Against America*) but the more everyday Nancy or Howie or Brad (*Everyman*)—or, ironically, in a kind of Beckettian reductionism, the erasure of a name, as that of the narrator of *Everyman*. The shouting, the way a Jew thinks, as Roth earlier wrote, had stopped.

But before he switched register and language, Roth had to exhaust his syntactically energized and diffuse style within the New Jersey *milieu*: *The Plot Against America* where threats to a New Jersey life in an altered America jeopardize not only life but language.[5] *The Plot* marks the end of Roth's exuberant style, functioning as a prelude to the return to his Jersey style. The language is serious, assuming a kind of moral responsibility for ordering American life in the face of widespread disorder. Roth stopped writing fiction in 2010 not because he had no more to say but because he had exhausted his language. The Jersey style had erased the need for flamboyance, lyricism, or high-octane writing and curtailed his storytelling. After the recovery of his Jersey style, there was no need for anything more.[6]

The Plot Against America (2004), a novel of the 1940s, was his second most popular work measured by sales. As he explained, the idea originated with a curious footnote that appeared in *A Life in the 20th Century: Innocent Beginnings, 1917–1950*, the historian Arthur Schlesinger Jr.'s autobiography, which said that some Republicans in 1940 considered nominating Charles Lindbergh for president. "What if they had?" was Roth's marginal annotation while reading the book. The question led to the novel, prompting his alternate history. He worked on the book from 2000 to 2004. He knew of Lindbergh's isolationism and anti-Semitism when he spoke for America First and so imagined the surprise defeat of Roosevelt in the 1940 presidential election. Even before Roth started school, he knew of Nazi anti-Semitism and how American anti-Semitism was being fueled by figures like Henry Ford and Lindbergh, as related to him by his father. The book's goal was to make the imagined history seem authentic.[7] It also gave him the chance to bring his parents back to life and show how they might respond to the pressure of a Jewish crisis in America addressing the problem of anti-Semitism. He presents them faithfully. But it is the victimized Wishnows (wish now) who become the most tragic figures, the mother murdered in Kentucky by a mob and the son suddenly orphaned but gallantly rescued by Herman Roth and his son, Sandy. Importantly, Roth represents history as the mundane, the everyday, as he depicts family life in 1940. History comes into and through the living room, *his* living room, as he re-creates his own family life, mixing history and memory. His mantra when writing the book, which he repeated often, was "Don't invent, just remember."[8] And his talent, as he outlined, was for imagining not on a grand scale, only on a small. Of course, Lindbergh did not become president, so Roth had to pretend that it happened and how his family would react. The menace of racist and isolationist Lindbergh and the pressure it put on family, especially his father, was the focus. It many ways family history trumps that of the U.S. Especially disturbing was having the young Roth watch his father break down and cry because he could not stop "the unforeseen" (PAA 113).[9]

Children are at the center of Roth's late work, first "Roth" in *Plot* at ages seven, eight, and nine, and then "Roth" as an adult looking back some sixty years later. Children or young adults will also be at the center of *Indignation* and *Nemesis*. In some ways, he was fulfilling an earlier realization: in March 1987, he admitted to his editor David Rieff that he felt stupid "at being childless."[10] In *Plot*, he balances the boy's and adult's perspectives. And to secure the fictionalized authenticity of the novel, Roth includes a twenty-seven-page reference guide containing a chronology, biographical guide, and sources, his first novel to do so. But as Roth repeats, what his text represents is the opposite of what it describes; in short, it did not, although it could, happen here.

The novel returns readers to pre–World War II America, where the pro-fascist Lindbergh's victory shatters any social or political innocence. Anti-Semitism and pogroms follow. The imagined past is as real as the present, creating a transhistorical link between fact and fiction, the imagined and the historical, with the destruction of civil liberties creating civil and social warfare. Rabbi Bengelsdorf, husband of Bess Roth's sister Evelyn, becomes head of Lindbergh's Jewish assimilation program, bringing anger to the doorstep of the Roths. In the direct manner of the Jersey style, appearing briefly throughout the novel, Roth writes, "Our homeland was America. Then the Republicans nominated Lindbergh and everything changed" (PAA 5).

Part of that "everything" that is the new America is the anti-Semitism that hovers over the country, its social impact vividly presented when the Roths visit the capital, where the contradiction between the ideal of America seen through its monuments and statues contrasts with the behavior of everyday people who have turned against the Jews, whether hotel managers or policemen. Roth is, here, expanding on an actual 1941 trip made to D.C. by his family. An important photo from the journey is the family in a semicircle at the Arlington Memorial Amphitheater at Arlington National Cemetery.

Why Roth wrote the novel at this time may have been in response to the fraught U.S. presidential election of 2000, with its Florida recount and Bush winning the Electoral College vote but losing the popular vote, or the Bush-led Iraq war of 2003 again exhibiting authoritarian power. The possibility of an earlier demagogue in America in Lindbergh was frightening. The re-creation of his childhood was the reestablishment of a secure and stable time with Roosevelt in charge and democracy but now threatened by fascist-like, anti-Semitic power. To renew the values of a democratic republic, he had to put his family (and readers) through the torturous threats to American freedom.

Expanding this new racist America is the violent, anti-Semitic riot that later traps Mrs. Wishnow, who has been transferred via the "Just Friends" scheme to Kentucky. The mob kills her, leaving her son Seldon an orphan (his father had died from cancer). But Herman Roth's moral responsibility compels him to rescue Seldon, driving down to Kentucky with Sandy to bring the boy back to Newark. At one point, Roth explained that the novel is actually about boys : Sandy and Philip, Seldon, and the son of the Cucuzzas.

Cousin Alvin in the novel, another orphan but an older boy and now a wounded war veteran with whom Philip shares a room, is another reminder of stunted heroism caused by outside forces. He had lost his left leg below the knee. The origin of the situation was Roth sharing his room with his dying Aunt Ethel when a teenager.

Guilt is an especially strong element of the novel, the older Philip recalling this period thirty years earlier and thinking in the text that he didn't mean for the Wishnows to move: "I didn't mean to make Seldon the target" (PAA 350). Roth feels responsible for much of the deceptions and tricks played on Seldon and indirectly responsible for Seldon and his mother being sent to Kentucky: he had ironically suggested this to his Aunt Evelyn who worked in the Lindbergh-Bengelsdorf relocation bureau. This personal domestic tragedy parallels that of America.

Story and plot control the book, something of an adventure novel in a genre—alternate history—not practiced by Roth, although he knew of Sinclair Lewis's *It Can't Happen Here* (1935) about a fascist takeover of the U.S. read by Herman Roth and referred to by Swede's father in *American Pastoral*. The style of *Plot* is direct, immediate, and almost melodramatic: "The round trip of fifteen hundred miles was the adventure of Sandy's lifetime. It was something more fateful for my father." This is the way Roth begins the rescue mission for orphaned Seldon (PAA 355). And his love of specifics remains: on the return, Roth itemizes the vestiges of nearly deserted industrial towns, allowing himself lengthy, descriptive sentences of an emptied America, filling the blight with prose (PAA 356). But the triumph, for the ill and physically depleted Herman, is his return, Philip proudly writing that his father "was a rescuer and orphans were his specialty" (PAA 358). In the shadows may be Telemachus's admiring relationship to his father, the heroic Odysseus, although the description also ironically applies to Roth, who repeatedly rescued women who thought of themselves as orphans.

Writing *Plot* allowed Roth to return to the world of his childhood and represent his parents as decent, resolute American Jews who would renounce neither their family nor their country. His father chose "resistance," unlike Rabbi Bengelsdorf, who chose "collaboration" (PAA 359). The plot of the novel also allowed Roth to restate the American identity of his American Jews and his idealistic belief that being a Jew was not a misfortune: "Being Jews issued from their being themselves, as did their being American," he declares (PAA 220). This affirmation of Judaism and Americanism is one of the achievements of the novel, but also a warning in that religious practice was not required to be identified as a Jew in Lindbergh's anti-Semitic nation (PAA 64–67). Yet the noble Herman Roth stands up to the hotel manager as well as the police, displaying an American heroism (PAA 68–70). But America remains a complicated world: even as Lindbergh reveals his biases against Jews, the young Roth does not want to give up his Lindbergh stamps, nor is Sandy prepared to sacrifice his portraits of Lindbergh that he has hidden under his bed.

The novel is an extension of Roth's American energy given impetus by his return to the U.S. in 1988 after years in England. He realized he had "a new subject that was an old subject, which was this country. . . . It was brand new to me in a strange way," yet he understood it because he was brought up there, as he explained to Jeffrey Brown in a PBS television interview.[11] Actual events in the text sometimes shift: Lindbergh gave his infamous Des Moines speech in which he blamed the Jews for pulling the U.S. into the European war in 1941; Roth places it in 1940. And the tone is cautious and careful with no monologist on a tirade and with the almost complete absence of irony replaced by pathos, as in a radio speech by Mrs. Lindbergh (PAA 317–18).

However, moments of stylistic and comic flair still exist, as when the distraught Seldon, missing his mother and not knowing her fate, calls Mrs. Roth in Newark where she successfully keeps the frantic child sane partly through restrained comedy (PAA 329–36). Such dystopian fiction, as J. M. Coetzee called it, succeeds on multiple, unexpected levels, although several characters simply disappear at the end.[12] Lindbergh departs into thin air as he takes one last ride in his Lockheed fighter, and Seldon disappears into darkest Brooklyn where he is taken to live with an aunt, while Alvin disappears into a world of anger-fueled petty crime.

Instrumental during the approximately three years it took to write the novel was Roth's relationship with Susan Fox Rogers, the grown daughter of close friends from the University of Chicago, Jacqueline and Tom Rogers. Initially it was a casual reconnection; Rogers had taught English at Bard since 2001 and often drove over to see Roth in Cornwall Bridge. He began to take an interest in her and soon an affair started, which surprised both of them because she was a lesbian and hadn't slept with a man since her early twenties. She was also a keen nature writer who would focus on women adventurers, Alaska, and outdoor writing. She enjoyed swimming, which Roth did daily.

When Rogers appeared, Roth was in the midst of a severe siege of back pain. He tripped on his studio step and cut his hand the first time she visited, the result of a momentary disorientation caused by the medication, which had happened to him once before in New York. At that time and during his current bout with back pain, Ross Miller assisted. But Roth was alone for much of that summer in 2001 and could not write for more than half an hour before he would have to lie on the floor. At his fall, Rogers surprised him by immediately offering to clean and bandage his cuts. He rarely expected to get assistance from a woman after his years with Bloom.

Roth's morale was sinking and he began to think about suicide brought on by the unremitting pain, as a female character does in *Everyman*. But Roth recalled something Nicole Prevatt said to him about prostitution which he related to suicide when the pain dominated his life: Don't think it didn't occur to me. Rogers sensed his despair and immediately and directly helped him through his depression, in contrast to Bloom whom, he believed, would repeatedly match incompetence with hysteria in a moment of need. But Rogers and Miller—one of the few times when Roth acknowledged Miller's positive help—were with him through this period of intense, disabling pain. This was in 2001, the year before Roth's first back surgery, preceded by a panoply of drugs recommended by his physician. The narcotic Vicodin was the most potent painkiller but also the most addictive. Four a day would provide almost ten hours of pain relief.

In a personal document, Roth records that Rogers had a female dean at Bard, where she had recently begun to teach, who had sexually harassed her, despite Rogers's breaking off their relationship. The incident forms part of *The Humbling*. Stalking was common and because Rogers worked out with the swim team, the dean began to show up at the pool and swim at the same time. Roth soon began to document the incidents in case legal action was necessary. He actually contacted his lawyer at Milbank Tweed, who had earlier advised him over the Bloom book, as to advice for Rogers. But the harassment stopped, so a visit to the lawyer, for which Roth would have paid, was unnecessary.

Walks together with Rogers near Lake Waramaug and the Housatonic River near his home were enjoyable; when pain free, he could maintain a quick pace for three to five miles. The routine was one of his pleasures and central to his enjoyment of living there. Because of his heart condition, he needed forty-five minutes of aerobic activity daily. Hence, the walking, swimming, and treadmill routines (he had treadmills in his Connecticut and New York studios). But the sieges of back pain depressed him not only because of the pain itself, but being incapacitated prevented him from the regular exercise prescribed for his heart: it was almost as if his body was preventing him from living. It also kept him from writing. His conscientiousness toward such obligations—both his health and his work—partially explains how he came to write thirty-one books. His diligence in keeping a cardiologist's diet and exercise program he kept to himself, causing Miller to believe he was just neurotic about his health.

Such diligence, Roth explains in his private document, coupled with thoroughness and perseverance, was what saw him through teaching Maggie's two children how to read, caring for his dying father, transferring money to twelve Czech writers, supervising Bloom's financial accounts (she had been more or less swindled by her second husband, the producer Hillard Elkins), and attending a series of Anna's recitals hoping that by doing so she would become less hostile to him.

Prolonging the back problems was Roth's general anxiety over back surgery going back to 1956 and the army. But after a CAT scan and X-rays, he understood clearly what the problems were; they included multilevel disc degeneration and multilevel stenosis with nerve impingement and scoliosis of the lumbar spine. Given this diagnosis, he believed that the back pain was just something he had to live with. At first he received injections into the spinal cavity followed by some drugs to relieve nerve pain and then an anti-inflammatory drug before being prescribed Vicodin, on which he became dependent, especially between a first and second back operation. His attempt to decrease his dependency resulted in extreme withdrawal symptoms. He became so jumpy and agitated at a lunch with Aaron Asher that he had to leave midway. Dinner, a concert, or a movie meant rationing the Vicodin for relief. A September trip to the Jersey Shore with Rogers was a success because he would take two pills in the morning and two in the afternoon. They had a room in a bed and breakfast in Spring Lake, New Jersey (where he went when Bloom's book came out), and, according to Roth, enjoyed every sensual moment. A highlight was dinner at a fish store and restaurant that had a dock overlooking Belmar's Shark River inlet, where he and his brother and father use to fish.

But during this period (December 2001 to April 2004), a series of heart problems began to signal that his condition was deteriorating and the stents implanted over the years were having only moderate success. Beginning in December 2001, he had an angioplasty and had actually suffered a silent heart attack that damaged the posterior wall of his heart. On 1 October 2003, he had a defibrillator installed, but three weeks later he was back at Lenox Hill Hospital for three stents. In April 2004, it was an angiogram. The urgency to write and complete his work intensified, as did his desperate attempt to do something normal. Living in New York just before his first back surgery, he asked Rogers to drive down so they could go to the Jersey Shore and take a walk along the boardwalk and eat again at their favorite fish restaurant. They did, but his pain was too great for him to drive; Rogers was at the wheel.

Rogers was with him during all these medical challenges, including his back surgery in March 2002, which was, and was not, a success (his second operation was three years later), although he befriended his Irish Mormon doctor.[13] Immediate pain was eliminated but new problems emerged, including Ross Miller who, Roth felt, believed Rogers was usurping his position with Roth. She, in fact, couldn't stand him; Julia Golier felt the same. Both thought he was trying to exert control over Roth.

During the latter part of Roth's time with Rogers, he continued to write portions of *The Plot Against America* and would ask her what Seldon Wishnow might say in certain situations. She answered on the spot and became a valuable sounding board for the novel as a whole. In appreciation of her emotional support and literary assistance, he dedicated the novel to her, many mistaking the initials SFR for his brother. She also accompanied Roth to the National Book Awards when he received a distinguished writer award.

At one point, when she was to go off to Estampe in France where her family had a summer home (her mother was French), he gave her a gift of $100,000 for improvements on her own home. At forty, she had little money and he felt he had too much. A year later, he gave her $40,000 to help pay off her mortgage and then bought her a used Volvo station wagon. *The Humbling* draws from his experiences with her. For example, she did not want her parents to know of their affair. Unlike Simon Axler in the novel and his relationship with Pegeen (he also knew her parents), Roth agreed. They did not pick up a girl and bring her home for a *ménage à trois,* which occurs in the novel. But she was certainly the victim of sexual harassment by a female colleague. At one point, to lift her spirits, he took her to buy clothes with Judith Thurman at an upscale New York thrift shop. Thurman had an eye for style.

Nevertheless, Rogers and Roth broke up in 2004 partly because of a three-month research trip to Antarctica, part of a special U.S. Antarctic Artists and Writers Program (2004–5) she joined. While away, she was supposed to communicate to Roth via email through Miller. She didn't write, or so he thought; Roth had suspicions that their affair might be ending. He later learned that she had emailed through Miller who, apparently, failed to pass on the messages, which might have been a way for him to undermine Rogers's place with Roth and restore his own privileged position. But the misunderstanding between Roth and Rogers could not be corrected.[14] And after *The Humbling* came out, all communication stopped.

Reaction to *The Plot Against America* when it appeared was strong: it made numerous bestseller lists despite serious competition from Marilynne Robinson's *Gilead*, Alan Hollinghurst's *The Line of Beauty*, John Grisham's *The Last Juror*, and Stephen King's *Song of Susannah*. But political works published that year—Bill Clinton's *My Life*, Woodward and Bernstein's *Plan of Attack* (on the Bush administration's decision to invade Iraq), and Ron Chernow's detailed *Alexander Hamilton* (2004)—also created interest in political fiction. With these works as background, the fearful portrait of fascist America in *The Plot Against America* found immediate resonance with readers nationally and internationally. And despite Roth's insistence not to read the text as a *roman à clef*, the public and reviewers could not resist making comparisons with the Bush administration. The novel received numerous awards, including one as the outstanding American historical novel for 2003–4.

Typically, Roth shunned the acclaim and publicity and remained in Cornwall Bridge, gradually entrapped by age and becoming more and more preoccupied by mortality, which he knew was inescapable. Journalists were alert to the new obsession: "Death versus Roth; Roth versus Death. He has managed to clear his life of everything that is not writing . . . but how much longer can he keep this up? Every novel might be his last. Death and Roth, Roth and death. That's what's happening up in Connecticut," wrote Keith Gessen in a lengthy commentary on Roth's next work, *Everyman* (2006), narrated by a dead man.[15]

At the time, Roth was encircled by death, beginning with his Litchfield physician and friend C. H. Huvelle in 2000, former publisher Robert Straus in 2004, Bellow in 2005, and then, in December that year, his friend Charles Cummings, the official historian of Newark and unofficial advisor to Roth on all things related to the city. Then William Styron died in 2006, and the painter R. B. Kitaj died in Los Angeles in 2007. Aaron Asher, friend and former editor, died in 2008. Capping this near decade of death was the loss of his brother, Sandy, in May 2009 at age eighty-one.[16]

Bellow's death hit the hardest, his loss at eighty-nine marking a turning point in Roth's belief in the conception and continuity of American (Jewish) writing. Bellow's fictional monologues by impatient and impassioned characters became a bellwether for Roth's writing, as did his characters: Herzog retreats to the Berkshires, as does Zuckerman. For better or worse, Bellow was the trailblazer whose literary successes marked the recognition of a writer who easily reached beyond a Jewish readership.

Roth never stopped admiring Bellow. He went out of his way to ensure Bellow's well-being during his visit to London in March 1986 to deliver a PEN lecture. The two began to relax their wariness, brought on by an implicit sense of competition. Bellow was seventy and starting over, depressed by the recent death of two brothers and the end of his fourth marriage. Roth helped him, first, by changing his hotel, moving him to the Royal Automobile Club where Roth was a member (because of their swimming pool). On a Sunday, Roth and Bloom took Bellow to a Borodin Quartet concert, but he remained morose partly because a week or so before his trip, Malamud had died of a heart attack. Later in his visit, Roth and Bloom gave a dinner party for him; Edna O'Brien and Timothy Garton Ash, the journalist, were present. Bellow was still morose, but O'Brien enlivened the gathering.[17]

At times, Roth felt that Bellow was remote but Roth never lost his respect for his writing. Janis Bellow believed that Martin Amis and Roth were the "twin pillars" of Bellow's last years.[18] Bellow's death was deeply felt by Roth, especially because in the last years of Bellow's life they had renewed their friendship partly through Roth's effort to do an extensive interview with the older writer, which became "Re-Reading Saul Bellow," in the 9 October 2000 issue of the New Yorker. By 2005, death had become inescapable and now encircled Roth.

Roth's second back surgery the same year as Bellow's death, 2005, intensified his feeling enfeebled. He had actually begun a book on an aging actor based on Bloom telling him about Ralph Richardson and his postperformance comment that he had lost the magic, but he soon put that aside to deal with the inescapable: death. Everyman, a work confronting the moral and physical cost of death, became his new focus and cemeteries his favored locale. They soon began to dominate his work, from the prolonged scene in The Anatomy Lesson to Sabbath's Theater and Everyman. Funerals became so frequent that even he could not face another hole in the ground, as his father told him when confronted with attending the death of his younger brother who died the same year as Roth's mother, 1981.[19] Everyman, suffused with death, opens with a funeral and then reverses time as the protagonist, and by extension Roth, engage with the inconvenience of death, which always arrives when "I had thee least in mind," as Everyman in the original morality play remarks. Roth believed it was the first great line in English drama

(EV 210).[20] He was also pleased that the black cover of the novel suggested a tombstone.

In the novel, as in *Sabbath's Theater*, one is repeatedly surprised at losing one's life when one least expects it. Yet the novel seems to restrain the honesty of its characters; for example, the red-haired nurse Maureen is prevented from talking with the bluntness fueled by her working-class, Irish-Slavic origins. The second wife of the protagonist, partially based on Ann Mudge, is in conflict with the narrator's perpetual quest for sex.[21] As another of Roth's narrators remarks, "Every mistake that a man can make usually has a sexual accelerator" (HS 35). Roth felt the nonallegoric work did not achieve its potential, admitting that he only conceived of the novel after he finished a rough draft of *The Humbling*. Still, Roth thought so highly of *Everyman* that he commissioned ten copies of a broadside poster containing the entire text laid out in micro-print in six columns as a gift to close friends. He signed every copy.

The Orthodox burial in *Everyman* adheres to tradition, the mourners dumping shovelfuls of dirt on the casket at the bottom of the excavated grave. This originated, Roth told Claudia Roth Pierpont, in his memory of Bellow's funeral, the scene parallel to one of workmen feeding fuel to a furnace. Bellow's funeral was held in the Jewish section of Morningside Cemetery in Brattleboro, Vermont; Martin Amis, Andrew Wylie, and Roth attended, along with Claire Messud, and the critics James Wood and Leon Wieseltier. Roth steadied a staggering Wieseltier when he went up to throw dirt on the coffin, Wieseltier later telling Bellow's biographer, with a good dose of sarcasm, that it was, as far as he knew, the only "known act of kindness in Roth's life."[22]

Ruth Wisse, Jewish studies scholar, was also present and thought Roth the most affected by the death, expressing more grief than anyone else there.[23] The opening burial in *Everyman*, with the protagonists' two sons, suggests Adam and Daniel Bellow at their father's funeral. Bellow's third son, Greg, describes the scene and the throwing of dirt on the casket in his memoir *Saul Bellow's Heart*.[24] At the grave, Roth told Wylie, "I wonder if the earth knows what it has just received."[25] But there are two burials in *Everyman*, one seemingly not enough: the protagonist and that of his father, the latter performed according to Jewish tradition, as was Bellow's.[26]

Researching *Everyman*, Roth actually spent time in a cemetery learning about grave digging, which becomes a poignant moment in *Everyman* when the protagonist encounters a gravedigger working, echoing the moment when Hamlet comes upon the gravediggers in Act V, Scene 1, Shakespeare a constant foil in Roth's work, most notably in *Exit Ghost*. In Roth, the amiable digger explains the details of making a grave and how it must be straight with a depth just so and a bottom so flat you can lay a bed on it (EV 171–80). Everyman learns this is the very man who dug his parents' grave. Everyman offers him a tip; the gravedigger refuses, but Everyman insists; and the man reluctantly accepts two fifty-dollar bills just as the narrator realizes that this person might someday dig his own grave. The encounter with friendly Death, described with deftness and yet gravity, forms the virtual conclusion to the novella. Only two pages remain.

But in Roth's late novels, undermining the encounters with death is a long-simmering anger. At their father's burial, the sons in *Everyman* seethe over their parents' divorce, precipitated by the father's affairs. What could he have done differently, the narrator asks himself, other than remain married, which he couldn't do (EV 94)? In *Indignation*, there is the constant anger of Marcus Messner's father over his work and his son's independence (leading to his mother's consideration of divorce), and in *Nemesis*, Cantor expresses anger about the many deaths caused by polio.

Exit Ghost, too, betrays a persistent if muted anger, but the main story is Eros tagging along after Thanatos—for Roth, the two always in conflict. Eros begins the story and sustains the seventy-one-year-old Zuckerman, but Thanatos catches up to him through illness and physical decline, causing his withdrawal to the country at the end. New York for Zuckerman becomes the world of Eros and youth, represented by the youthful writer Jamie Logan, Zuckerman's late infatuation. But to await death comfortably, the only remedy is the country. And the aging Amy Bellette, previously seen in *The Ghost Writer*, with her deep attachment to literature, now echoes Veronica Geng (and not Anne Frank). Both suffered from the same disease. Another critical figure in the novel is George Plimpton, with eight pages devoted to his life, death, and memorial service. Roth revealed that the original cover for *Exit Ghost* was to be a photograph of Plimpton at the center of a dinner party in a restaurant, literarily the life of the party.[27]

In the country, Zuckerman finishes the final scenes of a play he is writing entitled "He and She." In the last scene, Jamie agrees to visit him in his hotel room on a return visit, but a frightened Zuckerman peremptorily runs off, leaving the manuscript of Lonoff's supposed unfinished novel and six volumes of his published stories. The country is again refuge. The interplay between impotence and desire frames the novel, with a final abdication to youth in the face of an impotent old age.[28]

Impetus for the novel partly originated when Roth encountered Catherine Steindler; she was twenty-nine and Roth was seventy-two. They met at David Plante's Claremont Avenue apartment in New York. She was with her former boyfriend who was once a student of Plante's, then teaching at Columbia. This was in March 2005, two months before Roth's second back surgery, and he was in pain. Catherine had just read *American Pastoral* and spoke to him about it. He had no further contact with her until September 2005, when he was recovering and doing light exercises in the pool. To help him concentrate his mind while exercising, every day he focused on a different year since his birth and tried to remember everything that had happened in the world and America that year and in his life. He did this while swimming laps as well. He would also recite poetry he had learned in high school, beginning with the "Prologue" to the *Canterbury Tales*.

Catherine remained on his mind, and in early October he suggested to Plante that she join them at the Russian Samovar, "The Place of the Flavored Vodkas," on West 52nd and 8th for dinner. It was a well-known Russian restaurant created by eight Soviet emigrants in 1986, later joined as investors by Mikhail Baryshnikov and Joseph Brodsky. It was one of Roth's favorites; he attended their twenty-fifth anniversary party in June 2011, having become a friend of its owner, Roman Kaplan, who kept a photo of Roth and Nicole Kidman on a downstairs table. They had met during the filming of *The Human Stain*. Regular poetry readings took place for more than sixteen years there. Roth started to visit in the 1990s. And what did Roth and Kaplan talk about? "Death" was the quick reply by Judith Thurman who often joined the two.[29]

But in 2005, Roth and Catherine stayed talking for hours after Plante left. He then jumped into a cab with her, declaring, "I can't let you go," disregarding their forty-two-year age difference. He became quite enamored with her and at one point visited a geneticist to determine whether he could father a healthy child at his age, repeated in *The Humbling* when Simon Axler visits a fertility doctor. "I fell for her at dinner, as can happen to one outside of a novel as well as in," he admitted (NOT 308). The relationship ended a year later but not its impact. Jamie Logan, the married thirty-year-old writer in *Exit Ghost*, shares many attributes with Catherine. And in the novel, Zuckerman is seventy-one, Roth's age but one when he met her for the first time.

Later women had a similar impact on Roth's work and life. The first of two short-lived relationships was with a thirty-five-year-old Milanese lawyer

(Linda Berto) which started after his breakup with Steindler; next was a year-long affair with Kirby Woodson, whom he met when she provided materials about the Kincaid School in Houston, Texas, which he used as background for Jamie in *Exit Ghost*. Woodson was thirty-three; he was seventy-four. At the time, he was still involved with Catherine and forgot about Kirby until early 2007, when he called her to ask where to return the Kincaid yearbooks. He took her to dinner downtown, bringing a few pages of *Exit Ghost* dealing with the Kincaid School for her to review and correct. The next week, dinner and a movie and bed. She grew up in Texas and designed children's clothes in Paris before establishing her own graphics company in New York.

The forty-one-year age gap again did not matter: she was buoyant and attentive and accompanied him to Washington to the PEN/Faulkner awards for *Everyman* and to the PEN/Bellow award for fiction in New York. She joined Thurman for a seventy-fourth birthday party for Roth (a ploy to avoid a seventy-fifth party) and also accompanied him to Columbia for a seventy-fifth birthday celebration in 2008. But they separated later that year when she told him she wanted a husband and a family and he typically recoiled. He knew it was coming, Roth claims in "Notes for My Biographer."

During this period, Roth was finding life in New York easier than in Connecticut, especially in the winter. He was closer to his doctors, as well as the amenities of the city. But he wrote in both places, his expanded twelfth-floor apartment at 130 West 79th Street divided into a writing area and a living area separated by his black Eames chair that faced the windows which looked south over Midtown. Several desks, including a standing desk, dotted the 1,500-foot space, with his 1998 Pulitzer prominently displayed. The spacious apartment resulted from his combining two units in 2004. He had bought the first in 1989 for use as a writing studio.[30]

Indignation, written in five months in 2007–8, is a short work because he found the mental concentration required for a big book diminished. He had actually drafted it before *Exit Ghost* and edited it the summer before *Exit Ghost* appeared. The book required research. What did he know of kosher butchering, the trade practiced by the protagonist's father? As he did for his earlier novels, he researched, calling on a Weequahic High School classmate, Leonard Strulowitz, who once shared a school locker with Roth. Strulowitz's father owned the kosher Abe Strulowitz Butcher Shop on Bergen Street in Newark. Roth queried the son to learn all he could about the meat business and the operation of the store.[31] Leonard was happy to oblige, even recalling a number of stories about his father and incidents with the customers. Once as students, Roth recalled, he and the kosher Strulowitz accidentally mixed up their lunches, and Leonard ate Roth's shrimp sandwich. Roth generally avoided class reunions but did appear at his forty-fifth in 1996. The year after that, *American Pastoral* appeared, opening with a high school reunion.[32]

His small circle of readers, which had expanded to include Claudia Roth Pierpont, had reservations about *Indignation,* but he nonetheless let the novel appear, a modest work with an immediate historical context set by the opening sentence focusing on the Korean War in June 1950. The confrontation with the dean in the novel may echo Roth's memorable confrontation with the dean of men at Bucknell over a satiric edition of *Et Cetera* which might have meant expulsion. It was 1953 and he could have been drafted for the Korean War, precisely what will happen to Marcus Messner.[33] The idea of transferring Marcus to the fictitious Winesberg College partly resulted from his reading a new edition of Sherwood Anderson's short stories and his own experience of attending Bucknell in rural Pennsylvania.

Roth's final three novels do not renounce anger or discontent: old age, old grudges, and old habits, with the constant undertow of emotionally undernourished women, persist. They are all serious, earnest books embodying his austere subject, death and waning creative power, conveyed in a clipped, severe style. In *Indignation,* it is the anger of the father toward the independence of the son who is, himself, driven by guilt over his breaking away from his father and his romantic interest, Olivia Hutton. Echoing what Roth likely thought when he left Rutgers Newark for Bucknell, Marcus "wanted to do everything right. If I did everything right, I could justify to my father the expense of my being at college in Ohio rather than in Newark" (IND 34).[34] But the nice Jewish boy also needed to be free from "a strong, stolid father" fearful of a grownup son's independence (IND 34). The knives and meat cleavers are visual warnings of the punishment that occurs since the son will be killed by a bayonet in Korea. Echoes of the stubbornness of Roth's own father in responding to Roth's determination to grow up and leave Newark for Lewisburg can be seen in the novel.

Confronting the angry dean of his college, who cannot understand why Marcus does not attend chapel and moves dormitory rooms so often, Marcus stands up to him, though he also throws up on his carpet. But his impatience and fear of his father back in New Jersey do not stop Marcus's drive for freedom. His final escape is to the army, the conflict in Korea, and his death. But even he has an angry outburst when grilled by the dean about the apparent pregnancy of Olivia and her nervous breakdown. Challenging the dean, he angrily yells, "Fuck you," repeated when the dean makes a last effort to keep Marcus at the school if he writes a letter of apology to the president (IND 92, 231). The ransacking of his room by Bert Flusser, a former roommate, creates further havoc and anger, sustained at the end as the mortally wounded Marcus remembers his life through a morphine haze. The narrator reports how the news of Marcus's death in Korea angered and then devastated his father, who dies eighteen months after. The replacement of humor by anger surrounded by melancholy describes the book, whose title implies outrage against the damages life inflicts. Anger does not abate.

Ironically, in his engagement with death, Roth does not reveal, until approximately fifty pages in, that the narrator of *Indignation* has already died. Using the trope of *Everyman*, Roth's first-person narrator speaks from the grave. The novel is Marcus remembering, his displacement from college in Ohio recalling the displacement of Seldon Wishnow in *The Plot Against America*. Jewish boys—and Jersey boys—from Newark do not do well away from home. Yet the strength of Marcus is his uncompromising nature, refusing to attend chapel or acquiesce to the dean's demands to keep him in the college and out of the draft. And religion never helps, a long-standing Roth attitude. He prefers the position of a nineteen-year-old "rational atheist," the very argument Marcus presents to the dean. Roth sent a copy of the novel to the woman he credits with performing the only act of fellatio at Bucknell between 1950 and 1954. She went out with him only once.[35]

The Humbling displayed a different form of anger, partly generated because Roth was (typically) anxious over not having anything to write. "Without a novel I'm empty and not very happy," he told an interviewer in 1992.[36] During this time (2009–10), he was involved with several new women, notably Caro Llewellyn, met in March 2009 at the John Updike memorial at the New York Public Library. She was forty-four, Roth was seventy-six. She was nearly six feet tall with short blond hair, a powerful smile, remarkable blue eyes. Her mother was the poet Kate Llewellyn. Originally from Adelaide, Caro previously ran the Sydney Writers Festival but had been in New York three years, working with American PEN, running their annual Festival of World Voices, and assisting Salman Rushdie. She had recently left to organize activities and events for the New York Public Library's centenary in 2011 when she met Roth and they began to go out. But illness unexpectedly struck.

Six months after they met, while jogging in Central Park, the forty-four-year-old Llewellyn began to lose some feeling in her legs. She saw her doctor two days later, and he diagnosed early-stage multiple sclerosis. She was blindsided by illness, as are many of Roth's characters in his late fiction, suddenly discovering her vulnerability, as those in the fiction discover theirs. The news was devastating, made more so by her increasing inability to read because her eyesight constantly went in and out of focus. (After three years her vision came back.)

Ironically, she had grown up with disability: her father was paralyzed from the age of twenty due to polio. This detail may have contributed to Roth's decision to focus on polio in his final novel, *Nemesis*. Roth saw her in the hospital and afterward, and took her to Newark, where they joined the "Bus Tour of Philip Roth's Newark." He continued to see her, and she visited him on summer weekends in Connecticut and recuperated there for more than a week after stomach surgery.

During visits, he would always cook for her and encourage her to rest and even swim in his pool. On one occasion, he startled her by placing a small metal disc in her hand. It was his first defibrillator. It hadn't operated properly and he'd had a second implanted. The first rested on the kitchen table as a reminder of the fragility of the heart: it sometimes needs assistance. And when Llewellyn's insurance no longer covered her physical therapy sessions, he sent her a check unannounced to cover expenses. He looked after her. She eventually moved to Melbourne, where she became the engagement director of Museums Victoria and in 2019 published a memoir of her father and her diagnosis, *Diving into Glass*. In 2020 she became the director of the prestigious Wheeler Centre in Melbourne, promoting literary programs and administering literary prizes.[37]

The Humbling (2009) focuses on the failure of talent brought on by age, focusing on the inability to act on the stage. Even physical pleasure has declined, reignited only by Simon Axler's unexpected physical relationship with Pegeen, a professor from the nearby college and the grown daughter of early friends. His confusion over his dramatic parts and his inability to perform impedes his sense of self-confidence, which finds at least temporary renewal through Pegeen and renewed sexual escapades (HUM 6). His marriage to the dancer Victoria ended after Simon's on-stage collapse, leaving him alone in the country as thoughts of suicide begin, sending him to a hospital clinic where he befriends Sybil Van Buren, a depressed thirty-five-year-old who discovered her second husband abusing their eight-year-old daughter who now, in her rage, is looking for someone to murder him (HUM 10, 14–15). Suicide dominates, however, and Roth offers two pages of literary suicides, from Hedda Gabler to Konstantin in *The Seagull.* Throughout the short novel, anger is the undercurrent of Axler's depression.[38]

Pegeen permits the temporary abandonment of anger which, after she leaves him, returns with a vengeance, leading, in fact, to his suicide. Despair over the end of his career, despite the interlude with Pegeen, brings on the tragedy. Parallels with Susan Rogers, haunted herself by a dean, but open to other relationships, is evident.

Between 2008 and 2010, when Roth concluded his cycle of short books, illness and death never departed, the most important loss his brother, Sandy, who died on 6 May 2009 at eighty-one in Chicago of congestive heart failure (as would Roth nine years later). Five years older than Roth, Sandy was sympathetic toward his younger brother and Roth followed him everywhere, fascinated by his artistic abilities. Friends use to joke, "If Sandy stopped short, Philip's nose would go right up his ass."[39] The presence of art materials in their dining room showed Roth that there were fulfilling occupations beyond the law or business.

But as they matured, Sandy ran into personal and professional difficulties, especially after he gave up his career in advertising in 1983 to become a full-time painter. But Roth was there to help. By 2007, Sandy was facing a series of medical issues, including osteoporosis, losing seven inches of his height, which forced him to give up his teaching art and studio. The former six-footer now walked bent over. He had remarried but was finding it difficult to maintain his apartment and Chicago studio. Parallels to the narrator of *Everyman*, who also moved from advertising to painting, published the year before Sandy died, are apparent. Roth helped with expenses, as he also helped his two nephews, contributing to their education as they moved in and out of different careers, from photography to cooking.[40]

Roth was not satisfied with *The Humbling* and worked on it even after galleys went out to reviewers, who were generally not kind, one referring to the cold, calculating style used by Roth to chart the decline of Axler as almost clinical with a "sovereign decorum" for his sentences, while the sex scenes were "hilariously awful" and unbelievable.[41] *Nemesis* was even more problematic, with supposedly thirteen drafts.[42]

Before writing what would be his final novel, he reread Camus's *The Plague*, dealing with a widespread plague in the city of Oran in Algeria and with the character Joseph Grand also attempting to write a book. Grand is such a perfectionist, however, that he continually rewrites the first sentence, unable to find the words needed to express his meaning or get to sentence two.[43] But for the volunteers battling the plague, he became an unofficial general secretary recording the statistics of those who died. He is both witness and recorder, possibly influencing Roth's own conception of Bucky Cantor. Like Cantor, Grand becomes ill, but unlike Cantor, he makes a full recovery. Studying the book reintroduced Roth to Camus and in his research he may have seen Camus's headstone with its rough lettering, which he wanted duplicated on his own.

In October 2010, Roth explained to an interviewer that he came to write *Nemesis* because he wanted to mark the great menaces he knew as a child but also to face death again to show its indifference, striking children as well as adults. The novel was also a late-career exorcism of childhood fears; he addressed World War II in *Sabbath's Theater*, anti-Semitism in *The Plot Against America*, and a topic he had never written about before: polio. He did not know anyone who died from it but did learn of one boy in his neighborhood who got it, and it terrified all.[44]

After *Nemesis*, he had no other book on the horizon, despite making lists of possible subjects. He had published eight novels in the past ten years. He was seventy-six and unsure if, like Leopold Bloom on the Strand watching Gertie McDowell in the Nausicaa episode of *Ulysses*, he could still keep up such concentrated energy. But several sentences in the same episode by Joyce sum up Roth's feelings of fatigue and yet hope: "O! Exhausted that female has me. Not so young now. Will she come here tomorrow? Wait for her somewhere for ever."[45] The last sentence reconfirms the lasting desire of both Leopold Bloom and Roth regardless of age or situation.

The most significant public event of Roth's late career was his 2012 announcement in the weekly French cultural magazine *Les Inrockuptibles* that he would no longer write, a decision he had actually made in 2009 when, frustrated with his work after he spent 2008–9 struggling with *The Humbling* and then *Nemesis*, he had enough. In the French interview—Roth was seventy-eight at the time—in addition to his inescapable involvement with illness, he boldly, if ironically, renounced biography, repeating, as he did earlier in his career, that he did not think "the biography of a writer has anything to do with his books." Most of the time, he continued, "I write about things that didn't happen to me—because I'm curious." This is an unusual and comic statement since his most consistent subject was himself and he had arranged for an official biography first by Ross Miller and then by Blake Bailey.

Roth wanted the record to be clear, although he amusingly added that he anticipated at least 20 percent of the proposed biography, for which he was preparing documents, would be wrong, but "that's always better than twenty-two percent."[46] But he continued to exert control, fashioning a detailed contract with Bailey about what could and couldn't be said and the disposition of his personal papers after his death.

Specifically, he outlined that when Bailey had completed his work, his personal papers were to be destroyed and so instructed his trustees. The door to his past would be closed once an official account was offered, although Bailey has recently suggested this will not necessarily happen.[47] The hope of seeing into the personal, private side of Roth would be gone. If the documents have been deposited with his papers at the Library of Congress or another library, however, they would automatically be in the possession of the institution, which would have at least physical control over the materials and likely would resist any effort to destroy them. Roth's supposed reason for such a comment was that he didn't want his "personal papers dragged all over the place. No one has to read them."[48] On the question of not writing, he said, "I don't feel that fanaticism about writing that I felt all my life." But one of the first things he did after he decided to stop was to reread his work from the most recent to just before *Portnoy* to see if he had been wasting his time. He concluded that he did all right, citing the boxer Joe Louis and his remark "I did the best I could with what I had."[49]

Most readers did not believe Roth's declaration of retirement, and they were right. He did continue to write, but not fiction. He prepared several lengthy documents for Bailey, what he called in a 2013 interview "forensic writing," documenting his life.[50] The first, "Notes for My Biographer," consists of over three hundred typed pages, a refutation of Bloom's *Leaving a Doll's House*. Responding to distortions in interview tapes prepared by Miller, Roth arranged a second document. It was organized for the new authorized biographer, who at one point, at least in 2011, was to have been Hermione Lee.[51] When she declined, Roth selected Bailey after Bailey heard from James Atlas that Miller had been let go. Bailey had previously written a set of successful biographies including one of John Cheever. Andrew Wylie facilitated the arrangement, and after several meetings in 2012, Bailey and Roth formalized their agreement, Roth making it clear how the new life should be organized and what should, and should not, be in it.

Roth also composed a thirty-seven-page essay entitled "Money," again a response to inaccurate views about his use of money, especially concerning women, contradicting the view that it was only a tool to manipulate them. "Pain and Illness History" was another crucial document, written in July

2010, an ordered and detailed account of his health since the age of ten. A curious addition was proof from two psychiatrists that he was never diagnosed as schizophrenic or bipolar, refuting another claim by Miller. One document in two draft versions is a response to Bailey claiming that Roth would not accept blame for the dissolution of his two marriages and why.

Each of the hundreds of files sent to Bailey had meticulously typed memos attached on its contents, how they were to be used, and what to think about the material.[52] Roth was directing and even writing his biography, establishing credibility for its "authorized" status. After his death, it seemed, he would still be organizing the contents and narrative by proxy. These multiple documents would become testaments to his life in an effort to ensure, if not reclaim, his moral reputation, which he thought was badly damaged by Bloom and which he thought eliminated him from the Nobel Prize. Ironically, however, they may all be destroyed if the rumors of their ultimate disposition are true. But they are also score-settling accounts, acts of literary revenge. They confirm that Roth could not "get enough of getting even."[53]

These efforts to direct his biographer are part of ensuring that the unfinished business of life would be completed as he wanted. While the Library of America series of his writing exists in ten uniform volumes, the definitive story of his life has yet to be completed with the ending he proposed. In setting out his biographical program, Roth wanted to erase the uncertainty expressed by Malamud's hero in *Dubin's Lives*: "Life responds to one's moves with comic interventions."[54] Malamud's novel appeared in 1979, the year of *The Ghost Writer*. Farrar, Straus and Giroux published both books, and it is likely Roth read Malamud's latest work. The subject is a biographer who takes a young lover. At the end, Roth sought a life without comedy.

The goal was certainty and he hoped that the instructions, directives, files, and guidelines left for his biographer, and even for his funeral and memorial service, would stand unchallenged. Roth sought to complete his own unfinished life after he died through his directions.[55] He had an almost biblical belief that others would obey his written word. His edger, a tool used by the gravedigger in *Everyman*, is his instructions needed to square the hole of his life. He became the actor, director, and producer of his own story, his own ghost writer.

In the fall of 2016, as a kind of early postscript to his writing career, Roth gifted his personal library of over 3,500 books, many with annotations, to the Newark Public Library, which ensured that they would be housed in a separate, renovated library space. His original choice was Bucknell, but details, financial and otherwise, could not be worked out, so Newark stepped in. To facilitate the renovation and the move and installation of the books, he left them $2 million, supported by a grant from the Carnegie Foundation to assist in the transfer. As part of the announcement, he listed fifteen works of fiction he thought the most important in his life, along with the age at which he read them. They include Salinger's *The Catcher in the Rye*, read at twenty; Hemingway's *A Farewell to Arms*, read at twenty-three; Dostoevesky's *Crime and Punishment*, read at thirty-five; and Schulz's *Street of Crocodiles* read at forty-one.[56]

The books from his library would be shelved in broad categories, as Roth had them in Connecticut. There, he had a room devoted to nonfiction, with library shelves and library lighting. Fiction started in the living room and took up all the walls in a front study and overtook a guest bedroom upstairs. But he did group together, disregarding categories, those works that were helpful for his research on *Operation Shylock* and *The Plot Against America*.

To ensure his privacy and maintain the surrounding woods, over the years Roth had purchased various parcels.[57] In the town of Warren in Litchfield County, Roth's property consisted of a three-bedroom, two-and-a-half-story clapboard house originally built in 1790 and included a barn, an outdoor sunken swimming pool (which he added), and a two-room writing studio with two standing writing desks. Woods, ponds, and even pastures surrounded the main building, which contained a rustic great room with a vaulted ceiling and fieldstone floor. There were three fireplaces.

But Roth's home in the hamlet of Cornwall Bridge needed almost constant attention, and his caretaker, Russ Murdock, knew the two-hundred-year-old former dairy farm with its crisscrossed low stone walls well.[58] For nearly twenty years, he looked after the property year round, and among his various duties was to burn piles of pages in the backyard, presumably rough drafts of novels. Murdock, twenty-six years younger than Roth, was an unlikely friend but a likeable person. He always carried a pistol and listened dutifully to Rush Limbaugh, but there was often comedy between the two, some of it involving Eskimos. Murdock, with another property owner, yearly went fishing in Alaska. On one trip, he brought a load of Roth's winter clothes that were to be donated. Instead, they were given to the people in the Eskimo village where they stayed. Roth would no doubt be laughing at the thought that a group of Eskimos were now wearing his coats and sweaters, Murdock reported.

Murdock also confirmed that Roth borrowed aspects of the nearby village of Litchfield for his books, a number of the names of townspeople foremost, including the foreman of a local cutting crew eager to take down trees adjacent to Roth's property. Roth became incensed the morning they began, running out and berating everyone, who, it turned out, were also members of the fire department. For months afterward he was furious, until several friends told him that one day he might need the firefighters; reluctantly, he wrote an apology and delivered it by phone, speakerphone as he later learned, to the entire department. But in response, Roth named the truculent Vietnam vet in *The Human Stain* Les Farley; Les was the first name of the cutting crew's foreman. Roth liked to say, "If you sit by the river long enough, you can watch the bodies of your enemies float by."[59]

Other locals often became his sources of research. A neighbor named Dotty Ripley whose family ran a dairy farm became the informant on milking cows and farming used in *The Human Stain*. From Bob Ripley, once the president of *Playboy*, he learned about beekeeping. Curiosity led him to a character named Pat who wore a headband with branches stuck in it to ward off deerflies. Murdock revealed to an inquisitive reporter a year after Roth's death Roth's love of rural life, from the trails to the ponds, the villages, the history, and the people. To ensure continued exploring, Murdock made Roth a proper walking stick for his seventieth birthday, made from a woody shrub and called the Harry Lauder Walking Stick, named after the Scottish vaudevillian comic, a favorite of Herman Roth's.[60] But even in the country, Roth did not relax his wish to direct and ensure that things were to his liking: before coming up each summer, he drew diagrams for the exact positioning of the patio furniture and sent them to Murdock. They had to be just so. And after Claire Bloom left, he supposedly fumigated the house.

According to Murdock, in private Roth would reveal his vulnerability, sharing ailments with Murdock's father when they first met, and caring for his own father. But there were also darker feelings to offset the kindness and affection. One could not completely cancel the other out, as seen in the ambivalent portrait of his father in *Patrimony*, loved and criticized. He had an obsession with the procedures of death, after as much as before the end.[61] So it was no surprise that in either 2008 or 2009, Roth and Murdock went looking for a headstone for Roth on his property. They settled, however, not on a sizable rock but on his front step, a granite rectangle. When he asked Murdock to carve it, he knew exactly what he wanted: a simple statement of his name in rough lettering modeled after Camus. But after a fox "baptized" the step, Roth rejected it.

During this period, a series of women again played critically important roles, the two most important, perhaps, Julia Golier and Judith Thurman, the former a psychiatrist Roth met in the early 1990s at Silver Hill and soon after when she was just completing her residency. Tall and slender, she had been an English major at Barnard and was coming out of an unsuccessful long-term relationship. She was thirty and he was sixty-one; she lived in an unattractive apartment on Second Avenue which he transferred to the elderly Amy Bellette in *Exit Ghost*. They met by accident on Park Avenue when she was walking home from work at Mt. Sinai Hospital and he had just left the manuscript of *Sabbath's Theater* at Wylie's. Having once met, he located her again at a VA hospital in the Bronx to get information on posttraumatic stress and Vietnam veterans for what would become part of *The Human Stain*. Their 1994 meeting led to a relationship of almost four years, spending time together in Connecticut (she convinced him not to tear down the big house nor its surrounding trees because of its associations with Bloom) and the city. On Saturday nights, they would often listen to songs from the Big Band era played on WMNR radio, which found a place in *The Human Stain* linking Zuckerman and Silk. Golier stabilized his life after the turmoil with Bloom; Roth dedicated *American Pastoral* to her.

One new but common interest for both was learning to identify wildflowers, repeated in *American Pastoral* when Merry Levov attends the 4-H club in Old Rimrock, something Swede would recall. Golier also accompanied Roth to the Aix-en-Provence festival in 1999, to Washington when he received his National Medal of the Arts in 1998 from President Clinton, and in March 2011 when he received the 2010 National Humanities Medal from President Obama, joining Joyce Carol Oates and Sonny Rollins that year, among others. When the president unexpectedly entered the East Room of the White House to greet the recipients, Roth was the first person he saw, and he ebulliently called out "Philip Roth!" Roth, never missing a comic beat, duplicated the welcome with an equally enthusiastic "President Obama!," although with an undertone of comic disbelief.[62]

But despite his attachment to Golier, her wish for a family brought the relationship to a close. Nevertheless, they remained close friends after she married on 1 March 2002 and had twins, William and Amelia, in 2003.[63] Roth became quite attached to both children, but especially the daughter, who, after he retired from writing, wrote to ask if they could write a book together. The result was a set of children's stories written in tandem, each providing alternate lines by email. Subjects ranged from stars and snails to dogs, at one point Amelia putting Roth into their story about monkeys: he was a character writing a book about monkeys, a wonderful Rothian device turned upon himself.[64]

Speaking at Roth's memorial at the New York Public Library, Golier said she had tried to get him to change the title of *American Pastoral*, but he defended his choice, claiming he had earned it. She also claimed that the novel almost never got published because he had doubts and called Wylie, then in London, to halt publication. He was frustrated with writing and wanted no more of it. A long series of phone calls followed, and the novel did appear, going on to win a Pulitzer Prize.[65] Golier would become one of Roth's two end-of-life and hospital surrogates and one of his literary executors.

Judith Thurman, who began her career as a translator, first met Roth in 1982 when he wrote to her praising her biography of Isak Dinesen, which became the basis of Sydney Pollack's film *Out of Africa*. She was also a writer for the *New Yorker* beginning in 1987, where both her fashion columns and profiles of Hillary Clinton and Giorgio Armani appeared. She remained a close friend, reader, and confidante of Roth (in many ways supplanting Veronica Geng). He called her, for example, when he left the manuscript of *Deception* with Bloom to read, with the deceived wife then named "Claire." He anticipated Bloom's anger and asked Thurman what he should do. She told him to meet her on 57th Street with a credit card. They quickly went shopping and she helped him select the Bulgari snake ring made of gold and emerald he gave to Bloom. Thurman continued to comment on Roth's work throughout the remainder of his career, making important suggestions regarding *American Pastoral*, specifically that the Levovs should be shown having caring, companionable sex. Roth preferred passionate sex. He told her that the basis for the scene where Swede Levov accompanies his wife to a facelift originated with Bloom when she had a similar procedure to restore her beauty.

Thurman understood fashion as a certain language dealing with identities and image making and because of this, Roth often introduced her to many of his female friends.[66] Occasionally, the three of them went shopping for outfits. Thurman's sense of style was notable. And because of her close relation with Roth, he allowed her to publish in January 2017 "Philip Roth E-Mails on Trump," where he stated that *The Plot Against America* was not an allegory of Trump's government, at the same time indicting the new president and the dangers of his pseudo-leadership and unregulated worship of power. Outlining Lindbergh's essential heroism, Roth castigated Trump and his ignorance, referring to him as "just a con artist" and "humanly impoverished" with a vocabulary of only "seventy-seven words."[67] Other writerly acquaintances at this time included Zadie Smith, who gave the first Philip Roth Lecture at the Newark Public Library in October 2016; Nicole Krauss, who wrote Roth a letter in 2007 to which he responded with a letter of his own and his phone number, leading to an important friendship and a blurb by him on the cover of her novel *Forest Dark*; Louise Erdrich; and, again, Lisa Halliday.

Erdrich's friendship with Roth began, as it did with so many of his literary friends, with a letter received when she was twenty-nine and actually cooking dinner for several Dartmouth faculty members. A friendship soon developed, and she noted how he always bore down on a topic he didn't know much about. Early on it was curiosity about Native-owned casinos and tribal law, given her Native background. He considered her 2008 novel, *Plague of Doves*, a masterpiece (it was a finalist for a Pulitzer Prize) and constantly read her work. After he stopped writing, he showed her, she thought, the way to age: "Read your way up the mountain." She felt that "his work had blasted the doors off American fiction and other writers were stepping through."[68]

In retirement, Roth rediscovered the truth of the joke he gave to Zuckerman: "Other people. Somebody should have told me about them long ago" (AL 170). He formerly had a slogan when he became anxious writing, "The ordeal is part of the commitment," supplemented by another from the relief pitcher Bob Wickman: "You gotta trust your stuff." And finally, "Don't judge it, just write it." But when he retired, he attached a new note to his computer, which read "The struggle with writing is over," although he still believed that "the experience of contradiction *is* the human experience," recognizing at last, as Zuckerman finally realizes shortly before the end of *The Anatomy Lesson*, that "not everything has to be a book."[69]

But certain issues still rankled: in 2012 he published "An Open Letter to Wikipedia," correcting the error of what inspired *The Human Stain*.[70] But Wikipedia was partly right: Roth was slightly dissembling because in earlier letters he implied that Anatole Broyard was a partial inspiration for Silk. In two letters to John Updike, Roth notes Broyard's efforts at "passing" and his genius for mischief and deception.[71] Roth wanted an adjustment to the Wiki entry but was told that he was only the author and therefore not a credible source. They needed secondary sources. An astonished Roth took them to task, explaining the actual source of the event that ignited *The Human Stain* and altered the life of Coleman Silk. Anatole Broyard did not alone

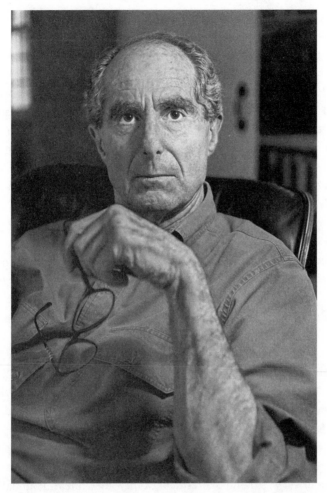

Figure 11.1 Portrait of Philip Roth in his studio, Cornwall Bridge, Connecticut, 2002. Credit: James Nachtwey/James Nachtwey Archive, Hood Museum of Art, Dartmouth College, Hanover, New Hampshire.

inspire the novel; it was Melvin Tumin, Newarker and sociology professor at Princeton and a friend of Roth. Roth goes into detail describing the 1985 incident where Tumin carelessly used the word "spooks" in class, not knowing that the errant students were Black. He then had to explain himself repeatedly to the university authorities, even though he was a distinguished scholar of the civil rights movement. The letter is a late and successful example of the thorough, logical, argumentative Roth, although after seven pages he refutes himself when he makes it clear that he did engage with Broyard and thought of him as "passing."

Judaism and the Jewish establishment made up to Roth when he received an honorary degree from the Jewish Theological Seminary in mid-May 2014, ironically four years to the day before his death, 22 May 2018. He was eighty-one and looked suspiciously gaunt and gray and used a walking stick, but he enjoyed the event, held in a tent with blue and white balloons. A klezmer band played, followed by two cantors (male and female) singing the national anthems of the U.S. and Israel. One attendee reported that Roth did not join others in singing "Hatikvah." What especially struck Roth was that the students applauded their parents who were made to stand to receive the honor, something Roth had never witnessed before. He talked to students who asked about *The Counterlife*, while he cited Bellow and Malamud. At the celebratory luncheon, he chatted and posed for photos, explaining to one young rabbi that he preferred not to be called a Jewish writer; he preferred to be called an American writer: Singer is a Yiddish writer, Amos Oz a Hebrew writer. Only a writer's language can define him.[72]

Another event during this time was his recurrent nemesis, the Nobel Prize. For years many rallied support for him directly and indirectly, Harold Bloom at one point organizing a nomination. But it always eluded him. Yet when called by a friend to commiserate over Bob Dylan's winning in 2016, Roth reportedly said, "No, its not bad, it's fun. [And] I've just been inducted into the Rock n' Roll Hall of Fame."[73]

A new and valuable late friend was Ben Taylor, met in 1994 at the sixtieth birthday party of Joel Conarroe held at the James Beard House on West 12th. Conarroe was then the president of the Guggenheim Foundation and a close friend of Roth from his days at the University of Pennsylvania. Roth and Taylor hit it off, although they did not reconnect until 1998, after Taylor sent his impressions of *I Married a Communist* to Roth. There was then a quick phone conversation, but not until 2001, after Taylor moved back to New York, did they have lunch together at a West Side Thai restaurant.

Roth had sent Taylor *The Dying Animal* and wanted to talk. Taylor cited a scene in Solzhenitsyn's *The Cancer Ward* analogous to Consuela showing Kepesh her doomed and cancerous breasts (DA 129–30, 132–34). Roth explained that "brain power has to do with *specificity*, life's proliferating details," not philosophical ideas. "I aim only at specifics."[74]

Accompanying Roth's maturity was a growing self-certainty, which Taylor later described as a self-confidence that did not permit his own faults, especially in relationships and his determination to find a biographer who would not be a Boswell nor a "ventriloquist's dummy."[75] He needed to be right, and if not right, to prevail. Old slights remained and he was determined to "even the score," even, surprisingly, after the antagonist had died.

The two began to meet and would speak frequently until Roth's death, Taylor supplementing the role once played by James Atlas, David Plante, and even Ross Miller. Their projects often overlapped: after Roth showed Taylor *The Plot Against America* in manuscript, Taylor read the next five books in their early stages, commenting and asking questions. In turn, Roth assisted Taylor with his edition of the letters of Saul Bellow published in 2010, in which Taylor refers to Roth as "a godfather to these pages."[76] Taylor told Roth of his summers at Indianola on Lake Mendota in Wisconsin, which Roth transformed into Camp Indian Hill in *Nemesis*. After publication, Roth received a letter from one of the two grown sons of the original director of Indianola asking how he could have known so much about the place, including that their father was a widower. Roth had actually imagined that part of the story.[77]

As their friendship deepened (and Roth persisted with calling at odd hours and frequently hanging up without saying goodbye), Roth not only passed on typescripts, proofs, and holograph leaves as gifts to Taylor but jokingly told him the items might have future value. Roth dedicated *Exit Ghost* to Taylor and offered editorial comments on Taylor's memoir about a year in his boyhood in Fort Worth, Texas, *The Hue and Cry at Our House: A Year Remembered* (2017), writing on almost every page of the draft.

Taylor interviewed Roth for the *Daily Telegraph* when he won the Man Booker International Prize in 2011. There, Roth explained how he researched historical events in his fiction, stating that he did his remembering while he was writing and didn't begin to read actual history until he was in his second or third draft: "I don't want to be caged in by reality, as it were."[78] As their friendship grew, Roth sent Taylor Philip Guston's illustrations for *The Breast*, eighty-five pages of handwritten notes for *Operation Shylock*, and "Marriage a la Mode" (2014), an annotated typescript in response to misleading statements concerning his marriages made by Ross Miller. In addition, there were numerous drafts, photographs, and personal records now at Princeton University.[79] The extensive autobiographical writings reveal Roth's determination to take control of the public and private narrative of his life and writing.

In his memoir, Taylor raises an important question: Why was the public "so exceptionally interested in his [Roth's] personal life," while his contemporaries, like E. L. Doctorow, Toni Morrison, and Don DeLillo, raise no such curiosity.[80]Witnessing a "Jewish good boy" undone by inner turmoil is Taylor's answer. Roth couldn't stay out of his own books or out of trouble, which sometimes came looking for him.[81]

In New York on the night of 29 April 2018, Roth's health suddenly turned worse. He called Taylor, who offered to stay the night with him at his apartment. A painful cry at 2:00 a.m. meant a 911 call: paramedics arrived and, after having trouble defibrillating his heart, transported him to Lenox Hill and then on to New York Presbyterian. For the next three weeks, Taylor visited every morning, greeted by Roth's "What news on the Rialto?," the question Salanio asks in Act I, Scene 3 of *The Merchant of Venice*.[82]

Taylor became an increasingly important confidant in Roth's last years, and Roth appointed him and Julia Golier his joint medical proxies. He also sent Taylor detailed burial and funeral instructions. Taylor was, in fact, the final speaker at the 25 September 2018 memorial for Roth at the New York Public Library, where he recalled Roth's humor creating imaginary relatives and answering arcane baseball questions—as well as an incident when he might have blurted out that he would never write again.

Taylor and Roth were dining at the West Street Grill on the village green in Litchfield on 22 August 2012. Roth had long been a fan of the small but well-appointed bistro-style restaurant, which opened in May 1990 with white tablecloths but a casual style and excellent American country-style food and a wall of horse photos. In 2010, when *Vanity Fair* invited Roth for an "Out to Lunch" interview, he chose the Grill. Charlie Kafferman (host) and James O'Shea (executive chef) were the co-owners and hosted not only Roth but for several years a weekly private luncheon group with Styron, Updike, Arthur Miller, Richard Widmark, and, of course, Roth. He and Mia Farrow (Kafferman first met her at Gatsby's in New York the night she became engaged to Frank Sinatra) would often dine there on Sunday nights, according to another regular, William O'Shaughnessy, a Litchfield resident. It was not unusual to have Bill Murray bring friends George Clooney and Wes Anderson for dinner.

At one point, O'Shaughnessy reported that when Roth was unable to receive an award, this time from the governor of Connecticut, he asked Charlie Kafferman to go and represent him. Kafferman agreed, and he and O'Shea drove to the ceremony and accepted a two-foot-high "winged victory" sculpture and carried it back to the Grill, where it remains. A few weeks later, Roth was off to the White House to receive the National Humanities Medal from President Obama. Coming in for dinner the week after, his friends naturally asked about the event. All was fine, Roth reported, until he went up to receive the medal. At that moment, the president leaned forward and whispered, "Where's Charlie?" He was disappointed, Roth laughed.[83]

Nemesis was to appear that October. But back in August 2012, at the Grill in Litchfield, after Roth and Taylor ordered, Roth froze, then fell forward into the gazpacho. He was rushed to the hospital in nearby Torrington while mumbling directives to the medics on how to do their job. Was this the end, wondered Taylor?[84]

At the hospital, an ER doctor explained that a reaction to one of the drugs Roth had been taking had caused his collapse. When Taylor entered to see him, the first words he heard from Roth were "No more books." Taylor did not understand at the time that this was Roth's retirement announcement. Roth then proceeded to tell the story of the wounded baseball player Eddie Waitkus, who, when shot on entering the hotel room of a slightly deranged lady admirer, could only say, "What'd you do that for, baby?," which became an ongoing joke between the two men.[85]

The humorous line recalls Roth telling Claudia Roth Pierpont that the greatest line in literature is when Raskolnikov's sister, Dunya, goes to see the villain Svidrigailov in his apartment and he corners her, threatening rape. About to make his move, she pulls a pistol out of her handbag and he mutters, "That changes everything."[86] Life can change in an instant. In a forum on Roth on 3 April 2019, Pierpont reported that she once asked him how long he could live without writing a book. "Psychologically, about two hours," he answered.[87]

Affiliated with Columbia University and the Weill Cornell Medical College on East 70th, New York Presbyterian Hospital had a renowned heart unit. During the first week Roth was there he had an attack of arrhythmia, and doctors discovered that he had several blocked stents from a previous angioplasty. They did another angioplasty to unblock the stents and thought he would recover and return home, but within a week, his kidneys began to fail, characteristic of late-stage congestive heart failure. On 20 May he decided he was done fighting and went into palliative care; on the 21st he asked to be taken off life support; on the 22nd he died.[88] The day was overcast with occasional showers and even fog.

Roth had suffered heart problems since 1982, when he was diagnosed with coronary artery disease; he was forty-nine. In 1989, he had his emergency quintuple bypass operation. When Blake Bailey began to interview him in 2012, Roth detailed his illness and reportedly said he would help Bailey for about a year and then would get out of his way. He lasted another six, maintaining a regimen of exercise and hiring a cook to prepare healthy meals. When he went to Cornwall Bridge, it was in the summer and always with a companion, since health problems necessitated assistance in one form or another.

As soon as friends learned Roth was again in the hospital with heart issues, numerous visitors streamed by: Judith Thurman, Blake Bailey, Julia Golier, Ben Taylor, Andrew Wylie, Lisa Halliday, Claudia Roth Pierpont, Barbara Sproul, Sean Wilentz, and more, including a number of old girlfriends. At one point, he supposedly whispered to Wylie, "You have to let me go," a revision of what he had said to his dying father in *Patrimony*: "Dad, I'm going to have to let you go" (PAT 233). And after a late outburst—"We're going to the Savoy!"—Philip Roth died.[89]

In his memorial remarks, Taylor acknowledged the self-protective Roth who, through his public persona and supportive friends, constructed a "remote citadel." But once you were permitted to enter, defensive Roth disappeared and a playful human figure emerged. He cared about the well-being of friends and at the end actually instructed others "in how to die," in many ways the epitome of the comedy of unhappiness.[90]

Taylor expands on these ideas in his emotional memoir of Roth, *Here We Are*, where he repeats conversations, jokes, and incidents from his long friendship with Roth and some of Roth's habits: how he enjoyed secrets and deceptions, but that there were also clear no-go areas: "there were rooms in the fortress of secrets marked P. Roth" he was excluded from. But Roth was also a remarkable student of the "inner lives" of others who created and sustained intimacy.[91] And he remained in control, at one point telling Taylor that if he became too disabled, he had pills in a safe in his New York apartment that would end his life. He knew that those who take too many barbiturates on an empty stomach throw up, so he also had Triscuits.

Roth's actions were always deliberate and well researched. Even at the end, which he knew was coming, he resisted the chance to go back to his apartment; it would suggest too much of life. And his request to be removed from life support was partly a response to a black comedy moment: an intern candidly told him that he would never be able to swim again; that was it. The next day he died. In Taylor's words, he decided "to make a rational exit."[92]

Taylor ended his comments at the memorial by recounting how Roth, asking to be alone with him a few moments, told him that he had seen the great enemy, death, and he was not to be feared. Taylor added that amid the sorrow of his final days, Roth was Socratic, educating those around him. Taylor concluded by reading the final, triumphant paragraph of Bucky Cantor unleashing his javelin skyward in *Nemesis*, but it may be Henry Zuckerman in *The Counterlife* who best captures Roth's singular achievement: "To be truthful, it wasn't a bad idea" (CL 217).

12

Coda: "It's a Miserable Life"

> To be a man of letters is an incurable disease.
>
> —Goethe, 1820

The title of Roth's last volume in the Library of America series is the rhetorical *Why Write? Collected Nonfiction 1960–2013*. It's an intriguing question after a career of thirty-one books and countless essays. But it's not far from what he expressed in a 2009 interview while struggling with *Nemesis*. To Eleanor Wachtel of CBC radio, he explained, "If I could live my life again I don't think I'd want to be a writer. There are many hard occupations to be sure—this is one of them. It's very grueling because you're always an amateur whenever you begin a new book."[1]

Just as Roth was candid with the faults and fissures in the life he saw around him, so, too, was he clear regarding the nuts and bolts of writing. Or as he explained to a server in a New York deli in 2012, two weeks before he publicly announced his retirement from writing, after the server had the courage to present Roth with his first novel, "It's a miserable life": "Quit while you're ahead. . . . It's an awful field. Just torture. . . . You write and write and you have to throw almost all of it away because it's not any good."[2] The young writer declared his perseverance, but Roth soon announced that he had stopped. Old age was a challenge and he used to joke that every year his age was "becoming more like the number of a house on a street than the age of a person."[3]

At first, Roth felt anxious about what he would do next but then found himself elated to experience the freedom of not needing to write. He could now read what he wanted, see whom he wanted, go anywhere he liked, and relax. He no longer had to invent, although at one point he said he would like to start a novel that would take the rest of his life to finish and hand it in just before he died. That way he would not have to bear the agony of starting again. "The work is difficult in the beginning," he once said. "It's also difficult in the middle and difficult in the end." And he could even happily quip to Claudia Roth Pierpont that one of the benefits of what would be his last stay in the hospital was that he wouldn't have to write about it.[4] Nevertheless, Roth admitted, "Without a novel, I'm empty and not very happy." At one of his first meetings with Nicole Krauss and after discussing the challenges of writing, he slipped her a piece of paper on which was written "IT'S NOT GOING TO GET BETTER. RESIGN YOURSELF TO THIS."[5]

In the spring of 2014, he wrote out what he had told Krauss in an elevator as they descended to the ground floor of his apartment building to say goodbye. It underscores his pleasure at discovering a new life in the moment: "I am struck by the fact that I'm still here. I become intensely aware of being aware of whatever I am reading, of whatever I am looking at, of whoever may be talking to me."[6] Krauss later introduced the eighty-one-year-old Roth on the occasion of his last public reading, held at the 92nd Street Y in New York on 8 May 2014. His text? *Sabbath's Theater* and the description of the chaos of grief when the family gets the news that, first, Mickey Sabbath's brother, Morty, was missing in action in the Philippines and then that he was shot down and killed at age twenty on 13 December 1944, eight months before the end of the war (ST 411–12). Roth followed this with Mickey's liturgy of gravestones as he tours a cemetery established by New Jersey seashore Jews and discovers his grandparents', his parents', and Morty's grave (ST 363–65, 370). Roth's vital reading, according to one who was there, brought "Jersey shore sunlight" to the dark passage.[7]

Roth now concentrated on maintaining his health, while accepting the occasional award. But what was he doing every day, now that the writing had stopped? He went to baseball games and chamber music concerts. And read. As he told Charles McGrath, his reading focused on history and contemporary social problems; he read three books by Ta-Nehisi Coates, Nell Irvin Painter's *The History of White People*, Edmund Morgan's *American Slavery, American Freedom* with further essays by Teju Cole, and Stephen Greenblatt's *The Swerve*. Lucretius, more Greenblatt (on Shakespeare), and a work that was surprisingly enjoyable, Bruce Springsteen's *Born to Run*. Further titles included a discussion of pogroms by Steven Zipperstein in *Pogrom: Kishinev and the Tilt of History*, followed by Yuri Slezkie's *The Jewish Century* before he picked up Isaiah Berlin's *Personal Impressions* with its startling account of Berlin's night with Anna Akhmatova in postwar Leningrad.[8]

Roth also spent time facing the past, completing selections for *Why Write?* The volume, with no editor listed, contains selections from *Reading Myself and Others* and *Shop Talk*, plus fourteen additional essays. In his "Preface," he notes that of his thirty-one published books, twenty-seven had been fiction and that his nonfiction, other than *Patrimony* and *The Facts,* resulted from "provocation" or a response to an interview or receipt of an award. That "provocation" should be first on his list underlines Roth's perpetual aggressiveness and persistent determination to set things right.

But as complications from his heart disease multiplied, he became more fearful that he would not finish his work, the undiminished goal he set for himself modeled on his father's determination to get the job done. Every day he would put his work in order, uncertain if he would return: At fifty-six, he had had his emergency bypass operation at New York Hospital, and his new strength and happiness contributed strongly to his literary rebirth. With that assurance, he could begin again. *Deception*, a slight work and more a signal to Bloom that their life together was over, was finished before his operation; what followed were his great, mature works. A new exuberance for life and the ability to create found expression in the post-1989 novels, but the litany of stents, angioplasties, and then, in September 2016, replacement of his aortic value always kept his enthusiasms in check.

Importantly, the final words of *Why Write?*, borrowed for the conclusion of his address at his eightieth birthday party at the Newark Museum on 19 March 2013, are "Here I am," in Hebrew, "Hineni," the forceful declaration of Abraham before God when he is about to sacrifice his son to demonstrate his faith stated by Sabbath at the end of his liturgy for the dead (WR404; ST 370).[9] It is an open, honest, undisguised statement of the naked self without deception or a mask. Before this moment, Roth read the long passage where Mickey Sabbath recites the names on the gravestones of a South Jersey Jewish cemetery as he searches for the graves of his grandparents, parents, and brother. Loss defines his world. But "Here I am" is a conclusive affirmation, not only of a son to his parents and brother but by the author of his undiminished presence, something Roth sought ever since he was a child. It is recognition of a sentence Bellow had written in *The Bellarosa Connection* (1989): "If you worked in memory, which is life itself, there is no retirement except in death."[10]

The Cornwall Bridge house, painted a pale blue-gray, went up for sale in the late summer of 2019, a little more than a year after Roth's death. Listed for $2.92 million, the property encompassed nearly two hundred acres, land acquired over the years since he originally bought the home for $110,000 in 1972. Before the sale, an auction of household items was held, which was an awkward moment for Russ Murdock, who quietly stood in the background. The auction mixed furniture with mementos: lamps, chairs, a Federal-style circular mirror, a 1963 Topps baseball card of Sandy Koufax, a record player, radio, carry-on suitcase with Roth's own hand-lettered nametag, Yogi Berra's baseball bat, a photo of Kafka from Roth's study, and his portable typewriter. The online and actual sale exceeded expectations: the portable Olivetti 32 typewriter (in its original case) sold for $17,500, the Samsonite roll-on suitcase bid up to over $550. And the baseball bat—Yogi Berra played for the Newark Bears before the New York Yankees—went for $4,000. Murdock said the left-handed Roth had it partly to discourage burglars.

Preceding the sale of his Cornwall Bridge home was that of Roth's New York apartment on the twelfth floor of his West 79th Street building, listed for $3.2 million. The 1,500-square-foot, two-bedroom condo was the result of combining two units with three balconies. His belongings still furnished the double unit when it first went on the market, including his 1998 Pulitzer Prize for *American Pastoral* and Saul Bellow's top hat, worn when he received the Noble Prize in 1976. A fax machine, Dell computer, thesaurus, and several books (including *Death and the Afterlife* by Samuel Scheffler) still dotted the apartment.

Roth's nondenominational funeral at Bard College on 28 May 2018 was fittingly, for this American writer, on an American holiday: Memorial Day. Several busloads of mourners attended. The location was a surprise to many, but Roth had quipped that he wanted to be with Jews he could talk to, notably the writer Norman Manea and Leon Botstein, president of Bard, who had indicated that they too would be buried there. One Jew he could already talk to was Hannah Arendt, an acquaintance from the 1970s, buried near her husband Heinrich Blücher in the Bard cemetery and not more than twenty paces from Roth.

He initially thought he would be buried near his parents in the Gomel Chesed Cemetery in Newark, where Allen Ginsberg's ashes rest alongside his parents, but the deterioration of the neighborhood and his inability to find an adjacent plot deterred him. The noise from a nearby highway and the proximity to the New York–Philadelphia train corridor and the Anheuser-Busch brewery on Route 1 also did not appeal. What kind of rest could anyone have between speeding trains and fermenting hops? For peace and quiet and space, Bard was best.

Roth had modest connections with Bard, receiving an honorary doctor of letters from the college in 1985 and teaching there in 1999 with Norman

Manea.[11] Friendships with Botstein and Manea solidified connections, and he confirmed with both that his preferred site would be the Bard cemetery. For his funeral, he made it clear beforehand that there were to be no religious rituals, no Mourner's Kaddish, although the day before the actual burial, a stone had been placed on the gravesite in accordance with Jewish tradition, memorialized in the graveyard visit of Sabbath at the end of his novel. Some sixty people attended the funeral, including, in addition to Botstein and Manea, Andrew Wylie, Ben Taylor, Julie Golier, Steven Zipperstein, Judith Thurman, and Blake Bailey. Instead of prayers, excerpts from his texts were read, one participant later remarking that it was more like the burying of texts than a person, alluding to the halachic prohibition against the destruction of Jewish prayer books and the need to bury them. But the last words were fittingly Roth's and no one else's. He was, as another friend wrote, "the master conductor of his final performance."[12]

Late in the afternoon on 25 September 2018, a memorial tribute to Roth took place at the New York Public Library on Fifth Avenue in the elegant Celeste Bartos Forum with its thirty-foot-high glass-domed ceiling, the room requested by Roth who also had precisely listed the speakers he wanted, their order of appearance, and the length of time for each, a sign of

Figure 12.1 Philip Roth's gravestone, 2020. Credit: Michelle Foster, New York.

his control even beyond the grave. He wanted the Russian Samovar on West 52nd to cater. The first speaker was his longtime friend and former president of the Guggenheim Foundation, Joel Conarroe, first met at the University of Pennsylvania and to whom Roth entrusted manuscripts, page proofs, and photographs, who began by noting that years earlier Roth had carefully outlined to him the details of such a service.[13]

Others who spoke included Edna O'Brien, Norman Manea, Andrew Wylie, Ben Taylor, Nicole Krauss, Julia Golier, Janis Freedman Bellow, Bernard Avishai, Claudia Roth Pierpont, and Judith Thurman, who recalled riding around Connecticut with Roth years earlier searching for a proper burial spot. Pierpont recalled how much Roth enjoyed New York, even greeting admirers accidentally met on the Upper West Side, at one point speaking to an admirer through his wife's cell phone.[14] Manea reported that he and Roth competed over the number of stents they had (Roth won), and Wylie related that Roth promised to marry Claire Bloom only when Nelson Mandela was released from prison; he was stunned to find himself forced by events to keep his word. Golier recounted their lengthy relationship, moving from romance to independent dependence.

Taylor offered final remarks and Conarroe concluded the memorial with a reading of excerpts from some of Roth's letters, the most revealing from 2013, when Roth, confronted by death, would tell himself "I'm here and it's now" to shutter away the darkness and enjoy the present. "So long as I'm alive I'm immortal, am I not?"[15] Music for the memorial, chosen by Roth, was Fauré's "Élégie" in C Minor, Op. 24, which ended the nearly two-and-a-half-hour ceremony. Salman Rushdie, Mia Farrow, Don DeLillo, Robert Caro, and hundreds of others were in the audience.

For months after Roth's death, when Russ Murdock went to Roth's house, he would speak to Roth out of frustration over his absence but with recognized familiarity, addressing him with their preferred phrase, "motherfucker."[16] Murdock was naturally invited to the memorial service held in September at the New York Public Library and Golier threatened that he might even have to speak. Reluctantly, and anxiously—he preferred not to be in a crowd of writers and intellectuals—he attended and prepared some remarks, but Golier happily skipped him.

As to the headstone: in October 2017, Murdock found a small boulder on the property, an uneven rounded trapezoid with a flat face perfect for carving. They exchanged ideas on the stone, which Roth approved, but he never made it back to Cornwall Bridge to oversee the carving of his name and dates. Following his death, Rogers and Golier came up to confirm Murdock's choice of the boulder. They agreed and work began on Murdock's first tombstone job. With advice from Trow & Holden, a Vermont company renowned for its stonemasonry, he began imitating the roughness of "Albert Camus" chiseled onto his unfinished stone as a guide. Roth told him he wanted it to look like you "dipped your finger in black paint and drew it on the stone."[17] The finished stone says simply "PHILIP ROTH" and on the next line, chiseled into the rock, "1933–2018" (Figure 12.1).

Murdock oversaw its installation on Roth's grave in the Bard cemetery in October 2018, returning months later for the unveiling with his wife Wendy and Mia Farrow, a longtime friend and neighbor of Roth. They stopped first at Roth's property to gather stones to place on his grave, a Jewish sign of remembrance, a revision of the ancient custom of placing heavy stones over the buried (originally placed in the ground without a casket) to prevent animals from digging up the remains. A less solemn folk tradition is that the stones prevent the souls of the dead from escaping.

At the unveiling, Murdock, like others, told several stories, one of them about Roth coming out to watch him restore a stone wall. Murdock told him it was like writing a book: I have to work in sections, but in the end, it's to look seamless. Roth returned the next day with a copy of what Murdock believed was *American Pastoral*. A plaque soon appeared on the exterior of The Austin, Roth's apartment building at 130 West 79th Street. It notes that more than half of his novels were written in the building and lists a swath of his many awards. It also celebrates his championing the work of other writers, from dissidents of Eastern Europe to overlooked artists of his own generation. The final sentence is "The writer was as fierce as the man was generous; an enemy of cant, and an advocate of freedom in all its guises, personal and political." The Historic Landmarks Preservation Center created the plaque.

Judith Thurman once remarked that biographies that cling only to the "shore of fact" sacrifice "something more vibrant and sensuous, which only comes through an imaginative connection."[18] Such self-invention is not only that of the subject but occurs when the biographer tries to get down the one or two sentences that explicitly say what the subject and writer have in common, "to give the subject a reality in the form of a sentence."[19] But what often happens is the creation of a countertext, a critical life that directly or indirectly opposes, or at least questions, the way the subject wants to be portrayed.

Roth, supremely alert to self-invention almost from the onset of his career, was always aware of the possible emergence of countertexts; not only had he written many, but he seemed to encourage them. To the Italian filmmaker Livia Manera, he explained in her 2013 film *Philip Roth: Unmasked* that in the coming years he had "two great calamities to face: death and biography. Let's hope the first comes first!" But at times, his own self-invention trapped him into becoming its victim, not only in *Operation Shylock* but in the entirely fabricated interviews with him published by Tommaso Debenedetti.[20] To curb, if not prevent, such counternarratives, Roth instructed his friends and literary trust to restrict access to materials and even instructed his trustees to destroy the personal documents written for his official biographer when he finished with them.[21]

His only satisfaction was that outsiders would likely continue to get his life wrong, no matter what materials would be available. Only his official life could possibly get things right, matching his strenuous efforts to get all of his work right, carefully researching, proofreading, and criticizing those who got any part of it wrong including himself (the reason he hired his own copy-editor). He possibly took uncomfortable pleasure in knowing, as did Mickey Sabbath, that "everybody got everything wrong"—all the time (ST 109).

What Roth undertook in his work and life was not only constant self-scrutiny and complaint but the filling of a vacuum. A passage read at his eightieth birthday party outlines his overall approach to living and dying. Describing Sabbath, he explained, "His refractory way of living, a life of unalterable contention, is the best preparation he knows of for death. In his incompatibility, he finds his truth" (PR80 60–61).[22] But this is only half the story.

The other half begins with a question: What was Roth searching for? Or, what did he do, as Zuckerman asks the aged Amy Bellette in *Exit Ghost* (EG 172)? The answer might be in his story "The Box of Truths," which appeared in Bucknell's undergraduate literary magazine *Et Cetera* in October 1952. The three-page story narrates a young author's anger at a rejection letter, the editor telling the new writer he does not yet have a subject: "You don't have anything to write about. It's as easy as that. You haven't lived."[23] The box of truths is empty because he has yet to write "searchingly" or "sympathetically" about real people, which remained a challenge throughout Roth's long career. But through opposition and rebellion, by the end of his life, he had filled the box.

Roth was a realist who laid bare the contradictions and struggles shared by all. He made readers uncomfortable, but with style; bad taste was his *métier*. And he probably wrote more about death than any other writer after Tolstoy.[24] But what Roth wrote was the "lived reality" of experience, a phrase he used after he cleaned up his father's mess in *Patrimony*. It was not symbolic; it just *was*: "nothing less or more than the lived reality" (PAT 176). With his comic style, hard truths appeared. He exposed the "lived reality" we all face but also seek to avoid.

"Philip Roth, Towering Novelist Who Explored Lust, Jewish Life and America, Dies at 85" was the headline in the *New York Times* on 22 May 2018. Flattering obituaries appeared worldwide with the same theme: a soaring American writer gone, the heir to Bellow and even James, but always just missing the grand prize, the Nobel. But a group in Sweden took action. On 10 December 2018, the very evening of the Nobel ceremony, a protest event was held in Stockholm by the Jewish/Swedish Society. The advertisement read "A Nobel Evening dedicated to Philip Roth." Adam Gopnik, Claudia Roth Pierpont, Bernard Avishai, Lisa Halliday, and Judith Thurman flew in from New York to participate. This literary protest was a vivid reminder to the Nobel committee of its failure to recognize Roth's literary achievements.

Articles continued to examine his life, question his attitude toward women, and compare his Newark to Faulkner's Yoknapatawpha County. They argue that his American Trilogy was a triumph, although in many of these accounts, sanctimony and piety, qualities Roth detested, reigned.

But what if Roth wrote his own obituary? In a sense he did, twice. The first was in *The Counterlife*. Immediately after Zuckerman's funeral, his brother Henry discovers that Nathan has secretly written his own eulogy, to be delivered at his own funeral: "The fiction and the man were one! Calling it fiction was the biggest fiction of all!" (CL 227). The second is when Mickey Sabbath composes his own satiric, epitaphic biography on a New York subway. Sabbath imagines that he has fallen from a window eighteen stories up. The cause was suicide, says Rosa Complicata, housekeeper, whom, the narrator adds, "Mr. Sabbath sodomized moments before taking his life" (ST 192). As the obituary concludes, we learn that he was haunted by the ghost of his mother and, in a final, ironic, footnote that he "did nothing for Israel" (ST 195).

But what if Roth's characters offered their own one-line tributes, a genuine Rothian gesture? Some samples:

Neil Klugman: "No fines. His books have been returned."

Ronald Patimkin: "Anything left in the fridge?"

Alex Portnoy: "Still shtupping?"

Nathan Zuckerman: "Freed at last from the tyranny of his intensity."

Maureen Tarnopol: "Miss me, motherfucker?"

Milton Appel: "Finally zipped it up?"

Alvin Pepler: "Gone or just hiding?"

David Kepesh: "Unhappy ending."

Smilesburger: "He took the money, no?"

Mickey Sabbath: "Another act?"

Drenka Balich: "You gave me a double life. I couldn't have endured with just one."

Eve Frame: "Liar!"

Coleman Silk: "Ready to dance?"

Simon Axler: "What took him so long?"

And Roth's own clarifying, three-word gift: "At it again."[25]

Acknowledgments

Many have assisted, directed, encouraged, and cajoled during the life of this project beginning with the late Mark Shechner and the late Derek Parker Royal, outstanding Roth scholars, who led the way for numerous followers. Jesse Tisch has been an exceptional, stimulating, resourceful, and critical voice sharing ideas, barbs, and insights on Roth in the late stages of the writing. He generously unpacked his remarkable Roth knowledge and provided valuable readings and suggestions, while reminding me of the importance of sticking to the subject. Jacques Berlinerblau similarly provided repeated reminders to speed up, while suggesting new leads and enthusiastic support, never letting me forget to probe, question, and think in original ways. Glenn Horowitz and Benjamin Taylor deserve special thanks for their guidance and suggestions of new directions, Glenn alerting me to shifts in the status of Roth archives and Ben generously allowing me to see his memoir of Roth before publication. Victoria Aarons, Aimee Pozorski, David Brauner, Steven Sampson, and Debra Shostak have similarly been helpful, offering positive criticisms and wise counsel, as has James Bloom, New Jerseyian through and through, ably assisted by Robin Beaty. Steven Zipperstein has also been a stimulating traveler on the road of Roth studies.

Others to be thanked include Claire Bloom, Robert Brustein, Jason Epstein, Alan Lelchuk, Maxine Groffsky, Ann Mudge, Jules Feiffer, David Rieff, Ivan Sanders, and the late James Atlas. Larry Peerce was especially helpful with details on filming *Goodbye, Columbus*. Ross Miller, Blake Bailey, Clarke Blaise, David Gooblar, Jack F. Knowles, Maggie McKinley, Bernard F. Rodgers, Matthew Shipe, and the late Philip Roth have all contributed in countless ways.

At the Newark Public Library, James Lewis, formerly of the library and curator of *Philip Roth Photos from a Lifetime*, assisted by Rosemary Steinbaum, a current trustee of the Newark Public Library, have generously helped. Tom Ankner, director of the Charles F. Cummings New Jersey Information Center at the Newark Public Library, has been especially supportive, as has Barbara Bair, historian, Manuscript Division, Library of Congress, and Jeffrey Flannery, head of Reference & Reader Services at the Library of Congress.

Both excelled in securing material during the Library's COVID closure. Alice Birney, previously responsible for the Roth archive at the Library of Congress, was also a wonderful guide. Shulamith Z. Berger, curator of Special Collections and Hebraica-Judaica, Yeshiva University Library, New York, has been of great assistance, as has Isabella O'Neill, head of Special Collections and university archivist, Bertrand Library, Bucknell University. Others include Cristina Zuccaro of the Centro Internazionale di Studi Primo Levi Centre, Turin, Italy, Luisa Fava of *La Stampa* and James Nachtway. Michelle Foster of New York generously photographed Roth's grave at Bard College.

In addition, Jeff Severs, Mike Zeitlin, and Judith Paltin at the University of British Columbia, Vancouver, have listened and offered helpful responses. Brendan O'Neill, formerly of Oxford University Press, and Norman Hirschy, editor *extraordinaire* and a man of great perseverance and good humor, are also to be thanked. In Singapore, Daniel Keith Jernigan, Kevin Riordan, Fredrik Tydal listened with patience. Michael Earley, currently of Singapore, has been a longtime and supportive friend, as well as a valuable *agent provocateur*.

The Newark Historical Society, the Berg Collection at the New York Public Library, as well as the Manuscript Division, plus the Rutgers University Library, J. P. Morgan Library, Bertrand Library at Bucknell University, the University of British Columbia Library, and the Vancouver Public Library all provided assistance. The Philip Roth Society has been a welcome and generous home and testing ground for various ideas through its conferences, journal and seminars. I am indebted to the Society and its members for encouragement and support.

More personally, this project could not have been undertaken nor completed without the love, support, and singular patience of Anne MacKenzie, a perceptive critic with a sharp eye, as well as my son, Ryan, and my daughter, Dara, along with Jon and their enthusiastic new readers, Gideon and Levi.

Notes

Preface

1. He dismissed the first because of distortions in the proposed narrative; after much scrutiny, he located a second.
2. Roth, "The Art of Fiction," CWPR 166.
3. Roth to Ted Solotaroff, 1983(?), cited in Jesse Tisch, "The Philip Roth Archive," *Tablet*, 21 May 2020, https://www.tabletmag.com/sections/arts-letters/articles/philip-roth-letters. "Candor is the passport to everything": Ben Taylor interview, 3 June 2020, Newark Public Library, webinar on his memoir, *Here We Are.*
4. Søren Kierkegaard, *Repetition and Philosophical Crumbs,* trans. Edward F. Mooney (Oxford: Oxford World's Classics, 2009) 60. Roth varies the line at the opening of *Operation Shylock* to read "Existence is surely a debate" (9).
5. Virginia Woolf, "Stopford Brooke," in *The Essays of Virginia Woolf,* vol. 2, ed. Andrew McNeillie (San Diego: Harcourt Brace Jovanovich, 1987) 184. Philip Roth in Bob Thompson, "Many Faces of Philip Roth," *Washington Post,* 18 November 2006.
6. Ben Taylor, *Here We Are: My Friendship with Philip Roth* (New York: Penguin, 2020) 21–22.
7. Roth to Rieff, 28 January 1987, Farrar, Straus and Giroux (hereafter FSG) Archive, NYPL.
8. Roth, "Just a Lively Boy," in *An Unsentimental Education: Writers and Chicago,* ed. Molly McQuade (Chicago: University of Chicago Press, 1995), 124.
9. Kafka to Max Brod in Gabriel Josipovici, *What Ever Happened to Modernism?* (New Haven, CT: Yale University Press, 2011), 4.
10. Roth in Tisch, "The Philip Roth Archive."
11. Roth, "The Art of Fiction," CWPR 165. Roth may be echoing Emerson, who in 1838 said, "Truly speaking it is not instruction, but provocation, that I can receive from another soul." Ralph Waldo Emerson, "Divinity School Address," 15 July 1838, American Transcendentalism Web, https://archive.vcu.edu/english/engweb/transcendentalism/authors/emerson/essays/dsa.html.
12. The essay was frequently taught by Professor Stuart Tave at the University of Chicago. See Molly McQuade, "Famous Writers' School," *Chicago Tribune,* 4 June 1995, https://www.chicagotribune.com/news/ct-xpm-1995-06-04-9506040297-story.html.
13. Alan Lelchuk to Roth, 29 July 1977, box 19, folder 10, Roth Papers, Library of Congress. Hereafter LC.
14. Early in the novel, the narrator asks if Ziff was really that good or "was he really that *bad,* and therefore very good, like Céline, driven by crazy, malevolent impulses." Alan Lelchuk, *Ziff: A Life?* (New York: Carroll & Graf, 2003), 6.

15. Lelchuk to the author, email, 13 June 2020.

16. Roth to Ben Taylor, quoted in Taylor, *Here We Are*, 54.

17. Roth originally made these statements in a 1984 interview in *Quinzaine Littéraire*, adding, "I feel called by his voice." Jean-Pierre Salagas, "Philip Roth," *La Quinzaine Littéraire*, 16 June 1984, quoted in Henri Godard, *Henri Godard Présente Voyage au bout de la nuit de Louis-Ferdinand Céline* (Paris: Gallimard, 1991), 190. An important survey of Céline and American writers is Alice Kaplan, "The Céline Effect: A 1992 Survey of Contemporary American Writers," *Modernism/Modernity* 3.1 (1996): 117–36. Norman Manea cites Roth saying "Céline is my Proust!" at their first meeting, at the Essex House in New York, after Manea gave him his short story entitled "Proust's Tea." Roth told Manea that he could not read Proust, leading to his outburst. Manea, "Nearby and Together: Norman Manea on His Friend Philip Roth," *Los Angeles Review of Books*, 23 June 2018, https://lareviewofbooks.org/article/nearby-and-together-norman-manea-on-his-friend-philip-roth/. Also see Adelaide Docx, "A Gentler Céline," *New Yorker*, 27 May 2013, https://www.newyorker.com/books/page-turner/a-gentler-cline.

18. Roth in Lee, "The Art of Fiction" (1984), CWPR 168; Roth in Alvin Sanoff, "Writers Have a Third Eye" (1987), CWPR 213.

19. Janet Hobhouse, *The Furies* (New York: Doubleday, 1993), 203, 197. Hobhouse also refers to his "obsession of secrecy" (195).

20. Flaubert to Gertrude Tennant, 25 December 1876, in *Correspondence, Quatrième Série (1869–1880)* (Paris: Louis Conard, 1910), 4:280.

21. Roth, "His Mistress's Voice," *Partisan Review* 53.2 (1986): 170.

22. In *The Facts*, Roth writes that "turning the flame up under my life" expressed in a non-fictional form brought him closer to felt experience (7).

23. Roth uses the "*stung* by life" phrase in "A Formidable Writer, an Exceptional Man: Philip Roth on Richard Stern," *Literary Hub*, 1 September 2017, https://lithub.com/a-formidable-writer-an-exceptional-man-philip-roth-on-richard-stern/.

24. In his 1998 novel *I Married a Communist*, he identifies her and her husband (in the novel an informer for an inflammatory anti-Communist publication, *Red Channels*) as the malicious Grants, who actually ghostwrite the inflammatory book by Eve Frame exposing Ira Ringold and titled *I Married a Communist* (187, 242). Its cover had a photo of Eve and Ira walking down West 11th Street in the Village, with his head circled in red. Ironically, it was the Grays who alerted Roth to the rural farm house in Cornwall Bridge that he bought in 1972.

25. Taylor, *Here We Are*, 31.

26. On *Sabbath's Theater* as a nervous breakdown, see Mark Shechner, *Up Society's Ass, Copper: Rereading Philip Roth* (Madison: University of Wisconsin Press, 2003), 146. On Roth's narcissism, see Jeffrey Berman, *Narcissism and the Novel* (New York: NYU Press, 1990) or David Foster Wallace, who dismissed Roth with Updike and Mailer as "the Great Male Narcissists who've dominated postwar realist fiction": Wallace, "John Updike, Champion Literary Phallocrat, Drops One," *Observer*, 13 October 1997, https://observer.com/1997/10/john-updike-champion-literary-phallocrat-drops-one-is-this-finally-the-end-for-magnificent-narcissists/. Wallace also writes that, to

women readers, Updike is "just a penis with a thesaurus." Any two pages of *Portnoy's Complaint* will also exhibit the narcissist at work, he adds.

27. Taylor, *Here We Are*, 159, 160.
28. Taylor, *Here We Are*, 63.

Introduction

1. Roth to Candida Donadio, 28 July 1967, box 7, MSS22491, Correspondence File, Ms. Division, Philip Roth Papers, LC.

2. On the struggle to write *Portnoy* and its various drafts, see, most recently, Scott Saul, "Rough: A Journey into the Drafts of *Portnoy's Complaint*," *Post 45*, 12 April 2019, http://post45.research.yale.edu/2019/04/rough-a-journey-into-the-drafts-of-portnoys-complaint/.

3. Roth's next story was "On the Air," about a talent agent seeking a new radio show who lit on the idea of Einstein as a guest. On a trip to find Einstein in Princeton, the promoter and family encounter a series of characters, "all fury," notably a gentile, ex-merchant seaman-bartender of Scully's Tavern, who might instantly take "their three heads" (Lippman, his wife, and his son) and smash them "together until they were just mush and blood and splinters of bone" (ONA 22, 23). As they prepare to leave, the bartender leaps over the bar to deliver a page-and-a-half angry screed essentially and comically on the corruption of the English language and his hearing problems (ONA 24–25). The bartender then becomes the angry police chief who threatens Lippman with a gun for "Reckless Accusations against Christians" (ONA 33–47). In his *Journals*, Alfred Kazin noted that showbiz soon succeeded socialism in importance in Jewish history. Kazin, *Alfred Kazin's Journals*, ed. Richard M. Cook (New Haven, CT: Yale University Press, 2011), 8 December 1968: 389.

4. The origin of the incident was Aaron Asher's mother, who had immigrated to America in the 1930s and, as Roth later explained, shows how for American Jews the Holocaust is always there, even if submerged or hidden. In the novel, Mrs. Zuckerman had grown up not in Europe but in New Jersey. Her son keeps the paper on which his mother had inscribed the word. For Roth's comments on the scene, see Claudia Roth Pierpont, *Roth Unbound* (New York: Farrar, Straus and Giroux, 2013), 130.

5. Hans J. Kleinschmidt, "The Angry Act: The Role of Aggression in Creativity," *American Imago* 24.2 (1967): 124, 125. For further research on the topic, see Matthijs Baas et al., "Creative Production by Angry People Peaks Early On, Decreases over Time, and Is Relatively Unstructured," *Journal of Experimental Social Psychology* 47.6 (2011): 1107–15.

6. Kleinschmidt, "The Angry Act," 126. There is a further parallel with Roth being locked out and Proust and his mother. As a young mother, Mme Proust refused and then granted a goodnight kiss from Proust at Auteuil. The opening of *Swann's Way* emphasizes the anticipation and sometimes denial of such nightly exchanges. At her death on 26 September 1905, Proust wrote that she had finally and fully accepted his caresses, although tomorrow she would be lost forever. Proust in George D. Painter,

Marcel Proust, A Biographer, vol. 2, rev. ed. (London: Chatto and Windus, 1989), 49. The relationship between mother and son was intense: Proust wanted simultaneously to be independent *and* to remain the little boy who was at the center of his mother's world (2: 69–71). Anger erupted at this dilemma after her death to such an extent that he supposedly gave his mother's furniture to a male brothel (Kleinschmidt 127). After her death, Proust said that she kept a lifelong air of absolute calm and that "none of us knows what she is thinking or suffering" (Painter 2: 48). Proust's mother (Jeanne Weil) was Jewish and did not convert to Catholicism. There may be a parallel here with Bess Roth, a similar model of equanimity, Roth writing in his "Notes for My Biographer" that his mother wasn't silent because she was subdued but because she knew when to be silent and saw no reason to speak when she had nothing to say (NOT 122). Michael Wood analyzes the love/hate between Proust and his mother in "Proust and His Mother," *London Review of Books* 34.6 (22 March 2012), https://www.lrb.co.uk/the-paper/v34/n06/michael-wood/proust-and-his-mother and begins with a commentary on Proust's angry fight with his parents in 1897, not unlike Roth's later quarrels with his father. Proust fictionalizes the battle in *Jean Santeuil*.

7. Pierpont, *Roth Unbound*, 24. In *Zuckerman Unbound*, Alvin Pepler, Newark nuisance, is part of a semicomic scheme to kidnap Zuckerman's mother and hold her for a ransom. Sensing a trick, Zuckerman doesn't pay.

8. Bellow offered friendly criticism of Roth throughout their friendship but stronger views in a distorted *People* interview from 1984 on the Zuckerman books. He also disliked *I Married a Communist* and told Roth. Carmen Callil offered public condemnation of Roth's misogyny, resigning from the prize committee after he won the Man Booker International prize; most recently, Joel Conarroe auctioned a series of manuscripts, correspondence, and photographs in March 2020, including a previously unknown fifty-three-page manuscript, a sequel to *The Breast* (1972). For a lively summary of the Bellow-Roth friendship, see David Gooblar, "Lesson from the Master," *Guardian*, 8 October 2005, https://www.theguardian.com/books/2005/oct/08/fiction.saulbellow.

9. In *Roth Unbound*, written with Roth's cooperation, Pierpont titles one of her late chapters "Betrayal." It deals with Bloom's *Leaving a Doll's House* and Roth's *I Married a Communist*. See Pierpont, *Roth Unbound*, 226–42.

10. Jeffrey Berman has written extensively on the Roth-Kleinschmidt connection. See *The Talking Cure: Literary Representations of Psychoanalysis* (New York: NYU Press, 1985), and, more recently, Paul Mosher and Jeffrey Berman, *Confidentiality and Its Discontents* (New York: Fordham University Press, 2015).

11. Roth, "Forty-Five Years On," WR? 389. The phrase "emotional history" is from Kleinschmidt's "The Angry Act," 118. The full and telling sentence is "As he denies his emotional history, he ignores his present emotional ties and substitutes for them distortions of potentially gratifying reality." Kleinschmidt is referring to an accomplished painter who is his patient, but the comments apply equally to Roth, his next example. Another patient of Kleinschmidt exposed to his theory of creativity and rage several years after Roth was the *New Yorker* writer Adam Gopnik. In 1998, he published an essay about his six-year treatment, which appeared the

year after the psychiatrist died. Characterized as Dr. Grosskurth, he is parodied as constantly citing his celebrity patients (Leonard Bernstein, Richard Avedon, and Susan Sontag were among them). See Adam Gopnik, "Man Goes to See a Doctor," *New Yorker* 24, 31 August 1998, 24. https://www.newyorker.com/magazine/1998/08/24/man-goes-to-see-a-doctor.

12. Homer, *The Iliad*, trans. Robert Fagles, intro. Bernard Knox (New York: Viking, 1990), 77, ll. 1–2.

13. Roth, "Forty-Five Years On," WR? 389.

14. Roth, "His Mistress's Voice," *Partisan Review* 52.3 (1986): 170.

15. NOT 244–48. Roth adds that Bloom saw anger everywhere and worked hard to placate her daughter so she would not become angry with her. Roth composed the document after 2010, the year he gave up writing fiction.

16. Roth to David Plante in Jennifer Senior, "Philip Roth Blows Up," *New York Magazine*, 1 May 2000, http://nymag.com/nymetro/arts/features/2983/.

17. Kazin, *Alfred Kazin's Journals*, 8 December 1968: 389.

18. The ending of *Portnoy* replays this condition when Portnoy, in response to Naomi, the Israeli Sabra, sees her as the embodiment of his mother, "a real-fault-finder, a professional critic of me. Must have perfection in her men" (PC 259). Roth, "His Mistress's Voice," 170.

19. Aaron Asher in Sean O'Hagan, "One Angry Man," *Guardian*, 26 September 2004, https://www.theguardian.com/books/2004/sep/26/fiction.philiproth.

20. Solotaroff in Senior, "Philip Roth Blows Up." An example of explosive Roth occurred at his eightieth birthday party at the Newark Museum. Seated next to Edna O'Brien and greeting well-wishers, he exploded when a photographer moved a water bottle set in front of him so he could have a clear picture. An angry Roth almost jumped out of his seat in response, shouting at the photographer for daring to move anything. The man and his camera slunk away. I witnessed the event.

21. Mailer makes this point in *Advertisements for Myself* (1959; Cambridge, MA: Harvard University Press, 1992), 93.

22. On not needing the city, see Michiko Kakutani, "Is Roth Really Writing about Roth?," *New York Times*, 11 May 1981, https://www.nytimes.com/1981/05/11/books/is-roth-really-writing-about-roth-114855.html.

23. One is reminded of Wallace Stevens's question. In "Esthétique du Mal" he writes, "out of what one sees and hears and out / Of what one feels, who could have thought to make / So many selves[?]" Stevens, *Collected Poems*, ed. John Serio and Chris Beyers (New York: Vintage, 2015), 343.

24. Kleinschmidt, "The Angry Act," 125.

25. See MM 5–6. Roth composed this eight-page essay between June and July 2014.

26. See NOT. The document is over three hundred pages long. He began to write it in November 2010 as a late refutation of Bloom's memoir, published in 1996. He subsequently prepared a longer document which challenged the contents of the limited interviews done by Miller. Roth's important late female relationships were with Maletta Pfeiffer, Susan Rogers, Julia Golier, and Catherine Steindler. With the last, he actually visited a geneticist to determine whether at seventy-two he could father a

healthy child. She was twenty-nine. In a document outlining his relationships, Roth was careful to indicate that he had had affairs with only three married women: Janet Hobhouse, Maletta Pfeiffer, and, in London the woman who was the source of his novel *Deception*.

27. Roth, "Imaging Jews," *New York Review of Books*, 3 October 1972, 254–55, https://www.nybooks.com/articles/1974/10/03/imagining-jews/.

28. Roth, "Critical Standards," *New York Review of Books*, 12 December 1974, https://www.nybooks.com/articles/1974/12/12/critical-standards/.

29. Pierpont, *Roth Unbound*, 50; John Updike, *Rabbit, Run* (New York: Ballantine Books, 1960), 140.

30. He first stated the claim in a 1988 interview with Asher Z. Milbauer and Donald G. Watson, adding, "Lowly life . . . so long as it doesn't tumble over into misery and horror, can still be entertaining and, for all its grittiness, strangely uplifting" (CWPR 252). He repeats it in NOT 245.

31. In 1998, Roth received a letter from Bellow castigating him for his anger: "One of your persistent themes is the purgation one can obtain only through rage." When Roth reviewed his interview to be included in his final Library of America volume, *Why Write?*, he removed his comment on the dirty little secret of hatred and rage. Bellow, "Letter to Philip Roth January 1st 1998," in *Saul Bellow Letters*, ed. Ben Taylor (New York: Viking, 2010), 541; WR? 153; cf. RMY 131.

32. Roth in Jan Dalley, "At Home with Philip Roth," *Slate*, 26 June 2011, https://slate.com/human-interest/2011/06/at-home-with-philip-roth-the-author-confesses-he-never-reads-fiction.html.

33. Having broken Zuckerman's jaw in *Everyman*, Roth told Hermione Lee that he knew what he was doing: "For a Jew a broken jaw is a terrible tragedy. It was to avoid this that so many of us went into teaching rather than prizefighting" (CWPR 181). On boxing and Roth, see John G. Rodwan Jr., "The Fighting Life: Boxing and Identity in Novels by Philip Roth and Norman Mailer," *Philip Roth Studies* 7.1 (2011): 83–96.

34. David Remnick, "Philip Roth's Propulsive Force," *New Yorker* 4, 28 May 2018, https://www.newyorker.com/magazine/2018/06/04/philip-roths-propulsive-force.

35. Roth in Taylor, *Here We Are*, 156–57.

36. In 1912, at the peak of his business career, Anderson had a breakdown that led to a rejection of his former life with a wife and three children and the beginning of a new life as a writer. Importantly, he reinterpreted the nature of his breakdown as a form of personal agency: "I wanted to leave, I had a plan, I craftily staged the entire affair." Once released from the hospital, he moved to Chicago, divorced his wife, and later married his mistress. But that did not last long; after a divorce in Reno, he married a woman he had been involved with before the divorce. That relationship, too, failed and he undertook a fourth marriage. His early success, the short stories in *Winesburg, Ohio*, was a precursor to *Goodbye, Columbus*.

37. On illness in the novel and in Roth's work at large, Susan Sontag's *Illness as Metaphor* (1978) is helpful. Roth seems to subscribe to her view that looking for meaning in disease is destructive. His characters have it, face it, and succumb to it, as did Roth. Sontag herself battled three illnesses: metastatic breast cancer in 1976, uterine cancer

in 1996, and finally leukemia in 2004, which she did not survive. Not yet fifty, Roth was beginning to write seriously about illness in his fiction with existential, realistic clarity. Illness, Sontag argued, should not be honored with metaphor.

38. It should also be noted that the Roth Literary Trust is managing access to such materials, at least until the authorized life appears. Copies of this material have been deposited as the Benjamin Taylor/Philip Roth Archive at the Firestone Library, Princeton University. But shortly after receipt and cataloguing, and a brief period of open access for research in the fall of 2018, it was closed. There is now a dispute between the Trust and the university as to accessibility. Highlights of the archive include "Marriage à la Mode," an eight-page essay; "Money," a thirty-seven-page essay; a detailed thirty-page "Pain and Illness History" with a preface of two and a half pages that lists Roth's medical history; "Notes for My Biographer," a lengthy commentary on the misstatements and interpretations in the interviews done by Ross Miller; and, finally, a lengthy list with commentary of his various female relationships. Taylor's memoir of Roth, *Here We Are*, appeared in May 2020.

39. The three forbidden to attend either his funeral or memorial service were Claire Bloom, Francine du Plessix Gray, and Ross Miller. Gray died in January 2018. The other two are very much alive. He also stipulated the sale of his 1,500-square-foot two-bedroom New York City condo with three balconies on the twelfth floor at 130 West 79th Street near Columbus Avenue ($3.2 million was the asking price) and his home in Cornwall Bridge, Connecticut ($2.92 million was the asking price). See Joyce Chen, "Former Upper West Side Apartment of Famed Author Philip Roth Hits the Market for $3.2 Million," *Architectural Digest*, 26 February 2019, https://www.architecturaldigest. com/story/former-apartment-famed-author-philip-roth-for-sale.

40. Henry Wadsworth Longfellow in James Marcus, "The Public Poet," *New Yorker*, 8 and 15 June 2020, 73.

Chapter 1

1. John Cunningham, *Newark* (Newark: New Jersey Historical Society, 1966), 244 quoted in Larry Schwartz, "Roth, Race and Newark," *Cultural Logic*, 2005, https://ojs. library.ubc.ca/index.php/clogic/article/view/191860.

2. Others born that year include Jayne Mansfield, Joan Rivers, Kim Novak, Joan Collins, and Willie Nelson.

3. Roth in Scott Raab, "Philip Roth Goes Home Again," *Esquire*, 7 October 2010. Also see Mark Di Ionno, "A Tour of Philip Roth's Newark Includes Surprise Visit by the Author," 18 October 2009, NJ.com. https://www.nj.com/njv_mark_diionno/2009/10/ a_tour_of_phillip_roths_newark.html.

4. David Hartman and Barry Lewis, *A History of Newark*, WNET TV, 2002, http://www. thirteen.org/newark/history3.html. This series, by the documentary filmmaker David Hartman and historian Barry Lewis, reveals important elements of Newark's past.

5. Linda Forgosh, author of *The Jews of Weequahic*, cites 35,000 Jews in Weequahic alone for the same year. Another 29,500 Jews lived in suburbs such as Irvington,

Hillside, the Oranges, Bloomfield, and Verona. Forgosh, *The Jews of Weequahic* (New York: Arcade, 2008) 10. William B. Helmreich, *The Enduring Community: The Jews of Newark and Metrowest* (Livingston, NJ: Transaction, 1998) 30.

6. Helmreich, *The Enduring Community*, 35.

7. Forgosh, *The Jews of Weequahic*, 8.

8. Roth, "'Here I Am': Philip Roth Reflects on His Half-Century Career as a Writer," *Library of America News*, 6 November 2017, https://www.loa.org/news-and-views/1347-here-i-am-philip-roth-reflects-on-his-half-century-career-as-a-writer.

9. Marcia Kahan Rosenthal to Roth, 22 January 1981, box 30, folder 9, LC.

10. Joachim Prinz, *Joachim Prinz, Rebellious Rabbi: An Autobiography—The German and Early American Years*, ed. Michael A. Meyer (Bloomington: Indiana University Press, 2008) 169.

11. Prinz, *Joachim Prinz*, 177.

12. Prinz, *Joachim Prinz*, 192, 195.

13. Prinz, *Joachim Prinz*, 202.

14. Prinz was an outspoken supporter of racial equality and marched with King in the famous 1963 March on Washington. But as Prinz would often recount, the association with King was not always a plus. When he was held up at knife-point by a Black hitchhiker he picked up while driving to synagogue in Newark, he recalled that when the knife was pointed at his throat, he boldly told his attacker, "Young man . . . I marched with Dr. King." The assailant answered, "Look man, I don't give a fuck who your doctor is; just give me your damn money!" (Prinz in Allan Nadler, "The Plot for America: Remembering Civil Rights Leader Joachim Prinz," *Tablet*, 25 February 2011, https://www.tabletmag.com/sections/news/articles/the-plot-for-america.

15. One of Prinz's reservations was because rabbis in America served at the pleasure of their synagogue boards. Their salaries were low and security uncertain. In Germany, rabbis were considered civil servants and officials of the entire Jewish community. In many German states, the government guaranteed their position and income, which was generous; it also ensured a pension. A government salary made the rabbi curiously independent from the Jewish community (Prinz, *Joachim Prinz*, 201). In America, often uninformed lay leaders controlled the salary and fate of the rabbi. On his acceptance of the Newark pulpit, see Prinz, *Joachim Prinz*, 211.

16. Prinz, *Joachim Prinz*, 55.

17. Prinz, *Joachim Prinz*, 215, 217–18.

18. Prinz, *Joachim Prinz*, 219.

19. Among numerous sources, such as Helmreich's *The Enduring Community*; Brad Tuttle's *How Newark Became Newark: The Rise, Fall and Rebirth of an American City* (New Brunswick, NJ: Rutgers University Press, 2009); Kevin Mumford, *Newark: A History of Race, Rights and Riots in America* (New York: NYU Press, 2007), Ezra Shales, *Made in Newark* (New Brunswick, NJ: Rivergate Books, 2010), and Michael Kimmage's literary study, *In History's Grip: Philip Roth's Newark Trilogy* (Stanford: Stanford University Press, 2012). The articles of Charles F. Cummings are helpful, especially "Jewish Population Rose and Fell over 150 Years," *Star-Ledger*, 23

May 2002 and "Jewish Community Creates Host of Venerable Institutions," *Star-Ledger*, 6 October 2005. His "Knowing Newark" columns are invaluable sources for Newark's social and cultural history. "More than anyone other than perhaps Mayor Sharpe James," Rutgers professor Clement Price said at a memorial service for Cummings on 18 January 2006, "Charles raised the art of hyperbole on matters relating to Newark to a higher and more persuasive level." Roth also spoke about Cummings and his life, from his birth in Puerto Rico in 1937 to his early years in Maine and Virginia and his arrival in Newark to take a job as a librarian in 1963. See Brad Parks, "Hundreds Honor Late Historian," *Star-Ledger*, 19 January 2006. Margalit Fox prepared the *New York Times* obituary: "Charles F. Cummings, Official Historian of Newark, Is Dead at 68," *New York Times*, 23 December 2005, https://www.nytimes.com/2005/12/23/nyregion/charles-f-cummings-official-historian-of-newark-is-dead-at-68.html. For a concise summary of Jewish life in Newark and the surrounding area, see Cummings, "From Humble Start, Jews Built Strong Institutions," *Star-Ledger*, 16 May 2002.

20. Topping the list of Newark's Jewish fighters were these ten, all of whom have been enshrined in the New Jersey Boxing Hall of Fame: Allie Stoltz, Abie Bain, Nat Arno, Lou Halper, Benny Levine, Hymie Kugel, Max Novich, Mickey Breitkopf, Maxie Fisher, Al Fisher. Arno was born to immigrant parents in the Third Ward as Sidney Abramowitz. "Arno," he thought, was a better name for a boxer.

21. Ellenstein, living in Paterson as a youth while working ten-hour days in a silk mill, turned to amateur boxing in his free time and won every one of his amateur bouts over two years as a 115-pound flyweight to become the Metropolitan Boys Champion in his weight class. In 1907, he decided to turn professional. After he fought his first pro fight as "Kid Meyer," he quit boxing at the urging of his widowed mother, who, then with five children, depended on her only son for his earnings.

22. See Warren Grover, "The New Minutemen," in *Nazis in Newark* (New Brunswick, NJ: Transaction, 2003) 39–71. For Herman Roth on Longy and the Jewish gangs, see PAT 203–4. Also useful is Arnie Bernstein, *Swastika Nation: Fritz Kuhn and the Rise and Fall of the German-American Bund* (New York: St. Martin's, 2013), 131–41. He titles the chapter "King of Newark."

23. Grover, "The New Minutemen," 26–33.

24. Helmreich, *The Enduring Community*, 22.

25. The author of this biography was also born in Beth Israel Hospital, but ten years after Roth, becoming the fourth "Ira" in the Rothian orbit.

26. Helmreich, *The Enduring Community*, 25.

27. Zwillman was a dominating 6 feet 2 inches. Roth, for comparison, was nearly the same.

28. Tuttle, *How Newark Became Newark*, 98

29. Helmreich, *The Enduring Community*, 29.

30. Even her sudden death at a restaurant was not disruptive. She simply slumped forward: "Didn't even fall. Made no trouble for anyone. The way she always did everything," Herman Roth recalled (PAT 36).

31. Roth in Patricia Cohen, "Philip Roth, Provocateur, Is Celebrated at 75," *New York Times*, 12 April 2008, http://www.nytimes.com/2008/04/12/books/12roth.html.

32. Roth, "How My Mother Taught Me to Type," Web of Stories, n.d., https://www.webofstories.com/play/philip.roth/52.

33. Tuttle, *How Newark Became Newark*, 8.

34. Nat Bodian in "Newark's Colorful Depression-Era Jewish Mayor," Old Newark Memories, n.d., http://www.oldnewark.com/memories/bios/bodianellen.htm. Bodian cites figures from the U.S. Census for 1933 under the category "Census of Religious Bodies."

35. Edward S. Shapiro, *A Time for Healing: American Jewry since World War II* (Baltimore, MD: Johns Hopkins University Press, 1992) 145.

36. Three homes within the radius of Weequahic High mark Roth's moveable life in Newark, to be extended by his parents when, in response to promotions for his father, his mother and father moved to Elizabeth, then Moorestown in South Jersey, and, finally, back to Elizabeth.

37. Roth in Scott Rabb, "Philip Roth Goes Home Again," *Esquire*, 7 October 2010.

38. Roth to Linda Forgosh in Robert Wiener, "Separating Fact from Fiction in Philip Roth's Latest Novel," *New Jersey Jewish News*, 10 November 2010, http://www.njjewishnews.com/article/2427/separating-fact-from-fiction-in-philip-roths-latest-novel#.UP8yGmeWN9Z.

39. Wiener, "Separating Fact from Fiction."

40. "Suppose entertainment is the Purpose of Life?" a character asks in the story, which appeared in *New American Review* 10 (7–49) but has never been reprinted.

41. Roth, "The Radio," Web of Stories, n.d., https://www.webofstories.com/play/philip.roth/47.

42. For Roth on music, especially chamber music, see Benjamin Ivry, "Philip Roth's Favorite Elegy—and His Lifelong Love of Chamber Music," *Forward*, 5 October 2018, https://forward.com/culture/411284/philip-roths-favorite-elegyand-his-lifelong-love-of-chamber-music/. Also see Pierpont, *Roth Unbound*, 169, 329–30, where she suggests that Roth's engagement with music was to psychoanalyze the composers. Updike also comments on musical Roth.

43. The name derives from a Native American group called Weequahic (*Wee-QUAY-ic*) that originally inhabited the area and were part of the larger Lenape tribal group that occupied parts of New York and Pennsylvania as well as New Jersey. Sherry B. Ortner, *New Jersey Dreaming* (Durham, NC: Duke University Press, 2003), 3. In her book, Ortner states that the school, built with WPA funds, opened in 1932. Other sources, such as Forgosh (*The Jews of Weequahic*, 9), cite 1933.

44. See Ralph Keyes, *Is There Life after High School?* (New York: Warner Books, 1977), 43. Roth on Ginsberg's aunt, in Howard Junker, "Will This Finally Be Philip Roth's Year?," *New York Magazine*, 13 January 1969, 20.

45. Details appear in a reproduction of his yearbook photo and caption on the back jacket of the first edition of *The Facts* (New York: Farrar, Straus and Giroux, 1988).

46. Source: Philip Roth, caption to photo of B. Swerdlow, Lowenstein (then age ninety) and Roth on display at the Newark Public Library, 18–19 March 2013.

47. Debra Rubin, "Seniors Recall Their School Years in Jewish Newark," *New Jersey Jewish News*, 27 September 2010, http://www.njjewishnews.com/article/1993/seniors-recall-their-school-years-in-jewish-newark#.UPnpN3eWN9Y.

48. For Roth on Lowenstein, see Roth, "Requiem for a Mentor," *Rutgers Magazine*, Spring 2013, http://urwebsrv.rutgers.edu/magazine/archive1013/features/spring-2013/requiem-for-a-mentor. Lowenstein graduated Rutgers with a BA in classical languages in 1928. He was born in Newark.

49. Roth to Del Tufo in Valerie Merians, "Philip Roth Begins Campaign for Next Nobel," *Star-Ledger*, 22 October 2009, http://www.mhpbooks.com/apparently-you-can-go-home-again/.

50. Roth, "How I Wrote *Portnoy's Complaint*," Web of Stories, n.d., http://www.webofstories.com/play/philip.roth/54;jsessionid=CFEE195DFE5E1BD218558967AAC5276B.

51. Leslie Fiedler, "The Image of Newark and the Indignities of Love: Notes on Philip Roth" (1959), in *Critical Essays on Philip Roth*, ed. Sanford Pinsker (Boston: G. K. Hall, 1982), 23.

52. Mark Shechner, "Philip Roth," in *Critical Essays on Philip Roth*, ed. Sanford Pinsker (Boston: G. K. Hall, 1982), 119. The essay first appeared in *Partisan Review* 41 (1974).

53. Fiedler, "The Image of Newark," 24. Fiedler would join Roth in Israel in 1963 for a conference and meeting with David Ben-Gurion.

54. Marking Roth's commitment to the library is the donation of his personal library to the institution and the establishment of a separate room on the second floor to house the nearly four thousand volumes, many with annotations and comments. A room at the back of his house in Connecticut contained nonfiction, while fiction started in the living room and took over a front study and a guest bedroom upstairs. Closets and the attic contained copies of his own books. See Charles McGrath, "A Scene Right Out of Philip Roth: His Books Come Home to Newark's Library," *New York Times*, 25 October 2016, https://www.nytimes.com/2016/10/26/books/philip-roth-newark-public-library.html.

55. Roth, in fact, spoke at Cummings's funeral in December 2005 and again at a memorial service for him held at the library on 18 January 2006.

56. Roth, "'A Great Newark Hero,'" *Star-Ledger*, 25 December 2005.

57. Roth in Carrie Stetler, "Return of the Native," *Star-Ledger*, April 1999.

58. The *New York Times* obituary notice for Herman Roth gives the date as 1964. "Herman Roth," *New York Times*, 27 October 1989, D19. The later date appears in the Roth Chronology that accompanies each of the Library of America volumes. See, for example, Roth, *Nemesis* (New York: Library of America, 2013), 449.

59. For more, see Helmreich, *The Enduring Community*, 35, 156. For Roth possibly seeing the 1949 film originally titled *I Married a Communist* and staring Robert Ryan and Laraine Day, but released in 1950 as *Woman on Pier 13*, see Ira Nadel, "*I Married a Communist*: The Book! The Movie! The Commie Threat!," *Philip Roth Studies* 16.2 (Fall 2020): 3–15.

60. See Ira Nadel, "Philip Roth and Film," in *Roth and Celebrity*, ed. Aimee Pozorski (Lanham, MD: Lexington Books, 2012), 47–65.

61. Robert Zecker, *Metropolis: American City in Popular Culture* (New York: Praeger, 2007), 212.

62. Joel Szasz's suggestive illustrations enhance the article.

63. On Roth and swimming, see Ira Nadel, "Aquatic Roth," *Philip Roth Studies* 14.1 (2018): 36–54.

64. From Di Ionno, "A Tour of Philip Roth's Newark."

65. Roth to Atlas, March 1980, Berg Collection, NYPL.

66. Roth in "*I Married a Communist* Interview," Houghton Mifflin, n.d., http://www.houghtonmifflinbooks.com/authors/roth/conversation.shtml.

67. Roth to Theodore Solotaroff, 5 October 1990, Ms. Collection, NYPL.

68. Walter Benjamin, "Theses on the Philosophy of History," in *Illuminations*, ed. Hannah Arendt (New York: Schocken, 1969), 257–58.

Chapter 2

1. The passage, from Mann's *A Sketch of My Life*, reads, "All actuality is deadly earnest; and it is morality itself that, one with life, forbids us to be true to the guileless unrealism of our youth." Two other passages follow, one by Simone Weil from *Gravity and Grace* and then lines from Wallace Stevens's "Esthétique du Mal," which begin, "It may be that one life is a punishment / For another."

2. Roth in Jeffrey A. Trachtenberg, "Roth on Roth," *Wall Street Journal*, 30 October 2009, http://online.wsj.com/article/SB10001424052748704500604574485623270549670.html.

3. Robert Wiener, "Remembering Newark Royalty," *Newark Jewish News*, 30 May 2018, https://njjewishnews.timesofisrael.com/remembering-newark-royalty/.

4. The big-name strippers of the 1930s and 1940s who played the Empire included Margie Hart, Lili St. Cyr in her bath routine, Rosita Royce with her trained doves covering her partial nudity, and the fiery red-headed sensation of the day, Georgia Sothern, aka "The Human Dynamo" because of her rapidly moving hips.

5. Rutgers Newark Course Catalogue, 1950. Special thanks to Carla Capizzi, assistant director, Office of Communications, Rutgers Newark, for her assistance.

6. Office of the University Registrar, Rutgers Newark, first term, 1950–51 as of 1 November 1950. Thanks to the Office of Institutional Research for supplying the data.

7. Roth in Roberta Plutzik, "Philip Roth, in the First Person," *The Record* (Bergen County, NJ), 14 April 1991, E 4. Roth had received the National Arts Club Medal of Honor for Literature the previous month as "the funniest serious writer in the world" (E1). *Patrimony* had recently been published.

8. Philip Roth, "Jack Wheatcroft," in *A Slant of Light: Reflections on Jack Wheatcroft*, ed. Peter Balakian and Bruce Smith (Lanham, MD: Rowman and Littlefield, 2018), 1–2.

9. Roth in *Bucknell University Award of Merit: Mildred Martin* (Lewisburg, PA: Appletree Alley Press, 1982), n.p.

10. In a manuscript letter of 8 January 1975 to Roth, Charlotte Maurer, wife of the young American literature instructor at Bucknell Robert Maurer, writes, "I'll never

forget the story you told us, just before you graduated, about how she [Mildred Martin] had you over for lunch (or was it tea?) and tried to get you to seduce her. That was very instructive to me! A horrible object lesson in how not to behave with younger men." Charlotte Maurer to Roth, 8 January 1975, box 23, folder 1, Roth Papers, LC.

11. For further details on her sexual interest in Roth and the possibility of the reverse, see Laura Cumming, "Do We Really Need to Know?," *Literary Review,* November 1988, https://literaryreview.co.uk/do-we-really-need-to-know.

12. Interview, Eloise Mallinson ('29), Women's Resource Center, February 1996. See Bucknell online: http://www.departments.bucknell.edu/WRC/history/1951to1955/1951-1955.htm. Mallinson returned to Bucknell as a graduate student in 1950.

13. Jesse Bier, "The Love of Truth," *Bucknell World,* 6 July 1995, n.p.; John Wheatcroft, "The Life of the Mind," *Bucknell World,* 6 July 1995, n.p.

14. Roth never forgot Bucknell and in 1993 established the Philip Roth Residency in Creative Writing for young poets or novelists, allowing a four-month residency in the so-called Poet's Cottage and a $5,000 stipend. Much later, Bucknell was his first choice for depositing his personal library, which eventually went to the Newark Public Library.

15. Special thanks to Crystal Matjasic, assistant curator, Special Collections/University Archives, Library and Information Technology, Bucknell University, for supplying much of this information.

16. Charles Simic in Molly McQuade, "Famous Writers' School," *Chicago Tribune,* 4 June 1995, https://www.chicagotribune.com/news/ct-xpm-1995-06-04-9506040297-story.html.

17. Harriet Monroe in Richard Christiansen, *A Theater of Our Own: A History and a Memoir of 1001 Nights in Chicago* (Evanston, IL: Northwestern University Press, 2004), 63; Hecht in Christiansen, *A Theater of Our Own,* 68–69.

18. Nelson Algren, *Chicago: City on the Make* (Sausalito, CA: Contact Editions, 1961), 100.

19. *University of Chicago Official Publications* 60 (1955–56). This was the university calendar. Nine courses would have composed the MA (actually called the A.M. program by the department), supplemented by independent work whether by a thesis or by completing term papers for three different instructors, the more popular method. A final comprehensive exam marked the conclusion of the program, an exam divided into criticism and the analysis of ideas. For this, the text was usually "a rhetorical or intellectual work or a history." Both texts were announced at least one quarter in advance. Passing grade for the exam was B–.

20. Patrick Hayes, *Philip Roth, Fiction and Power* (Oxford: Oxford University Press, 2014), 64.

21. For Roth's encounter with the Jamesian universe concerned with motives and "moral realism" (the phrase is Lionel Trilling's), see Theodore Solotaroff, "Philip Roth: A Personal View," in *The Red Hot Vacuum* (New York: Atheneum, 1970), 314–15.

22. Roth to Tom Appelo of Amazon.com. interview, box 14, folder 3, p. 4, Roth Papers, LC.

23. According to Stern, Steiner met only one possible "genius," and that was at a poker game: the young cartoonist Hugh Hefner, then planning a magazine called *Stag*, later called *Playboy*. Stern, "Scattered Memoires of the U. of Chicago English Department. 1955 et seq.," in *Still on Call* (Ann Arbor: University of Michigan Press, 2010), 225. Stern spent forty-six years in the English Department. For another view of the department from the student point of view, see Ted Solotaroff, "The Ivory Basement," in *First Loves: A Memoir* (New York: Seven Stories Press, 2003), 161–256. Roth met Starbuck when he was poetry editor of the *Chicago Review*, which published one of Roth's early stories, his first publication outside the Bucknell literary magazine.

24. Stern, "Scattered Memoires," 225.

25. Roth, "The Day It Snowed," *Chicago Review* 8 (1954): 34–44.

26. Among the works were "Philosophy, or Something Like That," *Et Cetera*, May 1952, 5+; "The Box of Truths," *Et Cetera*, October 1952, 10–12; "The Fence," *Et Cetera*, May 1953, 18–23; "Armando and the Fraud," *Et Cetera*, October 1953, 21+; and "The Final Delivery of Mr. Thorn," *Et Cetera*, May 1954, 20–28.

27. Others at the University of Chicago during this period were George Steiner ('48), Carl Sagan ('54), and Philip Glass ('56). There is some dispute whether Sontag, at twenty or so, was the unacknowledged coauthor of Philip Reiff's *Freud: The Mind of a Moralist* (1959). See most recently Benjamin Moser, *Sontag, Her Life and Work* (New York: Ecco, 2019) 120–31.

28. Long considered one of the finest literary editors in the country, Silvers died on 20 March 2017 after fifty-four years editing the *New York Review of Books*.

29. Solotaroff, "Philip Roth," 307. On the role of Jewish intellectuals and critics like Philip Rahv and Lionel Trilling in the revival of James and his importance in American literary study for students like Solotaroff and Roth, see David Gooblar, *The Major Phases of Philip Roth* (New York: Continuum, 2011), 38–41.

30. Roth, "Just a Lively Boy," in *An Unsentimental Education: Writers and Chicago*, ed. Molly McQuade (Chicago: University of Chicago Press, 1995), 127. Roth explains that he and a few others sought to join their humble origins and "blunt neighborhood style" with "high-minded pursuits" (128). Chicago permitted and encouraged raucousness with seriousness.

31. Solotaroff, "Philip Roth," 307.

32. Solotaroff, "The Ivory Basement," 192. For Solotaroff on such department members as Zabel, see 168–72.

33. Solotaroff, "The Ivory Basement," 191.

34. Solotaroff, "The Ivory Basement," 193.

35. Solotaroff, "The Ivory Basement," 199.

36. Sally was most likely Maggie Martinson Williams. She was older than Roth and had a difficult divorce and a more difficult custody battle over her two children. But then, Solotaroff says, their affair blew up and Roth moved on to the daughter of a Chicago businessman, likely Susan Glassman (Solotaroff, "The Ivory Basement," 199–200). Roth and Maggie would later reconnect.

37. Solotaroff, "The Ivory Basement," 200.

38. In 1958, it was Bernard Malamud, who met Bellow at Stern's Hyde Park apartment. Other visitors included Norman Mailer, Lillian Hellman, Flannery O'Connor, John Berryman, Kingsley Amis, and J. P. Donleavy.

39. Solotaroff, "The Ivory Basement," 199.

40. Solotaroff reported that "Defender of the Faith" came from an event in Basic Training experienced by Art Geffen ("The Ivory Basement," 207).

41. Solotaroff, "The Ivory Basement," 209.

42. Solotaroff, "The Ivory Basement," 216.

43. See *Chicago Review* 11.1 (Spring 1957). His third piece appeared in the following issue, Summer 1957. Entitled "Mrs. Lindbergh, Mr. Ciardi and the Teeth and Claws of the Civilized World," it satirizes the strong response to the poetry editor John Ciardi's negative review of Anne Morrow Lindbergh's *The Unicorn and Other Poems*. Ciardi had the temerity to pan the book, resulting in an outpouring of letters contradicting his reading. Roth satirizes those "critics" who accuse Ciardi of being "unchivalrous." See *Chicago Review* 11.2 (Summer 1957): 72–76.

44. Benjamin Balint, "Imaginative Assault," *Tablet*, 28 May 2010, https://www.tabletmag.com/jewish-arts-and-culture/books/34640/imaginative-assault.

45. Roth in Esther B. Fein, "Philip Roth Sees Double. And Maybe Triple Too," *New York Times*, 9 March 1993, C13.

46. George Plimpton in *The Paris Review . . . Early Chapters* (Checkerboard Films, 2001), DVD, which contains interviews with many of the key originators of the magazine.

47. Nelson Aldrich Jr., ed., *George Being George: A Biography of George Plimpton* (New York: Random House, 2009), 127.

48. William Styron, *Selected Letters of William Styron*, ed. Rose Styron with R. Blakeslee Gilpin (New York: Random House, 2012), 143. For an account of the origin of the *Paris Review*, see William Styron, "The Paris Review," in *This Quiet Dust and Other Writings* (New York: Random House, 1982), 295–98.This account first appeared in *Harper's Bazaar*, August 1953. Also useful are James L. W. West III, *William Styron: A Life* (New York: Random House, 1998), 215–17, and Alexandra Styron, *Reading My Father* (New York: Scribner, 2011), 104–6. Additionally, see section III of Aldrich, *George Being George*, 83–129. E. M. Forster agreed to be interviewed because Plimpton had known him while at Kings College, Cambridge.

49. "History," *Paris Review,* http://www.theparisreview.org/about/. To date, there is no comprehensive history of the *Paris Review*. For a political account of the magazine suggesting CIA ties, see Richard Cummings, "The Fiction of the State: The Paris Review and the Invisible World of American Letters," *Lobster* 50 (Winter 2005/06), https://www.lobster-magazine.co.uk/issue50.php.

50. For an account of her experiences, see Jeff Seroy, "Maxine Groffsky, The Art of Editing, 3," *Paris Review,* no. 222 (Fall 2017), https://www.theparisreview.org/interviews/7038/maxine-groffsky-the-art-of-editing-no-3-maxine-groffsky. Edited in Paris and New York, the magazine during her tenure was printed in Amsterdam, requiring Groffsky to regularly travel by train to oversee proofreading.

51. For a profile of Silvers, see Emily Stokes, "Lunch with the FT: Robert B. Silvers," *Financial Times,* 25 January 2013, http://www.ft.com/intl/cms/s/2/091ba1b6-6576-11e2-a3db-00144feab49a.html#axzz2J2zQPk5z.

52. Roth, "Philip Roth's Hadada Award Acceptance Speech," *Paris Review*, 2010, https://www.youtube.com/watch?v=cr_MirhjO10.

53. Roth to Robert Silvers, 25 July 1958, *Paris Review* file, box 9, MA 5040, J. P. Morgan Library, New York City.

54. Roth to Robert Silvers, 25 July 1958.

55. Martinson letters, box 22, folder 10, Roth Papers, LC.

56. Roth, "Juice or Gravy? How I Met My Fate in a Cafeteria," *New York Times Book Review,* 18 September 1994.

57. Richard Stern, *A Sistermony* (New York: Dutton, 1995), 101.

58. Solotaroff, "Philip Roth," 314.

Chapter 3

1. Roth to Solotaroff, 8 December 1984, Solotaroff Archive, Manuscript Division, NYPL.

2. Pierpont, *Roth Unbound,* 37. On Bellow and Glassman, see FAC 95–96 and James Atlas, *Bellow: A Biography* (New York: Random House, 2000), 299. For a recent account of Bellow and Susan Glassman, see Zachary Leader, *The Life of Saul Bellow: To Fame and Fortune 1915–1964* (New York: Knopf, 2015), 589–615 and *passim.* Claudia Roth Pierpont in her *Roth Unbound* whimsically asked Roth that if *he* had married Glassman rather than Bellow, how might they have turned out? Nonplussed, Roth admitted that he could never marry her because he would always be in her shadow (37–38).

3. Daniel Maurer, "Philip Roth's Early, Unhappy Days in the East Village," *Bedford + Bowery,* 24 May 2018, https://bedfordandbowery.com/2018/05/philip-roths-early-unhappy.

4. Roth to Solotaroff, 11 March 1959, Solotaroff Papers, Manuscript Division, NYPL.

5. Roth to Bailey, 4 December 2012, Taylor/Roth Archive, Princeton.

6. The Library of America chronology lists 21 February 1926 (see WR? 407), but Pierpont in *Roth Unbound,* 326 says 22 February 1927. U.S. Census records from 1930 indicate that Bess (Beatrice) Roth was twenty-three when she married, three years earlier, or 1927.

7. Physically, the petite Maggie contrasted with the tall Roth. In an April 1960 photograph standing alongside Roth at the Newark Public Library, she only comes up to his shoulder. With a round face and blond hair, she projects a midwestern aura. Modestly dressed in a suit with pearls, she looks directly at the camera with a half-smile and an air of confidence. Roth, looking large and uncomfortable in a tie and jacket, stares out of the frame.

8. Roth to Solotaroff, 23 October 1959, Solotaroff Papers, Manuscript Division, NYPL.

9. Roth went to Candida Donadio because she was Richard Stern's agent, as well as Tom Rogers's, another Chicago friend. At the time, Donadio was becoming one of the few and soon to be powerful female literary agents in New York. Her clients would

include Mario Puzo, William Gaddis, Joseph Heller, Bruce Jay Friedman, and Thomas Pynchon. According to one writer whom she did not take on, she was a "dark, melancholic, haunted and overweight" Italian figure. See Alice Denham, *Sleeping with Bad Boys* (New York: Cardozo, 2006), 97–98.

10. Roth to Starbuck, 28 June 1958, Houghton Mifflin Archive, Houghton Library, Harvard University.

11. Roth to Starbuck, 25 July 1958, Houghton Mifflin Archive, Houghton Library, Harvard University.

12. The title, while referring to the farewell anthem of Ohio State University's graduating seniors, had another possible source, although there is no direct evidence that Roth knew the song from the Yiddish theater of New York in 1926. The song, in Yiddish "Ikh for Aheym" or "I'm Going Home," has, as the first line of the concluding stanza, "Zay gezunt, Kolumbes," or "Goodbye, Columbus."

13. Brooks to Thompson, 25 July 1958, Houghton Mifflin Archive, Houghton Library, Harvard University.

14. Brooks to Thompson, 25 July 1958.

15. Starbuck to Roth, 30 July 1958, Houghton Mifflin Archive, Houghton Library, Harvard University.

16. Roth, "Just a Lively Boy," 127.

17. Roth to George Starbuck, 9 August 1958, Houghton Mifflin Archive, Houghton Library, Harvard University.

18. Roth in Joyce Carol Oates, "A Conversation with Philip Roth," in *Conversations with Philip Roth*, ed. George J. Searles (Jackson: University Press of Mississippi, 1992), 92–93. Oates's work appeared in 1974 in the *Ontario Review*. Cf. Hermione Lee's comments about reading a version of *The Counterlife* in 1985 (CWPR 261). James Atlas read a version of *The Ghost Writer*, Ross Miller a version of *The Facts* and made suggestions as to its ending. Woolf's "Reviewing" appears in *The Captain's Death Bed* (London: Hogarth Press, 1940).

19. Roth to Solotaroff, 31 July 1958, Solotaroff Archive, Manuscript Division, NYPL.

20. Roth to Solotaroff, 31 July 1958.

21. For Roth's emancipation quote, see Roth, "Just a Lively Boy," 123. Also see Jesse Tisch, "Not a Nice Boy," *Jewish Review of Books*, Summer 2020, https://jewishreviewofbooks. com/articles/8035/not-a-nice-boy/?utm_source=rss&utm_medium=rss&utm_ campaign=rss.

22. Roth to Starbuck, 23 May 1958, Houghton Mifflin Archive, Houghton Library, Harvard University.

23. See Usha Maya Wilbers, "Enterprise in the Service of Art: A Critical History of the *Paris Review* 1953–1973," Radbound University, 2006, 39. This dissertation charts the up-and-down career of the literary journal. A detailed and useful account of the early life of the *Paris Review*, it draws from interviews and archives. One detail: for the magazine to obtain legal status in Paris, all of the editors had to be residents of the city. Later, as Roth became more prominent, the journal listed him on the masthead as an advisory editor, although there is no evidence that he did

any editorial work. Such notice was considered a reward for the support of the magazine (85–86).

24. Documentation for these exchanges can be found in Nadel, "Roth @ 25, Publishing Goodbye, Columbus," *Roth after Eighty, Philip Roth and the American Literary Imagination*, ed. David Gooblar and Aimee Pozorski (Lanham, MD: Lexington Books, 2016) 19–27.

25. Roth to Starbuck, 25 February 1959, Houghton Mifflin Archive, Houghton Library, Harvard University.

26. Roth to Dorothy de Santillana, 24 March 1959, Houghton Mifflin Archive, Houghton Library, Harvard University. The return address reads 128 E. 10th Street, New York.

27. On Roth's relationship with *Commentary*, see Norman Podhoretz, "The Adventures of Philip Roth," *Commentary*, October 1998,https://www.commentarymagazine. com/articles/the-adventures-of-philip-roth/. Podhoretz claims that he discovered Roth as a writer in 1957 when he located and published "You Can't Tell a Man by the Song He Sings."

28. Rackman (1910–2008) had a law degree from Columbia (1933) and a doctorate in public law (1952). In 1934, he was ordained as a rabbi. He practiced law for nine years. During World War II, he was a chaplain in the air force assigned as a military aide to the European Theater Command as special advisor on Jewish affairs. His encounters with Holocaust victims caused him to reconsider his legal career and he returned to become a full-time rabbi. He also taught political science at Yeshiva University. Soon representing modern Orthodoxy, Rackman became the rabbi of the Fifth Avenue Synagogue in 1967, and then provost of Yeshiva University and, in 1977, the first American president of Bar Ilan University in Israel. One of his most controversial achievements was his efforts to aid the so-called chained women, women who could not get a religious release from their husbands to remarry. He established a special rabbinic court to annul such marriages, which the Orthodox community condemned.

29. Roth to Rabbi Rackman, 30 April 1959, box 30, folder 8, Roth Papers, LC.

30. Roth to Rackman, 30 April 1959.

31. Houghton Mifflin (possibly Paul Brooks) to Roth, 25 March 1959, Houghton Mifflin Archive, Houghton Library, Harvard University.

32. Starbuck to Roth, 26 March 1959, Houghton Mifflin Archive, Houghton Library, Harvard University.

33. Roth to Starbuck, 29 March 1959, Houghton Mifflin Archive, Houghton Library, Harvard University.

34. Roth to Connie(?), 4 June 1959, Houghton Mifflin Archive, Houghton Library, Harvard University.

35. Alfred Kazin, "Tough-Minded Roth," in *Contemporaries* (Boston: Little, Brown, 1962), 259. The review originally appeared in *The Reporter*, 28 May 1959, 42–43. Kazin's response no doubt incorporates his own encounter with Jewish soldiers when he was prevented from entering a displaced persons camp in Austria not far from Salzburg just after the war. Denied entry by a Jewish guard and told "Sightseers we don't need," Kazin promptly disobeyed and shortly after climbed a fence "and climbed

right into Eastern Europe." Kazin, *A Lifetime Burning in Every Moment, from the Journals of Alfred Kazin*, ed. Alfred Kazin (New York: Harper Collins, 1996), 88.

36. Kazin, "Tough-Minded Roth," 260.

37. Kazin, "Tough-Minded Roth," 262.

38. Saul Bellow, "The Swamp of Prosperity," in *Commentary* 28 (July 1959): 77, qtd. in *New York Times*, 9 August 1959.

39. The most extensive discussion of the incident is Julian Levinson, "Roth in the Archives: 'Eli, the Fanatic' and the Nitra Yeshiva Controversy of 1948," *American Jewish History* 101.1 (January 2017): 59–80. More specifically, Levinson suggests Roth read Herrymon Maurer's *Commentary* article "The Yeshiva Comes to Westchester," *Commentary* 8.1 (January 1949): 319–27. However, Roth likely saw through the pious philo-Semitism Maurer celebrated (see Levinson, "Roth in the Archives," 77).

40. Philip Roth, "Goodbye Newark: Roth Remembers His Beginnings," *New York Times*, 1 October 1989, https://www.nytimes.com/1989/10/01/books/goodbye-newark-roth-remembers-his-beginnings.html. The essay is his preface for the thirtieth anniversary edition of *Goodbye, Columbus*.

41. Roth and Richler would keep in touch with each other, writing sporadically in the 1960s and reconnecting in London in 1983 and in 1984. See their correspondence, box 30, folder 10, Roth Papers, LC.

42. See Steven J. Zipperstein, "Philip Roth's Forgotten Tape: The Beginnings of the Great American Writer," *The Forward*, 28 May 2018, https://forward.com/culture/books/401928/philip-roths-forgotten-tape-the-beginnings-of-the-great-american-writer/. Also helpful is Jesse Tisch, "The Philip Roth Archive," Tablet, 21 May 2020, https://www.tabletmag.com/sections/arts-letters/articles/philip-roth-letters.

43. Jason Rosenblatt in Jacques Berlinerblau, "Do We Know Philip Roth?," *Chronicle of Higher Education*, 7 April 2014, http://www.chronicle.com/article/Do-We-Know-Philip-Roth-/145671.

44. See Menachem Butler, "Philip Roth's 1962 Visit to Yeshiva," *The Commentator*, Yeshiva University, 6 December 2004.

45. Wilbers, "Enterprise in the Service of Art," 175.

46. Somewhat sensationally, Rivers said he thought the best thing Roth ever did was asking Groffsky to stand nude at the top of a staircase with her legs spread so he could crawl up slowly until he reached her. Rivers cited in Barbara Goldsmith, "When Park Ave. Met Pop Art," *Vanity Fair*, January 2003. Also see Larry Rivers and Carol Brightman, "The Cedar Bar," *New York Magazine*, 29 October 1979, for another account of Groffsky and Roth. For a profile of Maxine Groffsky, see Jeff Seroy, "Maxine Groffsky: The Art of Editing," *Paris Review* 222 (Fall 2017), https://www.theparisreview.org/interviews/7038/the-art-of-editing-no-3-maxine-groffsky.

47. See Edmund White, *City Boy: My Life in New York during the 1960s and 70s* (New York: Bloomsbury, 2009), 175–76, for an account of Groffsky and dance. Groffsky was White's agent. Her involvement with ballet led to her marrying the president of the ballet board, Winthrop Knowlton, in January 1983. In conversation (25 February 2013), Groffsky clearly believed she was the source for Brenda Patimkin in *Goodbye, Columbus*—although Roth notoriously blended many people into his

characters—and said to me in a tone of absolute assurance, "You know who I am, of course," while also repeating, "I don't want to talk about Philip." But when I mentioned that a photo of her and Roth from 1955 with Bob and Holly Hayman would be exhibited at the Roth @80 conference in Newark in March 2013, she asked for a copy. Also see Maxine Groffsky in Aldrich, *George Being George*, 156.

48. From the lawyers Goldberg and Hatterer, 13 April 1959, box 12, folder 13, Roth Papers, LC; Roth, "Goodbye, Columbus," *Paris Review* 20 (Autumn–Winter 1958–59): 71–179. The publication of the Houghton Mifflin volume would be 7 May 1959. Thanks to Jacques Berlinerblau for locating this material.

49. Corman became known for titles like *Swamp Women* (1956), *Naked Paradise* (1957), *Hot Car Girl* (1958), *The Wasp Woman* (1959), and *The Last Woman on Earth* (1960). For an account of Roth and film, see Ira Nadel, "Philip Roth and Film," in *Roth and Celebrity*, ed. Aimee Pozorski (Lanham, MD: Lexington Books, 2012), 47–65.

50. Roth to Solotaroff, 10 June 1959, Manuscript Division, NYPL.

51. Roth to Solotaroff, 25 October 1959, Manuscript Division, NYPL.

52. Pierpont, *Roth Unbound*, 32.

53. Roth, "Distracted and Unblessed," box 85, folder 3, p. 4, Roth Papers, LC.

54. Starbuck to Roth, 4 December 1959, Houghton Mifflin Archive, Houghton Library, Harvard University.

55. Starbuck to Roth, 4 December 1959.

56. West, *William Styron*, 312.

57. Wallace Stegner to Richard Scowcroft, 1 March 1960, in Page Stegner, ed., *Selected Letters of Wallace Stegner* (Washington, DC: Shoemaker and Hoard, 2007), 306.

58. Stegner, *Selected Letters*, 123.

59. Stegner to Roth, 11 September 1966, box 32, folder 7, Roth Papers, LC.

60. Roth, letter, 5 January 2014, Taylor/Roth Archive, Firestone Library, Princeton University.

61. Maggie Roth to Paul Brooks, 18 April 1960, Houghton Mifflin Archive, Houghton Library, Harvard University.

62. Roth to Dorothy de Santillana, 3 May 1960, Houghton Mifflin Archive, Houghton Library, Harvard University.

63. Roth to Starbuck, 14 May 1969, Houghton Mifflin Archive, Houghton Library, Harvard University.

64. Starbuck to Roth, 30 June 1960, Houghton Mifflin Archive, Houghton Library, Harvard University.

65. Paul Brooks to Roth, (?), July 1950, and Thompson to Donadio, 3 August 1960, Houghton Mifflin Archive, Houghton Library, Harvard University.

66. Paul Brooks to Evan Thomas, 9 November 1960, Houghton Mifflin Archive, Houghton Library, Harvard University.

67. William Styron, "Bennett Cerf," in *This Quiet Dust and Other Writings* (New York: Random House, 1982), 271.

68. Roth to Starbuck, 9 November 1960, Houghton Mifflin Archive, Houghton Library, Harvard University.

69. Roth to Paul Brooks, 21 September 1960, Houghton Mifflin Archive, Houghton Library, Harvard University.

70. "1960s," in *The Workshop: Seven Decades of the Iowa Writer's Workshop*, ed. Tom Grimes (New York: Hyperion, 1999), 135–6. For detailed description of the seminar process, see 7–10. Also revealing is David O. Dowling, *A Delicate Aggression: Savagery and Survival in the Iowa Writers' Workshop* (New Haven, CT: Yale University Press, 2019), which explores the impact of the writers' workshop on literary culture, locally and nationally, and how talent and ambition clashed as much as intersected.

71. Department of English, *General Catalog,* University of Iowa, 1960–61, 1961–62. Thanks to Denise Anderson, Special Collections, University of Iowa Libraries, for this information.

72. Dowling's *A Delicate Aggression* is especially clear on this aspect of the instruction.

73. Dowling, *A Delicate Aggression,* 1.

74. See Mark McGurl, *The Program Era: Postwar Fiction and the Rise of Creative Writing* (Cambridge, MA: Harvard University Press, 2010), 135.

75. Grimes, *The Workshop,* 741.

76. Eugene Garber, "Vance Bourjaily," in *A Community of Writers,* ed. Robert Dana (Iowa City: University of Iowa Press, 1999), 210. Flaubert also remarked, "You can depict wine, love, and women on the condition that you are not a drunkard, a lover or a husband." Quoted by James B. Hall, "Paul Engle," in Dana, *A Community,* 4.

77. On classroom practice at Iowa, see Blake Bailey, *A Tragic Honesty: The Life and Work of Richard Yates* (New York: Picador, 2003), 328–32.

78. Robert Dana, "Preface," in Dana, *A Community of Writers,* ix. For a strong sense of what a workshop might be like, see Richard Stern, "Ray B. West, Jr.," in Dana, *A Community of Writers,* 198–99.

79. Clarke Blaise to the author, International Short Story Conference, Lisbon, Portugal, 27 June 2018. On the matter of the early morning encounter with Roth, Blaise to the author, Portland, Oregon, 13 September 2018.

80. Dowling, *A Delicate Aggression,* 202.

81. Vonnegut in Dowling, *A Delicate Aggression,* 180.

82. Dowling, *A Delicate Aggression,* 229.

83. Roth would use the restaurant as the locale where Portnoy and the Monkey have some brandies just before they pick up the prostitute Lina for the second time in *Portnoy's Complaint* (PC 139). A few pages later, in a dream set in the Middle Ages, he is called "Mr. Porte Noir" (PC 149).

84. Cerf to Roth, 19 October 1960, Random House Archive, Columbia University.

85. See Cheever's note to Houghton Mifflin in Blake Bailey, *John Cheever* (New York: Knopf, 2009), 283. On the same page, Bailey provides additional details about the *Esquire* symposium. For Cheever's journal comment on Roth, see *Journals of John Cheever* (New York: Knopf, 1990), 190.

86. Nixon quoted in Thomas Mallon, "Wag the Dog," *New Yorker,* 4 February 2013, 72.

87. According to Styron, James Jones kept a copy of Mailer's *Advertisements for Myself* on a sideboard near his bar in his Paris apartment and asked guests who were cited

by Mailer to write scurrilous remarks in response. West, *William Styron*, 307–8. Both Jones and Styron, as well as many others, were admonished in the book.

88. Roth to Loomis, 2 December 1960, Random House Archive, Columbia University.

89. David Williams in Robert A. Cohen, "Papa Portnoy: Philip Roth as Stepfather," *St. Louis Jewish Light*, 3 September 1975, 7, 38. David was twenty-seven at the time of the interview and living in a suburb of St. Louis. He reveals that his mother was only eighteen and his father, Daniel Dwight Williams (a commercial artist and trombone player), only twenty when he was born. His sister Holly was born two years later, in September 1950. The parents divorced in 1955. His father and mother each remarried in 1959. David goes on to explain that his first real period with Roth began in 1961, when he was thirteen and they all spent a summer in East Amagansett, Long Island. He admitted he was a wild kid and if it wasn't for Roth and his positive influence, "I might be in jail today: I was that kind of kid.'" Roth helped prepare David for Morgan Park Academy, a Chicago private school from which he graduated at nineteen and began one year at Eastern Michigan University in Ypsilanti. Tutoring David in English for Roth meant putting aside *Letting Go*. He gave him a reading list and afterward they would sit at the kitchen table and review books; Roth taught him such concepts as allegory, metaphor, and foreshadowing. The reading included such popular fiction as *Fail-Safe* by Eugene Burdick and Harvey Wheeler and *Exodus* by Leon Uris. They also discussed the Nuremberg War Crimes Trials (Cohen, "Papa Portnoy," 7). David pointed out that there was no attempt to generate a father-son relationship. Roth did develop such a role with his sister, Holly, however, going on father-daughter trips: "They were extremely close." Holly at one point was quite interested in Judaism. Roth did educate David in sex, explaining that there was nothing wrong with masturbation; David recalled that Roth cited a Harvard study showing that 96 percent of everyone masturbates and another 2 percent lie. David also recalled discussing the title of *Letting Go* at the breakfast table and remembered reading "Defender of the Faith." On the breakdown of the marriage between Maggie and Roth, he observed that his mother, while sexy and intelligent, was also "very destructive. She tried to destroy everyone in her path." Yet Roth would defend her to David when he criticized her (Cohen, "Papa Portnoy," 7, 38). Later, she would complain that Lucy Nelson in *When She Was Good* was patterned after her own life, the young Lucy living with her alcoholic father until eighteen, David noting that his mother's father, "Red" Martinson, had a drinking problem and his mother had to call the police several times. He believed that Maureen and Lydia Ketterer in *My Life as a Man* were based on his mother.

90. Klopfer to Roth, 28 April 1961, Random House Archive, Columbia University.

91. Roth to Cerf, 19 June 1961, and Cerf to Roth, 21 June 1961, Random House Archive, Columbia.

92. Roth to Cerf, 21 September 1961, Random House Archive, Columbia University.

93. Roth to Fox, 9 October 1961, Random House Archive, Columbia University.

94. Roth to Fox, 29 November 1961, Random House Archive, Columbia University.

95. Roth to Cerf, 29 December 1961, Random House Archive, Columbia University.

96. "Sleeping with Bad Boys: A 1956 Playboy Model's Escapades," *Publishers Weekly*, 30 October 2006, https://www.publishersweekly.com/978-1-58042-206-2.

97. Denham, *Sleeping with Bad Boys,* 133, 107.

98. Denham, *Sleeping with Bad Boys*, 203.

99. Denham, *Sleeping with Bad Boys*, 204.

100. Denham, *Sleeping with Bad Boys*, 205, 206.

101. Denham, *Sleeping with Bad Boys*, 209, 208.

102. Denham, *Sleeping with Bad Boys*, 210.

103. The first was at Columbia in 1958.

104. Roth to Solotaroff, 19 November 1960, Solotaroff Archive, Manuscript Division, NYPL.

105. Roth to Solotaroff, 19 November 1960.

106. Roth to Solotaroff, 19 November 1960.

107. Roth, "Iowa: A Very Far Country Indeed," *Esquire*, December 1962, 242.

108. Roth, "Iowa," 247.

109. Roth in Grimes, *The Workshop*, 4.

110. *Sabbath's Theater* clocks in at 451 pages, *Operation Shylock* at 398, *The Plot Against America* at 391, *The Great American Novel* at 382, *My Life as a Man* at 330. Perhaps his shortest novel is *The Humbling* at 140. *The Breast*, while published separately, is a novella at 87 pages. All references are to first editions.

111. Roth to Cerf, 19 April 1962, Random House Archive, Columbia University.

112. Roth to Fox, 20 April 1962, Random House Archive, Columbia University.

113. Roth to Fox, 4 May 1962, Random House Archive, Columbia University.

114. Roth to Fox, 30 April [1962], Random House Archive, Columbia University.

Chapter 4

1. Irving Feldman, "*Letting Go* by Philip Roth," review, *Commentary,* September 1962, 33. https://www.commentarymagazine.com/articles/letting-go-by-philip-roth/.

2. Roth in Archibald Elias, "Roth: Passionate Interest in Arts Lacking," *Daily Princetonian,* 13 December 1962, 3.

3. Roth in Frank Burgess, "Students, Critics, Not Readers," *Daily Princetonian,* 13 March 1963, 3.

4. Charles Creesy, "Reactions to Roth Varied, Reserved," *Daily Princetonian,* 14 March 1963, 1.

5. John P. Kretzmann, "Author Downing Succeeds Leach as 150s Captain," *Daily Princetonian,* 4 December 1963, 8. Downing was a professor of English at Baltimore Community College for more than thirty years and a consultant in the area of faculty development and student success.

6. Atlas, *Bellow*, 179, 403; CWPR 22.

7. Martha L. Lamar, "Faculty Portraits: Dr. Melvin Tumin," *Princeton Alumni Weekly* 68 (21 May 1968): 14–15, 21.

8. According to Roth, Tumin inquired about two students who had not attended his class all semester, asking, "Does anyone know these people? Do they exist or are they spooks?" Unknown to Tumin, both students were African American. Since "spooks" can be a racial slur for Black people (in addition to meaning "ghosts" or "spies"), Tumin was subjected by the university to an inquiry into possible hate speech, described by Roth as a "witch hunt." Tumin eventually emerged blameless. Philip Roth, "An Open Letter to Wikipedia," *New Yorker*, 6 September 2012, https://www. newyorker.com/books/page-turner/an-open-letter-to-wikipedia; Roth in Wolfgang Saxon, "Melvin M. Tumin, 75, Specialist in Race Relations," *New York Times*, 5 March 1994, section 1, p. 12.

9. The other is the writer Janet Hobhouse, who died in 1991. Tumin died in 1994, the year before *Sabbath's Theater* appeared.

10. Roth, "Philip Roth Talks to Teens," *Seventeen*, April 1963, 170, 208.

11. David Williams in Robert A. Cohen, "Papa Portnoy: Philip Roth as Stepfather," *St. Louis Jewish Light*, 3 September 1975, 38.

12. R. S. (Bob) Baker to Roth, 28 July 1963, box 3, folder 2, Roth Papers, LC.

13. Roth to Bennett Cerf, (?), May 1963, Random House Archive, Columbia University.

14. Roth to Solotaroff, 31 July 1963, Solotaroff Archive, Manuscript Division, NYPL.

15. Philip Roth, *Photos from a Lifetime*, 19 March–31 August 2013, James Lewis, curator, Rosemary Steinbaum, guest curator, Newark Public Library, 14. Roth used Ben-Gurion's comment on a Jewish tree and a Jewish bird in CL 52.

16. *American Jewish Congress Bi-Weekly* 30.12 (16 September 1963): 21. Hereafter "Congress Transcript."

17. "Congress Transcript," 21.

18. "Congress Transcript," 28.

19. "Congress Transcript," 35.

20. "Congress Transcript," 37.

21. "Congress Transcript," 39.

22. "Congress Transcript," 61.

23. "Congress Transcript," 61.

24. "Congress Transcript," 72. Shifting to the question of readership and the dangers of philo-Semitism, which might mask anti-Semitism, Roth reports that young, would-be Jewish (male) writers tell the same story. At the Iowa Writers' Workshop, 25 percent of his graduate students were Jewish and told the same story. The details differed but not the situation of a young Jewish adolescent and his tense family relations. Resolution usually occurred via sex with the *shiksa* next door. The father and mother remain the same in all the stories, the father unable to speak to his son, the mother hovering and protecting. The femme fatale, importantly, is never in the mold of the mother or sister but always the *shiksa*, an inescapable, central Jewish fantasy and one Roth will elaborate in *Portnoy's Complaint* ("Congress Transcript," 73).

25. "Congress Transcript," 75.

26. Roth to Solotaroff, 31 July 1963, Solotaroff Archive, Manuscript Division, NYPL.

27. Roth to Solotaroff, 31 July 1961.

28. Bellow, *Seize the Day* (1956), in Saul Bellow, *Bellow, Novels 1944–1953* (New York: Library of America, 2003), 79.

29. Roth to Fox, 3 August 1963, and Fox to Roth, 7 August 1963, Random House Archive, Columbia University.

30. For an incisive commentary on the subject, especially "The Psychoanalytic Special" and feminism, see Maren Scheurer, "A Psychopathology of Everyday Women: Psychoanalytic Aesthetics and Gender Politics in *Letting Go* and 'The Psychoanalytic Special,'" *Philip Roth Studies* 13.1 (2017): 13–28.

31. Bruce Webber, "L. Rust Hills, Fiction Editor at Esquire, Dies at 83," *New York Times*, 13 August 2008, http://www.nytimes.com/2008/08/14/books/14hills.html. When Hills left in 1964 to go to the *Saturday Evening Post*, Mailer's novel *An American Dream* was being serialized in *Esquire*, bringing outright sexuality into the magazine for the first time. The year before, Hills conceived an entire literary issue of the magazine, which included stories but also interviews with writers; a photo essay on writers' lives and a snarky profile by Gay Talese of the circle surrounding Plimpton's *Paris Review*; and, most controversially, an illustrated diagram of "The Structure of the American Literary Establishment," identifying writers, agents, publishers, reviewers, and events that Hills determined to be at and around the "red-hot center" of American literary life. The issue and especially the map angered many who felt they ought to have been included and many who were; nonetheless, it entertained just about everybody else.

32. LeRoi Jones, "Channel X, a Reply," *New York Review of Books*, 9 July 1964, https://www.nybooks.com/articles/1964/07/09/channel-x-1/.

33. Roth, "Channel X," *New York Review of Books*, 28 May 1964, https://www.nybooks.com/articles/1964/05/28/channel-x-two-plays-on-the-race-conflict/.

34. See Walter R. Dean Jr., "Channel X," *New York Review of Books*, 9 July 1964, https://www.nybooks.com/articles/1964/07/09/channel-x-2/. Roth's reply is in the same issue.

35. Roth, "The Play That Dare Not Speak Its Name," *New York Review of Books*, 25 February 1965, https://www.nybooks.com/articles/1965/02/25/the-play-that-dare-not-speak-its-name/, originally sparked the outcry. See letters published in the *New York Review of Books* of 8 April 1965: https://www.nybooks.com/articles/1965/04/08/tiny-alice-3/.

36. "Tiny Alice," *New York Review of Books*, 8 April 1965, https://www.nybooks.com/articles/1965/04/08/tiny-alice-3/.

37. Roth, "Letters," *New York Review of Books*, 8 April 1965, https://www.nybooks.com/articles/1965/04/08/tiny-alice-3/.

38. Roth, "The Nice Jewish Boy," 8, 87, Perzigian Collection of Philip Roth, Special Collections Research Center, Regenstein Library, University of Chicago. On canceling the staged reading, see Roth in Pierpont, *Roth Unbound*, 44.

39. Robert Brustein, *Making Scenes: A Personal History of the Turbulent Years at Yale* (New York: Random House, 1981), 22.

40. Roth to Vernon Gibberd, 17 March 1967, box 11, folder 1, Roth Papers, LC.

41. Roth to Fox, 24 September 1964, Random House Archive, Columbia University.

42. Fingerhood practiced in New York. She later became a judge of the Civil Court and then of the State Supreme Court from 1979 to 1993. She died in December 2008.

43. Alfred Albelli, "Walked Out on the Platinum," *New York Daily News*, 14 April 1964, 135.

44. During a June court hearing to finalize the separation agreement, the issue became funds in a joint bank account. Maggie earned no money between June 1959 and the summer of 1963 but now claimed at least half of the funds from the account. The amount was $6,806.89, the balance of a check from his agent for $13,162.50 received in December 1959 for *Goodbye, Columbus*. Maggie testified that she charged everything she could between the date of their separation and the trial. But Roth's lawyer argued that the defendant now required the funds to pay her charges. Roth's lawyer stated that Maggie went to Roth's apartment supposedly to negotiate with him personally but on arrival she refused to discuss the financial matters that were at issue. She also refused to leave. Roth attempted to eject her and they quarreled. A few days later, she was hospitalized, but Roth does not believe their quarrel led to her hospitalization. He thinks that her hospital stay was caused by her reaction to the disapproval of her behavior by friends. But Roth did pay for her hospital expenses and medications. Fingerhood file, box 10, folder 1, Roth Papers, LC.

45. Roth was at Yaddo, the writer's colony, during many of these procedures.

46. Fingerhood to Roth, 26 October 1964, box 10, folder 1, Roth Papers, LC.

47. Twelve shares of AT&T stock, however, soon became contentious. Roth received the stock from his father at his marriage, but they were in his name only: it was not a marriage gift but a cushion against any unanticipated living expenses as a married man. They were not Maggie's or thought to be common property. His parents actually bought a set of Spode china dishes as a wedding gift, which Maggie now had. Nonetheless, to avoid further litigation, Roth agreed to transfer half of the AT&T stock to her. Roth to Fingerhood, box 10, folder 2, Roth Papers, LC.

48. Truman Capote, "Playboy Interview (1968)," *Playboy Magazine*, March 1968, https://scrapsfromtheloft.com/2016/11/16/truman-capote-playboy-interview/.

49. Brustein, *Making Scenes*, 44.

50. Albert Goldman, "*Portnoy's Complaint* by Philip Roth Looms as a Wild Blue Shocker and the American Novel of the Sixties" in Searles, *Conversations with Philip Roth*, 32. It originally appeared in *Life*, 7 February 1969, 58, 61–64.

51. Elizabeth Manus, "Lie Down Where Philip Roth Did: Swatting Flies at Literary Camp," *New York Observer*, 22 June 1998, http://observer.com/1998/06/lie-down-where-philip-roth-did-swatting-flies-at-literary-camps/. Also see Micki McGee, ed., *Yaddo: Making American History* (New York: Columbia University Press, 2008). The Yaddo archive is at the New York Public Library. Ironically, it would be the MacDowell Colony, a competitor to Yaddo, that would award Roth its MacDowell Medal, presented to him by Styron in 2001 for artistic achievement.

52. Brustein, *Making Scenes*, 85.

53. On Roth as an American rather than Jewish writer, see Adam Gopnik, "Philip Roth, Patriot," *New Yorker*, 6 November 2017, (https://www.newyorker.com/magazine/

2017/11/13/philip-roth-patriot) and Ira Nadel, "American Roth," *Fudan Journal of the Humanities and Social Sciences* 12.3 (2019): 493–510.

54. Roth to Fox, 29 January 1968, Random House Archive, Columbia University.

55. Fox to Roth, 24 October 1966, and Fox to Robert Scudellari, 24 October 1966, Random House Archive, Columbia University.

56. Fox to Robert Scudellari, 4 November, 1966, Random House Archive, Columbia University.

57. Roth to Fox, 21 April 1967, Random House Archive, Columbia University.

58. Roth to Fox, 5 August 1967, Random House Archive, Columbia University.

59. Fox to Roth, (?), January 1968, Random House Archive, Columbia University.

60. Solotaroff to Roth, 16 December 1966, Solotaroff Archives, NYPL.

61. Herbst to Roth, 15 May 1967, NYPL.

62. Wilfrid Sheed, "Pity the Poor Wasps," *New York Times,* 11 June 1967, http://movies2.nytimes.com/books/98/10/11/specials/roth-good.html.

63. Robert Alter, "When He Is Bad" (1967), in Pinsker, *Critical Essays on Philip Roth,* 42–6.

64. The phrase is Goldman's, "*Portnoy's Complaint* by Philip Roth Looms," 32.

65. Webster Schott, "And When She Was Right—Help!," *Life* 62.24 (16 June 1967): 8.

66. Ross Miller to the author, 22 May 2014, Washington, DC.

67. Roth to Fox, 13 June 1968; Roth to Fox, 23 December 1967 and 29 February 1968; Fox to Roth, 13 June 1968, all in box 10, folder 5, Roth Papers, LC. Joe Fox died on 29 November 1995, and a memorial service was held on 7 December. Roth attended the service (or at least had a copy of the program); others who attended were John Irving, Martin Cruz Smith, James Salter, and Peter Matthiessen.

68. Bernard Avishai, *Promiscuous: Portnoy's Complaint and Our Doomed Pursuit of Happiness* (New Haven, CT: Yale University Press, 2012), 177, 192–3; "Kleinschmidt, Hans," *New York Times,* 22 February 1997, section 1, p. 28. He retired from his practice at age eighty-two and died on 21 February 1997 at age eighty-three. His four children survived him.

69. Gopnik, "Man Goes to See a Doctor."

70. The list includes Nina and Herbert Schneider, Joe Fox, James Atlas, Francine du Plessix Gray, and Ross Miller, plus, of course, Claire Bloom, to name a few. Mailer, Malamud, and Updike could also be added. Balancing this were his lasting friendships with Richard Stern, George Plimpton, Ted Solotaroff, Saul Bellow, Aharon Appelfeld, Edna O'Brien, Joel Conarroe, Norman Manea, Hermione Lee, R. B. Kitaj, Veronica Geng, Alain Finkielkraut, Leon Botstein, Judith Thurman, Julia Golier, Claudia Roth Pierpont, and Benjamin Taylor.

71. Adam Gopnik in Avishai, *Promiscuous,* 193. Also see Gopnik, "Man Goes to See a Doctor." For a critic's encounter with Kleinschmidt, see Jeffery Berman, "Revisiting Roth's Psychoanalysts," in *The Cambridge Companion to Philip Roth,* ed. Timothy Parris (Cambridge: Cambridge University Press, 2007), esp. 96–100.

72. Gopnik in Avishai, *Promiscuous,* 195.

73. Avishai, *Promiscuous,* 179.

74. The essay will have a major role in Roth's *My Life as a Man*. See also Jeffrey Berman, *The Talking Cure: Literary Representations of Psychoanalysis* (New York: New York University Press, 1985), 239–69.

75. Harry Slochower, "Genius Psychopathology and Creativity," *American Imago* 24 (spring–summer 1967): 5.

76. Kleinschmidt, "The Angry Act," 99, 100.

77. Kleinschmidt, "The Angry Act," 101.

78. Kleinschmidt, "The Angry Act," 107, my italics.

79. Kleinschmidt, "The Angry Act," 111.

80. Kleinschmidt, "The Angry Act," 116. Art as anger is the core, as David Mamet understood: "Nobody with a happy childhood ever went into show business," he writes in *True and False: Heresy and Common Sense for the Actor* (New York: Pantheon, 1997), 87.

81. Kleinschmidt, "The Angry Act," 118.

82. Kleinschmidt, "The Angry Act," 123.

83. Kleinschmidt, "The Angry Act," 125.

84. Kleinschmidt, "The Angry Act," 125.

85. Jeffrey Berman in *The Talking Cure* shows the near identical passages in Kleinschmidt's essay and Spielvogel's interpretation of Tarnopol in *My Life as a Man* (264–65).

86. Kleinschmidt, "The Angry Act," 125.

87. Kleinschmidt, "The Angry Act," 125.

88. See Roth to Donadio, 28 July 1967, Box 7, MSS22491, Correspondence File, Ms. Division Philip Roth Papers, LC.

89. Berman, *The Talking Cure*, 268.

90. West, *William Styron*, 277.

91. Jane Troxell Stark, "Jacqueline Kennedy Inspires the International Look," *Look* 26.12 (5 June 1962): 73–78. Ann Mudge is one of the women photographed.

92. Roth in Goldman, "*Portnoy's Complaint* by Philip Roth Looms," 33.

93. Roth to Vernon Gibberd, 2 December 1967, box 11, folder 1, Roth Papers, LC. Roth was optimistic, however, regarding a new divorce law. New York State did not pass a no-fault divorce law until October 2010, one of the last in the nation. For a useful summary, see J. Herbie DiFonzo and Ruth C. Stern, "Addicted to Fault: Why Divorce Reform Has Lagged in New York," *Pace Law Review* 27.4 (2007): 559–603,https://digitalcommons.pace.edu/cgi/viewcontent.cgi?referer=https://www.google.com/&httpsredir=1&article=1135&context=plr, which, among other details, refers to a 1934 *New York Mirror* story entitled "I Was the 'Unknown Blonde' in 100 New York Divorces" and the practice of fraudulent adultery to gain a divorce.

94. Roth to Vernon Gibberd, 4 June 1968, box 11, folder 1, Roth Papers, LC.

95. David Williams in Cohen, "Papa Portnoy," 38.

96. Obituary, *New York Times*, 13 May 1968, 43.

97. Roth to Vernon Gibberd, 22 June 1968, box 11, folder 1, Roth Papers, LC.

98. Joan Crawford, Igor Stravinsky, Arturo Toscanini, George Gershwin, Irving Berlin, and Ayn Rand were also "guests" at one time or another.

99. Philip Roth to Claire Bloom, 7 February 1976, Bloom Archive, Boston University. Roth would later live on the same block as the funeral home.

100. Nina Schneider to Roth, 21 September 1988, box 30, folder 16, Roth Papers, LC.

101. R. S. (Bob) Baker to Roth, 15 June 1968, box 30, folder 2, Roth Papers, LC.

102. Roth to Vernon Gibberd, 22 June 1968, box 11, folder 1, Roth Papers, LC.

103. Mudge to Roth, undated, box 2, folder 13, Roth Papers, LC.

104. Roth to Jacob Epstein, 21 April 1969, Random House Archive, Columbia University.

105. Pierpont (*Roth Unbound,* 324) incorrectly gives 1968 as the year of their breakup. Roth told Pierpont that if he had not married Maggie, he likely would have married Ann; they probably would have had a child, he likely would have fooled around; and they would have divorced.

106. See Roth to Dr. Randall, 13 March 1969, written from Yaddo, box 30, folder 13, Roth Papers, LC.

107. Roth summarizes the event in "Notes for My Biographer," 196–97, Taylor/Roth Archive, Firestone Library, Princeton University. He composed this section in October 2010.

108. Roth to Herman and Nina Schneider, 29 April 1969, box 30, folder 16, Roth Papers, LC.

109. Roth to Kleinschmidt, 15 April 1969, box 17, folders 6 and 21, Roth Papers, LC. All further references are to this document.

110. Roth to Vernon Gibberd, 9 July 1969, box 11, folder 1, Roth Papers, LC. Alvarez, poet, critic, and later London friend of Roth's, went on to say that "being a writer is like being a psychoanalyst, but you don't get any patients."

111. Roth to Candida Donadio, 28 July 1967, box 7, folder 13, Roth Papers, LC.

112. Fox to Roth 9 August 1967, Random House Archive, Columbia University.

113. Roth to Fox, 13 June 1968, and Fox to Roth, 13 June 1968, box 10, folder 5, Roth Papers, LC.

114. There is a draft dated 27 August 1968, but the actual letter is dated 28 August. Fox to Roth, 28 August 1968, box 10, folder 5, Roth Papers, LC.

115. Jason Epstein to the author, 17 May 2012, New York City.

116. The titles were *Portnoy's Complaint* and years later *The Plot Against America* (Jason Epstein to the author, 17 May 2012).

Chapter 5

1. Viva in Victor Bockris, *Warhol: The Biography* (New York: Da Capo Press, 1989), 274.

2. Roth, "Civilization and Its Discontents," *New American Review* 3 (1968): 7–81.

3. Harry Golden's popular *Only in America* appeared in 1958, the year before *Goodbye, Columbus.* Leo Rosten's *The Return of Hyman Kaplan* (1959) was a finalist for the National Book Award for Fiction, won by *Goodbye, Columbus.* Herman Wouk, known for *Marjorie Morningstar* (1955), published *This Is My God: The Jewish Way of Life* also in 1959.

4. Scott Raab, "Philip Roth Goes Home Again," *Esquire*, October 2010, https://www.esquire.com/news-politics/a8604/philip-roth-interview-1010/.

5. It is no surprise that one of the most enterprising critical studies of the time was Richard Poirier's *The Performing Self* (1971), which dealt with pop culture, psychotherapy, educational reform, and neo-Marxist politics, developing the idea that each "performance is an exercise of Power" which "competes with reality itself for control." Richard Poirier, *The Performing Self* (New York: Oxford University Press, 1971), 86–87. And preceding *Portnoy* by three years was Susan Sontag's claim that "in place of a hermeneutics we need an erotics of art." Susan Sontag, "Against Interpretation," in *Against Interpretation and Other Essays* (New York: Farrar, Straus and Giroux, 1966), 104.

6. Lenny Bruce, *How to Talk Dirty and Influence People: An Autobiography of Lenny Bruce* (Chicago: Playboy Press, 1965), 5.

7. "B. B. King came to the Garden, and Al took me backstage to meet him just after *Portnoy's Complaint* came out. The girls were lined up around the block for B. B. King's dressing room, and in back with him he had a half a dozen or so acolytes in powder-blue suits, and we sat around and talked for a while. Then I went to get the seat while Al interviewed him further—and when I left, B. B. King looked at his boys in their powder-blue suits, rubbed my seat, and said, 'This guy just made a million dollars from *writin' a book*.'" Roth in Raab, "Philip Roth Goes Home Again." Many believed that Goldman, adjunct professor of English and comparative literature at Columbia, inspired David Kepesh, who appears in *The Breast, The Professor of Desire*, and *The Dying Animal*.

8. Goldman, "*Portnoy's Complaint* by Philip Roth Looms" 58. See CWPR 23–34. Also included in the article is the photo of Herman Roth standing behind Sandy and Philip taken at Bradley Beach in August 1937. Roth is four, his brother nine, Herman thirty-six. Roth used it as the jacket photo of *Patrimony*. Final photo in the article is Roth concentrating at his desk at Yaddo shown through a latticed window. His right hand holds his forehead, his left holds a pen. The photo was taken by Bob Peterson on special assignment for *Life*. See Derek Parker Royal, "Framing the Cusp of Celebrity: Bob Peterson's 1968 Photographs of Philip Roth," *Philip Roth Studies* 7.2 (2011): 121–44

9. Roth, "A Jewish Patient Begins His Analysis," *Esquire*, April 1967, 191.

10. Roth, "A Jewish Patient Begins His Analysis," 193.

11. For a detailed and useful account of the textual history of *Portnoy*, a five-year process with Roth "adrift" part of the time, see Scott Saul, "Rough: A Journey into the Drafts of *Portnoy's Complaint*," *Post45*, April 12, 2019. http://post45.org/2019/04/rough-a-journey-into-the-drafts-of-portnoys-complaint/. Saul summarizes Roth's disparate productivity as churning through a series of projects: "a Chekhovian play about a young couple in crisis; a whimsical novel built around a baby dropped off at a Jewish home for the elderly; a set of stories revolving around the patients of a single psychoanalyst; a serious-minded novel titled *Portrait of the Artist as a Young Jewish Man*, which later morphed into a semi-serious novel like text entitled *The Nice Jewish Boy*; and several stories revolving around sex-hungry Jewish men, with titles like 'The Sex Fiend' and 'The Age of Jane Fonda.'" One draft opening had Portnoy commenting on

an obscene slideshow with Dr. Spielvogel, the projectionist, focusing mostly on body parts: the body, for example, is nothing less than a pedestal for the penis, says the narrator.

A bibliography of the part-publication of *Portnoy*:

"A Jewish Patient Begins His Analysis," *Esquire*, April 1967, 104, 107, 191–93.
"Whacking Off," *Partisan Review* 34 (Summer 1967): 385–99.
"The Jewish Blues," *New American Review* 1 (September 1967): 136–64.
"Civilization and Its Discontents," *New American Review* 3 (1968): 7–81.
"Oh, to Be a Center Fielder," *Sport,* June 1969, 27.

The six sections of *Portnoy* as published:

"The Most Unforgettable Character I've Met"
"Whacking Off"
"The Jewish Blues"
"Cunt Crazy"
"The Most Prevalent Form of Degradation in Erotic Life"
"In Exile"

12. Henry Raymont, "To Philip Roth, Obscenity Isn't a Dirty Word," *New York Times,* 11 January 1969, 20. Ironically, the article appears next to a suggestive ad of a woman removing her sweater for Milos Forman's *Firemen's Ball.* See also Avishai, *Promiscuous,* 25.

13. West, *William Styron,* 366–69. West notes that *Nat Turner* generated $1 million for Styron *before* publication.

14. Roth to Epstein, (?), July 1968, Random House Archives, Columbia University.

15. Roth to Epstein, 13 July 1968, and 25 July 1968, Random House Archives, Columbia University.

16. Roth to Epstein, 27 July 1968, Random House Archives, Columbia University.

17. Epstein to Roth, 31 July 1968, Random House Archives, Columbia University.

18. Roth to Epstein, 9 August 1968, Random House Archives, Columbia University.

19. Roth has retold this story numerous times. See Pierpont, *Roth Unbound,* 68.

20. Avishai, *Promiscuous,* 25–26.

21. Roth in George Plimpton, "Philip Roth's Exact Intent" (1969), in Searles, *Conversations with Philip Roth,* 35.

22. Plimpton, "Philip Roth's Exact Intent," 38.

23. Plimpton, "Philip Roth's Exact Intent," 39.

24. Plimpton, "Philip Roth's Exact Intent," 39. The texts included "The Metamorphosis," *The Castle,* "In the Penal Colony," *Crime and Punishment, Notes from the Underground, Death in Venice,* and *Anna Karenina.* Chronologically, however, Roth is incorrect since he did not begin teaching at Penn until 1970.

25. Sproul to Roth, 31 May 1982, box 32, folder 3, Roth Papers, LC.

26. Pierpont, *Roth Unbound,* 67.

27. Random House advertisement, *New York Times,* 1 April 1969, 45; Editorial, *New York Times,* 1 April 1969, https://timesmachine.nytimes.com/timesmachine/1969/04/01/78334768.html?pageNumber=46.

28. Scholem in Alan Cooper, *Philip Roth and the Jews* (Albany: State University of New York Press, 1996), 110. Also see Gershom Scholem in Melody Barron, "Philip Roth: Life in the Shadow of Portnoy," The Librarians, National Library of Israel, 23 May 2018, https://blog.nli.org.il/en/philip_roth/. In a passage from Scholem, quoted from a manuscript of the outburst, he refers to Roth as a "highly gifted if perverted artist" who has the temerity to take "vengeance on his upbringing in the Jewish home . . . and going forth to lay *shikses* thereby freeing himself from his nightmare of [the *Yiddishe*] *mame*." The review was actually two letters to *Ha'aretz*.

29. Official publication date was 21 February 1969, but several critics jumped the gun. Geoffrey Wolff, *Washington Post*, 7 February 1969; Bruno Bettelheim, "Portnoy Psychoanalyzed: Therapy Notes Found in the Files of Dr. O. Spielvogel, a New York Psychiatrist" (1969), in *Surviving and Other Essays* (New York: Vintage, 1980), where in a preface Bettelheim claims his review is a satire; Gershom Scholem, "Some Plain Words" and "Social Criticism—Not Literary," in Scholem, "*Portnoy's Complaint*," trans. E. E. Siskin, *Central Conference of American Rabbis*, June 1970: 56–58; Marie Syrkin, "The Fun of Self-Abuse," *Midstream*, April 1969, 64–68; Diana Trilling, "The Uncomplaining Homosexuals," *Harper's*, August 1969. Some critics, like Isa Kapp, suggested that "what made *Portnoy's Complaint* a best-seller was not really the flamboyant vocabulary or the lurid sexual images, but the complaint itself, the encroachment of the Jewish family on the outlook and imagination of its vulnerable offspring." Kapp, "Zuckerman in Turmoil," *California Literary Review*, 5 November 2007, http://calitreview.com279. For another positive assessment of the novel, see Patricia Meyer Spacks, "About Portnoy," *Yale Review* 58 (1969).

30. Albert Goldman, "Boy-Man Schlemiel: The Jewish Element in American Humor," in *Freakshow* (New York: Atheneum, 1971), 176–77, 179. For the Heine reference, see 174.

31. Bettelheim, "Portnoy Psychoanalyzed," 387. Another hostile reaction was that of Saul Maloff in *Commonweal*: *Portnoy's Complaint* is "a desperately dirty novel; and that, like it or not, is its chief joy and aesthetic principle." Some might think this was a good thing. Maloff did not. Roth did. Saul Maloff, "Tropic of Conversation," *Commonweal*, 21 March 1969, 23–24.

32. Bettelheim, "Portnoy Psychoanalyzed," 388–89.

33. Bettelheim, "Portnoy Psychoanalyzed," 393.

34. Alfred Kazin, "Up Against the Wall, Mama!," *New York Review of Books*, 27 February 1969, https://www.nybooks.com/articles/1969/02/27/up-against-the-wall-mama/. Yates in Bailey, *A Tragic Honesty*, 124.

35. Judy Klemesrud, "Some Mothers Wonder What Portnoy Had to Complain About," *New York Times*, 31 March 1969, L42.

36. Herman Roth to Philip Roth, 15 March 1969, box 30, folder 1, Roth Papers, LC.

37. Herman Roth to Philip Roth, 4 March 1969, box 30, folder 1, Roth Papers, LC.

38. Herman Roth to Philip Roth, 15 March 1969; box 30, folder 1, Roth Papers, LC; Pierpont, *Roth Unbound*, 68.

39. Herman Roth to Philip Roth, 9 October 1969, box 30, folder 2, Roth Papers, LC.

40. Herman Roth to Philip Roth, 14 April 1969 and 13 May 1969, box 30, folder 2, Roth Papers, LC.

41. Larry Peerce to the author, 23 February 2018 and 9 March 2018.

42. Michael Meyers, *Goodbye Columbus, Hello Medicine* (New York: William Morrow, 1976). In Chapters 1 and 2 of his memoir, Meyers describes his disappointment and surprise at the success of his role. His medical career, however, was not as triumphant. Practicing medicine in California, Meyers developed a substance abuse problem that started in med school. A year later, when the film was released, he received acting offers and TV invitations and had to decide to return to med school or not. He returned, but his dependency on drugs grew until he realized his addiction was killing him. He began a recovery program in 1982 and recovered but was no longer permitted to practice medicine. By 1991, he was hosting a series for professionals on how to combat chemical dependency. He died on 14 September 2009, age sixty-three. See Susan King, "Dr. Michael Meyers: Addicted Now to Helping Others," *Los Angeles Times*, 9 June 1991, https://www.latimes.com/Paperss/la-xpm-1991-06-09-tv-712-story.html.

43. See "Hoo-Boy, Columbus," *Mad Magazine* 131 (December 1969): 42, 46. It was the "Back to College Issue." The subtitle of the comic strip was "The Gripes of Roth Department." Mort Drucker illustrated and Tom Koch did the script.

44. On the curious bibliographical history of the afterword—added, subtracted, and then added to the edition—see James Duban, "'Juice or Gravy?' Philosophies of Composition by Roth, Poe and Sartre," *Philip Roth Studies* 12. 2 (2016): 80n1.

45. John Updike in Mick Brown, "John Updike: The Descent of Man," *Daily Telegraph*, 24 October 2008, https://www.telegraph.co.uk/culture/donotmigrate/3562536/John-Updike-the-descent-of-man.html.

46. Philip Roth, "Old Books, New Thoughts," *New York Times*, 16 November 2014, https://www.nytimes.com/2014/11/06/t-magazine/pen-auction-philip-roth.html. Further quotations are to this source. In addition to a first edition of *Portnoy's Complaint* (1969)—signed twice with extensive annotations—there was a first of *American Pastoral* published in 1997. Even now, some fifty years after publication, the novel continues to attract attention, Bernard Avishai's enthusiastic and supportive study of the social impact of the novel, *Promiscuous: Portnoy's Complaint and Our Doomed Pursuit of Happiness* (2012), one of the most recent examples. Avishai's work benefits from his friendship with Roth by drawing on the teaching notes Roth prepared in 1999 when presenting the book in a course at Bard College (Avishai 8 ff.). Also of interest, from a Freudian and linguistic point of view, is Patrick Hayes, *Philip Roth: Fiction and Power* (Oxford: Oxford University Press, 2014), 90–108. And as if he cannot rid himself of the novel, in a 6 November 2017 interview for the Library of America, Roth explains that forty-two years after *Portnoy*, he imagined *The Dying Animal* where Kepesh becomes "Portnoy unPortnoyed, the complete libertine.... The Sixties do for Kepesh what Dr. Spielvogel could never begin to do for poor Portnoy." Roth, "'Here I Am': Philip Roth Reflects on His Half-Century Career as a Writer," Interviews, Library of America, November 6, 2017, https://www.loa.org/news-and-views/1347-here-i-am-philip-roth-reflects-on-his-half-century-career-as-a-writer.

47. Roth, "Old Books, New Thoughts."
48. Anticipating this is the moment in Roth's 1963 play "The Nice Jewish Boy" where the hero's father offers money to the son's possibly pregnant girlfriend Lucy in an attempt to buy her off. See Chapter 4.
49. Irving Howe, "Philip Roth Reconsidered" (1972), in Pinsker, *Critical Essays on Philip Roth*, 234, 230, 232. Countering this is Mark Shechner's balanced "Philip Roth" (1974), in Pinsker, *Critical Essays on Philip Roth*, 117–32. A recent supporter of Howe's perspective is Ruth Wisse, "The Exuberant Joylessness of Philip Roth," *Commentary*, July/August 2018, 41–49. Her premise is that Roth "never graciously accepted his designation as a Jewish writer" and distrusted his Jewishness (48).
50. Howe, "Philip Roth Reconsidered," 233, 236.
51. Howe, "Philip Roth Reconsidered," 237, 238, 239, 242.
52. Harvey Kurtzman and Will Elder, "Little Annie Fanny," *Playboy* 17.12 (December 1970).
53. Blake Bailey, "Philip Roth's America," *New Yorker Radio Hour*, 20 July 2018.
54. Roth to Epstein, 4 March 1969, Random House Archives, Columbia University.
55. He adds that this is "what Zuckerman should have done after *Carnovsky*—but he hung around, the fool, and look what happened to him. He would have enjoyed Yaddo more than he enjoyed Alvin Pepler. But it made *Zuckerman Unbound* funnier keeping him in Manhattan, and it made my own life easier, not being there" (RMY 135; CWPR, 176).
56. Philip Roth, "Will," box 9, folder 13, Roth Papers, LC.
57. Quoted in Pierpont, *Roth Unbound*, 73.
58. Roth to Jason Epstein, (?), 1968, from London, Random House Archives, Columbia University.
59. He detested the title "A Moral Position" for Roth's new novel and suggested "The Other Side of Love." "That says it without saying too much and avoids the stiffness of words like 'moral' and 'position.'" And it only took him one sleepless night to come up with it. Kleinschmidt to Roth, 27 August 1966, box 17, folder 6, Roth Papers, LC.
60. Kleinschmidt to Roth, 18 July 1968 and 31 July 1968, box 17, folder 6, Roth Papers, LC.
61. Kleinschmidt to Roth, 9 June 1974, Roth Papers, LC.
62. Roth, "Civilization and Its Discontents," 39.
63. Roth qtd. by Blake Bailey to Sandra Tropp, 17 December 2013, email.
64. Roth often exhibits a desire to be praised by the critics, and when he's not, he's resentful, as would later happen after Updike's reserved review of *Operation Shylock*, which created a rift between the two. See Updike, "Recruiting Raw Nerves," *New Yorker* 69.4 (15 March 1993): 109–12; Maloff, "Tropic of Conversation," 23–24.
65. Roth to Epstein, 28 March 1969, Random House Archives, Columbia University.
66. Roth to Epstein, 4 April 1969, Random House Archives, Columbia University.
67. Roth to Epstein, 21 April 1969, Random House Archives, Columbia University.
68. Roth to Kleinschmidt, 15 April 1969, box 17, f. 6, Roth Papers, LC. All further references are to this document.
69. Roth to Kleinschmidt, 15 April 1969, box 17, folder 6.

70. Roth to Kleinschmidt, 15 April 1969, box 17, folder 6.

71. Roth to Kleinschmidt, 15 April 1969, box 17, folder 6.

72. Both passages from Roth to Kleinschmidt, 15 April 1969, box 17, folder 6.

73. Roth to Kleinschmidt, 15 April 1969, box 17, folder 6.

74. Sproul to Roth, 21 April 1969, box 32, folder 2, Roth Papers, LC.

75. Lelchuk to Roth, 1969, box 19, folder 8, Roth Papers, LC.

76. In order to get additional funding from the Canadian Film Development Corporation, the setting moved from Chicago and New York to Toronto and New York, with principal photography in the Canadian city.

77. Peter Mark Richmond, *I Saw a Molten White Light: An Autobiography of My Artistic and Spiritual Journey* (Albany, GA: BearManor Media, 2018), n.p.

78. Mudge to Roth, undated, box 2, f. 13, Roth Papers, LC.

79. Mudge to Roth, undated, box 2, folder 13.

80. Pierpont, *Roth Unbound*, 46.

81. Roth to Kleinschmidt, 20 July 1969, box 17, folder 6, Roth Papers, LC.

82. Roth to Kleinschmidt, 20 July 1969, box 17, folder 6.

83. Roth to Lelchuk, undated. box 19, folder 2, Roth Papers, LC.

84. On Roth believing Barbara wanted a child with him, see Sproul, 1974, box 32, folder 2; on her sadness, see 9 March 1969, box 32, folder 2, Roth Papers, LC. On his need for solitude and security, see Roth's letter to Kleinschmidt, 15 April 1969, box 17, folder 6, Roth Papers, LC. On interruptions, Roth became so annoyed by Anna Steiger, Claire Bloom's daughter, and her friends when living with Bloom in London that he ordered the daughter out, giving Bloom an ultimatum: Either she goes or I go. See LDH 157–58.

85. Roth to Epstein, 15 April 1969, Random House archives, Columbia University.

86. Guston qtd. in Ross Posnock, *Philip Roth's Rude Truth* (Princeton, NJ: Princeton University Press, 2006) 244.

87. Roth, "Pictures by Guston," *Shop Talk* in WR? 286.

88. Roth to Vernon Gibberd, 4 June 1968, Roth Papers, LC.

89. Holly Williams to Roth, (?), 1969(?), box 36, folder 9, Roth Papers, LC.

90. This parallels a passage late in *Lolita* when the seventeen-year-old Lolita, married and pregnant, writes to Humbert Humbert asking for money. Humbert tracks her down and gives her the money.

91. Hatch Williams to Roth, (?) 1969(?), box 36, folder 16, Roth Papers, LC.

92. See the letter cited earlier in Chapter 2 from Maggie's father, "Red" Martinson, written ca. December 1955 or January 1956, to his wife Evelyn, with its enigmatic sentence on page 3 of the eight-page penciled note (box 22, folder 10, Roth Papers, LC).

93. Hannah, Alex's sister in *Portnoy's Complaint*, was older; Maggie was four years older than Roth, Bloom was two.

94. See Debra Shostak, "Roth/CounterRoth: Postmodernism, the Masculine Subject and *Sabbath's Theater*," *Arizona Quarterly* 54.3 (1998): 120.

95. Berlinerblau, "Do We Know Philip Roth?" Also see Berlinerblau, *The Philip Roth We Don't Know: From #Me Too to Metempsychosis* (Charlottesville: University Press of Virginia, 2021).

96. See R. L. Goldberg, "'Incest, Blood, Shame. Are They Not Enough to Make One Feel Sinful?' Miltonic Figurations of Incest and Disobedience in Philip Roth's *American Pastoral*," *Philip Roth Studies* 16.2 (2020): 33–52. On incest and collective fantasy, see 39; on incest and narcissism, 51n14.

97. A footnote to these and other examples in late Roth is when Simon Axler befriends Sybil Van Buren at a psychiatric hospital. She is there because of an attempted suicide, the result of catching her husband sexually abusing his eight-year-old stepdaughter. Some months later, he reads that she shot and killed her husband for his act, violence the only answer to such abuse.

98. Roth, "Foreword," in Fredrica Wagman, *Playing House* (Barnes & Noble, 1978), https://www.barnesandnoble.com/w/playing-house-fredrica-wagman/1008782594 (site discontinued).

99. Needing cash in 1988 following his return from London, Roth sold the manuscript for $15,000. He also sold a Persian carpet that had been in his 18 East 81st Street apartment in New York. He bought the rug in 1969; it, too, sold for $15,000. See Roth, "Money," n.d., Taylor/Roth Papers, Firestone Library, Princeton University. Roth wrote this essay of thirty-seven leaves in response to Ross Miller's claim that Roth tried to control people with money. In the document, Roth lists gifts or loans to friends from 1968 onward.

100. Otto Rank linked the incest theme and artistic creativity to an aesthetic working through of the Oedipus complex. Otto Rank, *The Incest Theme in Literature and Legend: Fundamentals of a Psychology of Literary Creation*, trans. Gregory C. Richter (Baltimore, MD: Johns Hopkins University Press, 1992), *passim*. Also helpful is James B. Twitchell, *Forbidden Partners: The Incest Taboo in Modern Culture* (New York: Columbia University Press, 1987), Peter Nesteruk, "The Incest Theme in American Writing: Two Hundred Years of a Literary Motif," *Borderlines: Studies in American Culture* 4.4 (1997): 358–80; Christine Grogan, *Father-Daughter Incest in Twentieth Century American Literature* (Madison, NJ: Fairleigh Dickinson University Press, 2016).

101. Alan Lelchuk confirmed Roth's penchant for picking up young girls, narrating a story of how the two of them took a young woman to a motel room, reconstructed in the *Humbling* when Simon Axler and Pegeen pick up a young female in a bar and excitedly end up in a bedroom. The incident leads to Pegeen's renewal of her lesbian desires with the woman. Shortly after, she leaves Simon. Gary Shteyngart told a similar story about Roth and a young girl with the added touch of Viagra. Shteyngart to J. Berlinerblau, told to the author, 19 September 2013. On Lelchuk's report, see Lelchuk, box 19, folder 12, Roth Papers, LC.

102. See Maud Ellmann, *The Hunger Artists: Starving, Writing and Imprisonment* (Cambridge, MA: Harvard University Press, 1993), *passim*. While reviewing the galleys of "A Hunger Artist" during his final illness, Kafka was, himself, unable to eat and starving. Tuberculosis of the larynx prevented him from swallowing and even taking liquids. See Ernst Pawel, *The Nightmare of Reason: A Life of Franz Kafka* (New York: Farrar, Straus and Giroux, 1984), 445.

103. Helpful on this topic is Cathy Caruth, *Unclaimed Experience: Trauma, Narrative, History* (Baltimore, MD: Johns Hopkins University Press, 1996) and Aimee Pozorski, *Roth and Trauma: The Problem of History in the Later Works (1995–2010)* (New York: Continuum, 2011).

104. Redheads and Roth: Maxine Groffsky, Edna O'Brien (reddish brown), Naomi in *Portnoy's Complaint*, Kathy Goolsbee in *Sabbath's Theater*, and the nurse Maureen in *Everyman*.

Chapter 6

1. See Roth's letter to Kleinschmidt of April 1969, discussed in the previous chapter. On the complicated question of Roth and his mother, see AL 47. The novel itself is something of a mother fiction, beginning with its opening sentence—"When he is sick, every man wants his mother"—and ending with reference to "the paternal bond to those in duress" (AL 1, 291).

2. Barbara Sproul to Roth, 21 April 1969 and Sproul to Roth, 1974(?), box 32, folder 2, Roth Papers, LC.

3. Sproul to Roth, 7 March 1969, box 32, folder 1, Roth Papers, LC.

4. Sproul to Roth, 22 March 1969, 31 March 1969, and 22 March 1969, box 32, folder 1, Roth Papers, LC.

5. Her example was apparently Alan Lelchuk, whom she strongly disliked as much as Roth liked him. See Roth letter, 20 May 2015, Taylor/Roth Papers, Firestone Library, Princeton University.

6. As they were separating and underscoring their travels together, she tells him that she will take the Thai mobile: "Having carried it so far, I thought I'd carry it a little further." Sproul to Roth, 1974(?), box 32, folder 2, Roth Papers, LC. Sproul went on to have relationships with Joseph Brodsky and others, and later sent Roth details about her marriage to the playwright Herb Gardner (*A Thousand Clowns*). She actually invited Roth to the wedding in 1978, but he did not attend, although over the years she sent him pictures of their two adopted sons, regular birthday cards, and updates of her involvement with Amnesty International. She also maintained a connection with George Steiner through Amnesty International and reported in 1975 on Roth's recent return from Prague and the overall Czech situation.

7. See Cecil Wolf and John Bagguley, eds. *Authors Take Sides on Vietnam* (New York: Simon and Schuster, 1967), 65–66. Date of Roth's contribution is 14 February 1967. Also in the collection are William S. Burroughs, Graham Greene, Hannah Arendt, W. H. Auden, Susan Sontag, James Baldwin, Simone de Beauvoir, Robert Brustein, Robert Creeley, Jules Feiffer, Lawrence Ferlinghetti, Joseph Heller, Norman Mailer, Marshall McLuhan, Bertrand Russell, William Styron, and Leonard Woolf.

8. Pierpont, *Roth Unbound,* 185, 304. Pierpont, commenting on Updike's summary of his disagreements with Roth in his autobiography, *Self-Consciousness,* cites Updike's references to the Weathermen and the Jains and that they try to hide the view that

to be alive is to kill. Prompting Updike's comments, titled "On Not Being a Dove," was the publication of *Authors Take Sides on Vietnam,* where his own truncated comment in defense of the war appears on page 73, sandwiched between Kenneth Tynan's and Gore Vidal's. The conjunction of subjects in Updike's text—Roth, Vietnam, the Weathermen, and the Jains—published five years before Roth's novel, is a startling coincidence, Pierpont observes (304).

9. Roth, "Interview," Amazon.com, August 2013: 65, Roth Papers, LC.

10. Mikhail Lermontov, "Author's Preface," in *A Hero of Our Time,* 2nd edition, n.d., https://www.ibiblio.org/eldritch/myl/hero.htm.

11. Roth, "On Our Gang," in RMY 46. The essay-interview originally appeared in the *Atlantic Monthly,* December 1971 and was reprinted as an afterword to the "Watergate Edition" of *Our Gang* (New York: Bantam, 1973).

12. Roth to Epstein, 16 April 1971, Random House Archives, Columbia University.

13. Jules Feiffer to Jason Epstein, no date; Burgess to Epstein, 25 August 1971; Macdonald to Epstein, no date, all box 8, folder 16, Roth Papers, LC.

14. *Time,* 25 October 1971; *New Republic,* 6 November 1971, 29; Dwight Macdonald, "Our Gang," in Pinsker, *Critical Essays on Philip Roth,* 61–64.

15. The two prefaces appear on pages 664–66 of the second volume of the Library of America's edition of Roth's works: *Novels 1967–1972* (New York: Library of America, 2005).

16. *Plot* spent fifteen weeks on the *New York Times* bestseller list, from 10 October 2004 to 16 January 2005, at one point rising to number 2. In the interval, his books received critical praise but only modest sales, even when praise was high, as with *The Ghost Writer* (1979), or controversial, as with *Sabbath's Theater* (1995). *My Life as a Man,* with nearly fifty thousand copies in print by June 1974, still did poorly. The warehouse overstock meant another remainder sale with copies offered to Roth at between 35 and 75 cents a copy (box 36, folder 2, Roth Papers, LC). Prize-winning titles also failed to give him the kind of sales numbers reached by a Herman Wouk or Chaim Potok. *American Pastoral* may have won the Pulitzer Prize for 1997, but John Grisham's *The Partner,* Thomas Pynchon's *Mason and Dixon,* and Charles Frazier's *Cold Mountain* overshadowed it on the bestseller lists. Peter Mayle, the advertising executive turned author, writing about his experiences in Provence in a series of autobiographical works and novels, far outsold Roth in the 1990s. *A Year in Provence* (1990) started the series, which continued through *Hotel Pastis* (1993) and *Chasing Cezanne* (1997) and ended with *Provence A–Z* (2006). Mayle's *A Good Year* (2004), appearing the same year as *The Plot Against America,* had an initial print run of 175,000, according to *Publishers Weekly,* http://www.publishersweekly.com/978-0-375-40591-4.

17. Aaron Asher and Martin Garbus, "The Letting Go of Random House by Philip Roth," *Book of the Month Club Newsletter* 1.3 (1972), Random House Archives, Columbia University.

18. Roth to Klopfer, 20 May 1972, Random House Archives, Columbia University.

19. Klopfer to Roth, 27 June 1972, Random House Archives, Columbia University.

20. Asher and Garbus, "The Letting Go of Random House by Philip Roth."

21. Alan Lelchuk, *American Mischief* (New York: Farrar, Straus and Giroux, 1973), 288. The murder scene occurs on pages 286–92; moments before he shoots him, the

narrator thinks, "Didn't I at least owe it to him to push the event to a Maileresque extreme?" (291).

22. Roth's *Esquire* piece was in response to the editor's 1972 request for a feature on older writers writing brief essays about authors under thirty-five they admired. Isaac Bashevis Singer, Leslie Fiedler, Mark Schorer, and Roth were asked to contribute. Roth chose Lelchuk, whom he had met at Yaddo. He had read *American Mischief* in manuscript.

23. Actually, it was Napier Wilt, Roth's former dean, who misheard a report of Roth's dying, writing a summary of his confusion in January 1974. The actual radio report dealt with Philip Rahv, who died on 22 December 1973. Both, however, had a contempt for provincialism. In a letter addressed to Roth, Wilt happily clarified his error, while recalling his pleasure at reading the manuscript of *Goodbye, Columbus* in the Dean's Office at the University of Chicago.

24. Alan Lelchuk, "The Godfather of the Literary World & A Young Offender," box 20, folder 10, p. 10, Lelchuk Papers, Boston University. This is an unpublished twenty-six-page manuscript.

25. Eric Pace, "Mailer Finds Book Is No Advertisement for Himself," *New York Times,* 18 October 1972, http://www.nytimes.com/1972/10/18/Paperss/mailer-finds-book-is-no-advertisement-for-himself-mailer-find. Rembar, quoted in the article, said they would charge Lelchuk with libel—Mailer would never act out of personal fear under any circumstances, as depicted in the passage—but that there would not be any legal action. Mailer only wanted Lelchuk to reconsider the section. Everyone got excited in the ensuing argument, the *Times* reported. For a short time, the incident became a feature of New York literary gossip. Interestingly, Boris Kachka omits the encounter in *Hothouse: The Art of Survival and the Survival of Art at America's Most Celebrated Publishing House, Farrar Straus & Giroux* (New York: Simon and Schuster, 2013).

26. Lelchuk, "The Godfather of the Literary World," 11.

27. Lelchuk, "The Godfather of the Literary World," 12, 14, 16, 22, 19.

28. Lelchuk, "The Godfather of the Literary World," 25.

29. Lelchuk will use this technique when he writes *Ziff: A Life?* (New York: Carroll & Graf, 2003), a semifictitious biography of Arthur Ziff, actually Roth. Comments on writing, biography, women, and life can all be linked to Roth. "No one messing seriously with the real, sometimes hot-potato facts, no separating the real from the fabricated in the Ziff fiction," was a proviso as easily offered by Roth as by Ziff. However, Lelchuk and Roth were on the outs at this point in their relationship (5). Emily Dickinson, "Tell All the Truth," in *Poetry: A Pocket Anthology*, 7th edition, ed. R. S. Gwynn (New York: Pearson, 2014), 163.

30. Lelchuk, *American Mischief,* 288–92. The details are graphic, with Lenny Pincus first wounding Mailer in the shoulder and then shooting him in the anus, the "last act violent and extraordinary enough . . . to satisfy his wild teachings" (292).

31. Mailer in Pace, "Mailer Finds Book Is No Advertisement for Himself."

32. Student to Roth, December 1972, box 36, folder 19, Roth Papers, LC.

33. Student to Roth, April/May 1973, box 36, folder 19, Roth Papers, LC

34. Roth in Sara Davidson, "Talk with Philip Roth," *New York Times Book Review*, 18 September 1977, 1, 51. *The Breast* appeared in 1972.
35. Ozick to Aaron Asher, 16 June 1972 and 19 June 1972, box 1, folder 2, Roth Papers, LC.
36. Rosalyn Drexler to Epstein, 24 July 1972, box 1, folder 2, Roth Papers, LC.
37. Jason Epstein to the author, June 2013, New York City. Epstein said that after *Portnoy*, Roth's satires and general titles sold poorly.
38. Roth's publishers and key editors in chronological order: 1959, Houghton Mifflin (George Starbuck); 1960, Random House (Joe Fox, Jason Epstein); 1972, Holt Rinehart and Winston (Aaron Asher); 1975, Farrar, Straus and Giroux (Aaron Asher, David Rieff); 1989, Simon and Schuster (Michael Korda); 1995, Houghton and Mifflin (John Sterling, Wendy Strothman).
39. In 1966 RCA had taken over Random House. At one point, while negotiating the contract for *When She Was Good*, Roth was offered RCA stock in lieu of a full advance from the publisher.
40. Philip Roth to Irving Howe, 1 December 1973, box 13, folder 1, Roth Papers, LC.
41. David Gooblar, *The Major Phases of Philip Roth* (New York: Continuum, 2011), 94–96.
42. Roth himself expanded the concept of narcissism to a national level when he told the *London Daily Telegraph* in 2002, "What we've been witnessing since September 11 is an orgy of national narcissism." Sam Leith, "Philip Roth Attacks 'Orgy of Narcissism' post Sept. 11," *Daily Telegraph*, 5 October 2001, 21.
43. Roth in Gooblar, *The Major Phases of Philip Roth*, 65. He earlier mentioned the phrase in his 1969 interview with George Plimpton.
44. To write such a book she must have been as angry as Roth but, unlike Roth, in need of money.
45. Cynthia Ozick to Philip Roth, 15 April 1974, box 26, folder 12, p. 1, Roth Papers, LC.
46. Ozick to Roth, 15 April 1974, 2.
47. Ozick to Roth, 15 April 1974, 2.
48. Ozick to Roth, 15 April 1974, 3.
49. Ozick to Roth, 15 April 1974, 3.
50. In an aside, she takes on Irving Howe and his earlier critique of Roth, noting that "it's no use saying this is a bad time for Jews, a bad time for women." And to claim it is a period of transition is feeble: "I'm persuaded it will *always* be a transitional time." Ozick to Roth, 15 April 1974, 3.
51. Ozick to Roth, 15 April 1974, 4. Among Segal's novels is *Her First American* (1985), an account of a Jewish refugee from Nazi Europe and her relationship with a middle-aged black intellectual, Carter Bayoux. In certain ways, it anticipates *The Human Stain* with Coleman Silk and his relationship with Faunia Farley. In a 2019 interview, Segal said that memory is "the artist's notebook," again an idea Roth has embodied. Cressida Leyshon, "Lore Segal on Memory as the Artist's Notebook," *New Yorker*, 18 March 2019, https://www.newyorker.com/books/this-week-in-fiction/lore-segal-03-25-19. Another aspect of the novel, although not one Ozick noticed, is the choice of Tarnopol as the protagonist's last name. Roth may have had in mind the town in western Ukraine variously known as Ternopil or, in Polish, Tarnopol. Dostoevsky and Tolstoy were also to play a larger role in early versions of the novel, going back to

1969, when Roth titled two chapters "A Karamazov Brother" and "Yasnaya Polyana," Tolstoy's home southwest of Tula, Russia, two hundred kilometers from Moscow. See box 143, Roth Papers, LC.

52. Berman, *Talking Cure,* 265.

53. Paul Mosher and Jeffrey Berman, "'The Angry Act': The Psychoanalyst's Breach of Confidentiality in Philip Roth's Life and Art," in *Confidentiality and Its Discontents* (New York: Fordham University Press, 2015), 71; Kleinschmidt, "The Angry Act." 124; Roth in Mosher and Berman, "'The Angry Act,'" 70. Compare with Roth, "The Jewish Blues," 145 and PC 51. For additional insight into Kleinschmidt and his practice, see Norma Stevens and Steven M. L. Aronsen, *Avedon: Something Personal* (New York: Spiegel and Grau, 2017), 382–93.

54. Kleinschmidt, "The Angry Act," 125.

55. Kleinschmidt, "The Angry Act," 101.

56. Kafka in Kleinschmidt, "The Angry Act," 101.

57. Kleinschmidt, "The Angry Act," 101.

58. Kleinschmidt, "The Angry Act," 101, 107, 116.

59. Kleinschmidt, "The Angry Act," 126, 127.

60. Harry Slochower, "Genius, Psychopathology and Creativity," *American Imago* 24.1 (Spring 1967): 5.

61. See especially the funeral of Zuckerman's mother in AL 237–38 and the persistent hovering (sometimes literally) of the mother throughout *Sabbath's Theater.*

Chapter 7

1. Mark Shechner, "Thickening the Culture," unpublished manuscript, 2007, 4. I'm indebted to the late Mark Shechner for sharing with me his important account of Roth and Mitteleuropa. Irving Howe advanced these views in his infamous attack on Roth in *Commentary*: Howe, "Philip Roth Reconsidered," *Commentary* 54.6 (1972): 69–77 rpt. in *Philip Roth*, rev. edition, ed. Harold Bloom (1986; New York: Chelsea House, 2003).

2. By the time he was four, writes his first biographer, James Atlas, Bellow could "recite whole pages of the book of Genesis, in both Yiddish and Hebrew" (*Bellow*, 13) Also see Bellow, *Letters*, ed. Benjamin Taylor (New York: Viking, 2010), xvii, 298. "French in the street, Yiddish at home" is Taylor's summary of Bellow's early linguistic enterprise (xvii).

3. Chile began its military dictatorship in 1973, as did Uruguay; Argentina's was in 1976. Vietnam in 1973 passed a set of decree-laws that allowed the police and military to shoot all who urged people to demonstrate, despite plans for a peace agreement signed in late January 1973, although bombing of North Vietnamese bases and supply routes in Cambodia resumed in February.

4. On this element of Roth's work, see Jack F. Knowles, "Philip Roth and the Struggle of Modern Fiction," PhD dissertation, University of British Columbia, 2020, 238–43, which pays particular attention to Czesław Miłosz's influence on *I Married a Communist* and argues that *The Plot Against America*, Roth's most national text, "is

conceived in relation to a European history that threatens to engulf it" and draws from Bruno Schulz (239, 242–43). Primo Levi was another influence on *American Pastoral*, according to Knowles, especially Levi's *The Monkey's Wrench* (248–51). For the 1972 first draft of *American Pastoral*, see box 39, Roth Papers, LC. For an interview with Roth on the series, see Roth, "Prague, Kafka, and more . . . ," Web of Stories,https://www.webofstories.com/play/philip.roth/19;jsessionid=72185416647F1CBEAEE45A C182905EC0, where he explains how he met the dissident writers following a meeting at his Czech publisher where one member of the editorial board confided to him at a lunch that a substratum of writers was suffering. His series essentially reprinted works that had already appeared in English but had disappeared. For the impact of the series and the Cold War, see Brian K. Goodman, "Philip Roth's Other Europe: Counter-Realism and the Late Cold War," *American Literary History* 27.4 (2015): 717–40.

5. Shechner, "Thickening the Culture," 7.
6. For a valuable survey, see Michal Sykora, "The Prague Orgy: The Life of Writers in a Totalitarian State according to Philip Roth," *Humanities* 8.2 (2019): 71ff, https://www.mdpi.com/2076-0787/8/2/71/htm. Sykora makes the interesting point that Roth's portrait of the dissident writers as bohemian, sexually liberated, and dissolute is similar to that of Communist propaganda, although he admires their commitment to artistic freedom. Also helpful is Martyna Bryla, "Understanding the Other Europe: Philip Roth's Writings on Prague," *Revista de Estudios Norteamericanos* 17 (January 2013): 13–24.
7. Roth in Al Alvarez, "Philip Roth," in *Risky Business* (London: Bloomsbury, 2007), 38.
8. Roth, "In Search of Kafka and Other Answers," *New York Times Book Review,* 15 February 1976, 6.
9. Roth, "In Search of Kafka and Other Answers," 2. Also useful is Roth, "A Czech Education," in WR? 368–70. The focus of this 2013 speech is Ivan Klíma.
10. Roth Interview with Klíma, SHP 53.
11. Shechner, "Thickening the Culture," 10.
12. Roth enlisted various writers to introduce the volumes. Jerzy Ficowski, Polish poet, writer, and translator, introduced the Schulz volume.
13. Roth in Pierpont, *Roth Unbound,* 92.
14. What may not be fantasy is the source of Lonoff's name. One of Roth's boyhood friends, who later owned an auto supply house and who as a child lived across the street from Roth when in grade school, was Lenny Lonoff. See PAT 78.
15. One of Rhoda's skills is as a puppeteer, anticipating the career of Mickey Sabbath in *Sabbath's Theater* (1995).
16. Roth, "Writers from the Other Europe," in Milan Kundera, *The Book of Laughter and Forgetting* (New York: Penguin, 1981), [3].
17. Roth, "Country Report # 1 Czechoslovakia," PEN American Center, August 1973, [1].
18. Roth, "Country Report," 2.
19. Milan Kundera, "Edward and God," *American Poetry Review* 3 (March–April 1974) 5–11; Jiří Weil, "Shanghai," "The Sheep from Lidice," *American Poetry Review* 3 (September–October 1974) 22–23, 23–24.
20. Roth met Weil's widow in 1973.

21. Anne Tyler, "Pursued by They," *New York Times*, 18 June 1989, 7:3, http://movies2. nytimes.com/books/99/02/28/nnp/weil-star.html. Roth wrote the Preface to the volume translated by Ruzena Kovarikova with Roslyn Schloss. Jiří Weil, *Life with a Star* (New York: Farrar, Straus and Giroux, 1989). Schloss was for years Roth's professional copyeditor.

22. Sproul in Geraldine Baum, "The Czech Connection: For Rita Klimova, Revolutionary Turned Ambassador, These Are Stellar Times," *Los Angeles Times*, 11 April 1990.

23. Milan Kundera to Roth, April 1988(?), box 17, folder 16, Roth Papers, LC.

24. Kundera to Roth, 1985(?), box 17, folder 16, Roth Papers, LC.

25. Kundera to Roth, box 17, folder 16, Roth Papers, LC.

26. Kundera actually has four titles in the series: *Laughable Loves, The Farewell Party, The Book of Laughter and Forgetting,* and *The Joke*. Roth provided an Introduction to the first, and an Afterword to the third.

27. John Updike, "Introduction," in *Sanatorium Under the Sign of the Hourglass*, trans. Celina Wieniewska (New York: Penguin, 1979), xvii, xviii.

28. Updike, "Introduction," xv, xix.

29. David Grossman, "The Age of Genius: The Legend of Bruno Schulz," *New Yorker*, 8 June 2009, 66+. In the novel, as told by the youthful narrator Momik, Schulz escapes his shooting to plot his own death and rebirth as a fish who wants to live in a world without memory.

30. Roth, "Introducing Milan Kundera," in *Laughable Loves*, trans. Suzanne Rappaport (New York: Penguin, 1975), xv.

31. In 1979–80, Penguin published a four-volume set from the series, containing work by Borowski, Kiš, Kundera, and Schulz. Roth provided an Introduction. See Velichka Ivanova, "Philip Roth, Editor of the 'Writers from the Other Europe' Series," *Philip Roth Studies Newsletter* 9, no. 1 (Fall 2011): 11–12.

32. William T. Vollmann, "Afterword," in Danilo Kiš, *A Tomb for Boris Davidovitch* (Chicago: Dalkey Papers, 2001), 136–45.

33. Krauss in *Philip Roth and World Literature*, Introduction by V. Ivanova (Amherst, NY: Cambria Pres, 2014); Krauss, "Preface," in *Best European Fiction 2012*, ed. Aleksandar Hemon (Champaign, IL: Dalkey Papers Press, 2011), xvii–xx.

34. Roth to Ivan Sanders, 15 February 1978, private collection. Ironically, in 1987 Roth did publish Konrád's *The Case Worker* in his series with (a further irony) an introduction by Irving Howe, satirized by Roth in *The Anatomy Lesson*, published in 1983.

35. Ivan Sanders, "Review of Hungarian Translation of Philip Roth's *The Humbling*," undated manuscript, 2, private collection.

36. Shechner, "Thickening the Culture," 14.

37. Roth, "2013 Literary Service Award Remarks," Pen America, May 21, 2013, http://www.pen.org/nonfiction/philip-roth-2013-literary-service-award-remarks#overlay-context=user.

38. See Bloom, boxes 1 and 2, Claire Bloom Collection, Howard Gotlieb Archival Research Center, Boston University. Bloom formed a special relationship with Boston University, attending the dinner to honor Howard Gotlieb, founder of their Special Collections, in October 2003.

39. Bloom, LA 160–63; Claire Bloom, "Notebook #1," box 1, [9], [27], Claire Bloom Collection, Howard Gotlieb Archival Research Center, Boston University.

40. James Atlas, "A Visit with Philip Roth," *New York Times*, 2 September 1979. For a later account of Roth's working space, notably his New York apartment, see Charles McGrath, "Goodbye, Frustration: Pen Put Aside, Roth Talks," *New York Times*, 17 November 2012. Litchfield County Auctions conducted an auction of household items on 20 July 2019, thirteen months after Roth's death. Various real estate sites listed the sale of his New York apartment at 130 West 79th Street in February 2019. See my "Preface" for details. For further details, see Matthew Ormseth, "Philip Roth, Novelist and Warren Resident, Remembered by Those Who Knew Him," *Hartford Courant*, 24 May 2018, https://www.courant.com/news/connecticut/hc-philip-roth-connecticut-20180523-story.html. Hartford is forty-five minutes from Cornwall Bridge and Warren. For details on Roth's house, listed for $2.925 million and with photos of the expansive interior and surrounding forest, see https://www.wsj.com/articles/connecticut-estate-where-philip-roth-penned-pulitzer-prize-winner-asks-2-925-million-11568035820. For further details on Roth's Connecticut home, see Tayla Zax, "Philip Roth Doesn't Live Here Any More: A Writer, a Stonemason, an American Friendship," *Forward*, 17 May 2020, https://forward.com/culture/446516/philip-roth-russ-murdock-grave-house-connecticut-litchfield/.

41. Claire Bloom to Roth, box 3, folder 11, Roth Papers, LC.

42. Roth to Roger Straus, 20 April 1982, FSG Papers, NYPL.

43. Don Miguel Ruiz, "Don't Take Anything Personally," in *The Four Agreements* (San Rafael, CA: Amber-Allen, 1997), 38–45.

44. Precipitating the matter were editorial problems concerning the inadequate preparation of *The Great American Novel* for volume 3 of the Library of America edition, which appeared in 2006. Roth found Miller's editorial work incompetent.

45. Janet Malcolm in Jesse Tisch, "The Philip Roth Papers," *Tablet*, 21 May 2020, https://www.tabletmag.com/sections/arts-letters/articles/philip-roth-letters#contact.

46. Nina Schneider to Roth, 21 September 1988 and Nina Schneider to Roth re Barbara Sproul, 8 December 1985, box 30, folder 17; Herman Schneider to Roth, [1981], box 30, folder 16; Roth to the Schneiders on the suicide attempt of Ann Mudge, 29 April 1969, box 30, folder 16, Roth Papers, LC. Herman Schneider died in 2003, Nina in 2007. The reference to Elise is to a New York friend from Vienna with an interest in psychiatry.

47. Roth to Rieff, 12 April 1984, FSG Papers, NYPL.

48. David Plante, *Becoming a Londoner: A Diary* (New York: Bloomsbury, 2013), 252. Other close London associates were Antonia Fraser, Gaia Servadio, and Deborah Rogers, Roth's first English agent.

49. Plante, *Becoming a Londoner*, 453.

50. David Plante, *Worlds Apart: A Memoir* (London: Bloomsbury, 2015), 63.

51. Plante, *Worlds Apart*, 63–65.

52. Plante, *Worlds Apart*, 65.

53. Plante, *Worlds Apart*, 63.

54. Plante, *Becoming a Londoner*, 459; Hermione Lee, "The Art of Fiction LXXXIV: Philip Roth," *CWPR* 162.

55. Robert McCrum, "Bye-bye . . . Philip Roth Talks of Fame, Sex and Growing Old in Last Interview," *Guardian*, 17 May 2014, https://www.theguardian.com/books/2014/may/17/philip-roth-retires-imagine-interview.

56. Plante, *Worlds Apart*, 415.

57. Roth added the second sentence in red ink to his notes to Lee's interview with him. Lee, "The Art of Fiction LXXXIV: Philip Roth," 12, Paris Review Papers, J. Pierpont Morgan Library. The quote "I'm American because I'm Jewish" is from Matthew Hoffman, "Profile: Philip Roth," *Independent* (London), 30 August 2003.

58. Roth in Plante, *Becoming a Londoner*, 501.

59. Hermione Lee, "'Life *Is and*': Philip Roth in 1990," *Independent on Sunday*, 2 September 1990, rpt. CWPR 262; Roth in McCrum, "Bye-bye."

Chapter 8

1. Al Alvarez, "Philip Roth," in *Risky Business* (London: Bloomsbury, 2008) 31. The essay on Roth first appeared in the *Guardian* in 2004, prompted by the appearance of *The Plot Against America*.

2. Roth said he thought about suicide during the worst of his back pain and then depression in the late 1980s, brought on partly by medications from his knee operation, but he had experienced serious depression as early as 1974. And sometimes thinking about it was enough.

3. For more on Roth and swimming, see Ira Nadel, "Aquatic Roth," *Philip Roth Studies* 14.1 (2018): 36–54.

4. Pierpont, *Roth Unbound*, 100.

5. Alvarez, "Philip Roth," 31.

6. Zax, "Philip Roth Doesn't Live Here Anymore."

7. Alvarez, "Philip Roth," 32.

8. Alvarez, "Philip Roth," 33.

9. Al Alvarez, *Where Did It All Go Right?* (London: Richard Cohen Books, 1999), 295.

10. Dongala met Roth and William Styron in 1980 at a party, brought to the gathering by Dr. C. H. Huvelle of Litchfield, Connecticut. Huvelle was physician for both Roth and Styron. Roth grew especially fond of Dongala and asked him to accept, on his behalf, the Karel Čapek literary prize presented to him by Václav Havel at a PEN conference in Prague. In 1997, with the aid of Leon Botstein, president of Bard College, Roth managed to get Dongala and his family out of the war-torn Republic of Congo. For more, see Julie Michaels, "Writer in Exile," *Boston Globe Magazine*, 6 February 2000, 12–31.

11. For the Antonia Fraser anecdote about Pinter and Roth, see Plante, *Becoming a Londoner*, 465–66.

12. Pierpont, *Roth Unbound*, 100.

13. Antonia Fraser, *Must You Go? My Life with Harold Pinter* (New York: Nan A. Talese, Doubleday, 2010), 124.

14. Ariel Dorfman, "How Harold Pinter's Kindness Saved My Play," *Telegraph* (UK), 12 October 2011, http://www.telegraph.co.uk/culture/theatre/theatre-features/8821715/Ariel-Dorfman-How-Harold-Pinters-kindness-saved-my-play.html.

15. When the heirs of Max Brod sold the handwritten manuscript of *The Trial* for $1.98 million to a West German book dealer supposedly acting for the West German government in November 1988, Roth angrily responded with a letter to the *New York Times*.

16. R. B. Kitaj, "Associating Texts with Paintings," *Cambridge Opinion* 37 (1964): 52–53.

17. For a reproduction of the drawing, plus the better known *Philip Roth, 1985*, a seated Roth with his left knee crossing his right and reproduced as the cover of the 2001 paperback edition of *Reading Myself and Others*, see Kitaj, *Confessions of an Old Jewish Painter*, Preface by David Hockney, ed. Eckhart J. Gillen (Munich: SchirmerMosel, 2017), 364–65. The image also appears as the frontispiece to Ben Taylor's *Here We Are: My Friendship with Philip Roth* (2020). What appears to be the casual 1985 sketch, however, took six sessions. During those meetings, and others, Kitaj became, in a sense, Roth's art tutor. See Julian Ríos, *Kitaj: Pictures and Conversations* (Harmondsworth, UK: Hamish Hamilton, 1994), 61.

18. Marco Livingstone, *Kitaj*, 4th edition (London: Phaidon, 2014), 259n114.

19. Kitaj, *Confessions*, 355.

20. Oates, postcard to Kitaj, 5 April 1995, and Eno and McCartney letters, R. B. Kitaj Papers, UCLA.

21. Kitaj quoted in a letter by Pete Townshend to Kitaj, 27 May 1997, R. B. Kitaj Papers, UCLA. Townshend was a student of Kitaj and in the classroom at the time.

22. Andrew Lambirth, *R. B. Kitaj* (London: Philip Wilson, 2004), 118.

23. Kitaj, *First Diasporist Manifesto* (London: Thames and Hudson, 1989), 31; John Russell, "Art View: An American Abroad Undertakes a Self-Excavation," *New York Times*, 30 July 1989, 2: 13, https://www.nytimes.com/1989/07/30/arts/art-view.html. Russell notes that Kitaj has been "admired and derided, idolized and detested."

24. Kitaj, *First Diasporist Manifesto*, 11.

25. Russell, "Art View."

26. Kitaj, *First Diasporist Manifesto*, 19, 37.

27. Another feature of the text is Kitaj's identification of other diasporists, notably Palestinians, while also citing an Africa diaspora occurring in Asia (*First Diasporist Manifesto*, 27). The Palestinian reference may have influenced Roth's decision to portray various Palestinian voices in *Operation Shylock* (1993).

28. Livingstone, *Kitaj*, 259n115, 51.

29. For an image of the page, see http://pinky.bol.ucla.edu/kitaj/3_tj/5_tj_roth.htm.

30. Marco Livingstone, "Knowing Kitaj," Phaidon Agenda, 8 July 2010, https://ca.phaidon.com/agenda/art/articles/2010/july/08/knowing-kitaj-marco-livingstone-on-his-friendship-with-the-artist/.

31. In "R. B. Kitaj, Obsessions," *The Economist*, 2 March 2013, https://www.economist.com/books-and-arts/2013/03/02/obsessions. Also cited in *Three White Leopards*,

blog, 27 March 2013, linked to image titled *Desk Murder*, https://ladyofsilences. blogspot.com/2013/03/.

32. Lambirth, *R. B. Kitaj*, 1.

33. John Ashbery, "R. B. Kitaj," in *Reported Sightings: Art Chronicles 1957–1987*, ed. David Bergman (New York: Knopf, 1989), 299.

34. Ashbery, "R. B. Kitaj," 306–7.

35. Kitaj, *First Diasporist Manifesto*, 79.

36. Commentary from Stephen Ongpin Fine Art, London. https://www.stephenongpin. com/object/790570/0/portrait-of-philip-roth. On the Roth drawing, see Marlborough Fine Art, *R. B. Kitaj*, exhibition catalogue (London, 1985), no. 73, illustrated p. 43; Andrew Brighton, "Conversations with R. B. Kitaj," *Art in America*, June 1986, 102; Kitaj, *First Diasporist Manifesto*, detail illustrated p. 8; Julián Rios, *Kitaj: Pictures and Conversations* (London: Hamish Hamilton, 1994), 62; Richard Morphet, ed., *R. B. Kitaj: A Retrospective*, exhibition catalogue (London: Tate Gallery, 1994), no. 74, p. 152. This is the principal catalogue of the 1994 London retrospective which went on to the Metropolitan Museum of Art in New York and the Los Angeles County Museum of Art. For a reproduction of "A Jew in Love (Philp Roth)," see Kitaj, *Confessions*, 364.

37. Roth in Charles McGrath, "Philip Roth's Final Interview: 'Life Can Stop on a Dime,'" *Irish Times*, 22 January 2018, https://www.irishtimes.com/culture/books/ philip-roth-s-final-interview-life-can-stop-on-a-dime-1.

38. Kitaj, *Confessions*, 286.

39. Michael Herr, *Dispatches* (1977; New York: Avon, 1981), 210.

40. Herr's scene with the map parallels the opening of Orwell's *Homage to Catalonia* where Orwell enters the barracks in Barcelona in December 1936 to find a bewildered Italian militiaman staring at a map that he does not understand.

41. For details on Herr in England, see John May, "Michael Herr: An Exclusive Tribute + Vietnam Books," *The Generalist*, 18 July 2016, http://hqinfo.blogspot.ca/2016/07/ michael-herr-exclusive-tribute-vietnam.html. The nonfiction novel phrase appears in Feliks Garcia, "Michael Herr . . . Dies Aged 76," *Independent*, 25 June 2016, www. independent.co.uk/news/people/michael-herr-dead-dispatches-apocalypse-now-full-metal-jacket-vietnam-war-a7103086.html; Michael Herr in Adam Bernstein, "Vietnam War Reporter Michael Herr . . . Dies at 76," *Washington Post*, 24 June 2016, https://www.washingtonpost.com/entertainment/books/michael-herr-who-wrote-powerfully-about-vietnam-in-dispatches-dies-at-76/2016/06/24/ac9c0e58-3a2e-11e6-9ccd-d6005beac8b3_story.html?utm_term=.27bc5645886a. Letters between Roth and Herr range from 1986 to 1998 in the Roth Papers at the Library of Congress.

42. Michael Herr in Eric James Schroeder, "We've All Been There," in *Vietnam: We've All Been There*, ed. Eric James Schroeder (Westport, CT: Praeger, 1992), 34. Also useful is Paul Ciotti, "Michael Herr: A Man of Few Words," *Los Angeles Times Magazine*, 15 April 1990, 22.

43. Roth alludes to this issue in his interview with Edna O'Brien in SHP 106–7: "You have to go if you find your roots too threatening, too impinging. . . . Writers are always on the run," she explains (107). There may also be a broad parallel with Gore Vidal, who

wrote his seven American novels, including *Burr, 1876, Lincoln,* and *Empire,* largely living in Ravello, Italy.

44. O'Brien in Dan O'Brien, "'A Harp in the Hallway': Edna O'Brien and Jewish-Irish Whiteness in *Zuckerman Unbound*," *Philip Roth Studies,* 12.2 (2016): 22n16. O'Brien points out that Edna O'Brien has not much mattered in Roth criticism, but Ronan Bennett, in a 4 May 2002 article in the *Guardian,* drew attention to important parallels between O'Brien and Roth: "dazzling, flamboyant, turbulent beginnings followed by restless middle periods in which the writer takes time (and books) to reconsider and recast, to work through what he has seen, what he has learned, and then arresting returns to form in which experience, style and subject successfully cohere." Bennett also writes that "with Roth, *American Pastoral* announced the overdue but triumphant maturation of Nathan Zuckerman, simultaneously kinder and crueller than his earlier incarnations, sadder but wiser. With O'Brien, the new phase became apparent in her 1990 collection of stories, *Lantern Slides.* Set mostly in Ireland, the stories show O'Brien at her best: empathetic, passionate, cool, and vivid. Like Kate and Baba, her characters are still looking for love—this is her real subject—but unlike the country girls, they now have a wisdom that is not just the instinctive understanding of bright young things but the self-knowledge that comes with wounds and experience." Ronan Bennett, "The Country Girl's Home Truths," *Guardian,* 4 May 2002, https://www.theguardian.com/books/2002/may/04/fiction.reviews1.

45. Edna O'Brien, *Philip Roth at 80* (New York: Library of America, 2014), 45.

46. Roth, "Conversation in London with Edna O'Brien," SHP 102. The interview originally appeared as "A Conversation with Edna O'Brien," *New York Times Books Review,* 18 November 1984, http://movies2.nytimes.com/books/00/04/09/specials/obrien-roth.html.

47. Bennett, "The Country Girl's Home Truths."

48. See O'Brien, "'A Harp in the Hallway,'" 21n4. Also see Dan O'Brien, *Fine Meshwork: Philip Roth, Edna O'Brien and Jewish-Irish Literature* (Syracuse, NY: Syracuse University Press, 2020).

49. Australia's National Literature Board of Review considered it obscene in March 1969 and banned its importation. Private imports of the book were confiscated. Only in August 1970 was restricted distribution permitted. See Amy Lay, "Portnoy's Complaint," Banned, May 1, 2013, http://blog.naa.gov.au/banned/2013/05/01/portnoys-complaint/.

50. Roth, "Foreword," in Edna O'Brien, *A Fanatic Heart: Selected Stories* (New York: Farrar, Straus and Giroux, 1984) vii.

51. Roth, "Foreword," in O'Brien, *Fanatic Heart,* viii, vii. Also see Rebecca Pelan, "Edna O'Brien's 'World of Nora Barnacle,'" *Canadian Journal of Irish Studies* 22.2 (1996): 49–61.

52. Roth, cover blurb, in Edna O'Brien, *Country Girl: A Memoir* (Boston: Little, Brown, 2012). Others who provided blurbs were Alice Munro, Judith Thurman, and Hilary Mantel. Hereafter C. Girl.

53. For O'Brien's introduction of Roth at the Newark birthday party, see O'Brien, "'A Harp in the Hallway,'" 5; O'Brien, *Philip Roth at 80,* 43–49.

54. O'Brien, *Country Girl*, 293.

55. O'Brien, *Country Girl*, 293.

56. Pierpont, *Roth Unbound*, 126.

57. O'Brien, *Country Girl*, 275–78.

58. Roth in Pierpont, *Roth Unbound*, 45.

59. Roth's other two collections of prose would be *Shop Talk* (2001), containing interviews with writers, and *Why Write? Collected Nonfiction, 1960–2013* (2017) in the Library of America series.

60. Once asked if he ever read anything frivolous in his childhood, the critic George Steiner answered, "Moby Dick." In *The Professor of Desire*, expressing his own sense of unhappiness and discontent, Roth writes, "To each angry man his own Melville" (PD 173).

61. Informed of his Hong Kong trip, Roth's former mentor at the University of Chicago, Napier Wilt, offered to help, telling him that he knew all the tourist haunts and how to avoid them. Wilt suggested that he and his partner Bill McCollum might meet Roth and Sproul there since they would be visiting on 15 March. Wilt to Roth, box 36, folder 17, Roth Papers, LC. Wilt admired *Our Gang*, calling it Swiftian. Wilt, Mildred Martin, and Robert Maurer were the dedicatees of the satire. Wilt also celebrated "Epstein" in *Goodbye, Columbus*, recalling that when he first read the manuscript of the collection, "Epstein" was his favorite.

62. Robert W. Straus to Roth, 23 August 1977, box 33, folder 2, Roth Papers, LC.

63. "The Professor of Desire," *Kirkus Review* 3 October 1977, https://www.kirkusreviews.com/book-reviews/philip-roth/professor-of-desire/.

64. An uncorrected proof has written on it "3 October 1977" as the publication date, although Vance Bourjaily, novelist and former Iowa colleague of Roth's, reviewed the book on 18 September for the *New York Times*.

65. "Chronology," WR? 407; Searle, *Conversations with Philip Roth*, 19. Additional details of his parents and grandparents appear on WR? 407. For photographs of the grandparents, see *Philip Roth: Photos from a Lifetime* (Newark, NJ: Newark Public Library, 2013), *passim*.

66. Roth in Sally Bedell Smith, "Philip Roth's Struggle to Make TV Film," *New York Times*, 7 February 1984, http://www.nytimes.com/2007/10/20/arts/20lantz.html.

67. The teleplay appears in ZB 507–93.

68. Roth, "The Prague Orgy, Television Adaptation," ZB 514. The freedom of adaptation Roth experienced a few years earlier working with Tristram Powell on a version of *The Ghost Writer* for the BBC in late 1983 encouraged his later attempts. He adjusted the structure, opening and closing with exterior shots of Lonoff's snowbound cabin. Flashbacks in the novella became foregrounded and presented as real time in the TV adaptation. His interest in adaptation goes back to 1963 with a movie scenario entitled "The Grimes Case" and another work entitled "The Penetrator."

69. Chronology, box 5, MC 1111, Janet Hobhouse Papers, Special Collections, Rutgers University Libraries, Rutgers University. The Papers include the papers of Hobhouse's mother with various detailed letters from Janet written from England to her mother

plus her mother's diaries. The source for the 1974 date is Roth, "Notes for My Biographer," 201. Taylor/Roth papers, Firestone Library, Princeton University.

70. Pierpont, *Roth Unbound*, 154.

71. Janet Hobhouse, *The Furies* (New York: Doubleday, 1993), 196.

72. Hobhouse, *The Furies*, 194, 196, 195, 196, 197.

73. Box 5, MC1111, Janet Hobhouse Papers, Special Collections, Rutgers University.

74. Hobhouse, *The Furies*, 199.

75. Roth to Janet Malcolm, 6 August 1994, YCAL MSS 935, Malcolm Papers, Beinecke Rare Book and Manuscript Library, Yale University.

76. Hobhouse, *The Furies*, 203, 199, 203–4.

77. In describing this event, Pierpont uses it to comment on Roth's own search for a cemetery and burial plot, which he will repeat in a series of his late fictions, notably *Everyman*.

78. Bruce Wolmer, "Janet Hobhouse Interview," *Bomb* 19 (Spring 1987), http://bombmagazine.org/article/910/janet-hobhouse. A. M. Homes, who knew Hobhouse at Yaddo in the summer of 1989, wrote that she was "the kind of woman everyone fell in love with, wild, brilliant, intimidating—and incredibly great fun." Homes fictionalizes some of their experiences at Yaddo in her short story collection, *The Safety of Objects*. See Jane Fine, "A. M. Homes," *Bomb*, 16 November 2012, http://bombmagazine.org/article/6951/a-m-homes.

79. Richard Stern, *A Sistermony* (New York: Donald I. Fine, 1995), 45.

80. Roth to Janet Malcolm, 6 August 1994, YCAL MSS 935, Malcolm Papers, Beinecke Rare Book and Manuscript Library, Yale University.

81. Roth, blurb for *The Furies*, New York Review of Books, http//www.nybooks.com/books/imprints/classics/the-furies/.

82. Pia Masiero, *Philip Roth and the Zuckerman Books* (Amherst, NY: Cambria Press 2011), 45.

83. Patrick O'Donnell, "The Disappearing Text: Philip Roth's *The Ghost Writer*," *Contemporary Literature* 24.3 (1983): 374. This self-criticizing technique appeared with Joan in *My Life as a Man* (see the Peppy section, 101–28) and again in *The Facts* with Zuckerman's concluding letter.

84. Roth, "The Ghost Writer: A Special Message to Members of the First Edition Society" (1979), in ZB 611.

85. Roth in Cynthia Haven, "'The Novelist's Obsession Is with Language': Philip Roth on Writing, the Future of Language and *The Ghost Writer*," *Stanford Report*, 3 February 2014, https://bookhaven.stanford.edu/2014/02/an-interview-with-philip-roth-the-novelists-obsession-is-with-language/.

86. See Steve Geng, *Thick as Thieves: A Brother, a Sister—A True Story of Two Turbulent Lives* (New York: Holt, 2007).

87. Veronica Geng to Philip Roth, 15 March 1979 and 5 April 1979, box 11, folder 1, Roth Papers, LC. All subsequent dates of correspondence refer to this source.

88. Geng to Roth, 5 April 1979.

89. Geng to Roth, 5 April 1979 and 23 April 1979, box 11, folder 1, Roth Papers, LC.

90. Geng to Roth, 25 May 1979, box 11, folder 1, Roth Papers, LC.

91. Geng to Roth, 4 June 1979, box 11, folder 1, Roth Papers, LC,

92. Roth to Straus, 25 February 1981, FSG Papers, NYPL.

93. Geng to Roth, 1 April 1980, box 11, folder 2, Roth Papers, LC.

94. Qtd. in Carrie Rickey, "Veronica Geng, Satirist and Writer Raised in Olney," *Philly. com*, 27 December 1997, http://articles.philly.com/1997-12-27/news/25556396_ 1_new-yorker-philip-roth-veronica-geng. For an additional critique, see Helen Schumacher, "Veronica in the Extreme," *This Recording*, 16 November 2011, http://thisrecording.com/today/2011/11/16/in-which-we-imagine-ourselves-as-veronica-geng.html.

95. Roth, "Veronica," box 11, folder 2, Roth Papers, LC.

96. Roth in Dinitia Smith, "Veronica Geng, 56, Parodist and Editor with Rapier Wit," *New York Times*, 26 December 1997, http://www.nytimes.com/1997/12/26/arts/ veronica-geng-56-parodist-and-editor-with-rapier-wit.html. Roth frequently relied on a small circle of readers to review his work before he sent the final copy to his editors. At times this included James Atlas, Hermione Lee, Veronica Geng, Judith Thurman, Ben Taylor, and others.

97. Ross Posnock's *Philip Roth's Rude Truth: The Art of Immaturity* (Princeton, NJ: Princeton University Press, 2006) explores this in detail, emphasizing their serious laughter and antipastoralism with a dollop of erotic play.

98. Asher to Roth, 16 February 1978, box 1, folder 3, Roth Papers, LC.

99. Frank Bruni, "The Literary Agent as Zelig," *New York Times Magazine,* August 11, 1996, https://www.nytimes.com/1996/08/11/magazine/the-literary-agent-as-zelig. html.

100. Barbara Sproul to Philip Roth, 31 May 1982, Taylor/Roth Papers, Firestone Library, Princeton University.

101. See Roth to Arline Kaufman, 26 October 2004, box 15, folder 3, Roth Papers, LC. Bess Roth's Marble Pound Cake recipe: "¾ c butter (1 stick = ¼ lb plus ½ of ¼ stick). 1½ c sugar. Cream together. Add 3 eggs (not separated). One at a time to mixture. Beat well after every egg. Add 1½ teasp vanilla—beat well. Add 3 c Presto Self-Rising Flour (sift). Add 1 1/8 c milk (1/2 of ¼). Beat together well. Take 3 tablsp. batter put in another bowl. Add 2 tablespoons of Hershey's Choc syrup. Mix well and add to batter once cooled already in baking pan. Swirl a knife through batter to marble. Bake at 350f for ca. 60 min. or until a wooden tooth-pick inserted into the center comes out clean. Cool in pan on wire rack about 10 minutes; remove from pan and continue to cool on wire rack." Reference to his mother's marble cake, "freshly baked in our oven that afternoon," appears in PAA 107.

102. Roth to Arline Kaufman, 26 October 2004, box 15 folder 3, Roth Papers, LC.

103. His paternal grandfather died from a stroke in 1942.

104. Taylor, *Here We Are,* 166.

105. Among his contemporaries, only Updike seems an exception. Roth spent time learning about glove manufacturing for *American Pastoral*, taxidermy for *I Married a Communist,* jewelry making and grave digging for *Everyman*, milking cows and running a dairy farm in *The Human Stain*. Russ Murdock, Roth's Connecticut caretaker, tells of Roth's consulting with his neighbor Dotty Ripley, whose family ran a

dairy farm. He interviewed her for hours, incorporating her details in *The Human Stain* related to Faunia Farley. Murdoch in Zax, "Philip Roth Doesn't Live Here Anymore."

106. Roth to Blake Bailey, 14 April 2014, Taylor/Roth Papers, Firestone Library Princeton University. Also see PIH *passim*.

Chapter 9

1. "Halcion is the brand name for triazolam. These tablets are taken orally and are most commonly prescribed to treat insomnia, although it is also common to prescribe Halcion for a number of mental and mood disorders. Halcion takes effect faster than most other benzos, slowing brain activity and making it easier to sleep. . . . Halcion targets neuroreceptors that regulate brain function. This slows hyperactive brain activity and promotes deeper sleep. The substance is sometimes referred to as the slang term 'Up Johns.' Halcion has a much shorter half-life than other benzodiazepines." Doctors rarely prescribe Halcion for more than ten days "because of the drug's potency and addictive potential. Halcion can stop working like it's supposed to after a week and may not be as effective the longer it's taken." This can lead users to increase their dose in an attempt to regain the drug's effects. "Halcion Addiction and Abuse," Addiction Center, n.d., https://www.addictioncenter.com/benzodiazepines/halcion/.

2. For the record, the Zuckerman texts, including those in which he appears only briefly, are *The Ghost Writer, Zuckerman Unbound, The Anatomy Lesson, The Prague Orgy,* and *The Counterlife,* followed by his narrative role in *American Pastoral, I Married a Communist, The Human Stain,* and finally *Exit Ghost.* He is incipiently present in the "Salad Days" section of *My Life as a Man,* where his father is described as a "dynamo of a protector" but also as "volcanic" (MLM 4, 5). In *The Facts,* Zuckerman discusses the text with the narrator.

3. Roth to Atlas, 3 March 1980, Berg Collection, NYPL. Despite their separation, Atlas recorded a sympathetic reminiscence of Roth for Audible, released in April 2019, entitled "Remembering Roth."

4. Roth to Atlas, 14 September 1981, Berg Collection, NYPL.

5. Roth to Atlas, 12 March 1982, Berg Collection, NYPL.

6. Roth to Atlas, 12 March 1982.

7. Anna Freud, who had given Masson permission to publish the complete Freud-Fliess letters, was also suddenly attacked by Masson, as was Eissler, all of this occurring against the background of Masson revising his own views of Freud's methods and conclusions dealing with the centrality of the unconscious. Malcolm at once point claimed that Masson even repudiated psychoanalysis. Janet Malcolm, "Trouble in the Archives," *New Yorker,* 5 December 1983, 80.

8. In the same letter, she writes, "We seem to be ruled by some sort of brutal inner economy that dictates how much we may give and then says no more." Malcolm to Roth, December 2012(?), YCAL MSS 935, Malcolm Papers, Beinecke Rare Book and

Manuscript Library, Yale University. Jesse Tisch best represents the Roth-Malcolm exchange in his essay "The Philip Roth Papers," *Tablet*, 21 May 2020, https://www.tabletmag.com/sections/arts-letters/articles/philip-roth-letters.

9. Cathleen Medwick, "A Meeting of Arts & Minds," *Vogue*, October 1983, www.vogue.com/article/philip-roth-1983-vogue-profile-claire-bloom. Photos are by Inge Morath, Arthur Miller's wife. The profile opens, "It is a soft, breezy day in north-western Connecticut. There is an old farmhouse, fronted by a sea of tall grass; beyond that, deep woods. Philip Roth walks quietly in his meadow."

10. "I knew what I was doing when I broke Zuckerman's jaw. For a Jew a broken jaw is a terrible tragedy. It was to avoid this that so many of us went into teaching rather than prizefighting." Roth to H. Lee, CWPR 181.

11. Kazin, "Look Back in Aggravation," box 92.5, Kazin Papers, Berg Collection, NYPL.

12. Plante, *Becoming a Londoner*, 459.

13. Plante, *Worlds Apart*, 87.

14. Plante, *Worlds Apart*, 102, 103.

15. Plante, *Worlds Apart*, 105.

16. Plante, *Worlds Apart*, 105.

17. Plante, *Worlds Apart*, 64.

18. Cynthia Ozick to Roth, 18 June 1986, box 26, folder 1, Roth Papers, LC.

19. Roth to Kazin, 21 April 1987, Berg Collection, NYPL. On the final page of *The Counterlife*, the narrator writes, "England's made a Jew of me in only eight weeks, which, on reflection, might be the least painful method. A Jew without Jews, without Judaism, with Zionism . . . a Jew clearly without a home, just the object itself, like a glass or an apple" (CL 324). Roth told Atlas in 1988 it was a great relief to be back in the States "where I can hate the whole spectacle rather than being in England where I have to defend this place from those idiots." Roth to Atlas, 29 August 1988, Berg Collection, NYPL. For a profile of Rieff, see Suzy Hansen, "Rieff Encounter," *The Observer*, 2 May 2005, https://observer.com/2005/05/rieff-encounter/.

20. Alfred Kazin, *Alfred Kazin's Journals*, ed. Richard M. Cook (New Haven, CT: Yale University Press, 2011), 496.

21. Richard Cook, *Alfred Kazin: A Biography* (New Haven, CT: Yale University Press, 2007), 390.

22. Kazin, *Alfred Kazin's Journals*, 384.

23. Kazin, *Alfred Kazin's Journals*, 390–91, 497.

24. Kazin, *Alfred Kazin's Journals*, 541.

25. Kazin, *Alfred Kazin's Journals*, 350.

26. Cook, *Alfred Kazin*, 411.

27. "American passion for newness was the source of his inspiration." Robert McCrum, David Hare, and Hannah Beckerman, "'I Did the Best I Could with What I Had . . .': Writers on the Philip Roth They Knew," *Observer*, 27 May 2018, https://www.theguardian.com/books/2018/may/27/writers-remember-the-philip-roth-they-knew-robert-mccrum-hannah-beckerman-david-hare.

28. See box 308, FSG Papers, NYPL.

29. FSG to Roth, 23 September 1986, box 308, FSG Papers, NYPL.

30. For the remarks by Primo Levi's son and Wiesel, see Diego Gambetta, "Primo Levi's Last Moments," *Boston Review*, 1 June 1999, http://bostonreview.net/diego-gambetta-primo-levi-last-moments.

31. Antonio Gnoli per Robinson, Gaia Servadio, "Una Vita Gaia," *Il repubblicia il Sole*, 12 September 2019, rpt. *Dagospia.com*, https://www.dagospia.com/rubrica-2/media_e_tv/vita-gaia-ndash-lsquo-rsquo-rsquo-italia-causa-suo-213506.htm. See also *Raccogliamo le Vele* (*Lower the Sails*), (Feltrinelli, 2014) reviewed by Ian Thomson, "As Decreed," *TLS*, 2015, https://www.the-tls.co.uk/articles/as-decreed/.

32. Marco Belpoliti, "The Writer and the Chemist," *Doppiozero*, 4 July 2018, https://en.doppiozero.com/materiali/history/philip-roth-interviews-primo-levi. Belpoliti edited the third volume of Levi's work, *Conversations, Interviews and Statements* published by Einaudi as *Opere complete III: Conversazioni, interviste, dichiarazioni* (2018). Importantly, Belpoliti identifies three versions of the Levi interview: the *New York Times*, *La Stampa* with certain details cut but with one added (a reference to his doctor, who was Natalia Ginzburg's brother, Ginzburg the important Italian novelist, essayist, and activist who also worked for the publisher Einuadi in Turin before moving to Rome in 1950), and a third version on Levi's computer, a longer master text which he sent to his publisher and remained in their files until recently but is now published in *Opere complete III*. The title is "Responses to Philip Roth." Roth's own corrected version is what appears in WR? 187–99.

33. Belpoliti, "The Writer and the Chemist."

34. See Pierpont, *Roth Unbound*, 163–66.

35. Roth to Kazin, 21 April 1987, Berg Collection, NYPL.

36. See Gambetta, "Primo Levi's Last Moments." Levi was not the only concentration camp survivor Roth met; two others were Ivan Klíma and Aharon Appelfeld, but Levi may have been the most eager to confront it through his writing.

37. Roth in John Freeman, "Philip Roth," in *How to Read a Novelist* (New York: Farrar, Straus and Giroux, 2013), 146.

38. Roth to Kazin, 28 July 1987, Berg Collection, NYPL.

39. Roth in Freeman, "Philip Roth," 147.

40. Roth reports this in Freeman, "Philip Roth," 151.

41. Martin Krasnik, "Philip Roth: It No Longer Feels a Great Injustice That I Have to Die," *Guardian*, 14 December 2005, https://www.theguardian.com/books/2005/dec/14/fiction.philiproth.

42. Krasnik, "Philip Roth."

43. Krasnik, "Philip Roth."

44. Krasnik, "Philip Roth."

45. Roth in a canceled passage from his interview with Primo Levi. See Belpoliti, "The Writer and the Chemist."

46. Roth to David Rieff, 31 March 1987, FSG Papers, NYPL.

47. Roth to David Rieff, 31 March 1987.

48. Roth to Atlas, February 1979(?), Berg Collection, NYPL.

49. Roth to Atlas, 1988(?), 7–8, Berg Collection, NYPL.

50. Roth to Atlas, 1990(?), Berg Collection, NYPL.

51. The five books are Basil, Judea, Aloft, Gloucestershire, and Christendom. Reference to Basel may allude to Theodore Herzl's organization of the first Zionist Congress, which took place in Basel in 1897.

52. See Roth to Rieff, 18 January 1987, FSG Papers, NYPL.

53. David Hare in McCrum, Hare, and Beckerman, "'I Did the Best I Could.'"

54. Susan Sontag to Roth, 5 October 1986, box 31, folder 20, Roth Papers, LC.

55. Roth, "An Exchange with Mary McCarthy," SHP 114.

56. Kachka, *Hot House*, 255.

57. See Benjamin Moser, *Sontag: Her Life and Work* (New York: Ecco, 2019), 508–9. Moser also outlines Wylie's protective but aggressive actions to secure Sontag's financial well-being (509–11). Authors always wanted more money and publishers always wanted to pay less, Moser writes (510).

58. Kachka, *Hot House*, 258.

59. Kachka, *Hot House*, 262.

60. See Wylie, box 676, FSG Papers, NYPL; Kachka, *Hot House*, 263.

61. Roger Cohen, "Roth's Publishers: The Spurned and the Spender," *New York Times*, 9 April 1990, C11, https://www.nytimes.com/1990/04/09/books/roth-s-publishers-the-spurned-and-the-spender.html. One rumor was that after Wylie's success, Roth walked around at a party with a hundred-dollar bill sticking out of his pants zipper.

62. Edwin McDowell, "Book Notes," *New York Times*, 16 August 1989, C20.

63. McDowell, "Book Notes," 20. For further details on how Wylie operated, convincing authors that they were selling themselves short by not keeping their copyright and not working to gain greater advances, see Lloyd Grove, "The World According to Andrew Wylie," *Portfolio*, 14 December 2007, http://www.portfolio.com/views/columns/the-world-according-to/2007/12/14/An-Interview-With-Andrew-Wylie/index.html. For additional information on Wylie, see Craig Lambert, "Fifteen Percent of Immortality," *Harvard Magazine*, July–August 2010, https://harvardmagazine.com/2010/07/fifteen-percent-of-immortality and Gideon Lewis-Kraus, "The Last Book Party," *Harper's Magazine*, March 2009, https://harpers.org/Papers/2009/03/the-last-book-party/7/.

64. Kazin, *Alfred Kazin's Journals*, 560.

65. The doubling may have been too puzzling or baroque for readers who could not easily tell one Philip Roth from another. It also became a threat to the actual Philip Roth in the story when he confronts his double when peering out of a doorway of his hotel bedroom as fact and fiction intersect and even suggests suicide. See OPS 179. For characteristic criticism that the novel is verbose and too "self-congratulatory," see D. M. Thomas, "Operation Shylock," *New York Times*, 7 March 1993, https://www.nytimes.com/1993/03/07/books/operation-shylock.html.

66. Dinitia Smith, "Claire Bloom Looks Back in Anger at Philip Roth," *New York Times*, 17 September 1996, https://www.nytimes.com/1996/09/17/books/claire-bloom-looks-back-in-anger-at-philip-roth.html; LDH 239. Vidal also asserted that she already had experienced Portnoy's complaint, her previous marriage to the Broadway producer Hillard Elkins (LDH 239). Bloom, of course, was not coy, having had

sustained relationships with Richard Burton, Laurence Olivier, Yul Brynner, and Anthony Quinn, plus marriages to Rod Steiger and Elkins before Roth.

67. Roth to Bloom, package 1, box 1, Claire Bloom Collection 1200, Gotlieb Archival Research Center, Boston University.

68. Roth to Bloom, 6 January 1976, package 1, box 1, Claire Bloom Collection 1200, Gotlieb Archival Research Center, Boston University.

69. Roth to Bloom, 21 April 1976, package 1, box 1, Claire Bloom Collection 1200, Gotlieb Archival Research Center, Boston University.

70. Roth to Bloom, 9 June 1976, package 1, box 1, Claire Bloom Collection 1200, Gotlieb Archival Research Center, Boston University.

71. Roth to Bloom, 23 June 1976, package 1, box 1, Claire Bloom Collection 1200, Gotlieb Archival Research Center, Boston University.

72. Roth to Bloom, 25 June 1976, package 1, box 1, Claire Bloom Collection 1200, Gotlieb Archival Research Center, Boston University.

73. Roth to Anna Steiger, 30 July 1986, package 1, box 1, Claire Bloom Collection 1200, Gotlieb Archival Research Center, Boston University. Ten years earlier he told Bloom that Anna was welcomed anytime to the house in Connecticut and that he would even arrange for someone to meet her at Kennedy Airport and drive her back (13 June 1976).

74. Maletta and Roth began their relationship in the late 1970s, their on-again-off-again affair flourishing for the next sixteen years or so, especially during the summers and when he was home from London and Bloom away on tour or in London with her daughter. Intimacy, not mothering, was the key to this long-standing relationship, he writes. The critical and intimate deathbed scene in *Sabbath* with Drenka dying of cancer is all Maletta, he explains (NOT 208–9).

75. Roth to B. Bailey, 18 May 2015, Taylor/Roth Papers, Firestone Library, Princeton University.

76. Roth to Bennington College, 17 June 1991, box 13, folder 13, Correspondence, Roth Papers, LC.

77. Roth to Updike, 19 January 1976, Updike Papers, Houghton Library, Harvard University. For the record, Roth was writing from 18 East 81st Street, New York 10028.

78. Roth in Adam Begley, *Updike* (New York: HarperCollins, 2014), 279. For a synoptic discussion of the Roth-Updike friendship and rivalry, see Charles McGrath, "Roth/Updike," *Hudson Review*, Autumn 2019, https://hudsonreview.com/2019/10/roth-updike/#.XlNTD0p7k2w. It begins, "At the end of the last long conversation I had with Philip Roth, we wound up talking about John Updike. This wasn't unusual." Roth's competitiveness was offset by Updike's productivity, one almost egging the other on.

79. John Updike, "Recruiting Raw Nerves," *New Yorker*, 15 March 1993, 111.

80. Updike in Mick Brown, "John Updike: The Descent of Man," *Daily Telegraph*, 24 October 2008, https://www.telegraph.co.uk/culture/donotmigrate/3562536/John-Updike-the-descent-of-man.html. In the same article, Updike said, "Sex is like money; only too much is enough."

81. For the Roth letter, see James Plath, "Philip Roth Takes NY Times to Task over Begley Review," John Updike Society, 10 April 2014, https://blogs.iwu.edu/johnupdikesociety/2014/04/10/philip-roth-takes-nt-times-to-task-over-begley-review/. Dated 9 April, the *Times* printed Roth's letter on the 10th with the headline "Philip Roth, Still Writing (Letters, at Least)," *New York Times*, 10 April 2014, https://www.nytimes.com/2014/04/11/opinion/philip-roth-still-writing-letters-at-least.html. In his review, Garner makes the important point that one of Updike's most un-American habits was that he hid his suffering. By contrast, Roth exposes his and his characters', suffering on almost every page. See Dwight Garner, "A Writerly Life, beneath the Surface," *New York Times*, 8 April 2014, https://www.nytimes.com/2014/04/09/books/updike-adam-begleys-look-at-a-novelists-career.html;   Updike, "Recruiting Raw Nerves," 109.

82. In Begley, *Updike* 280. Review reprinted in Updike, *More Matter: Essays and Criticism* (New York: Knopf, 1999), 9.

83. The history of facts is as uncertain as their treatment. They began in the Renaissance, although historians differ on their origin, one group claiming it was double-entry bookkeeping in late fifteenth-century Venice that created "the fact," as discussed by Mary Poovey in *A History of the Modern Fact: Problems of Knowledge in the Sciences of Wealth and Society* (Chicago: University of Chicago Press, 1998). Other scholars believe it was the introduction of laws of evidence, leading to corroboration and documentation that established, first in the courts, and then in society, the idea of a "fact." Barbara J. Shapiro develops this theory in *A Culture of Fact: England, 1550–1720* (Ithaca: Cornell University Press, 2000), arguing that legal discourse is the origin of the reliability and verifiability of fact. *How Well Do Facts Travel? The Dissemination of Reliable Knowledge*, edited by Peter Howlett and Mary S. Morgan (Cambridge: Cambridge University Press, 2011), pursues the life of facts. Earlier, Stephen Neale's *Facing Facts* (New York: Clarendon Press, 2001) untangled the philosophical issues surrounding representation and fact.

84. Roth, "A Bit of Jewish Mischief," *New York Times Book Review*, 7 March 1993, 1+.

85. On the narrative and postmodern elements of *Operation Shylock*, see Elaine B. Safer, "The Double, Comic Irony, and Postmodernism in Philip Roth's Operation Shylock," *Melus* 21.4 (1996): 157–72.

86. Taylor, *Here We Are*, 83, 84; OPS 183–84.

87. The fish store, at Amsterdam and 87th, where it's been for ninety years, was a Roth hangout, with its brown-and-beige wallpaper and pictures of old New Orleans. Its cold cases displayed gefilte fish, potato salad, blintzes, latkes, herring, and smoked fish, and its marble counters were piled up with bialys, babka, rugelach, and bagels, forming a Jewish paradise on the Upper West Side. Roth met the U.S. senator from New Jersey, Frank Lautenberg, there; other diners included Nora Ephron, Jerry Seinfeld, and Anthony Bourdain. When the current owner's grandfather shipped his smoked fish in the 1930s by U.S. mail, a label on the package said, "If Not Delivered in Three Days, Forget It." Reggie Nadelson, "The Store Where Philip Roth Ate Chopped Herring," *T, New York Times Style Magazine*, 4 June 2019, https://www.nytimes.com/2019/06/04/t-magazine/barney-greengrass.html.

Chapter 10

1. One of the two psychiatrists was Dr. William Frosch.
2. Vivian Gornick, *The Men in My Life* (Boston: MIT Press, Boston Review of Books, 2008), 118.
3. Vivian Gornick, "Why Do These Men Hate Women? American Novelists and Misogyny," *Village Voice*, 6 December 1976, 12–13, 15, rpt. *Essays in Feminism* (New York: Harper & Row, 1978), 189–99.
4. Gornick, *The Men in My Life*, 124, 125.
5. Roth's annotated document is forty-six pages long. Blake Bailey is the source for Roth's photo album of his girlfriends. See Bailey, 3 April 2019, "Roth Remembered," Levy Center for Biography, CUNY,https://www.youtube.com/watch?v=6Ke-wOLc8wo. James Atlas chaired.
6. Roth to Kazin, 31 October 1989, Berg Collection, NYPL.
7. Kazin, *Alfred Kazin's Journals*, 352.
8. Alfred Kazin, "Roth's Remarkable Patrimony: Comic and Heartbreaking Saga," 1991(?), Kazin Papers, Berg Collection, NYPL.
9. Roth, "Arena," BBC 2 TV, 19 March 1993. The show is 58 minutes 33 seconds long.
10. Alfred Kazin, "Arena," BBC 2 TV, 19 March 1993.
11. Robert Pinsky, "Letting Go," *New York Times*, 6 January 1991, http://movies2.nytimes.com/books/98/10/11/specials/roth-patrimony.html.
12. Kazin, ca. 1993, Berg Collection, NYPL.
13. *Diagnostic and Statistical Manual of Mental Disorders*, 3rd. ed., rev. (*DSM–III–R*) (Washington, D.C.: American Psychiatric Association, 1987), 347, 348–51. The *DSM–IV* appeared in 1994, the year after Roth's treatment.
14. Roth to Bloom, 5 April 1976 and 30 April 1993; Bloom to Roth, 31 August 1993, package 1, box 1, Claire Bloom Collection 1200, Gotlieb Archival Research Center, Boston University.
15. Bloom to Roth, 31 August 1993.
16. Roth to Bloom, September 1993(?), package 1, box 1, Claire Bloom Collection 1200, Gotlieb Archival Research Center, Boston University.
17. Roth to Janet Malcolm, 5 November 1993, YCAL MSS 935, Malcolm Papers, Beinecke Rare Book and Manuscript Library, Yale University.
18. Roth to Janet Malcolm. 5 November 1993.
19. Roth to Janet Malcolm, 5 November 1993.
20. Roth to Bloom, 19 October 1993, package 1, box 1, Claire Bloom Collection 1200, Gotlieb Archival Research Center, Boston University.
21. Roth to Bloom, 14 December 1993. package 1, box 1, Claire Bloom Collection 1200, Gotlieb Archival Research Center, Boston University.
22. Roth to Bloom, 14 December 1993.
23. Roth to Bloom, 14 December 1993.
24. Roth in Ben Taylor, *Here We Are*, 156. The individual was Dr. Julia Golier, who would in fact form a new "playful relationship" with Roth, who misleadingly suggested that they only met accidentally in New York in 1994. Golier alludes to an earlier meeting

without specifics before the New York sidewalk encounter. See Golier, *Philip Roth in Memory* (New York: Library of America 2019), 57.

25. Taylor, *Here We Are*, 158.

26. Maletta Pfeiffer to Roth, 30 October 1993, MC 704, folder 42, Honor Moore Papers, Schlesinger Library, Radcliffe Institute, Harvard University.

27. Roth to Bloom, 15 March 1995, 15 May 1995, Claire Bloom Collection #1200, Gotlieb Archival Research Center, Boston University. package 2, box 1.

28. Julia Golier ["Philip Roth"], *Philip Roth in Memory* (New York: Library of America, 2019), 58.

29. Roth to Bloom, 21 May 1995, Claire Bloom Collection #1200, Gotlieb Archival Research Center, Boston University, package 2, box 1.

30. "Anonymous letter," Malcolm Papers, YCAL MSS 935, Beinecke Rare Book and Manuscript Library, Yale University; Martin Garbus to Ms. Francine du Plessix Gray, 1 December 1993, Malcolm Papers, YCAL MSS 935, Beinecke Rare Book and Manuscript Library, Yale University. For a discussion of the impact of the letter in *The Human Stain* see José Carlos del Ama, "Everyone Knows: Public Opinion in Philip Roth's Contemporary Tragedy, *The Human Stain*," *Philip Roth Studies* 5, no. 1 (2009): 93–110.

31. Roth to Janet Malcolm, 6 August 1994, Malcolm Papers, YCAL MSS 935, Beinecke Rare Book and Manuscript Library, Yale University.

32. Roth to Bailey, 18 May 2015, Taylor/Roth archive, Firestone Library, Princeton.

33. Roth to Rachael Hallawell, 18 January 1988, package 1, box 1, Claire Bloom Collection 1200, Gotlieb Archival Research Center, Boston University. Like Anna, Hallawell became a singer and performed at Glyndebourne in the late 1980s.

34. Daphne Merkin, "Acting the Victim: Claire Bloom vs. Philip Roth," *New Yorker*, 4 November 1996, rpt. in *Dreaming of Hitler* (New York: Harcourt Brace, 1997), 195–204. Sarah Kerr, in an intriguing essay, compares the uncanny similarities between Bloom's autobiography and Mia Farrow's *What Falls Away: A Memoir* published in 1997. See Kerr, "Sisters Under the Mink," *Slate*, 5 March 1997, https://slate.com/culture/1997/03/sisters-under-the-mink.html. A further parallel is a possible connection between Roth's dumping Bloom and the situation of Harry Block and his ex-wife Lucy in Woody Allen's *Deconstructing Harry*, a parallel pursued by Alex Abramovich in "The Estranged Twins, Woody Allen and Philip Roth: Separated at Birth?," *Slate*, 22 August 2001, https://slate.com/culture/2001/08/the-estranged-twins.html. The malice of the Roth-Bloom divorce was in some ways duplicated by the Woody Allen–Mia Farrow split.

35. Zachery Leader, *The Life of Saul Bellow*, vol. 2: *Love and Strife 1965–2005* (London: Cape, 2019), 476; Saul Bellow, *Letters*, ed. Benjamin Taylor (New York: Viking, 2010), 467–68.

36. Pierpont, *Roth Unbound*, 283.

37. Bellow, *Letters*, 41; Leader, *The Life of Saul Bellow*, 2:608–9.

38. Saul Bellow, "I Got a Scheme!," *New Yorker*, 25 April 2005.

39. Roth, "On Our Gang," RMY 46.

40. Pierpont, *Roth Unbound*, 189–90.

41. Roth, *Sabbath's Theater*, boxes 202–19, Roth Papers, LC. In shaping his materials, Roth was not above drawing from actual sources. The letters written to Roseanna by her father before he killed himself were drawn from letters Maletta's father wrote to her (ST 250–54). The setting has changed but the content is similar.

42. Roth to Janet Malcolm, 6 August 1994, YCAL MSS 935, Malcolm Papers, Beinecke Rare Book and Manuscript Library, Yale University.

43. Kazin to Roth, 3 January 1995 and Roth to Kazin, 17 January 1995, Berg Collection, NYPL.

44. For reactions to *Sabbath's Theater*, see Harold Bloom, *Genius: A Mosaic of One Hundred Exemplary Creative Minds* (New York: Warner Books, 2003), 207; William Pritchard, "Sabbath's Theater," *New York Times*, 10 September 1995, https://www. nytimes.com/1995/09/10/books/sabbaths-theater.html; Frank Kermode, "Howl," *New York Review of Books*, 16 November 1995, https://www.nybooks.com/articles/ 1995/11/16/howl/. Kermode values the novel's energy and range, plus the depth of its obscenity. To read Roth's valedictory speech, including the passage from the novel, see PR80 51–71. On his final public lecture, see Jennifer Schuessler, "Philip Roth Says He Has Given His Last Public Reading," *New York Times*, 9 May 2014, https://www. nytimes.com/2014/05/10/books/philip-roth-says-he-has-given-his-last-public-reading.html. The actual date of Roth's talk was 8 May 2014.

45. David Lodge, "Sick with Desire," *New York Review of Books*, 5 July 2001, https://www. nybooks.com/articles/2001/07/05/sick-with-desire/. The essay is actually a review of Roth's *The Dying Animal*. Lodge admires Roth's productivity and energetic characters, noting that earlier the boastful Sabbath had "fitted in the rest of his life around fucking while most men do the reverse." Roth on retitling the novel in Schuessler, "Philip Roth Says He Has Given His Last Public Reading."

46. For Bellow's remark and the controversy see Leader, *Life of Saul Bellow*, 2:507–9; Bellow "Papuans and Zulus," *New York Times*, 10 March 1994, http://movies2. nytimes.com/books/00/04/23/specials/bellow-papuans.html. For James Atlas's comment on the comment which he recorded and printed and the misquotation, see Atlas, *The Shadow in the Garden: A Biographer's Tale* (New York: Pantheon, 2017), 178–79, 261–63.

47. Sam Lipsyte, "Philip Roth's 'Toxic Masculinity,'" *New York Times*, 23 May 2018, https://www.nytimes.com/2018/05/23/opinion/philip-roth-toxic-masculinity.html. For the phrase "dominating narcissism," see ST 91.

48. David Remnick, "Into the Clear: Philip Roth," in *Reporting, Writings from the New Yorker* (New York: Knopf, 2006), 121.

49. In the 1983 *Vogue* interview, Roth emphasizes that the only difference between a writer and anyone else is imagination. What separates him from others is that he can make things up. Having a self alone won't do it; you need that other thing, which he calls imagination, citing Tolstoy, who said, "You can see a street fight and write War and Peace." Medwick, "A Meeting of Arts & Minds."

50. Roth's anger at Gray may partly be jealously. Her Continentalism, good looks, and sense of style, plus her public identity as a fashionable, readable writer who exuded sophistication, may have contributed to his growing dislike of her, intensified by

her support of Bloom rather than himself. For many years she and her husband were close friends, but once she supported Bloom, she became Enemy Number One. For a profile of Gray, see Adam Gopnik, "Becoming Francine du Plessix Gray," *New Yorker,* 15 January 2019, https://www.newyorker.com/culture/postscript/becoming-francine-du-plessix-gray.

51. Just after Maggie's funeral in May 1968, Roth supposedly went to the spot in Central Park where she was killed to visit the scene of his release. Taylor, *Here We Are,* 55.

52. For the Roth-Updike exchange, see "Slight Revision," *New York Review of Books,* 4 March 1999, https://www.nybooks.com/articles/1999/03/04/slight-revision/.

53. See Christopher Bonanos, "Philip Roth's Biographer Has a Hair-Raising Claire Bloom Story to Share," *Vulture,* 29 May 2018, https://www.vulture.com/2018/05/philip-roth-biographer-has-a-hair-raising-claire-bloom-story.html.

54. Marion Winik, "Mrs. Portnoy's Complaint," *Los Angeles Times,* 13 October 1996, https://www.latimes.com/Paperss/la-xpm-1996-10-13-bk-53235-story.html. Bloom kept the ring and wore it for years, until a friend remarked that as long as she wore it, she would never be free. In response, she sold it almost immediately. Stuart Jeffries, "Screen Gods, Guilt and Glamour: Actor Claire Bloom on Her Life in the Limelight," *Guardian,* 23 December 2016, https://www.theguardian.com/film/2016/dec/23/screen-gods-guilt-and-glamour-actor-claire-bloom-on-her-life-in-the-limelight.

55. Zoë Heller, "An Emerald Ring, a Portable Heater and $150 an Hour," *London Review of Books* 19.4 (20 February 1997), https://www.lrb.co.uk/v19/n04/zoe-heller/an-emerald-ring-a-portable-heater-and-150-an-hour.

56. Roth to Kazin, 28 October 1996, Kazin Papers, Berg Collection, NYPL.

57. Roth to Kazin, 28 October 1996.

58. On parallels between Roth's novel, Eva's book, and Howard Hughes's 1949 movie, *I Married a Communist,* see Ira Nadel, "*I Married a Communist*: The Book! The Movie! The Communist Threat!," *Philip Roth Studies* 16.2 (Fall 2020): 3–15.

59. Other daughters who deconstruct male ideals of a virtuous or heroic past are Consuela in *The Dying Animal,* young enough to be Kepesh's daughter, and Marcia Steinberg in *Nemesis,* who encourages Bucky to become a counselor at Indian Hill camp, where he contracts polio. She is the daughter of Dr. Steinberg, who repeatedly offers advice to Bucky.

60. Roth, having explored the Amy-Lonoff connection in the novel, was shocked to learn from the Malamud biography that he in fact had had a long affair with a student. Two other Malamud habits: the writer asked his wife to prepare him half an egg, as Lonoff does, and during a visit to Malamud, Roth once glimpsed a young Bennington student sitting on a floor arranging his papers (Pierpont, *Roth Unbound,* 109–10). On the matter of Anne Frank, her diary, and her introduction to the novel, Roth prepared a seven-page letter to his friend Jack Miles (see Pierpont, *Roth Unbound,* 115–19). Malamud's daughter, Janna Malamud Smith, writes that even her mother had an affair at Bennington. Malamud's novel *Dubin's Lives* is about a married biographer who takes his young girlfriend to Venice, where he thinks he sees his daughter with an older man. He justifies his behavior with the idea that the age difference between his daughter and her lover is even greater than that between himself and his lover.

Malamud's daughter, a psychotherapist, said that her father constantly struggled with his life and that he wanted privacy: "One of the functions of writing is to transmute shame.... Writing was a way to cloak his shame." Dinitia Smith, "Bernard Malamud's Daughter Finally Tells His Secrets," *New York Times*, 9 March 2006, https://www. nytimes.com/2006/03/09/books/bernard-malamuds-daughter-finally-tells-his-secrets.html.

61. For the comment on Bellow and his wives, see Smith, "Bernard Malamud's Daughter."

62. When Lowenstein died, Roth spoke at his funeral and published "In Memory of a Friend, Teacher and Mentor" in the *New York Times* of 20 April 2013,https://www. nytimes.com/2013/04/21/opinion/sunday/in-memory-of-a-friend-teacher-and-mentor.html . Roth sent Lowenstein a final draft of *American Pastoral* so that he could correct any errors dealing with early twentieth-century Newark. In his piece, Roth also reminded many that Lowenstein was forced out of the Newark school system for six years as a result of an anti-Communist inquiry but that he was finally able to win reinstatement.

63. Philip Roth, "After Eight Books," RMY 86.

64. Robert Brown, "Philip Roth Gave Me an A Minus," *Pennsylvania Gazette*, 23 August 2018, www.thepenngazette.com/philip-roth-gave-me-an-a-minus.

65. Jill Haber Palone, "Philip Roth and Me," *Pennsylvania Gazette*, 28 August 2018, www. thepenngazette.com/philip-roth-and-me/.

66. Palone, "Philip Roth and Me."

67. She met Roth in 1999 outside Dodge Hall at Columbia when he was to be a visitor in David Plante's writing class. She guided him to the class, even though she wasn't in it, although she had permission to attend. She was noticeable for a number of reasons, not the least for her figure and breasts. A week later, Roth and Hooper met for breakfast. She was nearly six feet tall with red hair and twenty-four; Roth was sixty-six. She went to Australia and on her return, they became a couple. She had written a novel which he thought first-rate and showed it to his agent, Andrew Wylie, who loved it and sold American and English rights.

68. Prevatt was an unlikely Roth hero and romantic partner. She had experienced hardship, humiliation, and impoverishment. She was the mother of two children she had in her teens, brought up by her mother, who despised her. She was also an alcoholic and may have worked as a prostitute in Florida after running away from home. Roth met her in the Cornwall Bridge post office in 1999 when she was in her early thirties, running the office of a local electrician and working at a raw milk farm. With reddish brown hair and striking posture, she was stunning. He didn't like her male friends, however, collectively turning them into Les Farley and his Vietnam buddies in *The Human Stain*. She was not broken the way Maggie or Bloom were, he writes, but possessed a kind of animalistic sensuality. He also prevented her from a possible suicide: talking to him on the phone one evening, she told him she had a gun. He used a cell phone to call the state police. Yet she died alone in a Torrington, Connecticut, motel after serving six months in a women's prison for multiple drunk-driving offenses.

69. Coleman Silk in *The Human Stain* is also seventy-one; he has an affair with Faunia Farley, thirty-four, described by Silk as "an ignitable woman."

70. Lisa Halliday, *Asymmetry* (New York: Simon and Schuster, 2018), 5.

71. An early draft of the scene had the narrator succeed in connecting with the jogger; the finished draft shows that he failed to pick her up (NOT 239).

72. Halliday, *Asymmetry*, 33.

73. In Table 2 of his recent study *The Philip Roth We Don't Know: From #MeToo, to Race, to Metempsychosis* (2021), Jacques Berlinerblau lists what he calls "age-dissimilar romance" in Roth's novels from 1972 to 2009.

74. Roth to David Rieff, 31 March 1987, FSG Papers, NYPL. On the matter of children in Roth, Alan Lelchuk suggests that Roth may have developed Merry Levov in *American Pastoral* from Nugget in *American Mischief*. (Lelchuk to the author, 13–14 June 2020). Nugget is a fourteen-year-old virgin who joins a commune in Cambridge, Massachusetts, and becomes attached to the older Lenny Pincus, a radical. She suggests sexual abuse to Lenny in describing sitting on her father's knee when five. And in a sentence anticipating Merry in *American Pastoral*, Lelchuk writes, "She was so incredibly reticent and shy, except when speaking about her father; then confused fear wrinkled that small forehead." Lelchuk, *American Mischief*, 255, 272.

75. Roth in Charles McGrath, "Goodbye Newark, the Place Roth Never Left," *New York Times*, 21 March 2013, C1.

76. Christine Bohlen, "Rare Unfurling of the Reluctant Philip Roth," *New York Times*, 15 September 2011, https://www.nytimes.com/2011/09/16/arts/16iht-Roth16.html.

77. "On the Ghost Writer," WR? 376. Others have noted the American Roth. Ross Posnock in sections of *Philip Roth's Rude Truth* and Andy Connolly in *Philip Roth and the American Liberal Tradition* address links: the former partially considers Hawthorne, Emerson, and James within the larger theme of Roth's contested maturity as a writer, while the latter focuses on American political culture and its influence on Roth from the New Deal forward.

78. Roth in "Writers of the Century," in Debra Shostak, *Philip Roth: Countertexts, Counterlives* (Columbia: University of South Carolina Press, 2004), 236.

79. Saul Bellow, *Ravelstein* (New York: Viking, 2000), 23.

80. Nadine Gordimer to Roth, 17 June 2000, unprocessed, box 14, p. 2, Roth Papers, LC.

81. Roth to Gordimer, 9 July 2000, unprocessed, box 14, p. 1, Roth Papers, LC

82. Gordimer to Roth, 27 August 2000, unprocessed, box 14, p. 2, Roth Papers, LC.

83. Roth to Updike, 12 June 1996 and 28 June 1996, MS Am 1793, Updike Papers, Houghton Library, Harvard University.

84. Renata Adler, *Pitch Dark* (1983; New York: New York Review of Books, 2013), 144.

85. Judith Thurman, "Roth on Trump," *New Yorker*, 30 January 2017, https://www.newyorker.com/magazine/2017/01/30/philip-roth-e-mails-on-trump.

86. In the spring of 1994, Roth went down to the Jersey Shore to scout locations for Sabbath's trip home. He was in such pain, however, he could not drive himself and hired a driver to drive his car while he stretched out across the back seat. He walked as best he could when they got there; on the drive back to New York, he again rested

across the back seat. Roth, "Illness," 30, Taylor/Roth Papers, Firestone Library, Princeton University.

87. Pierpont, *Roth Unbound*, 271.

88. Roth and a partner regularly danced to Susan Kennedy's *Big Band Hall of Fame* on WMNR radio from Monroe, Connecticut, each Saturday night.

89. Roth in Sam Leith, "Philip Roth Attacks Orgy of Narcissism post September 11," *Telegraph*, 5 October 2002, https://www.telegraph.co.uk/education/4792421/Philip-Roth-attacks-orgy-of-narcissism-post-Sept-11.html.

90. Cynthia Haven, "On the Ghost Writer," in WR? 374–78.

91. Adam Gopnik, "The Patriot," *New Yorker*, 13 November 2017, 74–77.

Chapter 11

1. Suicide is a theme appearing as early as Lucy Nelson in *When She Was Good* and Ronald Nimkin in *Portnoy's Complaint*, echoed in *The Professor of Desire* in the attempted suicide of Elisabeth Elverskog, one of Kepesh's two Swedish girlfriends, and Millicent Kramer in *Everyman*. A section of *Portnoy's Complaint* even considers the possibility of suicide by a number of Portnoy's eligible women (PC 104–5). In *The Humbling*, Roth devotes several pages to suicide in drama recalled by Simon Axler (HUM 38–39). Roth himself considered it several times in the late 1980s because of his insufferable knee and back pain and revealed to Ben Taylor that in a safe in his New York apartment he had a drug and a rope in case things got desperate.

2. George Plimpton described the Jersey style in a 2003 interview, highlighting its "habitues": "The mob, great prizefighters, the prisons, the world of Far Hills, the gamblers, the shore, the corridor between Philadelphia and New York—there is this extraordinary framework that the state's writers have had throughout American history." Plimpton in Gregory Jordan, "A School of Literature That's Called New Jersey," *New York Times*, 3 August 2003, https://www.nytimes.com/2003/08/03/nyregion/a-school-of-literature-that-s-called-new-jersey.html.

3. "Overview," *New Jersey Department of Transportation Specification Style Guidelines*, 2007, https://www.nj.gov/transportation/eng/specs/2007/styleguide/styleguide.shtm. Also see Gregory Jordan and Ira Nadel, "Jersey Boys: Philip Roth and Bruce Springsteen: from American Pastoral to Born to Run," *Journal of English Language & Literature* 65.3 (Sept. 2019): 425–40. Plain-speaking, transparent writing focusing on the mundane might summarize the Jersey Style seen in the abbreviated, direct language of Herman Roth in *The Facts* or Swede Levov's father in *American Pastoral* lamenting in vivid but simple language the ruin of Newark (AP 164). The content of the Jersey Style is often the hard-working life of individuals surrounded by industrial skylines, not the landscape of Short Hills. Roth links the Jersey Style with symbols of larger American dilemmas.

4. Roth, of course, relied on other styles broadly defined as Jamesian when he started, overturned by the exuberant psychological outbursts of Portnoy and his successors,

including Mickey Sabbath. Zuckerman offered a slightly more expository method in *The Anatomy Lesson* and the American Trilogy, until a more diminished tone or minor key took over in the last three books.

5. Compare the sentence on Sandy and how he uses his allowance to obtain art supplies or the drama of Mr. Cucuzza and his gun in *The Plot Against America* (283–84) with the somewhat objective, distanced description of the kosher slaughtering of animals in *Indignation* or Bucky Cantor's disappointment over not going off to war, left to fight only on "the battlefield of his playground" in *Nemesis* (IND 158–59; NEM 173). Anguish has been tempered as tone manages energy. Replacing the violence and exuberance of Roth's earlier sentences is a less emotive and more managed style, intensified by Cantor, who "by and large ... had the aura of ineradicable failure about him as he spoke of all that he'd been silent about for years" (NEM 246).

6. Compare Roth's description of the New York deli at the end of *Operation Shylock* (378–79) with Mr. Messner's kosher butcher shop in *Indignation* (2–8) to distinguish the two Roth styles.

7. Roth, "The Story behind 'The Plot Against America,'" *New York Times Book Review*, 19 September 2004, https://www.nytimes.com/2004/09/19/books/review/the-story-behind-the-plot-against-america.html.

8. Jeffrey Brown, "The Plot Against America," *PBS Online NewsHour*, 27 October 2004, http://www.pbs.org/newshour/bb/entertainment/july-dec04/philiproth_10-17.html.

9. Imagining something that did not happen carries over to *Nemesis*: yes, there was a polio epidemic in America, but no, not in Newark.

10. Roth to David Rieff, 31 March 1987. Box 676, Farrar, Straus and Giroux archive, Ms. Division, New York Public Library.

11. Jeffrey Brown, "Conversation: Philip Roth," *PBS Online NewsHour*, 10 November 2004, http://www.pbs.org/newshour/bb/entertainment/july-dec04roth_11-10.html.

12. J. M. Coetzee, "Philip Roth, *The Plot Against America*," in *Inner Workings: Literary Essays 2000–2005* (New York: Vintage, 2007), 241.

13. Because Roth was curious about the Mormon religion, the doctor gave him the *Book of Mormon* and asked for his reactions. Three weeks later, Roth told him it was "soporific" and that he would rather read *Madame Bovary* every Sunday. The doctor explained that in the Mormon religion, one is reunited with one's parents for eternity after death. Roth's response? "Couldn't I just phone once a week?" See Roth, "Medical History," 23, Taylor/Roth Papers, Firestone Library, Princeton University.

14. The result of her Antarctica trip was *Antarctica: Life on the Ice* (2007). Her new work is an edited collection, *When Birds Are Near: Literary Bird Tales* (2020).

15. Keith Gessen, "His Jewish Problem," *New York Magazine*, 16 September 2004, http://nymag.com/nymetro/arts/books/reviews/9902.

16. Sandy had had a second emergency bypass operation in April 1997 in New York while visiting a grandchild. He recuperated in Roth's apartment. His first was thirteen years earlier, Roth told Bellow; the replacement valves usually lasted ten years. Roth to Bellow, 22 April 1997, box 3, folder 1, Roth Papers, LC. Ben Taylor was with Roth in Chicago when Sandy died after struggles with heart disease, prostate cancer, and osteoporosis (Taylor, *Here We Are*, 72). Roth at the time revealed that his brother

and first wife had adopted two boys and that Roth met with the birth mother of Seth, the elder of the two, and took the newborn to Sandy and Trudy, an event repeated in *Letting Go*.

17. See Leader, *The Life of Saul Bellow*, 2: 396.
18. Leader, *The Life of Saul Bellow*, 2: 607.
19. Pierpont, *Roth Unbound*, 284.
20. Krasnik, "Philip Roth."
21. Pierpont, *Roth Unbound*, 286–87.
22. Leader, *The Life of Saul Bellow*, 2: 641.
23. Leader, *The Life of Saul Bellow*, 2: 641.
24. Greg Bellow, *Saul Bellow's Heart: A Son's Memoir* (New York: Bloomsbury, 2013), 214.
25. Leader, *The Life of Saul Bellow*, 2: 641.
26. Roth's burial, on 28 May 2018 at Bard College, was not. He had died in Manhattan on 22 May.
27. Pierpont, *Roth Unbound*, 293–94.
28. As Taylor points out in *Here We Are*, Roth had in fact become impotent by 2007 as a result of his various drugs. I am indebted to Taylor for generously allowing me to see a galley of the book, which appeared in May 2020.
29. Molly Fischer, "The Place of the Flavored Vodkas," *Paris Review*, 1 June 2011, https://www.theparisreview.org/blog/2011/06/01/the-place-of-the-flavored-vodkas/.
30. Chen, "Former Upper West Side Apartment."
31. Roth also visited a kosher butcher in Brooklyn to observe the smells, the customers, and the conditions of the neighborhood. See Benjamin Taylor, "Philip Roth Interview," *The Telegraph*, 10 May 2011, https://www.telegraph.co.uk/books/authors/philip-roth-interview-dont-want-caged-reality/.
32. Robert Wiener, "Remembering 'Newark Royalty,'" *New Jersey Jewish News*, 30 May 2018, https://njjewishnews.timesofisrael.com/remembering-newark-royalty/.
33. Pierpont, *Roth Unbound*, 27.
34. In a different context, but with the same degree of guilt, was Bruce Springsteen's relation to his father, as he explained in *Born to Run* (2016), a book favored by Roth. Springsteen, in turn, praised the American Trilogy. See Ira Nadel, "Jersey Boys: Philip Roth and Bruce Springsteen from *American Pastoral* to *Born to Run*," *Journal of English Language & Literature* 65.3 (2019): 425–40.
35. Pierpont, *Roth Unbound*, 301.
36. Brown, "Conversation."
37. For details on Caro Llewellyn, see "Multiple Sclerosis Took Away Former Sydney Writers' Festival Director Caro Llewellyn's Ability to Read," Australian Broadcasting Corporation, 19 April 2019, https://www.abc.net.au/news/2019-04-20/caro-llewellyn-diving-into-glass-multiple-sclerosis-reading/11028444. For details of her time with Roth see Caro Llewellyn, "My Relationship with Philip Roth," *Sydney Morning Herald*, 5 March 2019, https://www.smh.com.au/entertainment/books/my-journey-with-philip-roth-i-loved-that-he-made-me-laugh-20190304-h1by7j.html.
38. In his account of his various women, Roth notes the prevalence of suicide: Ann Mudge attempted suicide, Maletta Pfeiffer's father committed suicide when she was

ten or twelve, while the London journalist's father committed suicide when she was a child; Barbara Sproul's father committed suicide when she was in college.

39. Roth, "My Brother Sandy," *Web of Stories*, 2011, https://www.webofstories.com/play/philip.roth/4.

40. Sandy Roth married in 1954 and shortly afterward adopted two boys, Seth and Jonathan. After his wife died in 1970, he struggled to raise his two sons, made more challenging by the move to Chicago in the mid-1970s. He remarried in Chicago.

41. Wieseltier, "The Explored Recesses," *The New Republic* 10 January 2010, https://newrepublic.com/article/72334/the-explored-recesses.

42. Pierpont, *Roth Unbound*, 311.

43. Roth owned two copies of the novel, one heavily annotated. Both will be in his personal library, soon to be available at the Newark Public Library. Rosemary Steinbaum, webinar on *Nemesis,* 25 June 2020, Newark Public Library.

44. Roth in John Heilpern, "The Gripes of Roth," *Vanity Fair*, 1 November 2010, https://www.vanityfair.com/news/2010/11/philip-roth-interview.

45. James Joyce, *Ulysses*, ed. Hans Walter Gabler (New York: Vintage, 1986). References are to the episode and line number: 13.746, 13.1253–54.

46. Roth in Nelly Kaprielian, "In Which Philip Roth Announces His Retirement (in English)," *Paris Review*, 13 November 2012, https://www.theparisreview.org/blog/2012/11/13/in-which-philip-roth-announces-his-retirement-in-english/. This is the full interview.

47. On Roth's supposed request to destroy his personal files, see Hillary Kelly, "Philip Roth's Empty Threat: 'Burn My Papers,'" *New Republic,* 14 November 2012, https://newrepublic.com/article/110151/phili-roth-empty-threat-b.

48. Roth in Kaprielian, "In Which Philip Roth Announces His Retirement."

49. Roth in Kaprielian, "In Which Philip Roth Announces His Retirement."

50. Roth in Josyane Savigneau, "Philip Roth," *Le Monde,* 14 February 2013, https://www.lemonde.fr/livres/article/2013/02/14/philip-roth-i-don-t-wish-to-be-a-slave-any-longer-to-the-stringent-exigencies-of-literature_1831662_3260.html.

51. Contents List, "Taylor Collection of Philip Roth materials," Finding Aid, C1609: 9, Dept. of Rare Books and Special Collections, Princeton University Library.

52. Blake Bailey, "Roth Remembered," Levy Center for Biography, CUNY, New York, 3 April 2019, https://www.youtube.com/watch?v=6Ke-wOLc8wo.

53. Taylor, *Here We Are*, 161.

54. Bernard Malamud, *Dubin's Lives* (New York: Farrar, Straus and Giroux, 1979), 65.

55. On Roth preparing documents for his official biographer, see Ian Burrell, "Philip Roth Reveals His Last Great Project—His Own Biography," *The Independent,* 19 May 2004, https://www.independent.co.uk/arts-entertainment/books/news/philip-roth-reveals-his-last-great-project-his-own-autobiography-9398912.html.

56. The list contains only one female author:

- *Citizen Tom Paine* by Howard Fast, first read at age 14
- *Finnley Wren* by Philip Wylie, first read at age 16
- *Look Homeward Angel* by Thomas Wolfe, first read at age 17
- *Catcher in the Rye* by J.D. Salinger, first read at age 20

- *The Adventures of Augie March* by Saul Bellow, first read at age 21
- *A Farewell to Arms* by Ernest Hemingway, first read at age 23
- *The Assistant* by Bernard Malamud, first read at age 24
- *Madame Bovary* by Gustave Flaubert, first read at age 25
- *The Sound and the Fury* by William Faulkner, first read at age 25
- *The Trial* by Franz Kafka, first read at age 27
- *The Fall* by Albert Camus, first read at age 30
- *Crime and Punishment* by Fyodor Dostoyevsky, first read at age 35
- *Anna Karenina* by Leo Tolstoy, first read at age 37
- *Cheri* by Colette, first read at age 40
- *Street of Crocodiles* by Bruno Schulz, first read at age 41

See Talya Zax, "At His Library in Newark, Philip Roth Names 15 of His Favorite Books," *The Forward*, 26 October 2016, https://forward.com/culture/352704/at-his-library-in-newark-philip-roth-names-15-of-his-favorite-books/.

57. He duplicated the process in New York when he purchased the apartment below and another studio adjacent to his to ensure some peace and quiet when he wrote.

58. These and other details are from Talya Zax's useful "Philip Roth Doesn't Live Here Anymore."

59. Roth in Zax, "Philip Roth Doesn't Live Here Anymore."

60. The woody shrub is also known as a Contorta, a variation of *Corylus avellana,* itself commonly known as the hazel or European filbert.

61. Murdock also reported that in Roth's bedroom was an original copy of *Portnoy's Complaint* inscribed "January 1969. To my mother and father. With all my love and filial gratitude." Zax's "Philip Roth Doesn't Live Here Anymore."

62. Pierpont, *Roth Unbound*, 322.

63. Curiously, she met her husband, William Bornmann, also on the street when they passed each other walking in opposite directions on East 91st. After some hesitation, he decided to turn around, run after her, and introduce himself. Two years later, they married. See "Weddings; Julia Golier, William Bornmann," *New York Times*, 10 March 2002, Section 9:10.

64. Julia Golier, ["Philip Roth"], in *Philip Roth in Memory* (New York: Library of America, 2019), 60–62.

65. Golier, ["Philip Roth"], 60.

66. Thurman's journalistic interests were initially biographical; she published her account of Isak Dinesen, for which she won a National Book Award, in 1982 and then *Secrets of the Flesh: A Life of Colette,* also praised by Roth, in 1999. Both works displayed intellectual and emotional acuity. She also maintained an interest in fashion and its relation to gender and sexuality, writing pieces on fashion for the *New Yorker* after she published her Collette biography. The collected essays appear in her volume *Cleopatra's Nose: 39 Varieties of Desire* (2007). For Thurman on fashion, see Francesca Ganata, "'Women's Work': An interview with Judith Thurman," *Design Observer*, 1 April 2013, https://designobserver.com/feature/womens-work-an-interview-with-judith-thurman/37799.

67. Judith Thurman, "Philip Roth E-Mails on Trump," *New Yorker*, 30 January 2017, https://www.newyorker.com/magazine/2017/01/30/philip-roth-e-mails-on-trump.

68. Louise Erdrich, "A Letter from Philip Roth," *New Yorker*, 24 May 2018, https://www.newyorker.com/culture/culture-desk/a-letter-from-philip-roth.

69. Charles McGrath, "Goodbye, Frustration: Pen Put Aside, Roth Talks," *New York Times*, 17 November 2012, https://www.nytimes.com/2012/11/18/books/struggle-over-philip-roth-reflects-on-putting-down-his-pen; AL 238, 281.

70. Roth, "An Open Letter to Wikipedia," *New Yorker*, 6 September 2012, https://www.newyorker.com/books/page-turner/an-open-letter-to-wikipedia.

71. Roth to Updike, 12 June 1996 and 24 June 1996, Box 371, MS Am 1793, Updike Papers, Houghton Library, Harvard University.

72. For a brief account of the event, see Judith Thurman, "Philip Roth Is Good for the Jews," *New Yorker*, 28 May 2014, https://www.newyorker.com/books/page-turner/philip-roth-is-good-for-the-jews.

73. Judith Thurman, "Remembering Roth," Levy Center for Biography, City University of New York, 3 April 2019, https://www.youtube.com/watch?v=6Ke-wOLc8wo. James Atlas chaired.

74. Taylor, *Here We Are*, 32.

75. Taylor, *Here We Are*, 51, 52.

76. Benjamin Taylor, "Editor's Note and Acknowledgments," in Saul Bellow, *Letters*, ed. Benjamin Taylor (New York: Viking, 2010), 557.

77. Taylor, *Here We Are*, 131.

78. Taylor, "Philip Roth Interview."

79. Taylor sold the material to Princeton, although there is currently a controversy over access to the Papers, the Literary Trust at odds with the university.

80. Taylor, *Here We Are*, 26–27.

81. Taylor says that when he and Roth decided to dine on the Upper East Side rather than the West because Roth thought he was less known there, a woman in the restaurant at the bar beckoned to Taylor and asked if that was Philip Roth. He nodded yes. She then gave him her card and said "Tell him I've got a classic six on Park and am available" (Taylor, *Here We Are*, 28).

82. Taylor, *Here We Are*, 136.

83. William O'Shaughnessy, "In Remembrance of Philip Roth," *Litchfield County Times*, 30 May 2018, http://www.countytimes.com/news/william-o-shaughnessy-in-remembrance-of-philip-roth/article_f1cec2b6-9022-52ab-9d82-f9c2a9bc21d5.html. The New York–born Charlie Kafferman, who worked in fashion before moving to Litchfield, died of cancer at eighty-eight on 6 July 2019. He and James O'Shea ran the West Street Grill for nearly thirty years. For Roth's lunch interview in October 2010 when he was seventy-seven, see Heilpern, "The Gripes of Roth." Prompting the meeting was the publication of *Nemesis*.

84. Taylor, *Here We Are*, 9–10.

85. Taylor, *Here We Are*, 11. Also see Benjamin Taylor, "Exit Ghost," *Harper's*, March 2019, https://harpers.org/Papers/2019/03/exit-ghost-philip-roth-benjamin-taylor/. This is a reprint of Taylor's remarks at the Roth Memorial of 25 September 2018 published in *Philip Roth in Memory* (New York: Library of America, 2019), 73–8.

86. Pierpont, *Roth Unbound*, 326.

87. Claudia Roth Pierpont, "Remembering Roth," Levy Center for Biography, City University of New York, 3 April 2019, https://www.youtube.com/watch?v=6Ke-wOLc8wo.

88. Eric Cortellessa, "The Story behind Philip Roth's Final Days," *Times of Israel*, 25 May 2018, https://www.timesofisrael.com/the-story-behind-philip-roths-final-days/; Taylor, *Here We Are*, 154.

89. Shortly after Roth's death, Taylor had to go to the Riverside Memorial Chapel, the Jewish funeral home at Amsterdam and 76th, to reidentify the body. There, he approached a serene-looking Roth, pulled up a chair, and said, "Here we are," here at the promised end. He instinctively wanted to tell him he was doing fine, "that he was a champ at being dead," bringing to it a professionalism equal to the way Roth had handled all his other tasks (*Here We Are*, 18).

90. Taylor, in *Philip Roth in Memory*, 74.

91. Taylor, *Here We Are*, 24.

92. Taylor, *Here We Are*, 156.

Chapter 12

1. Eleanor Wachtel, "The Incomparable Philip Roth," Writers & Company, CBC Radio (2009), 3 September 2017, https://www.cbc.ca/radio/writersandcompany/the-incomparable-philip-roth-looking-back-on-his-life-in-fiction-1.4270239.

2. Julian Tepper, "In Which Philp Roth Gave Me Life Advice," *Paris Review*, 25 December 2012, https://www.theparisreview.org/blog/2012/12/25/in-which-philip-roth-gave-me-life-advice/. Tepper later wrote a public apology admitting he was "setting himself up for a miserable existence." Tepper, "Julian Tepper: Leave Philip Roth Alone!," *Daily Beast*, 12 July 2017, https://www.thedailybeast.com/julian-tepper-leave-philip-roth-alone. In a 1983 *Vogue* interview, Roth explained, "The experience of writing is mostly saying, 'This is wrong. This word is wrong, this sentence is wrong, this page is wrong.'" Medwick, "A Meeting of Arts & Minds." William Carlos Williams, in a note about composing *Paterson* to his publisher James Laughlin, wrote, "I write and destroy, write and destroy" (27 December 1943). Hugh Witemeyer, ed., *William Carlos Williams and James Laughlin: Selected Letters* (New York: Norton, 1989), 95. Roth expressed a similar view in 2005 just before the appearance of *Everyman*. To a Danish journalist he conveyed anxiety over what might be his next book and said being a writer is a "horrible existence . . . filled with deprivation." Krasnik, "Philip Roth."

3. Caro Llewellyn, "My Relationship with Philip Roth," *Sydney Morning Herald*, 5 March 2019, https://www.smh.com.au/entertainment/books/my-journey-with-philip-roth-i-loved-that-he-made-me-laugh-20190304-h1by7j.html.

4. Roth on work in Nathan Heller, "Remembering Philip Roth, Literary Risk-Taker," *Vogue*, 23 May 2018, https://www.vogue.com/article/remembering-philip-roth-literary-risk-taker. Roth in Claudia Roth Pierpont, *Philip Roth in Memory* (New York: Library of America, 2019), 21.

5. Brad Parks, "Philip Roth's Newark Roots Inspired a Lifetime of Extraordinary Storytelling," NJ.com, 23 May 2018, https://www.nj.com/news/2018/05/philip_roth_whose_newark_roots_inspired_a_lifetime.html; Nicole Krauss, "The Presence of Philip Roth," *New Yorker*, 24 May 2018, https://www.newyorker.com/culture/culture-desk/the-presence-of-philip-roth.

6. Roth in Charles McGrath, "Goodbye, Frustration: Pen Put Aside, Roth Talks," *New York Times*, 17 November 2012, https://www.nytimes.com/2012/11/18/books/struggle-over-philip-roth-reflects-on-putting-down-his-pen.html; Roth in Krauss, "Presence." Roth continued, "It's an odd and comforting feeling of posthumousness, that all this is coming after my life but is still my life, a posthumousness achieved without dying. Maybe I'm saying that there is a renewed freshness enveloping me . . . a constantly recurring newness just on the brink of it's all disappearing. . . . One is always intermittently stunned to be alive. . . . I am to cease being in time and of time, which is the ultimate magic. My last moments in time. Maybe that's the ecstasy now."

7. Anne Margaret Daniel, "Philip Roth Reads One Last Time," *HuffPost*, 14 May 2014, https://www.huffpost.com/entry/philip-roth-reads-one-last-time_b_5308818.

8. Charles McGrath, "No Longer Writing, Philip Roth Still Has Plenty to Say," *New York Times*, 16 January 2018, https://www.nytimes.com/2018/01/16/books/review/philip-roth-interview.html.

9. The phrase is also the powerful conclusion to Leonard Cohen's 2016 song "You Want It Darker" from his late album of the same name. The specific lyrics, forming the chorus, are "Hineni, hineni / I'm ready my lord," preceded by

> It's written in the scriptures
> And it's not some idle claim
> You want it darker
> We kill the flame.

10. Saul Bellow, *The Bellarosa Connection* (New York: Penguin, 1989), 2.

11. For an account of the course, see Jonah Weiner, "Philip Roth Taught a Course at Bard; Did It Inspire *The Human Stain*?," *Slate*, 7 September 2012, https://slate.com/culture/2012/09/philip-roths-open-letter-to-wikipedia-another-possible-inspiration-for-the-human-stain.html. The course, in the fall of 1999, met twelve times to discuss six of Roth's books. Manea would teach one day and Roth would appear the next with Manea to discuss the text. The last class saw Roth bring transcripts from court proceedings against artists during the Stalinist purges to expose the dangers of institutional censure upon artistic freedom. Questions from the previous class either on *Sabbath's Theater* or *I Married a Communist* prompted Roth's lecture, or possibly the incident that starts *The Human Stain,* which appeared the following year. For generalized details of the Bard cemetery see Mikhail Horowitz, "Philip Roth Is Laid to Rest in Annandale," *hv1*, 29 May 2018, https://hudsonvalleyone.com/2018/05/29/philip-roth-is-laid-to-rest-in-annandale/.

12. On Roth as conductor of his own performance, see Caro Llewellyn, "My Relationship with Philip Roth," *Sydney Morning Herald*, 5 March 2019. https://www.smh.com.au/entertainment/books/my-journey-with-philip-roth-i-loved-that-he-made-me-laugh-20190304-h1by7j.html. A year and a half after Roth's death, a set of essays

appeared in *Post45*, a scholarly online journal dealing with post-1945 literature, entitled "Roth's Yahrzeit," a Yiddish term for "time of year," commemorating the one-year anniversary of someone's death and the beginning an annual prayer of remembrance. The articles published in the 4 December 2019 issue range from a detailed textual history of *Portnoy's Complaint* to a discussion of his late works entitled "Roth's Modest Phase" and the question of Roth's relation to Zion and Zionism. See http://post45.org/sections/contemporaries/roths-yahrtzeit/.

13. Bonham's auctioned Conarroe's Roth material on 6 March 2020. Among the items were an unpublished manuscript draft sequel to *The Breast*; an annotated manuscript copy entitled "Phallic Symbol" (April 1972), originally gifted to Barbara Sproul, which became the "My True Story" section of *My Life as a Man*; corrected galley proofs to both *The Anatomy Lesson* and *The Counterlife*; and almost sixty letters and notes from Roth to Conarroe. One of the interesting items is his praise for John le Carré's 1986 novel *A Perfect Spy,* which he calls "the best English novel since the war. Quite brilliant."

14. An earlier list of speakers included Saul Bellow and William Styron, but they predeceased him. The Library of America published a limited keepsake entitled *Philip Roth in Memory* with the remarks of the speakers (New York: Library of America, 2019). On the cell phone incident, see Pierpont, *Philip Roth in Memory* 19. For more on the memorial, see Lynne Schwartz, "Philip Roth Memorial at the New York Public Library, May 25, 2018," *Philip Roth Society Newsletter,* Fall 2019, 11–12.

15. Roth in Conarroe, *Philip Roth in Memory,* 81–82.

16. Zax, "Philip Roth Doesn't Live Here Anymore."

17. Roth had read Camus's *The Fall* when writing *The Dying Animal* and *The Plague* when writing *Nemesis* and may have researched details of Camus's life and death. Zax, "Philip Roth Doesn't Live Here Anymore."

18. Judith Thurman, "The Writer's Twin," *New Yorker,* 14 May 2012, https://www.newyorker.com/books/page-turner/the-writers-twin.

19. Thurman in Travis Nichol, "A Moment with . . . Judith Thurman Literary Critic," *Seattle Post Intelligencer,* 27 November 2007, https://www.seattlepi.com/ae/books/article/A-Moment-With-Judith-Thurman-literary-critic-1256980.php.

20. See Judith Thurman, "Counterfeit Roth," *New Yorker,* 27 March 2010 and "Debenedetti Confesses!," *New Yorker,* 24 June 2010. Tommaso Debenedetti published several fake interviews with Roth in Italian tabloids where accuracy was overlooked. He also published false interviews with Gore Vidal, Elie Wiesel, Paul Auster, and John Grisham.

21. In 2009, he exerted early control when he prepared questions for Harry Maurer and Lisa Halliday, who offered to conduct interviews about his life for him. He, of course, provided the list of approved interviewees.

22. The sentence before reads, "His refractory way of living—unable and unwilling to hide anything and, with his raging, satirizing nature, mocking everything, living beyond the limits of discretion and taste and blaspheming against the decent—this refractory way of living is his uniquely Sabbathian response to a place where nothing keeps its promise and everything is perishable."

23. Roth, "The Box of Truths," *Et Cetera*, October 1952, 11.
24. Christian Lorentzen, "There Were Many Philip Roths," *Vulture*, 23 May 2018, https://www.vulture.com/2018/05/philip-roth-obituary-appreciation-assessment.html.
25. And one more by Roth: "I am still amorphous Roth." The source for this is his 1981 interview with *Le Nouvel Observateur* reprinted in RMY 110.

Figure Credits

1.1. Philip Roth at four months old at Belmar, New Jersey, with his parents, Herman and Bess Roth, and his brother, Sandy, 1933. Credit: Newark Public Library.

1.2. Roth (fifth in on the right) with friends celebrating his high school prom at Billy Rose's Diamond Horseshoe Club, New York City, January 1950. Credit: Newark Public Library.

1.3. The main branch of the Newark Public Library, which opened in 1901. Building based on the fifteenth-century Palazzo Strozzi in Florence. Credit: Newark Public Library.

1.4. Philip Roth, age eight, at Bradley Beach with his brother, Sandy, 1942. Credit: Newark Public Library.

2.1. The Roth family on a trip to Washington, D.C., in the summer of 1941. Photo taken at the Arlington Memorial Amphitheater, Arlington National Cemetery. *Left to right:* Philip, Bess, Herman, Sandy. Credit: Newark Public Library.

2.2. Roth (*left*) in the office of Bucknell's literary magazine *Et Cetera* with Robert Pincus, 1953. Credit: Special Collections/University Archives, Bucknell University.

2.3. Roth (*right*) performing in *Death of a Salesman* at Bucknell, 1953. Credit: Special Collections/University Archives, Bucknell University.

3.1. Roth with his arms around Maggie on their wedding day, 22 February 1959, Yonkers, New York. Credit: Vernon Gibberd. Philip Roth Papers, Library of Congress.

3.2. An exuberant Roth in front of a furniture store on his wedding day, 22 February 1959, Yonkers, New York. Credit: Vernon Gibberd. Philip Roth Papers, Library of Congress.

3.3. Poster for Yeshiva University symposium, 29 March 1962, listing the three participants with the moderator. Credit: Yeshiva University Archives, Special Collections, Yeshiva University, New York.

3.4. Four Yeshiva University symposium speakers: (*left to right*) Pietro di Donato, Ralph Ellison, David Fleisher (moderator), Philip Roth. Credit: Yeshiva University Archives, Special Collections, Yeshiva University, New York.

3.5. Roth at the lectern speaking at Yeshiva University symposium, 29 March 1962. Credit: Yeshiva University Archives, Special Collections, Yeshiva University, New York.

3.6. Roth (*right*) with a smiling Richard Ellmann (*center*), winner of the Biography prize for his biography of James Joyce, and Robert Lowell (*left*), poetry winner for *Life Studies*. National Book Award ceremony, 23 March 1960, at the Astor Hotel. AP File.

3.7. Roth with his wife Maggie at the Newark Public Library, April 1960. She is holding a copy of the National Book Award winner, *Goodbye, Columbus*. Credit: Newark Public Library.

4.1. Roth with Maggie in Central Park, 1962. Credit: Carl Mydans, Getty Images.

4.2. Roth listening to David Ben-Gurion in Israel with other members of the 1963 delegation sponsored by the American Jewish Congress. To Roth's left, Margaret and Leslie Fiedler. Credit: Newark Public Library.

5.1. First-edition cover of *Portnoy's Complaint* by Philip Roth. Credit: Designed by Paul Bacon; published by Random House, January 1969.

5.2. Philip Roth and Ann Mudge at the country home of Vernon Gibberd in the U.K., 1968. Credit: Vernon Gibberd, Philip Roth Papers, Library of Congress, Washington, D.C.

6.1. Roth in New York, March 1973. Credit: Copyright Nancy Crampton.

7.1. Roth and Bloom walking down a Chelsea Street, London, 10 March 1990. Credit: Ian Cook, Getty Images.

7.2. Roth and Bloom at Bucknell University in 1979, when Roth received an honorary degree. Credit: Special Collections/University Archives, Bucknell University.

7.3. Roth listening to R. B. Kitaj in his London studio, 1985. Credit: Ian Cook/Getty Images.

8.1. Cover, *Sabbath's Theater*, 1995. Credit: Houghton Mifflin Publishers.

9.1. Roth and Bloom in their London home, March 1990. Credit: Ian Cook/Getty Images.

9.2. Roth and Primo Levi in Levi's study in Turin, April(?) 1986. Credit: Primo Levi Center, Turin; La Stampa.

10.1. Roth at his standing desk in his Cornwall Bridge studio, 2004. Credit: James Nachtwey/James Nachtwey Archive, Hood Museum of Art, Dartmouth College, Hanover, New Hampshire.

11.1. Portrait of Philip Roth in his studio, Cornwall Bridge, Connecticut, 2002. Credit: James Nachtwey/James Nachtwey Archive, Hood Museum of Art, Dartmouth College, Hanover, New Hampshire.

12.1. Philip Roth's gravestone, 2020. Credit: Michelle Foster, New York.

Index

For the benefit of digital users, indexed terms that span two pages (e.g., 52–53) may, on occasion, appear on only one of those pages.